D0166440

COMMON PLACES
Integrated Reading and Writing

Lisa Hoeffner

McLENNAN COMMUNITY COLLEGE

Kent Hoeffner

McLENNAN COMMUNITY COLLEGE

McGraw Hill Education

COMMON PLACES: INTEGRATED READING AND WRITING

Published by McGraw-Hill Education, 2 Penn Plaza, New York, NY 10121. Copyright © 2015 by McGraw-Hill Education. All rights reserved. Printed in the United States of America. No part of this publication may be reproduced or distributed in any form or by any means, or stored in a database or retrieval system, without the prior written consent of McGraw-Hill Education, including, but not limited to, in any network or other electronic storage or transmission, or broadcast for distance learning.

Some ancillaries, including electronic and print components, may not be available to customers outside the United States.

This book is printed on acid-free paper.

1 2 3 4 5 6 7 8 9 0 RMN/RMN 1 0 9 8 7 6 5 4

ISBN: 978-1-259-19223-4 (student edition)
MHID: 1-259-19223-7 (student edition)

ISBN: 978-1-259-19219-7 (instructor's edition)
MHID: 1-259-19219-9 (instructor's edition)

Senior Vice President, Products & Markets: *Kurt L. Strand*
Vice President, General Manager, Products & Markets: *Michael Ryan*
Vice President, Content Design & Delivery: *Kimberly Meriwether David*
Managing Director: *David S. Patterson*
Executive Brand Manager: *Kelly Villella*
Director, Product Development: *Meghan Campbell*
Senior Market Development Manager: *Suzie Flores*
Senior Marketing Manager: *Jaclyn Elkins*
Marketing Manager: *Nancy Baudean*
Executive Director of Development: *Lisa Pinto*

Director, Content Design & Delivery: Terry Schiesl
Program Manager: *Jennifer Gehl*
Content Project Manager: *Sandy Wille*
Buyer: *Susan K. Culbertson*
Design: *Trevor Goodman*
Content Licensing Specialists: *Shawntel Schmitt*
Cover Image: © *Fuse*
Compositor: *Laserwords Private Limited*
Printer: *R. R. Donnelley*

All credits appearing on page or at the end of the book are considered to be an extension of the copyright page.

Library of Congress Cataloging-in-Publication Data

Hoeffner, Lisa, author.
  Common Places : integrated reading and writing / Lisa Hoeffner, McLennan Community College ; Kent Hoeffner, McLennan Community College.
    p. cm
  Includes bibliographical references and index.
  ISBN 978-1-259-19223-4 (student edition : alk. paper) — ISBN 1-259-19223-7 (student edition: alk. paper) — ISBN 978-1-259-19219-7 (instructor's edition) — ISBN 1-259-19219-9 (instructor's edition) 1. English language—Rhetoric—Problems, exercises, etc. 2. Report writing—Problems, exercises, etc. 3. Reading comprehension—Problems, exercises, etc. 4. College readers. I. Hoeffner, Kent, author. II. Title.
  PE1413.H553 2015
  808'.042076—dc23
                                                                                          2014022177

The Internet addresses listed in the text were accurate at the time of publication. The inclusion of a website does not indicate an endorsement by the authors or McGraw-Hill Education, and McGraw-Hill Education does not guarantee the accuracy of the information presented at these sites.

ABOUT THE AUTHORS

Lisa Hoeffner

Lisa Hoeffner earned a PhD in English with a specialization in rhetoric from the University of Houston. She has taught a wide range of courses over the past twenty-five years, including English composition and rhetoric, reading, critical thinking, American and British literature, world literature, humanities, and business writing. Since 1998, Dr. Hoeffner has served in two positions—professor of English and professor of reading—at McLennan Community College in Waco, Texas.

In addition to her teaching role, Dr. Hoeffner is focusing on curricular redesign in developmental education. She serves as grant director for a Texas Higher Education Coordinating Board grant awarded for work on improvement and innovation in developmental education. With the advent of integrated reading and writing in Texas, she has provided leadership for colleges and universities across the state that are creating integrated reading and writing (INRW) programs. She has designed and led training workshops and webinars to prepare faculty to teach INRW and to help institutions create INRW programs. She has also provided leadership to public school districts implementing INRW programs as college preparatory classes.

Dr. Hoeffner has a passion for teaching and for innovative technologies. She designed and taught her first online freshman composition class in 1999 and has since developed and taught online courses for developmental students. She is thrilled that she is able to bring both passions to bear in her development of *Common Places* and the Connect IRW: *Common Places* Master Course.

Dr. Hoeffner is a recipient of several awards, including the National Institute for Staff and Organizational Development (NISOD) Excellence Award. She has written and published scholarly articles and poetry, and she has presented her work in developmental education nationally. A native Texan, Dr. Hoeffner enjoys exploring the flora and fauna of regional ecosystems, cooking, and dreaming about living off the grid.

Kent Hoeffner

Kent Hoeffner earned a BA from Texas A&M University in College Station, an MDiv from Golden Gate Seminary in Mill Valley, California, and a PhD from Southern Seminary in Louisville, Kentucky. Before working in higher education, Dr. Hoeffner was employed in the mental health field, working primarily with adolescents with social and emotional difficulties. During that time, he also taught adult basic education and GED preparation classes.

Dr. Hoeffner has served at McLennan Community College since 2001, first as the division director for liberal arts and currently as a professor of philosophy. In addition to teaching introductory courses in philosophy, he has also taught and developed courses in critical thinking and logic. In 2007, he developed McLennan's first online philosophy course, and since then he has continued to develop and teach various online courses.

Recently, Dr. Hoeffner renewed his long-standing involvement in academic advising by joining a group of faculty in a grant-funded intensive advising program focused on improving the success of developmental students. He regularly mentors students who need help in the areas of successful academic behaviors, self-advocacy, and the development of college-level reading and writing skills.

His background in foreign languages and logic contributed to his talents for creating the sentence-combining and grammar units in *Common Places*, and his expertise in teaching critical thinking and in student mentoring has helped to shape the text. When he is not teaching, advising, or writing, Dr. Hoeffner enjoys following the Dallas Cowboys, reading, and traveling.

BRIEF CONTENTS

PART 4   Additional Skills

Available only in **McGraw-Hill Create**™

Strategies for Reading and Writing Exams

PART 5   Well-Crafted Sentences

Available only in **McGraw-Hill Create**™

Editing and Revising Practice

PART 6   Thematic Anthology of Readings

Available only in **McGraw-Hill Create**™

**THEME   Television and Stereotypes
THEME   The Rules of Attraction**

CONTENTS

CHAPTER **7**

Organizing, Drafting, and Summarizing 222

CHAPTER **8**

Titles, Introductions, and Conclusions 247

CHAPTER **9**

Inferences and Tone 277

CHAPTER **10**

Revising and Editing 312

PART 3

Integrated Reading and Writing Projects

CHAPTER 11

Project 1: Working with Informative Texts 348

Social Media—For Better or Worse

Project 6: Reading and Writing Persuasive Responses

Prisoners and Education

PART 4
Additional Skills

CHAPTER 14

Using Sources 440

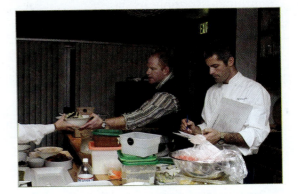

Available only in McGraw-Hill Create™

Strategies for Reading and Writing Exams

PART 5
Well-Crafted Sentences

Available only in McGraw-Hill Create™

Editing and Revising Practice

THE LEARNING SUPPORT SYSTEM OF *COMMON PLACES*

The *Common Places* Text

- Quick Start Guide to Integrated Reading and Writing Assignments: an overview of steps in the integrated reading and writing process
- Text chapters: fourteen foundational chapters, three handbook units, and four themed anthology sections available in the national edition

Connect Integrated Reading and Writing: The *Common Places* Master Course

Lisa Hoeffner has set up a master Connect IRW course with the following assignments to align with chapters in *Common Places*:

- *LearnSmart Achieve* topics
- Chapter quizzes
- Chapter vocabulary quizzes
- *Power of Process* assignments built around selected chapter readings
- Chapter Reading and Writing Assignments set up in *Power of Process* and *Writing Assignments*
- *PowerPoint* presentations for chapter concepts
- Discussion board prompts for chapter concepts

Teaching Resources and Digital Support

- *Annotated Instructor's Edition* with on-page teaching tips
- *Instructor's Manual*
- Handouts, exercises, and graphics
- Chapter quizzes and vocabulary quizzes
- Topical *PowerPoint* presentations

Create™ Options for a Variety of IRW Programs

- Additional content: four additional chapters, one additional handbook unit, and two additional themed anthology sections available through McGraw-Hill Create™ to shape course materials for various institutions' course sequences
- Expressbooks: pre-built versions of *Common Places* designed for different course sequences, including those defined by specific IRW states

PREFACE

Why *Common Places?*

Common Places teaches students to *read from a writer's point of view* by considering the choices writers make when presenting their content. It also encourages students to *write from a reader's point of view* as they face the same choices with their own writing. Students immediately and continually emulate recursive reading and writing processes as they work through the text. As the teaching of reading and writing is consolidated into one course on campuses across the country, reading and writing instructors are coming together in *common places* to find effective methods for teaching both sets of strategies as an interdependent reading and writing process. The title *Common Places* celebrates this interdependence and the thoughtful common ground that instructors are finding with this integration.

The *Common Places* Instructional Framework

A leader in developmental education redesign, Lisa Hoeffner has created for *Common Places* an innovative instructional framework that includes step-by-step modeling for integrated reading and writing processes, a unique series of purpose-oriented projects, a fresh approach to grammar, and a compelling set of thematic, leveled readings. Hoeffner incorporates the powerful concepts of metacognition, reflection, and critical thinking using practical exercises. Offering unsurpassable flexibility with customizable content, *Common Places* is backed by a thoughtful learning support system, envisioned and developed by Hoeffner.

Features of the Learning Support System of *Common Places*

Common Places and the components of Connect Integrated Reading and Writing (Connect IRW) address the specific needs of integrated reading and writing courses.

- **A fully integrated and flexible solution for the integrated reading and writing course.** *Common Places* provides a strong instructional framework for intertwining the skills of reading and writing. The Learning Resources in Connect IRW *LearnSmart Achieve* provide students with integrated skills instruction in the form of visual slides with narrated coach text and video resources, within an adaptive platform that targets areas in which students need remediation.

- **Multiple features to promote metacognitive skills.** These features, including Thinking from an Instructor's Point of View exercises and end-of-chapter activities in emotional intelligence, cultural literacy, critical thinking, and metacognition, help students develop an awareness of multiple points of view as readers, writers, students, and citizens. Features in Connect IRW *LearnSmart Achieve* and *Power of Process* assignments also support the development of students' metacognitive awareness.

- **A methodical, step-by-step approach for modeling integrated reading and writing processes.** The logical and clear framework presented in *Common Places* provides an abundance of models that help build students' confidence in their ability to master specific skills as they work through the chapters and the projects. The Learning Resources in Connect IRW *LearnSmart Achieve* display annotated examples as good models for students.

- **A fresh approach to grammar.** The handbook takes a positive, highly effective approach to grammar, with a strong emphasis on sentence combining and grammar in context. Grammar Focus features within chapters reinforce the integrated nature of reading and writing. Students have ample opportunity for additional, targeted grammar practice in any of the eighteen *LearnSmart Achieve* grammar and mechanics topics in Connect IRW.

- **Unique, purpose-oriented projects for upper-level and lower-level IRW courses.** Each project within the set emphasizes a particular writing purpose: to inform, to analyze and evaluate, or to persuade. Each upper-level project features four readings on a specific topic and requires students to read and analyze the selections and then integrate them effectively in their own source-based, documented essay. The lower-level projects, available only in Create™, require students to read critically a single source and complete a purpose-oriented writing assignment appropriate for the earlier course in the sequence. These assignments have been built into Connect IRW: *Common Places* Master Course using *Power of Process* to analyze these sources and the writing assignment toolset to support peer review and rubric grading of the writing projects.

- **The Quick Start Guide to Integrated Reading and Writing Assignments.** This brief guide at the start of the text articulates the steps in the reading and writing process and enables students to engage in the process immediately.

- **A wealth of highly engaging readings across a range of themes.** With fifty readings in *Common Places* and approximately 140 readings in Connect IRW *Power of Process*, instructors will find readings for any student audience or Lexile range. Themes and readings have all been chosen to include topics that are of high interest to students and most prevalently used in IRW courses. All readings come with a variety of assessments and assignments. Connect IRW *Power of Process* makes visible to students their own reading and writing process as they analyze readings within the toolset. Essay-writing assignments for each selection and reading-based writing assignments for each thematic collection may be assigned through the Connect IRW *Writing Assignment* toolset to support rubric assessment and peer review.

- **Examples of how purpose and patterns work together.** *Common Places* treats patterns of development (rhetorical modes) as tools for creating support in texts, not as ends in themselves. Students are guided to select and combine patterns of development that fit writing purposes—informing, analyzing, evaluating, and persuading—and provide the best support for particular audiences. For instructors who teach only particular text patterns, *Common Places* Chapter 6 may be customized to include only the text patterns desired.

- **An abundance of opportunities to practice skills.** *Common Places* provides students with extensive practice in reading and writing skills. Exercises interspersed throughout the text build individual skills, and more-comprehensive activities appear at the end of each chapter. Connect IRW *LearnSmart Achieve* provides additional practice of those skills in an adaptive, individualized learning experience. *Power of Process* supports more holistic practice and assessment of the integrated reading and writing process.

Flexible Content for Any IRW Program and Course Sequence

After closely studying numerous statewide and department curriculum frameworks and student learning outcomes (SLOs) for integrated reading and writing courses, the authors designed *Common Places* as a program of content flexible enough to align with various SLOs and course configurations. As an alternative to this national text, instructors may use McGraw-Hill Create™ to arrange chapters to align with their syllabus, eliminate chapters they do not wish to assign, and add any of the *Common Places* content available only in Create™ to build one or multiple print or e-book texts—including Connect IRW access codes—for their integrated reading and writing courses. With additional content available only in Create™, *Common Places* offers the full breadth of content needed to craft customized texts for the entire sequence of IRW courses or for a single course. The content available only in Create™ includes a chapter on taking reading and writing exams, three alternative lower-level projects (Project 4: Reading and Writing Summaries, Project 5: Reading and Writing to Solve Problems, Project 6: Reading and Writing Persuasive Responses), two additional thematic anthology units ("Television and Stereotypes" and "The Rules of Attraction"), and an editing practice unit. Through Create™, instructors may also add their own material, such as a course syllabus, a course rubric, course standards, and any specific instruction for students.

Within McGraw-Hill Create™, the ExpressBooks offer a simple solution to order alternative tables of contents that present *Common Places* content for two or three course sequences with just a couple of clicks.

McGraw-Hill Create™ is a self-service Web site that allows instructors and departments to create customized course materials using McGraw-Hill's comprehensive, cross-disciplinary content and digital products. Instructors can even access third-party content, including readings, articles, cases, and videos, and select and arrange the content to match the scope and sequence of courses. After personalizing the book with a cover design, instructors choose the best format for their students: e-book, color print, or black-and-white print. Once they have customized their course materials, instructors receive a PDF review copy in just minutes!

Teaching Resources

As an early adopter of Connect Integrated Reading and Writing, Dr. Hoeffner created the annotations in the *Annotated Instructor's Edition*, as well as all the textbook supplements. Dr. Hoeffner has also built a Connect IRW: *Common Places* Master Course to facilitate instructors' full integration of Connect IRW and *Common Places*.

Connect IRW: *Common Places* Master Course

In this master course, which you can copy to your own Connect account and adapt as you wish, you will find pre-built assignments aligned with every chapter of the text; you will also find various Connect IRW assignment types that complement the *Common Places* text and accelerate learning. Dr. Hoeffner sets up *LearnSmart Achieve* topics, quizzes, vocabulary practices, vocabulary quizzes, *Power of Process* assignments, *Writing Assignments*, concept *PowerPoint* presentations, and Discussion board prompts for every chapter of the text. Contact your local McGraw-Hill representative to copy the course to your Connect account.

Connect IRW addresses the specific needs of integrated reading and writing courses and various redesign models of instruction. It teaches reading and writing skills as a *complementary* process by contextualizing the material within thematic disciplinary readings and authentic writing models. In addition to the innovative content, revolutionary learning technology drives the integration of reading and writing skills through a selection of corresponding toolsets:

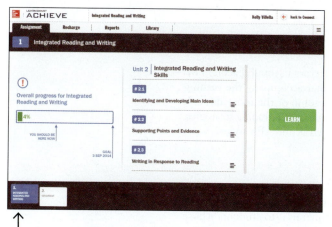

- *LearnSmart Achieve* offers students an adaptive, individualized learning experience designed to ensure the efficient mastery of reading and writing skills in tandem. By targeting students' particular strengths and weaknesses, *LearnSmart Achieve* customizes its lessons and facilitates high-impact learning at an accelerated pace.

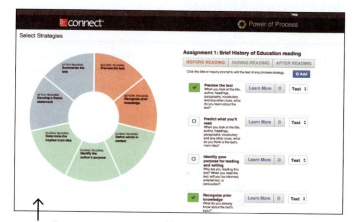

- *Power of Process* guides students through performance-based assessment activities using the pedagogy of strategies instruction, in which students use strategies to read and respond to the text, and then instructors can assess students' depth of engagement with the text.

- *Writing Assignments* with **Outcomes Based Assessment** allow instructors and departments to assess written assignments with custom rubrics built around learning outcomes and to generate detailed reports that support formative assessment and improve efficacy at the student, section, and program levels.

- **A thematic, leveled e-book reader and question bank** provide approximately 140 compelling readings and assessment options that instructors can incorporate into their syllabuses. Four pre-built assessments, aligned with the same topics and learning objectives in *Learn-Smart Achieve*, may be used as static pre- and posttests for lower- and upper-level courses.
- **McGraw-Hill Campus** is a Learning Management System (LMS) integration service that offers instructors and students universal single sign-on, automatic registration, and gradebook synchronization of McGraw-Hill Connect products.
- Connect Insight™ is an analytics tool that provides a series of visual data displays—each framed by an intuitive question—to provide instructors at-a-glance information regarding how their classes are doing

Annotated Instructor's Edition: On-Page Teaching Tips

The author draws on her extensive experience in the classroom—as well as the experiences of many other seasoned IRW faculty—to offer pedagogical ideas that are effective and easy to use. Marginal tips suggest innovative ways to present the topics in each chapter. The *Annotated Instructor's Edition* also alerts instructors to teaching resources such as handouts, quizzes, and *PowerPoint* presentations, as well as to assignments and resources in Connect IRW.

The following teaching resources are downloadable from www.mheducation.com/hoeffner1e. Please contact your local McGraw-Hill representative for the username and password to access these resources.

Instructor's Manual

The *Instructor's Manual* is written with the diverse needs of IRW instructors in mind. Faculty new to teaching reading will appreciate the brief presentations of theory that accompany the reading pedagogy in the textbook, as well as the suggestions for how to teach some of the more difficult reading skills. Faculty new to teaching writing will find helpful the suggestions for grading strategies, managing the paper load, addressing grammatical issues, and teaching MLA and APA styles.

Handouts, Exercises, and Graphics

These documents may be used for in-class, hands-on practice. These copy-and-go pages make preparing for class easier, and they give instructors a way to present material to students whose learning styles benefit from kinesthetic activities.

Chapter Quizzes

The chapter quizzes test students' literal comprehension of chapter content. They can be used to motivate students to read the chapters, and they were designed to be easily administered and graded.

Topical *PowerPoint* Presentations

The *PowerPoint* presentations for *Common Places* are short, fun for students, and powerful. Unlike traditional textbook-supplied *PowerPoint* presentations that simply provide chapter outlines, *Common Places* presentations are topical and highly visual. For instance, the *PowerPoint* presentation "Broad or Narrow?" starts with photos and transitions to text in order to teach students to recognize differences in the breadth of ideas.

A Word from the Lead Author, Lisa Hoeffner

Integrating the teaching of developmental reading and writing courses simply makes sense. Many of the learning objectives for each course mirror each other: identify a thesis statement/ write a thesis statement, identify various types of support/create various types of support, and so on. The natural way to integrate is to teach the reading skill and then teach the mirrored writing skill. Nonetheless, when I began teaching the course, I could not find a textbook that presented true integration.

The problem with trying to teach integrated reading and writing with a textbook that is not fully integrated is that you really end up teaching two courses in one semester—and in half the time. The only way to make integrated reading and writing courses work is to use time-saving integration strategies. Instead of spending a week on identifying minor supporting details and then another week on paragraph development, for example, a truly integrated pedagogy addresses those topics together in the same week.

This point is important to me as an instructor. We have so little time to remediate in so many areas that I needed a book that would really support an integrated process to accelerate student learning. With that need in mind, I began writing *Common Places*. Throughout the process of developing this book, the driving question was always *How can we present this topic in a truly integrated way?* My hope is that *Common Places* provides the best integration of reading and writing possible and that it makes the learning of both subjects not only feasible in a shorter time frame, but also enjoyable.

To write a book is a humbling experience. The process reminded me of just how much I am indebted to all the people around me who have stimulated my thoughts, shared their own great ideas, and encouraged me to keep going. I would like to thank a few people without whom this book simply would not exist. I am entirely grateful for Paul Banks and the faith he had in this project from the beginning. Also, *Common Places* owes much of its visionary content to Kelly Villella. She has been a dynamic source of ideas, energy, and drive and has often been the engine that has propelled me forward. And I cannot imagine finding a more personable, professional, and gifted editor than Linda Stern. Linda has a real knack for seeing the possibilities in a text and making them come to life. Lisa Pinto has also been crucial to our team; her calm, can-do attitude and logical ideas have brought reassurance to our team meetings. I am also grateful for the many people who worked tirelessly and cheerfully on various aspects of *Common Places*: Wes Hall, who managed the text permissions; Shawntel Schmitt, who handled the photo program; Trevor Goodman, who created the beautiful cover and design; Dana Wan, who handled administrative details; Judith Riotto, who copyedited the manuscript; Debra DeBord and Martha Ghent, who proofread the pages; Nancy Ball, who prepared the index; Suzie Flores, who managed market development activities; Jaclyn Elkins and Nancy Baudean, who carefully crafted marketing plans; and Sandy Wille, who oversaw the entire production process masterfully.

To my colleagues at McLennan, I owe a debt of gratitude. In particular, Linda Crawford, Lorraine Stansel, Charlotte Laughlin, Bill Matta, and Fred Hills have not only offered great ideas, but have been supportive of this project from the beginning. I would also like to thank the crucial work of all the faculty reviewers. Without their guidance and creativity, *Common Places* would be a different book: Susan Achziger, *Community College of Aurora*; Marian Anders, *Alamance Community College*; Joe Antinarella, *Tidewater Community College–Chesapeake*; Deva Arumugam, *El Centro College*; Jenny Beaver, *Rowan Cabarrus Community College*; Erica Bertero, *Del Mar College*; Michael Boyd, *Illinois Central College*; Kimberly Britt, *Horry Georgetown Technical College*; Robyn Browder, *Tidewater Community College–Virginia Beach*; Sarah Bruton, *Fayetteville Technical Community College*; Kellie Cannon, *Coastal Carolina Community College*; James Carranza, *College of San Mateo*; Judith Carter, *Amarillo College*; Susan Chism, *Greenville College*; Thomas Connolly, *Suffolk University*; Michael Cox, *Mitchell Community College*; Christy Cutshaw, *Allen County Community College*; JoAnn Davis, *Saint Philips College*; Patricia Davis, *Houston Community College–Southwest*; Kelly Dedmon, *Isothermal Community College*; Brian Dickson, *Community College of Denver*; Alicia Dominguez, *Saint Philips College*; Tammy Donaldson, *Del Mar College*; Barbara Doyle, *Arkansas State University–Jonesboro*; Mary Dubbe, *Thomas Nelson Community College*; Patricia Dungan,

Austin Community College–Rio Grande; Christi Duque, *Tarrant Community College;* Justin Eatmon, *Coastal Carolina Community College;* Crystal Edmonds, *Robeson Community College;* Jason Ellis, *Cincinnati State Technical and Community College;* Dell Smith Enecks, *Beaufort Community College;* Ruth Engel, *Tarrant Community College;* Betty Evans, *University of Arkansas–Monticello;* Ellen Feig, *Bergen Community College;* Marianne Friedell, *College of the Mainland;* Jacquelyn Gaiters-Jordan, *Pikes Peak Community College;* Julie Garner, *Tri-County Community College;* Debbie Gilmore, *Temple College;* Brent Green, *Salt Lake Community College;* Dustin Greene, *Caldwell Community College;* Karen Hackley, *Dominican College;* Beth Hammett, *College of the Mainland;* Curtis Harrell, *Northwest Arkansas Community College;* Michelle Hawkins, *Bryant and Stratton College;* Michael Hedges, *Horry Georgetown Technical College;* Kathleen Hickey, *Dominican College;* Amy Holly, *Front Range Community College–Fort Collins;* Judy Hubble, *Austin Community College–Round Rock;* Elizabeth Hudspeth, *Northeast Lakeview College;* Jill Hughes, *Casper College;* Blanche Hunt, *Arkansas Northeastern College;* Sharyn Hunter, *Sinclair Community College;* Janis Innis, *Houston Community College–Southwest;* Danen Jobe, *Pikes Peak Community College;* Alyssa Johnson, *Horry Georgetown Community College;* Leah Jones, *College of the Albemarle;* Kimberly Koledoye, *Houston Community College–Northwest;* Mary Ann Landino, *Housatonic Community College;* Jeff Landon, *John Tyler Community College;* Kina Lara, *San Jacinto College–South;* Alice Leonhardt, *Blue Ridge Community College;* Thomas Lilly, *Georgia Gwinnett College;* Tiffany Lofton, *Horry Georgetown Technical College;* Breanna Lutterbie, *Germanna Community College–Locust Grove;* Carol Manciel, *Wayne County Community College–Western;* Elizabeth Marsh, *Bergen Community College;* Lori Massey, *Tarrant County College;* Brook Mayo, *Asheville Buncombe Technical Community College;* Kathy McCoskey, *Butler Community College;* Kerry McShane-Moley, *Cape Fear Community College–North Camp;* Kim Meeks, *Oconee Fall Line Technical College–Dublin;* Marti Miles-Rosenfield, *Collin College Plano;* Kathleen Mollick, *Tarleton State University;* Robbi Muckenfuss, *Durham Technical Community College;* Maureen Murphy-Smolka, *Sussex County Community College;* Alice Newsome, *Tarleton State University;* Hilda Ollmann, *Austin Community College–Eastview;* Diane Payne, *University of Arkansas–Monticello;* Emily Peebles, *San Jacinto College–Pasadena;* Betty Perkinson, *Tidewater Community College–Portsmouth;* Cara Potter, *Durham Technical Community College;* Jeanni Pruitt, *Northeast Texas Community College;* Sandra Reinhardt, *Catawba Valley Community College;* Nancy Risch, *Caldwell Community College;* Jackie Roberts, *Richland Community College;* Kathleen Ross, *Asheville Buncombe Technical Community College;* Kay Ruth, *Wake Technical Community College;* Maria Salinas, *Del Mar College;* Robert Sandhaas, *San Jacinto College–South;* Esther Sapell Rachelson, *Devry University–South Florida;* Tracy Schneider, *Solano Community College;* Jim Schrantz, *Tarrant County College;* Linda Shieff, *Wake Technical Community College;* Mary Sizemore, *Lamar State College–Orange;* Debra Slaton, *Cisco College–Abilene;* Cheryle Snead-Greene, *Prairie View A&M University;* Mae Spicer, *Richland College;* Tanya Stanley, *San Jacinto College–Pasadena;* Kelly Terzaken, *Coastal Carolina Community College;* Alexandr Tolj, *John Tyler Community College–Midlothian;* Ernie Tsacalis, *San Antonio College;* Joan Valichnac, *Northland Pioneer College;* Dustin Wenrich, *Wright State University–Dayton;* Tina Willhoite, *San Jacinto College–South;* Katherine Winkler, *Blue Ridge Community College;* Michelle Zollars, *Patrick Henry Community College.*

I am grateful for the contributions of my brother, Richard Wright, my mother, Gail Wright, and my sister-in-law, Margie Hoeffner. For bearing with Kent and me throughout the process of "the book," I must also thank our kids, Abby, Hannah, and Seth, and our parents, Richard and Gail Wright and Vondee Hoeffner. Our families have patiently stood by us, offering encouragement and helping us as they could.

Finally, I must thank my husband and coauthor, Kent Hoeffner. I now look back with fondness at the many days we sat in our study researching together, writing and rewriting, fussing, and laughing. Kent's incredible writing gifts, intelligence, and creativity mark many of the pages of *Common Places*, and his constant encouragement brought this project to fruition.

Lisa Hoeffner

QUICK START GUIDE
to Integrated Reading and Writing Assignments

This brief reference guide will walk you through the integrated reading and writing process so that you have guidance for your reading and writing assignments from the first day of class. The first column lists the tasks as steps. The second column briefly explains each task. While these steps are listed in order, most people go back to previous steps during the reading and writing process. For instance, the first step—analyze your assignment—is something you will likely do more than once. Reviewing the assignment at various points in the process will help guide your reading and will help keep you on track as you write. Notations suggest steps to review if you need more ideas, support, or information as you work.

Not all assignments require you to use every step presented here. Choose the steps that will best help you complete each assignment.

GETTING STARTED

Analyze your assignment.	Ask yourself: Is the assignment clear and complete? Is research required? What are the formatting and length guidelines? Highlight or underline key words. For additional clarity, reword the topic as a question to be answered.
Identify your purpose.	Ask yourself: What is my purpose as I read the assigned texts? When I write, will my purpose be to inform, to entertain, to evaluate or analyze, or to persuade?

WORKING WITH READINGS

Preview the reading and think about the topic.	Examine the title, headings, illustrations, and context to determine the topic. Make a guess about what the writer will say about the topic. Consider how the new information will fit into what you already know about the topic.
Read and annotate the text.	Annotate the thesis statement, major supporting points, and supporting details. Annotate any key words associated with the issue. Mark at least three potential quotes.
Outline and summarize each reading.	Write a brief outline that includes the thesis statement and major supporting points. Summarize the article in two or three sentences. In your summary, include the source's bibliographic information (author's name, title, and publication information), the topic, the writer's main idea, the major supporting points, and the significant supporting details.

(continued)

Prepare an information sheet for each reading.

List the source's bibliographic information and any other general notes. Add your outline, your brief summary, a list of issues addressed in the reading, a list of key words, and the quotes you have identified.

For more ideas, go back to "Read and annotate the text" and "Outline and summarize each reading."

DEVELOPING YOUR ESSAY

Synthesize your sources.

If you are using several sources, organize the ideas from all the sources. Determine the points the sources have in common and where the sources differ. Use a graphic organizer, such as a chart, to categorize and organize the ideas.

Prewrite to develop your ideas.

Use prewriting strategies (discussion, simple listing, clustering, journalistic questions, freewriting, and freetalking) to come up with topics, major supporting points, and supporting details.

For more ideas, go back to "Analyze your assignment."

Construct a thesis statement.

Write a thesis statement, a complete sentence in which you articulate your topic and your main point about the topic. Check that your thesis statement is not a statement of fact, a question, or an announcement and that it is not too broad.

Develop support for your thesis statement.

Determine your major supporting points. Develop supporting details for each major supporting point as content for your essay. Select text patterns (narration, definition, illustration, classification, comparison-contrast, cause and effect, process analysis) and features (such as examples and facts) to express the supporting details.

For more ideas, go back to "Prewrite to develop your ideas."

Create an outline to organize your essay.

Start with your topic and thesis statement. Express each major supporting point in a complete sentence. Add supporting details. Jot down ideas for the introduction and conclusion.

Add source materials to your outline.

Add to your outline references to where you might use information from the summaries you wrote, the quotes you identified, and any other source information you plan on using.

For more ideas, go back to "Read and annotate the text" and "Prepare an information sheet for each reading."

Write a complete draft of your essay.

Using your outline for guidance, write an introduction, body paragraphs, and a conclusion. Use the major supporting points as topic sentences for body paragraphs. Write as many paragraphs as you need to develop fully the essay's main idea. Decide where to place your thesis statement. Keep your audience's needs in mind as you write. Frequently reread your paper from the beginning to check the flow of ideas, to add needed information, and to reword passages for clarity.

(continued)

| Integrate ideas and quotes from sources correctly. | Follow these rules: (1) Copy direct quotations exactly from the source. (2) Integrate a quoted fragment grammatically into a complete sentence. (3) Use an attributive tag to integrate a quotation into your writing. (4) Start and end a quotation with quotation marks. (5) Place the sentence's period inside the quotation marks; if a parenthetical reference ends the quotation, place the period after the reference.

For more ideas, go back to "Read and annotate the text" and "Prepare an information sheet for each reading." |

FINISHING YOUR ASSIGNMENT

| Check that you have met assignment requirements. | Review your annotated assignment to make sure the content of your essay meets the requirements of the assignment.

For more ideas, go back to "Analyze your assignment." |

| Revise for organization and unity. | Ask yourself: Is the essay's organization logical? Do all the paragraphs relate to the main idea? Have I used transitions effectively? Make any necessary changes.

For more ideas, go back to "Create an outline to organize your essay." |

| Revise for development. | Ask yourself: Have I answered readers' potential questions? Have I included enough support for my thesis statement? Have I explained unfamiliar terms? Make any necessary changes.

For more ideas, go back to "Prewrite to develop your ideas." |

| Revise for clarity. | Ask yourself: Are the words I use concrete and specific? Is the tone appropriate? Are all pronoun references clear? |

| Create a works cited or references list. | If you used sources, create an MLA works cited list or an APA references list.

For more ideas, go back to "Integrate ideas and quotes from sources correctly." |

| Check for plagiarism. | Make sure you have given credit to sources: (1) Check that each summary, quotation, and idea from a source is credited with an attributive tag (*Jones said, . . .*) or a parenthetical reference. (2) Check that each source cited in your essay is listed correctly in the works cited or references list. |

| Edit your essay using SMART TRACS. | Check for grammatical errors that you have had trouble with in the past. Run a spell-checker. Use other methods, such as SMART TRACS, to find errors.

S = Spelling   T = Tense consistency
M = Missing words   R = Rhythm
A = Accurate punctuation   A = Active voice
R = Repeated words   C = Confusing words
T = Terminal punctuation   S = Sources |

| Put your essay in the proper format. | Follow your instructor's directions for formatting your paper in MLA style or APA style. |

QUICK START GUIDE
to Integrated Reading
and Writing

GETTING STARTED

- Put your essay in the proper format.
- Edit your writing using SMART TRACS.
- Check for plagiarism.
- Create a works cited or references list.
- Revise for clarity.
- Revise for development.
- Revise for organization and unity.
- Check that you have met assignment requirements.

FINISHING YOUR ASSIGNMENT

- Integrate ideas and quotes from sources correctly.
- Write a complete draft of your essay.
- Add source materials to your outline.
- Create an outline to organize your essay.
- Develop support for your thesis statement.
- Construct a thesis statement.
- Prewrite to develop your ideas.

DEVELOPING YOUR ESSAY

- Select memorable quotes from each reading.
- Summarize each reading.
- Outline each reading.
- Read and annotate for main ideas and supporting details.
- Preview readings for context and topic.

WORKING WITH READINGS

- Identify your purpose.
- Analyze your assignment.

PART 1

Planning for Success

Many students juggle a variety of responsibilities—working, studying, parenting—and try to fit in time for relaxation. What challenges do you face? How can you develop the skills you need and create a plan for success that will help you achieve your academic goals?

Critical Thinking Skills and Success Strategies

What are the two most important skills needed for success in college and at work? Computer literacy? A good attitude? A knack for doing research?

These skills are important, but they are not the *most* important ones. To succeed in college and at work, you must be able to read critically and write clearly. Every college course requires reading, and often your knowledge and abilities are assessed through writing assignments. Additionally, most jobs require employees to read carefully and critically, and many jobs require competent writing ability. In short, your ability to read and write well is a life skill.

The foundation for strong reading and writing skills is the ability to think clearly and critically. As you develop your critical thinking ability, your reading and writing skills will also improve. Picture thinking, reading, and writing as connected skills that continually reinforce one another:

- The more you practice critical thinking, the better you can read critically.
- The more you read critically, the better you can write.

Success in college and at work depends on building and improving these important skills.

CHAPTER OBJECTIVES

After completing this chapter, students will be able to do the following:

- **Explain the importance and interdependence of critical reading and writing skills.**
- **Define and practice critical thinking.**
- **Describe the foundations for college success.**

Connect IRW LearnSmart Achieve: Assign the topic "Reading and Writing as Complementary Processes" for adaptive learning to accompany the chapter.

Teaching Resources: See the Chapter Quiz.

READING CRITICALLY TO WRITE WELL

Reading critically—that is, reading the way students are expected to read in college—goes beyond basic reading in a number of ways. Reading critically means understanding relationships among the elements in a text. For example, when you read a chapter in a college textbook critically, you must determine which ideas are more important and which ideas are less important. You must also figure out whether ideas are contradictory or similar, and whether they are related. More complex tasks, such as understanding **inferences** (the unstated but suggested ideas in a text), are also part of critical reading. These are only a few of the important reading skills you will develop as you practice reading critically.

Strong writing skills are also necessary for college and career success. Your writing is often the primary way professors get to know you and your work. In a business class, for example, your instructor might come to know you by reading your ideas for improving a failed business. In a nursing class, your instructor might get to know you by reading the annotations you write on a patient's chart. The ability to write well often makes a difference when employees are considered for promotions. More importantly, strong writing reflects clear thinking. Because people get to know us through our writing, clear thinking and competent writing can profoundly affect our lives, choices, and opportunities.

How exactly does reading critically help you write better?

- When you read critically, you no longer see a static page of words: reading becomes a dialogue between you and the writer. Likewise, your own writing becomes a conversation between you and your reader. As a reader, you become aware of the information you need a writer to supply. For example, if a writer does not provide enough background information about a topic, you may feel frustrated.

- As you read critically, you begin to think about your needs as a reader. Thus, as you become more aware of what it takes to communicate with a reader, you write texts that better meet your reader's needs and expectations.

- When you read critically, you develop vocabulary skills. You learn new words and new forms of expression that you can employ later on in your own writing. As your vocabulary develops, your ability to think and write about complex issues increases.

- When you read critically, you learn to distinguish between more effective and less effective writing. You can tell whether writers have successfully made their points—or not. In turn, you become more adept at assessing the effectiveness of your own writing.

Teaching Resources: See the worksheet "Reading Critically" on reading literally vs. reading critically.

I like the way the writer explains the background information.

I'm going to explain some background information readers might need to know.

■ Reading critically leads to writing more carefully and competently.

■ When you look at the same city from two different perspectives, what insights can you gain?

• When you read critically, you discover models for good writing. As you become a more critical reader, you find writing techniques worth emulating in your own writing. For example, after noticing how convincingly a writer has used a comparison to make a point, you may decide to use a comparison in an essay of your own.

Learning to read critically takes practice. It helps to set aside regular times to read and to make sure your surroundings are comfortable and free of distractions. Keep reading material with you when you travel so that you can practice reading in spare moments. Remember to ask yourself questions as you read, and if possible, read with a pencil in hand and take notes. Finally, also take the time to read for fun—even magazines, gossip Web sites, and graphic novels.

Like reading, writing is a skill that is developed through practice. Many people think that writing well is a mysterious ability possessed from birth by lucky people like novelists and scholars. Anyone who has struggled to get words down on a page has had days when the words seem barely to drip out. Those same people, however, also experience times when the words seem to pour onto the page without effort. Even the best writers have both types of days. The more time you spend practicing writing, the more comfortable you will get with the ebb and flow of ideas. You will eventually develop a writing process that works—whether you are having a good day or a bad day.

By focusing on texts from the perspectives of both a reader and a writer, we become better thinkers in general. And when we think more critically, we understand and communicate better.

PRACTICE ❶ Predicting Reading and Writing Tasks for Your Future Career

Make a list of five careers you think might be interesting, such as being a national park ranger, a veterinarian, a small business owner, an event planner, or an environmental activist. On a separate sheet of paper, jot down the reading and writing tasks that might be involved in each career. If you cannot identify possible reading and writing tasks, discuss the career with someone in the field. Alternatively, consult the US Bureau of Labor Statistics' *Occupational Outlook Handbook* (available online) to determine the duties involved in each career.

Answers will vary.

1. _____

2. _____

3. _____

4. _____

5. _____

WHAT IS CRITICAL THINKING?

Critical thinking is the practice of forming and asking key questions about the texts you read and the situations you encounter in life. Critical thinkers go on to answer these key questions in order to form rational judgments and find creative solutions to problems.

One way to understand critical thinking is to consider examples of thinking that are *not* critical. For example, anyone who has children knows that kids do not always think critically, as the following dialogue illustrates:

Teaching Resources: See the *PowerPoint* presentation (PPT) "Understanding Critical Thinking."

TIMMY:	Mommy, I want this toy. Why can't I have it?
MOM:	I don't have the money for it.
TIMMY (digging through his mother's purse):	Look! Here's your credit card! You *do* have money, Mommy!

It's easy for adults to chuckle at this scene. Timmy is hopelessly naive about how money works. He assumes that having a credit card means having money. He cannot even think of the right questions—Will we have money to pay the credit card bill? Does the credit card even "work"?—much less ask them.

As adults, however, we can be equally naive. You would be in a situation similar to Timmy's. If you did not know that the amount of random access memory (RAM) in a computer affects the tasks it can accomplish, you would not know to ask about a computer's RAM. Similarly, if you had not figured out the tasks you would be doing on the computer, you could not ask the right questions about the components the computer should have.

An Example of Critical Thinking

While critical thinking sometimes relies on having background knowledge, it also involves being able to predict difficulties, question assumptions, and solve problems. In the workplace, being able to think critically often separates managers from lower-level employees.

Consider this scenario: Monica is a clerk at a rental car agency. It is a busy Friday afternoon, and lines of people are waiting to pick up rental vehicles for weekend travel. Monica's supervisor, Fred, who is the store manager, has to leave suddenly to handle a family emergency. Monica and Jill, another entry-level employee, are the only rental clerks available. They are managing to keep the lines moving and keep customers happy, much to Monica's relief.

A customer whom Monica recognizes—an administrative assistant for the local university's sports program—comes in the door. He greets Monica by name; he has done so much business with the rental agency that he has developed a warm relationship with all the employees. In fact, the agency relies on the university's business to meet its sales goals each month.

He bypasses the line of customers and asks to have a private word with Monica. An unexpected situation has come up, he says, and the basketball team needs three vans immediately. Monica doesn't even have to look at her computer to know that the agency's last three vans have already been reserved by customers who are waiting in line. She checks anyway, and sure enough, the vans are reserved. Pulling Jill aside, she asks her advice. Jill has no idea what to do. Monica texts Fred, but she gets no answer. She calls a nearby agency, but they have no vehicles of any sort available.

What should Monica do? Should she lease the vans to the loyal university customer and turn away the people who already have reservations? Surely, the company would do better financially to retain the university's business than to satisfy three casual customers. But would such an action be fair? What would her boss do, she wonders? What are the things she should consider to make this decision? What Monica needs is the ability to think critically—to weigh all of her options, think creatively about possible solutions, predict the consequences of her actions, and make an informed decision.

Teaching Resources: See the Instructor's Manual (IM) for critical thinking teaching ideas and see the "Critical Thinking Scenarios" worksheets.

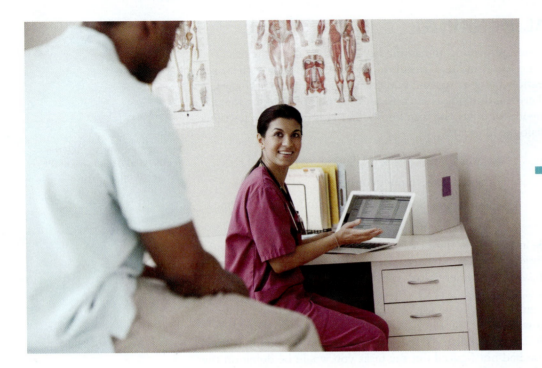

Health-care professionals use critical thinking to ask questions that lead them to a correct diagnosis. For example, if a patient presents with seizures, a nurse or physician's assistant might ask him whether he has taken drugs or has a history of neurological disorders. Knowing the right questions to ask requires critical thinking.

This same kind of thinking is required in college courses. Sometimes courses will require you to simply memorize information, a task that does *not* involve thinking critically. Often, however, your instructors will push you to think critically by requiring you to use that information in unpredictable ways. For example, on a math test, you may see problems that are not like the ones you studied and reviewed but whose solutions are possible if you apply the knowledge you have learned. In applying your knowledge to solve these problems, you are thinking critically, the way Monica has to think.

How Critical Thinking Affects Reading and Writing Skills

Just as there is more to running a rental car agency than following a list of instructions for checking out cars, there is more to comprehending a text than merely understanding its literal meaning. Critical reading requires us to ask questions: What does this writer want me to believe? How might this writer benefit if I believe what he has to say? What assumptions is he making? Do I agree with those assumptions?

Good writing also depends on critical thinking. We can teach a computer to construct grammatically correct sentences, but a computer cannot write convincing essays. It cannot analyze its audience, and it cannot analyze its own assumptions. It cannot think of the critical questions that need to be asked. Such questions include much more complex inquiries than simply "How many pages should this essay be?" Effective writers ask a variety of questions that help them focus their writing. For example, a writer might ask herself whether she should use the term *woman* or *lady* in a composition. She might wonder if an audience is likely to respond more positively to one term than the other. Her analysis can help her choose the more appropriate term for her purpose. This kind of critical questioning will help her anticipate readers' responses and consequently become a better writer. Just as Monica's questions can help her determine the right course of action, critical thinking about your writing will help you determine how to word your ideas and communicate your thoughts effectively. Practice your critical thinking skills by completing the exercise that follows.

PRACTICE 2 Thinking Critically

The following passage describes a scheduling problem for Lin, a freshman in college. Read the passage, and then use critical thinking to answer the questions on a separate sheet of paper.

Answers will vary.

> Lin lives with his parents and is in his second semester in college. He is considering renting an apartment with his best friend. The apartment is within walking distance from campus, so Lin believes he will save on gasoline and make better use of campus resources if he lives in the apartment. Lin would need to work about twenty-five hours a week to afford the apartment and related expenses. His part-time job offers him only fifteen hours a week, but he plans to ask his supervisor for more hours. He has three weeks to decide whether he wants to rent the apartment or remain at his parents' house.

1. List the questions Lin should ask before making this decision.
2. List the potential problems that could arise if Lin were to rent the apartment with his friend.
3. Which of these potential problems could Lin prevent or overcome?
4. If these problems were to occur, how would they affect Lin?
5. Based on your critical thinking, is this a risk worth taking? Why or why not? What advice would you give Lin? Explain in a paragraph.

THE FOUNDATIONS FOR COLLEGE SUCCESS

Researchers who study the reasons for college success and the obstacles preventing it have identified several characteristics of successful students:

- Students who succeed are self-directed.
- Students who succeed use resources effectively.
- Students who succeed manage their time well.
- Students who succeed are self-reflective.

Students Who Succeed Are Self-Directed

People who are self-directed are in charge of their own learning experiences. They find a way to learn. They do not depend solely on a textbook or on an instructor or on having the perfect learning situation. They do not wait for an instructor's advice to go to a tutoring center. They take the initiative to find the resources they need for success.

Consider, for example, the situation of Jenny, a self-directed learner. She makes sure to buy her textbooks before the semester begins so she is prepared for class, and she reviews her class notebook or folder before each class session. This semester Jenny is taking an algebra class. She begins to realize that every time her instructor discusses multiplying and dividing fractions, she gets lost. As a self-directed learner, Jenny goes to the library, checks out a book on basic mathematics, and reviews the rules for working with fractions. She could also do a quick Internet search for information, visit a learning center, or talk to her instructor.

One way to work on being self-directed is to use a learning journal. A **learning journal** is a place to record your thoughts and goals, any obstacles to those goals, and new insights. By writing down these reflections, you are better able to analyze them. Journaling is a way to think about the things that happen to you, beyond just experiencing them. It is a way to take a step back and view yourself as a learner.

The goal in keeping a learning journal is to reflect on the concepts you are encountering and to learn about yourself. The goal is not to write perfect sentences, so do not be overly concerned with grammar. To start a learning journal, find a dedicated space to keep your writing, such as a spiral notebook or a computer file. Some students use smartphones with digital voice recording to keep track of their thoughts. By periodically reviewing your journal, you will become aware of just how much you are learning in college.

Students Who Succeed Use Resources Effectively

Resources are the tools that are available to you as you work on a task. To succeed in college, you need to use a variety of tools: your textbooks, the learning labs on campus, your supportive friends and family, computer software, Web sites, and so on. Identifying the correct tools to use for academic tasks requires careful thinking, and it also requires that you know what tools are at hand. Two categories of tools, in particular, can assist your journey through college: human resources and content resources.

Human Resources

Human resources are the people around you who can provide help:

- Your instructors are your best resources. Do not hesitate either to visit your instructors during their office hours or to e-mail them. Professors welcome their students' questions and office visits.

- Look around your classes to identify peers with whom you might be able to connect. Consider swapping e-mail addresses with one or two classmates so you can discuss assignments or keep up with class notes in case of absences. Of course, always use care about giving your personal information to anyone. A campus e-mail address is a fairly safe way to chat with a classmate, but it might *not* be wise to give out your phone number or address.

■ We learn from tutors in many areas of our lives. Find a tutor with whom you feel comfortable, and develop a working relationship with him or her.

- You can also form study groups to discuss course assignments. Such groups can meet on a regular basis or only when necessary.
- Lab instructors or tutors can also be excellent resources for professional feedback on papers or for help with complex assignments.
- If your campus has a writing center, use it. Writing center instructors or tutors are specially trained to help with reading and writing assignments. Do not hesitate to ask a writing center instructor for help with your reading course.
- Additionally, student success counselors and librarians have been trained to help students succeed.

Once you have identified the available human resources on your campus, take the next step—use them! Regularly interacting with instructors and others on campus who are there to help will make a significant difference to your academic success.

PRACTICE ❸ Finding Human Resources

Using college directories, the Internet, and conversations with your instructors and classmates, construct a list of human resources available to you.

Answers will vary.

Consider starting with a class discussion on how to locate resources.

Type of Resource	Name	Phone/E-mail	Hours/Location
Instructor			
Classmate			
Librarian			
Tutor			
Lab instructor			
Others			

Content Resources

Textbooks, library reference books, *YouTube* and *TeacherTube* videos, reading comprehension Web sites, online writing labs (OWLs), and search engines are only a few of the content resources that can help you succeed in college. These resources can often help you with questions you have about coursework and careers. Librarians can help you locate a wealth of valuable content resources. In addition, writing textbooks and carefully chosen Internet sites can be useful.

When choosing Internet content resources, be careful. Some Web sites that appear at first to be helpful are actually commercial sites that exist to sell educational products—or plagiarized essays. Use these principles to guide your search for credible Internet study resources:

- **Check to see whether the Web site is associated with a college or university.** Usually, *.edu* in a Web address tells you the source is housed at a college or university. Often instructors post helpful study information on their personal college Web pages. Be aware, though, that student Web sites may also have an *.edu* address; these sites are less likely to provide credible resources than instructor-created Web pages.
- **Use the online resources that are available from your textbook publisher.** Many publishers make available study resources on the Internet free of charge. For example, if you search for "sentence fragments" and "McGraw-Hill" (the publisher of this textbook), you will find a variety of Web resources, such as tutorials, *Power-Point* slides, and practice quizzes.

Purdue OWL: **Sentence Fragments**
owl.english.purdue.edu › OWL › General Writing › Mechanics ▾
Feb 21, 2013 - This handout provides an overview and examples of
sentence fragments.

Sentence Fragments - Guide to Grammar and Writing
grammar.ccc.commnet.edu/grammar/fragments.htm ▾
Sentence Fragments: How to Find and Repair them.

■ A search on *Google* for "sentence fragments" brings up a long list of sites. The information in the Web addresses can help you identify credible and potentially helpful Web sites.

PRACTICE ④ Finding Online Resources

Using a computer search engine such as *Google* or *Yahoo,* find a Web site that provides the particular type of information listed for each item.

Answers will vary. See the IM for Web searching tips, and suggested Web sites.

Information Needed	Web Site You Found	Features of Web Site
For a psychology class: help understanding a reference to "Pavlov's dogs"		
For a geology class: help understanding how the Richter scale works		
For a health careers class: practice quizzes to help you learn medical terminology		
For a math class: a video that reviews exponents		

- **When you open a Web site, click on a few items to see how thoroughly the information is covered.** For example, students post questions to social media sites, but the answers are often not very helpful, as you will see when you read the postings. Look for Web sites that do not allow users to post their own answers to questions.

Students Who Succeed Manage Their Time Well

Time management is a necessity in almost every area of life. Good time management starts with assessing your time commitments honestly and carefully. Logging your commitments on a calendar—whether on paper, on a computer, or on your smartphone—is one way to realistically view what you need to get done. There are a variety of ways to sync online calendars to smartphones. Use technology to help you when possible, but make sure that you manage your electronic devices and that they do not manage you:

- Turn off your phone when you study.
- Use your phone's alarm and calendar to keep track of due dates.
- Reward yourself with *Facebook* and other social media *after* you have finished your course work for the day.

To make a time management system, use a simple chart that lists the days of the week and the hours of each day. Input your commitments, and schedule your study time.

Teaching Resources: See the IM for research and teaching ideas about the effects of multitasking.

Teaching Resources: See the reproducible "Time Management Chart."

Time	Sun.	Mon.	Tues.	Wed.	Thurs.	Fri.	Sat.
Dana's Time Management Plan							
6 a.m.							
7							
8							
9							
10							
11							
Noon							
1 p.m.							
2							
3							
4							
5							
6							
7							
8							
9							
10							

KEY
- Class
- Family/children
- Lab/study time
- Study time
- Work

Be sure to leave some hours open for flexibility. Also, be aware of your habits and preferences. If you are not a "morning person," do not schedule study time before morning classes. For example, see Dana's Time Management Plan above, which was created by a student who works part-time and is also a parent.

Another way to make sure you have time for everything in your life is to predict the circumstances that will affect your time and inhibit your success. For example, commitments to children, spouses, and employers can unexpectedly interfere with your best intentions to study. By predicting these situations, you can find ways to deal with them. One way to make sure you have uninterrupted study time is to be intentional about constructing a plan that allows time for each aspect of your life, and then stick to your plan. Make others aware of your plan so they can help you follow it.

Making small changes can be a good strategy for improving time management. You may not be able to spend three hours each day studying, but you may be able to find an hour in the morning and an hour at night. Similarly, if you have downtime during your day—for example, waiting in line to pick up children or commuting to work on public transportation—use it to read and work on assignments. Keep energy bars, earplugs, and any other helpful items in your backpack so that you can make the most of your time. Planning ahead and using your time wisely can result in major benefits.

PRACTICE 5 Creating a Time Management Plan

Follow these directions to create a time management plan.   *Answers will vary.*

1. On a separate sheet of paper, list small changes that will help you be a successful student.

(Continued)

2. Choose two or three of these changes, and come up with an action plan to implement them. Some examples are waking up earlier, studying during a certain time period every day, packing a lunch for the day, and avoiding procrastination.

3. Fill in the chart with the changes you selected and how you will make them.

Small Change	How I Will Make This Change

Students Who Succeed Are Self-Reflective

Reflecting is simply taking time to think about something in order to understand it or learn from it. *Self-reflection* is looking at your behaviors and feelings from the outside so that you can see yourself more objectively.

We can all think of someone—perhaps an acquaintance, a friend, or even a family member—who makes the same mistakes repeatedly. Perhaps this person is always late or cannot maintain a relationship. It is easy to see the person's faults, and most likely, we can see what causes his failures. But it is much more difficult for us to view ourselves as objectively. Self-reflection is an attempt to do just that.

To practice self-reflection, imagine yourself floating to the top of a room and looking down at yourself, noting the things you are saying and doing. The goal is to be able to see yourself as others see you. Think about yourself as a student. Which of your behaviors sabotage your success? Which behaviors work for you? Self-reflective analysis will help you view your strengths and weaknesses more objectively so you can become the kind of learner and person you want to be.

Writing a Self-Reflective Analysis

One way to become a successful learner is to use self-reflection to assess your strengths and weaknesses. Below is a list of questions that one student, Monty, used as a guide in writing a self-reflective analysis.

QUESTIONS FOR SELF-REFLECTION

1. How would you describe your personality?
2. Think of three previous instructors you have had. How might each instructor describe you as a learner?
3. When you reflect on yourself as a learner, do you find yourself agreeing with your former teachers' descriptions? If not, what would you say these teachers did not know about you?
4. How would you describe yourself—at your best—as a student?
5. At your worst, what kind of student are you?
6. How would you finish the following sentence? "[Your name] will be very successful in college and in life if [she/he] . . ."

What follows is the self-reflective analysis written by Monty in response to these questions. Notice how most of Monty's analysis is written in third person. Instead of saying "I" or "me," he writes from the perspective of another person so that he can see himself more objectively.

■ According to Plato, the ancient Greek philosopher Socrates said that "the unexamined life is not worth living." What do you think Socrates meant?

Teaching Resources: See the IM for ideas about using self-reflective journal assignments, creating blogs for self-reflection, and using Connect IRW for self-reflective assignments.

Monty's Self-Reflection

1. Monty is a really nice guy. He is easy to get along with and funny sometimes, and he will offer help to anyone who needs it. He has never been afraid of hard work, although he likes to be lazy on the weekends. He is a great Web page designer, a good driver, and a pretty good cook.

2. Previous teachers might describe Monty like this:

   • "He is shy when it comes to answering questions in class or even asking questions. He is not shy about cracking a joke and can make us laugh sometimes."

   • "He is an average student, but he does not always turn in his work on time. I know he could make higher grades if he took more interest in the subject and turned work in on time."

   • "I like Monty but wish he would take school more seriously."

3. I would agree with most of the teachers' statements, but I would disagree about not being interested in the subject. I am usually interested but just do not have the confidence to speak up in class, or maybe I just have not done all the reading, so I do not feel very sure of myself. I do not want to be asked questions. The last teacher's comment is right: I could take school more seriously.

4. At best, Monty is a great student. He does the reading for class, gets to every class on time, listens to everything the teacher says, and does not cut up in class too much.

5. At worst, Monty can almost be depressed. He can oversleep and stay in bed too long, put off doing his homework assignments, and feel as if college does not matter.

6. Monty will be very successful in college and in life if he takes college seriously and does the things he knows he should do—study, wake up on time, be in class, and maybe ask questions or make comments in class on occasion. He will also be more successful if he limits his time creating Web pages, his favorite hobby.

Complete the following exercise about Monty's self-reflective analysis. Then use Monty's questions to write your own analysis.

PRACTICE ⑥ Writing a Self-Reflective Analysis

Write a self-reflective analysis about yourself as a student, using Monty's analysis as a guide.   Answers will vary.

1. To begin, answer the following questions about Monty's analysis.

   a. Which strengths does Monty identify about himself?

   b. Which weaknesses does Monty identify about himself?

   c. Does Monty's self-reflection seem believable? In other words, does it seem as though he is being truly honest about his strengths and weaknesses? Why or why not?

   d. What can Monty learn from his self-reflection? What would be the best insights he could gain from it?

2. Now, using Monty's self-reflection as a model, compose your own. Use the same questions and instructions Monty used to compose his analysis.

CHAPTER ACTIVITIES

A READING AND WRITING ASSIGNMENT

The critical thinking, reading, and writing skills we discuss in this text not only apply to college success but also affect workplace success. What follows is an article entitled "Employability Skills: Your Trump Card." As you read the article, underline at least three important pieces of advice that you will use to prepare for a future career. A writing assignment follows the article.

Employability Skills: Your Trump Card

Lexile: 1030L

Two guys—let's call them Ace and Joker—have associate's degrees from the same community college. They have obtained basically the same level of academic knowledge and the same technical skills. They both held jobs while in high school and in college. Yet Ace is a much more attractive job candidate to managers who are recruiting workers. Why?

Everyone would agree that having basic knowledge and stock technical abilities is essential for career readiness. However, in addition to academic and technical competencies, a third category of abilities is critical for career readiness: employability skills.

Employability skills, sometimes called *work-readiness* or *job-readiness skills,* are a set of competencies and behaviors that are necessary for *every* type of job. Acquiring them *and* being able to demonstrate to prospective employers that you possess them are crucial to employment success.

Foundational Skills

Being a good employee depends on some very basic, foundational skills. While these qualities may seem too obvious to be highlighted, employers express frustration at how few workers possess them.

Joker pads his time sheet by adding a half-hour here and fifteen minutes there. Ace is totally honest about the hours that he works.

Honesty and trustworthiness are indispensable qualities in the workplace. If an employer cannot trust a worker, every aspect of the work environment becomes overly complicated.

Ace shows up for work on time every single day. Joker comes in on time some days but straggles in a few minutes late about as often. Ace finishes his assignments on time; Joker frequently has excuses about why he was unable to get an assigned project completed by the deadline.

Dependability is vital. Employees need to show up on time every day (unless they have a valid excuse). Completing every task is another dimension of dependability. A staff member who completes tasks as assigned, without prompting and by the deadline, is a very valuable employee.

When Ace goofs up, he admits it; when he borrows an idea from coworkers, he gives them credit. Joker, on the other hand, frequently tries to blame others when things go wrong, and he regularly takes credit for the insights and accomplishments of others.

Employers greatly appreciate staff members who take responsibility for their own decisions and actions. If you make a mistake, own it. If someone else came up with a worthwhile idea, give credit where credit is due.

Ace is aware of the benefits of his job, and he remembers all too well the frustration and discouragement he felt when he was unemployed. Joker, on the other hand, seems to consistently see only the negative side of his job.

Having a positive attitude toward work is a wonderful characteristic. You don't have to "whistle while you work," but being upbeat matters. Nobody relishes working with a grumbler; coworkers and supervisors alike appreciate someone with a can-do attitude.

Joker catches on to new tasks quickly, but he often tires of doing the work and fails to complete assignments. If Joker is the hare, Ace is the tortoise. He sees every project through to the end.

Workers need to exert high levels of effort and persistence. Working hard and keeping at it will not only enable you to accomplish more, but your persistence will be noticed by colleagues and superiors. To some employers, a college degree is more important as evidence of perseverance than of knowledge.

Whenever an unexpected crisis occurs, Joker freaks out and has a hard time recovering. Ace, however, rolls with the punches; he is able to adjust on the fly.

Flexibility is highly valued by employers. Many of us like routine; however, in every work environment, unanticipated events occur, often upsetting the regular order of affairs. Workers who can adapt to changing situations are especially valuable.

Ace "looks the part." He comes to work dressed and groomed appropriately. Joker, conversely, will often show up for work looking disheveled, lacking some part of his uniform, and generally resembling a slob.

Understanding and following the dress code or uniform guidelines should be a given in every work context. Employees must always be presentable and pay attention to personal hygiene.

Interpersonal Skills

In most work environments, there are three groups with whom a person interacts: customers or clients, coworkers or colleagues, and managers or supervisors. Relating well to all three groups is vital for success in the workplace.

Many of Joker's customers view him as a jerk. Ace's goal, on the other hand, is to help all his customers feel better about their day after their encounter with him.

Anyone who works with customers must be friendly and polite and must respond appropriately to their requests. Although it is not always the case that "the customer is always right," that assumption is an excellent beginning point in dealing with customers.

Everybody likes a team player, and that is how Ace's colleagues characterize him. Joker's associates, in contrast, comment about how they often have to do his part of an assignment.

Good employees respect and work well with coworkers, even those they do not like. It's crucial to be compatible enough with everyone in the workplace to make a successful team. Consider basketball as an analogy. Although it would be great if the players on a team liked one another, it is not really necessary. As long as they communicate with one another and each player performs his or her role, they can be successful as a team.

Joker always seems to be in conflict with his supervisor. Different jobs, different managers—it doesn't seem to matter; there's always tension between Joker and his boss.

The manner in which employees relate to their supervisors is absolutely critical to job success. Employees must treat their supervisors with respect, despite their personal feelings toward them. As an employee, you must respect the *role* even if you do not respect the *individual*.

If Ace's boss tells him that he could do better work, Ace views it as a "gift" from his supervisor. Ace wants to be better at what he does, so he appreciates guidance in that regard—even if he doesn't necessarily enjoy being corrected.

Effective employees take constructive criticism to heart and consider it carefully. No one enjoys being criticized, but effective employees understand that their supervisors offer criticism to guide, not to insult. Good workers don't reflexively reject criticism. Rather, they use it to gain insight and improve their performance on the job.

Whether relating to customers, coworkers, or supervisors, employees inevitably encounter conflict at work. Being able to resolve conflict successfully is a very important interpersonal skill. The successful resolution of conflict lies between two extremes. One extreme is to react to a clash defensively and aggressively. The other extreme is to respond by withdrawing and acting as though no issue exists. Neither of those reactions is productive. If conflict is respectful, honest, sincere, and kind, then it isn't confrontational at all—and it can be very fruitful!

Problem-Solving Skills

Every job involves problem solving: How can we produce our goods or provide our services faster, better, more efficiently? How do we address the roadblocks that inevitably arise? It's not surprising that problem-solving skills routinely rank at the top of the list of desirable traits for prospective staff members. Problem solving involves both critical thinking and creative thinking.

When Joker sees a problem at work, he criticizes his supervisors for not having solved it. On the rare occasions when Joker has a suggestion, he throws out an idea without having thought it through. He skips steps—he tends to go from A to C without explaining how to get there, and then he is unhappy when no one thinks his plan is worthwhile. Ace constructs a plan with his audience in mind— whether that is customers or his boss or someone else. He realizes that they cannot fill in unexplained gaps.

Critical thinking involves recognizing and clarifying a problem. What issue, precisely, is it that needs to be addressed? Identifying possible solutions and then ranking them in terms of preferability is a next step. Constructing a step-by-step explanation as to how the approach selected would be implemented is the final stage. (You can see how courses in math and science provide students with training in critical thinking;

although the particular issues in a job setting may not be algebra problems or chemistry experiments, the *method* learned in these academic courses can be applied in a multiplicity of situations.)

> *Joker never seems to come up with any fresh ideas. He offers the same, tired approaches even when they have not worked in the past or when new issues arise on the job. Ace, in contrast, thinks creatively.*

While critical thinking emphasizes the rigorous, analytical type of thinking that we associate with math and science, creative thinking is just as important. Innovative thinking is highly valued in most work environments. Just as the relationship between critical thinking and courses in math and science is clear, so too is the parallel between creative thinking and "artistic" academic courses. Courses in the visual and performing arts—drama, music, art, dance—provide examples of how artists conceive new and imaginative creations. Moreover, academic study in areas less commonly thought of as creative can be very helpful as well. Engineering, marketing, and education courses—to name a few—promote innovative thinking, too.

Conclusion

The skills described here are the attributes that workforce managers repeatedly indicate they desire in their employees. People who are looking for employment opportunities—or better jobs than they currently hold—must possess both employability skills and specific job skills. Additionally, when applying for a job, people need to convey their employability skills in the application process. Employability skills can be added to a résumé, discussed in an interview, or demonstrated while networking. Perhaps most importantly, a person who demonstrates these employability skills in every aspect of his life will impress potential employers as unique.

> Who would not want to hire Ace?

Questions for Consideration

1. What are employability skills? Write two to three sentences defining them.
2. How do employability skills differ from academic and technical skills?
3. Read through the section describing the foundational skills employees should have. In what other contexts are these skills important? Explain.
4. On the left side of a sheet of paper, list all the employability skills discussed in the article. Next to each skill, write a sentence explaining whether you possess the skill, are working on acquiring the skill, or have not developed the skill yet. How would an employer view your abilities as a potential employee on the basis of the list you created? Which of these skills do you plan to work on developing? Explain in a paragraph.

Responding to the Reading

1. Reread Monty's self-reflection. Compare his strengths and weaknesses to the employability skills discussed in "Employability Skills: Your Trump Card." If Monty had to choose two areas to work on immediately, which two should they be? Write

Questions for Consideration

1. Employability skills go beyond job or academic skills and include thinking critically, working well with others, having personal integrity, and taking responsibility for one's actions.
2. Academic skills include reading, writing, and solving problems. Technical skills are specialized job-related abilities (knowing how to weld, administer medication, or program a computer). The need for technical and academic skills may differ, but everyone needs employability skills.
3. Employability skills are important in nearly every situation; e.g., dependability is important no matter what the task.
4. Answers will vary.

Answers will vary.

two or three paragraphs defending your answer. Use the Quick Start Guide to Integrated Reading and Writing Assignments for guidance.

2. Choose three employability skills that you need to develop more fully. Write a paragraph about each skill in which you do the following:

   • Explain why you believe you need to develop the skill.
   • Provide an example of a time when you would have been more successful if you had possessed the skill.
   • Finish the paragraph with ideas for how you can develop the missing skill.

3. Using the "Employability Skills" article for ideas, write an essay in which you identify the top five employability skills required for a job in which you are interested. Explain why each skill is important for the job you choose. For example, if you would like to be a nurse, you might discuss the importance of problem solving.

THINKING FROM AN INSTRUCTOR'S POINT OF VIEW

Answers will vary.

Instructors know they are preparing students not only for academic success but also for proficiency in the workplace. Consequently, most instructors expect workplace behaviors from their students. The behaviors employers expect from workers include the following:

• Arrive on time to work and stay until the shift is finished.

• Listen carefully to directions.

• Do the work correctly.

• Stay focused and productive (no personal calls, texts to friends, or excessive conversing with coworkers).

• Use a respectful tone and respectful language.

You can probably think of several other behaviors that employers expect. Now, try thinking from an instructor's point of view. You are responsible for teaching your students the course content, but you also want to prepare them for workplace success. Additionally, you want your students to use behaviors that will help them succeed in college.

If you were an instructor, what kinds of policies would you create to make sure your students' behaviors contributed to their learning and to their future workplace success? Answer in three or four paragraphs, explaining how each of your ideas would contribute to success in college and at work.

ADDITIONAL ASSIGNMENTS

Answers will vary.

1. Think of a job or a class you had in the past in which discipline and behavior were not good. What was the problem? What could your employer or instructor have done differently to make student or worker behaviors more acceptable? Write two or three paragraphs to explain.

2. Think of a time when you made a decision without thinking critically about it. Perhaps you told a lie to a person you loved or bought something expensive on an impulse. What decision did you make? What process did you use to make the decision? Why do you think you made the decision without thinking critically? What steps should you have taken to make a better, more-informed decision? Write two or three paragraphs to explain.

3. If you made a time management chart in response to Practice 5, exchange charts with a classmate. Ask your classmate questions that might help her think critically about her time planning. For example, if you notice she has scheduled a study

session from 5:00 a.m. to 6:00 a.m., you might ask her if such an early hour is reasonable for her. (Some people could not consistently wake up that early, while others are naturally early risers.) Find potential areas of time conflict, and ask her about them. Have your classmate do the same for you. Revise your time management chart as needed.

4. Earlier in this chapter, you read about four characteristics that make students successful. Here is a restatement of the list:

   - Students who succeed are self-directed.
   - Students who succeed use resources effectively.
   - Students who succeed manage their time well.
   - Students who succeed are self-reflective.

For each of these four characteristics, write a brief paragraph in which you do the following:

   a. Explain what the characteristic means. For example, what does it mean to be self-directed?
   b. Make a judgment about yourself regarding the characteristic. To what extent are you self-directed?
   c. Provide an example of a time you exhibited the characteristic. When were you self-directed?
   d. Finally, describe one way you plan to exhibit the characteristic this semester. For example, you might say that this semester, if you receive a failing grade on an assignment (or a grade you do not like), you will figure out why you received the grade and will make a plan to do better on the next assignment.

 EMOTIONAL INTELLIGENCE

We all have good moods and bad moods. People who are "emotionally intelligent" can explain their moods and the likely reasons for them. They can do something else, as well: they can find ways to regulate their moods when doing so is desirable. Psychologists suggest that people who can control their moods have much better relationships and are happier and more successful than people who cannot. Have you ever intentionally *controlled* a mood? For example, perhaps you went to work one day feeling irritated and snapped at your coworkers. Realizing the effects of your mood on others, you decided to breathe deeply, relax, and say only kind things the rest of the day. If you have managed to control a mood, what methods worked for you? What might have happened if you had not taken control of your mood? Explain in a paragraph.

Answers will vary.

 CULTURAL LITERACY

A culture consists of the behaviors, expectations, customs, and rules (both written and unwritten) of a group of people. Colleges have their own cultures. Think about your college. What are some ways students are expected to act? What are some unwritten rules and behaviors on campus? Here are some examples:

Answers will vary.

- In college, students take out their class materials without being instructed to do so by the professor.
- Most college students act more politely in class than many high school students do.

Make a list of at least five behaviors, expectations, customs, or rules you have found in the culture of your college.

CRITICAL THINKING

Attending college is an experience that many students find new and challenging. Nevertheless, college is in some ways similar to each of the situations below—although some of the comparisons are better than others. Think about each of the following comparisons. Which is most likely to help you succeed in college? Why?

Answers will vary.

- Going to college is like going to high school.
- Going to college is like going to a job.
- Going to college is like going to prison.
- Going to college is like going to a doctor.

Write a few sentences explaining your answer.

METACOGNITION

Think about a college or high school class that you found very difficult. Imagine that you can watch a video of how you behaved (studied, attended, listened, questioned, spoke, read, and so on) during that class. What would the video show you doing? Describe the video in a paragraph. What insight can you gain by looking at yourself *from outside*?

Answers will vary.

PART 2

Reading and Writing as Integrated Processes

One way to learn new skills and techniques is to emulate the skills and techniques of experts. What skills—physical or mental—have you practiced or even perfected by observing other people at work?

Annotating Texts and Developing Vocabulary

The writer Stephen King has said, "If you don't have time to read, you don't have the time (or the tools) to write. Simple as that." What King means is that to become a good writer, you have to read. And the more you read, the better you can write.

Why does reading play such a significant role in writing ability? Reading and writing processes are two sides of the same coin. When we read actively and critically, paying close attention to the text, we cannot help but learn how writing works.

To help with paying close attention, we can use annotation—making notes on a text. In addition, we can use strategies to develop our vocabulary. These two techniques—learning to annotate and building vocabulary—are foundational for becoming both a better reader and a better writer.

CHAPTER OBJECTIVES

After completing this chapter, students will be able to do the following:

- **Use reading to improve their writing.**
- **Annotate a text for its content and features.**
- **Determine the meanings of words and build vocabulary.**

Connect IRW LearnSmart Achieve: Assign the topics, "Reading and Writing as Complementary Processes" and "Reading, Vocabulary, and Study Skills" for adaptive learning to accompany the chapter.

Teaching Resources: See the Chapter Quiz.

USING READING TO IMPROVE WRITING

Whether we are reading for analysis or for pleasure, reading has an effect on our writing ability through unintentional and intentional emulation. *Emulation* means doing the same thing as someone else. A high school basketball player, for example, may emulate the moves of his favorite NBA star.

Unintentional Emulation

When you read, you begin to understand on an unconscious level how language works. Have you ever started using a word you learned from a friend?

If so, you probably did not make an intentional decision to use that word; the word just began to appear in your vocabulary. Although you are not consciously aware of it, your brain records information such as words and phrases. (Think about all the clichés you have learned unintentionally—for example, *seeing eye to eye, easy as pie, love is blind.*)

Our brain also records information about the features of texts we read. For example, if we read several texts that begin with questions, we sometimes find ourselves writing a text that starts with a question. This process is called **unintentional emulation.** People who read frequently often write well because they have a wealth of information to draw on from unintentional emulation.

Intentional Emulation

We can also use our reading to study texts purposefully and use them to become better writers. This method is **intentional emulation.** It involves carefully analyzing the techniques writers use to communicate effectively. Once we analyze the techniques, we can then practice using them in our own writing. The purpose of intentional emulation is to develop a toolbox of writing strategies we can use as we compose our own texts.

Imagine you are taking a business communications class. Your instructor asks you to read and analyze a memo, which you will then use as a model for a writing assignment. In the memo, a company is recalling an unsafe product. To use the memo as a model, you would start by noticing its key features and the kinds of information it includes.

Recall Notice	Title
Industrial Food Products, Inc.	Company name
January 16, 2014	Date
Name of product: Industrial Honey Mustard, 12-oz. plastic bottles	Name of product and important descriptive information
Hazard: The sealing mechanism on certain bottles of mustard did not work properly, posing a risk of contaminated product.	Reason for recall
Remedy: Consumers should immediately stop using Industrial Honey Mustard if purchased in 12-oz. plastic bottles between June 15, 2013, and January 16, 2014. Consumers may obtain a full refund by returning the product to the place of purchase or by contacting Industrial Food Products.	What consumers should do
Consumer Contact: Industrial Food Products, 11114 Ellison Blvd., Hannington, IL 56565. Toll-free number: (800) 555-0199 from 8 a.m. to 5 p.m. CST, Monday through Friday.	Contact information

Vocabulary Collection Word:
mechanism

Your in-context definition:

_____

_____

A dictionary definition:

_____

_____

Try your hand at intentional emulation by completing the following practice exercise.

PRACTICE ① Using Intentional Emulation

Imagine your company, Eft Toy Company, has created an unsafe product, the Tough and Ready Tool Belt. The belt has small parts that can come off and pose a choking hazard to young children. The toy was sold at Aim retail stores between June 13, 2013, and October 15, 2013.

Answers will vary.

Using the model from Industrial Food Products, write a memo issuing a product recall notice for Eft Toy Company, 14500 Nelson Dr., Winnipeg, LA 87777, phone 800-555-0199, hours 8 a.m. to 5 p.m. CST, Monday through Friday.

DEVELOPING ANNOTATION SKILLS

Like most people, you read for a variety of reasons: to find an answer, to study, to learn, to relax, and to be entertained. Developing your reading and writing skills for college requires you to go a step beyond casual reading: it requires you to practice reading critically. Reading critically is reading to determine not only *what* writers are saying but also *how* they communicate their messages.

One way to start reading critically is to begin annotating. **Annotation** is reading a text and marking points that are important and items about which you have questions. Most students have experience highlighting words or phrases. While this is one way to annotate, it is not the only way or even the best way. Annotating is a way of reading actively. When you read actively, or critically, you are engaged in a conversation with the writer. Think of annotation as a way to deepen that conversation.

Annotation Tips

Many of the annotation tips shown here require that you write in your books. You may not be comfortable writing in books because you have always been told that marking books ruins them (true for a library book!), but writing in your books is one of the best ways to make sure that you're getting the most out of the time you spend reading.

Tips for Annotating Readings	
Mark new information	Mark only information that is new to you. If you already know something, there's no need to mark it.
Use highlighters sparingly	If the page is covered with yellow by the time you're done reading, the important information won't stand out. Only about 20 percent of a page should be annotated, and even less than that should be highlighted.
Focus on vocabulary	Save the yellow highlighter for definitions. That will make them really stand out. Circle words you do not know. Look them up and write the definition in the margins.
Use different colors	Use different colored pens for different types of information. For example, underline the main idea of a paragraph in red and write "main idea" in the margin. Use a blue pen to write your questions in the margins.

Teaching Resources: See the *PowerPoint* presentation (PPT) "Annotation Strategies That Work."

(continued)

Tips for Annotating Readings *(continued)*	
Talk to the text	Ask the writer questions: "Why true?" "Always the case?" Note when you agree or disagree with the text. Make connections between different parts of a text: "Said something different on p. 50." Make connections between the text and your experience: "Just like M's habits."
Make comparisons	Start a dialogue between the text you are marking and others you have read. Do the authors agree with one another? Make shorthand notes in the margins about other writers' views: "Smith disagrees; says air pollution is only getting worse."
Develop a system of codes	Use a question mark for something you aren't sure about, an exclamation point for something you find particularly interesting, and a star next to the main idea.
Use sticky notes	Write a word or two on a sticky note so you can quickly find the important information you have flagged: "Stats about pollution." Use these sticky notes sparingly, like a highlighter. Too many notes make it hard to identify what is important.
Summarize	When you're finished reading, put the main ideas in your own words. Summarizing is an excellent way to make sure you've understood what the reading is about.

Think about how convenient it would be to have the writers of the texts we read sit next to us during the reading process. We could ask a variety of questions, such as these:

- What did you mean by that phrase?
- How do you know this information?
- Why did you choose to include an example in this spot but not in this spot?
- Is this story true?
- Would you please define that term for me?

These are the kinds of questions it is valuable to think about and note in the margins of the texts you read. By "voicing" your questions in annotations, you become more aware of needing answers to those questions; consequently, you will be more likely to look for possible answers as you continue reading. Marking significant features or content in a text will also help you remember those items.

Connect IRW Power of Process Assignment: See the Connect IRW *Common Places* Master Course for pre-loaded PoP annotation assignments.

PRACTICE ② Assessing the Value of Annotations

Look at each example of annotation below, and determine whether the annotation is likely or unlikely to be useful to you as you learn the material. Explain your reasoning.

1. Is this annotation useful? Explain why or why not. This annotation is helpful because it makes a connection between information.

Teaching Resources: See the Instructor's Manual (IM) for the worksheet "Practicing Annotation Skills."

The amygdala is the part of the brain responsible for processing and regulating emotions and for storing and retrieving memories. Part of the limbic system, the amygdala is located deep within the two hemispheres of the brain. It is a small, almond-shaped mass of tissue.

Isn't the limbic system related to nerves? (go back and check)

(continued)

2. Is this highlighting useful? Explain why or why not. No. Too many words are highlighted.

The amygdala is the part of the brain responsible for processing and regulating emotions and for storing and retrieving memories. Part of the limbic system, the amygdala is located deep within the two **hemispheres** of the brain. It is a small, almond-shaped mass of tissue.

Vocabulary Collection Word:
hemisphere

Your in-context definition:

_____

_____

3. Is this annotation useful? Explain why or why not. Yes. Annotation points out the two functions of the amygdala.

A dictionary definition:

_____

_____

The amygdala is the part of the brain responsible for processing and regulating emotions and for storing and retrieving memories. Part of the limbic system, the amygdala is located deep within the two hemispheres of the brain. It is a small, almond-shaped mass of tissue.

Amygdala
1. regulates emotions
2. retrieves memories

4. Is this annotation useful? Explain why or why not.

Yes. Annotation defines the amygdala.

The amygdala is the part of the brain responsible for processing and regulating emotions and for storing and retrieving memories. Part of the limbic system, the amygdala is located deep within the two hemispheres of the brain. It is a small, almond-shaped mass of tissue.

DEF:
Amygdala: part of brain, processes emotions/memories/ almond shaped/deep inside 2 hemispheres

Annotating a Text's Content

Annotations that concern the **content** of a text are about the ideas the writer presents. Your primary responsibility as a reader is to understand the content of the text. It is usually a good idea to start the reading process with these questions in mind:

- What is this text about? (What is the topic?)
- What is the writer's main point?

As you think about the topic and the writer's point, you may also wonder *why* the topic is important or *how* the content of the text relates to you. When you are reading for a particular assignment, you will probably also wonder which parts of the reading are more important than others. These are additional content questions to keep in mind as you read. When you find an answer to such a question, jot down an annotation.

Content annotations concern anything in the text that helps you understand its meaning. For example, if the first paragraph defines a term, make a note of the definition in the margin. You will probably need to know that term as you read through the text. If you find an idea later in the text that you believe is important, make an annotation by jotting down "impt. idea" or putting a star in the margin. If a part of the reading is confusing, jot down a question mark or simply note "confusing." Later you can reread the confusing sections and see if they make more sense or ask for help in understanding them. These kinds of content annotations will help you better understand and remember the text.

The following example shows how Zoe, a student, annotated a textbook passage for content. The passage is from *Foundations of Parasitology*, 9th edition, by Larry Roberts, John Janovy, Jr., and Steve Nadler.

Parasitology is largely a study of symbiosis, or, literally, "living together." Although some authors restrict the term symbiosis to relationships wherein both partners benefit, we prefer to use the term in a wider sense, as originally proposed by the German scholar A. de Bary in 1879: Any two organisms living in close association, commonly one living in or on the body of the other, are symbiotic, as contrasted with free living. Usually the symbionts are of different species but not necessarily.

Symbiotic relationships can be characterized further by specifying the nature of the interactions between the participants. It is always a somewhat arbitrary act, of course, for people to assign definitions to relationships between organisms. But animal species participate in a wide variety of symbiotic relationships, so parasitologists have a need to communicate about these interactions and thus have coined a number of terms to describe them.

DEF *parasitology* (like parasites)
DEF: symbiosis (a relationship where both parties get something/ depend on the other)
A. de Bary (1879) (gave def.)

Def: symbionts—the organisms in the symbiotic relationship
Parasitology: study of symbiotic relationship (betw 2 symbionts)

Huh? the nature of the interactions?
What does this mean?

(random)

Animals (organisms) have parasitic (symbiotic) relationships with other animals (organisms).

Zoe annotated definitions, made note of a question she had, and summarized her understanding of the passage. Notice how she reserved yellow highlighting only for definitions. She used green highlighting for material that she did not fully understand. Developing a simple system will help ensure that your annotations make sense to you when you go back to review them later.

Annotating a Text's Features

Annotating a text's features makes you more aware of the choices a writer has made to communicate her message. This awareness of writing features, in turn, can open up a world of possibilities for your own writing.

Writers make choices about the ways they communicate their messages to particular audiences. They may use **analogies** (comparisons), **anecdotes** (stories), **rhetorical questions** (questions for which the writer provides an answer or for which the answer is obvious), and other techniques to communicate their points. The chart Common Text Features presents some of the features often used by writers. Don't worry if you do not know what all of these are. As you learn more about the features of texts, you will feel more comfortable finding these features and using these terms.

Common Text Features	
Main ideas	**Thesis statement:** The main idea of an essay. **Topic sentence:** The main idea of a paragraph.
Organizing strategies	**Conclusion:** One or more paragraphs at the end of an essay that bring the essay to a close. **Introduction:** One or more paragraphs at the beginning of an essay that introduce the topic and create interest in the reader. **Sequence of information:** Use of time, space, and level of importance to organize information.
Details and text patterns	**Analogy:** An example that explains something unfamiliar by comparing it with something more familiar. **Anecdote:** A brief story that illustrates a specific point. **Cause and effect:** How one circumstance brought about or resulted from another. **Comparison and contrast:** How one item or event is similar to or different from another. **Concrete example:** Specific information that helps the reader understand the writer's point. **Definition:** An explanation of the meaning of a word or concept. **Explanation:** A description of how something is constructed, how a task is performed, or how something works. **Hypothetical example:** An example that asks the reader to imagine something that is not currently true. **Use of sources:** Citing experts so the reader knows where the information is coming from and can evaluate its validity.
Language features	**Questions:** Use of questions to focus readers' attention or engage their emotions. **Repetition:** Use of a word or a phrase several times for emphasis. **Rhetorical question:** A question that the writer asks to make a point but does not expect the reader to answer. The answer may be provided in the text, or it may be self-evident. **Sentence variety:** Use of sentences of different lengths and types to create interest. **Tone:** Use of specific language to convey the emotion the author feels or wants the reader to feel. **Transition:** A word, phrase, or sentence that moves the reader from one idea to another, such as *first, next,* and *after that.* **Wit, sarcasm:** Use of humor to get the point across. Sarcasm is a kind of humor that relies on saying one thing and meaning the opposite.

Annotating features means looking not so much at *what the text says* but at *how the writer writes.* The more you learn about the strategies writers use to convey their ideas in texts, the more you will find to annotate. The passage that follows, called "Why I Am a Vegan," presents one of the major supporting reasons the author decided to change her diet. This passage has been annotated in different colors to point out the text features. (Your annotations as a student should look more like the sample annotations shown earlier in the chapter—and you might not annotate every feature indicated in this example. The color annotations shown here are used throughout the text to demonstrate important points in the examples.)

Why I Am a Vegan

I did not begin my life as a vegan. Like many other children, I dutifully drank the creamy white milk my mother poured for me at breakfast. Rarely did my family not have a

Introduction paragraph

Detail: example of childhood eating habits

(continued)

steaming, beautifully prepared platter of meat on the dinner table. And an unusual occasion it would be when that platter was not licked clean—sometimes literally. Three growing boys made certain of that.

It was in the years after college that I decided I could no longer eat meat. I have come to believe that we harm our planet when we eat animals. As the demand for meat and animal products increases, the environment suffers. Vast rain forests in Brazil have been cleared, their ancient and priceless trees cut to the ground, to provide grazing land for cattle. This is happening all over the world.

If losing our rain forests is not enough, then consider the effects of feeding cattle. Growing grain and transporting it to ranchers across the country requires fuel, creates pollution, and ties up even more land in service to the cattle industry. And when cattle eat, they also create waste. How much animal waste can our streams and rivers withstand? We already know that the amount of methane gas cattle produce has had an effect on the ozone layer. That's a lot of cattle!

Detail: example of concrete, specific image
Tone: light-hearted, conversational
Organized by time periods: childhood, after college
Writer's main point
Detail: description of how rare these trees are
Transition: uses "if . . . then" sentence to move from one idea to the next
Detail: discussion of causes and effects
Rhetorical question: used to make a point

The annotations reveal features such as the use of concrete examples, rhetorical questions, and time order. While you may not yet be aware of all the strategies and features writers use, you can still start annotating the features you find in texts.

Teaching Resources: See the IM for the worksheet "Identifying Text Features."

Connect IRW Power of Process Assignment: See the Connect IRW *Common Places* Master Course for pre-loaded PoP assignments that lead students to identify text features.

PRACTICE 3 Annotating and Highlighting Texts

Highlight content and features in this brief passage from the textbook *Principles of Environmental Science* by William Cunningham and Mary Ann Cunningham. Use the tips for annotating readings presented earlier in this chapter. Write your questions in the margins. Circle words you need to look up in the dictionary. Underline the writer's main idea if you can determine it. Make a comment about the textbook's Fig. 10.17 (on the next page). Don't worry about finding every single feature; just mark those you can identify.

Metals

Many metals, such as mercury, lead, cadmium, and nickel, are highly toxic in minute concentrations. Because metals are highly persistent, they accumulate in food chains and have a cumulative effect in humans.

Currently the most widespread toxic metal contamination in North America is mercury released from incinerators and coal-burning power plants. Transported through the air, mercury precipitates in water supplies, where it bioconcentrates in food webs to reach dangerous levels in top predators. As a general rule, Americans are warned not to eat more than one meal of wild-caught fish per week (Fig. 10.17). Top marine predators, such as shark, swordfish, bluefin tuna, and king mackerel, tend to have especially high mercury content. Pregnant women and small children should avoid these species entirely. Public health officials estimate that 600,000 American children now have mercury levels in their bodies high enough to cause mental and developmental problems, while one woman in six in the United States has blood-mercury concentrations that would endanger a fetus.

(continued)

YOUR ANNOTATIONS

Vocabulary Collection Word:
minute

Your in-context definition:

_____

_____

A dictionary definition:

_____

_____

FISH CONSUMPTION ADVISORY

Fish from these waters contain chemicals.
Eating too much may be harmful,
especially for pregnant women and children.

■ Mercury contamination is the most common cause of impairment of U.S. rivers and lakes. Forty-five states have issued warnings about eating locally caught freshwater fish. Long-lived, top predators are especially likely to bioaccumulate toxic concentrations of mercury.

Teaching Resources: See the PPT "Analyzing Visual Aids."

Emulating a Text's Features

Once you identify strategies writers use to convey their messages, you can practice using those strategies yourself. In ancient days, students would actually copy—word for word—the texts of good writers, not to plagiarize, but to practice and **internalize** the writing styles and strategies of skilled writers. A version of that old activity is to practice writing by intentionally emulating the features another writer uses.

The writing you produce from an emulation exercise will *not* be an original, creative work. Emulation exercises are like paint-by-number artwork. Someone else has already created the picture, chosen the paints, and provided the instructions so you can complete the painting. The painting you produce will not be your original work.

If you were to emulate another writer and turn in your work as if it were your original work, you would be guilty of plagiarism. **Plagiarism** is the act of passing off another writer's words or ideas as your own. Just as it would be wrong to present your paint-by-number artwork as your original creation, it would be wrong to present the writing you do in an emulation exercise as if it were your original creation.

The following chart displays Amber's intentional emulation of parts of "Why I Am a Vegan." In this exercise, Amber was assigned a similar topic: "Why I Am a Recycler." Notice how Amber uses the annotated model to word her ideas so that she can practice using the original writer's techniques.

Vocabulary Collection Word:
internalize

Your in-context definition:

_____

_____

A dictionary definition:

_____

_____

Teaching Resources: See the PPT "What Is Plagiarism?"

Using "Why I Am a Vegan" as a Model

ORIGINAL MODEL: "WHY I AM A VEGAN"	AMBER'S PRACTICE SENTENCES	EXPLANATION
I did not begin my life as a vegan. Like many other children, I dutifully drank the creamy white milk my mother poured for me at breakfast.	I have not always been a recycler. We threw away everything. Two-liter bottles, junk mail, cardboard, and aluminum cans all went into the trash can.	Amber emulates the writer's beginning strategy by explaining that she has not always been a recycler, just as the writer was not always a vegan. But she phrases her opening sentence differently. Next, Amber gives details about what her family used to throw away, just as the writer gives examples of the animal-based food she used to eat.

(continued)

Using "Why I Am a Vegan" as a Model   *(continued)*

ORIGINAL MODEL: "WHY I AM A VEGAN"	AMBER'S PRACTICE SENTENCES	EXPLANATION
I have come to believe that we harm our bodies and our planet when we eat animals.	I now understand why recycling is important.	Amber emulates the writer's focus on her changed thinking, but she uses different words.
Growing grain and transporting it to ranchers across the country requires fuel, creates pollution, and ties up even more land in service to the cattle industry.	Filling up acres and acres of landfill with plastic products that could be recycled will have an effect on our children and our grandchildren.	Amber moves from the personal (her own history of not recycling) to the general (the impact on the world of not recycling), emulating the writer, who discusses the environmental impact of raising meat for food.

DEVELOPING YOUR VOCABULARY

We are constantly exposed to new words, both in what we read and in what we hear. An unfamiliar word is an opportunity to learn and develop your vocabulary. Three ways to learn a new word are to consult a dictionary, to use word parts to determine the word's meaning, and to use context clues to **speculate** as to what the unfamiliar word means.

Using Dictionaries

The quickest and easiest way to learn the definition of a word is to use a dictionary. These days, online dictionaries are more commonly used than printed versions. When you do an online search for a word's definition, you will get a lot of results. As with many online searches, not all results are equally valuable. Look for dictionary sites that provide multiple definitions of the word, a pronunciation guide, examples of how the word can be used in a sentence, and information about the word's history. These three online dictionaries are all good choices: *Merriam-Webster*, *Oxford Dictionaries*, and *American Heritage Dictionary*.

Regardless of the type of dictionary, the entries will typically look about the same. A quick review of dictionary features will help you understand some of the helpful dictionary elements you might overlook. See the sample dictionary entry that follows.

Vocabulary Collection Word:
speculate

Your in-context definition:

_____

_____

A dictionary definition:

_____

_____

SAMPLE DICTIONARY ENTRY

The word and its phonetic pronunciation → **cache (kæsh)**

Syllables

Part of speech indicator → **cach•ing**

n. **1. a.** a hiding place for valuable or useful items.
b. a stockpile of valuable or useful items.
2. COMPUTING A portion of random access memory set aside for high-speed use.
v.t. **3.** to store in a cache.

How the word is used in a special way for a field of study

Online dictionaries allow you to click on this icon to hear the word pronounced.

The primary definitions are identified by numbers. Further clarifications are indicated by letters.

Each element of a dictionary definition helps you learn particular information about the word. First, the word appears and is followed by **phonetic** symbols. Most online dictionaries also provide an audio button that you can click to hear the word pronounced.

On the next line of the sample dictionary entry, the dot between letters shows readers where the word breaks into syllables.

The italicized abbreviations (*n.*, *v.t.*) indicate parts of speech for the word. Some words can function as more than one part of speech. For example, *spot* can be used as a noun (*n.*): *There is a spot on my blouse.* It can also be used as a verb (*v.*): *I can spot the boat from the shore.*

The numbers *1*, *2*, and *3* indicate that there are three different definitions of the word *cache*. When used as a noun, *cache* has two main meanings, one of which is specific to how the word is used in the field of computing. As a verb, *cache* has one meaning.

Knowing which meaning to choose is a crucial part of using a dictionary correctly. To choose the correct meaning, first determine the word's part of speech in the sentence.

Example: We found a *cache* in the wall. We speculated that outlaws used the *cache* to hide money and weapons.

In this example, *cache* is functioning as a noun (a person, place, thing, idea, or quality).

Next, consider the definitions listed under the correct part of speech. For the word *cache* as a noun, we are presented with three definitions. Read the definitions, and find the one that fits the word as it is being used in its context. For the example above, the best definition is the first one given, that is, "a hiding place for valuable or useful items."

To get the most out of dictionaries, read definitions slowly and carefully. Don't skip over the information about the part of speech. It can help you think more clearly about the word itself as well as remember the word's meaning.

PRACTICE ④ Using a Dictionary Effectively

Complete the definition exercises that follow.

1. Word: *geocaching.* Find the word in a dictionary, and then answer these questions:

   a. How many parts of speech are listed for this word? _____

   b. How many definitions are listed? _____

2. Word: *transient*. Find the word in a dictionary, and then answer these questions:

   a. How many parts of speech are listed for this word? _____

   b. How many definitions are listed for this word? _____

3. Read the following sentence:

   The lobby was filled with beautiful flowers and with the *exquisite* aroma of rich perfume.

   a. What do you think *exquisite* means? _____

   b. Divide the word into syllables. _____

   c. Check your definition in a dictionary. What is the dictionary definition?

   _____

   _____

Answers will vary according to the dictionary consulted.

Vocabulary Collection Word:
transient

Your in-context definition:

_____

_____

A dictionary definition:

_____

_____

Using Word Parts

One way to increase your vocabulary is to learn the meanings of individual word parts. You already know many word parts. For example, *-ology* is an ending with which you are familiar. Considering words like *astrology*, *geology*, and *biology*, what do you think *-ology* means? (Check a dictionary to see if you are correct!) You will be surprised at how many word parts you already know. If you memorize the word parts in the Common Prefixes, Common Suffixes, and Common Roots charts, you will be well equipped to figure out the meanings of many of the new words you encounter.

Prefixes and **suffixes** are syllables that can be added to a word to change its meaning; prefixes and suffixes cannot stand alone as complete words. Prefixes appear at the beginning of a word, and suffixes appear at the end of a word. **Roots** are syllables that convey the basic meaning of a word. They can appear in the beginning, middle, or end of a word, and sometimes they can stand alone as complete words.

Example of a Word with a Prefix, Root, and Suffix		
Word: microscopic		
Prefix: micro- **Meaning:** small, tiny	**Root:** scop **Meaning:** to see	**Suffix:** -ic **Meaning:** relating to, characterized by
Definition: Relating to something too tiny to be seen by the unaided eye.		

Study the charts of common prefixes, suffixes, and roots, and complete the practice exercises that follow.

Common Prefixes

See the Connect IRW *Common Places* Master Course for practice quizzes on prefixes, suffixes, and roots.

PREFIX	MEANING	EXAMPLE
anti-	against, opposite	antisocial
auto-	self	autobiography
bi-	two	bicycle
com-, con-	with, together	communicate, context
dis-	not, opposite of	dislike
em-, en-	to cause to be, to put into or onto, to go into or onto	embattle, enable
ex-, exo-	out of, from	exoskeleton
fore-	earlier	foreshadow
hom-, homo-	same	homogeneous
hype-	over, too much	hyperactive
im-	not	impatient
in-, il-, im-	not	insufficient, illiterate, immature
inter-	between	interstate
micro-	small, tiny	microchip
mid-	middle	midline
mis-	bad, wrong	misbehave

(continued)

Common Prefixes   *(continued)*

PREFIX	MEANING	EXAMPLE
neo-	new, recent, revived	neonatal
poly-	many, much	polygon
pre-	before	premarital
pro-	forward	proceed
quad-	four	quadrilateral
re-	again, back	rejoin
retro-	back, backward	retroactive
se-	apart	separate
semi-	half	semisolid
sub-	under, beneath, secondary	subterranean
super-	above, on top of, beyond	superimpose, superintendent
tele-	far, distant	telephone
trans-	across, change, through	transfer, transmit
tri-	three	tricycle
un-	not, opposite of	unhappy
uni-	one, single	unicycle

Common Suffixes

SUFFIX	MEANING	EXAMPLE
-able, -ible	can be done	laughable, edible,
-age	result of an action/collection	manage
-al, -ial	related to, characterized by	parental, trivial
-an, -ian	one having a certain skill, relating to, belonging to	artisan, Haitian
-ation, -ion, -ition, -tion	act of, state of	graduation, isolation
-en	made of, to make	brighten, wooden
-ence, -ance	act or condition of	governance
-ent, -ant	an action or condition, causing a specific action	obedient, inhabitant
-er, -or	person connected with, comparative degree	competitor, greater
-fy	to make, to form into	liquefy
-hood	state, quality, condition of	adulthood
-ic	relating to, characterized by	historic
-ice	state or quality of	cowardice
-ide	chemical	peroxide

(continued)

Common Suffixes *(continued)*

SUFFIX	MEANING	EXAMPLE
-ish	like, having the characteristics of, inclined or trending to	childish
-ity, -ty	state of, quality of	beauty, prosperity
-ive, -ative, -tive	inclined or tending toward an action	active, inquisitive
-ize	to make, to cause to become	energize
-less	without	homeless
-logy, -ology, -ologist	science of, study of, one who studies	psychology, ecologist
-ment	act, process	torment, replacement
-ness	condition, state of	happiness
-ous, -eous, -ious	full of or characterized by	joyous, rambunctious
-ward	characterized by a thing, quality, state, or action	backward, inward
-ways	in what manner	sideways

Common Roots

ROOT	MEANING	EXAMPLE
amo, amatum	love	amorous
aqua	water	aquatics
aud, audi, aus	to hear, listen	audiophile
bene, boun, bon	good, well	benefit
biblio	book	bibliography
bio	life	biological
chrom, chron	time	synchronous
dico, dictum, dict	to say, tell, speak	dictation
fact	make, do	manufacture
geo	earth, ground, soil	geological
graph	writing	biography
inter	between	interrelated
junct	join	junction
log, logos	word or study	dialogue
magnus	large	magnificent
meter, metron	measure	thermometer
path, pathos	feeling, suffering	sympathy
phone	sound	phonetics
populous	people	population
pro	for	proponent
scribe, script	to write	transcribe
sol	sun	solar

(continued)

Common Roots   *(continued)*

ROOT	MEANING	EXAMPLE
sonus	sound	sonogram
spectro, spect, spec	to see, watch, observe	prospect
struct	to build	destruction
syn, sym	the same, alike	sync, synonym
terra	land	subterranean
trans	across	translate
visum, video	to see	videographer
vivo	live	vibrant

PRACTICE ⑤ Using Word Parts to Speculate about Meanings

Use the Common Prefixes, Common Suffixes, and Common Roots charts to make an educated guess about the meaning of each of the following words. Write the meaning in the provided space. Then consult a dictionary, and write the dictionary meaning in the appropriate space.

1. Word: *bioconcentrates*

   Your best guess: Answers will vary.

   Dictionary definition: The buildup of chemicals in an organism's tissues to a higher level than in the surrounding environment.

2. Word: *excommunicate*

   Your best guess: Answers will vary.

   Dictionary definition: to take away a person's ability to participate in a specific church or religious community.

3. Word: *contamination*

   Your best guess: Answers will vary.

   Dictionary definition: The introduction of harmful impurities into a substance or an environment.

4. Word: *benefactor*

   Your best guess: Answers will vary.

   Dictionary definition: A person or entity that supports another person or entity with donations, usually of money.

5. Word: *transcribe*

   Your best guess: Answers will vary.

   Dictionary definition: To create a written copy of spoken material, or to write down the score of a musical composition.

Using Context Clues

A **context** is an environment. The context of a particular word is the sentence in which it appears and sometimes the sentences nearby.

You may have already noticed Vocabulary Collection Words in the margins of this chapter like the example shown at the right. This feature is designed to call attention to words you

Vocabulary Collection Word:
mechanism

Your in-context definition:

_____

_____

A dictionary definition:

_____

_____

may not know. When you see a vocabulary box for a word in the text, first attempt to figure out the word's meaning using the context clues described in the steps that follow. Finish the paragraph you are reading, and then fill in the definitions for the word in the vocabulary box.

These three steps can help you use context clues effectively to determine definitions.

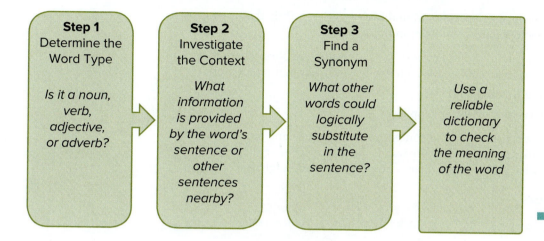

Step 1
Determine the Word Type

Is it a noun, verb, adjective, or adverb?

Step 2
Investigate the Context

What information is provided by the word's sentence or other sentences nearby?

Step 3
Find a Synonym

What other words could logically substitute in the sentence?

Use a reliable dictionary to check the meaning of the word

■ Using context clues to determine a word's meaning

Context Clue Step 1: Determine the Word Type

The sentence in which the word appears and the surrounding sentences are context clues. The first point to notice when you are using context clues is the *type of word*. In the following example, we will consider the word *precipitates*, a word unfamiliar to many people.

Example: Transported through the air, mercury *precipitates* in water supplies . . .

Precipitates describes something that mercury *does*, so it is an action word. Thus, *precipitates* is a verb.

Context Clue Step 2: Investigate the Context

Now that you know the word is a verb, think of other verbs you are familiar with, such as *jumps*, *runs*, and *sits*. Can you come up with another verb that might mean the same thing as *precipitates*? To do so, investigate in more depth to determine what happens before mercury precipitates.

Example: Currently the most widespread toxic metal contamination in North America is mercury released from incinerators and coal-burning power plants. Transported through the air, mercury precipitates in water supplies, where it bioconcentrates in food webs to reach dangerous levels in top predators.

- Since mercury is released from incinerators and coal-burning power plants, it is not on the ground: it is coming out of smokestacks. Thus we can conclude that the mercury is in the air.

- The word *transported* gives us another clue: mercury moves through the air before ending up in water supplies.

- The mercury *precipitates* from the air into water supplies. That must mean it somehow gets from the air into the water below.

- You may already be familiar with a similar word, *precipitation*, which is often used in weather forecasts. You know *precipitation* means rain. Rain is a *thing*—the actual water that falls from the sky—but *to rain* is a verb. Precipitation is a thing—the actual wet weather—but it can also be used as a verb, *to precipitate*. Thus, maybe *to precipitate* is like *to rain*.

- Conclusion: *Precipitates* very likely means "falling from the sky like rain."

Context Clue Step 3: Find a Synonym

Once you have used the context to understand the writer's point, you can find a synonym to help you define the new word. A **synonym** is a word that means the same thing as another word. For example, *house*, *home*, and *residence* are synonyms; all three words mean roughly the same thing.

Take the unfamiliar word out of the sentence, and plug in other words that might make sense. Think through each potential synonym in this way.

Example: Transported through the air, mercury _____ in water supplies, where it bioconcentrates in food webs to reach dangerous levels in top predators.

Try this: Mercury *falls* into water supplies.

Or this: Mercury *rains down* into water supplies.

If the synonym makes sense *and* if it fits in the context of the sentence and paragraph, you may have found the word's meaning. The only way to be sure is to use a dictionary to check your hunch. Here's what part of a dictionary entry for *precipitate* might look like.

---

pre•cip•i•tate ◁») (pri-'si-pə-tāt)

v. **1. METEOROLOGY** To cause water to condense and fall from the air in the form of rain, snow, sleet, or hail.
2. CHEMISTRY To cause a solid to separate from the solution in which it is contained.

Precipitate means "to condense and fall from the air." That is exactly what the mercury is doing. There is also a second definition from chemistry that fits: mercury, which is a solid, is being separated from the smoke released from incinerators and coal-burning power plants and falling into the water. The context clues were successful in leading us to the right meaning. Context clues will not always lead you to the exact meaning of a word, but they can help you get close.

Try your hand at using context clues to figure out the meanings of unfamiliar words by completing the following exercise.

PRACTICE ⑥ Using Context Clues

Use context clues to guess the meaning of each of the *italicized* words in the passages below. Follow the three context clue steps described above. Next, use a dictionary to see if your definition is correct. Record your answers.

1. Mike, the lodge owner, gave us a *convoluted*, hand-drawn map that was impossible to follow.

   Context-based guess: Answers will vary.

   Dictionary definition: Complex; difficult to follow

   Teaching Resources: See worksheet "Using Context Clues."

2. The map was intended to lead us to a gold mine that had long been abandoned by *prospectors*.

   Context-based guess: Answers will vary.

   Dictionary definition: People who are in search of minerals or valuable goods

   Teaching Resources: See the mini-quiz "Using Context Clues." Also, see the Connect IRW *Common Places* Master Course for a practice quiz.

3. After hiking for half an hour, we decided that the *pragmatic* thing to do would be to walk back to the lodge and ask for clearer instructions.

   Context-based guess: Answers will vary.

   Dictionary definition: Sensible; reasonable

4. Mike laughed and gave us a list of *enumerated* instructions. We could easily follow the ten instructions he gave us.

   Context-based guess: Answers will vary.

   Dictionary definition: Listed by number

Acquiring New Vocabulary

You now have three tools—using a dictionary, using word parts, and using context clues—to help you understand unfamiliar words you encounter as you read. These tools are great at leading you to a temporary understanding, but to actually acquire new vocabulary that you will remember, you have to be much more intentional than merely noting a definition.

The key to expanding and adding to your vocabulary is *using* the words you learn. One way to do this is to keep a log of all the vocabulary words that are new to you. You can keep the log in a notebook or, better yet, on note cards. Make a note card each week with new vocabulary words. Include the words that are annotated as vocabulary words in each chapter of this textbook, and add any other new words you find in your reading. Your vocabulary log will give you a collection of words to study and to practice using in daily conversation and writing.

- When you write e-mails, use as many of the words on your note card as you can.
- Think about situations in your life that would provide the right context for the new word. For example, if the new word is *stringent* ("strict; severe"), a discussion about rules or laws may be a good situation in which you can use the word *stringent*.
- When you write assignments for your classes, find a way to weave in new vocabulary words.

At the end of each chapter, you will find an Adding to Your Vocabulary activity that will challenge you to use the new vocabulary from the chapter in your day-to-day activities.

CHAPTER ACTIVITIES

READING AND ANNOTATING

As you know, intentional and unintentional emulation help us learn new skills. However, emulation alone is not always enough to help us become fully competent in a new craft or skill. Perhaps the most important ingredient in accomplishing any goal is motivation.

In the selection that follows, you will read about how motivation and emulation led Frederick Douglass to true accomplishment. Douglass was born into slavery around 1818 in Maryland. Around the age of twelve, his master's wife began teaching him the alphabet. After being reprimanded by her husband, she stopped her lessons, but Douglass was determined to read. In his remarkable story, he explains how learning to read and write was a major factor in his desire to become free. Douglass eventually escaped slavery and became a greatly respected thinker, speaker, and writer. In addition to other writings, lectures, and accomplishments, he told the story of his life in *My Bondage and My Freedom* (1855) and *Life and Times of Frederick Douglass* (1881).

What follows is a paraphrase of a passage from *Narrative of the Life of Frederick Douglass, an American Slave*, published in 1845 by the Anti-Slavery Office in Boston. Read and annotate the paraphrased selection. As you read, think about the character traits Frederick Douglass had. He was a very patient man, but he had many other character traits that helped him succeed in life. Make notes about these traits when you read about Douglass's strategies to learn to read and write.

This selection is a paraphrase of chapter 7 from Frederick Douglass's text. It divides the content into more paragraphs than the original and eliminates archaic words and constructions. For instructors who wish to use the original text, a reproducible copy of the original is available in the IM. "Also, the IM contains instructions for uploading Douglass's text using Power of Process.

Learning to Read and Write

By Frederick Douglass

I lived in Master Hugh's family about seven years. During this time, I succeeded in learning to read and write. In order to accomplish this, I was compelled to resort to various strategies because I had no regular teacher.

YOUR ANNOTATIONS

Lexile: 990L

The plan which I adopted, and the one by which I was most successful, was that of making friends of all the little white boys whom I met in the street. I "converted" as many of these boys as I could find into "teachers." With their kind assistance, obtained at different times and in different places, I finally succeeded in learning to read.

When I was sent to run errands, I always took a book with me and by doing one part of my errand quickly, I found time to get a lesson in before my return. Bread was always available to me at the house but not so for many of the poor white children in our neighborhood. So I would bring extra bread with me on my errands and give some to these hungry little urchins. In return, they gave me the much more valuable bread of knowledge.

I am strongly tempted to give the names of two or three of those little boys as a testimonial of the gratitude and affection I have toward them. However, I believe it is wiser not to do so—not because so doing would injure me but because it might embarrass them in that teaching slaves to read is an almost unpardonable offense in this Christian country. It is enough to say of the dear little fellows that they live on Philpot Street, very near Durgin and Bailey's shipyard.

On occasion, I would sometimes talk the matter of slavery over with them. Sometimes I would tell them that I wished I could be as free as they would be when they became men. "You will be free as soon as you are twenty-one, but I am a slave for life! Do I not have as much right to be free as you have?" These words troubled them; they would express deep sympathy for me and console me with the hope that something would occur by which I might be free.

At this point I was about twelve years old, and the thought of being a slave for life began to weigh heavily on my heart. Just about this time, I obtained a book entitled *The Columbian Orator.* I read it at every opportunity. Among its many interesting ideas, I discovered in it a dialogue between a master and his slave. The slave had run away from his master three times. The book presented the conversation that took place between the two of them after the slave was recaptured the third time. In this exchange, the master presented every pro-slavery argument, and the slave addressed every point. The slave was characterized as saying some very smart, impressive things in reply to his master. The slave was both surprised and delighted regarding the effect of the argument he presented—the master decided voluntarily to emancipate the slave!

In the same book, I encountered some of the powerful arguments that Richard Sheridan made regarding the oppression of Catholics in Britain. I read his ideas over and over again because they were so interesting. He expressed some of my own thoughts, which had frequently flashed through my mind but which died away because I could not put them into words. The key insight that I gained from his works was that truth could have power over even the conscience of a slaveholder. What I learned from Sheridan was a bold denunciation of slavery and a powerful vindication of human rights.

Reading these documents enabled me to express my own thoughts and to address the arguments offered for the continuation of slavery. While they relieved me of one difficulty, they brought on another even more painful understanding. The more I read, the more I was led to abhor and detest my enslavers. I could regard them as nothing other than a band of successful robbers, who had left their homes, gone to Africa, and stolen us from our homes, reducing us to slavery in a strange land. I loathed them as being the meanest as well as the most wicked of men.

The Columbian Orator was a collection of poems, political essays, and other writings. It was widely used in American schoolrooms in the early nineteenth century to teach reading and speaking.

After the Reformation in Great Britain, Roman Catholics were subjected to many restrictions. They could not own land, hold government offices or seats in Parliament, or practice their religion freely without being fined or prosecuted. Richard Sheridan was a writer and member of Parliament who actively supported the expansion of rights for British Catholics.

As I writhed under this pain, I would at times feel that learning to read had been a curse rather than a blessing. Learning to read had given me a view of my wretched condition but without any cure. It opened my eyes to the horrible pit of my circumstances but offered no ladder with which I could get out. In moments of agony, I envied the unawareness of my fellow slaves. I have often wished that I myself were an animal and thus ignorant of my plight. I thought that I would prefer to be the lowliest reptile rather than myself. Anything—no matter what—to escape from thinking! The contemplation of my situation tormented me. There was no getting rid of it. It was pressed upon me by every object within sight or hearing, animate or inanimate. The silver trumpet of freedom had roused my soul to eternal wakefulness. Freedom now appeared, to disappear no more forever. It was heard in every sound and seen in every thing. It was ever present to torment me with a sense of my wretched condition. I saw nothing without seeing it; I heard nothing without hearing it; and I felt nothing without feeling it. Freedom—it looked from every star, smiled in every calm moment, breathed in every wind, and moved in every storm.

I often found myself regretting my own existence and wishing that I were dead. If it had not been for the hope of being free, I have no doubt but that I would have killed myself—or done something for which I would have been killed. While in this state of mind, I was eager to hear anyone speak about slavery. I was a ready listener. From time to time, I would hear a reference to the "abolitionists." However, it was some time before I learned what the word meant. It was always used in a context that caused it to be an interesting word to me. If a slave ran away and succeeded in getting clear, or if a slave killed his master, or set fire to a barn, or did anything very wrong in the mind of a slaveholder, it was referred to as the fruit of abolition. Hearing the word in this connection very often, I set about to learn what it meant. The dictionary offered me little help. I found it was "the act of abolishing," but then I did not know what it meant for something to be abolished. So I was perplexed.

I did not dare to ask anyone about its meaning, for I was confident that it was something they wanted me to know very little about. After waiting patiently, I came across one of our city newspapers that contained an account of the number of petitions from the North pleading for the abolition of slavery in the District of Columbia and of the slave trade between the States. From this time forward, I understood the words "abolition" and "abolitionist" and always drew near when that word was spoken, expecting to hear something of importance to myself and fellow-slaves. The light broke in upon me by degrees.

One day I went down on the wharf, and seeing two Irishmen unloading stone from a scow, I went, unasked, and helped them. When we had finished, one of them came to me and asked me if I was a slave. I told him I was. He asked, "Are ye a slave for life?" I told him that I was. The good Irishman seemed to be deeply bothered by the statement. He said to the other that it was a pity that so fine a little fellow as I should be a slave for life. He said it was a shame to hold me. They both advised me to run away to the North; they said that I would find friends there, and that I would be free. I pretended not to be interested in what they said and acted as though I did not understand them because I feared they might be treacherous. White men have been known to encourage slaves to escape, and then, to get the reward, catch them and return them to their masters. I was afraid that these seemingly good men might use me so; but I nevertheless remembered their advice, and from that time onward I resolved to

Scow: a large flat-bottomed boat.

run away. I looked forward to a time at which it would be safe for me to escape. I was too young to think of doing so immediately; besides, I wished to learn how to write, as I might have occasion to write my own pass. I consoled myself with the hope that I should one day find a good chance. Meanwhile, I would learn to write.

The idea as to how I might learn to write was suggested to me by being in Durgin and Bailey's shipyard. I would frequently see the ship carpenters, after hewing and getting a piece of timber ready for use, write on the timber the name of that part of the ship for which it was intended. When a piece of timber was intended for the larboard side, it would be marked thus—"L." When a piece was for the starboard side, it would be marked thus—"S." A piece for the larboard side forward would be marked thus—"L. F." When a piece was for starboard side forward, it would be marked thus—"S. F." For larboard aft, it would be marked thus—"L. A." For starboard aft, it would be marked thus—"S. A." I soon learned the names of these letters and understood their meaning when written on a piece of timber in the shipyard. I immediately began copying them and in a short time was able to make these four letters.

After that, whenever I met any boy whom I knew could write, I would tell him I could write as well as he. The next word would be, "I don't believe you. Let me see you try it." I would then make the letters which I had been so fortunate as to learn and ask him to beat that. In this way I got a good many lessons in writing, which I could not possibly have gotten in any other way. During this time, my copy-book was the board fence, brick wall, and pavement; my pen and ink was a lump of chalk. With these, I learned how to write.

I continued by copying the advanced spelling words in *Webster's Spelling Book* until I could make them all without looking at the book. By this time, my little Master Thomas had gone to school and learned how to write and had filled a number of copy-books with his handwriting. He had brought these home and shown them to some of our near neighbors and then laid them aside. My mistress would leave the house every Monday afternoon and require me to take care of the house. While she was gone, I used the time writing in the blank spaces left in Master Thomas's copy-book, copying what he had written. I continued to do this until I could write in a manner very similar to that of Master Thomas. Thus, after a long, tedious effort for years, I finally succeeded in learning how to write.

Hew: to cut wood coarsely.

Copy-book: a blank tablet for practicing handwriting.

Master Thomas: the child of Frederick Douglass's master.

Questions for Consideration

1. What effect did reading have on Frederick Douglass initially?
2. Why was Douglass so motivated to learn to read? Why was he motivated to learn to write?
3. What role did emulation play in Douglass's education?
4. In what ways was Douglass's reading of *The Columbian Orator* important in his intellectual and emotional development?
5. How did reading and writing separate Douglass from the other slaves?
6. Write a paragraph in which you speculate about what life would have been like for Frederick Douglass had he never learned to read or write. Use your imagination.
7. Why do you think slave owners prohibited slaves from learning to read and write?

USING MODELS TO PRACTICE COMPOSING

Shaun read Frederick Douglass's "Learning to Read and Write" in his English class and was given an essay assignment. Read Shaun's assignment on the next page and notice his annotations.

Questions for Consideration

1. Initially, Douglass was exhilarated by reading, but he eventually became miserable because of the insights he gained about his plight as a slave.

2. He was motivated by curiosity and the belief that he might one day be able to write his pass to freedom.

3. He emulated letters on timber, copied from *Webster's Spelling Book,* and mimicked the writing found in copy books.

4. He was moved by a scene depicting a slave and master arguing over slavery's injustice. The slave's argument convinced the master, and Douglass himself was influenced by the slave's powerful argument.

5. Enlightenment made Douglass more miserable. Slaves who could not read or write were less likely to question their enslavement and could more easily accept their situations.

6. Answers will vary.

7. Answers will vary.

Essay Assignment

In "Learning to Read and Write," we learn not only how Frederick Douglass became literate, but also about the character traits that helped him eventually become a free man. Write an essay in which you discuss the character traits that drove Douglass to become literate. Discuss at least three character traits and their effects on Douglass's life in your essay. Use examples from the reading to support your discussion.

SHAUN'S ANNOTATIONS

Assignment turned into a question: What are the character traits that drove Douglass to become literate?

Discuss character traits (3 or more).

Discuss their effects.

Use examples from the reading.

To respond to the assignment, Shaun reread the narrative and marked every possible character trait he could think of. Here are the first four paragraphs Shaun annotated with Douglass's character traits.

I lived in Master Hugh's family about seven years. During this time, I succeeded in learning to read and write. In order to accomplish this, I was compelled to resort to various strategies because I had no regular teacher. — **Determined**

Resourceful → The plan which I adopted, and the one by which I was most successful, was that of making friends of all the little white boys whom I met in the street. I "converted" as many of these boys as I could find into "teachers." With their **Flexible & persistent** → kind assistance, obtained at different times and in different places, I finally succeeded in learning to read. — **Friendly**

Hardworking → When I was sent to run errands, I always took a book with me and by doing one part of my errand quickly, I found time to get a lesson in before my return. Bread was always available to me at the house but not so for many of the poor white children in our neighborhood. So I would bring extra bread with me on my errands and give some to these hungry little urchins. In return, they gave me the much more valuable bread of knowledge. — **Creative**

— **Cooperative**

Thankful → I am strongly tempted to give the names of two or three of those little boys as a testimonial of the gratitude and affection I have toward them. However, I believe it is wiser not to do so—not because so doing would injure me but because it might embarrass them in that teaching slaves **Aware, concerned for others** → to read is an almost unpardonable offense in this Christian country. It is enough to say of the dear little fellows that they live on Philpot Street, very near Durgin and Bailey's shipyard. — **Wise**

When Shaun finished annotating the entire reading, he made a list of all the character traits he found. Next, he grouped together character traits that were similar, as you can see from the circled numbers in this excerpt from Shaun's prewriting.

In this book, we discuss the main lines of support as major supporting points rather than topic sentences. We do this because often—especially in professional readings—a major supporting point is expressed in more than one body paragraph. In chapter 5, students will learn about this distinction. For additional explanation about the terms used in this text, see the IM.

Character Traits

(2) determined   thankful
(1) resourceful   (1) creative
    friendly   (2) hardworking (diligent)
(1) flexible   cooperative
(3) persistent   wise
(3) patient   concerned for others

After identifying the character traits he would discuss in his essay, Shaun wrote a simple outline that included his thesis statement and the major supporting points he planned to use. He decided his essay would be structured like this:

Introduction paragraph

Thesis statement: Frederick Douglass's success in learning to read and write was a result of his resourcefulness, diligence, and persistence.

Major supporting point 1: Without resourcefulness, Douglass would probably not have ever become literate.

Major supporting point 2: While resourcefulness was necessary, diligence and hard work were also important.

Major supporting point 3: Most importantly, Douglass's persistence is the character trait that eventually gave rise to his success.

Conclusion paragraph

After drafting his essay, Shaun revised and edited it, making sure he gave credit to the sources he used. Notice the features of Shaun's writing in the first body paragraph of his essay.

Body Paragraph 1 from Shaun's Essay

Without resourcefulness, Douglass would probably not have ever become literate. Douglass had to come up with his own teachers and his own materials. With the exception of learning the alphabet from his master's wife, every bit of Douglass's reading education was a result of his own resourcefulness. For example, Douglass would get the boys in his neighborhood to teach him by giving them bread and befriending them. He used both bread and the young boys as resources for education. To learn to write, Douglass had to be especially resourceful. Noticing the letters used on wood in the shipyard, Douglass began to copy the letters by writing them with chalk on sidewalks and fences. Another example of Douglass's resourcefulness was in his use of the young Master Thomas's educational materials. Douglass would wait until his	Main idea of the paragraph (a topic sentence) Detail: resourcefulness required to learn to read Example Detail: resourcefulness required to learn to write Example Example

(continued)

mistress left the house and would then use blank spots in Master Thomas's used spelling-books. Because Douglass was resourceful, he was able to use non-traditional methods for learning to read and write.

A READING AND WRITING ASSIGNMENT

Try your hand at writing the remaining paragraphs of Shaun's essay. Using the first body paragraph Shaun wrote as a model, write the remaining two body paragraphs based on Shaun's outline. Alternatively, choose two other items on Shaun's prewriting list to write about. Add an introduction paragraph and a conclusion paragraph to complete the essay. Use the Quick Start Guide to Integrated Reading and Writing Assignments for assistance.

Connect IRW Writing Assignment: Use the tools in Connect IRW to set up this writing assignment for peer review and for rubric-based grading. Alternatively, this assignment is pre-loaded in the Connect IRW *Common Places* Master Course.

⊙ THINKING FROM AN INSTRUCTOR'S POINT OF VIEW

Emulation exercises like the one in this chapter based on "Why I Am a Vegan" can sometimes be worrisome for instructors. No instructor wants to convey the idea that it is OK to use another writer's composition after changing a few words. However, many writing instructors understand the importance of using models for study and practice.

Think about this issue from the perspective of an instructor for a moment. What is the difference between plagiarizing and practices like the emulation exercise in this chapter? How would you explain the difference to students? Write two or three paragraphs in which you answer these questions.

⊙ ADDING TO YOUR VOCABULARY

This chapter's vocabulary words appear below.

Teaching Resources: See the Connect IRW *Common Places* Master Course for vocabulary study practices that accompany this chapter, as well as a chapter vocabulary quiz.

mechanism	hemisphere	minute
internalize	speculate	transient

Choose five of the vocabulary words from this chapter that you would like to add to your vocabulary, and think about how you can use them this week. For example, one of this week's words is *speculate*. You can often substitute *speculate* for *guess*, as in the examples that follow.

Example: I don't know if this soup is fattening, but I'd *guess* that it is because it tastes so good.

I don't know if this soup is fattening, but I'd *speculate* that it is because it tastes so good.

List each of the five words you plan to use this week, and make note of a context in which you could use each word.

Example: *Speculate.* I can use this word when I predict what will be on tests or what we'll do in class.

⊙ ADDITIONAL ASSIGNMENTS

1. Reading and writing were arguably the most important skills Frederick Douglass ever acquired. Being literate opened new worlds for Douglass, and eventually he found a way to free himself from slavery. Think about your own life. Have you developed a skill that has made a difference in your world? Perhaps you have developed a friendship that has been highly influential, or maybe you have had an experience—such as a job or a vacation—that had a profound effect on you. Write two or three paragraphs about a positive, powerful influence you have had in your life. Explain why this influence affected you, and provide examples of its positive influence.

1. Answers will vary.

2. Using Frederick Douglass's essay and your own life experiences, reflect on these questions: What were the effects of hardship on Douglass? What have been the effects of hardship in your life? Write a few paragraphs in which you explain your answer.

2. Answers will vary.

3. In a variety of career fields, emulating the skills of others is a way to learn. For example, nursing students spend time as interns emulating the skills of professional nurses in clinics and hospitals. In disciplines such as music, art, and theater, students learn by emulating the masters of their crafts. And in sales and marketing, students learn by emulating the successful techniques of those in the field. Choose a career in which you are interested. How might emulation help you master the content or skills required in this career? Write two or three paragraphs to explain.

3. Answers will vary.

EMOTIONAL INTELLIGENCE

One skill that is important for getting along with others is social awareness. Management experts have defined social awareness as "the ability to perceive and understand the social relationships and structures in which you and those around you are operating. It involves being able to understand how other people are feeling—and validating those feelings. . . . And it means understanding that individual happiness is dependent upon assisting others to achieve their own happiness as well."

Answers will vary.

Write two or three paragraphs explaining what social awareness is. Put the ideas into your own words. Provide an example of a person who is socially aware in a particular situation. Provide another example of a person who is socially *unaware* in a particular situation. For example, a socially aware person may recognize that when the conversation turns to romantic relationships, one of her friends becomes uncomfortable. A person who is socially *unaware* might speak too loudly in class or might dominate a conversation without knowing how he is being perceived by those around him. Finish by offering suggestions for becoming more socially aware.

Instructors may wish to emphasize that the examples can be hypothetical.

CULTURAL LITERACY

"Learning to Read and Write" is chapter 7 of Frederick Douglass's story. The entire text is available at www.gutenberg.org/ebooks/23. Select at least one additional chapter from Douglass's narrative. Read the chapter and write a paragraph in which you summarize the information it presents. Use the Quick Start Guide for assistance.

Answers will vary.

CRITICAL THINKING

A valuable way to use critical thinking is to analyze the models we emulate, especially the people in our lives. It's easy to identify the emulation mistakes of other people. We have all observed a young person who falls in with the wrong crowd and makes poor choices. Seeing our own emulation mistakes, however, requires critical thinking about our lives.

Think about the people you have emulated—whether consciously or unconsciously. Often, they are the people closest to you, such as parents, friends, and relatives. Some people even emulate celebrities. Select the person who has had the greatest effect on you. Has it been a wise choice to emulate this person? Why or why not? Write two or three paragraphs that reveal critical thinking about your conscious or unconscious emulation of this person.

Answers will vary.

Teaching Resources: See the IM for a model response.

METACOGNITION

What do you remember after having read this chapter? Without looking back at the chapter, list the major topics this chapter covered. Then review the chapter to see what you missed. Write a short paragraph about how well you remembered the content for each topic.

When you finish, assess your understanding and memory of this chapter. Was it difficult to recall the information you read? Why? What particular material did you remember from the chapter? Why do you think you remembered those items and not others? Did you remember what you annotated better than what you did not annotate? What strategies might you use in the future to better remember the contents of what you read?

Answers will vary.

3

In many careers, previewing materials is essential to getting a job done well. Previewing strategies also help readers and writers keep focused as they work with and create texts.

Previewing Texts and Working with Topics

Sometimes the way you do a job really affects the final result. For example, a high school senior decided to paint his old worn-out car. Not being the mechanical—or artistic—type, he washed his car and dried it, and then he painted it with nine cans of red, high-gloss, bargain-brand spray paint. You can probably imagine the outcome. The painting process he used resulted in the creation of what he and his friends came to call The Bloodmobile. Indeed, the process he used affected the quality of the outcome.

The same principle is true for reading and writing. The early steps are important. Carefully following these steps will help you confidently begin the integrated reading and writing journey.

CHAPTER OBJECTIVES

After completing this chapter, students will be able to do the following:

- **Examine a reading's context.**

- **Preview a reading to identify its topic.**

- **Work with assigned writing topics.**

- **Develop and narrow a topic for an essay.**

- **Use prewriting strategies to generate ideas.**

Connect IRW LearnSmart Achieve: Assign the topics "Reading, Vocabulary, and Study Skills" and "Writing Process" for adaptive learning to accompany the chapter.

Teaching Resources: See the Chapter Quiz.

EXAMINING A READING'S CONTEXT

When we **preview** a reading, we look it over and notice key elements rather than read it word for word. One key element is the reading's context. The context of a reading consists of *where* it was published, *who* wrote it, and *for whom* it was written. Let's consider some specific types of texts, their characteristics, and the insights we can gather from their contexts.

Types of Text

	NEWSPAPER ARTICLES	ARTICLES IN GENERAL-INTEREST MAGAZINES	ARTICLES IN SPECIAL-INTEREST MAGAZINES	ARTICLES IN ACADEMIC JOURNALS	BOOKS
Author	Journalists, whose primary task is to report news and ideas	General-interest writers who are not necessarily subject experts	People with experience or background in the subject	Highly qualified experts with extensive background in the subject	Experts and nonexperts
Audience	General public	Wide range of readers	Readers interested in the subject	Experts in the subject	General or specialized audiences
Purpose	To inform or analyze (news articles) or persuade (editorials)	To inform, analyze, evaluate, or persuade	To inform, analyze, evaluate, or persuade	To inform, analyze, evaluate, persuade, or present new research	Varied purposes
Length	Often short	Varied	Varied	Varied, but generally long (3,000+ words)	Varied
Language and style	Journalistic (multiple short paragraphs)	Very little jargon or technical language, always explained and defined	Likely to include jargon and technical language	Likely to include jargon and technical language	Classifiable into genres (novels, textbooks); may use jargon and technical language
Examples	Articles in *The New York Times, The Washington Post,* and *The Wall Street Journal*	Articles in *Time, Newsweek, The Atlantic,* and *Salon.com*	Articles in *Psychology Today, Fortune,* and *Scientific American*	Articles in *American Journal of Nursing* and *Journal of Engineering and Technology Research*	*The Grapes of Wrath* by John Steinbeck; *Managerial Accounting,* 14th ed., by Ray Garrison

Vocabulary Collection Word:
editorial

Your in-context definition:

_____

_____

A dictionary definition:

_____

_____

By thinking about the publication, its intended audience, and the writer's purpose, you can develop insights about texts before reading them.

Practice examining contexts by completing the following exercise.

Teaching Resources: See the *PowerPoint* presentation (PPT) "Analyzing Contexts."

PRACTICE ① Examining the Contexts of Readings

Read the titles of the publications in the left column, and read the descriptors in the right column. Match each publication to the correct descriptor.

__g__ **1.** Journal: *Journal of Chemical Physics*

__e__ **2.** Book: *Money Management Principles That Work*

__c__ **3.** Journal: *Journal of Applied Psychology*

__f__ **4.** Newspaper: *The New York Times*

__d__ **5.** Specialty magazine: *Wine Enthusiast*

__a__ **6.** Newspaper: *The Loyaltown Gazette*

__h__ **7.** Book: *Invisible Man* by Ralph Ellison

__b__ **8.** Specialty magazine: *Texas Monthly*

a. Source most likely to report a Labor Day parade

b. Source most likely to appeal to regional readers

c. Source most likely to use technical jargon for mental health professionals

d. Source most likely to appeal to a hobby or interest group

e. Source most likely to provide practical advice to a general audience

f. Source most likely to offer high-quality news for a general but educated audience

g. Source most likely to require readers to know scientific concepts

h. Source most likely to provide pleasurable reading for a general audience

PREVIEWING A READING TO IDENTIFY ITS TOPIC

A careful preview of the reading can help you figure out what the reading is about—its **topic.** Being able to determine the topic of a reading is one of the most important reading skills. The topic can be expressed in a word or a short phrase. It will not be a complete sentence because a topic does not express a complete thought; it is only the subject or content with which the text is concerned.

> **Example of a topic:** iPads in education
>
> **Not a topic:** Although many schools are rushing to purchase iPads for their students, little research shows that learning on iPads is more effective than other methods of learning.

The second example is not a topic because it is a complete thought and is thus presented in a complete sentence.

A few techniques can help you determine the topic of a reading.

Teaching Resources: See the PPT "Identifying Topics."

Connect IRW Power of Process Assignment: See the Connect IRW *Common Places* Master Course for pre-loaded PoP assignments to give students practice in identifying topics.

Consider the Reading's Title

A title like "Five Weight-Training Techniques" is very helpful, as it clearly describes the topic of the reading. Not all titles, however, are as revealing. A title like "Alternatives" does not give us much information about the topic.

Examine the Reading's Headings

Flipping through the text to examine its headings and subheadings will give you clues about the topic. Consider the textbook chapter headings in the illustration that follows.

2 Environmental Systems: Connections, Cycles, Flows, and Feedback Loops

Chapter Title

2.4 Energy for Life ← Heading

Green plants get energy from the sun ← Subheadings

How does photosynthesis capture energy?

The title tells us that the chapter is about environmental systems. Since section 2.4 is about energy, we can reasonably conclude that energy is an environmental system or is part of an environmental system. Looking at the subheadings, we have good reason to expect to learn about the connection between green plants and the sun. More specifically, we will learn about photosynthesis.

Teaching Resources: Consider explaining that new information is more easily understood when we link it to what we already know. See the Instructor's Manual (IM) for more information.

Look at the Reading's Illustrations

A preview should also involve looking at any photos or illustrations. The illustration labeled "Figure 2.2" (below) from the same textbook chapter can help us predict content. Reading the caption is a quick way to see how the illustration connects to the headings and subheadings. In this case, the illustration gives us an example of a food chain. This picture helps us get a better idea of what the chapter title means when it refers to "environmental systems."

From a simple preview of the chapter, we know we will be learning about systems such as those involving photosynthesis and the food chain. We can then think about what we already know about photosynthesis and the food chain so that when we encounter new information about those systems, we can have a frame of reference for the new knowledge, a place to plug the information into what we already know.

Figure 2.2 A system can be described in very simple terms.

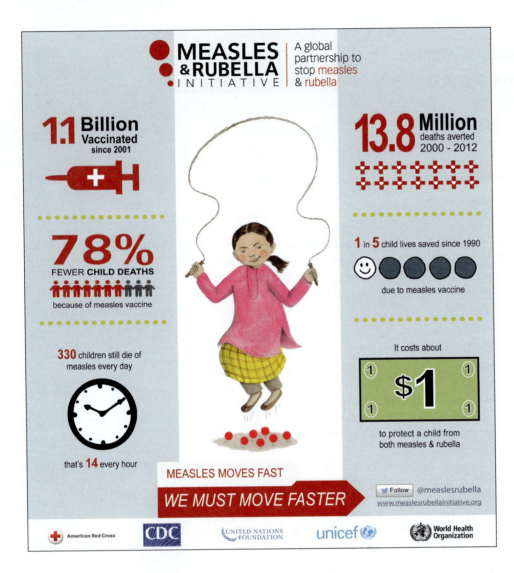

■ If you found this infographic in a text, what would you think the text's topic might be?

As you preview readings, you may find **infographics,** which are illustrations that combine artwork and text to convey information or explain topics. Maps are a common type of infographic. When you find infographics, take a minute to read through them. Look at the infographic "Measles & Rubella Initiative." A good infographic can provide quality information about a text's content.

To preview an infographic, you can use strategies similar to those that you use for text.

- **Read the title and subtitle for a clue to the topic.** In the infographic the title is followed by a subtitle, "A global partnership to stop measles & rubella." What clues do the title and subtitle give you about the topic?

- **Notice the different visual elements.** How are the elements grouped together? Do they have explanatory captions or headings?

- **Check how colors and sizes are used.** Bright colors and large shapes are often used to draw the reader's attention to aspects of the graphic that the creator thinks are important. Notice the use of the color red in this graphic. Why do you think red is used for some information?

- **Identify familiar images and what they mean.** One image used in the graphic is a syringe. What might readers think of when they see this image? What other images do you see? Do these images help you understand the graphic's content and meaning?

- **Look for elements that are essentially traditional charts and graphs in disguise.** For example, the graphic that shows a row of children and has "78%" written above it could be expressed as a statistic on a chart.

PRACTICE ② Previewing a Textbook Chapter

Study the title, headings, and photo below, taken from a chapter of a textbook entitled *Criminal Investigation*. Then answer the questions that follow.

CHAPTER OUTLINE

Introduction

Class versus Individual Characteristics

Comparison Samples

Soil and Pollen

Footwear, Foot, and Tires: Prints and Impressions

Paint

Glass

Fiber, Cloth Fragments, and Impressions

String, Cord, Rope, and Tape

Fingerprints

Forensic Odontology

Hair

Blood

Lip Cosmetics, DNA, and Lip Prints

Firearms

Tool Marks

Questioned Documents

Chapter 4 PHYSICAL EVIDENCE

▶**FIGURE 4-21**
Bite mark in food
A partially eaten "Moon Pie" bitten by one of the suspects in a double homicide. From the bite marks it can be determined that the individual making them had two non-equally protruding upper front teeth. Such information can play an important role in determining probable cause for arrest and/or search warrants. (Courtesy Dr. Richard R. Souviron, DDS, ABFO, Chief Forensic Odontologist, Dade County Medical Examiner Department, Miami, Florida)

1. **What do you think this chapter is about?**

   The types of physical evidence found at crime scenes.

2. **For whom do you believe this book is written?**

   Students studying criminology or law enforcement.

3. **What do you think the purpose of this chapter is?**

   To familiarize students with the types of physical evidence found at crime scenes and how the evidence is handled.

4. **The chapter outline lists a number of items, such as hair, blood, and lip cosmetics. What are these? What information do you think the chapter will present about these items?**

   These are types of physical evidence. The chapter will probably explain what they are, where they are found, why they are important, and how investigators will handle them.

Once you've skimmed over the graphic, you should be able to identify its topic. How does the topic of the infographic relate to the topic of the entire reading? Use the other information you've gleaned from previewing the reading to answer that question.

Look for Repeated Words and Phrases

Another method for identifying the topic is to briefly scan the reading. *Scanning*, or *skimming*, simply involves glancing at each paragraph, perhaps reading a sentence or two on each page, and getting a sense of the kind of content and the kind of writing in the text. As you scan the reading, note any words that come up again and again. Look also for synonyms. Imagine skimming over an article and seeing these words constantly repeated:

flying	phobia	fear	nervousness
flights	paranoia	calm	worry
fear of flying	travel	anxiety	uneasiness

These words suggest that the reading's topic is the fear of flying. Notice that some of the words are synonyms. *Anxiety, worry, uneasiness, nervousness, fear*—these words are all somewhat related in meaning. Finding the recurring words and synonyms will help you identify the topic at a glance.

Find Common Ideas

Some readings present a number of different elements, any one of which could be the topic. In such readings, asking what all these elements share may give you the topic of the reading. For example, consider these subheadings from a magazine article:

Biodiesel Engines

Hydrogen-Based Automobiles

Natural Gas Vehicles

Electric Cars

All the subheadings refer to vehicles that use alternative forms of energy. Thus the topic of the article is likely to be alternative-fuel vehicles.

PRACTICE **3** Identifying Topics

Read each passage that follows, and identify its topic. Use the context information to help you, and circle any repeated words and synonyms.

1. Context: A short paragraph found in a community newspaper's opinion section. The writer is a citizen of the community.

   Our town is woefully ill-prepared for flash floods. We do not have a recycling program. Our library has struggled to keep its doors open and has not had funds for new books for two years. In spite of these facts, the City Council is considering installing a new, expensive fence around the city park baseball field. The projects we need the most are not even being discussed. City Council members need to get their priorities in order and consider projects that will benefit all of the citizens in our town, not just sports enthusiasts.

   What is the topic? Deciding on town projects

2. Context: A short reading from a general-interest magazine.

   Although anxiety disorders are common, they often go undiagnosed for years. One reason for this delay in diagnosis is that the symptoms of anxiety can appear to be symptoms of other illnesses.

   In particular, anxiety disorders often produce physical symptoms such as intestinal discomfort, nausea, dizziness, shortness of breath, hyperventilation, and rapid heartbeat. Since these symptoms *can* be caused by physical ailments, people with anxiety often assume their disorder is physical. This assumption can lead them to even greater anxiety and worry because they fear there is something wrong with them and that they may die.

   All of the physical symptoms of anxiety—racing heartbeat, shortness of breath, hyperventilation, dizziness, nausea, and intestinal cramps—can converge on a sufferer at one time. This onslaught of physical symptoms can be terrifying. It can be hard for the victim to believe that the cause is "only anxiety" since the physical symptoms are so real.

   What is the topic? Physical symptoms of anxiety

WORKING WITH ASSIGNED WRITING TOPICS

Much of the writing you will do in college and the workplace will be based on topics assigned by your instructors or supervisors. Sometimes you will receive very specific topic information. For other writing assignments, you may be given a range of topic choices and will need to narrow the topic you choose. You will also encounter writing assignments that require you to supply your own topic.

In some ways, when an instructor selects the topic, the writing process is easier since the first step has already been completed for you. Nonetheless, you should plan to use four strategies to make sure that the paper you write fits the assignment.

Teaching Resources: See the IM for the worksheet "Interpreting Assignments."

Create an Assignment Page

Ideally, you will be provided with written instructions that tell you exactly what the topic is and how to approach it. If you do not have written directions, then you need to create your own page of instructions. Record all of the information about the assignment available to you. Here are some questions you should use to collect information for your assignment sheet:

Teaching Resources: Consider giving students oral instructions for a hypothetical assignment and having them create an assignment page based on your instructions. For more details, see the IM.

- What is the topic?
- Is research required? If so, what kind of research is expected?
- Is research (or the use of sources such as the Internet) prohibited?
- What is the writing purpose—to inform, to analyze and evaluate, or to persuade?
- What is the due date?
- What is the length requirement?
- What formatting is expected? Has the instructor specified font type and size, spacing, and heading format? Do you need to include a word count? Do you need to use a particular documentation style, such as MLA (Modern Language Association) style or APA (American Psychological Association) style?

Finally, take note of who will be reading your paper. You will need to consider your audience as you make decisions about what to include and how to word your ideas. Often with academic writing tasks, the instructor is the only person who will read what you write. Even though the instructor is just an audience of one, keeping in mind that you are writing for your professor is very important, as it will help you choose content, terminology, and a style appropriate for academic writing. Academic writing assignments always require formal writing, so avoid contractions and slang, use correct grammar and mechanics, and use third person.

Read and Reread the Assignment

A common writing mistake is to write about something that does not address the topic well enough. Understanding the assignment is imperative. Read the assignment instructions twice, making annotations to highlight each particular requirement. Merely reading through assignment instructions in a cursory fashion can lead to disastrous results. For example, students in a writing class were asked to write an essay about the morality of physician-assisted suicide. One student wrote a paper on why physicians' assistants should not commit suicide. A second reading of the assignment instructions would have helped this student avoid the embarrassment of misunderstanding the topic and, as a result, receiving a low grade.

Vocabulary Collection Word:
cursory

Your in-context definition:

_____

_____

A dictionary definition:

_____

_____

State the Paper's Topic in the Form of a Question

If the topic is not offered to you in the form of a question, transform the instructions into a question, as in the following example.

> **Original instructions:** Write an essay in which you examine how credit card companies exploit college students. Include a consideration of the various problems that result for students as a consequence of this exploitation.

> **Instructions reworded as a question:** How do credit card companies exploit college students, and what are the problems that result from this exploitation?

Seek Help If You Need It

The best way to find help is to talk to your instructor. If your instructor is not available, work with a staff member at a writing lab or tutoring center. If you are confused about the topic or unsure how to begin, seek help before you go any further with your writing.

DEVELOPING AND NARROWING A TOPIC FOR AN ESSAY

Some assignments require you to generate your own topic. The best place to start this process is on a blank sheet of paper. Brainstorm about the subject by writing down everything that comes to mind. Do not evaluate your ideas at this time. Just allow yourself the freedom to write them down.

Brainstorming for Topics

On the next page are some strategies you can use to brainstorm ideas for possible topics.

Teaching Resources: Some students do not like to read (or write) because they have little intellectual curiosity. Consider talking about the value of intellectual curiosity. Ask each student to write a question about which he or she is curious and conduct an Internet search to find its answer. See the IM for more suggestions to foster intellectual curiosity. Also, see the assignment "Are Your Curious?" in the Connect IRW *Common Places* Master Course.

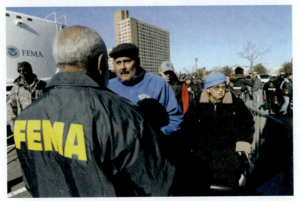

■ One way to find a topic is to consider an interesting scene, such as a photo of a street in New York City (top), and think of a question like "What advantages are there to living in a major city?" As you look at these photos, what questions come to mind? Can you think of a question that would lead you to a good essay topic?

- **Start with your own interests.** If you were not writing this paper, what would you be doing right now? What are your interests? What are you passionate about? Make a list.

- **Free your imagination.** If you had the time, money, energy, and ability, what activities would you pursue?

- **Reflect on the world around you.** Which world events affect or interest you? Are there issues about which you are passionate? Could you write an essay on one aspect of a particular world event?

- **Think about your life and your history.** You have a history of experiences and memories. What are some of these experiences or memories that are worthy of being recorded? Does your family tell the same stories again and again because they are fun to listen to? Have you learned lessons about life that might interest or benefit readers?

- **Visit your college's writing lab or tutoring center or your college library.** Librarians can help by guiding you to the resources that are available for topic selection. Some librarians will even help you think through topics that interest you and that would be suitable for your writing assignment. Writing center and tutoring center staff members are also good resources for topic development.

- **Use an online database available through your college library.** An **online database** is a collection of articles, studies, and other types of research information. Often, databases will also offer topic guides, such as "hot topics" or "current issues." Ask a reference librarian where you should start. Remember that you are using the database for ideas about subjects, not to find actual sources. If you use an actual source, you must give credit to the source in your essay. Unless your instructor requires you to find a source, use the database for topic searches.

- **Use an Internet search engine like *Google* or *Yahoo*.** Search engines can be powerful and quick tools for generating information. However, be aware that information found on the Internet is not always reliable. Avoid sites that offer papers for sale. Those kinds of Web sites often pop up when you are browsing for topics. Your instructors are familiar with the kinds of papers these Web sites sell or give away, and using a paper written by someone else for your writing assignment is plagiarism.

PRACTICE ④ Finding Topics of Interest

Imagine that your writing instructor asks you to choose a current event or issue that is important for your classmates to consider. The assignment is to select the issue and write an informative essay about it. What event or issue would you choose? Use one or more of the topic-selection techniques to choose a topic.

Answers will vary.

1. Your topic: _____

2. What process did you use for choosing this topic? Explain in one or two sentences:
   _____
   _____

Narrowing Topics

The topic you choose for an essay or other writing assignment (and sometimes even a topic that is assigned to you) needs to be adequately narrowed. For example, Raphael was considering majoring in music. When his instructor asked students to write an essay that discusses the daily activities involved in a job of interest to them, he decided to write about a job in the music industry. Though Raphael plays several instruments, he did not want to pursue a career as a performer. So he focused on finding jobs that do not include performing music.

Students often have trouble discerning whether an idea is narrow or broad. The ability to make such distinctions affects both reading and writing skills. Consider introducing the skill of identifying broader versus narrower ideas at this point.

To narrow the topic, Raphael started by breaking the subject into parts or types.

Next, he chose one type of music career—being a teacher—to discuss in his essay. After choosing "teacher," Raphael identified the following three kinds of teachers.

Teaching Resources: See the PPT "Broader or Narrower?"

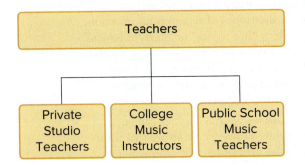

At this point, Raphael determined that these topics could be narrowed even further. Thus he identified three types of "college music instructors."

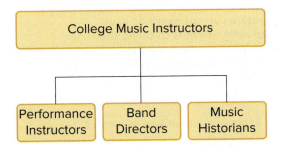

Raphael was then able to choose a narrower topic—the daily job activities of a band director—that was suitable for his assignment. To check whether he had sufficiently narrowed his topic to fit the scope of an essay, Raphael asked himself the questions that follow:

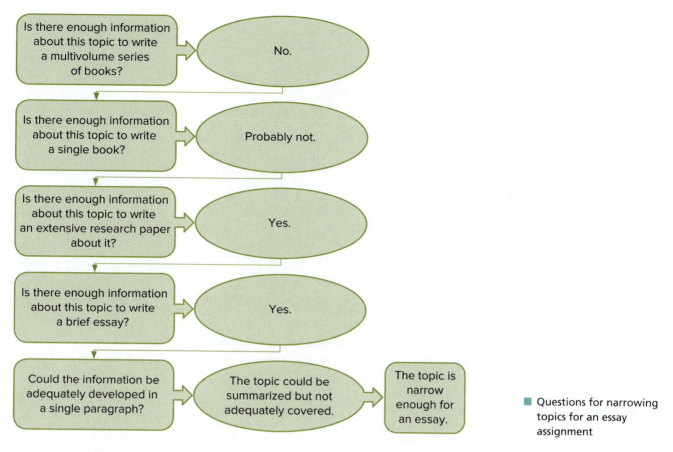

As Raphael did, you can use these questions to determine whether the topics you select are suitable for essays.

■ Questions for narrowing topics for an essay assignment

Teaching Resources: See the IM for a reproducible handout of this graphic. The oval shapes on the handout include blank spaces for student responses.

PRACTICE ⑤ Narrowing Topics for Essays

Use the "Questions for Narrowing Topics for an Essay Assignment" to consider each topic that follows. If the topic is suitable for an essay, write "Suitable for an essay." If the topic is too broad, narrow it so that it would be suitable for an essay.

1. The programming on cable television

Suitable for an essay

2. The importance of healthy lunches for schoolchildren

Suitable for an essay

3. Dentistry

How dentists can make patients feel comfortable

4. Why teens drop out of high school

Suitable for an essay

5. Sleep

Why people should take getting enough sleep more seriously

6. Stress

Methods for combating stress at work

7. Homelessness

How Seattle has dealt with homelessness

Note that some of these topics can be used for several genres (books, essays, paragraphs). Consider talking through other potential answers to help students see the thought process that goes into determining a topic's breadth and appropriateness for particular genres.

(continued)

8. Why tattoos are so popular

Suitable for an essay

9. Religious tolerance in the United States

Religious tolerance of Mormon missionaries in the southern United States

10. Cell phones

Why the extra price for smartphones is justified

USING PREWRITING STRATEGIES TO GENERATE IDEAS

Writers do not start at the beginning, go through the middle, and then finish at the end all in a straight line. They might get partway through the writing process only to realize they need to return to an earlier step to clarify their ideas.

Masterful writers go back and forth constantly, often throwing out entire paragraphs or pages as they figure out what they want to say and how they want to say it. Sometimes they go back to texts they were reading to gather more ideas. As you compose, be willing to go back and revise, rethink, and rewrite when your paper would benefit from your doing so.

Prewriting strategies—methods for coming up with ideas—are particularly useful techniques to employ again and again. Once you determine a topic, you can use prewriting to generate ideas. You may find yourself returning to different prewriting strategies to develop more ideas as you write.

As you experiment with prewriting methods, suspend judgment; that is, do not be critical about what you write. Write everything that comes to mind. You can weed out unsuitable ideas after you finish prewriting.

Practice using the following prewriting methods to find one or two of them that work well for you. You might find that some strategies work better than others for a particular topic.

Prewriting Strategy: Discussion

Discussing ideas with others can be a useful prewriting strategy. Meet with other students—in person, online, or by phoning or texting—and talk about your ideas for the assignment. While classmates make good discussion partners, family members and friends can also help you with ideas. Tell your discussion partners about your writing task, and ask them how they would proceed. Take notes so that you can revisit the ideas later when you are developing an outline.

PRACTICE 6 Using Discussion for Prewriting

Imagine your task is to write an essay about a current trend, such as getting a tattoo or wearing a certain style of clothing. You must determine why the trend is popular and how it developed. Use discussion to (1) identify a trend, (2) make a list of the possible reasons for its popularity, and (3) determine, if possible, how the trend developed. Jot down your answers on a separate sheet.

Answers will vary.

Teaching Resources: See the PPT "Student Prewriting Responses" for actual prewriting examples from students responding to Practices 6–11.

Prewriting Strategy: Simple Listing

Some people love to make lists. Even if you are not one of those people, you might still find that **listing** is a helpful prewriting strategy. The best way to use listing is to first turn the topic into a question.

For example, Luisa's topic for a writing assignment was the following: *strategies for increasing exercise.* First, she rewrote the topic as a question: What are some ways people can get more exercise? Next, she simply made a list of ways people could increase the amount of their daily exercise. Notice how her list, which follows, includes a wide variety of items. She did not censor any ideas at this stage; she wrote them all down and chose the best ones later on.

What are some ways people can get more exercise?

- go for a walk every day
- park farther away from entrances
- take stairs when possible
- join a gym
- join a community team (such as volleyball, baseball, and so on)
- find an exercise partner
- let their children be their "trainers"
- buy an exercise machine, such as an elliptical or treadmill
- buy a video and exercise with it
- use an online program for motivation
- hire a personal trainer
- do chores that require physical exertion, such as washing a car by hand
- find activities that combine exercise with fun, such as visiting and hiking in parks
- do the things they liked in childhood, such as bike riding, playing kickball, and so on

PRACTICE 7 Using Listing for Prewriting

Drawing on your own experience as a student or a parent, think about the following question: "What changes could be made in the public school system to increase student learning?" On a separate sheet, list at least ten ideas in response to the question.

Answers will vary.

Prewriting Strategy: Clustering

Clustering, or *mapping,* is a visual method of prewriting, illustrated on the next page. To use clustering, draw a circle in the middle of a sheet of paper, and in that circle write your paper's topic. As you think of an idea related to the topic, put the new idea in a new circle. Use lines to show relationships among ideas. Do not censor any ideas during this process, and do not worry if your result is messy. The example on the next page shows how Samuel used clustering for an essay about common rites of passage for American youth. (A *rite of passage* is an event or ritual that marks the change from one life stage to another.)

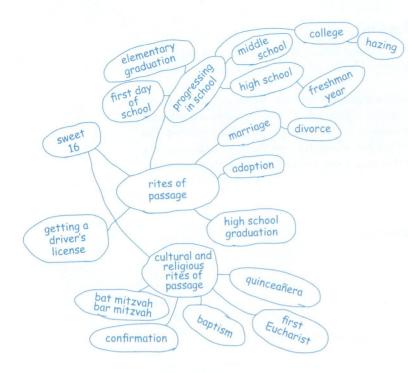

PRACTICE **8** Using Clustering for Prewriting

Use clustering to come up with examples or illustrations for an essay. The topic for this essay is *family traditions*. On a separate sheet, draw a clustering chart to prewrite about this topic. Some items you might consider are types of traditions, problems with traditions, and feelings about traditions.

Answers will vary.

Prewriting Strategy: Journalistic Questions

The six **journalistic questions** used by reporters can help you generate ideas about your topic. Think about your topic, and then consider these questions:

Who?   What?   Where?   When?   Why?   How?

Prewriting for essay due 4/25

Topic: The effects of battle on a soldier

Who? Soldiers, their families, health-care workers

What? Veterans often come back with depression,

anger, a sense of worthlessness, guilt, and extreme stress.

All of these symptoms are part of post-traumatic stress disorder.

Where? I will focus on veterans who returned from Afghanistan.

When? When we are at war.

Why? Extreme stress of war, not having enough mental

health resources, feeling that warriors/soldiers should

not have mental issues

How? I will focus on how these effects are recognized and treated.

PRACTICE (9) Using Journalistic Questions for Prewriting

Consider the issue of cheating on tests. Use the six journalistic questions to explore this issue. Write your answers for the following questions on a separate sheet.

Answers will vary.

Topic: Cheating on tests

1. Who is involved?
2. What happens?
3. Where does it happen?
4. When does it happen?
5. Why does it happen?
6. How does it happen?
7. What can we do to prevent it?

Keep in mind that you may not need to use all the information these questions will produce. At this stage, do not censor any information. If you wish, use a computer to type in your ideas. The example below shows Carolina's questions and answers about a particular topic.

Prewriting Strategy: Freewriting

Freewriting is one of the simplest prewriting methods. To freewrite, simply think about your topic and write everything that comes to mind for a limited period of time, such as three minutes. You do not need to write in complete sentences; it is fine to jot down phrases and words that come to mind. If you cannot think of anything to write, then type or write the topic's key words over and over. The point is not to censor ideas during this stage of writing. The example below shows Anita's freewriting. Notice how she simply recorded everything that came to mind.

Topic: sleep **deprivation**

makes it hard to concentrate, makes it hard to stay awake at work and school, can't live life well if you don't get enough sleep, must take time for yourself, set a good example for your kids by going to bed on time, sleep, sleep, deprivation, not enough of it, why, because too much is going on, eat dinner too late, too many activities, maybe should cut down on activities, eat a simple dinner like sandwiches, make a time you must go to bed every night, stick to it, teach kids the same, sleep, make room comfortable, nice atmosphere, comfy bed, fluffy pillows

Vocabulary Collection Word:
deprivation

Your in-context definition:
_____
_____

A dictionary definition:
_____
_____

PRACTICE (10) Using Freewriting for Prewriting

Imagine that you are required to write an essay about the decline of manners in public. Give yourself two to three minutes to freewrite. On a separate sheet, write down everything that comes to mind during this time period. If you get stuck, write a key word like *rude* or *polite* or *manners* over and over until you think of new ideas.

Answers will vary.

Prewriting Strategy: Freetalking

Freetalking is just like freewriting, except you use speech instead of a pen and paper. For two to three minutes, simply talk out loud to yourself about the topic. Consider using a cell phone that records your voice or a small digital recorder. Take your time and think out loud. It might be helpful to imagine you are talking to a friend about the topic. If you get stuck, repeat the topic over and over again. Jot down new ideas as they come to mind.

PRACTICE ⑪ Using Freetalking for Prewriting

Find a quiet place where you can talk to yourself or to your cell phone or digital recorder without distraction (or embarrassment!). Imagine that you have been assigned a paragraph or an essay on a social issue about which you are very concerned. More specifically, your assignment is to explain why this issue is worth our time and our attention. Examples of such issues are global warming, the eradication of poverty in a certain place, and the improvement of every elementary school. Use freetalking to explore why your chosen social issue is important. Write down at least three ideas you discover.

Answers will vary.

Vocabulary Collection Word:
eradication

Your in-context definition:

_____

_____

A dictionary definition:

_____

_____

CHAPTER ACTIVITIES

READING AND ANNOTATING

Below is a passage from the textbook *Environmental Science: A Study of Interrelationships* by Eldon Enger and Bradley Smith. This is the kind of textbook reading you will frequently encounter in college courses. Using the strategies in this chapter, preview the passage and jot down what you think the passage will be about. As you preview the text, identify the topic and try to predict what the main idea of the passage will be. Use annotations to mark key ideas. Additionally, mark any ideas that you find interesting. You will use your annotations for a later assignment.

Teaching Resources: Students can use the Power of Process tool in Connect IRW to analyze this reading. See the IM for instructions, or see this assignment pre-loaded into the *Common Places* Master Course.

Your Observations from Previewing

_____

_____

_____

_____

Lexile: 1340L

Potential Consequences of Global Warming and Climate Change

It is important to recognize that although a small increase in the average temperature of the Earth may seem trivial, such an increase could set in motion changes that could significantly alter the climate of major regions of the world. Computer models suggest that rising temperature will lead to changes to the hydrologic cycle, sea level, human health, the survival and distribution of organisms, and the use of natural resources by people. Furthermore, some natural ecosystems or human settlements will be able to withstand or adapt to the changes, while others will not.

YOUR ANNOTATIONS

Vocabulary Collection Word:
hydrologic

Your in-context definition:

_____

_____

A dictionary definition:

_____

_____

Poorer nations are generally more vulnerable to the consequences of global warming. These nations tend to be more dependent on economic activity that is climate-sensitive, such as subsistence agriculture, and lack the economic resources to adjust to the changes that global warming may bring. The Intergovernmental Panel on Climate Change has identified Africa as "the continent most vulnerable to the impacts of projected changes because widespread poverty limits adaptation capabilities."

Disruption of the Hydrologic Cycle

Among the most fundamental effects of climate change is disruption of the hydrologic cycle. Rising temperatures are expected to result in increased evaporation, which will cause some areas to become drier, while the increased moisture in the air will result in greater rainfall in other areas. This is expected to cause droughts in some areas and flooding in others. In those areas where evaporation increases more than precipitation, soil will become drier, lake levels will drop, and rivers will carry less water. Lower river flows and lake levels could impair navigation, hydroelectric power generation, and water quality and reduce the supplies of water available for agricultural, residential, and industrial uses.

Some areas may experience increased flooding during winter and spring, as well as lower supplies of water during summer. In California's Central Valley, for example, melting snow provides much of the summer water supply; warmer temperatures would cause the snow to melt earlier and thus reduce summer supplies, even if rainfall increased during the spring. More generally, the tendency for rainfall to be more concentrated in large storms as temperatures rise would tend to increase river flooding, without increasing the amount of water available.

Rising Sea Level

A warmer Earth would result in rising sea levels for two different reasons. When water increases in temperature, it expands and takes up more space. In addition, a warming of the Earth would result in the melting of glaciers, which would add more water to the oceans. Rising sea level erodes beaches and coastal wetland, inundates low-lying areas, and increases the vulnerability of coastal areas to flooding from storm surges and intense rainfall. By 2100, sea level is expected to rise by 15 to 90 centimeters (6–35 inches). A 50-centimeter (20-inch) sea-level rise will result in substantial loss of coastal land in North America, especially along the southern Atlantic and Gulf coasts, which are subsiding and are particularly vulnerable. Many coastal cities would be significantly affected by an increase in sea level. The land area of some island nations and countries such as Bangladesh would change dramatically as flooding occurred. The oceans will continue to expand for several centuries after temperatures stabilize. . . .

Changes to Ecosystems

Some of the most dramatic projections regarding global warming involve natural systems:

- Geographic distribution of organisms could be significantly altered by climate change. As climates warm, organisms that were formerly restricted to warmer regions will become more common toward the poles. The tundra biomes [habitats] of the world will be greatly affected because of the thawing of the permafrost, which will allow the northward migration of species. Similarly, mountainous areas will have less snow and earlier melting of the snow that does accumulate during the winter.

YOUR ANNOTATIONS

Vocabulary Collection Word:
subsistence

Your in-context definition:
_____
_____

A dictionary definition:
_____
_____

Vocabulary Collection Word:
storm surge

Your in-context definition:
_____
_____

A dictionary definition:
_____
_____

- Coral reefs are especially challenged because they are affected both by an increase in water temperature and by an increase in the acidity of the ocean. When carbon dioxide dissolves in water, it forms an acid. An increase in acidity would cause the skeletons of corals and the shells of many other organisms to tend to dissolve. This would make it more difficult for these organisms to precipitate calcium salts from the ocean to construct their skeletons and shells.

- Low-lying islands and shorelines will be especially impacted by rising sea level. Mangrove forests and marshes will be inundated and subjected to violent weather and storm surges.

Challenges to Agriculture and the Food Supply

Climate strongly affects crop yields. Yields will fall in regions where drought and heat stress will increase. In regions that will receive increased rainfall and warming temperatures, yields should increase. However, episodes of severe weather will cause crop damage that will affect yields. A warmer climate would reduce flexibility in crop distribution and increase irrigation demands. Expansion of the ranges of pests could also increase vulnerability and result in greater use of pesticides. Despite these effects, total global food production is not expected to be altered substantially by climate change, but negative regional impacts are likely. Agricultural systems in the developed countries are highly adaptable and can probably cope with the expected range of climate changes without dramatic reductions in yields. It is the poorest countries, where many already are subject to hunger, that are the most likely to suffer significant decreases in agricultural productivity.

Questions for Consideration

1. What is the topic of this textbook passage—global warming or rising sea levels? Explain and defend your answer in a paragraph.
2. How can global warming affect the growth of crops? Explain your answer in a paragraph.
3. Why should we be concerned with the issues raised in this reading? Explain your answer in two or three paragraphs.
4. What is the *hydrologic cycle*? Explain it in a paragraph.
5. What do the writers want students to know after reading this passage? Make a list of important items.

USING MODELS TO PRACTICE COMPOSING

The model essay that follows was written by Kendra, a student in an environmental science class. Kendra's assignment was to select a topic the instructor discussed in class and to explain why people should know more about that topic. Kendra remembered her instructor's discussion of the effects of rising sea levels and chose to write her essay on why people need to know about rising sea levels. For support, she planned to use information from her in-class lecture notes and information from her textbook. The passage "Potential Consequences of Global Warming and Climate Change" you read in the Reading and Annotating activity is from Kendra's textbook.

Follow the instructions below to see how Kendra used her text to write an essay.

Questions for Consideration

1. Global warming. Sea-level rise is one result of global warming.

2. In some areas, drought will be a problem and will affect agriculture. In other places, flooding will damage crops. Cropland near coasts may be damaged due to rising sea levels.

3. Every environmental change has effects on other parts of the environment. Some of those effects will matter to us, such as the loss of coastlines due to sea rise and the increase in famine in some countries across the world.

4. It is the process by which water evaporates and turns into clouds and then is dropped again to the earth as precipitation.

5. Global warming will affect "the hydrologic cycle, sea level, human health, the survival and distribution of organisms, and the use of natural resources by people. Furthermore, some natural ecosystems or human settlements will be able to withstand or adapt to the changes, while others will not."

1. Read the textbook selection below that Kendra used as a source, observing the types of annotations she created.

Potential Consequences of Global Warming and Climate Change
from *Environmental Science: A Study of Interrelationships*

KENDRA'S ANNOTATIONS

Rising Sea Level

A warmer Earth would result in rising sea levels for two different reasons. When water increases in temperature, it expands and takes up more space. In addition, a warming of the Earth would result in the melting of glaciers, which would add more water to the oceans. Rising sea level erodes beaches and coastal wetland, inundates low-lying areas, and increases the vulnerability of coastal areas to flooding from storm surges and intense rainfall. By 2100, sea level is expected to rise by 15 to 90 centimeters (6–35 inches). A 50-centimeter (20-inch) sea-level rise will result in substantial loss of coastal land in North America, especially along the southern Atlantic and Gulf coasts, which are subsiding and are particularly vulnerable. Many coastal cities would be significantly affected by an increase in sea level. The land area of some island nations and countries such as Bangladesh would change dramatically as flooding occurred. The oceans will continue to expand for several centuries after temperatures stabilize.

2 reasons for rising sea levels: expanding water, melting glaciers

Negative effects (good quote)

√ Prediction (good info)

Result: loss of land in North America (good quote)

Flooding and loss of land in other areas

2. Kendra wrote the following essay. Read Kendra's essay and the supplied annotations, which point out content and features. Insert your own annotations to mark writing strategies you would like to use in your essay.

Hayworth 1

Kendra Hayworth

Dr. Miller

INRW 0402

13 November 2013

The Effects of Rising Sea Levels

Somewhere in the world a steady *drip, drip, drip* sound can be heard. The sound comes from a massive glacier, slowly melting as

Introduction paragraph

Hayworth 2

the sun's rays penetrate the thinning ozone layer and warm the ice. How can a little drip hurt? Multiply that single drop by millions across the world and soon the melting ice will form enough water to cause problems. In fact, scientists predict that the sea level will rise by 6-35 inches by 2100 (Enger). *Information from textbook* Global warming has already begun to increase the sea levels, and more people should be concerned about this potentially deadly phenomenon. *Kendra's thesis statement*

As sea levels rise, beaches and their communities are affected. *Major supporting detail 1: coastal regions affected* An increase in sea level "erodes beaches and coastal wetland, inundates low-lying areas, and increases the vulnerability of coastal areas to flooding from storm surges and intense rainfall" (Enger). *Quote: used as support* Beaches are thin strips of land. It does not take much erosion to cause a narrow strip of land to disappear completely. Sand dunes can be washed out when sea water rises, and then sea water can easily flood the low-lying areas. *Explanation* When Hurricane Sandy hit the eastern region of the United States, entire beach communities were destroyed. *Example*

While the human cost of this destruction is apparent, there is also an ecological cost. *Transition sentence* When marshes and wetlands disappear, the species that live in those areas are threatened. *Major supporting detail 2: species threatened* As Dr. Miller has explained, whenever one species decreases, there are chain reactions such as increases in other species. For example, if marsh birds disappear because the environment has changed, mosquito populations could increase. Eventually, the spread of diseases would *Explanations and examples*

*Margin labels:*

- Information from textbook
- Kendra's thesis statement
- Major supporting detail 1: coastal regions affected
- Quote: used as support
- Explanation
- Example
- Transition sentence
- Major supporting detail 2: species threatened
- Explanations and examples

Hayworth 3

also increase since mosquitos carry disease. Ultimately, human life would be affected by these changes.

Rising sea levels will be a challenge for cities on the coast. In the United States, many major cities are on coastlines. Miami, New York, Los Angeles, New Orleans, Houston, Boston, and Seattle are among many cities that would be impacted by a rise in sea level. An increase in sea level of 20 inches "will result in substantial loss of coastal land in North America, especially along the southern Atlantic and Gulf coasts, which are subsiding and are particularly vulnerable" (Enger).

The impact of sea level rise could be devastating for coastal cities. The costs of relocating coastal populations and industries would be enormous, not to mention the social upheaval such changes would cause.

A rising sea level may not sound as alarming as a potential nuclear disaster or the threat of a disease like avian flu. However, the increase in sea level that is occurring right now is quite serious. More people need to know about the dangers that await if the government does not make changes to stop the rise of the oceans.

Major supporting detail 3: major cities on coasts threatened

Examples: cities on coastlines

Quote: used as proof

Causes and effects

Conclusion paragraph

A READING AND WRITING ASSIGNMENT

Using Kendra's essay as a model, write your own essay about a topic you have recently learned about in one of your classes and consider important. Consult your textbook for that class as a source.

Alternatively, use a different portion of the textbook passage "Potential Consequences of Global Warming and Climate Change" as a source for an essay on another aspect of climate change about which people should be concerned.

Refer to the Quick Start Guide to Integrated Reading and Writing Assignments for help as you write this essay.

Teaching Resources: See the Connect IRW *Common Places* Master Course for additional readings on the topic of climate change. Also, this writing assignment has been pre-loaded into the Connect IRW *Common Places* Master Course.

THINKING FROM AN INSTRUCTOR'S POINT OF VIEW

In a classroom setting, listening is important in at least two ways. For one, students have to focus on their instructors to learn the content covered in the course. Also, students must understand the instructions for assignments—what to read for homework, what to do for the next class, and so on. These tasks require basic listening tasks, yet some students have trouble with them.

If you were a college instructor, how would you help students learn to listen? Consider this scenario. The semester is fifteen weeks long, and it is week 9. Each week you have talked about the research essay due in week 10. There is a "no late work" policy in your class, so it is really important that students understand the assignment and its due date.

You leave some time during the last class of week 9 to answer students' last-minute questions. A few students stay after class to get clarification about the assignment.

On the research essay's due date, seven students out of twenty-five turn in their papers. That means only seven students will be eligible to pass because submitting the research essay is a requirement for passing. What follows are tears, apologetic e-mails, explanations about elderly relatives who died, and so on.

You do not want students to fail, but on the other hand, learning to listen and follow instructions is such an important life skill that you cannot send students the wrong message about listening. How do you proceed?

Write a paragraph or two explaining what you would say to students who failed to turn in their research papers. Write another paragraph or two presenting what you would say to your supervisor to explain why more than half your class failed.

ADDING TO YOUR VOCABULARY

This chapter's vocabulary words appear below.

Teaching Resources: See the Connect IRW *Common Places* Master Course for vocabulary study practices that accompany this chapter, as well as a chapter vocabulary quiz.

editorial	cursory	deprivation	eradication
hydrologic	subsistence	storm surge	

Choose five of the vocabulary words from this chapter that you would like to add to your vocabulary, and think about how you can use them this week. For example, one of this chapter's words is *cursory*. You can often substitute *cursory* for *hasty*, as in the examples that follow.

Example: I didn't have time to study, so I looked over my notes in a *hasty* fashion.

I didn't have time to study, so I looked over my notes in a *cursory* fashion.

List each of the five words you plan to use this week, and make note of a context in which you could use the new word.

Example: *Cursory.* I can use this word to teach my kids the difference between cleaning their room thoroughly and cleaning their room in a *cursory* way.

⊙ ADDITIONAL ASSIGNMENTS

1. In Practice 7, you wrote down ideas in response to this question: "What changes could be made in the public school system to increase student learning?" Using your prewriting, select two to four changes you believe would transform public education. Write an essay in which you present your ideas.

2. Study the infographic "Measles & Rubella Initiative," which appeared earlier in this chapter. First, determine its topic. Then complete the following assignments.

   a. Why is measles and rubella prevention important enough for the federal government to create posters and campaigns? Use a prewriting method to generate a page of thoughts to answer this question.

   b. Select a health or environmental issue you believe people should be concerned about. Create your own infographic poster in which you present the topic, your point about the topic, and information to help you prove your point. Use color and images to emphasize information. For additional infographic models, go to www.google.com, click on "images," and type in "infographics." Hit the enter key and you will see a screenful of various infographics you can use as models.

1. Answers will vary depending on each student's responses in Practice 7.

2. The topic is preventing measles and rubella.

   a. The topic is important because so many children die unnecessarily from these preventable diseases. The government wants parents to know that vaccinations are inexpensive and effective.

   b. Answers will vary.

EMOTIONAL INTELLIGENCE

A recent experiment shows the importance of *optimism,* a tendency to feel hopeful and positive about the future. A psychologist tested students at the University of Pennsylvania to determine whether optimism had an effect on grades. The experiment showed that by analyzing the level of optimism students had, researchers could more accurately predict the students' college success than by analyzing their SAT scores! Students who were on the optimistic end of the scale earned better grades than did students who were pessimistic.

Think about optimism, pessimism, and how they affect a person's success. Think of someone you know who is always optimistic. Has optimism made this person a better student or worker? Think of a pessimistic person you know. Has pessimism decreased this person's effectiveness? Write a paragraph in which you speculate on this topic.

Answers will vary.

CULTURAL LITERACY

Many of the readings in this book concern issues in the fields of psychology and interpersonal communications. What are these two fields? Do some Internet research to determine what experts in these areas study. Write a paragraph explaining what the experts in each field focus on. Give credit to the sources you consult.

The field of interpersonal communications involves the study of how individuals communicate with others and within groups. To study this kind of communication, a knowledge of and focus on psychology is needed. Psychology is the study of the mind and human behaviors.

CRITICAL THINKING

To find the best solution to a problem, we must consider all of the possible solutions. An enjoyable way to practice this kind of critical thinking is to find an answer to a problem.

To start, select a simple but irritating situation that needs a solution. For example, a disorganized pile of papers in your house might be a problem. How could you solve the problem? What solutions might you use that would help you eliminate the problem? Cleaning up the pile of papers is a good start, but it is not a permanent solution to the problem. Keeping the pile from coming back requires a daily organization routine.

Answers will vary.

Find a minor problem in your life that needs a solution. Think critically and creatively about how you might be able to solve the problem. If you wish, work with a classmate and see how many creative solutions you can devise. Write a paragraph in which you explain the problem and the solution you believe will work.

METACOGNITION

Answers will vary.

Did you know that students can change their learning ability over time? If you were never successful in math in the past, that does not mean you cannot learn to do math well now. Your ability to learn can develop and increase over time. What seemed unattainable last year might prove quite achievable this year.

Make a list of your assumptions about your strengths and weaknesses as a learner. Note any subjects about which you have thought, "I'm just not good at that." Next, think of a skill you found difficult at one time but later came to master. Write a paragraph explaining how you learned the skill. Finally, write a paragraph about whether you believe you can learn one of the weak subjects or skills you listed earlier. In your paragraph, explain the reasons for your beliefs.

If you were blindfolded and could touch only one part of an elephant—trunk, tusk, or leg, for example—what would you guess you were touching?

Main Ideas

In an old parable from India, several blind people each examine a single part of an elephant. Unable to see the whole, the person examining the tail assumes that the item in question is a rope. The person examining a tusk, meanwhile, determines that he is feeling a spear. The body is thought to be a wall, the trunk is mistaken for a snake, and the legs are assumed to be tree trunks. Without any knowledge of the whole—the elephant!—the investigators are led astray.

A written text can also be seen as a whole made up of various parts. While appreciating the individual parts is important, grasping how the parts make up the whole message—the writer's main idea—is crucial to comprehension.

Both reading and writing require us to work with main ideas. In reading, we must be able to identify main ideas, and in writing we must be able to communicate them. Our focus in this chapter is to see how the identification of particular parts of a reading can lead us to an understanding of the whole—the reading's main idea.

CHAPTER OBJECTIVES

After completing this chapter, students will be able to do the following:

- Identify topic sentences and implied main ideas in paragraphs.

- Compose topic sentences for paragraphs.

- Identify main ideas in essays.

- Find implied main ideas in essays.

- Compose effective thesis statements.

- Use parallel structure in thesis statements.

Connect IRW LearnSmart Achieve: Assign the topic "Identifying and Developing Main Ideas" for adaptive learning to accompany the chapter.

Teaching Resources: See the Chapter Quiz.

IDENTIFYING TOPIC SENTENCES AND IMPLIED MAIN IDEAS IN PARAGRAPHS

The purpose of a paragraph is to communicate a main idea to the reader. The main idea of a paragraph is expressed in a **topic sentence,** and additional sentences in the paragraph are called **supporting sentences.** These additional sentences provide explanations, examples, and other kinds of support to help readers understand the topic sentence.

A topic sentence generally has these characteristics:

- **A topic sentence expresses the most important point in the paragraph.** If a writer could point to only one sentence that communicates her message, it would be the topic sentence.

- **A topic sentence presents an idea that requires support.** The idea is complex enough to require additional explanation.

  Acceptable: High blood pressure can do more damage to health than many people realize.

  What damage can high blood pressure cause? We need more information.

  Inadequate: Many people have high blood pressure.

  This simple fact does not require any more explanation.

- **A topic sentence expresses an idea that is broader than the ideas in supporting sentences.** To support a topic sentence, other sentences must provide narrower and more detailed information.

  Topic sentence: High blood pressure can do more damage to health than many people realize.

  Supporting sentences: *In the supporting sentences, the writer will describe the specific types of damage high blood pressure can cause, such as weakening of arterial walls, enlargement of the heart, and scarring of the kidneys.*

- **A topic sentence is not a question.** A topic sentence makes a **claim**—an assertion that requires support—and that claim is backed up by details in the other sentences in the paragraph.

Keeping in mind these characteristics will help you both identify and compose topic sentences.

Identifying Topic Sentences

In addition to recognizing topic sentences based on their characteristics, you can also identify topic sentences by means of this four-step process.

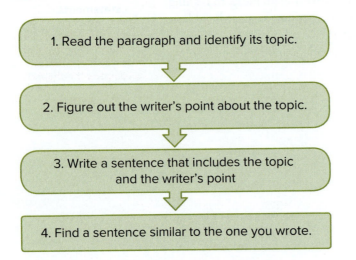

1. Read the paragraph and identify its topic.

2. Figure out the writer's point about the topic.

3. Write a sentence that includes the topic and the writer's point

4. Find a sentence similar to the one you wrote.

Teaching Resources: See the PowerPoint presentation (PPT) "Identifying and Composing Topic Sentences."

For an activity on identifying topic sentences, try this: Have students create a table with three columns to use when analyzing readings. In the first column, they write the topic; in the second, the writer's point about the topic. In the third column, students write a topic sentence using the info from the first two columns. Students then look through the reading to find a sentence similar to the one they wrote.

Example:

Topic	Point about the Topic	Topic Sentence

■ Steps for identifying topic sentences

Study the following paragraph to see how the four-step process works. The **bold** print shows repeated words that suggest the topic.

Stress management is an emotional intelligence skill that increases the value of employees in a workplace. Personnel who have methods for relieving **stress** are much less likely to lash out at either coworkers or customers. Additionally, the ability to **control stress** helps workers be more efficient because they are not distracted by tension and worry. Staff who are successful at **keeping their stress levels down** will often rise to a higher level and become especially valued employees.

> Topic: stress management
>
> Detail: makes people less likely to lash out
>
> Detail: helps with efficiency
>
> Detail: makes employees more valued

Since managing stress is repeatedly mentioned in the paragraph, we can reasonably guess that the topic of the paragraph is stress management. The details in the paragraph suggest that stress management has benefits for employees. Once we identify the topic and the details about the topic, we can use the four steps to identify the topic sentence.

1. Read the paragraph and identify its topic.
   Topic: stress management

2. Figure out the writer's point about the topic.
   Writer's point: importance of stress management skills for workers

3. Write a sentence that includes the topic and the writer's point.
   Your sentence: Stress management is important for workers.

4. Find a sentence similar to the one you wrote.
   Topic sentence: Stress management is an emotional intelligence skill that makes employees valuable.

By using these four steps, we created a sentence with a meaning similar to the sentence we found in the original paragraph. If you can correctly identify the topic and the point the writer is making about the topic, you can find the paragraph's topic sentence.

Additionally, you can check to see whether the sentence you've identified has the qualities that topic sentences generally have. In this case, the sentence we have identified has the following characteristics.

Characteristics of an Effective Topic Sentence

- It expresses the most important point in the paragraph.
- It presents an idea that requires support.
- It expresses an idea that is broader than the ideas in supporting sentences.
- It is not a question.

In this example, the topic sentence is the first sentence in the paragraph. While a topic sentence is often placed first, it does not have to be. It may be placed in the body of a paragraph or even at the end. The key to finding a topic sentence is not to focus on where it is placed; rather, you need to put the main idea communicated in the paragraph into your own words and then find a sentence that corresponds to that idea. Complete the following exercise to see if you can find the topic sentence of a paragraph.

PRACTICE ❶ Finding Topic Sentences

Annotate the following paragraph to determine its main idea and topic sentence. Fill in the answers below.

What is the difference between a credit card and a debit card? Both can be used instead of cash or checks to make purchases online as well as at places of business. Debit cards are often associated with major credit card companies such as MasterCard

YOUR ANNOTATIONS

Topic

Similarity

(continued)

and Visa. Yet debit cards function quite differently from credit cards. The fundamental difference is that when you use a credit card, you are actually borrowing money from a bank (the credit card company). That money must be paid back at the end of the grace period (usually about a month), or interest will be charged to you on the amount of the loan. With a debit card, you are spending your own money. Most often the money comes directly out of your checking account. <u>While there are other dissimilarities, the principal difference between a credit card and a debit card is the difference between taking out a loan and spending money that you already have "on hand."</u>

Difference

Difference

Topic sentence

Teaching Resources: See the Instructor's Manual (IM) for the worksheet "Identifying and Composing Main Ideas in Paragraphs."

1. Read the paragraph and identify its topic.

   Topic: <u>Differences between credit and debit cards</u>

2. Figure out the writer's point about the topic.

   Writer's point: <u>Credit cards are a loan; debit cards are a way of spending your own money.</u>

3. Write a sentence that includes the topic and the writer's point.

   Your sentence: <u>Credit cards and debit cards may seem similar, but they are actually very different: credit cards are a way of borrowing money, while debit cards allow you to spend your own money.</u>

4. Find a sentence similar to the one you wrote.

   <u>While there are other dissimilarities, the principal difference between a credit card and a debit card is the difference between taking out a loan and spending money that you already have "on hand."</u>

Conclusion: If your analysis is correct, you have very likely identified the topic sentence. <u>The last sentence is the topic sentence. It is the main idea of the paragraph.</u>

Finding Implied Main Ideas in Paragraphs

Some paragraphs do not include a stated topic sentence. In such paragraphs, the main idea is **implied**—suggested by the ideas in the paragraph but not explicitly stated. Readers must figure out the main idea and put it into their own words. When they do so, they are composing an **implied topic sentence.** Use this modified four-step process to identify the implied main idea, put it into your own words, and create an implied topic sentence.

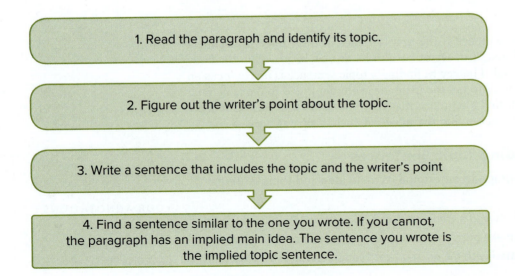

1. Read the paragraph and identify its topic.

2. Figure out the writer's point about the topic.

3. Write a sentence that includes the topic and the writer's point

4. Find a sentence similar to the one you wrote. If you cannot, the paragraph has an implied main idea. The sentence you wrote is the implied topic sentence.

■ Steps for identifying an implied topic sentence

What follows is a paragraph from a psychology textbook. This paragraph does not have an explicit topic sentence. To find the paragraph's implied main idea, we must first identify the topic. The repetition, in **bold** print, of the terms *middle school* and *children* suggests that the topic involves middle school children. The terms *obsess, being scrutinized, being judged,* and *self-consciousness* help sharpen the focus of the topic. Other details will help us determine the writer's point about the topic.

In the **middle school** years, **children** may obsess over perceived personal flaws such as their height, weight, hair color, style of clothing, and even the types of music they choose. They believe that they are being scrutinized by everyone around them, and many **middle school children** feel that they are constantly being judged by their peers. **Children** in **middle school** can focus so much on their image that their grades suffer, they get depressed, or they are unable to maintain friendships. This self-consciousness can also result in dangerous or tragic behaviors, such as experimenting with drugs or harming themselves.

Topic: middle school children

Detail: They obsess over perceived personal flaws.

Detail: They believe they are being watched.

Detail: They feel they are being judged.

Effect: Their self-focus can have negative results.

Effect: Their self-consciousness can even have dangerous effects.

We can use the four-step process to figure out the implied main idea and to write an implied topic sentence.

1. Read the paragraph and identify its topic.
   Topic: the self-consciousness of middle school children

2. Figure out the writer's point about the topic.
   Writer's point: detrimental effects self-consciousness can have

3. Write a sentence that includes the topic and the writer's point.
   Your sentence: Middle school children may experience detrimental effects due to extreme self-consciousness.

4. Find a sentence similar to the one you wrote. If you cannot, the paragraph has an implied main idea. The sentence you wrote is the implied topic sentence.
   There is no similar sentence in the paragraph. Thus, the sentence from step 3 is the implied topic sentence.

Teaching Resources: See the PPT "Finding Implied Main Ideas in Paragraphs."

Notice that each of the sentences in the paragraph above presents a type of difficulty middle school children experience. No single sentence sums up these difficulties, so the main idea is implied, not stated. We could write the implied topic sentence in a variety of ways, each of which is effective:

- Middle school children are at a difficult stage of life because of social stress.
- The extreme self-consciousness of middle school children makes this stage of life a challenge.
- The middle school years present social challenges for children because of self-consciousness.

When you encounter a paragraph with an implied topic sentence, write your own implied topic sentence in the margin. You will then be able to go back to the paragraph and read your implied topic sentence to get a quick summary of the paragraph's point.

A well-written paragraph always has a main idea. It may be stated explicitly in a topic sentence, or it may be implied, in which case you will have to write the implied topic sentence in your own words. Practice determining topic sentences in the exercise that follows.

PRACTICE 2 Finding Implied Main Ideas in Paragraphs

The following paragraph has an implied main idea, not an explicit topic sentence. Use annotations to determine the topic and the writer's point, and then compose your own topic sentence for the paragraph.

Banks frequently make credit cards available to college students. Some people are critical of this practice, pointing out that many college students are not mature enough—in terms of financial wisdom—to handle the borrowing potential that easy credit offers. Despite these criticisms, such cards do offer benefits to college students. Having a credit card can provide a student with an emergency fund. Not many college students have the luxury of a robust savings account. In the event of an emergency, such as a serious health issue, a wrecked vehicle, or stolen textbooks, having a credit card might be a real advantage. Having a credit card also enables a student to begin the process of building credit, which can have long-term benefits. The careful use of credit cards throughout college may mean the student will have built enough credit history to qualify for a home mortgage after graduation.

YOUR ANNOTATIONS

Topic

One advantage of credit cards

Another advantage of credit cards

1. Read the paragraph and identify its topic.

   Topic: Making credit cards available to college students

2. Figure out the writer's point about the topic.

   Writer's point: Credit cards offer some benefits.

3. Write a sentence that includes the topic and the writer's point.

   Your sentence (implied topic sentence): Giving credit cards to college students can be a good idea because credit cards can serve as an emergency fund, and they can also help students build credit.

Finding Topic Sentences in Journalistic Style Paragraphs

Articles that appear in newspapers and popular magazines often have many very short, often single-sentence, paragraphs, even when the content could logically be combined into one longer paragraph. The use of short paragraphs is a feature of journalistic writing—a less formal style of writing intended to be read by a **diverse** general audience.

When you read essays that contain short, journalistic style paragraphs, group together the paragraphs that address the same topic. Use the grouped set of paragraphs to determine the explicit or implied topic sentence. For example, consider these paragraphs from a college newspaper article.

Vocabulary Collection Word:
diverse

Your in-context definition:

_____

_____

A dictionary definition:

_____

_____

One program that is funded by the student use fee at Suntown College is the Academic Tutoring Project.

Students can enroll in Academic Tutoring and do not have to pay anything out-of-pocket for the services.

The student use fee is also used to help fund the Suntown Mental Health Clinic, a resource students can use free of charge for counseling and other mental health services.

Detail: Student use fee pays for tutoring.

Detail: Tutoring is free.

Detail: The student use fee funds Mental Health Clinic.

Detail: Counseling is free.

Although this passage consists of three very short paragraphs, these paragraphs are unified. They are all about the student use fee, and they all answer the question "What does the student use fee cover?"

Topic: student use fee

Writer's point: what the student use fee is used for

Your sentence: The student use fee at Suntown College funds free tutoring and free mental health services for students.

After you group together short paragraphs that are related, use the four-step process for finding the topic sentence. Keep in mind that the topic sentence may be explicit (stated) or implied (unstated).

Connect IRW Power of Process Assignment: See the Connect IRW *Common Places* Master Course for a pre-loaded PoP assignment that asks students to analyze journalistic style texts.

PRACTICE ③ Analyzing Journalistic Style Paragraphs

Read and annotate the paragraphs that follow. Determine the topic sentence. If the topic sentence is stated, underline it. If not, write it in your own words.

Apartheid was a legal system of segregation and institutionalized racism in South Africa. It began officially in 1948, although South Africa had discriminated against people of color since the Dutch colonial period.

One of the most prominent and influential critics of apartheid was Nelson Mandela. Born in 1918, Mandela came of age during the institutionalization of apartheid.

Mandela practiced nonviolent resistance to apartheid. He was a natural leader.

Although he spent twenty-seven years in prison for an alleged plot to overthrow the racist government, he eventually became president of South Africa in 1994. Nelson Mandela was instrumental in ending apartheid in South Africa.

YOUR ANNOTATIONS

Topic: apartheid and Mandela

Topic sentence

1. Topic: Apartheid and Nelson Mandela

2. Writer's point: What Mandela did about apartheid

3. Topic sentence or implied main idea: Nelson Mandela was instrumental in ending apartheid in South Africa.

COMPOSING TOPIC SENTENCES FOR PARAGRAPHS

As you use the four-step process to identify topic sentences in readings, you are—at the same time—learning how to write topic sentences. When you compose a topic sentence, it should have the same four characteristics we described earlier.

- A topic sentence expresses the most important point in the paragraph.
- It presents an idea that requires supporting sentences.
- It expresses an idea that is broader than the ideas in supporting sentences.
- It is not a question.

You can follow a three-step process, shown on the next page, for composing a topic sentence.

■ Steps for composing a topic sentence

For example, suppose you are assigned an essay in which you are to identify and discuss the core college courses that are most important for being a well-informed person in today's world. You decide to consider three courses—World Geography, Public Speaking, and American Government. Here's how you might compose a topic sentence for your paragraph on the geography course.

1. Write down your topic.
   Topic: college course in World Geography
2. Write down the point you wish to make.
   Your point: what taking World Geography means for understanding world events
3. Write a sentence that combines your topic and your point.
   Your topic sentence: Because it is so important for understanding world events, World Geography should be a required course for all college students.

You can check the quality of your topic sentence by considering whether it has the characteristics of topic sentences.

• **Does it express the most important point in the paragraph?** Yes. The other sentences will help prove the point that college students should take World Geography.

• **Does it present an idea that requires supporting sentences?** Yes. Readers will want to know why the course is so important.

• **Does it express an idea that is broader than the ideas in supporting sentences?** Yes. The supporting sentences will give specific reasons why the course is important enough to be required of all college students.

• **Is it a question?** No.

Practice writing your own topic sentences in the exercise that follows.

PRACTICE ④ Writing Topic Sentences

Below you will find sets of topics and points about those topics. For each set, write a topic sentence by combining the topic and the point to be made about it. Use the characteristics of topic sentences to check your work.

1. Topic: choosing a career

   Point: how aptitude tests can help

   Your topic sentence: Aptitude tests can help people choose careers.

2. Topic: home water filters

   Point: how they help the taste of tap water

   Your topic sentence: Home water filters can improve the taste of tap water.

(continued)

3. Topic: easing mental depression

Point: how a new hobby can help

Your topic sentence: Taking up a new hobby can help ease depression.

4. Topic: volunteering

Point: four steps for choosing appropriate volunteering opportunity

Your topic sentence: Following four steps can help people choose appropriate volunteering opportunities.

You can also practice composing topic sentences as you analyze readings. This kind of practice helps you understand what you are reading. Making it a habit to write out the topic sentences of the paragraphs you read yields two additional benefits. First, you improve your ability to write your own topic sentences. Second, you can use the topic sentences you write to grasp the broader idea that unites all of the paragraphs, as you will see later in this chapter.

PRACTICE **5** Identifying and Writing Topic Sentences

The following textbook passage contains three body paragraphs. For each body paragraph, identify the topic and the writer's point about the topic. Write a sentence that combines the topic with the writer's point. If the main idea is expressed in a topic sentence, write the topic sentence.

PARAGRAPH A

Guilt both alerts us to and motivates us to correct a wrong we have committed. Guilt is a lot like pain. When you cut yourself, you feel pain at the site where the injury occurred. The pain motivates you to repair the injury before it becomes infected and festers. Guilt also motivates us to avoid harming ourselves and others. We refrain from cheating on an exam or from stealing someone's laptop—even when no one is around to see us take it—because the very thought of doing so makes us feel guilty.

1. Topic: Guilt

2. Writer's point: What guilt does

3. Topic sentence in your words: Answers will vary.

4. Topic sentence from paragraph or implied topic sentence: Guilt both alerts us to and motivates us to correct a wrong we have committed.

PARAGRAPH B

Guilt is frequently regarded as a barrier to personal freedom and happiness. Some of us respond to guilt with resistance, either trying to ignore it entirely or getting angry at the person who "made" us feel guilty. But at the same time, we generally regard a person who feels no guilt—such as a sociopath—as inhuman and a monster.

(continued)

1. Topic: Guilt

2. Writer's point: Attitudes toward guilt

3. Topic sentence in your words: Answers will vary.

4. Topic sentence from paragraph or <u>implied topic sentence:</u> While we know guilt can be good for us, we often resent its presence.

PARAGRAPH C

Guilt is often broadly defined to include shame. However, the two are different. Guilt results when we commit a moral wrong or violate a moral principle. Shame, on the other hand, occurs as a result of the violation of a social norm, or not living up to someone else's expectations for us. Teenagers who are lesbian, gay, or bisexual may feel shame for not living up to the expectations of their family, church, or society—but they may not feel moral guilt. Rather than motivating us to do better, shame leaves us feeling inadequate, embarrassed, and humiliated. As good critical thinkers, it is important that we distinguish between guilt and shame.

1. Topic: Guilt and shame

2. Writer's point: The difference between guilt and shame

3. Topic sentence in your words: Answers will vary.

4. <u>Topic sentence</u> from paragraph or implied topic sentence:

   As good critical thinkers, it is important that we distinguish between guilt and shame.

IDENTIFYING MAIN IDEAS IN ESSAYS

Just as a paragraph is a group of sentences that expresses and supports one main idea, an *essay* is a set of paragraphs that work together to support a main idea. Essays can take many forms, including magazine articles, scholarly journal articles, brief academic papers, and personal reflections.

Essays vary widely in depth, coverage, and use of technical language, depending on their context, purpose, and audience. An essay written for a medical journal, for example, is likely to be a well-researched piece of writing because of the expectations of its readers—doctors and professors—who require proof of careful research and reasoning in the essays they read. On the other hand, an essay written for an introductory biology course will be much shorter and will not go into much depth. The instructor will expect far less research and detail since the students reading the piece are just beginning to study the subject.

A common thread uniting all essays is that each one uses multiple paragraphs to communicate a main idea to an audience. Usually, a writer introduces the topic, states the main idea, supports or explains the main idea in a series of paragraphs, and offers a conclusion. Not all essays follow this pattern, but most essays include all four elements:

- Introduction
- Statement of the main idea (thesis statement)
- Supporting paragraphs
- Conclusion

Teaching Resources: See the PPT "Identifying and Composing an Essay's Thesis Statement."

Theorists in reading and writing disciplines sometimes differ in the terminology used to describe ideas. For an explanation of the terms used in this text, see the IM.

Recognizing the Characteristics of Thesis Statements

The main idea of an essay is its **thesis statement.** The thesis statement provides the writer's topic and the point the writer wishes to make about the topic. Often, a thesis statement is expressed in a single sentence, but sometimes it will span two or three sentences. To help readers understand or accept a thesis statement, the writer must provide support. Each of the body paragraphs in an essay provides such support.

Like a topic sentence, a thesis statement has particular characteristics.

- **A thesis statement expresses the most important point of an essay.** While an essay may contain a great deal of information, all of that material is used to support a central point: the thesis statement.

- **A thesis statement presents an idea that requires support.** The idea or opinion demands explanation, evidence, or discussion in the essay.

  Acceptable: The Americans with Disabilities Act (ADA) has significantly helped disabled people, but more changes are needed to ensure that equal opportunities are available for people with disabilities.

  How has the ADA helped people, and what changes still need to be made? The thesis statement needs support to answer these questions.

  Inadequate: Some college students have physical disabilities.

  This simple fact does not require any more explanation.

- **A thesis statement expresses an idea that is broader than the ideas in supporting paragraphs.** To support a thesis statement, narrower and more detailed information is required.

  Thesis statement: The Americans with Disabilities Act (ADA) has significantly helped disabled people, but more changes are needed to ensure that equal opportunities are available for people with disabilities.

  Supporting paragraphs: *The writer will use some supporting paragraphs to discuss areas in which the ADA has improved life for disabled people, such as public transportation and access to public places. In other supporting paragraphs, the writer will discuss the changes that still need to be made, such as greater employment opportunities and more independent living options.*

- **A thesis statement is not a question.** A thesis statement makes a point that the writer believes and wants readers to believe or understand; thus, a thesis statement will not be a question.

Comparing Thesis Statements and Topic Sentences

You may have noticed that the characteristics of thesis statements are similar to those of topic sentences. In fact, thesis statements and topic sentences are similar in that they both communicate main ideas. The difference between them lies in their functions within an essay. If you have only a single paragraph, you will have only one single main idea, expressed either in an explicit topic sentence or in an implied topic sentence. You already know the purpose of the topic sentence: it tells you the most important point of the paragraph.

What happens when paragraphs are put together in an essay? These paragraphs still have topic sentences, and each topic sentence still tells the reader the most important point of its paragraph. However, the paragraphs in an essay serve to support the thesis statement. In the case of the thesis statement concerning the Americans with Disabilities Act given earlier, we might write four paragraphs to support the thesis statement. Each paragraph's main idea, stated in its topic sentence, would provide evidence for the thesis statement, as the diagram on the next page shows.

Thesis statement: The Americans with Disabilities Act (ADA) has significantly helped disabled people, but more changes are needed to ensure that equal opportunities are available for people with disabilities.

Body paragraph 1	Body paragraph 2	Body paragraph 3	Body paragraph 4
Topic sentence:	Topic sentence:	Topic sentence:	Topic sentence:
The ADA has improved the public transportation opportunities for people with disabilities.	Additionally, the ADA has given people with disabilities improved access to public places.	However, employment opportunities are still hard to find for many people with disabilities.	Also, people with disabilities continue to need better housing options.

Notice how the thesis statement in the preceding illustration presents a broader idea than each of the topic sentences. Just as a topic sentence presents a broader idea than the supporting sentences in a paragraph, the thesis statement of an essay presents a broader idea than the topic sentences of the supporting paragraphs. Try your hand at distinguishing thesis statements from topic sentences by completing the exercise that follows.

PRACTICE ⑥ Distinguishing Thesis Statements from Topic Sentences

In each group below, you will find a thesis statement and several topic sentences. Put an X in the blank for the sentence that is the thesis statement.

1. _____ Cooking at home saves money.

   __X__ Knowing how to cook is advantageous in terms of savings, food safety, nutrition, and relaxation.

   _____ Cooking can be a relaxing activity.

   _____ The nutritional value of homemade meals is superior to that of fast food.

   _____ Home cooks can be assured their food is safely prepared.

2. _____ Some people take risks because of a need for sensory stimulation.

   _____ Risk taking is associated with aggression and hostility.

   _____ People who are impulsive are more likely to be risk takers.

   __X__ Risk taking is a result of a complex set of human needs, behaviors, and emotions.

3. _____ Attending college with people of all backgrounds helps ease social tensions between groups.

   _____ Diversity on campus leads to diversity in the workforce, which has been shown to benefit businesses.

   _____ As individuals become more educated, their income generally rises.

   __X__ Supporting affirmative action in college admissions is in the national interest.

Identifying the Thesis Statement in an Essay

Like topic sentences, thesis statements express a main idea by providing the *topic* and the *writer's point about the topic*. Thus, you can use a process for finding thesis statements that is similar to the one you used for finding topic sentences. These five steps will help you identify thesis statements.

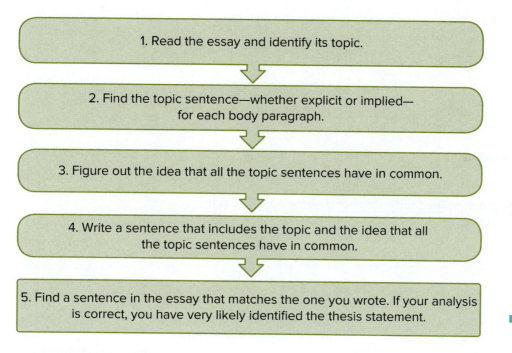

1. Read the essay and identify its topic.

2. Find the topic sentence—whether explicit or implied—for each body paragraph.

3. Figure out the idea that all the topic sentences have in common.

4. Write a sentence that includes the topic and the idea that all the topic sentences have in common.

5. Find a sentence in the essay that matches the one you wrote. If your analysis is correct, you have very likely identified the thesis statement.

■ Steps for identifying a thesis statement

Now we will examine in more detail each step in the process of identifying thesis statements.

Step 1: Read the essay and identify its topic.

Identify the essay's topic by analyzing the title, introduction, and context of the publication. Titles often reveal the writer's focus. We can guess reasonably well the topic of an essay entitled "The Benefits of Acupuncture." Of course, such guesses can be wrong, so it is important to follow guesses with a close reading of the essay.

Sometimes introduction paragraphs provide important clues to the topic of the essay. If "Surprises in Vermont" begins with a story of a couple finding gold in their backyard, you might reasonably guess that the surprise in question is that gold exists in Vermont.

Consider also the context of the reading. If an article titled "A Step Forward in New Mexico" is published in a journal written for high school principals, you might guess the article would concern good things happening in education in New Mexico. Reading the introduction paragraph would help confirm your guess.

Step 2: Find the topic sentence—whether explicit or implied—for each body paragraph.

Each body paragraph in an essay will have a main idea—either expressed in a topic sentence or implied. Read and carefully annotate each body paragraph, underlining the topic sentence or expressing the implied topic sentence in your own words.

Earlier in this chapter, we found an implied main idea in the paragraph about middle school children (see "Finding Implied Main Ideas in Paragraphs"). Now we will return to that paragraph and put it into the context of an essay. The paragraph about middle school children is only one of four body paragraphs in an essay about the theories of Jean Piaget, a well-known Swiss psychologist. By examining the topic sentences for all of the paragraphs, you can figure out the idea that unites them. The example below displays the topic sentence for the paragraph about middle school children. It also displays the topic sentences for the other three body paragraphs, with student annotations.

Topic sentence of body paragraph 1: According to Jean Piaget, in the <u>first stage of development,</u> which occurs in infancy and toddlerhood, children **experience** challenges in their motor development and language **acquisition**.

First stage (motor and language challenges)

Topic sentence of body paragraph 2: In the elementary school years, which Piaget designates as the <u>second stage of development,</u> children learn to think more logically and **practice** more independence from parents.

Second stage (logical thinking and more independence)

Implied main idea of body paragraph 3: <u>Middle school children</u> may **experience** <u>extreme social stress.</u>

Third stage (social stress)

Topic sentence of body paragraph 4: <u>The fourth stage of development</u> occurs in high school when children's **experiences** can have profound effects on their lives as adults.

Fourth stage (experiences with profound consequences)

Once you have determined the topic sentence for each paragraph in an essay, highlight ideas and words (including synonyms) they have in common, as the example above illustrates.

Step 3: Figure out the idea that all the topic sentences have in common.
Reread the topic sentences, asking yourself, "What point do all of these sentences support?" In the paragraphs shown in step 2, the topic sentences all concern *chronological stages* in a child's development. Additionally, the topic sentences focus on what children *experience* during these stages.

Step 4: Write a sentence that includes the topic and the idea that all the topic sentences have in common.
Now you are ready to combine the essay's topic and the common point made by the supporting paragraphs into one sentence.

> **Topic:** Jean Piaget's description of children's life stages
>
> **Writer's point:** each stage and the experiences in it
>
> **Your sentence combining the topic and the writer's point:** Children progress through four developmental stages and have different experiences in each stage, according to Jean Piaget.

Step 5: Find a sentence in the essay that matches the one you wrote. If your analysis is correct, you have very likely identified the thesis statement.
Read through the essay looking for a sentence that, like your sentence, contains the essay's topic and the writer's point about the topic. Do not expect the sentence you find to match your sentence precisely. In fact, sometimes you will find the thesis statement and then realize that the sentence you wrote was off-track. The goal is to identify the writer's point about the topic. When you understand the writer's point, you will be able to determine the thesis statement.

Vocabulary Collection Word: acquisition

Your in-context definition:

_____

_____

A dictionary definition:

_____

Connect IRW Power of Process Assignment: PoP assignments can be set up so that students focus exclusively on finding the topic and/or thesis statement and/or major supporting points. See the Connect IRW *Common Places* Master Course for pre-loaded assignments that require students to analyze PoP readings by finding topic sentences and thesis statements.

PRACTICE ⑦ Using Topic Sentences to Find the Main Idea of an Essay

Below you will find an essay's topic sentences. Use the topic sentences to make an educated guess about what the essay's thesis statement might be. Put the thesis statement into your own words.

Topic sentence of body paragraph 1: Movement—physical activity of any kind—changes the brain's structure and reduces depression.

Topic sentence of body paragraph 2: Certain types of therapy, especially cognitive behavioral therapy, can help with depression.

Topic sentence of body paragraph 3: Learning a new skill, even something as minor as using a new recipe, can lessen depression.

Topic sentence of body paragraph 4: Biofeedback, meditation, and deep breathing contribute to a calmer, less depressed mood.

Write the main idea in a complete sentence: Mild depression can be managed in a variety of ways.

Answers will vary. A sample answer has been provided.

Vocabulary Collection Word:
cognitive

Your in-context definition:
_____
_____

A dictionary definition:
_____
_____

Example of Identifying an Essay's Thesis Statement

The following essay contains a paragraph you analyzed earlier in this chapter. Read the essay to see how one student, Sarit, uses the steps you just learned to identify the main idea and thesis statement of the essay.

First, Sarit determines what the essay's topic is by highlighting key words in the title and words that are repeated throughout the essay. Then she identifies and underlines the topic sentence of each paragraph.

Why Emotional Intelligence Matters—At Work

Do you know anyone who is not necessarily the smartest member of a work group but who is a great team player and always seems to contribute significantly? On the other hand, do you know someone who is "book smart" but seems to have a difficult time getting along with coworkers? The first person has high "emotional intelligence." The second person does not. Emotional intelligence (EI) refers to how well people understand their own feelings as well as the emotions of others. Surprisingly, perhaps, being "book smart" is not sufficient for career success. We have learned in recent years that successful employees—those who move the most quickly up the ladder—possess greater emotional intelligence skills than their coworkers.

Awareness of your emotions is one way EI makes you a better employee. Intentionally thinking about how you are feeling is a crucial skill. For example, if you are irritable, you may have a harder time with a planning session at the office than you otherwise would. Realizing that you are grumpy does not instantly make you happy, but it does give you a heads-up that you need to be especially careful as you relate to your coworkers or customers or supervisors. Sometimes people with low emotional intelligence will think their moods justify bad behavior. You may even have heard comments like "Don't mind Jessica; she's always moody." The truth is, Jessica won't be the one getting the promotion.

Sarit's Annotations

Step 1—Identify topic.
Emotional intelligence?

Can't be thesis statement—these are questions.

Definition. Maybe the entire essay's main idea is to define emotional intelligence.

Topic—EI and career success?

Step 2—Find the topic sentences.

Topic sentence

Topic:—being a better employee??

Emotional intelligence again—topic?

(continued)

Empathy means putting yourself in another person's shoes emotionally. Beyond being self-aware, employees who interpret the emotions of others by being empathetic are assets in the workplace. Can you imagine how the other person feels in a given situation? If one of your colleagues has just come from an evaluation with his supervisor and snaps at you when you say "Hello," he might be feeling upset because of what his boss had to say. Recognizing your coworker's emotional situation would help smooth over hurt feelings. Similarly, a salesperson who can empathize with customers will have more pleasant interactions with them; as a consequence, she might even make more sales!

Topic sentence

A benefit of emotional intelligence

Stress management is another EI skill that makes employees more valuable. A person who has methods for relieving her stress is much less likely to blow up at a coworker or a customer. One who can control her stress is also a more efficient employee because she is not distracted by the tension that has built up inside her psyche. Controlling stress is not always an easy thing to do; people who are successful at keeping their stress level down can rise above their colleagues and become more valued employees.

Topic sentence

Topic—how emotional intelligence benefits you?

Unpleasant or difficult situations inevitably occur in the workplace. Workers who are able to adapt fairly quickly when frustrations or disappointments occur will be able to proceed with occupational tasks. Employers can trust employees who are adaptable; such employees will make the adjustments needed to get the work done. Workers who are prone to "drama" over frustrations or disappointments will be labeled "difficult" and will not be the ones on the promotion list. Employees who have emotional flexibility are considered more dependable than those who do not.

Topic—emotional intelligence at work?

Topic sentence at end of paragraph

Teamwork is crucial in almost every vocation, and EI makes employees better team players. Working well with clients or customers is also critically important in many occupational settings. Being able to recognize and relate to the feelings of others and being aware of your own feelings will increase your ability to work well with others. That is why people with high EI are more successful in their careers than people with low EI.

Topic sentence

EI is tied to career success.

Sarit must now figure out what all the topic sentences have in common. Her annotations show her that two principal things are going on in this essay:

- The topic sentences discuss four components of emotional intelligence: awareness of emotions, empathy, stress management, and emotional flexibility.
- The topic sentences also show that emotional intelligence is valuable to employees because workers who have EI skills are more valuable than those who lack them.

Thus, Sarit has found both the topic—components of emotional intelligence—and the writer's point: that these components make workers more valuable.

With this information, Sarit continues with the fourth step—combining the topic and the point made by the topic sentences. Here is the sentence she wrote:

Having emotional intelligence skills helps people in their careers.

        Topic   *Writer's point about the topic*

To complete the last step, Sarit rereads the essay to find a sentence that matches the main idea she has identified. She is able to locate two sentences that match the main idea. One is in the introduction:

We have learned in recent years that successful employees—those who move the most quickly up the ladder—possess greater emotional intelligence skills than their coworkers.

And one is in the conclusion:

> That is why people with high EI are more successful in their careers than people with low EI.

Sarit decides that the first statement, which more fully expresses the main idea, is the thesis statement and that the sentence in the conclusion simply **reiterates** the main idea.

Not all essays will include repeated thesis statements as this example does. As a flexible reader, you need to be aware that essays do not follow a strict formula. Some writers will place the thesis statement in the middle of an essay, and sometimes the thesis statement occurs only at the very end.

Vocabulary Collection Word:
reiterate

Your in-context definition:

_____

_____

A dictionary definition:

_____

_____

PRACTICE 8 Finding the Thesis Statement of a Textbook Passage

Read and annotate the following passage from *Lesikar's Business Communication,* a textbook by Kathryn Rentz, Marie Flatley, and Paula Lentz. Use your annotations and the five-step process for identifying a thesis statement. Fill in the answers below.

The Importance of Communication Skills to You

<u>Because communication is so important in business, businesses want and need people with good communication skills.</u> Evidence of the importance of communication in business is found in numerous surveys of executives, recruiters, and academicians. Without exception, these surveys have found that communication (especially written communication) ranks at or near the top of the business skills needed for success.

For example, NFI Research, a private organization that regularly surveys over 2,000 executives and senior managers, recently found that 94 percent of the members "rank 'communicating well' as the most important skill for them to succeed today and tomorrow." A study of skills and competencies needed by accountants strongly supports the value of writing, speaking, and listening, and Deloitte & Touche, ranked by *BusinessWeek* in 2007 as the best place to launch a career, cited communication skills as the "most desirable trait" in a job candidate. Employers surveyed for the National Association of Colleges and Employers' *Job Outlook 2009* also cited "communication skills" and the related traits of "a strong work ethic, ability to work in a team, and initiative" as highly prized qualities in job applicants. Recruiters who participated in *The Wall Street Journal*'s latest ranking of MBA programs agreed. They rated "interpersonal and communication skills, a teamwork orientation, personal ethics and integrity, analytical and problem-solving abilities, and a strong work ethic" as most important.

Unfortunately, business's need for employees with good communication skills is all too often not fulfilled. Most employees, even the college trained, do not communicate well. In fact, surveys show that, in the opinion of their employees, even managers and executives who think they communicate well actually fall short. Effective communicators are, therefore, in high demand. Not surprisingly, there is a high correlation between communication skills and income. Even among college graduates, those with higher scores in literacy (use of printed and written information) earn significantly more than lower scoring graduates earn. A study by Office Team revealed that technology magnifies the exposure of one's communications skills, forcing workers to communicate more effectively and articulately because these skills will be showcased

(continued)

YOUR ANNOTATIONS

The first sentence could be the thesis statement, but the very last sentence of the essay could also.

Implied topic sentence: Research shows that business leaders rank communication skills very highly.

Implied topic sentence: Most employees do not communicate well, so effective communicators are in high demand.

more. Email often results in a sender's language skills being placed in front of different people simultaneously, while audio and video will reveal the caliber of one's verbal and diplomacy strengths as well.

The communications shortcomings of employees and the importance of communication in business explain why you should work to improve your communication skills. Whatever position you have in business, your performance will be judged largely by your ability to communicate. If you perform and communicate well, you are likely to be rewarded with advancement. And the higher you advance, the more you will need your communication ability. <u>The evidence is clear: Improving your communication skills improves your chances for success in business.</u>

Thesis statement

1. Write the essay topic: Importance of communication skills in business

2. Underline the topic sentence for each paragraph, or write the implied topic sentences here: See above.

3. Write the idea that all the topic sentences have in common: _____

    The need for good communication skills in employees

4. Write your own sentence that includes the essay topic and the idea that the topic sentences have in common: Answers will vary.

5. Underline the thesis statement and write it here: See above.

FINDING IMPLIED MAIN IDEAS IN ESSAYS

Just as some paragraphs do not have explicit topic sentences, some essays do not contain explicit thesis statements. The main idea—and thesis statement—in such essays is implied. Readers must figure out the main idea through the essay's content. We can use steps from the same process to find implied thesis statements as we use to find explicit ones.

Lucas needs to analyze an essay to determine its thesis statement for an assignment in his sociology class. He determines that the essay is on the topic of learning disorders in children. To identify the writer's point about the topic, he first annotates the function of each topic sentence.

Teaching Resources: See the PPT "Finding Implied Thesis Statements."

Topic sentence for paragraph 1: Parents often notice <mark>physical difficulties</mark> with fine motor skills first.

One symptom of a learning disorder

Topic sentence for paragraph 2: <mark>Trouble in particular classes</mark>—such as math or reading—is a symptom that may indicate particular learning disabilities.

Another symptom of a learning disorder

Topic sentence for paragraph 3: Some learning disabilities are identified by a child's <mark>social behaviors.</mark>

Social behaviors—also symptoms

Topic sentence for paragraph 4: <mark>Language difficulties</mark> can also signal learning disorders.

Language difficulties—another symptom

By looking for a common point that unites all four paragraphs, Lucas can see that they all concern symptoms of learning disorders. Now he is ready to write a sentence combining the writer's topic and main point. Here is Lucas's statement of the essay's implied main idea:

<u>Four types of symptoms are associated with</u> <u>learning disorders in children.</u>
     Writer's point about the topic   Topic

Lucas's sentence expresses the implied main idea of the essay. When the thesis statement is implied, write out the thesis statement yourself, as Lucas did. You will have an easier time remembering the essay's main idea if you write it down in your own words.

Connect IRW Power of Process Assignment: Assign PoP readings with implied main ideas to give students extra practice. See Connect IRW *Common Places* Master Course for pre-loaded PoP readings that require students to find implied thesis statements.

PRACTICE 9 Finding an Implied Thesis Statement in an Essay

The following essay has an implied main idea. Annotate the essay to determine its topic and topic sentences. On the basis of your analysis, complete the questions that follow.

Summer. The Kenai Peninsula. Wow.

When we leave Dallas, it is 98°F. It is an amazing 68°F when we land in Alaska. It's almost midnight when we pick up the rental car. We proceed to drive the length of the Kenai Peninsula, from Anchorage to Seward, amazed by the amount of daylight. On summer evenings in this part of the world, the sky never grows entirely dark. The sun dips just below the horizon, creating a lingering dusk, and then an hour or two later, the sun gradually peeks above the horizon again. Dusk and dawn are buddies, pals, hanging out together.

<u>Green—everything is green.</u> The mountains are green; the valleys are green; even the water in the dozens of lakes and rivers and creeks that we drive past is emerald green. The mountaintops are the only exception: they are white. Even in July, the mountain crests are still covered with glistening snow.

<u>Salmon are running in the creeks.</u> We stop along the highway and take a few steps to a stream to watch them. In water that is only a couple of feet deep, we see dozens, scores, hundreds of salmon struggling upstream to spawn. During their trek from the ocean, the color of their bodies has been transformed from silver to deep scarlet.

More than once, we come around a curve and happen upon moose beside the road. The size of these animals is startling. They just chew their cud and watch us go by.

At one point, we exit the highway. <u>We drive a few miles and come face-to-face with an ancient—millions of years old—glacier</u> and the icebergs that it calves. We see icebergs as big as houses in a just-above-freezing lake within walking distance of the highway.

Alaska. The Kenai Peninsula. Summer. Wow.

(continued)

YOUR ANNOTATIONS

Implied topic sentence: We arrive in Alaska and drive, noticing that the sun never seems to set.

Topic sentence

Topic sentence

Implied topic sentence: The moose are intriguing.

Topic sentence

1. Write the essay topic: The Kenai Peninsula in summer

2. Underline the topic sentence for each paragraph or write the implied topic sentences here: See above.

3. Write the idea that all the topic sentences have in common: Amazing natural scenes

4. Write your own sentence that includes the essay topic and the idea that the topic sentences have in common: Sample answer: In summer, the Kenai Peninsula is a land of amazing natural scenes.

COMPOSING EFFECTIVE THESIS STATEMENTS

When you put the main idea of a reading into your own words, you are not only learning how to find thesis statements; you are also learning how to write them. Remember that to find the thesis statement of an essay, you must focus on determining the topic and identifying the point the writer is making about the topic. Similarly, when you compose a thesis statement, you write a sentence that includes your topic and your point about the topic.

Thesis Statements That Are Too Narrow or Too Broad

Because a thesis statement provides the main point of an essay, it must be broad enough to cover everything the writer will include in the essay. For example, imagine you are writing an essay about ways to conquer stage fright. In the essay, you plan to discuss how practice, relaxation techniques, and planning for mistakes can help a person conquer stage fright. If the thesis statement focuses on only one of the suggestions you will be discussing in your essay, the thesis statement will be too narrow.

Teaching Resources: See the IM for the worksheet "Identifying and Composing Thesis Statements in Essays." and see Connect IRW *Common Places* Master Course for additional exercises.

Overly narrow thesis statement: Stage fright can be conquered by setting aside time each day to practice.

Effective thesis statement: Stage fright can be conquered by practicing, using relaxation techniques, and planning for mistakes.

Thesis statements can also be too broad. "Stage fright is a very common experience," for example, is too broad to really focus in on your main idea—that there are several specific ways to conquer stage fright. The key is to write a thesis statement that is just broad enough to cover every point you will be making in your essay.

PRACTICE ⑩ Creating Effective Thesis Statements

Below are sets of topic sentences that go with the body paragraphs of different essays. Construct a thesis statement for each set of topic sentences, making sure your thesis statement is neither too broad nor too narrow.

Answers will vary. Sample answers are provided.

(continued)

EXAMPLE

Topic sentences:

- A common effect of recession is unemployment.
- Additionally, businesses lose money in recessions.
- In a recession, most people have less money to spend.

Your thesis statement: *Recessions have negative effects on businesses and individuals.*

SET 1

Topic sentences:

- Online courses require students to be self-motivated.
- Additionally, online classes are best for students who have a functional knowledge of computer operations.
- Students who take online courses should have a learning style that is consistent with independent learning.

Your thesis statement: Students who enroll in online classes should be self-motivated, knowledgeable about computers, and independent in terms of learning style.

SET 2

Topic sentences:

- Studying economics results in greater knowledge about how consumer goods are priced.
- A course in economics also benefits students by showing how financial decisions have long-term consequences.
- An economics course provides an understanding of how investments work.
- Studying economics helps students understand the **implications** of political decisions on the economy.

Your thesis statement: Students who take economics courses develop an important knowledge base that will be relevant to their personal lives.

Vocabulary Collection Word:
implications

Your in-context definition:

_____

_____

A dictionary definition:

_____

_____

SET 3

Topic sentences:

- Students need basic Internet skills to be able to succeed in college.
- Students need to know how to do word processing for a variety of tasks.
- The ability to use e-mail and to handle e-mail attachments is another requirement for students.

Your thesis statement: To succeed in college, students must have basic Internet skills, know word processing, and be able to use e-mail.

Prewriting and Thesis Statements

You have already learned some methods for prewriting. Prewriting will help you generate ideas about topics, and from your prewriting, you can decide on the main idea you want to communicate. Prewriting will also help you determine the ideas you will use to support your thesis statement.

In the example of prewriting that follows, we see a list of ideas generated by Ben, a student in a writing class, in response to an essay assignment. He has crossed out the ideas he does not want to address and has made notes next to the ones he will include in his essay.

Assignment: Write an essay in which you discuss how failure can be a positive experience.
Ideas from prewriting:

- helps people learn about their strengths and weaknesses   (helps people with self-discovery)

- ~~teaches people to not give up can be motivational~~

- ~~makes people stronger~~

- is actually a way we learn new skills   (bike riding, for example)

- teaches people life lessons   (when people fail because of not listening to wise advice or by breaking the law)

Because of his prewriting, Ben knows what he wants to discuss in his essay. He is ready to write a thesis statement. To write a thesis statement, Ben can follow these steps.

1. Write down the topic.

2. Write down the point you wish to make about the topic.

3. Write a statement that combines the topic and your point.

4. Check that your statement has all the characteristics of an effective thesis statement.

■ Steps for composing a thesis statement

Here's what Ben did to compose his thesis statement.

1. Write down the topic.
   Topic: the value of failure

2. Write down the point you wish to make about the topic.
   Ben's point: encourages self-discovery, is a way of learning new skills, teaches life lessons

3. Write a statement that combines the topic and the point you wish to make.
   Ben's thesis statement: Failure is valuable because it encourages self-discovery, provides a way to learn new skills, and teaches life lessons.

Ben believes that in the long run, it is more important for people to learn life lessons, so he decides to emphasize that idea by putting it last. In his thesis statement, he puts the ideas in the order in which he will present them in the essay.

Ben's thesis statement provides the main idea of the essay. It also gives readers a clue to the kind of information the essay will contain and the order in which it will be presented.

To make sure his thesis statement is acceptable, Ben must do one more task. He needs to make sure his thesis statement has all the characteristics of an effective thesis statement.

> **Characteristics of an Effective Thesis Statement**
>
> - It combines the topic of the essay with your point about the topic.
> - It expresses the main idea you are making in the essay.
> - It requires supporting details, supplied in the essay's paragraphs.
> - It is broad enough to unify the ideas in the supporting paragraphs.
> - It is a statement, not a question or an announcement.

After evaluating his thesis statement, Ben finds that it has the characteristics of an effective thesis statement. Refer to this list of characteristics to complete the following exercise.

PRACTICE 11 Critiquing Thesis Statements

Imagine you are guiding Sharon, who is writing an essay about why people choose to be vegetarians. She plans to discuss these three reasons:

- Some people believe vegetarian diets are healthier than meat-based diets.
- Others choose vegetarianism because of their ethical beliefs regarding the treatment of animals.
- A third reason for choosing a vegetarian diet is concern about the effects of meat production on the environment.

Sharon has written several sentences and wants to know which one would make the best thesis statement, based on the characteristics of thesis statements. Read each numbered sentence, and explain why it would or would not be the best thesis statement. Finally, write your own thesis statement for Sharon's essay.

1. Why is it a good idea to be a vegetarian?

   Your comments: This is the question the essay is going to answer, so it is not a good thesis statement. A thesis statement should be an assertion, not a question or an announcement.

2. Because a vegetarian diet is healthier than a meat-based diet, becoming a vegetarian is a good idea.

   Your comments: This is just one point about the topic, so it is not broad enough to be a thesis statement.

3. People must decide for themselves whether a vegetarian diet is the right choice.

   Your comments: This is a very broad statement; it is not specific enough to be a thesis statement.

4. Your thesis statement: People choose vegetarianism because they believe it is a healthier diet, is more ethical than eating meat, and is better for the environment.

Open and Closed Thesis Statements

Not all thesis statements are explicit about the support the writer will present. Some thesis statements lead the reader to expect to learn about "several reasons" or "important aspects," or they use some other phrase to let the reader know the essay will address a variety of similar elements. These kinds of statements are **open thesis statements.**

> **Example:**   Making firearms illegal on college campuses is the right policy.

We call this an open thesis statement because it does not reveal the writer's reasons for his position or the kinds of support he will present in the essay. The rest of the essay is left *open*, so to speak.

On the other hand, **closed thesis statements** tell the reader exactly what support will be used in the essay.

> **Example:**   Making firearms illegal on college campuses will reduce the potential for violence, keep campuses focused on education, and foster a community of trust.

Closed thesis statements reveal the reasons or supporting points that will be in the essay; thus, the essay is *closed* to other reasons or support.

Open thesis statements are appropriate for essays with body paragraphs that are similar to one another in function. For example, an essay setting out causes of **insomnia** lends itself to a thesis statement such as this one.

Open thesis statement: <u>Insomnia</u> can be caused by a variety of conditions.
           Topic   Writer's point about the topic

The following chart gives examples of open thesis statements.

TYPE OF ESSAY	OPEN THESIS STATEMENT
An essay showing how the differences between the public school systems of the United States and Canada affect learning	A comparison of the public school system in the United States with the public school system in Canada reveals significant differences that affect student learning.
An essay offering solutions to the problem of homelessness	Communities can reduce the negative consequences of homelessness by using six strategies that have been proved effective.
An essay in support of making college education free	Making a college education free and available to all citizens makes sense for several reasons.

Vocabulary Collection Word:
insomnia

Your in-context definition:

_____

_____

A dictionary definition:

_____

_____

Teaching Resources: See the handout "Writing Open and Closed Thesis Statements."

Closed thesis statements are appropriate when it is important or helpful to readers to reveal the content of the essay in advance. The disadvantage is that such thesis statements can be difficult to compose since they list the specific support that will appear in the body paragraphs. For instance, to convert the open thesis statement about reasons for insomnia to a closed thesis statement, we would need to include particular causes of insomnia.

Closed thesis statement: Insomnia can have many causes, but the most common ones are stress, medications, and environmental distractions.

The topic is insomnia, and the three causes presented in this closed thesis statement are stress, medications, and environmental distractions.

One key to writing a good closed thesis statement is using parallelism. The Grammar Focus that follows will help you write closed thesis statements that demonstrate parallelism.

■ The design of this room demonstrates parallelism in that both of the columns are parallel to each other. Can you find other elements that are parallel?

 Parallelism

Teaching Resources: See the worksheet "Creating Parallelism in Sentences."

Thesis statements often contain a series of elements that are part of the writer's main idea. For example, in the thesis statement that follows, three phrases are used to communicate parents' responsibilities.

Parents' primary duties are to nurture, to protect, and to educate their children.

The sentence lists three duties in a series connected by and. *Notice that each item in the series takes the form* to + *main verb.*

In the following thesis statement, a series of elements is presented in parallel form.

Life coaches should model successful living, provide good advice, and teach effective planning to their clients.

Each item in the series consists of a verb and an object:

model (*verb*) ⟶ successful living (*object*)

provide (*verb*) ⟶ good advice (*object*)

teach (*verb*) ⟶ effective planning (*object*)

The sentence contains a series of three verbs (model, provide, teach). Each verb is followed by an adjective that modifies a noun (successful living, good advising, effective planning).

Parallelism is the use of consistent structure for all elements in a series of two or more elements. (Hint: Look for a conjunction such as *and* that links the items.)

Bullying in schools is a serious problem because it can cause extreme anguish to victims *and* result in serious physical harm.

The two reasons for the seriousness of bullying are presented in parallel form.

(continued)

Knowledge of geography is <u>necessary for jobs in commerce</u>, <u>important for careers in sales</u>, and <u>essential for careers in international business</u>.

The three items in the series are presented in parallel form; each contains an adjective followed by a prepositional phrase.

Because thesis statements often present series of elements, always check to ensure that your thesis statement is in parallel form. While parallelism is especially important in thesis statements, *every* sentence that presents a series of elements should reflect parallel form.

To use parallelism in sentences, follow these guidelines:

- Identify items in the sentence that could be put in parallel form, usually a series of two or more similar elements joined by a coordinating conjunction (*for, and, nor, but, or, yet, so*).

- Make sure the items in the series are alike in their parts of speech.

  Example: During college, Micah liked <u>skiing</u>, <u>jogging</u>, and ~~to skateboard~~ <u>skateboarding</u>.

- Make changes in wording, if necessary, to achieve parallelism.

  Example: Trinity teaches special-needs adults to manage their money, practice good hygiene, and ~~the ability to make breakfast, lunch, and dinner~~ prepare their own meals.

COMBINING SENTENCES

The examples that follow show how to combine ideas to create thesis statements with parallelism.

Ideas to combine:

- <u>Time</u> is required to open a new business.
- Having <u>patience</u> is part of opening a business.
- Opening a business requires <u>an initial investment</u>.

Parallel thesis statement: To open a business requires <u>time</u>, <u>patience</u>, and <u>money</u>.

Ideas to combine:

- <u>A college education should be free in the United States</u>.
- An alternative to making college free is <u>making student loans available to anyone who wants one</u>.

Parallel thesis statement: Either <u>a college education in the United States should be free</u> or <u>student loans should be available to anyone who wants one</u>.

EXPANDING THE CONCEPT

Parallelism is used in sentences, but it is also used in headings and lists, in sets of instructions, and within paragraphs and compositions.

Connect IRW Grammar Assignment: Assign "Parallelism in Context."

EXERCISES

Combine each set of sentences below into a thesis statement that demonstrates parallelism.

Answers will vary. Sample answers provided.

(continued)

1. Ideas to combine:

- Global warming affects sea levels.

- Global warming creates changes in precipitation patterns.

- Ecosystems are also affected by global warming.

    Answer: Global warming affects sea levels, precipitation patterns, and ecosystems.

2. Ideas to combine:

- One reason to require college algebra for college degrees is to teach students to think **sequentially**.

- The improved use of logic in thinking is another reason college algebra should be required.

- Algebra also creates more flexibility in the way people think.

    Answer: College algebra should be required in college because it teaches students to think more sequentially, logically, and flexibly.

Vocabulary Collection Word:
sequentially

Your in-context definition:

_____

_____

A dictionary definition:

_____

_____

3. Ideas to combine:

- The use of drones reduces casualties for the military that uses them.

- The cost of military engagement is decreased when drones are used.

- Drones do less damage to cities than traditional warfare does.

    Answer: Using drones in warfare results in fewer troop casualties, lower costs for military engagement, and less damage to cities.

4. Ideas to combine:

- Because tablet computers are more expensive than desktop computers, schools should purchase desktop computers rather than tablets.

- Regular desktop computers offer greater functionality than tablets.

- Tablets are much more likely to be stolen than desktop computers.

    Answer: Schools should buy desktop computers rather than tablets because tablets cost more, offer less functionality, and are more likely to be stolen.

PRACTICE 12 Writing Parallel Closed Thesis Statements

Combine each of the essay topics below with the point being made about the topic to write a parallel closed thesis statement.

Answers will vary. Sample answers provided.

1. Topic: learning a new skill

    Writer's point: helps you grow intellectually, can discover new talents, can be fun and relaxing.

(continued)

Closed thesis statement: Learning a new skill is worthwhile because doing so can foster

intellectual growth, reveal hidden talents, and provide fun and relaxation.

2. Topic: wind technology

Writer's point: advantages—it is renewable; cost of energy production is relatively low; environment is not harmed

Closed thesis statement: The advantages of wind technology are that it is renewable,

inexpensive, and environmentally friendly.

3. Topic: reasons to shop in thrift stores

Writer's point: fun, save money, might be rewarded by finding valuable items

Closed thesis statement: Shopping in thrift stores is fun, economical, and potentially

rewarding.

4. Topic: advantages of using e-mail instead of other forms of communication

Writer's point: can control your emotional responses to ideas, time is available to think about the ideas involved, discussion of the issue is recorded in the e-mail

Closed thesis statement: Using e-mail to communicate results in the writer's having greater

control over emotional responses to ideas, more time to process the ideas involved, and a

clearer record of the discussion of the issue.

CHAPTER ACTIVITIES

READING AND ANNOTATING

The following is an excerpt from a brief essay published in the journal *Perspectives in Biology and Medicine*. Like many professional essays, this one includes a wide variety of support.

1. Analyze the body paragraphs. Some of the body paragraphs are quite short, so when necessary, use the strategies provided in this chapter for finding the topic sentences for journalistic paragraphs.

2. Identify the topic sentences—whether explicit or implicit—for each paragraph (or set of journalistic paragraphs) in this article.

3. Use the five-step process described in this chapter to determine the essay's main idea. Find the thesis statement in the text, or if the thesis statement is implied, write it in a sentence.

Be sure to annotate the essay as you read.

Connect IRW Power of Process Assignment: This reading and annotating assignment is pre-loaded in Power of Process in the Connect IRW *Common Places* Master Course.

Adapting to the Situation
by Peter J. McDonnell, MD

> Be yourself; everybody else is already taken.   —Oscar Wilde
> Whatever you do, don't be yourself.   —Unknown

Many years ago, one of my younger sisters worked for a U.S.-based international corporation. It's an enormous company; they make all kinds of things. You probably have something made by them around your house.

To develop (and test) their young executives, the company would send them to head up a division in another country. If they performed well, they were brought back to the United States in a few years and moved into a high-level position at corporate headquarters.

Mary was sent to Europe and was doing very well in a glamorous but high-pressure position despite all the cultural and linguistic challenges.

"Running a business here in Europe is very different [from] back home," she told me.

I, of course, was proud of her. During a visit to Europe, Mary and I celebrated her success. We had dinner at a wonderful restaurant in Munich, enjoying the fantastic draft beer and delicious German sausages. There was a musician playing a guitar and singing Simon and Garfunkel songs.

A terrible singer myself, I admire people who are talented at it. "He is really good," I said to my sister, who agreed and suggested that I tell him. Mary laughed, as it was clear the musician had absolutely no idea what I was saying.

"There are musicians like this all over Europe," she said, "unable to understand a word of English but singing American songs as though they had grown up in New Jersey."

I was reminded of this story recently while attending a U2 concert. To me, the lead singer, Bono, sings pretty much without a discernible accent, but when he speaks to the audience between songs he sounds like the quintessential boy from the streets of Dublin. A couple weeks after the concert, I did an experiment with someone who has had a lot of musical training, but whose taste runs to classical and jazz (but not rock).

"I'll give you $20 if you can tell me what country this singer is from," I said.

"America?" was the guess.

Behaviors and Mannerisms

My thought is that really talented musicians are so adaptable that they can learn new manners of speech to entertain their audiences better. Similarly, successful businesspeople learn what it takes to be successful in whatever situation they find themselves. Physicians also do the same, as they adopt certain mannerisms and speech patterns to meet their patients' expectations.

Sir William Osler, MD, a famous American physician, wrote a book called *Aequanimitas.* In it, he argued that physicians should cultivate a persona of cool detachment from patients and calmly accept what comes, so that the difficulties and sufferings of patients do not cause emotional reactions and cloud the physician's scientific judgment.

Some have criticized Dr. Osler and this approach as reducing physicians' empathy for patients. Right or wrong, it suggests that good physicians can serve their patients best by adopting behaviors that might be different from their normal attributes in the rest of their lives.

The bottom-line impression I have is that success in many fields involves being good at pretending to be someone or something you are not.

Questions for Consideration

1. The writer thinks pretending can be a useful method for adapting to different situations. Think of someone you know who is successful—perhaps a relative, a friend, a teacher, or a doctor. In what ways do you think this person has used *pretending* as an effective strategy? Explain in a paragraph.

2. We all know people who try to excuse bad behaviors or bad habits by saying, "That's just how I am." Consider a situation in which saying, "That's just how I am," would have negative effects. Reflect on job situations, college responsibilities, and relationships. Write a paragraph in which you examine a particular situation.

3. Think about the career you aspire to have. In what ways might pretending help you when you start this career? For example, when teachers begin their careers, they have to project confidence in the classroom. Most inexperienced teachers are worried and insecure about their ability to teach well, especially in the first year. When teachers project confidence, parents and students can relax, believing that the teacher has everything under control. In what way will pretending help you adapt to the career you plan to pursue? Write a paragraph to explain.

4. Although we may be unaware of it, we adapt to situations all the time. If we feel ill, for example, and a coworker asks, "How are you?" many of us will say, "Just fine." These minor acts of pretending make interactions with colleagues more positive. In what ways have you pretended today or in the last few days? Why did you pretend? Did it help your relationships with others go more smoothly? Describe one of your experiences in a paragraph.

Questions for Consideration

1. Answers will vary.

2. Answers will vary. Sample answer: A student does not like to type, but her instructors insist that she hand in assignments. Turning in handwritten assignments and saying, "That's just how I am," would result in poor grades.

3. Answers will vary.

4. Answers will vary.

USING MODELS TO PRACTICE COMPOSING

What follows is a model essay written by Xavier, a student in an English class. Read through the assignment instructions that Xavier's professor provided.

> **Essay assignment:** In the conclusion paragraph of Peter J. McDonnell's essay "Adapting to the Situation," the author writes, "The bottom-line impression I have is that success in many fields involves being good at pretending to be someone or something you are not."

To start this assignment, Xavier used the prewriting technique of clustering as a method for considering new situations that many people experience.

Next, Xavier chose a topic derived from his prewriting and examined how pretending might be advantageous and disadvantageous in his particular context. He used prewriting to make lists.

Situation: Death of a loved one

Benefits of pretending:

- Pretending life is normal helps you do the necessary things (wake up, get ready for work, deal with children, go to the job site).

- Pretending can help your kids feel like their lives are in control, even if you don't feel in control.

- Pretending will give you more privacy; other people won't always be asking if they can help or what is wrong.

Disadvantages of pretending:

- Pretending takes a lot of energy and effort.

- Pretending might keep you from grieving and experiencing the sorrow so that you can work through it.

- Pretending might set a poor example for children by teaching them to cover up their feelings of sorrow.

Once Xavier finished his prewriting, he created a brief outline that included his thesis statement and the topic sentences for each of his body paragraphs. Notice that he chose not to include all the advantages and disadvantages that he came up with.

Thesis statement: Pretending is a way to adapt to the loss of a loved one, and as a coping strategy, it offers advantages as well as disadvantages.

Body paragraphs:

1. Topic sentence: Pretending life is normal helps parents do the things necessary for everyday life (wake up, get ready for work, deal with children, go to the job site).

2. Topic sentence: By pretending everything is okay, parents can provide a more stable living environment for their children.

3. Topic sentence: Pretending might set a poor example for children by teaching them to cover up their feelings of sorrow.

4. Topic sentence: Pretending takes a great deal of energy and effort.

After creating an outline that includes his thesis statement and topic sentences, Xavier drafted his essay, revised it, and checked it for errors. Read Xavier's final essay, and annotate at least three features in the essay. For example, if you see sentences that demonstrate parallelism, annotate them. If you find a passage that you believe is worded particularly well, annotate it. Also, annotate the thesis statement and notice where it is placed, and mark the topic sentences.

Lewis 1

Xavier Lewis

INRW 0402

Dr. Wright

20 February 2014

The Role of Pretending in Times of Grief

New situations can easily throw us off balance. A new job, a new baby, or a new living situation can be hard to handle. However, most people find methods for adjusting to these new circumstances. One method that can be helpful is pretending. Sometimes by pretending, people can reduce the stress involved in making the transition to a new situation. This is especially true in the case of grief. Pretending is a way to adapt to the loss of a loved one, and as a coping strategy it offers advantages, although there are disadvantages as well.

Pretending that everything is normal helps a grieving person do the things necessary for dealing with everyday life. By pretending that nothing is out of the ordinary, a person is more likely to wake up on time, bathe, tend to chores, go to work, and so on. Pretending, in this case, is a good way to deal with grief. It keeps the grieving person busy, and it allows him or her to do the things that have to get done. Without pretending that life is normal, grieving people might merely stay in bed and cry or quit their jobs out of despair. These actions would add even more complications to adjusting to life without the loved one. Therefore, pretending that nothing has changed is a good way to keep going.

Pretending can help children feel that their lives are in control, even if their parents don't feel in control. Children need stability in

Answers will vary. See the IM for teaching suggestions regarding this exercise and for a fully annotated version of Xavier's essay.

Parallelism

Thesis statement

Topic sentence

Topic sentence

YOUR ANNOTATIONS

their lives. This need for stability doesn't change, even though a parent's life may have drastically changed with the loss of a loved one. Parents who recognize their children's need for stability can use pretending as a way to keep their children on an even keel. When parents act as if life goes on as usual, continuing with typical daily activities, children can be comforted and can continue their own lives with fewer disruptions.

While pretending is helpful in many ways, people who are adjusting to grief must realize that pretending, if not used carefully, can have some disadvantages. For one thing, pretending might set a poor example for children by teaching them to cover up their feelings of sorrow. While children need the stability that comes from pretending life is normal, children also need to know it is OK to feel sorrow and to grieve. Therefore, pretending should be used to help life go on, but it should not be used so extensively that there is no room for sorrow.

Topic sentence

In addition, pretending takes a lot of energy and effort. It is hard to act as if everything is OK when everything in life has changed so drastically. There must be times of release when those who are grieving can take off the mask of pretending and admit they are exhausted and sad. Having periods of sorrow and periods of productive pretending helps those who are grieving. By reserving energy and effort for only those times when pretending to be normal is necessary, people can reap the advantages of pretending without the disadvantages of it.

Topic sentence

No one asks for the sorrow that death brings, but most people go through it sometime in their lives. By pretending that life is normal, people who are grieving can find a way to go on with life—until life really does become normal again, or at least as normal as it can be after a deep loss.

A READING AND WRITING ASSIGNMENT

Now that you have read and annotated Xavier's essay, use the same assignment instructions Xavier received to write your own essay on the topic. Follow these steps.

1. Reread Xavier's assignment from "Using Models to Practice Composing," repeated here:

   In the conclusion paragraph of Peter J. McDonnell's essay "Adapting to the Situation," the author writes, "The bottom-line impression I have is that success in many fields involves being good at pretending to be someone or something you are not."

2. Use prewriting to think about situations in which a person could benefit from using pretending as a coping strategy.

3. Choose one of those situations, and use a prewriting method to determine ways in which pretending might be advantageous and disadvantageous.

4. Use prewriting to write a thesis statement and compose topic sentences for body paragraphs. Plan as many paragraphs as you need to support your thesis statement.

5. Using Xavier's essay as a model, write a complete essay, including an introduction paragraph, body paragraphs, and a conclusion paragraph. Use the thesis statement and topic sentences you have already composed.

6. Follow the Quick Start Guide to Integrated Reading and Writing Assignments to help you with this process.

Connect IRW Writing Assignment: Use Connect IRW to guide students through writing this essay and using peer review.

Connect IRW Power of Process Assignment: This reading and writing assignment is pre-loaded in Connect IRW *Common Places* Master Course.

⊙ THINKING FROM AN INSTRUCTOR'S POINT OF VIEW

One method for understanding assignments is to look at them from your instructor's point of view. Focus on getting inside your instructor's mind. Your instructor cares about your learning. She has written assignments so that you can demonstrate your progress. When you read an assignment, ask yourself, "How will this assignment enable me to demonstrate my knowledge and skills?"

In the exercise below, excerpts from a possible essay assignment are provided. Read each excerpt and ask yourself, "What does my instructor want me to do when she says . . . ?" The first exercise has been completed as an example. Remember, you don't have to actually do the assignments in the left column. Your task is to interpret the assignments and to write about how you think the instructor wants you to respond to them.

WHAT MY INSTRUCTOR WROTE	WHAT I THINK MY INSTRUCTOR MEANS OR WANTS FROM ME
Example: While you may not be familiar with additional parts of the writing process, such as choosing supporting details and writing effective introductions and conclusions, try your hand at writing a complete essay by doing the assignment that follows.	**Example:** *She wants me to write an entire essay without worrying too much about the parts we have not covered.*
Write an essay in which you choose a situation in your life that required adaptation. In your essay, write about your own experiences with adjusting to this situation.	Answers will vary.
In the conclusion, comment on this statement in Peter J. McDonnell's essay "Adapting to the Situation": "The bottom-line impression I have is that success in many fields involves being good at pretending to be someone or something you are not." From your experience, is he correct? Why or why not?	Answers will vary.
Next, write a closed thesis statement that makes use of your prewriting ideas and categories. Be sure to combine the topic and your point about the topic into your thesis statement, and be sure your thesis statement demonstrates parallelism.	Answers will vary.
For examples of complete essays, look through this chapter.	

⊙ ADDING TO YOUR VOCABULARY

This chapter's vocabulary words appear below.

diverse	acquisition	cognitive	reiterate
implication	insomnia	sequentially	

Teaching Resources: See the Connect IRW *Common Places* Master Course for vocabulary study practices that accompany this chapter, as well as a chapter vocabulary quiz.

Choose five of the vocabulary words from this chapter that you would like to add to your vocabulary, and think about how you can use them this week. For example, one of this chapter's words is *diverse*. You can often substitute *diverse* for *varied* or *assorted*.

Example: This college offers a *varied* course selection.

This college offers a *diverse* course selection.

List each of the five words you plan to use this week, and make note of a context in which you could use each word.

Example: *Diverse.* I can use this in talking about the career opportunities in my field.

⊙ ADDITIONAL ASSIGNMENTS

1. Look up the word *adaptation* in a dictionary. You will find more than one definition for this term. Which definition of *adaptation* is the most appropriate one for the term as Peter McDonnell uses it in his essay?

2. Reread the textbook passage entitled "The Importance of Communication Skills to You" in Practice 8 in this chapter. After you reread it, focus on this excerpt:

A study of skills and competencies needed by accountants strongly supports the value of writing, speaking, and listening, and Deloitte & Touche, ranked by *BusinessWeek* in 2007 as the best place to launch a career, cited communication skills as the "most desirable trait" in a job candidate. Employers surveyed for the National Association of Colleges and Employers' *Job Outlook 2009* also cited "communication skills" and the related traits of "a strong work ethic, ability to work in a team, and initiative" as highly prized qualities in job applicants. Recruiters who participated in *The Wall Street Journal*'s latest ranking of MBA programs agreed. They rated "interpersonal and communication skills, a teamwork orientation, personal ethics and integrity, analytical and problem-solving abilities, and a strong work ethic" as most important.

List the qualities employers value. Which of these qualities do you have? Which ones do you lack? Explain actions you can take so that you will have all the qualities employers desire. Write a paragraph or two presenting and explaining your answers.

3. Consider the qualities you explored in assignment 2 above. Now imagine you are writing an essay in which you present four qualities you would like to develop while you are in college. Write a thesis statement for an essay in which you combine the following ideas.

Topic: qualities employers desire in workers

Your point about the topic: qualities you would like to develop for your own advancement

You may write an open or closed thesis statement.

1. *Adaptation* means "to change your behavior so that it is easier to live in a particular place or situation" (*Merriam-Webster*).

2. Answers will vary.

3. Answers will vary.

EMOTIONAL INTELLIGENCE

Earlier in this chapter, you read "Why Emotional Intelligence Matters—At Work." In that essay, you read about emotional flexibility. How is emotional flexibility like adaptation? How is it different? Write a paragraph explaining your answers.

Emotional flexibility is a type of adaptation. In some situations, you can adapt over time. Emotional flexibility requires a more immediate adaptation response.

CULTURAL LITERACY

Some of the readings in this chapter come from the fields of psychology, sociology, and economics. What is the focus of each of these fields? How are they different, and how are they similar? Skim over the readings in this chapter. Name one reading that comes from each of the three fields. (Not all of the readings in this chapter come from these fields.)

Psychology is the study of the mind and how it influences our behaviors. Sociology is the study of how humans react to one another in groups. Economics is the study of wealth and how it is produced and used.

CRITICAL THINKING

Figuring out implied main ideas requires critical thinking. You have to look at clues and contexts, and you have to read critically. Analyzing cartoons and examining advertisements are two ways to practice identifying implicit main ideas. Both cartoons and advertisements are intended to communicate an idea without stating it explicitly. What is the implied main idea of the advertisement that follows? Explain your answer in a paragraph.

Answers will vary.

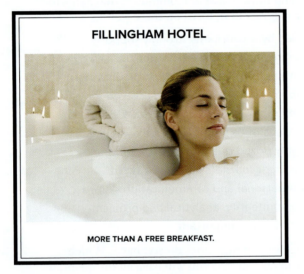

FILLINGHAM HOTEL

MORE THAN A FREE BREAKFAST.

METACOGNITION

One way to learn about your strengths and weaknesses as a student is to analyze your graded exams. Find a graded exam on which you received a lower grade than you had expected. On a separate sheet of paper, answer these questions about that exam.

Answers will vary.

1. What study methods did you use to prepare for the exam?
2. Based on your exam grade, did your study methods work?
3. Look at the questions you missed on the exam. Do the question types have anything in common? For example, on a math test, perhaps you missed the word problems or the problems that require multiplying fractions. On a history test, you may have missed questions based on instructor lectures.
4. Based on the type of questions you missed, what study strategies might have helped you prepare better for these questions?
5. In general, what can you do differently next time to earn an even higher grade?

The Capital Gate Building in Abu Dhabi leans an incredible 18°, which makes it the world's farthest leaning building, according to Guinness World Records. How do you think Capital Gate manages to remain upright? In what ways are texts—such as essays and books—like Capital Gate?

Support for Main Ideas

At about the age of four, children begin to ask a particular question: "Why?" If you have spent much time with four-year-olds, you probably know the frustration of having to explain *everything:* why broccoli is green, why cars need gasoline, why dinosaurs no longer exist, why it is not OK to talk with your mouth full of food. A part of the maturation process is to wonder about the reasons for things. Curious children need more than a main idea; they need support for that idea, and they will ask "Why?" until they get that support!

As adults, we are not all that different from these curious four-year-olds. We may recognize a writer's main idea, but we may not fully understand why the writer believes as he or she does. We may not understand why the main point is important. We may not even entirely understand the main point unless the writer gives us explanations and examples. A major responsibility for writers is to provide the support needed to communicate their ideas effectively. Readers must also be able to identify supporting details in order to understand a writer's main point correctly.

CHAPTER OBJECTIVES

After completing this chapter, students will be able to do the following:

- **Recognize major supporting points and supporting details in texts.**
- **Use outlining or graphic organizers to identify major supporting points and supporting details.**
- **Identify and use transitions.**
- **Use specific types of supporting details in writing.**

Connect IRW LearnSmart Achieve: Assign the topic "Supporting Points and Evidence" for adaptive learning to accompany the chapter.

Teaching Resources: See the Chapter Quiz.

RECOGNIZING MAJOR SUPPORTING POINTS AND SUPPORTING DETAILS IN TEXTS

The thesis statement of an essay is a strong sentence because it provides the writer's main idea. However, it cannot stand on its own. It requires support, and this support comes in the form of body paragraphs.

Support consists of all the information readers need to fully understand a writer's main idea. Supporting details come in a variety of types: examples, analogies, explanations, short anecdotes (stories), reasons, statistics, quotations, and so on. The support you choose depends on your thesis statement and writing purpose. If you are informing readers, you might use *data* and *explanations* to support your thesis statement. If your purpose is to define a term, you will probably use *definitions* and *examples*.

To be a critical reader, you must be able to identify the supporting materials in texts. This identification begins with a clear understanding of how support provides the structure for an essay.

Major Supporting Points in Essays

In an essay, the **major supporting points** are the ideas that explain, develop, or prove the thesis statement. A common way writers structure essays is to create a paragraph of support for each major supporting point.

For example, in "Four Ideas for How Obama Could Really Transform the Cost of College," an essay by Bryce Covert, the thesis statement lists the writer's "four ideas." These four ideas are the major supporting points of the thesis statement, and each is discussed in its own body paragraph. Moreover, the topic sentence for each paragraph states the major supporting point that is explored in the paragraph.

The diagram that follows illustrates the support structure for Covert's essay. Notice that each body paragraph presents a different major supporting point—one of the writer's four ideas—for the thesis statement.

Thesis statement: There are four ideas for how to radically transform the way Americans pay for college that stand a chance of truly shaking up the system.

| Paragraph 1 Major supporting point 1 Topic sentence: First, we should allow graduates to discharge student loans in bankruptcy. | Paragraph 2 Major supporting point 2 Topic sentence: A second significant idea is to encourage and finance college savings accounts. | Paragraph 3 Major supporting point 3 Topic sentence: Third, we should cover the cost of tuition with an income-based payment plan post-graduation. | Paragraph 4 Major supporting point 4 Topic sentence: And finally, we could simply make college free. |

Supporting Details in Essays

Within each of Covert's paragraphs, other sentences help readers understand the major supporting point (topic sentence). These other sentences provide supporting details that relate directly to the topic sentence. The supporting details offer further information (examples, explanations, statistics, quotations, anecdotes, and facts) for the topic sentence.

Teaching Resources: See the *PowerPoint* presentation (PPT) "Identifying and Creating Support for Ideas."

Here is one of the body paragraphs of Covert's essay. Notice that some supporting details are themselves expanded upon by additional sentences with details.

> Third, we should cover the cost of tuition with an income-based payment plan post-graduation. In July, Oregon passed a bill that allows students to attend a community college or public university at no cost if they agree to pay a certain portion of their income after they graduate. One model proposed that for 20 years after graduation, community college students would have to pay 1.5 percent of their incomes and four-year public university students would pay 3 percent. Those are much more favorable terms than what many go through with student loans. And while income-based repayment plans exist for student loans, the Consumer Financial Protection Bureau has found that few are making use of them.

Major supporting point (topic sentence)

Supporting detail: presents Oregon's bill as a solution

Details: info about Oregon's bill

Supporting detail: makes a new point to support the topic sentence

One way to visualize the support structures of an essay is to label them in a diagram.

■ Major supporting points can have varying numbers of supporting details.

Now that you are familiar with the levels of support used in essays, read Covert's essay and study the annotations that point out the various types of support in it.

Four Ideas for How Obama Could Really Transform the Cost of College
by Bryce Covert

As part of his summer bus tour, President Obama will be making speeches this week that will include proposals for tackling the problem of college affordability. As the *New York Times* reports, ahead of those speeches he told supporters in an email, "To create a better bargain for the middle class, we have to fundamentally rethink about how higher education is paid for in this country. We've got to shake up the current system."

The value of a college degree is clear: University graduates make 85 percent more than high school graduates on average and have just a 3.8 percent unemployment rate, compared to 7.6 percent for those with high school degrees. The factors behind the sharp increases in college tuition and mounting load of student debt are complex.

In this essay, each major supporting point is addressed in only one body paragraph. Thus, each topic sentence happens to be a major supporting point. Later in this chapter, students will see essays in which major supporting points are developed in more than one paragraph. In those essays, the topic sentences are not always major supporting points. It may be helpful to point out this distinction here so that students are prepared for the later material.

(continued)

But tinkering with student loan rates, while important, doesn't actually change the way Americans pay for higher education. There are four ideas, however, for how to radically transform the way Americans pay for college that stand a chance of truly shaking up the system.

First, we should allow graduates to discharge student loans in bankruptcy. While nearly all forms of debt can be discharged in bankruptcy proceedings, letting a borrower start anew financially, rules put into place by Congress in the 1970s make it nearly impossible to do so with student loans. Joe Valenti and David Bergeron of the Center for American Progress have proposed changing this system by allowing loans with unbearable repayment conditions or taken out to attend schools with poor track records on graduates finding employment to be eliminated in bankruptcy. This would not only combat the sky-high default rate and give graduates a way to build back their finances, it would incentivize lenders to offer better terms and schools to improve the employment prospects for students.

A second significant idea is to encourage and finance college savings accounts. The Assets and Education Initiative at the University of Kansas has proposed a plan that would automatically enroll every child in a college savings account at birth, publicly finance initial deposits, and provide public matching funds to help families pay for college costs. This would allow many more families to pay for the costs out of pocket and rely less on student loans that have to be paid back with interest. But doing so wouldn't just make college more affordable—it would make it vastly more accessible to many people. The report notes that while just 45 percent of high school students without college savings ever enroll, nearly three-quarters of those with savings do. Meanwhile, just seven percent of those without savings will graduate compared to a third of those who have them. Even college savings of less than $500 means low- and moderate-income students will be three times as likely to enroll and four times as likely to graduate.

Third, we should cover the cost of tuition with an income-based payment plan post-graduation. In July, Oregon passed a bill that allows students to attend a community college or public university at no cost if they agree to pay a certain portion of their income after they graduate. One model proposed that for 20 years after graduation, community college students would have to pay 1.5 percent of their incomes and four-year public university students would pay 3 percent. Those are much more favorable terms than what many go through with student loans. And while income-based repayment plans exist for student loans, the Consumer Financial Protection Bureau has found that few are making use of them.

And finally, we could simply make college free. It may sound like a radical idea, but it wouldn't have to be a huge expense. The Roosevelt Institute's Mike Konczal ran the numbers and found that the government already spends $22.75 billion through tax breaks and incentives that are aimed at making student loans or the cost of college more manageable. The government also spends $104 billion on student loans. The cost of providing free public higher education has been estimated to come to $127 billion—not far from what it's already shelling out. Not only would this create an entirely affordable and accessible option for all students, but private universities would likely be pressured to reduce costs to better compete with the free option.

Thesis statement

Major supporting point 1 (topic sentence)
Supporting detail: background info

Supporting detail: a proposal

Detail: info about proposal

Vocabulary Collection Word:
initiative
Your in-context definition:

_____

_____

A dictionary definition:

_____

_____

Major supporting point 2 (topic sentence)

Supporting detail: Univ. of Kansas plan

Details: info about Kansas plan—results, statistics

Supporting detail: general statistic

Supporting detail: general statistic

Major supporting point 3 (topic sentence)

Supporting detail: Oregon's bill

Details: info about Oregon's bill

Supporting detail: other plans

Major supporting point 4 (topic sentence)

Supporting detail: view of cost

Details: facts about cost

Supporting detail: effects on private universities

To distinguish the types of support in a paragraph, keep in mind that secondary support always elaborates on the idea provided in primary support. Here is a very simple example:

Major supporting point (topic sentence): Our cafeteria serves great Italian food.

Supporting detail: The homemade lasagna is one of the specialties.

Additional details: Rachel, the head cook, uses her own family recipe to make the lasagna, and she uses herbs from her own garden!

To distinguish major supporting points from supporting details, examine the relationships the idea has with the ideas around it.

PRACTICE **1** Recognizing Major Supporting Points and Supporting Details in Essays

In the following essay, the thesis statement has been annotated for you. Read the essay, and underline the topic sentences (major supporting points) of the body paragraphs. Highlight or underline the supporting details that go together.

The Footprint That Does Not Fade

Anyone who uses a cell phone, posts to social media sites such as *Facebook* or *Twitter*, posts comments on Web sites, uploads photos, or even uses a credit or debit card has a digital footprint—a trail left behind by all of the digital activity in which the person has been involved. A digital footprint provides small bits of information about a person, and all of that information—together—is used to generate a picture of the person's character. Should people be concerned that this information is so readily available to almost anyone who wants it? Probably. Digital footprints can affect a person's reputation, opportunities in life, and personal safety.

The nature of social networking encourages people to freely post their on-the-spot and **off-the-cuff** comments or photos without thinking carefully about what the information they post says about them. Postings can have serious consequences for one's reputation. For instance, Fox News reported that Janet Dudley-Eshbach, president of Salisbury University, was recently embarrassed by photos she had posted from a personal vacation. One of the photos showed her daughter close to a man, both smiling, and Dudley-Eshbach coming toward the man with a stick. She had included a caption saying she had to "beat off Mexicans because they were constantly flirting with my daughter." The photo and caption—as well as numerous stories about the issue—can still be found on the Internet, although Dudley-Eshbach has pulled her Facebook profile. Another high-profile person affected by his digital footprint is Anthony Weiner, former US representative from New York. Weiner sent "sexts" (sexually explicit texts, including explicit photos) to several women, and when confronted, he originally denied the accusations. Wiener eventually confessed—ashamedly—for both lying and having sent the photos and texts, according to CNN. The scandal ultimately resulted in his resignation as a congressman.

YOUR ANNOTATIONS

Thesis statement

Vocabulary Collection Word:
off-the-cuff

Your in-context definition:

_____

_____

A dictionary definition:

_____

_____

Major supporting point (topic sentence)

Dudley-Eshbach example

All of the supporting details go together since they all develop the Dudley-Eshbach example.

Weiner example: details for major supporting point

(continued)

In addition to affecting one's reputation, a digital footprint can have serious implications for a person's opportunities in life. It is now commonplace for employers to check out the *Facebook* pages or *Twitter* histories of potential employees. A photo that was meant for only friends to see or an offhand comment about hating one's job can give potential employers an impression that can be damaging. Ashley Payne, a twenty-four-year-old teacher in Georgia, recently lost her job when a parent complained about a photo Payne posted of herself holding a glass of wine and a mug of beer, says CBS News. Payne said she tried to make the photo private when she posted it on Facebook but apparently did not succeed. Payne's situation demonstrates how simple postings can have disastrous results.

> *Major supporting point (topic sentence)*

> *Photos can have serious effects on one's job.*

Perhaps more frightening than the potential for damaged reputations or the loss of a job is the possibility of losing one's life. Alicia Ann Lynch, a twenty-three-year-old from Michigan, made the unfortunate choice to dress up for Halloween as a victim of the Boston Marathon bombing. After she posted a picture of herself in "costume" on *Tumblr*, outraged people sent her death threats, dug up and circulated nude photos she had posted on the Web, and even harassed her parents. "I've had voice mails where they want to slit my throat and they want to hang me and tear off my face," Lynch said in the *New York Daily News*. Lynch also lost her job, and she probably will not have an easy time finding another one because of the infamous digital footprint she now has.

> *Major supporting point (topic sentence)*

> *Lynch example: details for major supporting point*

Educators are now beginning to teach children from a young age to guard their digital footprint. Before the Internet, people could erase their history and start anew. Photos could be ripped up and destroyed; people had the chance to change their reputation if they had made mistakes in the past. These days, a thoughtless posting or photo may be on the Web forever. It is far easier to protect one's reputation than to re-establish it. *Caveat usor* [Latin for "user beware"].

Multiparagraph Support

So far, we have seen how an essay might be structured by presenting each major supporting point in its own body paragraph. What happens, however, if one of the major supporting points requires more than one paragraph of explanation?

In professional essays, writers sometimes use several paragraphs to explain one of the major supporting points. For example, one of the major supporting paragraphs in Covert's essay proposes the use of income-based payment plans for college graduates. The paragraph discusses Oregon's bill for such a plan. The writer could also discuss another state's ideas to provide further explanation of income-based payment plans. If he chooses to talk about another state's income-based payment plan, he would very likely create another paragraph. The new paragraph would *not* be a new major supporting point. It would simply be a continuation of the point that income-based repayment plans are a good idea.

For the sake of example, we can write a hypothetical paragraph to show what an additional support paragraph might look like. The first paragraph below is from Covert's essay. The second paragraph shows what an additional paragraph with new details might look like. (The details in this example are purely fictional.)

Teaching Resources: See the exercise "Finding Major Supporting Points."

Covert's paragraph:

Third, we should cover the cost of tuition with an income-based payment plan post-graduation. In July, Oregon passed a bill that allows students to attend a community college or public university at no cost if they agree to pay a certain portion of their income after they graduate. One model proposed that for 20 years after graduation, community college students would have to pay 1.5 percent of their incomes and four-year public university students would pay 3 percent. Those are much more favorable terms than what many go through with student loans. And while income-based repayment plans exist for student loans, the Consumer Financial Protection Bureau has found that few are making use of them.

Major supporting point 3 (topic sentence)

Supporting detail: Oregon's bill

Details: info about Oregon's bill

Supporting detail: other plans

Hypothetical additional paragraph:

Another example of an income-based repayment plan has been proposed in Montana. The Montana plan would require graduates to pay a small percentage of their yearly taxable wages as part of their annual state taxes for a period of either ten or twenty years. Graduates would be able to choose the repayment period. Montana's plan has the additional advantage of making the collection of repayments easier since it would be built into the state tax system.

Supporting detail (topic sentence): Montana's bill

Details: info about Montana's bill

Notice that while the topic sentence in Covert's paragraph is a major supporting point, the topic sentence in the paragraph that we have added is just a supporting detail, like this.

Major supporting point: Third, we should cover the cost of tuition with an income-based payment plan post-graduation.

- Supporting detail: In July, Oregon passed a bill that allows students to attend a community college or public university at no cost if they agree to pay a certain portion of their income after they graduate.

- Supporting detail: And while income-based repayment plans exist for student loans, the Consumer Financial Protection Bureau has found that few are making use of them

- Supporting detail: Another example of an income-based repayment plan has been proposed in Montana.

Writers provide an additional paragraph of supporting details when the point they are making needs significant explanation or discussion. Try your hand at identifying different types of support by completing the following exercise.

PRACTICE ② Identifying Support in Essays

Read the following essay, which provides an opinion on tar sands oil. You will notice that the thesis statement has been identified. The essay presents three major supporting points, but you will find more than three body paragraphs. Figure out where each major supporting point is, and put brackets around the paragraphs that provide support for the major supporting point.

To encourage critical thinking, have students analyze some of the counterarguments found in the exercises in the Grammar Focus in this chapter.

(continued)

The Most Deadly Oil Yet

The United States is **on the cusp** of an oil-importing contract that will provide us with endless gallons of cheap crude oil, and we won't have to depend on oil from Saudi Arabia, Venezuela, or other oil-rich countries with whom we have tenuous relationships. How will we make this miracle happen? The answer, we have been told, is to import tar sands oil from our neighbor and friend, Canada. Tar sands oil has been touted as the answer to our oil problems. A close look at what tar sands oil is and the devastation it wreaks, however, will reveal the truth: the use of tar sands oil is an impending disaster, not a miracle.

Canada's countryside, particularly in Alberta, is full of oil. The trouble is that the oil is trapped in sand. Extracting oil from sand is an extremely dirty and environmentally harmful process. To free the sticky oil from the sand, vast amounts of steam (and sometimes toxic solvents) are used. It is a process that increases greenhouse gases by 5%–15%, according to IHS CERA, a research firm. Burning tar sands oil has been shown to produce 20% greater emissions, according to David Strahan.

In addition to the environmental price of tar sands oil, people and animals also pay a high price—with their health, and sometimes with their lives. A number of substances that are linked to cancers and serious diseases, volatile organic compounds, have been found in the area of tar sands oil production at levels of six thousand times normal, according to Think Progress. Cancer levels in the area of tar sands production are now higher than normal, and the Athabascan people who live north of the vast area of tar sands oil production are fearful for their health.

While people worry about cancer, the animals in the area are sick and dying. Kevin Timoney writes in a peer-reviewed article that in the tar sands oil-production areas, large numbers of animals died between 2000 and 2008, including black bears, deer, red foxes, coyotes, and moose. The National Wildlife Federation points out that the tar fields are directly in the path of scores of migratory birds, including American songbirds and the endangered whooping crane. The Athabascans will not eat the local fish because of the potential that the fish contain toxins.

If devastating the environment, endangering animals, and causing cancers in humans is not enough, the dangers posed by transporting tar sands oil might be. TransCanada Corporation, a major producer of tar sands oil, has petitioned the United States to allow the development of a pipeline that would sends tar sands oil components from Canada to Port Arthur, Texas, to be refined. This pipeline would literally run through the backyards of thousands of Americans. It would intersect major rivers and the Ogallala **Aquifer**, a water supply that is used by one-fourth of the irrigated land in America and provides drinking water for two million people, according to Friends of the Earth.

YOUR ANNOTATIONS

Vocabulary Collection Word:
on the cusp

Your in-context definition:

_____

_____

A dictionary definition:

_____

_____

Thesis statement

To help students integrate reading and writing skills, use prediction exercises. Ask students to jot down their predictions of the kind of support they will find in a reading. (Students will need to know the thesis statement first.) As you present the reading, ask students to judge whether their predictions were correct.

Background information

Major supporting point

Statistics: details for major supporting point

Major supporting point (and topic sentence)

Facts about toxins and Athabascan example: details for major supporting point

Facts about animal deaths: details for major supporting point

Major supporting point (and topic sentence)

Facts about pipeline and water supply: details for major supporting point

Vocabulary Collection Word:
aquifer

Your in-context definition:

_____

_____

A dictionary definition:

_____

_____

(continued)

What would happen if the pipeline leaked or a major break occurred? The oil sands product flowing in the pipeline is a heavy, sludgy material, Friends of the Earth points out. If a leak occurs in water, the oil sands material will sink, unlike traditional crude oil. Cleanup efforts would be extremely costly and complicated. Our supply of water may become more valuable than oil itself.

It would be wonderful to do business with our Canadian neighbors and solve our oil problems at the same time—but not at the risk of ruining the environment and endangering our lives and livelihood. The ecological and human costs far outweigh any of the touted benefits of this deadly oil.

Hypothetic example of pipeline leak: detail for major supporting point

USING OUTLINING OR GRAPHIC ORGANIZERS TO IDENTIFY MAJOR SUPPORTING POINTS AND SUPPORTING DETAILS

One of the best ways to visualize a reading's support is to create a simple outline. The outline should include the reading's title and author, thesis statement, major supporting points, and supporting details. What follows is an informal outline of Bryce Covert's essay on college costs from earlier in this chapter.

Title: "Four Ideas for How Obama Could Really Transform the Cost of College" by Bryce Covert

Thesis statement: "There are four ideas, however, for how to radically transform the way Americans pay for college that stand a chance of truly shaking up the system."

Major supporting point 1: "First, we should allow graduates to discharge student loans in bankruptcy."

Supporting detail: Bankruptcy law now

Supporting detail: What the Center for American Progress proposes—allowing bankruptcy forgiveness

- Would lower **default** rate
- Would benefit graduates
- Would incentivize lenders to offer better loan terms
- Would encourage colleges to develop career-placement strategies

Major supporting point 2: "A second significant idea is to encourage and finance college savings accounts."

Supporting detail: Example—University of Kansas Assets and Education Initiative

- Would allow families to rely less on student loans and would provide other benefits

Teaching Resources: See the exercise "Fill-in Outline."

Vocabulary Collection Word:
default

Your in-context definition:

_____

_____

A dictionary definition:

_____

_____

(continued)

Supporting detail: Savings accounts associated with higher graduation rate

Supporting detail: Even low savings associated with higher graduation rate

Major supporting point 3: "Third, we should cover the cost of tuition with an income-based payment plan post-graduation."

    Supporting detail: Introduces Oregon's income-based payment plan

- Details of Oregon's plan
- Comparison of Oregon's plan to existing student loan repayment plans

    Supporting detail: Few make use of existing income-based repayment plans.

Major supporting point 4: "And finally, we could simply make college free."

    Supporting detail: Would be more affordable than appears

- Roosevelt Institute cost data
- Comparison of Roosevelt data with current costs
- Projections based on Roosevelt data

    Supporting detail: Results—college available for all; private universities may reduce costs.

Notice that the outline includes complete sentences for each of the major supporting points. If the major supporting points are stated directly in the reading, you can simply copy them into your outline. Always use quotation marks around any words you quote directly so that you can easily tell which words are from the source and which are yours. If a major supporting point is implied, you will have to use your own words to express it. For each supporting detail, write a short phrase or sentence summarizing the idea. The goal is to express—very briefly—what these details say.

An outline allows you to reduce the content of a reading into a short, easy-to-read map. In fact, some people create actual maps or graphic organizers to take the place of an outline. If you prefer a more visual representation of the information in a reading, you can create a simple graphic organizer. What follows is a graphic organizer showing the ideas used to support the first major supporting point.

> **Major supporting point:**
> First, we should allow graduates to discharge student loans in bankruptcy.

> **Supporting detail:**
> Bankruptcy law now

> **Supporting detail:**
> What the Center for American Progress proposes—allowing bankruptcy forgiveness

> **Results:**
> Would lower default rate, benefit graduates, incentivize lenders to offer better loan terms, and encourage colleges to develop career-placement strategies

■ To create a graphic organizer of a paragraph, write the major supporting point in a box at the top of the page. Place the major supporting details in the next row of boxes. Place any additional details below. Attach all the boxes with lines to show how they are connected.

The purpose of a graphic organizer is to show the relationships among supporting details. Because each essay presents ideas in its own unique way, graphic organizers will not look the same. For example, the graphic organizer for an essay with six major supporting points will look different from one for an essay with four major supporting points.

Hand-drawn graphic organizers are effective for showing relationships among ideas, and they are easy to draw. The hand-drawn organizer below demonstrates the relationships among ideas in a essay on the benefits of encouraging farmers' markets. Notice that the student found it easier to draw the diagram from left to right rather than from top to bottom.

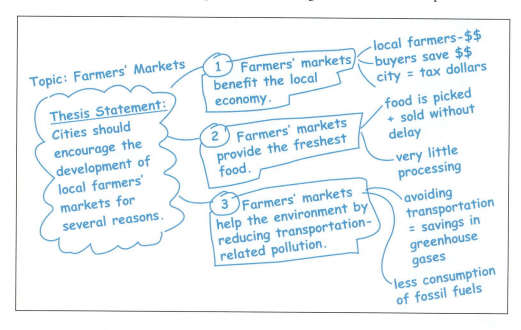

An especially good occasion for using outlining is when you are reading complex material and studying. By putting a reading's major supporting points and supporting details in order, you will be better able to understand the relationships among ideas and remember them later for tests.

PRACTICE **3** Outlining a Reading

Earlier in this chapter, you read "The Footprint That Does Not Fade." Create an outline or graphic organizer for this essay. Use the outline or a graphic organizer presented in this chapter as a model.

Answers will vary.

GRAMMAR FOCUS   **Transitions**

In good writing, the sentences used for support are clearly related to one another. One way to make sure that the relationships between sentences are evident is to use words or phrases that help readers follow the ideas in a text and help writers move smoothly from one idea to another. Notice how the use of the phrase *for example* helps readers see the relationship between the two following sentences.

Even cell phone use leaves a digital footprint. For example, a person's cell phone records can reveal that he was traveling between Austin and San Antonio on May 15, 2014, when he made a phone call.

Teaching Resources: See the exercise "Using Transitions."

(continued)

The phrase for example *reveals that the second sentence is meant to elaborate on the first sentence.*

Words and phrases that help the reader move from one sentence to another or from one paragraph to another are called **transitions.** Transitions also help readers recognize a sequence of ideas. If each major supporting point in a text starts with a transition, it is easy to recognize the points. Note the transitions (underlined) in the following example.

Three factors are important to consider in choosing a career. The <u>first</u> factor to consider in choosing a career is personal interest. . . .

The <u>second</u> factor is aptitude. . . .

The <u>third</u> factor that comes into play is the training and education requirements of the career. . . .

When sentences related by transitions indicate a series, the sentences often function in the same way. In this case, the sentences are all major supporting points.

Often, the logic of the supporting details is easier to follow when transitions are used, as in this example.

Good reasons exist on both sides of the debate about whether it is wise to take out student loans. <u>On the one hand,</u> taking out student loans seems logical. College graduates, <u>after all,</u> statistically earn much more than those who do not have degrees. <u>Thus,</u> it seems likely that college graduates will be able to pay off their loans. <u>On the other hand,</u> taking out student loans is fraught with risk. <u>Clearly,</u> college students cannot be certain they will find good jobs after graduation. <u>Additionally,</u> even if they do find good jobs, their entry-level salaries may not be high enough for both a comfortable life and the repayment of student debt.

Transitions show the logical relationships among ideas in this supporting paragraph.

One way to think about transitions is to identify them by their functions, as this table demonstrates.

COMMON TRANSITION WORDS AND PHRASES

CLARIFICATION		
for example	in reality	to demonstrate
for instance	put another way	to explain further
indeed	that is	to illustrate
in fact	to clarify	simply stated
in other words		specifically

SEQUENCES OR TIME ORDER		
about	immediately	previously
after	in the future	simultaneously
as	later	soon
as soon as	meanwhile	to begin
at the same time	next	until
during	now	when
final	often	while
first, second, . . . last	one, another	

(continued)

COMMON TRANSITION WORDS AND PHRASES

SIMILARITY OR ADDITION

additionally again along with also another as well besides	equally important for another thing for example for instance furthermore in addition	in the same way likewise moreover next plus similarly

CONTRAST

although conversely counter to despite even though however	in spite of this nevertheless on the contrary on the one hand, on the other hand	otherwise still yet

CONCLUSION OR SUMMARY

accordingly in closing in short	in summary in the end lastly	the bottom line the final point to conclude

CAUSE AND EFFECT

as a consequence as a result at last	because consequently resulting in	so then therefore thus

DIRECTION

above across against behind below beyond	here nearby next to opposite over	overhead there to the left to the right

SENTENCE COMBINING

The example that follows shows the major supporting points that appear as topic sentences in an essay. Notice how the added transitions clarify that these sentences are giving the three main ideas in the essay. In some cases, the writer has to rewrite the sentences slightly to make the transitions work.

Main supporting points needing transitions:

- Using tar sands oil will reduce the US presence in the Middle East. Canada will provide the majority of the oil the country imports.

- Developing tar sands oil production will greatly benefit the economies of both Canada and the United States.

- Innovations in its production are reducing the potential environmental effects of manufacturing it.

(continued)

Main supporting points using transitions:

- One reason to support using tar sands oil is that it will reduce the US presence in the Middle East; indeed, Canada will provide the majority of the oil the country imports.

- An equally important reason for developing tar sands oil production is that it will greatly benefit the economies of both Canada and the United States.

- A final reason for using tar sands oil is that innovations in its production are reducing the potential environmental effects of manufacturing it.

In the following example, the sentences give the supporting details for the final major supporting point of the essay. Notice how the added transitions connect the sentences to one another and provide clues about meaning. Note also that while transitions most commonly appear at the beginning of a sentence, they can also be effective in the middle or even at the end of a sentence.

Supporting details needing transitions:

- Innovations in its production are reducing the potential environmental effects of manufacturing it.

- Producers use less water now. A process that used to take ten barrels of water to produce a barrel of bitumen (the valuable product that is turned into oil) now takes about half of that.

- Some companies plan to recycle water. They plan to share water among themselves to protect the area's aquifer.

- Extraction companies are now beginning to use another method of reaching the bitumen. This method, called THAI (toe-to-heel air injection) does not affect the water supply.

Supporting details using transitions:

- A final reason for using tar sands oil is that innovations in its production are reducing the potential environmental effects of manufacturing it.

- To begin, producers use less water now. A process that used to take ten barrels of water to produce a barrel of bitumen (the valuable product that is turned into oil) now takes about half of that, for example.

- Additionally, some companies plan to recycle water. They plan, in fact, to share water among themselves to protect the area's aquifer.

- Moreover, extraction companies are now beginning to use another method of reaching the bitumen. This method, called THAI (toe-to-heel air injection) does not affect the water supply.

Try your hand at using transitions to add clarity to supporting ideas.

EXERCISES

Insert appropriate transitions into the sentences that follow. Reword the sentences if necessary.

Answers will vary. Sample answers are given.

1. Major supporting points (topic sentences) needing transitions:

   a. Federal student loans are a good financing option. College graduates have the choice of not repaying them. Graduates can work in the Peace Corps. They can participate in Teach for America. They can take part in other loan-forgiveness programs.

(continued)

b. Students do not have to pay back federal student loans immediately. Students can wait until after graduation.

c. Federal student loans do not start **accruing** interest immediately. Interest begins when the student graduates.

d. The interest rate on federal student loans is generally 3 to 7 percent. This is much lower than that of private student loans.

Answers:

a. One reason federal student loans are a good financing option is that college graduates have the choice of not repaying them. Instead, they can work in the Peace Corps, participate in Teach for America, or take part in other loan-forgiveness programs.

b. Additionally, students do not have to pay back federal student loans until after graduation.

c. Yet another reason to consider a federal student loan is that the loan does not start accruing interest until the student graduates.

d. Finally, the interest rate on federal student loans is generally 3 to 7 percent, much lower than that of private student loans.

2. Supporting details needing transitions:

a. There is a Teacher Loan Forgiveness Program. It is a way to help teachers pay back student loans. Not every teacher is eligible for the program.

b. The program is available only to teachers. Only teachers with Stafford Loans can participate.

c. There are eligibility requirements. A teacher must have worked for five years at a school. The school must be eligible to participate in the program.

d. The teacher must have taken the student loan prior to or during the five years of teaching.

Answers:

a. The Teacher Loan Forgiveness Program is a way to help teachers pay back student loans; however, not every teacher is eligible for the program.

b. More specifically, the program is available only to teachers with Stafford Loans.

c. Moreover, to be eligible, a teacher must have worked for five years at a participating school.

d. The teacher must also have taken the student loan prior to or during the five years of teaching.

3. Sentences needing transitions:

a. Over-the-counter medication can be abused. Many people fail to understand this fact.

b. Sleep aids are a commonly purchased over-the-counter item. They are abused.

c. Sleep aids are addictive. People who abuse sleep aids can become dependent on them and unable to sleep without them.

d. Over-the-counter substances that promise to deliver energy are popular. People can abuse these products. They use caffeine-laden products to help them stay awake.

e. Many over-the-counter products can cause dependencies. People should be careful with over-the-counter medication.

Answers:

a. Over-the-counter medication can be abused. Nevertheless, many people fail to understand this fact.

b. For instance, one type of commonly purchased over-the-counter medicine is sleep aids. Often they are abused.

Vocabulary Collection Word:
accruing

Your in-context definition:
_____
_____

A dictionary definition:
_____
_____

(continued)

c. Simply stated, sleep aids are addictive. People who abuse sleep aids can, in fact, become dependent on them and unable to sleep without them.

d. Likewise, over-the-counter substances that promise to deliver energy are popular. Yet people can also abuse these products. That is, they use caffeine-laden products to help them stay awake.

e. In short, many over-the-counter products can cause dependencies. Consequently, people should be careful with over-the-counter medication.

4. Sentences needing transitions:

a. The new law will allow students to graduate from high school with fewer mathematics courses than previous classes of high school students. The law requires only two years of high school math.

b. College students whose college entrance scores are too low will not be able to take math at the college level. These students will have to master high school math skills at off-campus facilities. They will then be allowed into college math classes.

c. Students should learn how much mathematics preparation they will need for college. They may have to add semesters to their degree plans. This may be the only way for them to finish their math requirements.

Answers:

a. The new law will allow students to graduate from high school with fewer mathematics courses than previous classes of high school students. That is, the law requires only two years of high school math.

b. As a result, college students whose college entrance scores are too low will not be able to take math at the college level. Instead, these students will have to master high school math skills at off-campus facilities. They will then be allowed into college math classes.

c. Therefore, students should learn how much mathematics preparation they will need for college. They may otherwise have to add semesters to their degree plans. In reality, this may be the only way for them to finish their math requirements.

USING SPECIFIC TYPES OF SUPPORTING DETAILS IN YOUR WRITING

Although you may not be aware of it, you use supporting details in your conversations all the time. For instance, in a casual conversation with a friend, you may comment about a movie you saw: "That movie was fantastic!" Your friend is likely to ask why you liked it so much. Your response will include supporting details. Notice how your conversation can be outlined in a way similar to an essay.

Thesis statement: That movie was fantastic!

Why?

Support:

- It was a classic epic. (*classification of the movie type*)
- It was so much better than the first movie in the series because the main character, Kudu, didn't win every battle. He seemed much more realistic. (*comparison*)
- The whole movie was in sepia-colored tones, which really added to the oddness of the scenery. (*description*)

We use support without even thinking about it. Moreover, these supporting details come in a wide variety of types.

Teaching Resources: See the PPT "Types of Support."

Recognizing Types of Supporting Details

As you read, become aware of the various types of support writers use and that you have available to you as a writer. The chart that follows lists some of the most common types of supporting details.

Common Types of Supporting Details	
Analogy	An example that explains something unfamiliar by comparing it with something more familiar
Cause and effect	How one circumstance brought about or resulted from another
Comparison and contrast	How one item or event is similar to or different from another
Concrete example	Specific information that helps the reader understand the writer's point
Definition	An explanation of the meaning of a word or concept
Description	Sensory information that helps the reader understand a thing or concept
Explanation	A description of how something is constructed, how a task is performed, or how something works
Fact	A statement that is verifiably true
Figurative language	Language that expresses ideas in an indirect way, such as metaphors, similes, personification, and hyperbole
Hypothetical example	An example that asks the reader to imagine something that is not currently true
Observation	An account of phenomena or field research
Reason	The rationale or justification for an assertion or claim
Rhetorical question	A question that the writer asks to make a point but does not expect the reader to answer; the answer may be provided in the text, or it may be self-evident
Summaries	A brief recounting of the content of a source
Steps, stages, or phases	A discussion of sequential actions or time periods to depict a process
Testimony	A person's firsthand account of something
Use of sources	Citing external sources, often to prove something: • Citing experts or authorities so the reader knows where the information is coming from and can evaluate its validity • Citing reference books so the information can be considered factual • Citing statistics to provide mathematical information or proof • Citing witnesses to provide evidence or acknowledgments
Visual aid	A photo, diagram, chart, cartoon, or any other graphic representation of content

It's helpful to teach audience analysis while teaching students to select appropriate support for their ideas. One way to do this is to present a thesis statement and to discuss how different types of support would be used for different audience demographics. See the IM for additional ideas about teaching audience awareness.

Writers select the type of supporting details to use based on the point they are making. To develop supporting details, think about each major supporting point as if you were the reader, not the writer. What questions would you have? What information would you want the writer to add to the paragraph?

For instance, to show that a movie is worth seeing, you might provide a brief *summary* of the plot, *compare* the movie to another movie, and *cite* the reviews of expert film critics. You would probably *not* use statistics, visual aids, or hypothetical examples. The following guidelines may help you select appropriate and effective details.

- Use concrete examples of real events and situations to convey trustworthiness.
- Use hypothetical examples—that is, fictional examples—to illustrate a point.
- Use short narratives—stories—to make a point.
- Imagine a reader who says "So what?" Make sure you show the importance of the point you are making.
- Use journalistic questions to think of content: who, what, where, when, why, and how. Only include the information generated by these questions if that information is relevant and truly strengthens the major supporting point.

Let's examine the kinds of support used in a specific essay. Below you will find the first part of an article written by a senior journalism major, Brittany Horn, at Penn State University. Horn does not provide a direct thesis statement, but an implied thesis statement might be worded like this: "In certain villages in China, pollution is causing cancer, and little is being done to change the situation." Read Horn's article, paying particular attention to the support she uses. The supporting details are highlighted, and they are annotated in the right column.

Recovery Is Slow in Rural China's "Cancer Villages"
by Brittany Horn

NANMEN, China—In this small village about 25 miles from Shanghai, the smell of paint and gasoline hangs heavy in the stagnant afternoon air. Small dogs run in streets wide enough for only a small car. Children with worn Disney backpacks walk home from school, avoiding the trash tossed into the street gutters.

It seems to be a village much like any other in rural China. But there is something different about Nanmen that weighs on villagers' minds.

Nanmen is one of more than 400 so-called "cancer villages," areas so polluted by waste and factory runoff that its citizens are in danger of contracting the deadly disease. The villages are part of the dark underside of China's industrial might—places that critics, environmentalists and foreign experts believe the government has sacrificed in its rush to prosperity.

"Many cancer villages can be proven, even though the government may choose to not acknowledge it," said Dong Jiang, an environmental activist who has studied the link between pollution and cancer in places like Nanmen.

Annotations
Example (Nanmen as an example of a cancer village)
Description
Comparison and contrast
Definition
Citation from environmental activist offered as proof

In the first four paragraphs, Horn uses an example, a description, comparison and contrast, a definition, and a quote from an environmental activist. These forms of support are all appropriate, yet diverse. The rest of the article appears in the practice below.

Vocabulary Collection Word: activist

Your in-context definition:

_____

_____

A dictionary definition:

_____

_____

PRACTICE ④ Identifying Types of Supporting Details

Identify the support in the remainder of Horn's essay. Underline each supporting detail and identify its type in the column on the right.

The term "cancer village" is not widely recognized by the academic world, but it's a phrase that's been used by the media, citizens and, most recently, the Chinese government to describe the poor living conditions.

Government officials and some academic experts argue that because the exact causes of cancer are so difficult to trace, there's no direct correlation between the cancer in rural villages and pollutants. But environmentalists like Dong say that the connection is clear, if people look.

And for those who've lost loved ones, there is no doubt.

It's been more than two years since Wang Qin said goodbye to her 22-month-old daughter, who died five months after she was diagnosed with leukemia. A day doesn't pass, Wang Qin said, when she doesn't think of her baby.

"I think of my lovely daughter all the time," she said. "She could say (the words) mom and dad, grandpa . . . she was quite smart."

Wang and her husband, Lu Weiming, spent thousands of dollars in medical bills and travel expenses to get their daughter, Wang Bole, the care she needed. But nothing worked. Their daughter slipped away in front of them, never recovering from the fever that took her life.

Today, more than two years later, Wang is still fighting the Chinese government for compensation for her loss and for recognition that a nearby waste collection factory be held accountable for its pollution.

She remembers the man who became blistered and fainted soon after touching the runoff water from the factory. Wang said the elderly are most susceptible, as the government can often overlook their deaths or blame them on natural causes. Other families tried to move away before the disease could take them, too, but not all were that lucky.

Part of Wang's struggle is getting the government and the scientific community to acknowledge the relationship between specific pollutants and cancer villages like Nanmen.

Professor Song Weimin, of Fudan University in Shanghai, said the connection between the cancer villages and pollutants is hard to prove, as the list of physical, chemical and biological factors continues to grow. Song, who specializes in environmental health, also said that the Chinese government is investigating the village pollution but hasn't released any official statistics as of yet.

"It's hard to find evidence," Song said. "Some organizations are afraid of getting in trouble because if they find that a factory is linked to cancer, it will lead to a lawsuit."

Activists like Dong Jian, vice president and secretary general of the Future Green Youth Leadership Council, say the proof exists, but the government chooses to ignore it.

"There is a direct connection," Dong insisted. "You have to compare the cancer rates before the factory has been built versus after the factory was built. Then you can see the rise."

YOUR ANNOTATIONS

Definition

Cause and effect

Some of the supporting details can be classified in more than one way. For instance, Qin's story is an example, but it also illustrates cause and effect and includes testimonial information.

Example of Wang Qin

Connect IRW Power of Process Assignment: Assign PoP to apply these strategies to analyze the support in this reading, or see the IM for alternative readings to assign within PoP.

Wang Qin's testimony about others.

Cause and effect

Citation of expert on cause and effect

Citation of expert on cause and effect

Citation of expert on cause and effect

(continued)

Progress may be slow, but there has been some movement. In a report released Feb. 20 by the Ministry of Environmental Protection, the government for the first time acknowledged the existence of cancer villages clustered around the outskirts of major cities and factories.	Citation of acknowledgment
Dong says it's not enough. "Although the government has the responsibility to acknowledge cancer villages and pollution, sometimes they don't do what they say they will," he said.	Citation of expert
Nanmen villagers know this story well. A village that was once removed from the rest of China became suddenly transformed into a place filled with pollution and disease.	Description
Villagers first noticed a change in 2002, when a small landfill began to take shape in the middle of Nanmen and soon gave way to a waste collection factory that virtually appeared overnight, Wang said.	Cause and effect
"The water was colorful, all kinds of colors," Wang said. "The water smelled terrible. Creatures couldn't live there anymore."	Description
The Zhaohong waste collection factory moved out more than two years ago, but Dong Jian said the negative effects on the environment and people remain.	Cause and effect
Take Wang Qin's elderly father. He can't afford to move from the village, nor does he want to. The streets he has called home since he was a child aren't something he's ready to give up for the sake of his health.	Example
The pond that once housed fish and wildlife is now home to a toilet basin with thick, black mud and leftover trash. Residents can no longer swim in the polluted water that scarcely resembles the place Wang Qin once swam.	Description
Villagers say conditions are getting better, but the effects of the longtime pollution are hard to gauge. Trees are only beginning to resume growth two years after the factory's removal, and the site where the Zhaohong waste collection factory once stood is barren and avoided.	Cause and effect
Home is no longer a place Wang Qin can stomach.	Cause and effect

Student Example: Selecting Appropriate Types of Support

To determine the best types of support to use in your own writing, use the three-step process shown here.

1. Write down the point that needs support.

2. Make a list of the types of details that could reasonably support your point.

3. Choose the types of details you believe will best meet the needs of your audience.

■ Steps for selecting types of support

We will follow the writing process of Trey, a college student writing an essay for a biology class. Trey's assignment is to select an issue in biology that affects public health, to form an opinion on the issue, and to write an essay expressing his opinion. He must offer solid support for his point of view.

Trey goes through the steps of analyzing his assignment, reading and annotating sources for ideas, and prewriting to develop his ideas. As a result of his prewriting, he chooses to write about the reasons why antibacterial products should no longer be sold to the general public, and he constructs a thesis statement.

Write Down the Points That Need Support

Trey decides to use four major supporting points to support his thesis statement.

Thesis statement: The sale of antibacterial products to the general public should be prohibited.

Major supporting points:

- First, the widespread use of antibacterial products is helping superbugs get stronger.
- Second, antibacterial products prevent helpful bacteria from doing their jobs, which results in a weakened immune system.
- Third, antibacterial products are no more effective at killing bacteria than regular soap and water.
- Finally, scientists now believe that antibacterial agents have negative health effects on people, especially pregnant women and children.

Now Trey must figure out the best types of details to use for each major supporting point.

For an in-class activity on selecting appropriate support, offer a claim and ask students what kind of support they would need to believe the claim. For example, you might ask them to discuss the kind of support they would need to believe this claim: "Getting a tattoo is a bad idea."

Biology public health essay - Microsoft Word

References   Mailings   Review   View

Point: First, the widespread use of antibacterial products is helping superbugs get stronger.

Support types I can use

- Cause and effect (explanation of process)
- Citation of expert (researcher in biology) or professional studies
- Comparison and contrast: could compare bacteria growth before antibacterial agents were used and now
- Example (could share a research study)
- Facts about how microbes adapt and change
- Figurative language: could use a metaphor or simile to describe this process
- Hypothetical example: make up an example of a situation in which microbes developed into superbugs, causing an untreatable flu
- Short summary: could summarize a research study and explain the way microbes gain resistance in steps or phases

List Details That Could Support the Points

Trey decides to do more prewriting, so he opens a document on his computer and creates a simple list for his first major supporting point.

Teaching Resources: See the exercise "Supplying Appropriate Support."

Choose Details That Will Best Meet the Audience's Needs

Trey knows that he cannot use all of these different types of support. He must choose the ones that will be most convincing to his audience, and he should choose the details he has learned the most about. After thinking about his list, Trey decides to use the following supporting details:

- Cause and effect (explanation of process). *This detail will give readers the information on how antibacterial agents can cause antibiotic-resistant microbes.*

- Citation of expert (researcher in biology) or professional studies. *This information will lend credibility to Trey's ideas.*

- Hypothetical example: make up an example of a situation where microbes developed into superbugs, causing an untreatable flu. *This information will help readers see how serious an issue antibacterial resistance is.*

When you are selecting types of support for a point you are making, use the same three-step process as Trey did. Always keep in mind how your audience will respond to the support you plan to offer. Choose the most compelling support available to you.

PRACTICE ⑤ Selecting Appropriate Types of Support for Your Writing

What follows is a simple essay outline containing a thesis statement and the major supporting points to develop the thesis statement. For each major supporting point, determine the best types of supporting details to use. Jot down your ideas in a fashion similar to Trey's. Use a bullet point for each type of supporting detail you will use.

Answers will vary. Sample answers are provided here.

Topic: College instructors carrying firearms on campus

Thesis statement: Instructors should not have the option of bringing their personal firearms to campus.

Major supporting points:

1. Most teachers do not have enough training to use a firearm with the kind of precision required to stop an attacker.

    Support: Facts about becoming an accurate marksman Citation of expert (policeman, for example) Hypothetical story

2. The more weapons that are on campus, the more dangerous campus will be.

    Support: Comparison: countries where carrying guns is legal and countries where it is not; comparison of death by gunshot Fact: instructors can also be violent Hypothetical situation: student angry at his grade, armed instructor, possibly armed student Anecdote about an accidental shooting

3. Other solutions to campus violence are better options.

    Support: Examples: metal detectors, security teams, security processes Facts and statistics about effectiveness of prevention programs Citation of expert on dealing with mental health issues in schools

Student Example: Developing an Essay from Prewriting to Outlining

Creating the kind of support that will help readers fully understand your thesis statement is an essential part of writing an essay. Usually, when you generate ideas in prewriting, you are already beginning to think about the kinds of information you will use in your body paragraphs. What follows is an example of how Sienna, a freshman writing student, generated supporting details for her assignment.

Analyze the Assignment

Sienna is taking a class in anthropology, and her instructor has given the class an essay assignment. Sienna's first task is to fully understand the assignment. She reads the assignment and makes annotations.

Assignment: Write an essay in which you *discuss* a rite of passage you have experienced; *show* readers *why* this rite of passage was significant.

SIENNA'S ANNOTATIONS

What is this?

By reviewing her class notes, she learns that a rite of passage is an important transitional experience in a person's life, such as marriage, graduation, childbirth, divorce, or even a particular birthday celebration. That information helps her rephrase the assignment as a question.

Sienna's question: What significant rite of passage have I experienced, and why was it important?

Identify the Purpose

Three other words in the assignment that Sienna annotated are *discuss*, *show*, and *why*. From these terms she concludes that the purpose of her essay is to tell about her rite of passage and discuss the reasons it was important. Moreover, she is not to discuss just any rite of passage. She must choose one from her own experience. So her purpose is to *inform* her readers about a rite of passage she experienced and *evaluate* its importance.

Prewrite to Develop Ideas

From class discussions, Sienna discovers that a rite of passage consists of three phases:

Separation

Transition

Reincorporation

Because she recently gave birth to a daughter, Sienna decides to write about how having a baby is an important rite of passage. With that in mind, Sienna rewrites the question her essay will answer.

Sienna's revised question: Why was giving birth to my daughter a significant rite of passage?

Then, using the three phases of a rite of passage, Sienna does some *freewriting*—writing quickly on a subject without pausing to make corrections. During her freewriting, she comes up with ideas about how having a child was a significant experience for her. Afterward, rereading her freewriting, she underlines the important details for each phase. She realizes that the last line of her freewriting answers the question "Why?" so she highlights that line.

Why was giving birth to my daughter an important rite of passage?

Separation: When I was pregnant, I didn't "party" anymore; didn't hang out with the same people; spent more time with my family, especially my mom and husband; entered a new world of doctors, hospitals, and *pain*! I was so sick when I was pregnant.

Transition: When I gave birth, I came home and took care of the baby on my own. Was tired all the time. No peace and quiet! Less money—everything cost so much. No time to shop, go out to eat, exercise. It seemed like work, work, work. Husband was always tired because he helped w/the baby every night and worked all day the next day. We fought. No time for myself. Emotional issues. Sad about losing my freedom and old body! I wasn't sure I was capable of raising a baby. Everything was scary. Read a million Web sites to try to figure it all out.

Reincorporation: One year later, I'm very happy in general. Different expectations. Not a lot of sleep is OK. Learned how to find some time for myself. Have a great daily routine. Feel like I am a competent mom now. Body/weight are adjusting. Feel changed forever—more mature and more like a woman and not a girl.

Construct a Thesis Statement

Using the material she developed in her prewriting, Sienna constructs a thesis statement.

> **Thesis statement:** The birth of my first child was a rite of passage that changed me forever.

Notice that Sienna has written an *open thesis statement:* it does not reveal an explicit plan for her essay. Sienna also considered this *closed thesis statement,* which lists the stages she will discuss in each major supporting point:

> The birth of my first child was a rite of passage that involved the stages of separation, transition, and reincorporation.

Develop Support for the Thesis Statement

Sienna plans to use each stage in her rite of passage as a major supporting point. Her next task is to create topic sentences for each major supporting point.

Writing Topic Sentences for Major Supporting Points Using the three rite of passage phases from her prewriting, as well as the details she developed in the prewriting, Sienna writes topic sentences for her major supporting ideas.

> **Thesis statement:** The birth of my first child was a rite of passage that changed me forever.
>
> **Major supporting point 1 (topic sentence):** When I became pregnant, I found myself separated from my old life.
>
> **Major supporting point 2 (topic sentence):** After I gave birth to my daughter, I entered into a tough transition period.
>
> **Major supporting point 3 (topic sentence):** Fortunately, today I am slowly beginning to see myself in a new way.

Sienna uses transitions while she writes her topic sentences. Notice her use of *When, After, Fortunately,* and *today.* These transitions help signal to readers the major phases through which Sienna passed. We also see some similarity in wording:

When . . . I found myself . . .

After . . . I entered into . . .

Fortunately, today I am slowly . . .

Both the transitions and the similarities in wording tell readers that these details are the major phases in Sienna's rite of passage.

Anticipating an Audience's Questions Sienna needs to make sure the supporting details she has developed in prewriting will provide enough information to meet the needs of her readers. One way to do this is to spend time thinking about what readers might want or need to know. By putting herself in the place of the reader, she can predict some of the needs of her audience. The chart below shows some of the audience questions Sienna asks herself about her second major supporting point.

Topic sentence for major supporting point 2: After I gave birth to my daughter, I entered into a tough transition period.	
Supporting details:	**Audience questions:**
• Emotional issues—sad about loss of freedom, body image adjustments, marriage was more difficult	• What do you mean by "loss of freedom"? Can you provide an example? What kind of freedom will/lose if/when I have children? • How did your body change? How much weight did you gain? • Why was your marriage more difficult? Can you provide an example?
• Physical difficulties, never getting enough sleep	• What do you mean by "physical difficulties"? • Couldn't you find a way to get more sleep?
• Had financial difficulties (baby-related costs)	• How much does it cost to have a baby? Do you mean an extra $50/month, or do you mean more like $300–$500/month?
• Believed I was not a competent mother	• Why were you so down on your mothering abilities? • What tasks were you particularly concerned about?

Listing and Choosing Supporting Details for Each Major Supporting Point Sienna returns to her prewriting to find effective supporting details. Although Sienna has already identified some of the supporting details she will use—personal anecdotes and facts about money—she finds even *more specific* examples as she continues thinking about her audience's needs. She plans to add a very short anecdote and some concrete examples to make her essay more informative and enjoyable.

Create an Outline to Organize the Essay

Sienna now writes a simple outline for her essay. She jots down her three major supporting points—written out as full topic sentences. Under each point, she adds the supporting details she will use. When the supporting details themselves need more explanation or support, she adds them as "details."

Sienna's Simple Outline

Title: Giving Birth: My Rite of Passage

Introduction paragraph

Thesis statement: The birth of my first child was a rite of passage that changed me forever.

Major supporting point 1: When I became pregnant, I found myself separated from my old life.

    Supporting detail: Did not go partying with old friends

        Detail: Was not interested in the same things anymore

    Supporting detail: Spent more time with family and less time doing the things I used to do

Major supporting point 2: After I gave birth to my daughter, I entered into a tough transition period.

    Supporting detail: Emotional trials

        Detail: Sad about loss of freedom, body image adjustments, marriage was more difficult

    Supporting detail: Had financial difficulties

        Detail: Living on one income

        Detail: Paying baby-related costs

    Supporting detail: Afraid I wasn't a competent mother

        Detail: Needed constant reassurance

        Detail: Worried about accidentally hurting the baby

Major supporting point 3: Fortunately, today I am slowly beginning to see myself in a new way.

    Supporting detail: Am a good mother

        Detail: Developed routines that work for the baby

    Supporting detail: More emotionally stable

        Detail: Wake up happy most days

        Detail: Have more confidence and less anxiety

    Supporting detail: See myself as grown up

        Detail: Can handle what other women handle

        Detail: Hang out with new group of people, women with children

Conclusion paragraph

Notice that not all of the body paragraphs have the same number of details. Some writers aim to have supporting paragraphs that are roughly the same length, and that is a good goal. However, body paragraphs can have minor variations in the number of details they include and still be effective.

Notice also how coming up with supporting details leads naturally into creating a simple, informal outline for your writing. It is always wise to create an outline before drafting.

PRACTICE 6 Planning Support Paragraphs for an Essay

Using Sienna's work as a model, generate ideas and an outline for an essay on a rite of passage you have experienced. You will use your outline in a later assignment to draft the essay. Follow these instructions.

1. **Start by reading the assignment.** For this assignment, you will write an essay in which you discuss a rite of passage you have experienced; your essay must show readers why this rite of passage was significant. For details, see A Reading and Writing Assignment at the end of this chapter.

2. **Prewrite to develop your ideas.** Choose a prewriting method, such as listing or freewriting, and use it to generate ideas for the topic. First, prewrite about some of the experiences in your life that were rites of passage. Write down each experience, and note why it was significant to you. Do this for at least three experiences.

   Once you have written about three or more rites of passage, choose one to discuss in an essay. If you need to, spend more time prewriting to think of the ways this experience changed you.

3. **Construct a thesis statement.** Write a sentence in which you express the main point you wish to make about the rite of passage you selected for your essay.

4. **Develop support for your thesis statement.** Write a topic sentence for each major supporting point. Consider creating a major supporting point for each significant effect this rite of passage had. Once you have written topic sentences for your major supporting points, list the questions a general audience might have about them. Next, jot down the minor supporting details that would help readers understand each of your major supporting points.

5. **Create a simple outline to organize your essay.** Use Sienna's outline as a model. Include your thesis statement, major supporting points, and supporting details.

CHAPTER ACTIVITIES

READING AND ANNOTATING

What follows is a brief essay about male rites of passage. It begins with an extensive example; the second half of the reading is an explanation of the phases of a rite of passage.

Preview the essay. What point do you think the writer is making about rites of passage? Make some notes based on your observations from previewing. Then read the essay, and annotate the major supporting points. Hint: the essay starts with a major supporting point. You may have an easier time analyzing this essay if you identify the major supporting points before you try to figure out the thesis statement.

When you are finished, answer the questions that follow.

Your observations from previewing:

_____

_____

_____

_____

Many students will find it challenging to differentiate the thesis statement from the major supporting details in this essay. Consider using the PPT "'Coming of Age'" as a guide for reading the essay together as a class. Or you might have students try to find the thesis statement and major supporting points on their own or in groups, and then use the PPT to help them assess their insights.

Lexile: 1090L

YOUR ANNOTATIONS

Coming of Age: The Importance of Male Rites of Passage

by Brett and Kate McKay

The elders of the tribe stood in front of the hut and beckoned for the young man to come out and begin the festivities of the special day. The young man had barely slept the night before, anxiously anticipating the tests he would soon be called to endure. As he rose to meet the elder, he was aware of a great gnawing in his stomach; he had had nothing to eat for the last three days as he purged his body of impurities.

The ceremony soon began. The elders of the tribe pierced his chest, shoulder, and back muscles with large wooden splints. Ropes, which extended from the roof of the hut, were then attached to the splints, and the young man was winched up into the air, his whole body weight suspended from the ropes. Agonizing pain coursed through the young man's body, but he gritted his teeth and tried not to cry out.

While hanging in the air, more splints were hammered through his arms and legs. Skulls of his dead grandfather and other ancestors were placed on the ends of the splints. All the while, the young man cried aloud to the Great Spirit for courage to endure. Eventually, the young man fainted from the loss of blood and the sheer pain of the torture. When the elders were sure he was unconscious, he was lowered down and the ropes were removed. Yet the splints were left in place.

When the young man recovered consciousness, he offered his left pinky to the tribal elders to be sacrificed. He placed his finger on a block and had it swiftly chopped off. This was a gift to the gods and would enable the young man to become a powerful hunter.

Finally, the young man ran inside a ring where his fellow villagers had gathered. As he ran, the villagers reached out and grabbed the still embedded splints, ripping them free. The splints weren't allowed to be pulled out the way they had been hammered

This story serves as a major supporting detail for the statement that comes later.

in, but had to be torn out in the opposite direction, causing the young man even greater pain and worse wounds. This concluded the day's ceremony.

The young man was exhausted and bloodied, but euphoric. He had been beyond glad to participate in the ritual. This was the greatest day of his life; today he was a man.

While the coming of age ceremony of the Mandan tribe is a particularly gruesome example, peoples and cultures from prehistoric times onward created rites of passage to initiate boys into manhood. Today, such rites of passage are almost extinct. Boys lack clear markers on their journey to becoming a man. If you ask them when the transition occurs, you will get a variety of answers: "When you get a car," "When you graduate from college," "When you get a real job," "When you lose your virginity," "When you get married," "When you have a kid," and so on. The problem with many of these traditional rites of passage is that they have been put off further and further in a young man's life. Fifty years ago the average age an American man started a family was 22. Today, men (for ill or good) are getting married and having kids later in life. With these traditional rites of passage increasingly being delayed, many men are left feeling stuck between boyhood and manhood. College? Fewer men are graduating. And many that do "boomerang" back home again, spending another few years figuring out what the next step in their life should be. As traditional rites of passage have become fuzzier, young men are plagued with a sense of being adrift.

Of course the process of becoming a man, ceremony or not, does not happen in a single moment. But rites of passage are important in delineating when a boy should start thinking of himself as a man, when he should start carrying himself as a man, when the community should start respecting him as a man, and when he should start shouldering the responsibilities of a man. Lacking these important markers, many young men today belabor their childhood, never sure of when they've really "manned up."

WHAT IS A RITE OF PASSAGE?

Sociologists have identified three phases that constitute a proper rite of passage: separation, transition, and re-incorporation.

Separation: During this phase an initiate is separated in some way from his former life. In the case of the Mandan tribe, the young man was isolated from the village in a hut for three days. In other tribes, boys' heads were shaved and they were ritually bathed and/or tattooed. In a more modern example, when a man has just enlisted in the military, he is sent away to boot camp. His former possessions are put aside, his head is shaved, and he is given a uniform to wear. During the separation phase, part of the old self is extinguished as the initiate prepares to create a new identity.

Transition: During this phase, the initiate is between worlds—no longer part of his old life but not yet fully inducted into his new one. He is taught the knowledge needed to become a full-fledged member of that group. And he is called upon to pass tests that show he is ready for the leap. In tribal societies, the elders would impart to the initiate what it meant to be a man and how the boy was to conduct himself once he had become one. The initiate would then participate in ritual ceremonies which often involved pain and endurance. In the case of the new soldier, he is yelled at, prodded, exercised, and disciplined to prepare him to receive a rank and title.

YOUR ANNOTATIONS

Major supporting point: Rites of passage were important for young men in the past. (The story at the beginning of the essay is the support for this point.)

Major supporting point: For young men today, rites of passage are almost extinct. (The content of this paragraph provides support for this point.)

Thesis statement

Major supporting point

Re-incorporation. In this phase, the initiate, having passed the tests necessary and proving himself worthy, is re-introduced into his community, which recognizes and honors his new status within the group. For tribal societies, this meant a village-wide feast and celebration. The boy would now be recognized by all tribe members as a man and allowed to participate in the activities and responsibilities that status conferred. For the soldier, his boot camp experience would come to an end and both his superiors and his family would join in a ceremony to recognize his new status as a full-fledged member of the military.

During all the phases of the process, the men who have gone through the ritual themselves guide the young initiate on his journey. By controlling the rite of passage, the men decide when a boy becomes a man.

Questions for Consideration

1. Some people have called modern body piercing or tattooing a rite of passage. They believe body piercing and tattooing are very significant experiences that often mark the beginning of adulthood. Do you agree? Why or why not? If you have a piercing or tattoo, did your experience make you feel different about yourself? Was it a true rite of passage? If you do not have a piercing or tattoo, would you predict getting one would be a meaningful rite of passage? Explain in one or two paragraphs.

2. The passage you read concerns male rites of passage. What female rites of passage exist in our society? Make a list. Do each of these rites of passage have a separation phase, a transition phase, and a reincorporation phase? Explain in one or two paragraphs.

3. Find a person who is much older than you are. Interview the person to find out whether he or she can recall a rite of passage that was significant. You may need to explain what a rite of passage is. Take notes from your interview. Using your notes, write one or two pages about this person's rite of passage.

4. Some rites of passage seem violent or destructive. Think about the ways young men and women in your culture prove they are moving from adolescence to adulthood. Are any of these ways violent or destructive? Write a paragraph explaining one such rite of passage.

USING MODELS TO PRACTICE COMPOSING

Earlier in this chapter, you read about the steps Sienna took as she worked on a writing assignment. Below you will find the essay Sienna wrote. Read the essay, and annotate any of the writing features you think are effective. Circle the transitions you find. Be mindful of the support Sienna used. Note any areas where you think she should have included more support.

Questions for Consideration

1. Answers will vary, but students should address whether the act of getting a piercing or tattoo was truly meaningful in terms of their self-identity.

2. Answers will vary, but students may list physical changes such as the onset of menstruation (menarche), loss of virginity, giving birth, and menopause. Though these are physical "events," they can be accompanied by societal changes and even ceremonies of various kinds. Students may also mention quinceañera and sweet sixteen celebrations.

3. Answers will vary, but students may interview a grandparent about making the transition as a soldier, leaving home for the first time, getting married, or any other event that may have been a rite of passage. Students may also mention religious rites of passage, such as confirmation.

4. Answers will vary. Examples are joining a gang, drinking or taking drugs, and even committing crimes to gain acceptance into a particular social group.

Mendez 1

Sienna Mendez

INRW 0402

Ms. Cassidy

15 November 2014

Childbirth as a Rite of Passage

There are two worlds—the one before having children, and the one afterward. Most young people, however, do not know about these two worlds. Regardless of how much I read about what it is like to have a child, I was not truly prepared for the world I entered after childbirth. Having a baby is a true rite of passage. It is a challenging moment in life, but it also comes with blessings. The birth of my first child was a rite of passage that changed me forever.

When I became pregnant, I found myself separated from my old life. After my long shifts as an emergency room clerk, I used to go out for bar food and drinks with a group of nurses and clerks. When I could not drink anymore, and when I could not stay awake long enough to have fun with the girls, I eventually stopped going. Plus, none of them had children—or wanted children. I still loved my friends, but being pregnant just made things different. I spent far more time with my family than I used to, and gradually my circle of friends became smaller.

After I gave birth to my daughter, I entered into a tough transition period. I was beginning to see what a life change I was in for. I had always been a calm, easygoing person, but I surprised myself with fits of crying or anger. At times I felt really happy, but there were other times when I was sad about losing my freedom, my thin, sexy body, and the fun times my husband and I used to have without the responsibility of a baby.

YOUR ANNOTATIONS

Sample answers are given.

Metaphor of two worlds

Transitions (all double-underlined, but not every one is marked)

Thesis

Major supporting point (topic sentence)
Personal anecdote

Major supporting point (topic sentence)

Mendez 2

In addition to those challenges, money problems began to appear. Life just became hard. I had made the choice to quit my job for two years to stay home with our child, but I hadn't realized how different it would be to live on one income instead of two. Baby supplies were so expensive!

Also, I was constantly worried and anxious. I needed reassurance every day, and I spent most of my free time searching for information on the Web or calling my mother in tears. I worried the most about accidentally hurting my child. Were the bottles washed well enough? Was she breathing? I could hardly sleep at night sometimes because of my worrying.

Fortunately, today I am slowly beginning to see myself in a new way. I truly am a different person than I was a year ago. I have slowly come to believe that I am a good mother. I am not perfect, but no mother is. By developing routines with my baby, I have learned how to manage my day more effectively, even fitting in more time to focus on my coursework.

Better yet, I have become much more emotionally stable. I no longer have fits of tears or anger, and most days I wake up happy and ready to face life. I have far less anxiety about being a mom, and I have developed the belief that now I am really a different person. I am no longer a child. I am proving myself capable of handling what other grown women handle. And even more impressively, I have a group of new friends, mothers with children. I am one of them now.

The transition was not easy, and it is not over. I have a feeling that being a parent will involve many rites of passage. After all, some day my child will leave, and I imagine that that day will be just as hard as the last year has been. With luck, it will result in the same joy.

Topic sentence

More info needed: how expensive?

Topic sentence

Rhetorical questions

Topic sentence

Cause and effect

Topic sentence

A READING AND WRITING ASSIGNMENT

Using Sienna's essay as a model and the material you developed in Practice 6, complete the following assignment:

> Write an essay in which you discuss a rite of passage you have experienced; show readers why this rite of passage was significant.
>
> A rite of passage is usually an event or a short period of time in a person's life that is particularly important and results in personal growth. For example, taking care of a loved one who is dying might trigger a reappraisal of life. For the caregiver, this task may be a rite of passage into new insights and a new way of living. Other rites of passage are more formal, such as getting married, having a child, and getting divorced. Think of an event or time in your life from which you emerged changed in some way: perhaps you became "older and wiser," or maybe you had insights that changed the way you live or that helped you mature. You may structure your paper around the ways this rite of passage has affected you, or you may write about each of the three phases Sienna included in her essay planning.

Use the Quick Start Guide to Integrated Reading and Writing Assignments to help you with this process. Be sure to reread your essay carefully for errors.

⊙ THINKING FROM AN INSTRUCTOR'S POINT OF VIEW

A *rubric* is a detailed grading sheet. Instructors create rubrics to help them grade assignments. One way to create a rubric is to analyze an assignment's instructions and turn them into *objectives* for the rubric. Each objective is then assigned a point value. The process looks something like this.

How Instructors Create Grading Rubrics

1. Analyze the assignment, and take apart the instructions piece by piece as the highlighting here shows.

   Example: Read the article called "Rehab for Bullies." Write an essay in which you argue whether the writer's thesis—that bullies should be put into rehabilitation programs—is a good idea or not. Compose a sound thesis statement, and offer supporting reasons, hypothetical examples, and discussions of how "bully rehabilitation" might affect children who experience it. When you refer to ideas from the article, be sure to use an appropriate method for giving credit to the source.

2. Turn each instruction into a learning objective.

   Examples: Learning objective: The student's essay shows that he or she read the article "Rehab for Bullies."

   Learning objective: The student's writing is an essay, and it addresses the topic (whether bully rehab is a good idea).

   Learning objective: The student takes a position on the question and writes a sound thesis statement. . . .

3. Assign a point value to each learning objective on the basis of how important the objective is.

   Examples: 10 points—Learning objective: The student's essay shows that he or she read the article "Rehab for Bullies."

   10 points—Learning objective: The student's writing is an essay, and it addresses the topic (whether bully rehab is a good idea).

   15 points—Learning objective: The student takes a position on the question and writes a sound thesis statement. . . .

Connect IRW Writing Assignment: Use Connect IRW to guide students through writing this essay and using peer review. This reading and writing assignment is pre-loaded in Connect IRW *Common Places* Master Course.

Consider having students provide you with an assignment sheet from another of their classes. Analyze the assignment sheet in class and create a rubric for the assignment. Have students participate in the process.

Here is an example of the first part of an actual grading rubric for a specific essay assignment.

EASY 1 RUBRIC / GRADE SHEET		ENGL 1301 Dr. Herze
Learning Objective/Points Possible	Comments about Student's Performance	Points Scored
1. Critical reading and understanding as demonstrated in student writing (Instruction from assignment: "Read and analyze the article, 'Light on the Horizon.' Use the article as a starting point for your own ideas on the topic.")	Lydia—You did a nice job showing you understood the main ideas and major supporting details. Work on understanding the writer's tone.	**Possible points: 20** Score: 17
2. Student's essay provides an appropriate response to the writing prompt. (Instruction from assignment: Write an essay that responds to this question: "Does 'Light on the Horizon' offer a convincing argument for changing immigration laws?")	Nice job staying on topic and fully considering each of the issues raised in the article.	**Possible points: 20** Score: 20

Using the information from the rite of passage essay assignment in Practice 6, create a grading rubric you believe would be an appropriate tool for assessing student essays. When you are finished, write a paragraph explaining what you learned from this activity.

Teaching Resources: See the handout "Rubric for Rite of Passage Essay."

⊙ ADDING TO YOUR VOCABULARY

This chapter's vocabulary words appear below.

initiative	default	accruing	activist
on the cusp	off-the-cuff	aquifer	

Teaching Resources: See the Connect IRW *Common Places* Master Course for vocabulary study practices that accompany this chapter, as well as a chapter vocabulary quiz.

Choose five of the vocabulary words from this chapter that you would like to add to your vocabulary, and think about how you can use them this week. For example, one of this chapter's terms is *off-the-cuff*. This term describes something that is said without forethought or preparation. You can often substitute *off-the-cuff* for *unplanned*.

Example: I didn't know my instructor would call on me to explain last night's reading, so I just gave my best *unplanned* answer.

I didn't know my instructor would call on me to explain last night's reading, so I just gave my best *off-the-cuff* answer.

List each of the five words you plan to use this week, and make note of a context in which you could use each word.

Example: *Off-the-cuff.* When I am explaining something to family members but do not have time to get into great depth, I'll let them know my explanation is off-the-cuff.

⊙ ADDITIONAL ASSIGNMENTS

1. Practice audience analysis skills by reading the following paragraph. As a reader, what information would you expect the writer to provide? Has the writer of this paragraph met those needs? Analyze the paragraph, and then write a list of recommendations for how the writer could change or add supporting details to meet readers' needs.

1. Answers will vary, but some possible questions audiences may have are

- What kind of things go on?
- Why did you call a certain prisoner "Diva"? Why did you choose that name?
- How did she change the perfectly ordinary Monday?
- Why is it so memorable to you?
- What did she do that was haunting?
- What kind of visitors did the other prisoner have?
- How did she look that made you think she would not have been a criminal?

No one would believe the kinds of things that go on in women's prisons. As a prison guard, I have had the opportunity to get an inside glimpse into the lives of this very isolated world. One prisoner, whom I will call Diva, changed a perfectly ordinary Monday into a day I will never get out of my mind. I am still haunted by that day. Another prisoner had the most unusual visitors, and from the way she looked, you would never have guessed she was the criminal type. My experience as a prison guard has been exceptional.

2. Choose one of the following thesis statements. If you were writing an essay, what major supporting points would you use to effectively demonstrate the thesis statement you selected? What kinds of supporting details would provide evidence for your major supporting points? Write an informal outline or graphic organizer for the thesis statement you chose.

   a. All US citizens should have to serve two years in the military.

   b. Making US citizens serve a mandatory period of two years in the military is a bad idea.

3. The list of prewriting ideas that follows was generated by Neil, a reading and writing student, in response to the following assignment: Write an essay in which you discuss the college courses that you think will be the most important ones to prepare you for your future career.

   a. Neil wants someday to own his own child-care center, so he wrote down all of the things he thinks he will need to know for this career. Read through Neil's prewriting, and put his ideas into categories.

   b. For each category, determine a college course that might help him learn the information he would need to know for his career.

Most important course: Child-Care Center Administration

- My future job: run a child-care center
- Need to know about costs involved in running a center
- Need to know how to advertise
- Need to know what to teach children at different ages
- Need to know about health laws
- Need to know about safety laws
- Need to know about how to buy a facility
- Need to know how to make a profit
- Need to know how to take care of emergencies
- Need to know how to deal with parents
- Need to know how to get start-up money to open a center
- Need to know what kinds of requirements we should have for child-care workers
- Need to know how to relate to children in a kind and friendly way
- Need to understand the psychological needs of children
- Need to know what parents want in a child-care center
- Need to know how to deal with sick children
- Need to know the kinds of toys and equipment to buy
- Need to know how to hire employees

2. Answers will vary, but some ideas follow:

All US citizens should have to serve two years in the military.

- We will have a stronger military with this requirement.
- People will be less likely to send our troops into war unless it's really necessary.
- Military experience will teach young people responsibility and will help them mature.

Making US citizens serve a mandatory period of two years in the military is a bad idea.

- Not all citizens agree with the military/government's ideals.
- Such a requirement is an infringement on human freedoms.
- Some people are not cut out for military work but could be well-suited for studying science or mathematics in college and could help our country in other ways.

3. A variety of categories can be constructed. Here are some suggestions.

- Legal issues (business law course)
- Money issues (business finance course)
- Procedural issues (business management course)
- Employee issues (human resources course)

- Need to know about government programs that affect child-care centers
- Need to plan food/dining/sanitation issues
- Need to make policies for employees
- Need to make policies for parents/children
- Need to know how to give employees health insurance
- Need to know if there are state laws about hiring child-care workers

EMOTIONAL INTELLIGENCE

In some ways, starting college is a rite of passage. Think about the three phases of rites of passage: separation, transition, and reincorporation. Think about your experience as a college student. In what ways does becoming a college student require you to experience separation? What kinds of transitions are required of college students? When you finish college, what kind of reincorporation do you expect? Explain in a paragraph or two.

Answers will vary, but students might write some of the following:

Students separate from their families and from high school friends to go to college. They make the transition to being a college student by learning how to navigate around campus, how to register for classes, and how to pass classes. They reincorporate into the community later after they complete their degrees.

CULTURAL LITERACY

One part of cultural literacy is having a knowledge of the key issues people are debating today. Two of the issues raised in this chapter—digital footprints and tar sands oil—are in the news often and are important to many people. Choose a reliable news Web site such as CNN, NPR, or *The New York Times.* Browse through the site and skim the articles you find. What are some of the national issues people are discussing today? Make a list of five issues. Next, choose one issue about which you are concerned. It may be one of the five on your list, or it may be a separate issue. Write a paragraph in which you present the issue and discuss your concerns.

Answers will vary.

CRITICAL THINKING

One of the characteristics of critical thinkers is open-mindedness. Some people are so strongly opinionated that they have difficulty even listening to the views of others. Critical thinkers can also be strongly opinionated, but they have learned how to put their opinions aside and listen—openly and genuinely—to other viewpoints. Critical thinkers are willing to change their viewpoints if another point of view is convincing.

Have you ever thought a particular way about an issue and, having heard convincing information, changed your mind on that issue? If so, write a paragraph explaining how you kept an open mind and the process that led to your changing your position. If not, write a paragraph about a time when your closed-mindedness was not a good thing.

Answers will vary. If students cannot think of an instance in which they were persuaded to change their views, prompt them to think about beliefs they had as children that they changed over time.

METACOGNITION

Think of a skill you possess that you had to learn. For example, perhaps you know how to work on automotive engines, or maybe you are a great cook, a fabulous guitarist, or a pretty good point guard. Now, think back to a time when you were *not* good at that skill. How did you learn the skill? What did you do in the beginning of the learning process? Did you learn by imitating someone else? Did someone specifically show you what to do? Did you read? Did you talk about the skill? Write a paragraph explaining the way you learned to be good at your skill. Reflect on why that learning method worked for you.

Answers will vary.

6

Can you identify the animals that made these tracks? Patterns help us know what to expect, not only in the wild, but also in texts.

Text Purposes and Text Patterns

Every text has a purpose. In fact, you could probably think of a long list of writing purposes: to reflect, to memorialize, to define, to entertain, to list, to vent frustration, and to make a plea, just to name a few. Most of the texts you encounter in your college and work life will have one or more of these writing purposes: to inform, to analyze, to evaluate, and to persuade.

To compose texts that effectively fulfill their purposes, writers often use text patterns. **Text patterns**—narration, definition, illustration, classification, comparison-contrast, cause and effect, process analysis, and argument—are modes of thought that communicate ideas. For example, to write an informative article about glaciers melting as a result of global warming, a writer may use a *cause and effect* text pattern. To evaluate alternative forms of energy, a writer may use a *comparison-contrast* text pattern. Writers choose text patterns on the basis of their topics and their writing purposes.

Text patterns help us both as readers and as writers. As readers, we recognize text patterns and expect them to present information in specific ways. As writers, we use text patterns to communicate our thoughts.

In this chapter, we focus on the four writing purposes and learn how text patterns can be used to fulfill these purposes.

CHAPTER OBJECTIVES

After completing this chapter, students will be able to do the following:

- **Identify the purposes of texts—to inform, to analyze, to evaluate, and to persuade.**

- **Connect purposes and text patterns.**

- **Recognize eight text patterns—narration, definition, illustration, classification, comparison-contrast, cause and effect, process analysis, and argument.**

- **Analyze these eight text patterns as they appear in readings.**

- **Use these eight text patterns to compose paragraphs and essays.**

- **Recognize mixed text patterns in a reading, and use mixed text patterns in writing.**

Connect IRW LearnSmart Achieve: Assign the topics "Recognizing and Applying Organizational Structures" and "Identifying and Applying Patterns of Development" for adaptive learning to accompany the chapter.

Teaching Resources: See the Chapter Quiz.

IDENTIFYING THE PURPOSE OF A TEXT

An important part of exploring a text is to ask yourself, "What is the writer's purpose?"

- Does the writer plan *to inform* readers about a particular subject?
- Does the writer plan *to analyze* a particular situation or course of action?
- Does the writer plan *to evaluate* an idea, proposal, or situation?
- Does the writer plan *to persuade* readers of the appropriateness of a particular idea or proposal?

Knowing the writer's purpose helps you determine the text's meaning and decide on the text's effectiveness.

Writing to Inform

Informative texts are straightforward: they tell readers about a subject. Newspaper articles are usually informative, as are textbooks, reference books, travelogues (travel writing), factual magazine articles, reports, and many scholarly journal articles.

You can identify informative writing by its characteristics:

- It exists to deliver information.
- It uses facts and may include data and statistics.
- It often includes citations from sources.
- It does *not* present the author's opinion; thus, it is unbiased.

Writing to Analyze

To **analyze** is to examine a subject, an event, an object, or a possibility very carefully. Analysis requires that we break a subject into its component parts. To analyze the engine of a car, you would look carefully at the individual parts under the hood. The same principle is true of analytical writing: it requires us to look at the individual components of a subject.

We might also use analysis to understand how past events, such as the Civil War, came to be. We might use analysis to examine current events, such as the privacy threats we face when we use the Internet. We might analyze an object, such as a smartphone or a tablet computer. And we might analyze future actions, such as proposals to change voter registration laws or the potential effects of buying oil from a particular country.

You can identify analytical writing by its characteristics:

- It explains or describes the parts of something.
- It explains or describes how something works or could work.
- It explains or describes how something happened or what might happen.
- It uses facts and credible information.
- It presents the topic in a fair and unbiased way.

Writing to Evaluate

Evaluative texts come to a conclusion about the value or effectiveness of a particular thing, idea, or course of action. Evaluation includes analysis. To evaluate the usefulness of a particular smartphone, for instance, you must first analyze it. You can then evaluate its worth. You might even compare it with another smartphone to make your evaluation.

Teaching Resources: This chapter is very long because it presents several text patterns. Instructors often pick and choose particular patterns to present. Alternatively, instructors might use a brief presentation of each pattern and discuss its role in mixed pattern essays (a topic covered at the end of this chapter.) See the Instructor's Manual (IM) for ideas about how to select the information in this chapter that is most appropriate for your course's focus.

Because evaluation means making a judgment, it usually involves setting up criteria. Suppose you live in a part of the country where tornadoes are common and you have decided to buy a storm shelter. To evaluate the available shelters, you would first analyze them. You might ask questions such as "What is it made of?" "How large is it?" "Is it inside the home or outside?" "Does it have features such as carpeting" and "What does it cost?" After completing your analysis, you would decide which criteria are important to you. You may realize that you want a shelter that is inside your home, costs under $3,000, and is made of steel. In this case, your criteria are location, cost, and material. By using these criteria, you will be able to evaluate your options and choose the shelter that best meets your requirements.

Teaching Resources: See the worksheet "Identifying a Text's Purpose."

You can identify evaluative writing by its characteristics:

- It is based on analysis.
- It generally presents subjects in a fair and unbiased way.
- It uses a fair and clearly stated appraisal process.
- It uses criteria for weighing choices.
- It makes a judgment.

Writing to Persuade

The goal of a great deal of writing is **persuasion.** Some texts that aim to persuade provide explicit arguments; that is, these texts make it clear that they want readers to buy into the point of view they offer. For example, editorials are brief articles written by newspaper editors. Their purpose—by definition—is to persuade readers of a particular point of view. For example, an editorial may describe an editor's opinion about immigration reform with the goal of persuading readers.

Some texts that aim to persuade are more subtle. For example, a Web site may appear to provide information about a product, but when you analyze the site in depth, you may find that the information is just a means to an end: the site's real purpose is to convince readers to buy the product. Persuasive writing is found in almost every genre of writing: fiction and nonfiction books, magazine articles, some newspaper articles, editorials, Web pages, and so on.

You can identify persuasive writing by its characteristics:

- It attempts to sway readers' opinions on a topic.
- It provides evidence for the writer's opinion.
- It is generally written from a biased (opinionated) point of view.
- It appeals to logic, emotions, and credibility to influence readers.

These four writing purposes—to inform, to analyze, to evaluate, and to persuade—will help you understand the choices writers make in their texts.

PRACTICE ● Determining a Text's Purpose

Read each text description and make an educated guess about the writer's purpose. Each description presents a different purpose: to inform, to analyze, to evaluate, or to persuade.

1. An article in a newsmagazine titled "Fences Won't Stop Illegal Immigration"

   Purpose: To persuade

2. "The iPhone versus the Android: Which One Is Best?"—an article in a computer magazine

   Purpose: To evaluate

(continued)

3. An article in a newspaper titled "Entire City Installs Solar Panels on Its Homes"

   Purpose: To inform _____

4. "Current Trends: The Decline of Marriage"—an article in a popular science magazine

   Purpose: To analyze _____

CONNECTING PURPOSES AND TEXT PATTERNS

In both oral and written communication, we depend on recognized patterns of thought to communicate ideas. When you read the phrase "for instance," you realize that you are about to be presented with an example that will help you understand another point the writer is making. When you read "Once upon a time," you mentally prepare to hear a story. These patterns that we use to communicate ideas are text patterns.

The most common text patterns are narration, definition, illustration, classification, comparison-contrast, cause and effect, process analysis, and argument. Often when we communicate, we use more than one text pattern. Consider the paragraph that follows, noticing the variety of text patterns that come into play.

An eclipse is an astrological event that occurs when one object gets in between you and another object and blocks your view. From Earth, we routinely experience two kinds of eclipses: an eclipse of the Moon and an eclipse of the Sun. Sometimes, as the Earth orbits the Sun, it comes between the Sun and the Moon. When this happens, the Earth throws a dark shadow across the Moon. This is known as an eclipse of the Moon, or a lunar eclipse. Sometimes, the Moon passes between the Earth and the Sun. The Moon blocks the light of the Sun and a shadow of the Moon is cast on the Earth's surface. This is an eclipse of the Sun, or a solar eclipse.	Definition Classification Cause and effect Definition Definition

Text patterns can be used for single pieces of support, as the paragraph above demonstrates, or they can be used to structure an entire essay. A writer who wants to discuss the causes and effects of eclipses in more depth could devote an entire essay to the subject. In such an essay, the writer could use cause and effect as the basic text pattern for the entire text, elaborating on particular causes and effects in each paragraph, for instance.

In the pages that follow, you will learn how to use text patterns in two ways: as supporting details and as the organizational framework for your writing.

Narration

Narration is simply storytelling. Everyone likes a good story. That's why people who are good at writing speeches or sermons frequently add interesting stories to their texts. Have you ever wondered why we enjoy listening to stories? Sometimes the answer is that the stories themselves are simply fun to hear. Perhaps they are funny, or maybe they retell an event that people enjoy recounting.

Another reason we use narration is to make a point or teach a lesson. Aesop's fables are narratives that communicate moral principles. If you have read "The Tortoise and the Hare," you know that the point of the story is to not give up. Because of his persistence, the slow tortoise wins the race.

When writers use narratives, they often do so to make a point. Even if the writer does not explicitly tell readers the point, the narrative should. The narrative should be such a good story and so well told that readers intuitively understand the writer's point in using it. Writing a good story can be challenging. Not only must the story be compelling, but the writer must choose words carefully so that readers can infer meanings.

See the IM for a PowerPoint (PPT) presentation called "Writing an Interesting Narrative Essay."

THE REPUBLICAN HARE AND THE DEMOCRATIC TORTOISE.
The Tortoise.—If that chap only goes to sleep, I'll win out by a mile.

A political cartoon published on the cover of a July 1908 magazine shows William H. Taft, a Republican hare, racing William Jennings Bryan, a Democratic tortoise, for the presidency. The caption reads, "The Tortoise: If that chap only goes to sleep, I'll win out by a mile." What message was the artist sending with this depiction of a well-known fable? At the time, the artist could not have known that Taft would go on to win the presidential election.

RECOGNIZING THE NARRATION PATTERN IN READINGS

Narrative essays usually present one story that is significant enough to be worthy of its own essay. In a narrative essay, the story *is* the sole content: it speaks for itself.

To identify the narration pattern in a text, look for these characteristics and key words.

CHARACTERISTICS OF THE NARRATION PATTERN

- A meaningful story is told.
- The story has a plot with a beginning, middle, and end.
- The story is told in first-person or third-person point of view.
- Chronological transitions are used to indicate the passing of time.
- Description is used to convey mood, develop characters, create settings, and convey information.

Key Words for the Narration Pattern			
after	as soon as	before	during
finally	first, second, third . . .	following	immediately
initially	later	meanwhile	next
not long after	now	once	soon
then	today	until	when

Narration in Supporting Details

In academic writing, a narrative used as a supporting detail usually takes the form of an *anecdote*—a short, interesting story. Anecdotes are often used as a type of evidence. For example, a veterinarian may write an informative essay about what daily life is like for her. She would very likely use short narratives about different medical cases to help readers get a clear picture of what her days are like.

Narration can also provide a lesson, identify a truth about life, or help readers understand the seriousness of an issue. For example, a writer may tell the story of a soldier who overcomes war injuries to show how success over trauma is possible. Another writer might underscore the dangers of texting and driving with the stories of real people who have lost their lives because of this lethal combination of activities.

Personal stories might also be used as subjects for analysis. For example, researchers often want to analyze personal stories for their research. Hospital researchers may listen to patients' stories to analyze how they can improve their services. These stories can also be used to evaluate hospital programs and make changes. Personal stories and experiences can be valuable bits of research.

In addition to providing material for analysis and evaluation, stories can be persuasive. Suppose the US Congress is considering the passage of a stronger gun control law. Advocates for such a law would be likely to tell their personal stories of tragedy and loss to make their arguments more compelling. These stories can be effective in persuading members of Congress to vote for or against the proposed law.

Finally, short stories are sometimes used to introduce essays. For instance, a writer may use the story of a person who triumphed over obesity to start an essay about effective methods of weight loss. The partial outline that follows demonstrates how narrative can be used as a supporting detail in an essay.

Using Narration as a Supporting Detail

Topic: Why people should work on anger management

Thesis statement: Anger issues should be addressed because they can result in lost jobs, broken relationships, and even death.

Consider having students craft a short fictional anecdote as Micah's story.

INTRODUCTION

Paragraph 1: Introduction

Paragraph 2: How anger issues can result in lost jobs (tell Micah's story) . . .

Narration as a Text Pattern

When a writer has a long story that makes a point, the story becomes the focus of the entire essay. In such an essay, narrative is used as a text pattern.

To write a compelling narrative essay, you will need to find a story worth telling, a story that not only is meaningful to you but that you predict others will find meaningful. Remember that you are writing for a general audience. You may love NASCAR, but your readers may not. Similarly, the story of your wedding is probably not going to capture readers' interest unless something unusual happened. Think about the stories you enjoy hearing. What makes them enjoyable? Often these stories appeal to our curiosity about how other people live, help us imagine what being in a particular situation would be like, or describe events that we can relate to.

To use narrative as a text pattern, writers employ features that are common to all narratives. The **plot,** or structure, of the story usually has these elements:

- A beginning
- Rising action that leads to a **climax,** or high point in the action
- The climax itself (usually a conflict)
- Falling action that leads to a resolution of the conflict
- The resolution itself and the ending

Additionally, the narrative should include the details readers expect. Readers want to know information about the characters involved: how old are they? where do they live? what are they like? Not knowing when an event happened, or not having a clear idea of the order of events in a story, can leave readers confused and dissatisfied. In narrative writing, it is important to include the details that contribute to a story's meaning but to exclude mundane or boring details.

ANALYZING A NARRATIVE TEXT

As you read the narrative essay that follows, "The Chosen One" by Laura Cunningham, see whether you can recognize some of the features of narrative writing. Cunningham's careful choices about plot, time order, details, and wording make her narrative essay particularly effective. As you read, notice the significant features of narrative writing that the annotations point out.

Teaching Resources: See the IM for a graphic organizer students can use to analyze narratives or plan their own.

For all the text patterns except narrative, essays are broken into their component parts (introduction, body, conclusion), and each part is discussed separately. The narrative example is given in its entirety with annotations for its parts and features.

The Chosen One
by Laura Cunningham

A year ago, I boarded a flight to Shanghai during a gale force wind. The plane shivered and taxied back to the hangar twice before takeoff. It is testimony to my anxiety about the purpose of my journey that I felt no fear of flying. I carried with me an empty infant car bed (aptly named the Dream Ride), a three-week supply of diapers, wipes, pediatric antibiotics, bottles and disposable nipples. I was on my way to adopt one of the tens of thousands of baby girls abandoned in China each year.

Today as I write, my 1-year-old daughter sleeps in a crib in the next room. She lies in the position of trust—on her back, her arms widespread, her face tip-tilted as if for the next kiss.

A happy ending, so far, for my darling Chinese daughter, and for me. But the journey to Shanghai has somehow not ended. Many nights, I wake at 3 A.M.—yanked from my dream, my heart hammering alarms. At that silent, moonlit time, I remember my choice.

Teaching Resources: See the IM for a completely annotated version of this essay.

Chronological transition: helps readers follow the story

Plot element: rising action

Chronological transition

Foreshadowing: The writer jumps to the end of the story and then returns to tell the story from the beginning.

(continued)

I am embarrassed now to recall the doubt that accompanied me to China. The orphanage had sent a fax (yes, in the new China, orphanages send faxes): "We have a baby for you. We would have taken her picture but it was too cold."

My concern, if I can articulate the chill gut slide of panic as a "concern," was that somehow I would walk into the orphanage and fail to respond to the baby; that somehow she would not feel like "the right one." I would have to go ahead with the adoption out of momentum, some grim sense of decency, but without the hoped-for love at first sight.

The baby, it seemed from the fax, was already chosen. And while I claimed to love all babies, in my secret, cowering heart I had to admit that I was more drawn to some babies than to others. It wasn't beauty or even intelligence that I required of a baby, but some sign of being, well, simpatico.

I could not see her until the orphanage opened Monday morning. I had arrived in Shanghai on Saturday night. The interval was the high tide of my fear—suspense seemed hydraulic; blood rushed through me at unprecedented speed.

Until Monday I had only the ambiguous answers of Ms. Zhang, the orphanage's emissary who had greeted me at the airport. When I asked: "How old is the baby? How big?" Ms. Zhang answered only with another question:

"What size baby clothes have you brought with you?"

Her response raised some possibility of control, or at least influence. Maybe the baby was not yet chosen. In my sneaking secret chicken heart, I could still pick the best and the brightest star of abandoned baby girlhood in Shanghai.

Passing the time until I could meet "my baby," I met another baby at the hotel, already adopted by a single man. (China permits adoptions by foreigners, whether married or unmarried. Its adoption policy is unusual in that citizens, as well as foreigners, must be at least 35 years old to adopt.) She struck me, however, as not meant to be my baby. She did seem just right for her new father, an American psychologist, who carried with him a sitcom's supply of baby paraphernalia.

Next, I went to the nearest tourist attraction, the Temple of the Jade Buddha, where there was said to be a Buddha to whom mothers pray for a good baby.

The Buddha glowed in the dim temple. It wasn't jet lag that sent me reeling to my knees before the Buddha. Half-Jewish, half-Southern Baptist, all doubt, I knelt in truest prayer. Let the baby be one I can truly love.

At 9 sharp the next morning I waited in the orphanage, wearing my winter coat indoors (now I understood the fax). Even in midwinter there was no heat. Vapor rose from the thermoses of hot tea carried by the female employees. The translator announced that the baby was being carried in from the nursery building.

"You will have a choice," she said.

I looked out the window as she pointed across a courtyard filled with dead bamboo and gray laundry. The window itself was grimy, but through it I saw two women in blue smocks, running toward me. Each held a bundle. There were two babies.

They were swaddled in comforters, their heads completely draped in towels. The first baby was unveiled. There was a staccato of Chinese, translated as: "Pick this one. She is more beautiful. She is more intelligent." Baby No. 1 was the nurses' favorite, a 2-month-old of unsurpassed good looks and robust health. She smiled.

Margin annotations:

Chronological transition

Plot element: The conflict starts to build.

More conflict: expression of anxiety about adopting the right baby

Plot element: Story approaches its climax—seeing the baby and learning whether she has a choice.

Chronological transition

Chronological transition

Plot element: start of the story's climax section. Notice that this very important sentence stands as its own paragraph.

(continued)

But I could not take my eyes from the second baby, who was revealed almost as an afterthought. She was thin, piteous, a green-complexioned elf, with low-set ears that stuck out. She wheezed. In the pocket of my coat, I held a vial of antibiotics, carried on good advice from a friend.

> Plot element: another crucial moment in the story's climax

I had no choice. The second baby was sick. I had medicine impossible to obtain here. I accepted the tiny green baby, gasping and oozing, into my arms. I noticed she also had a bald spot, from lying unmoved in her crib.

> Climax: The writer makes a choice.

Shame over my earlier indecision blew from the room like the fetid draft of disease and poverty.

Was it love at first sight? I knew in that instant that we were at the start of our life together.

Love overtakes you at odd moments. I was trying to collect a urine sample, required for a medical test. I held her, her little purple fanny over a rice bowl, in my arms all night. I drew the blankets around us both as a tent to keep away the cold. We waited, silently, all night, until she took a literal "tinkle." Her eyes met mine, on the other side of the world, and I knew Little-Miss-Ears-Stick-Out, With-Tears-in-Her-Eyes was mine, all right.

> Plot element: Falling action begins.

Within 24 hours, the medicine had taken effect: she turned ivory pink; her eyes cleared. She was beyond my dreams, exquisite, a luminous old soul with contemporary wit. I gazed at her and saw the fatefulness of every mother's choice. It is not the beautiful baby who is chosen, but the chosen baby who becomes beautiful.

> Chronological transition

> Thesis statement: the moral of the story

To enter a house filled with unwanted babies is to pass through a door that you can never shut. At 3 A.M., I see the others—the aisles of green cribs holding bundled babies. I try to close my eyes to them, but they refuse to disappear. They are lying there. They are cold; they are damp. I see one baby girl especially. She had an odd genetic defect: the skin of her body was coal black, but her face had no color. She looked as if she were wearing the white theatrical mask of tragedy.

Last Christmas, I was able to choose the green, sick baby over the laughing, healthy one. Would I have had the courage to take one of the others? Would someone? I wake up and see the small faces. They are lying there waiting, waiting to be chosen.

> Plot element: resolution. Notice that the resolution leaves readers not totally satisfied. This is intentional.

PRACTICE ● Analyzing a Narrative Text

On a separate sheet, answer the following questions about "The Chosen One" by Laura Cunningham.

1. Do you believe this story would be enjoyed by a wide variety of people? If so, why? What are the features that make it appealing? If not, why not? Explain.

2. The writer does not present the story in straight chronological order. Review the story and describe the order in which Cunningham relates the events.

3. What do you think Cunningham means when she writes that her baby appeared "a luminous old soul with contemporary wit"?

4. Cunningham uses figurative language to make her writing vivid and interesting. For instance, she says she is looking for "the brightest star of abandoned baby girlhood." Find two additional passages that use language in a nonliteral way. For each passage, write a few sentences explaining the effect Cunningham's words may have on readers.

5. In what way does the end of the story *not* present a perfect resolution? Why is the tone at the end of the essay not joyous? Explain in a paragraph.

1. Answers will vary.
2. She starts with the present, and then she goes back and recounts the past. She ends in the present and asks readers to consider the future.
3. Answers will vary.
4. Some examples are "a sitcom's supply of baby paraphernalia," "the interval was the high tide of my fear," "my heart hammering alarms," and "my sneaking secret chicken heart."
5. Answers will vary.

USING NARRATION IN YOUR WRITING

The following steps can guide you through writing your own narrative essay.

1. **Select a story suitable for your narrative essay.** The story you choose for your essay is the most important element of this assignment. You may use a story in which you were involved, or you may tell a story about someone else. Above all, find a story that a general audience will enjoy. Many stories that we personally find entertaining might make a general audience ready for a good long nap. Here are some examples of the types of stories that may be interesting to a general audience.

   - **Stories about ordinary events (like a graduation ceremony or the birth of a child) if the event is unusual in some way.** *Interesting example:* Your high school graduation night when you had a near-fatal car accident. *Not so interesting:* Your high school graduation night when you went to a party with your friends.
   - **Stories that tap into something most people are curious about.** *Interesting example:* What it is like to live in a house you believe is haunted. *Not so interesting:* How you rented your first apartment.
   - **Stories about something that could happen to the reader but is rare enough to be compelling.** *Interesting example:* What it is like to work in a funeral home. *Not so interesting:* What it is like to work in a clothing store.
   - **Stories that give the reader insight into your unique world.** *Interesting example:* How you learned to live with a disability or chronic disease. *Not so interesting:* How you and your sister fight all the time.
   - **Stories you find compelling enough to remember.** *Interesting example:* Dad's encounter with a crocodile in Australia. *Not so interesting:* How you found a baby bird on a sidewalk.
   - **Stories you yourself would like to read.** *Interesting example:* A story about the variety of cases you have seen in your job as an emergency room technician. *Not so interesting:* A story about how you met and fell in love with your significant other.

2. **Determine the order in which to tell your story.** *How* you tell the story can help readers experience the story in a particular way. Use the order of events to set up tension, anxiety, or any other emotion you would like readers to experience. Sometimes, writers use **foreshadowing**—a hint about events to come in a narrative—to keep readers' interest. Early on in "The Chosen One," the author gives us a clue to how her story resulted in a "happy ending," but we must read to the end of the story to find out what happened.

3. **Create a simple narrative plan, or outline.** Include your thesis statement in your plan. Decide on the major events of the story and the order in which you will tell them, and create a simple outline like the one that follows. Use plot elements—beginning, rising action, climax, falling action, resolution—to structure your narrative.

Consider distributing 2 or 3 index cards to each student and asking students to write a story topic on each card, e.g., "a story about fly fishing." Collect the cards and shuffle them. Ask students to form groups and talk about whether they find the stories on the cards interesting. Students might even rank the story topics in order of their group's interest.

A Simple Outline for a Narrative Pattern Essay

Thesis statement: Meeting my birth parents was the fulfillment of a dream I have had for a long time. At the same time, it was entirely depressing.

INTRODUCTION: Provide background
Rising action:

- Details about my adoption
- Description of my good life with my adopted family and my persistent longing to meet my birth parents
- Arrangement to meet my birth parents when I turned nineteen
- Anxiety and expectations

Climax: The disappointing encounter with my birth parents

Falling action: The flight back home and the thoughts I had

Conclusion (resolution): Final thoughts

4. **Use creative wording. Figures of speech**—imaginative comparisons between different things—can help readers understand the ideas you wish to convey. For example, instead of just telling readers a room is cold, comparing the room to a meat locker would more effectively convey the same idea. Several figures of speech in particular are useful for writers: personification, metaphor, and simile.

Teaching Resources: See excercise/handout "Figurative Thinking Exercises."

FIGURE OF SPEECH	DEFINITION	EXAMPLE
Personification	Giving human qualities to inanimate things	*Every plant in his yard had seen better days.*
Metaphor	Comparing two unlike things	*Her life is a constant soap opera.*
Simile	Using *like* or *as* to compare two unlike things	*My favorite chair is like a big marshmallow.*

5. **Use descriptive details to create the story's setting.** Descriptive language provides sensory information for readers. By using description, readers can imagine what something looks, sounds, smells, tastes, or feels like. In narrative writing, description helps readers understand characters better. It also helps writers convey a particular mood. For instance, description may convey a sense of eeriness or a sense of peacefulness. Writers also depend on description to create the setting of a story and to render the plot events in a story effectively. In "The Chosen One," Cunningham uses this description, "the tiny green baby, gasping and oozing," to convey the baby's fragility, sickliness, and even lack of appeal.

6. **Make intentional decisions about details and pace.** Cunningham left out details that were mundane so that her story would move at the perfect pace to keep her readers interested. Ask yourself whether the details in your story are necessary. Include details that add value but do not bog down its pace. Use chronological transitions so that readers can keep track of time.

7. **Be very careful about how you word your thesis statement and where you place it.** The thesis statement should not interrupt the narrative. Sometimes placing the thesis statement in the conclusion is an effective strategy for narrative writing since the thesis statement might give away the story's ending if it is placed earlier.

Teaching Resources: See "Choosing Narrative Details," a peer review exercise.

Connect IRW Power of Process Assignment: See the IM for a list of readings in PoP students can use to analyze narrative text patterns. The Connect IRW *Common Places* Master Course contains pre-loaded PoP narrative analysis assignments.

Students may need to be reminded not to share overly personal information in narrative essays.

PRACTICE — Using Narration in Your Writing

Use the preceding steps to write a narrative essay. Choose one of the following topics, or select your own.

A. Write about a time you witnessed someone acting especially kindly—or especially cruelly—toward another person.

B. Think of an event from your childhood that had an impact on you. Write a brief narrative detailing the event and your feelings about it.

C. Relate a story that your family particularly enjoys retelling. The story might concern something funny that happened, or it might recount a traumatic event that ended well, for example.

If none of these topics appeals to you, come up with your own topic for a narrative essay. Ask classmates or your instructor to give you an honest prediction of how interested (or uninterested) a general audience might be in the story you propose.

Answers will vary.

Connect IRW Writing Assignment: Set up the Practice assignments in Connect IRW to give students access to peer review tools. When you set up the assignment, you can create a rubric for easier grading.

These assignments are pre-loaded in the Connect IRW *Common Places* Master Course.

GRAMMAR FOCUS   Verb Tense Choices

As a writer, you must choose the verb tense you will use to convey information. Verbs express more than the action that happens in a sentence. Verb tenses tell when the action takes place—past, present, or future. For example, in each of the following sentences the tense of the underlined verb expresses the timing of the nurse's action.

Past: Earlier this morning, the nurse <u>examined</u> the patients' charts.

Present: The nurse always <u>examines</u> the patients' charts at 10 a.m.

Future: Tomorrow morning the nurse <u>will examine</u> the patients' charts.

Even without the phrases *Earlier this morning* and *Tomorrow morning,* readers would know which action already happened (past) and which action will happen (future) because of the verb tense.

For the most part, verbs in a text should remain consistent in tense, although there are places where tenses can change. Follow these guidelines to select the best tense for the information you are conveying.

1. USE PAST TENSE FOR NARRATIVE

Most narratives recount events that have happened. So when writers tell a story, they most commonly use past tense. Note this example from Laura Cunningham's "The Chosen One."

Example: "A year ago, I <u>boarded</u> a flight to Shanghai during a gale force wind. The plane <u>shivered</u> and <u>taxied</u> back to the hangar twice before takeoff."

Present tense is less useful for narratives and is best avoided. If we substitute present tense in the Cunningham quote, the passage is confusing. An essential element of the story is expressed in the phrase *A year ago,* but the present tense verbs conflict with that phrase.

Faulty: A year ago, I <u>board</u> a flight to Shanghai during a gale force wind. The plane <u>shivers</u> and <u>taxies</u> back to the hangar twice before takeoff.

For most verbs, we add *-ed* to the present tense to form the past tense. Some verbs, however, have special forms for the past tense: for example, *bring/brought, drink/drank, eat/ate, feel/felt, is/was, think/thought.* Still others keep the same form in the present and past tenses: for example, *cost/cost, cut/cut, hit/hit.* Consult a dictionary if you are unsure of the past tense form for a verb.

2. USE PRESENT TENSE FOR MOST ACADEMIC WRITING

For almost all academic writing, present tense is the correct tense, even when you are writing about the views of a person who died hundreds of years ago. Note the present tense used in this quotation from *Physical Science,* by Bill W. Tillery.

Example: "Newton's first law of motion <u>is</u> also <u>known</u> as the law of inertia and <u>is</u> very similar to one of Galileo's findings about motion."

However, when the goal is to compare historical events or beliefs, use past tense, as in this excerpt from *American Authors in the Nineteenth Century.*

Example: "In the nineteenth century, social changes and the rise of new media <u>revolutionized</u> the way people <u>discovered</u> and <u>read</u> literature. As a result,

(continued)

the audience for American literature <u>grew</u> tremendously, and many authors <u>became</u> celebrities."

Another exception is the use of past tense to describe research processes or studies. Notice the verb tenses in this quotation from "Detroit Exposure and Aerosol Research Study" on the US Environmental Protection Agency's Web site.

Example: "The Detroit Exposure and Aerosol Research Study <u>was</u> a three-year study conducted by the U.S. Environmental Protection Agency (EPA). Its primary objective <u>was</u> to investigate the relationship of select air pollutant concentrations and their sources measured at community air monitoring stations in comparison to those measured in various neighborhoods in Wayne County, Michigan."

3. AVOID UNNECESSARY SHIFTS IN TENSE

Generally, verbs should remain in the same tense throughout a passage. Notice how the shifts in tense in this example are unnecessary and even confusing. In the first sentence, the verbs are in the present tense (*claims, change, processes*), while the verbs in the second sentence are in both the past tense (*wrote*) and the present tense (*act*).

Faulty shift in tense: Margaret Trent <u>claims</u> that social media <u>change</u> the way the brain <u>processes</u> information. She <u>wrote</u> that social media <u>act</u> as "catalysts of neural development."

Corrected: Margaret Trent <u>claims</u> that social media <u>change</u> the way the brain <u>processes</u> information. She <u>writes</u> that social media <u>act</u> as "catalysts of neural development."

Sometimes shifts in tense are acceptable or even necessary, such as when a writer changes from a narrative to another type of writing. Consider this passage from *Physical Science* by Bill W. Tillery. It incorporates the initial sentence we quoted earlier as an example of present tense in academic writing.

Example: "Newton's first law of motion <u>is</u> also <u>known</u> as the law of inertia and <u>is</u> very similar to one of Galileo's findings about motion. Recall that Galileo <u>used</u> the term inertia to describe the tendency of an object to resist changes in motion. Newton's first law <u>describes</u> this tendency more directly."

Notice that the writer uses mostly present tense (*is known, is, describes*) but switches, appropriately, to past tense (*used*) to explain a historical event.

SENTENCE COMBINING

The example that follows shows how to take sentences that use a variety of tenses, combine them to make smoother and longer sentences, and correct the verb tenses for consistency and appropriateness.

Ideas to combine and correct:

- Benjamin Franklin is a scientist and a writer.
- He wrote *Poor Richard's Almanac.*
- He was known for his autobiography.
- Franklin signed the three most important documents of the revolutionary era: the Declaration of Independence, the peace treaty with Britain that ended the Revolutionary War, and the Constitution.
- He is the only person to sign all three.

(continued)

Consistent and appropriate verb tenses: Benjamin Franklin, a scientist and a writer, wrote *Poor Richard's Almanac* and is known for his autobiography. Franklin also was the only person to sign the three most important documents of the revolutionary era: the Declaration of Independence, the peace treaty with Britain that ended the Revolutionary War, and the Constitution.

EXERCISES

Combine each set of sentences to make smoother, longer ones. Change verb tenses as necessary for consistency and appropriateness. You may change the wording as much as you like as long as you communicate the same ideas.

Answers will vary. Sample answers are provided.

1. Ideas to combine and correct:

    - I stepped onto the train.
    - From the moment I did, I felt something was not right.
    - An older woman was bundled from head to toe in black.
    - She stared at my old suitcase.
    - "That's my suitcase!" she exclaimed loudly.

    Answer: From the moment I stepped onto the train, I felt something was not right. An older woman, bundled from head to toe in black, stared at my old suitcase. "That's my suitcase!" she exclaimed loudly.

2. Ideas to combine and correct:

    - Werner Heisenberg was a German theoretical physicist.
    - He discovered the Uncertainty Principle.
    - The Uncertainty Principle concerns subatomic particles.
    - It claims that we can know the position of a particle or its momentum, but not both.

    Answer: Werner Heisenberg, a German theoretical physicist, discovered the Uncertainty Principle, which concerns subatomic particles. It claims that we can know the position of a particle or its momentum, but not both.

3. Ideas to combine and correct:

    - The proposed bill will affect each state.
    - It will require each state to offer free preschool education.
    - According to the bill, any child in a school district will be eligible to attend preschool in the district.

    Answer: The proposed bill will require each state to offer free preschool education. According to the bill, any child in a school district will be eligible to attend preschool in the district.

Definition

To *define* is to express the meaning of a term or concept. In textbooks, you will often come across definitions that briefly explain the meaning of a word. These short definitions are a type of support that enable the writer to continue making a larger point.

Other texts, however, focus primarily on defining a term or concept. As a text pattern, **definition** implies going beyond dictionary explanations and providing a more meaningful or important interpretation. For example, a writer may create an entire essay to explain his personal definition of what it is to be a good parent. Such essays use definition, sometimes called *extended definition*, as a text pattern, not merely as a supporting detail.

Teaching Resources: See PPT called "The Many Uses of Definitions."

RECOGNIZING THE DEFINITION PATTERN IN READINGS

Both uses of definition share some characteristics and key words.

CHARACTERISTICS OF THE DEFINITION PATTERN

- A term or phrase is defined.
- When used as support, a sentence provides a definition. Explanatory sentences may follow.
- When used as a text pattern, the thesis statement concerns the definition in question. Body paragraphs help support the writer's point about the definition.

Key Words for the Definition Pattern		
consists of idea is known as redefine	define involves meaning of refers to	entails is characterized by means term

Definition in Supporting Details

As a type of support, definitions may appear in any paragraph in an essay. Whenever readers may need help understanding a term or concept, a writer may insert a simple definition. For example, a writer may wish to convince readers that the United States needs to invest more time and effort into safeguarding the Internet. One of the writer's reasons may be that cyberterrorism is a real and dangerous threat. Knowing that not all readers will understand what cyberterrorism is, the writer may define the term and provide an example of how cyberterrorism works. The partial outline that follows shows where a writer may use a definition as a type of support.

Using Definition as a Supporting Detail

Topic: Safeguarding the Internet

Thesis statement: The United States needs to invest more time and effort in safeguarding the Internet.

INTRODUCTION
   Paragraph 1

BODY
   Paragraph 2: One of the most serious problems the Internet poses is cyberterrorism.

(continued)

- Definition: Cyberterrorism is . . .
- An example of cyberterrorism is . . .
- Explanation of example

Paragraph 3: The reason cyberterrorism is such a threat is . . .

Definition as a Text Pattern

When definition is used as the focus of an essay, it becomes a text pattern. Writers use the definition text pattern for a variety of reasons. First, definition is helpful in explaining new concepts or terms. For example, not all readers know what urban legends are; thus, a writer may help readers get a clear understanding of urban legends by writing an essay that offers an extended definition.

Second, definition allows writers to create their own, unique meanings for terms or concepts. Phrases such as *common sense* or *the American dream* mean different things to different people. A writer may create his own definition of one of these expressions and present it using the definition text pattern.

Third, definition enables writers to analyze the various ways a particular term or concept has been defined. For example, in the history of law, the term *temporary insanity* has been defined differently over time.

And finally, definition is useful for arguing that an ambiguous or controversial term should be defined in a particular way. Some definition essays focus on defining debatable terms or concepts such as *torture*.

An essay that uses a definition text pattern will have a thesis statement that presents the writer's point about the definition. The body paragraphs will include supporting details that work together to convey the writer's point about the definition. The outline that follows shows definition being used as a text pattern. In the example, the writer is presenting her own definition of *family*, and she wants to persuade readers that her definition is sound.

A Simple Outline for a Definition Pattern Essay

Topic: Defining *family*

Thesis statement: A family is a group of people who are committed to and love one another.

INTRODUCTION

    Paragraph 1: How some people and institutions have defined family narrowly

    Paragraph 2: Thesis statement—writer's definition of *family*

BODY

    Paragraph 3: First characteristic—family members are committed to one another

        Paragraph 4: Additional definition—what *committed* means

        Paragraph 5: Examples of committed families—nuclear family, single-parent family, nontraditional family

    Paragraph 6: Second characteristic—family members *love* one another

        Paragraph 7: Additional definition—what *love* means in a family context

        Paragraph 8: Examples of families that demonstrate love—nuclear family, single-parent family, nontraditional family

CONCLUSION

    Paragraph 9: Why defining the family in a broad way is good for society

We emphasized throughout that the number of body paragraphs and their functions depend on a writer's thesis statement and the support needed to develop it. Students may find it helpful to be reminded of the diverse strategies they can use to organize their writing.

ANALYZING A DEFINITION TEXT

In "What I Really Meme Is . . . Anatomy of a Happenin' Thing," author Mary Ann Bell defines a term that is unfamiliar to many people: *meme*. Because the concept of memes is complex, Bell has written an entire essay on the topic. We will examine the components of her essay.

A Definition Text: Introduction and Thesis Statement

Definition texts often begin with an introduction to the term or concept being defined. Bell starts her essay with a definition from *Wikipedia* and then elaborates on that definition.

After students read the selection, consider asking them to find an example of an Internet meme and to write a paragraph on how the example fits Bell's definition.

Introduction Paragraph of "What I Really Meme Is . . . Anatomy of a Happenin' Thing" by Mary Ann Bell

Not long ago, I was relaxing in the den with my daughter and a friend of hers. Out of the blue, my daughter asked, "What is a meme anyway? I keep hearing about them and don't know what they are!" Her friend, a creative writing major, exchanged looks with me. We both knew what the word meant but found it hard to explain. "Well, a meme is, uh," I started. "Never mind!" she replied, "I'll Google it!" Of course, the first hit was from Wikipedia. Also not a surprise, the description there was spot on. Here is what she read to us: A meme is "an idea, behavior or style that spreads from person to person within a culture." It occurred to me that if the three of us with six university degrees between us could not come up with a good definition, then there might be others out there hazy on the concept too—hence, this column.

Thesis statement: The essay starts with a definition from *Wikipedia* and goes on to explain the definition.

A Definition Text: Body Paragraphs and Their Organization

Body paragraphs provide information about the definition the writer is proposing. Writers can include many different types of information in the body paragraphs of definition essays. Here are just a few ways writers can elaborate on and provide support for definition texts:

- Dictionary definition of term or concept
- Competing definitions
- History of term or concept
- Example
- Explanation
- Comparison
- Description
- Characteristics

In her article on memes, Mary Ann Bell writes body paragraphs that provide examples, explanations, additional definitions, and historical information about the term.

Since Bell uses a definition from *Wikipedia*, this might be a good time to discuss with students when (if ever) *Wikipedia* is an acceptable source of information. Students often do not understand the collaborative and open-ended nature of wikis.

Body Paragraphs of "What I Really Meme Is . . . Anatomy of a Happenin' Thing" by Mary Ann Bell

One of the easiest and most tempting ways to define "meme" is to offer examples. The ones most readily recognized are those from popular culture. Here are some recent examples that keep cropping up on social networking sites such as Facebook:

- LOLCats/I can has cheezburger?
- Binders of women
- Gangnam-style dancing
- Call me maybe?
- Hey girl (featuring Ryan Gosling)
- Sad Big Bird

Examples: elaboration of the definition

In today's social networking environment, the potential is tremendous for an idea, trend, rumor, meme, or anything catchy to spread very quickly. This is the phenomenon we call "going viral," and it is happening every day. Memes can rise up spontaneously or can be intentionally launched. The day after the second presidential debate in 2012, the phrase "binders of women" and iterations thereof spread overnight across the Internet.

Another meme from the campaign is what I call "Sad Big Bird." During the first presidential debate, Mitt Romney said that PBS's funding should be cut to reduce the deficit, even though he "loved Big Bird" as much as anybody. And so, with lightning speed we were treated to pictures of Big Bird standing in welfare lines, looking dejected with friends, and, in general, tugging at the heartstrings of PBS/Sesame Street fans. People wearing Big Bird suits started showing up at campaign rallies. There were people who admitted they remembered very little from the debate other than the threat to off Big Bird.

Another example

Similarly this past year, Gangnam-style dancing went viral. And it goes without saying that gorgeous pictures of actor Ryan Gosling, a library fan, offering various completions to the line "Hey girl . . ." are loved by librarians. You can see the collection of these pictures on the site called Hey Girl. I Like the Library Too (librarianheygirl .tumblr.com).

More examples

Memes such as these are visual and have a picture or video as the focal point. From these, captions and knockoffs abound. Some hang around for years, such as LOLCats, while others are relatively short-lived. My guess is that "binders of women" will not last far beyond the next months, as the campaign and Mitt Romney's candidacy fade from popular memory. But I am hoping Ryan Gosling does not go away for a very long time.

WHO SAID THAT?

How long has this been going on? The term "meme" is actually a coined one, which makes me think it might make it an example of its own definition. As a matter of fact, this term can be tracked back to its originator, Richard Dawkins, and he is alive and well and following memes to this day.

History of the term and concept

Here is a quotation from an article where he explains: "Our cultural life is full of things that seem to propagate virus-like from one mind to another: tunes, ideas,

(continued)

catch-phrases, fashions, ways of making pots or building arches. In 1976 I coined the word meme (rhymes with cream) for these self-replicating units of culture that have a life of their own." . . .

| | Quotation: traces term to its origin and offers another definition |

Remembering back to 1976 and forward, I can think of a number of memes that are still lodged in my brain and, perhaps, in yours as well, if your age allows you to remember that far into the past. One example that I remember in particular is the use and overuse of the phrase "Where's the beef?" The meme stems from TV commercials starring a loveable old lady trying to find a decent meat patty in a fast-food hamburger and promoting Wendy's restaurants. Like all good memes, this one has its own Wikipedia article.

| | Examples that go further back in history |

A Definition Text: Conclusion

Once the definition of the term or concept has been thoroughly explained and supported, writers conclude their essays. Mary Ann Bell concludes by calling attention to the fact that memes are constantly changing and evolving.

Connect IRW Power of Process Assignment: See the IM for a list of readings in PoP students can use to analyze definition text patterns.

The Connect IRW *Common Places* Master Course contains pre-loaded PoP assignments that require students to analyze definition text patterns.

Conclusion Paragraph of "What I Really Meme Is . . . Anatomy of a Happenin' Thing" by Mary Ann Bell

Since the advent of the Internet, the sources, subjects, and recipients have increased exponentially. By making it so easy to combine, change, personalize, and otherwise adapt Internet postings, memes now grow and evolve in countless iterations that can go their merry ways, further mutating along the way.

| | More explanation: how memes reproduce and mutate |

PRACTICE ● Analyzing a Definition Text

On a separate sheet, answer the following questions about "What I Really Meme Is . . . Anatomy of a Happenin' Thing" by Mary Ann Bell.

1. What is the purpose of the article?

2. After reading her definition of *meme,* do you have a good understanding of what memes are? If so, what type of body content helped you understand the best? Examples? Explanations? History? Explain. If not, what else could Bell have included to help you understand more clearly?

3. What does Bell mean when she says that memes evolve and change over time?

4. Without looking back at Bell's article, define *meme* in your own words. Provide an example that Bell did not include in her article, if you can think of one.

1. The purpose is to define *meme.*

2. Answers will vary.

3. People change the meme and attach different sayings and meanings to it. This is especially true of Internet memes.

4. Answers will vary.

USING DEFINITION IN YOUR WRITING

When your task is to present the meaning of a term or concept, you can use the definition text pattern to structure your writing. The following guidelines can help you through the process of using definition in your writing.

1. Select a topic, and determine your purpose for writing. If you are choosing your own topic for an essay, consider defining a term that may be new to readers, as Mary Ann Bell did when she defined *meme*. Choose a term that will interest readers.

Another approach to finding a topic is to think about terms whose meanings are debated. For example, what does it mean to be *moral*? How do you define *adultery*? You can also choose to define terms that are not necessarily debatable but tend to be defined in personal ways. For example, what does *physical beauty* mean to you? What does *success* mean to you?

If your instructor gives you a term to define, you can move to the next step, determining your writing purpose. Does your assignment tell you whether you are writing to inform, analyze, evaluate, or persuade? Do you want to persuade readers that your definition is the best? Do you want to analyze the way the word has been defined throughout history? Once you are certain about the purpose of the assignment, you can make specific decisions about how you will define the term or concept.

2. Start your prewriting by creating a formal definition that includes term, class, and characteristic. The **term** is the word you are defining, the **class** is the category into which the word fits, and the **characteristic** is simply the quality of the term on which you are focusing, as in the Definition Model diagram.

| **[DEFINED TERM]**
Freedom | is | **[CLASS]**
a right | that | **[CHARACTERISTIC]**
comes with
responsibilities |

■ Definition Model

Here are two more examples:

Friendship is a kind of relationship that endures through the ups and downs of life.
   term   class   characteristic

A solar panel is a technological device used to generate electricity from the sun's heat.
   term   class   characteristic

We can expect that an essay using the definition of *friendship* shown above will give the reader evidence about how friends stand by one another through difficult times.

3. Consider describing the history or background of the term. Unless you are writing a historical analysis, this part of your essay need not be long or extensive. Including a bit of history can make your essay more interesting and can sometimes provide helpful background information. Give credit to any sources you use.

4. Consider using negation in your definition. **Negation** is a way of defining a term by including an explanation of what the term is *not*. Here is an example from Berkeley's Greater Good Web site:

> Psychologists generally define forgiveness as a conscious, deliberate decision to release feelings of resentment or vengeance toward a person or group who has harmed you, regardless of whether they actually deserve your forgiveness.

Just as important as defining what forgiveness *is*, though, is understanding what forgiveness is *not*. Experts who study or teach forgiveness make clear that when you forgive, you do not gloss over or deny the seriousness of an offense against you. Forgiveness does not mean forgetting, nor does it mean condoning or excusing offenses.

Notice how the definition by negation in the second paragraph of the example helps us understand some of what the author means by *forgiveness*.

5. Determine how you will support your extended definition. Some ideas are providing examples of the way the term has been (or is being) used, citing experts about their definitions of the term, and offering reasons why your definition is appropriate or superior to others. Many types of support can be used to help you make your point. Remember, a definition essay will include a definition, but it will also rely on other support to convey your message.

6. Check your definition for circularity. A **circular definition** includes the term being defined and does not elucidate or clarify meaning.

> **Ineffective:** A Senate committee is a committee composed of members of the Senate.

> **Effective:** A Senate committee is a group of current senators that has specific responsibilities—for example, drafting legislation—regarding a particular area, such as the Armed Services.

7. Write a thesis statement, and construct a simple outline. Remember that although your focus is to define a term, you will need to include support in body paragraphs. The support you choose will help you establish your definition or make your point about the word you are defining.

PRACTICE ● Using Definition in Your Writing

Use definition as a supporting point in a paragraph and as a text pattern for an essay by completing these two assignments.

1. Write a paragraph in which you define what *social media* are. Provide examples to help readers understand your definition.

2. Use the definition text pattern to write an essay on one of the topics below. Use the Quick Start Guide to Integrated Reading and Writing Assignments for assistance.

   • Define what it means to be educated.

   • Define *egocentrism*. (Note: This definition will require the use of sources. Consult the Quick Start Guide for information about giving credit to every source you use.)

   • Define *freedom of speech*. Provide examples of what the concept means and what it does not mean.

Answers will vary.

See the IM for additional source-based essay assignments that require the use of definition as a text pattern.

Connect IRW Writing Assignment: Set up these assignments in Connect IRW to give students access to peer review tools. When you set up the assignment, you can create a rubric for easier grading. These assignments are pre-loaded in the Connect IRW *Common Places* Master Course.

Illustration

Much of the support we use to communicate our thoughts consists of **illustrations**—different types of examples. We frequently use illustrations as supporting details in essays. Occasionally, an essay will present an idea almost exclusively through the use of examples. In such cases, writers support their thesis statement by using illustration as a text pattern.

RECOGNIZING THE ILLUSTRATION PATTERN IN READINGS

Whether used as a supporting detail or as a text pattern, illustration can be identified by its characteristics and key words.

CHARACTERISTICS OF THE ILLUSTRATION PATTERN

- Illustrations are often used with vague, complex, or broad ideas that are hard to understand.
- Illustrations are more concrete and specific than the ideas they explain.
- Illustrations may appear as examples, visual aids, sample quotes, sample statistics, or other concrete samples.
- Illustrations that are examples can be true or hypothetical.
- Illustrations are often followed by explanations.

Teaching Resources: See the PPT "Illustrations Are Everywhere."

Key Words for the Illustration Pattern		
consider	for example	for instance
imagine	like	such as
support	to clarify	to explain

Illustration in Supporting Details

Illustrations are commonly used as support in essays of all sorts and for all purposes. Any time a concept could be made easier to understand with an example, a graphic, or a sample of some sort, it is appropriate to use illustration. Here is an example of an illustration (underlined) used in an informative text:

> Having the right tools on hand makes the process of completing a difficult task easier. <u>For example, if you are moving everything you own across town, renting an appliance dolly will make moving day less burdensome.</u>

Illustrations can also be actual visuals—graphs, charts, tables, photos, and drawings. Here is an example of an illustration accompanied by a graph in a persuasive text. Note that an explanation of the graph helps readers understand the illustration's significance.

> One reason for the decline in sales is that a new superstore opened down the street, as the graph below shows. After the competition's superstore was built in 2008, sales profitability dropped from a high of $3.9 million in 2008 to below $2 million in 2013.

The partial outline that follows includes an example (underlined) as an illustration of the writer's point.

Using Illustration as a Supporting Detail

BODY

Paragraph 1: One of the most serious problems the Internet poses is cyberterrorism.

- Definition: Cyberterrorism is . . .
- An example of cyberterrorism is . . .
- Explanation of example

Paragraph 2: The reason cyberterrorism is such a threat is . . .

Illustration as a Text Pattern

Usually, illustration is used as a type of support in an essay rather than as the text pattern for an entire essay. However, writers sometimes depend on illustrations as primary support for their ideas.

When writers attempt to explain a complex idea to an audience with limited knowledge of the subject, illustration can be a useful text pattern. For example, a physics textbook chapter on Newton's first law of motion may use an illustration text pattern. Notice how this excerpt from *Physical Science*, a textbook by Bill W. Tillery, depends heavily on illustration. The illustration in the text has been highlighted, and a diagram used as an illustration has been included.

Newton's First Law of Motion

by Bill W. Tillery

Newton's first law of motion is also known as the *law of inertia* and is very similar to one of Galileo's findings about motion. Recall that Galileo used the term *inertia* to describe the tendency of an object to resist changes in motion. Newton's first law describes this tendency more directly. In modern terms (not Newton's words), the first law of motion is as follows:

Every object retains its state of rest or its state of uniform straight-line motion unless acted upon by an unbalanced force.

This means that an object at rest will remain at rest unless it is put into motion by an unbalanced force; that is, the net force must be greater than zero. Likewise, an object moving with uniform straight-line motion will retain that motion unless a net force causes it to speed up, slow down, or change its direction of travel. Thus, Newton's first law describes the tendency of an object to resist *any* change in its state of motion.

Think of Newton's first law of motion when you ride standing in the aisle of a bus. The bus begins to move, and you, being an independent mass, tend to remain at rest. You take a few steps back as you tend to maintain your position relative to the ground outside. You reach for a seat back or some part of the bus. Once you have a hold on some part of the bus, it supplies the forces needed to give you the same motion as the bus and you no longer find it necessary to step backward. You now have the same motion as the bus, and no forces are involved, at least until the bus goes around a

Hypothetical example: The example starts here and continues through the paragraph.

(continued)

curve. You now feel a tendency to move to the side of the bus. The bus has changed its straight-line motion, but you, again being an independent mass, tend to move straight ahead. The side of the seat forces you into following the curved motion of the bus. The forces you feel when the bus starts moving or turning are a result of your tendency to remain at rest or follow a straight path until forces correct your motion so that it is the same as that of the bus.

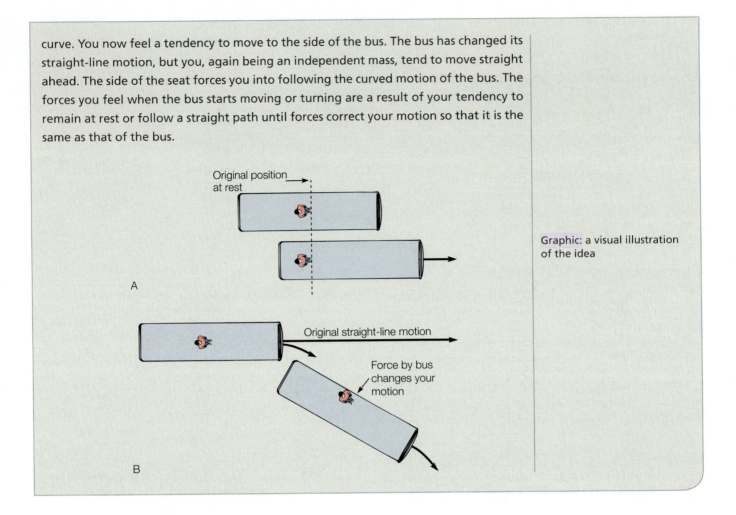

Original position at rest

A

Graphic: a visual illustration of the idea

Original straight-line motion

Force by bus changes your motion

B

This textbook selection provides a long hypothetical example. A **hypothetical example** is one that a writer makes up; it is fictional. As an educated guess, a hypothetical example is based on things that could very likely happen. Even though it is fictional, the example must be realistic: it must portray something that would be typical or likely, not something unlikely to happen. In the selection above, the hypothetical example asks readers to imagine being in a bus in motion. Because we can easily imagine standing on a bus, the example—although fictional—is credible and helps the writer make his point.

The type of illustration used depends on the writer's purpose. In an essay whose purpose is to analyze or evaluate, illustrations would likely come from the idea or object being analyzed. For instance, an essay that analyzes a new type of smartphone and evaluates its worth would include examples of the smartphone's features. A writer might analyze the apps built in to the phone and provide an example of one of them, or the writer might include a photo as an illustration of the phone's sleek profile.

In persuasive writing, illustrations can be used as proof. Suppose a writer wants to prove that studying math in college results in real-life benefits. One way to prove this point would be to provide specific examples of how mathematical knowledge benefits us in life.

The outline that follows on the next page demonstrates how a writer can use illustration as a text pattern for an essay by making illustrations (underlined) the primary method for supporting the thesis statement.

See the IM for the handout "Creating Good Hypothetical Examples."

A Simple Outline for an Illustration Pattern Essay

Topic: Choosing a career

Thesis statement: One way to choose a career is to find one that is personally interesting, that harmonizes with one's personality, and that fits one's lifestyle.

INTRODUCTION

Paragraph 1: Introduction and thesis statement

BODY

Paragraph 2: In general, the best way to start analyzing careers is to consider personal interests and to find careers that match them.

- Job satisfaction tied to interest
- Chart: shows job satisfaction is tied to interest level
- Anecdote: Leah's choice to quit teaching and open a restaurant
- Need to think creatively about potential jobs
- Example: interest in art, could consider merchandising, industrial painting, even cake decorating or making prosthetics

Paragraph 3: While a satisfying career will be personally interesting, it should also be a good fit for one's personality.

- Consider whether you like working with people.
- Explanation: introvert/extrovert
- Anecdote: Maddie's first job didn't match her personality.
- Examples: good fit for introverts—programmer, writer, chemist
- Examples: good fit for extroverts—activity director, salesperson, trainer

Paragraph 4: Finally, finding a fulfilling career requires choosing a job that matches one's lifestyle preferences.

- Examples of lifestyle issues: traveling, hours of work per week, flexibility
- Anecdote: Andre's story about traveling
- Quote: Andre
- Example of lifestyle fit: Cara's flexible job/parenting

CONCLUSION

Paragraph 5: Concluding thoughts

Notice that the essay will include lots of examples, as well as a chart that illustrates a point, anecdotes used as illustrations, and a quote from Andre, a person whose career choices are used as an illustration.

ANALYZING AN ILLUSTRATION TEXT

In the next reading selection, "Life with Asperger's Syndrome," the writer uses illustration as a text pattern. Notice that while illustration is the main method used for evidence, the writer also includes other types of support in the essay.

An Illustration Text: Introduction and Thesis Statement

One way to begin an essay is to use an example followed by an explanation that is tied to the thesis statement, as the writer does in the introduction to "Life with Asperger's Syndrome" on the next page.

Introduction Paragraphs of "Life with Asperger's Syndrome"

Eleven-year-old Paul paced nervously back and forth at the bus stop. His school bus is supposed to arrive every morning at 7:04. Usually Paul could see the bus coming down the street at 7:03, but this morning, at 7:03, there was no bus. A feeling of panic washed over him. When his watch said 7:04, tears began to stream down his face. The bus was not on time. By 7:05, he could not stand it any longer and ran home.	Example
If Paul had not been diagnosed with Asperger's syndrome, his mother would probably have been puzzled by this behavior, but she was not shocked. Because he has Asperger's syndrome, Paul is not like other children.	Explanation
Asperger's syndrome is a type of autism. Many people have heard of autism before, but not many know about Asperger's syndrome. Autism comes in many forms, some very severe and some quite mild. People who have Asperger's are considered to be on the mild "high functioning" side of the autism range. People with classic autism are often unable to talk and do not like being touched, while many of those with Asperger's can function fairly normally in these areas.	Definition followed by explanation
However, there are some challenges for those who have Asperger's syndrome, and some of these challenges are significant.	Thesis statement

Examples are often followed by explanations. Readers need to know why they are reading about a particular example, and explanations tie the example to the broader point—the thesis statement or topic sentence—the writer is making.

An Illustration Text: Body Paragraphs and Their Organization

Examples and explanations are the staples of illustration texts. Notice how the body paragraphs below are composed primarily of these features.

Body Paragraphs of "Life with Asperger's Syndrome"

First, those who have Asperger's have a really hard time interacting with other people.	Major supporting point
While most people can read body language, those with Asperger's ("Aspies," as they are sometimes called) cannot. For example, when people are aggravated, they might roll their eyes, cross their arms, or smirk. These are all body language clues that convey a sense of aggravation.	Examples
When they use this kind of body language, people expect others to step back and proceed with caution. Aspies are often not able to read such body language. Thus, they may respond inappropriately in social situations.	Explanation
Another problem is being able to use body language themselves. One mother recounts how her daughter Chrissy wanted to learn to roll her eyes.	Example
Unable to really master the eye roll, and unaware of when eye rolling is an appropriate gesture, Chrissy finally (to her mother's relief) stopped trying to do it.	Explanation
Aspies may cross their arms and impatiently tap their feet, not being aware of the message they are sending.	Example
Those with Asperger's can be taught how to read body language; however, social interactions are still often difficult because of this aspect of Asperger's syndrome.	Explanation
Another tendency shared by those with Asperger's is literal thinking. Language meant to be understood literally should be interpreted to mean exactly what the words denote.	Major supporting point
For example, interpreted literally, the phrase *money talks* would mean that	Example

(continued)

money actually has a voice and audibly speaks. Much of our language is not meant to be interpreted literally. Kevin Leary recounts a moment when Ryan, his eight-year-old son with Asperger's, was playing with cousins. An adult in the family said to one of the children, "You have ants in your pants!" Ryan ran to the boy and started helping him take off his pants, unaware of the non-literal nature of the comment. Young Aspies are especially literal-minded because they have not had enough experience with the world to understand which phrases are meant figuratively. For example, if a person were to tell Ryan that he will get a popsicle "in a minute," Ryan may watch the clock and be upset if he does not receive his treat in 60 seconds. It is a challenge for Asperger's children to learn to be less literal-minded.

A third characteristic of those with Asperger's is inflexibility. People with Asperger's syndrome find comfort in fixed routines and rules. They find it extremely agitating when the rules change or when routines must shift. Suppose you are the parent of a child with Asperger's. Every change you make—such as getting a haircut, putting your car keys in an unusual spot, buying your Aspie a new pair of shoes—can be the basis for true psychological distress for children with Asperger's. If a tantrum results, the child is not being bratty. Rather, the Asperger's brain sends distress signals when routines are broken or change occurs. Not all changes elicit the same reaction, so parents have to learn what sets off their particular child. When presented with such change, the Aspie may throw a fit or may stay awake crying all night. Even making a change that is as minor as moving furniture around may be extremely unsettling for those who have Asperger's syndrome. Learning to be flexible is another of the major challenges those with Asperger's face.

While Asperger's syndrome makes life different and sometimes difficult for those who have it, there are a number of coping mechanisms those with the syndrome can develop in order to function well. Therapists and physicians are becoming more familiar with Asperger's syndrome now as increasing numbers of diagnoses have been made in the last twenty years. (See chart.) Many people with Asperger's syndrome live typical lives. However, being able to adjust to the way neurotypical people think—especially with regard to social interaction—requires effort and diligence.

Margin annotations:
- Explanation
- Example
- Hypothetical example
- Major supporting point
- Examples
- Explanation
- Example
- Major supporting point: discussion of prognosis
- Chart used as illustration

Identified Prevalence of Autism Spectrum Disorders ADDM Network 2000–2008 Combining Data from All Sites				
SURVEILLANCE YEAR	**BIRTH YEAR**	**NUMBER OF ADDM SITES REPORTING**	**PREVALENCE PER 1,000 CHILDREN (RANGE)**	**THIS IS ABOUT 1 IN X CHILDREN…**
2000	1992	6	6.7 (4.5–9.9)	1 in 150
2002	1994	14	6.6 (3.3–10.6)	1 in 150
2004	1996	8	8.0 (4.6–9.8)	1 in 125
2006	1998	11	9.0 (4.2–12.1)	1 in 110
2008	2000	14	11.3 (4.8–21.2)	1 in 88

Source: Centers for Disease Control and Prevention

Notice that the last body paragraph is a single paragraph of discussion. Because the writer is making a point about increases in autism diagnoses in the United States, the perfect illustration is a chart showing this increase. Not only does the chart illustrate the writer's point, but it also lends credibility to the writer's point since the chart comes from an authoritative source, the Centers for Disease Control and Prevention.

An Illustration Text: Conclusion

The function of any conclusion paragraph is to bring closure to the topic. In this essay, the writer brings closure by ending the story about Paul that began the essay.

Conclusion Paragraph of "Life with Asperger's Syndrome"

> Paul did not get to school on time on the day he walked home from the bus stop. After his mother talked with him about the need to be flexible regarding time, Paul was able to calm down and eventually go to school. With time and maturity, Paul will learn how to deal with such situations. While life with Asperger's will present challenges, many of those who have it have proven that these challenges will not keep them from living happy, productive lives.

Example

Conclusion: presents good news

The conclusion provides the good news about Asperger's syndrome: that Aspies can learn methods for living happily. This ending is intended to leave readers with a feeling of hope and optimism for those who struggle with Asperger's.

Connect IRW Power of Process Assignment: See the IM for a list of readings in PoP students can use to analyze illustration text patterns. The Connect IRW *Common Places* Master Course contains pre-loaded PoP assignments that require students to analyze illustration text patterns.

PRACTICE ● Analyzing an Illustration Text

On a separate sheet, answer the following questions about "Life with Asperger's Syndrome."

1. The writer used a character—Paul—as an example. In which paragraphs does the writer mention Paul? Why do you think the writer uses Paul in these particular paragraphs?

2. Paul's case is not the only example the writer uses. Where are other examples used? List the examples used in the essay. Are the other examples of children with Asperger's based on real children, or are they hypothetical examples?

3. Is there a pattern to the writer's organization? For example, does the writer start body paragraphs with examples? When does the writer use explanations?

4. Read each paragraph in the essay but skip over the examples. As a reader, how would you experience the essay if the writer had *not* included examples? Explain your answer.

1. Paul is used in the introduction and conclusion paragraphs. (Details will vary.)
2. The writer uses the examples of "one mother," "Chrissy," "Kevin Leary," and "Ryan." The text presents these as if they are real examples, but we cannot tell whether they are. Other examples show actions and situations and are not tied to specific children.
3. Generally, the examples come after the topic sentences. Most of the examples are followed by explanations.
4. Answers will vary.

USING ILLUSTRATION IN YOUR WRITING

The key to using illustration effectively is to consider readers' needs. Has an instructor ever returned to you a writing assignment with the word "Explain" in the margin? If so, you are not alone. Because you already know the point you are communicating, it is easy to make the mistake of thinking your readers also know the point. The best way to guard against this mistake is to put yourself in the place of your readers and ask yourself, "What information might my readers need explained in more depth?" or "What background information do *I* know that my readers may not know?"

With your audience in mind, you can work through the process of composing an illustration text or selecting illustrations as supporting details. The guidelines that follow can guide you in your illustration writing.

1. Ask yourself how illustration suits your topic and purpose. Some topics lend themselves to illustration more than others do. The key to using illustration as a text pattern is to determine whether illustration will be sufficient support for your point. For example, an essay about how people are judged by their appearances could be developed by providing illustrations. Body paragraphs may include examples of particular ways of dressing or particular hairstyles and the messages those appearances might convey.

On the other hand, an essay explaining how crude oil is refined might not lend itself to the use of examples. Rather, such an essay would more readily be organized by steps or stages.

2. Consider using real examples. If you have access to real-life examples, use them. In "Life with Asperger's Syndrome," the writer uses the examples of Paul, Chrissy, and Ryan. Provide enough information so that readers will know the examples are from real life.

3. Consider using hypothetical examples. Hypothetical examples can be just as effective as real-life examples, but hypothetical examples must be believable and likely to happen.

4. Consider using concrete details. Concrete details help us communicate concepts more clearly. For example, a writer might say that her dorm room is uninviting. She might even explain that an uninviting room is one that a person is not attracted to, a room that does not make a person want to enter it. Yet the term *uninviting* still does not create a clear picture for readers. Concrete details about the room—descriptions of fluorescent lights, gray carpet, gray walls, and a mattress on a simple metal frame—can communicate what *uninviting* means and help readers picture the room more clearly.

Teaching Resources: See the PPT "Distinguishing Concrete and Abstract Language."

5. Consider using an extended example. An extended example is carried through an entire essay. In "Life with Asperger's Syndrome," the writer could have used an extended example by talking about Paul, the boy in the first paragraph, throughout the essay.

6. Consider using visual aids, facts, data, and statistics. You can illustrate a point in a variety of ways. One way is to provide actual visual aids. In many textbooks, visuals such as charts, photos, and graphics are used frequently. Why? One reason is that visuals explain some kinds of information more effectively than words do. A chart or graph is a way to combine data—such as facts and statistics—that can help readers see your point quickly. Remember also that any data you use must come from a reliable source, and you must give credit to the source.

7. Write a thesis statement, and construct a simple outline. Unlike definition essays whose thesis statements are likely to concern a definition the writer is offering, thesis statements for illustration essays vary widely. A writer may use illustration to argue that Ireland is the most beautiful place on earth, or a writer may use illustration to prove that persistent exposure to a certain chemical is associated with cancer. In any case, an illustration essay will primarily be developed by use of examples and presentation of visual illustrations such as charts, graphs, and art.

PRACTICE ● **Using Illustration in Your Writing**

Write an essay in which you use illustration as the dominant text pattern. Choose one of the following topics, or select your own.

A. Select an economic principle you believe is important to follow in your financial life. For example, one principle is to not keep a balance on credit cards. Another is to buy only items you can afford to pay cash for. Write an essay in which you use illustrations to show the importance of the economic principle you have chosen.

B. Choose a person you admire, explain why, and give examples to show the person's good qualities or actions. The person can be someone you know, a historical figure, or a well-known contemporary.

C. What are the characteristics of a good employee? Explain your view, and give examples to support your ideas.

Answers will vary.

See the IM for additional source-based essay assignments that require the use of illustration as a text pattern.

Connect IRW Writing Assignment: Set up these assignments in Connect IRW to give students access to peer review tools. When you set up the assignment, you can create a rubric for easier grading. These assignments are pre-loaded in the Connect IRW *Common Places* Master Course.

Classification

One of the ways we make sense of the world is to use **classification.** To classify is to create categories for groups of items that are similar. For example, scientists would classify a particular volcano as one of several types: cinder cones, composite volcanoes, shield volcanoes, or lava domes. Biologists classify microbes into archaea, bacteria, fungi, protista, viruses, or microbial mergers. Political scientists might put voters into several different categories—gender, race, age, and so on—depending on the needs of a survey or study.

As a text pattern, classification often informs readers about the characteristics of each category of information. An essay about social media, for example, might classify social media into four categories: social networks, blogging Web sites, media-sharing sites, and news-sharing sites. To further explain these categories, a writer might provide the characteristics of each type of social media. While the purpose of such an essay would be to inform, classification is also used to analyze, to evaluate, and to persuade.

Teaching Resources: See the PPT "Classification: Everything Fits Somewhere."

RECOGNIZING THE CLASSIFICATION PATTERN IN READINGS

Whether classification is used to present details in a reading or as the basic text pattern for a reading, it can be recognized by its characteristics and key words.

CHARACTERISTICS OF THE CLASSIFICATION PATTERN

- Classification presents information in types, groups, or categories.
- It includes discussion of the features associated with each type, group, or category.
- Classification writing often includes examples of the items of each type or in each group or category.
- Classification writing often includes discussion of the similarities and differences of each type, group, or category.

Classification is often used in the prewriting process—for a variety of essay types—to group together similar types of information. See the IM for an exercise that leads students through prewriting about a topic and then classifying the ideas they generate into categories.

Key Words for the Classification Pattern			
characteristic	classify	cohort	distinguish
feature	group	identify	kind
quality	section	sort	species
subtype	trait	type	variety

Classification in Supporting Details

Sometimes classification is used to provide helpful information or background knowledge about a subject. Suppose a writer is arguing that adult-onset diabetes can be reversed (an idea that is debatable). One way to begin the discussion would be to provide some background information on diabetes. To do this, the writer might start by classifying diabetes as a metabolic disease. In a body paragraph, she may divide the disease into its two main types: juvenile diabetes and adult-onset diabetes. In this way, classification becomes one of several patterns the writer will use to develop her essay, as this partial outline shows.

Using Classification as a Supporting Detail

Topic: Reversibility of diabetes

Thesis statement: With certain behavioral adjustments, Type II diabetes is reversible for some people.

(continued)

INTRODUCTION
    Paragraph 1

BODY
    Paragraph 2: Classifying diabetes
    - Classification of diabetes as a metabolic disorder
    - Explanation of metabolic disorders
    - Division of diabetes into types:
        ○ Type I diabetes
        ○ Type II diabetes

    Paragraph 3: Weight loss and its effect on Type II diabetes
    - Studies from Centers for Disease Control and Prevention
    - Cause-effect discussion

When classification is used as a supporting detail, the discussion of an item's classification is limited, as this outline demonstrates.

Classification as a Text Pattern

While classification can be used as a supporting detail, it can also be the primary function of a text. Classification is often used to inform or to analyze. Informative texts can employ classification to present information so that readers more easily understand it. For example, an introductory biology textbook might include an informative presentation of biological taxonomy—a ranking system for organisms that includes kingdom, phylum/division, class, order, family, genus, and species. A music education textbook might categorize the different types of instruments in symphony orchestras as woodwinds, brass, percussion, and strings, as in the Classification Model diagram.

■ Classification Model

While sorting information is a main focus of classification texts, the classification text pattern can also be used to analyze, to evaluate, and to persuade, as these examples demonstrate.

To inform: A magazine article classifying types of financial aid

To analyze: A marketing report presents a breakdown of the types of customers who buy a particular product.

To evaluate: A scholarly journal article on the types of treatment for a psychological disorder evaluates which type helps more people.

To persuade: An essay argues that certain groups of people—such as those with a criminal past or with certain diagnosed mental conditions—should not be allowed to own firearms.

Students can practice classification skills every time they use prewriting. The set of disparate information they generate in prewriting can be classified into categories.

As a text pattern, classification is used to present types, classes, varieties, or groups. Often classification texts are structured so that each type is presented separately, one after another. The discussion of each type or variety includes characteristics that describe the type. The outline below shows how an essay on the types of financial aid available for students might be organized. Notice how each type of financial aid includes a definition, examples, and a discussion of characteristics.

A Simple Outline for a Classification Pattern Essay

Topic: Financial aid available for students

Thesis statement: Three types of financial aid available to college students are scholarships and grants, loans, and work-based aid.

INTRODUCTION

Paragraph 1: General information about college costs; thesis statement

BODY

Paragraph 2: First type—scholarships and grants

- Definition of scholarship and grant
- Examples of scholarships and grants
- Characteristic 1: does not require repayment
- Characteristic 2: is usually competitive and more difficult to get
- Characteristic 3: may be awarded to members of a particular group
- Characteristic 4: might have restrictions on how or where one can use it

Paragraph 3: Second type—loans

- Definition of loan
- Examples of loans
- Characteristic 1: must be repaid
- Characteristic 2: can defer repayment until after college
- Characteristic 3: easy to qualify
- Characteristic 4: can use at any college or university

Paragraph 4: Third type—work-based aid

- Definition of work-based aid
- Examples of work-based aid
- Characteristic 1: usually does not have to be repaid
- Characteristic 2: sometimes covers more than just tuition and fees
- Characteristic 3: must meet particular requirements to qualify
- Characteristic 4: may be tied to a particular college or university

CONCLUSION

Paragraph 5: Conclusion

ANALYZING A CLASSIFICATION TEXT

The ideas in a classification text must be presented in an order that makes sense for readers. In the preceding example of the types of financial aid, the essay might present types of aid in the order of how easy (or difficult) each type is to obtain or how relevant each is for most students. The writer of the outline above chose to discuss the most desirable type of financial aid first. In a discussion of communicable diseases, a writer may start with the least serious type and progress to the most serious type. The key to determining the order in which to present types is to consider whether audiences might benefit more from one order than another.

A Classification Text: Introduction and Thesis Statement

In an essay that relies primarily on classification for support, the subject being classified is usually presented in the introduction paragraph, and sometimes the thesis statement contains the categories into which items are placed. In the example that follows, the writers tell readers what they will be classifying (types of workers to fire), but they do not reveal the specific categories until the body of the essay.

Introduction Paragraphs of "Three Types of People to Fire Immediately" by G. Michael Maddock and Raphael Louis Vitón

> We (your authors) teach our children to work hard and never, ever give up. We teach them to be grateful, to be full of wonder, to expect good things to happen, and to search for literal and figurative treasure on every beach, in every room, and in every person.
>
> But some day, when the treasure hunt is over, we'll also teach them to fire people. Why? After working with the most inventive people in the world for two decades, we've discovered the value of a certain item in the leadership toolbox: the pink slip.
>
> Show of hands: How many of you out there in Innovationland have gotten the "what took you so long?" question from your staff when you finally said goodbye to a teammate who was seemingly always part of problems instead of solutions? We imagine a whole bunch of hands. (Yep, ours went up, too.)
>
> These people . . . passive-aggressively block innovation from happening and will suck the energy out of any organization. When confronted with any of the following three [types of] people—and you have found it impossible to change their ways—say goodbye.

Introduction: leads up to the thesis statement

Rhetorical question: shows that authors are not merely coldhearted executives who like to fire employees

Clue that essay will classify types of employees

Thesis statement

A Classification Text: Body Paragraphs and Their Organization

Body paragraphs in a classification text present the categories, types, or groups into which the writer divides the subject. In the example that follows, the writers create three types of employees to fire immediately: the victims, the nonbelievers, and the know-it-alls. Notice how the body paragraphs include the characteristics or traits of each type of employee.

Body Paragraphs of "Three Types of People to Fire Immediately" by G. Michael Maddock and Raphael Louis Vitón

1. THE VICTIMS

"Can you believe what they want us to do now? And of course we have no time to do it. I don't get paid enough for this. The boss is clueless."

Victims are people who see problems as occasions for persecution rather than challenges to overcome. We all play the role of victim occasionally, but for some, it has turned into a way of life. These people feel persecuted by humans, processes, and inanimate objects with equal ease—they almost seem to enjoy it. They are often angry, usually annoyed, and almost always complaining. Just when you think everything is humming along perfectly, they find something, anything, to complain about. At Halloween parties, they're Eeyore, the gloomy, pessimistic donkey from the *Winnie the Pooh* stories—regardless of the costume they choose. Victims aren't looking for opportunities; they are looking for problems.

2. THE NONBELIEVERS

"Why should we work so hard on this? Even if we come up with a good idea, the boss will probably kill it. If she doesn't, the market will. I've seen this a hundred times before."

We love the Henry Ford quote: "If you think you can or think you cannot, you are correct." The difference between the winning team that makes industry-changing innovation happen and the losing one that comes up short is a lack of willpower. Said differently, the winners really believed they could do it, while the losers doubted it was possible.

In our experience, we've found the link between believing and succeeding incredibly powerful and real. Great leaders understand this. They find and promote believers within their organizations. They also understand the cancerous effect that nonbelievers have on a team and will cut them out of the organization quickly and without regret.

If you are a leader who says your mission is to innovate, but you have a staff that houses nonbelievers, you are either a lousy leader or in denial. Which is it? You deserve the staff you get. Terminate the nonbelievers.

3. THE KNOW-IT-ALLS

"You people obviously don't understand the business we are in. The regulations will not allow an idea like this, and our stakeholders won't embrace it. Don't even get me started on our IT infrastructure's inability to support it. And then there is the problem of . . ."

The best innovators are learners, not knowers. The same can be said about innovative cultures; they are learning cultures. The leaders who have built these cultures, either through intuition or experience, know that in order to discover, they must eagerly seek out things they don't understand and jump right into the deep end of the pool. They must fail fearlessly and quickly and then learn and share their lessons with the team. When they behave this way, they empower others around them to follow suit—and presto, a culture of discovery is born and nurtured.

In school, the one who knows the most gets the best grades, goes to the best college, and gets the best salary. On the job, the person who can figure things out the quickest is often celebrated. And unfortunately, it is often this smartest, most-seasoned employee who eventually becomes expert in using his or her knowledge to explain why things are impossible rather than possible.

Type 1: Headings list types of employees. Alternatively, a topic sentence could introduce each type. The presentation of Type 1 is the writer's first major supporting point.

Hypothetical quotation: follows each heading

Characteristic: Victims feel persecuted.

Characteristic: Victims are often angry, annoyed, and complaining.

Characteristic: Victims look for problems.

Type 2: The presentation of Type 2 is the writer's second major supporting point.

Hypothetical quote

Characteristic: Nonbelievers lack willpower.

Characteristic: Nonbelievers are doubters.

Characteristic: Nonbelievers have a negative effect on teams.

Type 3: The presentation of Type 3 is the writer's third major supporting point.

Hypothetical quote

Characteristic: Know-it-alls are not learners.

Characteristic: Know-it-alls do not seek out new information.

Characteristic: Know-it-alls do not want to fail and relearn.

Characteristic: Know-it-alls can be very smart and seasoned yet have a negative effect.

(continued)

This employee should be challenged, retrained, and compensated for failing forward. But if this person's habits are too deeply ingrained to change, you must let him or her go. Otherwise, this individual will unwittingly keep your team from seeing opportunity right under your noses. . . .

Characteristic: Know-it-alls may or may not be able to change.

A Classification Text: Conclusion

In this essay, the writers use a very short conclusion paragraph. The first sentence is a restatement of the main idea.

Connect IRW Power of Process Assignment: See the IM for a list of readings in PoP students can use to analyze classification text patterns. The Connect IRW *Common Places* Master Course contains pre-loaded PoP assignments that require students to analyze classification text patterns.

Conclusion Paragraph of "Three Types of People to Fire Immediately" by G. Michael Maddock and Raphael Louis Vitón

You don't want the victims, nonbelievers, or know-it-alls. It is up to you to make sure they take their anti-innovative outlooks elsewhere.

Conclusion: restatement of main idea

PRACTICE ● Analyzing a Classification Text

On a separate sheet, answer the following questions about "Three Types of People to Fire Immediately" by G. Michael Maddock and Raphael Louis Vitón.

1. Read through the paragraphs describing "the victims." Besides providing characteristics of this type of employee, what other information do the writers supply? Examples? Explanations? Comparisons? Statistics?

2. Explain this statement: The description of know-it-alls differs from the other two descriptions in that we have to infer their characteristics.

3. The writers use headings to list the three types of workers. Write a topic sentence for each of these types to replace each heading.

4. What is the purpose of this essay? To inform? To analyze? To evaluate? To persuade? (There can be more than one purpose.) Explain your answer.

1. The passage starts with a hypothetical quote from a victim. Support also includes explanations of how victims act and react to situations.
2. The text actually tells us what know-it-alls are *not*; we have to infer the negative qualities of know-it-alls.
3. Answers will vary.
4. The essay informs and analyzes, and it evaluates the effectiveness of different types of workers. It also argues that certain types of workers should be fired.

USING CLASSIFICATION IN YOUR WRITING

You can use classification as a text pattern for your writing whenever putting information into categories helps you achieve your writing purpose. The guidelines that follow will help you use the classification text pattern in your writing.

1. Ask yourself whether classification suits your purpose. Not all subjects can be classified. If you have been given an assignment, analyzing the assignment will help you determine whether classification will help you organize your text.

A simple way to think of a classification essay topic is to fill in this sentence:

My topic involves types of _____.

Classification skills have real-life benefits for students. Consider assigning a classification task that helps students organize their school work for all of their classes.

Start with your major. If you are a nursing major, you might choose types of nurses. If you are an education major, you might consider types of teaching jobs. Alternatively, think of a subject or hobby that interests you, and consider how you might divide it into groups such as types of movies, types of wind instruments, or types of alternative fuel vehicles.

For an even more relevant topic, choose to write about something that will help you solve a problem. For an example, one student, Hector, used the topic of financial aid; you saw the outline he created earlier in this chapter. He chose to write about types of financial aid because he needed to know more about how he could afford his college tuition. If you can find a topic that piques your interest and fits the assignment requirements, use it!

2. Use prewriting to determine the items you will classify and to group them into categories. For his essay classifying financial aid, Hector started by listing the aid that he knew was available. He realized that his list included three types of financial aid—scholarships and grants, loans, and work-based aid—and that these types provided convenient categories for classification. His annotated list is shown here.

Financial Aid Available

Scholarship —→
- Follow the Dream Art Scholarship at Westview Blayne College
- "Free tuition" work-and-study colleges ←
Loan —→
- The Bill Davenport loan
- Employer-sponsored tuition reimbursement grants for workers

Work-based aid —
- Educators Federation Credit Union Loan for older students
- Work-study funding
- Federal financial aid loans ←

Work-based aid →

Loans →

- A scholarship at Tennadi University for returning adults
- The Forty-Plus Scholarship at University of the North
- Veterans' education benefits

Scholarships

3. Write a thesis statement that uses the classification pattern. Include the groups or categories in your thesis statement. Be sure to arrange the groups in the same order you plan to use in your essay.

4. Write topic sentences for each group or type you are presenting. Use the body paragraphs to present and discuss the characteristics of each category or type. Plan to devote at least one body paragraph to each type or category. You may even need to use two or more paragraphs for the discussion of characteristics.

As shown in Hector's simple outline for an essay on financial aid, the first body paragraph will be rather long. If he ends up using two paragraphs for the first category, he can consider using two paragraphs for each of the remaining categories. Doing so would make his essay more balanced, but it is not necessary. As a general principle, use the number of body paragraphs required to successfully communicate your point.

As you draft, read back over your essay continually so that you can see your writing from a reader's point of view. Make any changes necessary to clarify your ideas and to make your sentences say exactly what you want them to say. Be certain that, after finishing your essay, readers will be able to correctly list the types or groups you discuss. Make sure your writing is clear enough so that they can easily remember the main characteristics of each type.

PRACTICE ● **Using Classification in Your Writing**

Use the preceding steps to write a classification essay. Choose one of the following topics, or select your own.

A. Along with all of the benefits we get from the Internet, we also see that some people use the Internet to harm others. What types of Internet abuse can you think of? Write an essay in which you present them.

B. Write an essay classifying one of the following:

- Types of bosses or managers
- Types of vacations
- Types of child care available in your city
- Types of opportunities for volunteering
- Types of poverty
- Types of diets

Answers will vary.

See the IM for additional source-based essay assignments that require the use of classification as a text pattern.

Connect IRW Writing Assignment: Set up these assignments in Connect IRW to give students access to peer review tools. When you set up the assignment, you can create a rubric for easier grading. These assignments are pre-loaded in the Connect IRW *Common Places* Master Course.

Comparison-Contrast

Comparing and contrasting are mental activities we do every day. We compare new information we learn in class with information we already know; we contrast a new law with an old law; we take stock of ourselves by comparing and contrasting our qualities with the qualities of others. We also use comparison and contrast to structure our thoughts as we communicate with others in writing.

Technically, to **compare** means to look at the *similarities* between two or more things; to **contrast** means to look at the *differences*. Sometimes, however, people use the term *compare* to mean both: to identify both the similarities and differences. Additionally, comparison-contrast writing always looks at things that are in the same general category. For example, comparing the tourist attractions of one city with those of another is a fair comparison, but comparing the tourist attractions of a city with those of an entire state is not.

Teaching Resources: See the PPT "Basic Principles of Comparing and Contrasting."

RECOGNIZING THE COMPARISON-CONTRAST PATTERN IN READINGS

To identify the comparison-contrast pattern in a text, look for these characteristics and key words.

CHARACTERISTICS OF THE COMPARISON-CONTRAST PATTERN

- Two or more elements are involved in the comparison and contrast.
- The text presents the differences and/or similarities of these items.
- The text presents an analysis of the items being compared and/or contrasted.

See the discussion of persuasion later in this chapter for a detailed explanation of constructing fair comparisons.

Key Words for the Comparison-Contrast Pattern			
although	but	by the same token	criteria
different	dissimilar	equal	however
in comparison	likewise	nonetheless	on the contrary
on the other hand	otherwise	point	similar

Comparison-Contrast in Supporting Details

We make comparisons so often that we are almost unaware we are making them. Think of the times you have been asked a question and used a comparison to answer.

- Oh, my new job? It's different from my old one because I have to answer phones all day.
- This sandwich tastes as if it's been sitting in a car for hours.

A similarity or a difference can be used as a supporting detail in an essay. Suppose, for example, that you are writing an essay to persuade people that it is morally reprehensible to park illegally in handicapped spots. To bring home your point, you may wish to ask readers to compare their health with the health of someone who needs a handicapped parking spot. You might ask readers to put themselves in the place of a person who uses a wheelchair, a person who just had knee surgery, or an elderly person who cannot walk very far. In an outline like the one on the next page, you might plan to use these kinds of comparisons.

Using Comparison-Contrast as a Supporting Detail

Topic: Respecting handicapped status

Thesis statement: Illegally parking in spaces designated for handicapped people is a reprehensible act; it shows no empathy for those who need handicapped spaces, does not provide much benefit for the person who does the illegal parking, and shows disrespect for the law.

INTRODUCTION
  Paragraph 1

BODY
  Paragraph 2: A person who takes a handicapped parking space without good cause has no empathy for the people who really need such spaces.
  - Types of conditions that merit handicapped parking spaces
  - Comparison: a person in good health vs. a person who just had knee surgery
  - Why people should try to empathize

  Paragraph 3: Another reason no one should illegally park in handicapped spaces is that doing so provides very little benefit to the healthy person and significant hardship to the truly disabled person.

  . . .

A comparison or contrast used as support can take up an entire paragraph or as little as one or two sentences.

Comparison-Contrast as a Text Pattern

Sometimes we write essays that provide extended comparisons or contrasts. For example, a writer may compare and contrast buying a car with leasing a car. In such an essay, the writer is likely to present the factors that are important to consumers, such as monthly payments, mileage limits, warranty considerations, and ownership.

For each writing purpose—that is, to inform, to analyze, to evaluate, and to persuade—comparison-contrast can be an effective choice. Comparison-contrast may be used in a history textbook to inform readers about the different capabilities of the Confederate Army and the Union Army during the Civil War, for example.

The writer of an analysis essay can also use comparison-contrast. For instance, the writer may analyze the differences and similarities between two potential careers. If the writer chooses, she can use her analysis to evaluate the two careers and determine which one is best for her. Thus, comparison-contrast can also lead to making evaluative judgments.

Persuasive writing also makes use of comparison-contrast. Arguments about whether to legalize recreational marijuana, for instance, often compare marijuana and alcohol. They may also compare the United States' laws on marijuana use with the laws of other countries. However, writers use comparisons only if doing so will help their side of the argument.

An essay that uses comparison-contrast as a primary text pattern can be organized in one of two ways: block (subject-by-subject) arrangement or point-by-point arrangement. Both arrangements depend on having two or more subjects to compare and particular points of comparison for each subject.

In the **block arrangement,** the writer organizes the discussion by subject, covering all the relevant points first for subject A and then for subject B. In the **point-by-point**

Students often have trouble establishing the points of comparison. Consider having students brainstorm about the potential issues to consider in a comparison-contrast, and then have students classify these factors into categories. This activity is especially effective after students have just finished working on classification text patterns.

arrangement, the writer organizes the discussion by the points of comparison, writing about the first point for both subjects A and B, then about the second point for both subjects A and B, and so on.

For example, we have noted that to compare two subjects—buying a car versus leasing a car—a writer could talk about these points: monthly payments, mileage limits, warranty considerations, and ownership. A circular graphic shows how a block arrangement of ideas would work.

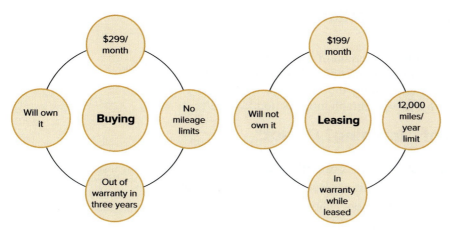

■ In this block arrangement graphic, each subject is in the center of its circle.

The sample outlines that follow highlight the differences between the block and point-by-point arrangements.

Block Arrangement	**Point-by-Point Arrangement**
INTRODUCTION	**INTRODUCTION**
Body	**Body**
Subject 1: Buying	**Point 1:** Monthly payments
• Monthly payments	• Buying
• Mileage limits	• Leasing
• Warranty	**Point 2:** Mileage limits
• Ownership	• Buying
Subject 2: Leasing	• Leasing
• Monthly payments	**Point 3:** Warranty
• Mileage limits	• Buying
• Warranty	• Leasing
• Ownership	**Point 4:** Ownership
	• Buying
	• Leasing
Conclusion	**Conclusion**

The block arrangement can result in some very long body paragraphs if a writer tries to cover all of the points for one subject in a single paragraph. Thus, writers sometimes devote individual paragraphs to each of the points for each subject. Nonetheless, the block arrangement is not always the best choice to discuss subjects that include several points of comparison.

ANALYZING A COMPARISON-CONTRAST TEXT

When you read a comparison-contrast text, clearly identify the subjects being compared and the points of comparison. Sometimes the introduction paragraph will help you identify these elements.

A Comparison-Contrast Text: Introduction and Thesis Statement

Comparison-contrast texts often begin with a discussion of the subjects being analyzed. Each subject is introduced, and enough information is provided so that readers understand why the writer is comparing and contrasting the two subjects. The essay that follows, "Teaching? Or Not," starts with a two-paragraph introduction.

Introduction Paragraphs of "Teaching? Or Not"

The United States is in an educational crisis. We constantly hear about schools that do not make the mark, students who graduate without learning to read, and countries that have far better educational systems than we do. Politicians wring their hands and propose new policies and new laws, but nothing seems to really change.

While many issues plague public K–12 education, the problem of attracting talented professionals to pursue teaching careers is a significant problem. One way to understand why is to think like a college student who is deciding whether to major in education. Following Laura—a hypothetical college student—through the process of deciding whether to major in education or accounting will reveal some of the reasons why, for so many college students, teaching pales in comparison with other careers.

The first paragraph of the introduction gives readers the broad context: public education is in crisis.

The second paragraph narrows the topic to attracting talented students to teaching careers.

Thesis statement: The essay compares and contrasts two subjects, (A) majoring in teaching and (B) majoring in accounting.

A Comparison-Contrast Text: Body Paragraphs and Their Organization

The writer has decided to organize her essay using the point-by-point arrangement. What follows are the body paragraphs, each of which addresses a point of comparison.

Teaching Resources: See the IM for graphic organizers students can use for comparison-contrast essays.

Body Paragraphs of "Teaching? Or Not" (Point-by-Point Arrangement)

Laura is in her sophomore year and is great at math. She is considering majoring in education and becoming a high school math teacher. Another possibility for Laura is to work in accounting. She aces her accounting classes and finds the work enjoyable.

The first point Laura considers is how many semesters each program—education or accounting—will require before she can graduate. In Laura's state, students who want to teach high school have to complete a degree in their educational field (such as math, English, or science) and then complete the education courses required for teacher certification. What that would mean for Laura is an extra year of college (at a cost of several thousand dollars) to meet the education requirements. In accounting, students have to complete only a four-year degree before going right to work. Also, to

Background

Point 1: educational requirements. Point 1 is a major supporting point for the essay.
Subject A (teaching): educational requirements
Details
Subject B (accounting): educational requirements
Details

(continued)

get a teaching degree, Laura would have to spend time in public schools as an intern—in addition to her classes on campus. Accounting requires no on-the-job training, so finishing an accounting degree would be easier than finishing an education degree.

Another issue important for Laura is vacation time and work hours. Teachers' generous vacation time during the summer and holidays is very attractive to Laura. However, she knows that summer vacation time has greatly decreased because of required teacher training activities during the summer break. Laura also knows what the average workday is like for a teacher because both of her parents are teachers. Rising at 5:30 a.m. to be at school for bus duty by 6:45, teaching until 3:30, staying the mandatory one hour after students leave, and then coming home with papers to grade until 8:00 p.m. makes for a long day. Accountants generally get less vacation time than teachers, but at a successful firm, Laura could expect days off for the major holidays and eventually several weeks of vacation. If Laura chose to set up her own accounting practice, she would ultimately be the one to decide her holidays. Laura could likely find a job as an accountant that enabled her to have a typical 8:00 to 5:00 workday. She could go home and not have to think about work until the next morning.

While Laura is not motivated solely by money, salary is an important consideration. The average starting salary for public school teachers is much lower than entry-level salaries for many other professions. In Laura's city, the starting salary for teachers is $28,000. Laura worries that the salary would not enable her to afford a nice apartment, pay off her student loans, and live the way she would like to live. By contrast, people who graduate with a degree in accounting can find entry-level jobs with salaries of about $35,000 where Laura lives. Laura has read that some accountants in her area start at even higher salaries. Potentially, she could start with an entry-level salary of $38,000. That is $10,000 more per year than entry-level teaching salaries in her town, and it would enable her to pay her debts and live the way she would like.

Point 2: vacation time and work hours. Point 2 is the writer's second major supporting point.
Subject A (teaching): vacation time
Details
Subject A (teaching): work hours
Subject B (accounting): vacation time
Details
Subject B (accounting): work hours
Point 3: salary. This is the writer's final major supporting point.
Subject A (teaching): teachers' salaries
Details
Subject B (accounting): accountants' salaries
Details

Suppose the writer had decided to use a block (subject-by-subject) arrangement rather than a point-by-point arrangement. How would the body paragraphs differ? Notice that in the following brief example featuring a block arrangement, the essay includes six body paragraphs—three "point" paragraphs for each subject.

Body Paragraphs of "Teaching? Or Not" (Block Arrangement)

Subject A: teaching major

Body paragraph—point 1: educational requirements

First, in Laura's state, students who want to teach high school have to complete a degree in their educational field (such as math, English, or science) and then complete the education courses required for teacher certification. What that would mean for Laura is an extra year of college (at a cost of several thousand dollars) to meet the education requirements. Because Laura is eager to get out of college and into the workforce, the extra year of education makes an education degree less attractive than an accounting degree.

Subject A: teaching major
Point 1: educational requirements for a teaching major

(continued)

Body paragraph—point 2: vacation time and work hours

Body paragraph—point 3: salary

Subject B: accounting major

Body paragraph—point 1: educational requirements

The educational requirements for an accounting degree would enable Laura to graduate more quickly than the requirements for an education degree would. For an accounting degree, Laura would need to complete four years of college work with accounting as her major. She could graduate "on time" (after four years) if she were to major in accounting. Also, accounting students are not required to complete internships, so Laura would have to worry only about getting her college work done—not also about working in an internship on the side.

Body paragraph—point 2: vacation time and work hours

Body paragraph—point 3: salary

> Subject B: accounting major
>
> Point 1: educational requirements for an accounting major

A Comparison-Contrast Text: Conclusion

As is true for any text, the writer must bring the essay to a satisfactory conclusion. One way to conclude would be to tell readers the decision Laura made—and that's exactly what the writer of this essay chose to do. Alternatively, comparison-contrast essays may conclude by letting the reader determine which of the compared items is preferable. The conclusion to the sample essay follows.

> Connect IRW Power of Process Assignment: See the IM for a list of readings in PoP students can use to analyze comparison-contrast text patterns. The Connect IRW *Common Places* Master Course contains pre-loaded PoP assignments that require students to analyze comparison-contrast text patterns.

Conclusion of "Teaching? Or Not"

Making the choice to teach is not easy. Compared with other jobs, a career in teaching means additional training and a lower paycheck. While those who choose to teach do get a few extra rewards, such as personal satisfaction and summer vacation time, the rewards are just not enough for many people. In the end, Laura decided to become an accountant because, in her words, "I just couldn't afford to be a teacher."

> Conclusion: ends with a quote

PRACTICE   Analyzing a Comparison-Contrast Text

On a separate sheet, answer the following questions about "Teaching? Or Not."

1. Which arrangement—point-by-point or block (subject-by-subject)—do you think would work best for an essay comparing two restaurants? Explain your answer.

2. In "Teaching? Or Not" the writer chose three points to consider: educational requirements, vacation time and work hours, and salary. Make a list of four additional points the writer could have used to compare and contrast teaching and accounting.

3. If you were asked to compare and contrast two different homes and then choose the home you liked best, what three points of comparison would be most important to you? Explain why.

4. Remember that one guideline is to compare and contrast things in the same category. Imagine an essay in which a writer claims that Beau's Restaurant—a very expensive steakhouse—is the best place to eat in town. To prove his point, the writer compares Beau's Restaurant with the local McDonald's and Wendy's. Why would such a comparison be unfair?

1. Answers will vary.

2. Answers will vary, but other factors are passion, personal interest and aptitude, personality (whether one is an introvert or extrovert), and job satisfaction (whether teaching would be more rewarding than accounting work).

3. Answers will vary.

4. It would be unfair because a fast-food restaurant should be compared to other fast-food restaurants, and an expensive restaurant should be compared to other expensive restaurants.

USING COMPARISON-CONTRAST IN YOUR WRITING

To use the comparison-contrast text pattern in your writing, follow these guidelines.

1. Ask yourself how classification suits your purpose and topic. While classification can be used to accomplish each writing purpose, it must also be appropriate for the topic you select. If showing the similarities and/or differences between two or more subjects is the primary way you will support your thesis statement, comparison-contrast should be the right text pattern to use for your essay.

2. Determine the specific subjects you will compare or contrast. Be precise about the subjects you are analyzing. If you are comparing high school with college, for example, narrow the subjects to make your topic more manageable. Comparing high school students' attitudes with college students' attitudes is a more precise topic and is more easily planned than a broad comparison of high school and college.

3. Make sure your comparison is fair. It is unfair to compare items in two different categories. Suppose a writer attempts to convince readers that crack cocaine should be a legal recreational drug because some states are making marijuana a legal recreational drug. Many people would say that the drugs are in different categories because crack cocaine is highly addictive and has other attributes that put it in a category of more dangerous drugs. To use comparison persuasively, make sure to choose subjects that are in the same category.

Teaching Resources: See the PPT "Making Fair Comparisons."

Teaching Resources: See the exercise "Creating Fair Comparisons."

4. Determine whether you will compare your subjects (analyze similarities), contrast them (analyze differences), or do both. Very often, comparison-contrast texts include both similarities and differences. Some writing tasks, however, may require you to choose either to compare or to contrast. For example, a geology assignment may require students to write about the differences in the types of rocks found in their hometowns. Because recognizing the differences is the skill the instructor is trying to help students develop, the focus of the assignment will be on contrasting rather than comparing.

5. Determine the points of comparison you will analyze. To determine the points of comparison and contrast, think about your writing purpose. To compare two potential careers, the essay in this section uses the comparative points of educational requirements, vacation time and work hours, and potential salary. The points you choose should be the most pertinent points in the discussion. For example, one could compare the type of clothing teachers can wear to work with the type of clothing accountants can wear to work, but this point would not be as important as other points of comparison.

6. Decide whether to use a block arrangement or a point-by-point arrangement. If you are comparing two subjects and have multiple points of comparison, a point-by-point arrangement will usually be more effective. If you are comparing multiple subjects and have only a few points of comparison, a block arrangement will work well.

Arrangements for a Comparison-Contrast Essay	
Block (Subject-by-Subject) Arrangement: Best for just two subjects with multiple points of comparison	Point-by-Point Arrangement: Best for multiple subjects with only a few points of comparison
Subject A • Point 1 • Point 2 • Point 3 • Point 4	Point 1 • Subject A • Subject B • Subject C

(continued)

Arrangements for a Comparison-Contrast Essay *(continued)*	
Block (Subject-by-Subject) Arrangement: Best for just two subjects with multiple points of comparison	Point-by-Point Arrangement: Best for multiple subjects with only a few points of comparison
Subject B • Point 1 • Point 2 • Point 3 • Point 4	Point 2 • Subject A • Subject B • Subject C Point 3 • Subject A • Subject B • Subject C

NOTE: The actual number of subjects and points will vary, as the arrangements above demonstrate.

7. Write a thesis statement, and construct a simple outline. The thesis statement you write should indicate the two subjects being compared. If you choose to write a closed thesis statement, include the points of comparison, like this:

> Determining whether to buy or lease a vehicle requires considering monthly payment, mileage limit, warranty, and ownership status.

Connect IRW Writing Assignment: Set up the Practice assignments in Connect IRW to give students access to peer review tools. When you set up the assignment, you can create a rubric for easier grading.

PRACTICE ● Using Comparison-Contrast in Your Writing

Use the preceding steps to write a comparison-contrast essay. Choose one of the following topics, or select your own.

A. Select two potential career fields. Choose points of comparison that are important to you, such as salary, type of work, job satisfaction, and typical work hours. Write an essay in which you compare both career fields.

B. What are the differences between courses that require you to master a skill—such as a writing or welding course—and courses that require you to think about information, such as history or sociology? Write an essay in which you discuss at least three points of comparison.

C. Write an essay in which you compare and contrast two movies in the same genre. For example, you could compare two horror movies you have seen. Choose appropriate points of comparison, such as the actors' performances, the plot, and special effects.

Answers will vary.

See the IM for additional source-based essay assignments that require the use of classification as a text pattern.

Connect IRW Writing Assignment: Set up these assignments in Connect IRW to give students access to peer review tools. When you set up the assignment, you can create a rubric for easier grading. These assignments are pre-loaded in the Connect IRW *Common Places* Master Course.

Cause and Effect

What caused a bridge to collapse? What are the effects of illiteracy? What will happen if the Arctic ice cap melts? These kinds of questions require that we assess causes and effects. Many subjects lend themselves to thinking about cause and effect; thus, it is common to read analyses of *why* something happened or *what will happen if* certain actions are taken. A discussion of causes and/or effects is called a *causal analysis*.

Teaching Resources: See the PPT "Causes, Effects, and Critical Thinking."

■ Figuring out causes and effects is not always easy. Scientists may agree that climate change is happening, but world governments cannot agree on the actions that will effectively avert its consequences.

RECOGNIZING THE CAUSE AND EFFECT PATTERN IN READINGS

To identify the cause and effect pattern in a text, look for these characteristics and key words.

CHARACTERISTICS OF THE CAUSE AND EFFECT PATTERN

- The text primarily concerns causes, effects, or both.
- The text concerns phenomena or events.
- The text makes predictions or attempts to explain causes of past events.
- The text examines one cause and/or effect, multiple causes and/or effects, or chains of causes and/or effects.

Key Words for the Cause and Effect Pattern			
as a result consequently since	at last effect so	because of for that reason therefore	cause if . . . then thus

Cause and Effect in Supporting Details

An analysis of cause and effect often answers the questions "Why?" and "What if?" In some texts, the writer may use the discussion of a cause or effect (or both) as one type of support among others.

Suppose the United States is considering sending troops to the aid of a foreign country in turmoil (let's call this country Otherland). A reporter is writing an article to evaluate all of the options the United States has. The reporter can provide some background about what *caused* the unrest in Otherland so that readers learn why the United States is considering intervening in the first place. After discussing the causes of the unrest, the reporter can describe the effects of the current situation and then discuss the possible types of action the United States could take. Used in this way, the cause and effect discussion becomes a supporting detail in the reporter's article; other details are likely to be other options that the United States should consider. A partial outline for such an article might look like this.

Using Cause and Effect as a Supporting Detail

Topic: Intervening in Otherland

Thesis statement: The United States needs to consider every possible option before intervening in Otherland.

INTRODUCTION
   Paragraph 1

BODY
   Paragraph 2: History of the problem

   • What *caused* the unrest
   • Current situation (effects of the fighting, turmoil, etc.)

   Paragraph 3: Option 1—The United States could wait and do nothing for the time being.

   Paragraph 4: Option 2—The United States could send troops.

The article is structured around a list of possible actions; thus, the reporter will likely discuss the potential effects of each action, along with other information, such as the cost of the action, public opinion about the action, and so on.

Cause and Effect as a Text Pattern

Discussions of causes and effects can be complicated. For instance, what causes a recession? Economists can find so many possible causes that figuring out the most likely ones is truly difficult.

Because cause and effect relationships are so complicated, it is not unusual to see entire essays (and books) devoted to explaining these relationships. Such texts are often organized using cause and effect as a text pattern. The cause and effect text pattern may also be used to explain the *domino effect*, a chain reaction that occurs when one effect causes another effect, which causes another effect, and so on. For example, drought causes the price of hay and corn to increase. The increase in hay and corn prices drives up the cost of beef. The increase in the cost of beef is passed along to consumers, and the net result is that consumers have less money after paying for groceries. An essay that discusses a domino effect might be organized chronologically so that the writer begins with the first cause, moves to its effect, discusses the effect as a new cause, and continues this pattern.

Essays that present causes and effects can achieve a variety of writing purposes. Informative writing often presents causes, effects, or both. For example, a business textbook chapter might explain the positive effects of Internet marketing. An essay on a successful business might present the good decisions that caused the business to succeed.

Analysis is always required for writing about cause and effect relationships, and sometimes analysis is the primary purpose for writing. An essay that presents an environmental problem, such as the rise of sea levels, might present an analysis of its causes and effects.

Sometimes the goal of a causal analysis is to evaluate. For example, a writer may evaluate different options for helping needy children receive free lunches during the summer. In such an essay, the writer will probably evaluate the potential effects of a number of solutions and will determine the solution that would work the best.

Finally, cause and effect is used extensively in persuasive writing. Any time a writer advocates a certain action, a discussion of that action's effects can be used for support. For example, a writer may argue that buying American-made products benefits American workers. To support that argument, the writer would probably present the effects on workers when Americans buy (or fail to buy) American-made products.

Persuasive writing can also focus on causes. What is causing decreases in the honeybee population? The causes are widely debated; thus, a persuasively focused paper could use a cause and effect text pattern to present a writer's belief—based on evidence—about causes for this phenomenon.

Depending on the number of causes and effects under consideration, a writer can use several different methods of organization, as the cause and effect models show.

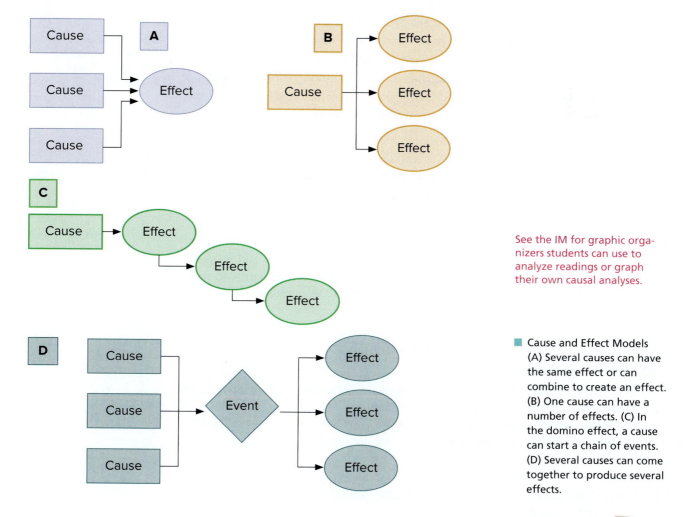

See the IM for graphic organizers students can use to analyze readings or graph their own causal analyses.

■ Cause and Effect Models (A) Several causes can have the same effect or can combine to create an effect. (B) One cause can have a number of effects. (C) In the domino effect, a cause can start a chain of events. (D) Several causes can come together to produce several effects.

ANALYZING A CAUSE AND EFFECT TEXT

The writers of effective cause and effect essays organize text elements in the way that best suits the subject, purpose, and reader.

A Cause and Effect Text: Introduction and Thesis Statement

In essays developed through a discussion of causes and effects, introductory paragraphs commonly use key words that focus readers' attention on causal analysis. While some writers provide a thesis statement early on, others first demonstrate the causes and/or effects and end their essay with a thesis statement that summarizes the text's information. In either case, the thesis statement will consist of the causes, the effects, or both causes and effects.

The following selection from *Natural Disasters*, a science textbook, demonstrates how the cause and effect pattern can be used to inform. Notice that the writer provides the topic but waits until the conclusion paragraph to offer the thesis statement.

Consider bringing the reading to life by pulling up some dust storm images on a computer if you live in an area where students are unfamiliar with such storms.

Introduction Paragraph of "US Dust Bowl, 1930s" by Patrick Leon Abbott

Might the worst conditions of the recent past serve as a prologue to the future? One of the greatest weather disasters in US history occurred during the 1930s, when several years of drought turned grain-growing areas in the center of the nation into the "Dust Bowl." Failed crops and malnutrition caused abandonment of thousands of farms and the broad scale migration of displaced people, mostly to California and other western states. This human drama was captured in many articles and books, including *The Grapes of Wrath* by John Steinbeck:

Now the wind grew strong and hard, it worked at the rain curst in the corn fields. Little by little the sky was darkened by the mixing dust, and the wind felt over the earth, loosened the dust and carried it away.

Introduction

Causes (failed crops, malnutrition) and effects (abandonment, migration) are summarized.

Note that the thesis statement does not appear in the introduction.

The introduction presents two effects of the Dust Bowl: failed crops and malnutrition. These, in turn, caused additional effects: people abandoned their farms to move West. In the body of the selection, we can expect the writer to elaborate on these causes and effects.

A Cause and Effect Text: Body Paragraphs and Their Organization

In the body paragraphs that follow, the writer first explains a cause in a long paragraph and follows with an explanation of the effects in another long paragraph. In the third body paragraph, the writer presents an alternative explanation of the cause of the Dust Bowl and shows why he rejects the explanation.

Body Paragraphs of "US Dust Bowl, 1930s" by Patrick Leon Abbott

What happened to cause the drought? Recurrent large-scale meanders in the upper-air flow created ridges of high pressure with clockwise flows resulting in descending air. The upper-level high-pressure air was already dry, but as it sank, it became warmer,

First major supporting point (implied): The Dust Bowl was caused by particular weather events.

(continued)

thus reaching the ground hot, dry, and thirsty. As the winds blew across the ground surface, they sucked up moisture, killing plants and exposing bare soil to erosion. Wind-blown clouds of dust built into towering masses of turbulent air and dust called rollers. When they rolled across an area, the Sun was darkened, and dust invaded every possible opening on a human body and came through every crack in a home. Dust even blew as visible masses across East Coast cities and blanketed ships at sea.	Domino effect: One natural event caused another, leading to drought. Effects: Drought affected human life.
The drought began in 1930, a particularly bad time. Only months before, in October 1929, the US stock market had crashed, and the nation's economy began sinking into the Great Depression. By 1931, farmers were becoming desperate. For example, a group of 500 armed farmers went to the town of England in Arkansas to seek food from the Red Cross. They were denied aid, so they went to the town's stores and took the food they needed. The event drew worldwide attention. Here were farmers from the US heartland who had helped feed the world during the early 20th century and through the ravages of World War I; now they could not even feed themselves.	Cause: The drought and the stock market crash made the Dust Bowl events even worse. This is the second major supporting point.
The dust storms became even worse in 1934 and 1936. Some of the blame for the Dust Bowl was heaped onto the farmers for plowing deeply through drought-tolerant native grasses and exposing bare soil to the winds. The plowed lands were sowed with seeds of plants that could not handle drought and thus died, exposing more soil. The farming practices were not the best, but they did not cause the drought; they just accentuated its effects. Evidence showing that droughts are common is found in the archaeological record. For example, droughts in the past probably led to the downfall of the Anasazi civilization of the southwestern United States and the migration of its people to areas with more dependable water supplies.	Effect Third major supporting point (implied): The cause was not plowing practices. Alternative explanation of cause Alternative explanation rejected

Notice that as the writer discusses the causes and effects of the Dust Bowl, he also comments about the events that made the Dust Bowl's effects even worse—the stock market crash and the drought. The last body paragraph rejects a proposed cause of the drought.

A Cause and Effect Text: Conclusion

In this particular text, the writer saves the thesis statement for the conclusion paragraph. Thus, the conclusion serves both to provide the writer's main point and to end the selection.

Conclusion Paragraph of "US Dust Bowl, 1930s" by Patrick Leon Abbott

The Dust Bowl drought affected more than just local agriculture. Combined with the stock market crash, it caused fundamental changes in the economic, social, and political systems of the United States.	Two-sentence thesis statement: summarizes the causes and effects presented and functions as the conclusion

PRACTICE ● Analyzing a Cause and Effect Text

On a separate sheet of paper, answer the following questions about "US Dust Bowl, 1930s."

1. What caused the Dust Bowl?

2. What are the relationships among the drought, the stock market crash, and the Great Depression?

3. One body paragraph describes the natural domino effect that created the drought. Was the effect on people part of the domino effect? Why or why not?

4. Think of a weather event that occurred during your lifetime. What were the effects of this event on people and the environment? Write a paragraph to explain.

1. The Dust Bowl was caused by years of drought.
2. The drought occurred almost the same time as the stock market crash, so farmers were affected by both events. The Great Depression was a result of the stock market crash.
3. Yes, the effect on people was caused by the drought, and the drought was caused by the weather events.
4. Answers will vary.

USING CAUSE AND EFFECT IN YOUR WRITING

Many subjects require that writers address causes and effects. If you are writing a paper and think cause and effect may be a helpful text pattern to use, follow these steps.

1. Ask yourself how cause and effect suits your topic and purpose. Will a discussion of causes and/or effects be the primary focus of your topic? If so, a cause and effect text pattern is appropriate. Events from the past may leave us wondering about their causes, so they are good subjects to consider for such an essay. A topic that prompts us to analyze future effects is also appropriate for the cause and effect text pattern.

While some cause and effect essays consider the past and others consider the future, another option is to think of issues that affect us now and to ask questions about their causes and/or effects. For example, with all of the information available about the harm of smoking cigarettes, many people still smoke them. Why? What causes people to continue a habit they know is dangerous to their health? Find a topic in which you are interested and ask, "Why did this happen?" or "What will be the effects of this event?"

2. Analyze the causes and/or effects of your topic. Use questions to help you determine causes and effects.

- What possible causes (or effects) can you think of for the questions you asked in step 1 above? List them. List as many as you can without censoring your ideas.
- Looking back at the causes (or effects) you have listed, ask, "Which of these are the *least* likely or *least* important causes or effects?" Go back to the list and cross out those that are least likely or least important. If a domino effect is involved, write out each cause and effect in the process.
- Select the most likely causes (or effects) to present in your essay.

3. Analyze the logic of the causes and/or effects you will present. It is, unfortunately, common to make logical errors when you are determining causes and effects. Three common errors are confusing correlations with causes, making faulty predictions, and oversimplifying possible causes.

- **Pitfall 1: Confusing correlations with causes. A correlation** is simply a relationship between two things. For example, we have evidence that eating fast food is correlated with having poor health. Imagine, for example, that your friend who eats only fast food (burgers, fries, and shakes, for example) develops a brain tumor. Can we say there is a causal relationship between eating fast food and developing a brain tumor?

Connect IRW Power of Process Assignment: See the IM for a list of readings in PoP students can use to analyze cause and effect text patterns. The Connect IRW *Common Places* Master Course contains pre-loaded PoP assignments that require students to analyze cause and effect text patterns.

Although some research shows that fast food and poor health are related, we do not have enough research to know whether eating fast food specifically *causes* brain tumors. In your friend's case, we see a correlation between eating lots of fast food and developing a brain tumor. However, we cannot prove one caused the other.

Teaching Resources: See the worksheet "Avoiding Cause and Effect Thinking Errors."

The correlation pitfall occurs when we assume that because two things appear to be related, one must have caused the other. If you do not have clear evidence linking a cause to an effect, you cannot assume a causal relationship.

- **Pitfall 2: Making faulty predictions.** When we consider taking an action, being able to make accurate predictions is important. Consider drinking and driving. We cannot say that a person who drinks and drives will definitely be involved in an accident. However, we know from evidence that a high percentage of auto accidents involve a driver who has been drinking alcohol. Thus we *can* say that a person who is driving under the influence of alcohol is *more likely* to be in a car accident than a driver who has not been drinking.

  Sometimes it is tempting to make predictions without much evidence because those predictions might help us win an argument or make a point. For example, someone might claim that if Americans agree to gun control laws, then eventually the government will take away people's guns. This is an *unreasonable prediction* because it is not based on evidence. Often, unreasonable predictions are attempts to make the listener fearful and to thus believe the speaker.

  To avoid making faulty predictions, keep the following questions in mind: "How do you know?" and "Would a reasonable person agree with this prediction?" You can avoid this pitfall by making sure you have sound reasons for your predictions, being certain your predictions would be acceptable to a general audience, and having proof to support them.

- **Pitfall 3: Oversimplifying possible causes.** Failing to consider all the possible causes for an event often results in oversimplification. For example, if you come down with a head cold after flying on a plane, you may blame the head cold on your air travel. This thinking, however, has oversimplified the situation. Touching such objects as doorknobs, grocery carts, and escalator rails can introduce germs that cause illnesses like colds. However, colds take several days to incubate. So if you get a head cold two days after flying, it is likely to have been caused by contact with germs before your flight.

  The best way to determine the cause of an event or phenomenon is to make a list of all the possible causes, cross out the causes that are not applicable to the situation, and try to find a cause that is reasonable.

4. Use very careful language to express causes and effects. After finding a reasonable cause, you will then need to use precise language to express the causal connection you have found. Consider this statement of cause:

Jana's decision to quit her job is probably what made her depressed.

By using *probably*, the writer acknowledges that there may be other causes. Thus, the writer is more accurate, precise, and careful in her language, and this care shows she has thought critically about possible causes.

Discussing qualifiers can lead to a discussion of why using absolute statements is often problematic. You can introduce the idea of generalizations since using qualifiers will help students avoid overgeneralizing.

One way to use more precise language is to use qualifiers, words like *may have*, *might*, and *likely*. Using qualifiers like these when appropriate will help you make more precise statements about causes and effects.

Common Qualifiers			
a few	all	always	commonly
could	entirely	few	many
may	might	never	possibly
seems	seldom	some	sometimes
suggests	the majority	unlikely	usually

5. Write a thesis statement, and construct a simple outline. Determine the best way to present the causes and/or effects you will be discussing. Create an outline in which you detail the specific causes and effects you will address and the order in which you will address them.

PRACTICE ● Using Cause and Effect in Your Writing

Use the preceding steps to write a cause and effect essay. Choose one of the following topics, or select your own.

A. Write an essay in which you discuss a trend—for example, an increase or decrease in crime on your campus or in your neighborhood—and the causes (or effects) of that trend.

B. Write a cause and effect essay about a good decision you made in life. Explain what caused you to make the decision and the effects of having made the decision.

C. Write an essay in which you discuss the causes or effects of one of the following: alcoholism, faith, a particular disease or condition, worry, a social problem, volunteering, living in a clean (or messy) place.

Answers will vary.

See the IM for additional source-based essay assignments that require the use of cause and effect as a text pattern.

Connect IRW Writing Assignment: Set up these assignments in Connect IRW to give students access to peer review tools. When you set up the assignment, you can create a rubric for easier grading. These assignments are pre-loaded in the Connect IRW *Common Places* Master Course.

Process Analysis

Perhaps at some point in your life, you struggled to make sense of the driving directions someone gave you. Or maybe you tried following a bread recipe, only to find that the result was an inedible lump of dough. These kinds of experiences emphasize how important it is to explain processes clearly and accurately.

The **process analysis** pattern usually presents the stages, steps, or phases of a process in a particular order. It can also be used to show how a particular historical event or discovery came about. Certain key words and transitions are often used in process analysis texts.

RECOGNIZING THE PROCESS ANALYSIS PATTERN IN READINGS

To identify the process analysis pattern, look for these characteristics and key words.

CHARACTERISTICS OF THE PROCESS ANALYSIS PATTERN

- Process analysis texts provide discussion of a process, procedure, method, course of action, or protocol.
- These texts present a sequence of steps (*first*, *second*, *third*, or some other sequencing indicators).
- Process analysis texts provide explanations about how the steps work or how to follow them.

Teaching Resources: See the PPT "Analyzing and Communicating Processes."

Key Words for the Process Analysis Pattern				
after	before	finally	first, second, third . . .	later
meanwhile	next	now	phase	stage
step	then	to begin	to continue	to end

Process Analysis in Supporting Details

A writer might briefly explain a process in a body paragraph of an essay to give the audience background information. Suppose a writer is composing a narrative essay to tell the story of someone who immigrated to the United States. The writer may devote a paragraph to explaining the process of becoming an American citizen if this information is necessary for readers to understand the immigrant's story. The partial outline that follows shows where a writer may use a brief explanation of a process as a type of support.

Using Process Analysis as a Supporting Detail

Topic: An immigrant's story

Thesis statement: Despite seemingly insurmountable odds, Robbie Kam-Lin realized his dream of American citizenship.

INTRODUCTION
    Paragraph 1

BODY
    Paragraph 2: Problems in his native land
    Paragraph 3: Getting to the United States
    Paragraph 4: The long path to citizenship
       - The process of becoming an American citizen

What Should I Expect From the Naturalization Process?

Preparing to Apply

- Read *A Guide to Naturalization.*
- Complete the Naturalization Eligibility Worksheet.
- Get an "Application for Naturalization" (Form N-400).
- Visit our website at **www.uscis.gov**.

Completing Your Application and Getting Photographed

- Complete your application.
- Get two passport-style photographs taken.
- Collect the necessary documents.
- Send your application, passport-style photographs, documents, and fee (DO NOT SEND CASH) to the appropriate Lockbox Facility or Service Center.
- Keep a copy of everything you send to USCIS.

Getting Fingerprinted

- Receive an appointment letter from USCIS.
- Go to the fingerprinting location.
- Get your fingerprints taken.
- Mail additional documents if USCIS requests them.
- Wait for USCIS to schedule your interview.

Being Interviewed

- Receive an appointment for your interview.
- Go to your local USCIS office at the specified time.
- Bring state-issued identification, Permanent Resident Card, and any additional documents specific to your case.
- Answer questions about your application and background.
- Take the English and civics tests.
- Receive case status.

Taking the Oath

- Receive a ceremony date.
- Check in at the ceremony.
- Return your Permanent Resident Card.
- Answer questions about what you have done since your interview.
- Take the Oath of Allegiance.
- Receive your Certificate of Naturalization.

Process Analysis as a Text Pattern

Process analysis can be used for a variety of purposes. For instance, when the sole purpose of an essay is to describe how an event came about or to explain how to perform a task, a writer can use process analysis as a text pattern. In *A Guide to Naturalization,* a brochure published by the US Citizenship and Immigration Services, shown above, process analysis is used to outline the steps a person must take to apply for and acquire US citizenship. Process analysis can also be used to explain a process a writer is proposing, such as a new way to handle incoming orders to improve speed and efficiency. Often the purpose of process analysis texts is to inform. An explanation of how global warming works, for example, could be presented using process analysis.

Explaining a process can also be part of an analysis. A scholarly article in an engineering journal might use process analysis to examine the method used to build a bridge that failed. The purpose of such a discussion may also be to evaluate: by examining processes, one can evaluate the best process to use for a given procedure.

Sometimes writers argue about processes to determine which processes are appropriate, which work the best, or which are the most ethical. For example, what is the best process to use to reunite an adopted child with a birth parent? What process should doctors and hospital staff use to determine whether a person is legally dead? What process should hospitals use for organ donation? These are debatable issues that are appropriate for process analysis papers.

Most process analysis papers can be organized by the stages or phases of the process being described. The outline that follows presents an example of how process analysis can be used to structure an informative essay.

A Simple Outline for a Process Analysis Pattern Essay

Topic: Creating a plan to improve customer service

Thesis statement: Any business can improve customer service by using a five-step process.

INTRODUCTION
   Paragraph 1: Introduction and thesis statement

BODY
   Paragraph 2: Stage 1—Examining the situation

   Paragraph 3: Stage 2—Exploring solutions

   Paragraph 4: Stage 3—Implementing a solution

   Paragraph 5: Stage 4—Assessing the solution

   Paragraph 6: Stage 5—Adjusting or creating a new solution

CONCLUSION
   Paragraph 7: Conclusion

ANALYZING A PROCESS ANALYSIS TEXT

Some specific features are typically found in the introduction, thesis statement, body paragraphs, and conclusion of process analysis texts.

A Process Analysis Text: Introduction and Thesis Statement

The introduction paragraph of a process analysis text states the topic and usually includes the thesis statement. The example below is a brief article from the New Jersey Department of Education that presents steps for making schools less violent.

Introduction Paragraph from "School Safety: Three Steps to Make the Peace"

Recent tragic school shootings remind us of the important role each child and each adult has in maintaining the safety of a school. There are three actions children, youth or adults can take to improve the safety of their learning community.	Simple introduction Thesis statement

A Process Analysis Text: Body Paragraphs and Their Organization

The body paragraphs of a process analysis essay describe the steps, phases, or stages of the process in question. Often, each body paragraph presents one particular step, phase, or stage, as in the example that follows.

Body Paragraphs from "School Safety: Three Steps to Make the Peace"

Treat each other with respect. Encourage, teach and above all role model respectful behavior. Identify acts of kindness, give attention to positive and cooperative behavior. Encourage children and youth to "make the peace" in their classroom and hallway. Many districts teach all students conflict resolution skills and train students to be peer mediators to help resolve conflicts. Address name-calling and bullying directly. Both students and staff can say clearly that name-calling and intimidation are not appropriate "in our school." Staff can help to change the climate of harassment by giving positive attention to the person being bullied. Publicly and directly tell the person who has been bullied that what happened to them was not OK, and check to see if there is any assistance you can give them. After an intervention with name-calling, acts of intimidation or harassment, check back in with both the victim and the offender to see if the offending behavior has stopped.	First step (major supporting point 1)

Second step (major supporting point 2) |
| Take threats seriously. If a student or an adult says they are thinking of harming themselves or others, tell a trusted adult. As a student, ask an adult to help you talk with the person who is making threats. As a staff person, work with both student support staff, administration and law enforcement to determine the seriousness of the threat. Work to address the needs of people affected or made fearful by a threat. | Third step (major supporting point 3) |
| For adults, there is an additional action step: keep weapons away from children and youth. Through newsletters, announcements at PTA/PTSO [parent teacher association/ parent teacher student organization] meetings and at parent/teacher conferences, at ball games and concerts, remind adults that if they own a gun, to be sure that the weapon is disassembled, locked away and that the ammunition is locked in a separate place. | An additional step for adults (major supporting point 4) |

A Process Analysis Text: Conclusion

The function of the conclusion paragraph is to add any remaining explanations, to comment on the process, and to end the text.

Conclusion Paragraph from "School Safety: Three Steps to Make the Peace"

In spite of incidents like school shootings, schools remain one of the safer places a child or adult can attend in our society. A person is three times more likely to be struck by lightning than to be shot in school. By working together, and supporting one another, parents, students and staff can make the school safe for everyone.	Simple conclusion: provides closure; includes information to help readers

PRACTICE • Analyzing a Process Analysis Text

On a separate sheet, answer the following questions about "School Safety: Three Steps to Make the Peace."

1. What is the writer's purpose? Explain.

2. Do you believe the steps the writer gives for keeping the peace in schools are effectively discussed and explained? Could the writer have presented them in a more convincing way? If so, how?

3. For whom is this article written? How can you tell?

4. How does the fourth step differ from the other steps? Do you think the writer's presentation of the fourth step is effective? Explain.

1. The purpose is to inform by providing information.
2. Answers will vary.
3. It was written for parents, students, and staff. The paragraph that starts "Take Threats Seriously" reveals the intended audiences.
4. The fourth step is directed to parents. (The remaining part of the answer will vary.)

USING PROCESS ANALYSIS IN YOUR WRITING

You can use process analysis to structure an essay when you want to guide readers through the steps of a process (such as applying for citizenship) or when you want to describe the stages of an event or phenomenon (such as photosynthesis). The guidelines that follow will help you plan a process analysis essay.

1. Determine whether process analysis will fit your topic and your purpose. Process analysis is effective only for papers that present, analyze, evaluate, or make arguments about processes. If you believe your topic is appropriate, determine what you hope to accomplish by presenting the process. Is your goal to present a simple overview of the process? Is the purpose of your writing to teach readers to use the process you will describe? Keep your purpose in mind as you select the types of details to include in your paper.

2. Carefully and critically consider your audience and what your audience needs to know as you explain the process. When explanations of processes go wrong, the reason is usually a failure on the part of the writer to think about the needs of the audience. If you can clearly identify your audience, think about the particular knowledge this audience already has. A general audience cannot be expected to have specific knowledge of specialized subjects. For example, while you can expect a general audience to know that refining oil is an industrial process, you cannot expect such readers to know anything specific about the process.

3. Use prewriting to determine the particular steps of the process you will discuss. Prewriting can help you determine the stages, steps, or phases involved in the process. Read through your prewriting critically to decide the best way to arrange your information. For example, determine whether each step needs its own paragraph or whether some steps belong in a paragraph together. Also, make sure you do not leave out any steps. Thinking like a reader will help you anticipate your readers' needs.

4. Write a thesis statement, and create a simple outline. Choose the best order in which to present each step or stage. Usually, steps or stages are presented in chronological order.

5. Have someone read over your rough draft, looking for missing steps. If you are familiar with the process you are describing, you may forget to include small, but important,

See the IM for a "Process Analysis Worksheet," an exercise that helps students differentiate the stages or steps in a process.

Connect IRW Power of Process Assignment: See the IM for a list of readings in PoP students can use to analyze process analysis text patterns. The Connect IRW *Common Places* Master Course contains pre-loaded PoP assignments that require students to analyze definition text patterns.

Teaching Resources: See the PPT "Making an Omelet."

steps. For example, a chef knows that to make an omelet, she needs to grease an omelet pan; because she is so familiar with the process, she may leave out this step, thinking readers will certainly know to grease the pan. Make sure you include all the necessary steps in your essay.

PRACTICE ● Using Process Analysis in Your Writing

Use the preceding steps to write a process analysis essay. Choose one of the following topics, or select your own.

A. Write about a process you have mastered. For example, if you know how to make tamales, you might write an essay explaining the process. If you understand the way an internal combustion engine works, you might write an essay about it. Write with the idea that your essay will be read by someone who knows nothing about the process you are describing.

B. How does online dating work? Describe the process in steps. Alternatively, what is the process many people use to find a life partner?

C. Write an essay in which you discuss how parents can build their children's self-esteem. Alternatively, write an essay about the stages teens go through as they become young men and young women.

An enjoyable exercise is to have students create from memory—as carefully as they can—instructions for how to make a particular recipe. Students then trade recipes and try them out at home, following the instructions to the letter and video-taping the process. Students can post their videos as discussion board links in Connect IRW and discuss where the instructions needed clarification.

Answers will vary.

See the IM for additional source-based essay assignments that require the use of process analysis as a text pattern.

Connect IRW Writing Assignment: Set up these assignments in Connect IRW to give students access to peer review tools. When you set up the assignment, you can create a rubric for easier grading. These assignments are pre-loaded in the Connect IRW *Common Places* Master Course.

Recognizing and Using Mixed Text Patterns

Most professional writers use a mixture of patterns as supporting details in their writing. When you read an essay, mark the types of supporting details you find. If most of the supporting details are one particular type, the essay may be written using a single text pattern. For example, an essay that presents primarily causes and effects is likely to be written using the cause and effect text pattern. If the types of supporting details vary, the writer is probably using a mixture of text patterns to support his thesis statement.

In a mixed pattern essay, a writer may devote a few sentences to offering a definition. She may then discuss a cause or an effect or make a brief comparison. The writer chooses the type of supporting detail to use based on her writing purpose.

To analyze mixed pattern essays, ask yourself what the writer is doing in each body paragraph. More specifically, ask questions such as these:

- Is the writer telling a short *story*?
- Is the writer giving an *example* or providing an *illustration*?
- Is the writer *defining* a term or concept?
- Is the writer putting information into a *category*?
- Is the writer explaining a *cause* or *effect*?
- Is the writer making a *comparison*?
- Is the writer explaining the stages, phases, or steps of a *process*?

In addition to finding these text patterns used as support, you may also find other supporting elements, such as *rhetorical questions* (questions to which the writer knows the answer), the use of facts and data, descriptions, summaries of other people's ideas, and explanations. By analyzing each body paragraph and jotting down the type of support the paragraph contains, you will be able to more easily identify the writer's thesis statement and major supporting points. Additionally, you will recognize how writers use mixed patterns and will be able to emulate the strategy of mixing text patterns in your own essays.

What follows is a humorous essay that includes a variety of types of support. As you read it, notice the annotations about the support the writer uses.

Teaching Resources: See the PPT "Mixing It Up."

Students often have difficulty identifying mixed types of support. One way to practice this skill is to start each class session by analyzing the support in a brief article from the daily news.

How to Plan a Vacation

My wife and I were brainstorming recently about what our next vacation should involve. As she talked about shopping in little boutiques along a flower-lined road, it became clear to me that her idea of a vacation was nowhere near my idea. I realized then that I needed to put my analytical prowess to good use.

Anecdote

First, we had to agree about what *vacation* means. Being the geeky type, I dusted off our ancient dictionary and thumbed my way to the *V* section. "A vacation," I read to my wife as she looked at red purses on a Web site, "is a period of time that a person spends away from home." That was not a very satisfactory definition. After all, shopping in precious boutiques is time away from home. I'd have to do more analysis.

Definition

My wife, having happily agreed to spend a vacation "away from home," kept browsing. I decided to add to the definition. "Additionally," I said, "a vacation cannot involve business or work—or the use of computers." I reasoned that not having a computer would make my wife less likely to find those cute boutiques she imagined dragging me to. Again, she happily agreed with my definition.

Definition

(continued)

Maybe this wouldn't be such a difficult process after all. The next thing to decide was where to go. I identified the two chief issues that mattered to us: temperature (cold-weather versus warm-weather settings) and activity level (primarily active versus principally relaxed agendas). In analyzing our options, I came up with four possible combinations: cold and active, cold and relaxed, warm and active, warm and relaxed. Now we were getting somewhere!

Process

Classification

A "cold active" vacation might involve downhill skiing, snowshoeing, or cross-country skiing. A "cold relaxed" retreat could include reading by a roaring fire, soaking in hot springs or a hot tub outside, chatting and sipping hot drinks while looking out on a beautiful landscape and watching the snow fall. A "warm active" holiday might consist of snorkeling at a coral reef, fishing on a chartered boat, or spending time at a jumbo water park. A "warm relaxed" vacation might entail sunning at a beautiful beach, whale-watching, or taking a cruise. The best part about all of these ideas? They could all be in the countryside, and we wouldn't have to shop!

Illustrations

I wrote down all of the options, and I even did some pricing. Noticing that my wife was no longer looking at red purses on the Internet, I thought maybe it would be a good time to present my ideas. I showed her all of my analysis and described the four types of vacations we might take. Her eyes lit up at the prospect of lying in a hammock on a tropical beach and watching sunsets. "I would feel like a different person if I could just lounge on a beach," she said. She came up with some even better ideas than I had: she suggested we add a few active activities to our otherwise relaxing vacation by going snorkeling and taking a deep-sea fishing trip! That sealed the deal for me. We ultimately decided on the Florida Keys.

Cause and effect

Cause and effect

Having finally come to a decision, she gave me a quick kiss. "You know that the Keys have some of the most beautiful conch pearl jewelry, don't you?" she asked with a wink.

PRACTICE ● Analyzing a Mixed Pattern Essay

On a separate sheet, answer the following questions about "How to Plan a Vacation."

1. The title suggests the essay might present a process. Does it? Explain your answer.

2. The annotations point out some of the major types of support the writer uses. Can you find additional types of support in the essay? If so, explain what they are and where they are used.

3. Could the writer have presented this information using a single text pattern? Why or why not?

4. In what way does the writer use classification? Explain.

1. The essay does present a process, although the steps involved are not prescriptive—they are not steps that everyone should necessarily take.

2. The fifth paragraph compares and contrasts vacations in the four identified categories. The essay also uses dialogue and humor.

3. The writer could have made the "process" more dominant, but then the essay might not have had the humorous tone that the writer aimed for.

4. The writer uses classification to create four possible vacation combinations of temperature and activity level.

Connect IRW Power of Process Assignment: See the IM for a list of readings in PoP students can use to analyze mixed text patterns. The Connect IRW *Common Places* Master Course contains pre-loaded PoP assignments that require students to analyze readings that contain a mix of text patterns.

MIXING TEXT PATTERNS IN YOUR WRITING

When you plan an essay, consider whether you can best communicate your main idea by using a single text pattern to organize your thoughts or by using a variety of text patterns as support. We will follow the process used by Marcus as he composes an essay using mixed text patterns.

Marcus is writing an essay for his biology class. The instructor has asked each student to write an informative essay about a particular illness. Each student has been assigned a particular disease and has received an information sheet about it. After students submit their work, the instructor will make copies of each student's essay to distribute to the class: the essays must help students learn enough about each illness to be able to answer questions about it on a test. Thus, Marcus's essay needs to include enough information to give his classmates a thorough understanding of the illness.

What text pattern or patterns should Marcus use in his essay on his assigned subject, mononucleosis? Clearly, he will need to *define* the illness because readers will want to know what the disease is. But readers will have other questions as well. Marcus makes a list of the questions readers may have, and then he jots down the kinds of information that will help him answer those questions.

Readers' Potential Questions about Mononucleosis

1. What is it?   definition
2. How do people get it? Is it contagious?   cause and effect
3. How serious is it?   cause and effect
4. What does it "look" like? Can you see it (like measles?)   description
5. What does it feel like?   illustration
6. What are its symptoms?   part of definition, illustration
7. What parts of the body does the disease affect?   cause and effect
8. Does the disease have long-lasting effects?   cause and effect
9. How long does it take to get rid of it?   cause and effect
10. How is it treated?   process analysis
11. How can people prevent it?   cause and effect

Marcus realizes that his essay does not fit into one text pattern. Rather, he will be using a variety of text patterns as supporting details.

What is the logical way to organize these patterns? To answer this question, Marcus determines what readers need to know first: most likely, they need a definition of mononucleosis. A description of the illness and examples of symptoms will enhance the definition, so he places those items together. Next, Marcus plans to talk about the causes and effects of mononucleosis and the process of treating it. Since understanding causes and effects is yet another way of getting a basic idea of what mononucleosis is, Marcus decides to discuss those as the second major supporting point in the essay. The final major supporting point is the treatment process, so he places that last. He also creates a thesis statement that unifies the major supporting points.

Thesis statement: Mononucleosis is a serious illness, but it is fairly common and is very treatable.

Major supporting point 1: Definition, description, and examples of symptoms

Major supporting point 2: Causes and effects

Major supporting point 3: Treatment process

To finish the outline, Marcus needs to include the supporting details he will use in each section of the body of his essay. At this point, Marcus consults the disease information handout his instructor provided. Using it, he finds specific information to plug into his outline. (He will give credit to the source of this information in his essay.) Here is how he organizes the supporting details (shown in italics).

A Simple Outline for a Mixed Pattern Essay

Thesis statement: Mononucleosis is a serious illness, but it is fairly common and is very treatable.

Major supporting point 1: Definition, description, and examples of symptoms

Definition: "Infectious mononucleosis (IM) is a disease that occurs in older children and adolescents when they develop a primary EBV infection" (Pediatrics).

Description and symptoms:
- *Usually appears in teens*
- *May not look sick but do feel sick*
- *Those infected may seem to simply be tired or lazy*
- *A rash can develop*
- *Pharyngitis*
- *Fever*
- *Profound fatigue*
- *Lymphadenopathy (swollen, enlarged lymph nodes)*

Major supporting point 2: Causes and effects
- *What causes it*
- *What causes it to spread*
- *What body parts it affects*
- *What serious damage it can cause*
  - *Short-term*
  - *Long-term*

Major supporting point 3: Treatment plan (process)
- *Rest (disease resolves on its own)*
- *No contact sports*
- *Over-the-counter medicines for pain and symptom relief*

Marcus can use his simple outline to draft paragraphs for his essay. Additionally, by noting the particular details he will use from his source, Marcus can take these details from his outline and integrate them into his essay, taking care to use the appropriate methods for giving credit to the source.

Complete the practice exercise that follows to try your hand at using mixed text patterns in an essay.

PRACTICE   ●   Selecting Text Patterns for a Mixed Text Pattern Essay

Follow these steps to select text patterns and create an outline for an essay responding to the question, what is a "good parent"? Then write an essay in which you answer this question.

1. Use a prewriting process to create ideas about what makes a good parent.
2. Determine which ideas from your prewriting you would like to include in your essay.
3. Identify the best text pattern to use for presenting each idea.
4. Using the outline for the essay on mononucleosis as a model, write an outline for your essay.
5. Using your outline, compose the essay. Refer to the Quick Start Guide to Integrated Reading and Writing Assignments if you need assistance.

Answers will vary.

See the IM for additional source-based essay assignments that require the use of mixed text patterns.

Connect IRW Writing Assignment: Set up these assignments in Connect IRW to give students access to peer review tools. When you set up the assignment, you can create a rubric for easier grading. These assignments are pre-loaded in the Connect IRW *Common Places* Master Course.

The Basic Elements of Argument

The word *argument* has a bad reputation. When we hear the word, we often think of an unpleasant disagreement or confrontation. We might think of a shouting match or an emotionally charged exchange of words between two angry people. Certainly, these kinds of exchanges are indeed arguments.

However, as the term is used academically, an **argument** is simply an opinion supported by evidence. The word is used in the same way that we use the word *viewpoint*, except that by definition, argument rests on supporting reasons whereas a person's viewpoint may not be as clearly supported. Thus, without any unpleasantness or rancor, a college professor may present her argument on an issue and may ask students to present their arguments on that issue.

IDENTIFYING THE PURPOSE OF ARGUMENT TEXTS

Unlike essays that are written to inform, to analyze, or to evaluate, the goal of an argument essay is to **persuade** a reader to accept a particular position or point of view. In college, you will read many written arguments, and you will also hear many oral arguments. Additionally, you will sometimes be required to write your own argument papers.

As a reader, when you approach argument texts, your goal is to determine the writer's main point and to find the support he uses to back up that point. You should also be able to evaluate the effectiveness of the support the writer uses. For example, a writer claims that Windows-based computers are better than Macs, and he bases that claim on the fact that he had a Mac once and did not like it, whereas he had a Windows-based computer and thought it was great. As a critical reader, you will recognize the weakness of the writer's evidence. He has only one piece of evidence about the quality of Windows-based computers—his own experience! He needs far more evidence to be able to prove persuasively that Windows-based computers are better than Macs. Ultimately, to assess the quality of an argument, you will need to analyze the writer's support and determine the weaknesses and strengths of the writer's argument.

Being able to read arguments critically will help you write better arguments, for you will know where potential weaknesses can lurk in your reasoning and can make sure you present the most convincing case to support your claim. To create a convincing case, you will need to have done enough reading and thinking to form and support a sound argument. Almost always, the grade you receive on an argument paper will be based on the quality of your argument, not on the particular opinion you express. Learning how to construct a sound argument is the aim. Ultimately, the goal of education is for students to think clearly and independently about issues; reading and writing arguments help develop this skill.

We have provided a very brief presentation of argument theory. See the IM for additional materials for teaching argument, including additional explanations and exercises for these topics:

- The three appeals: ethos, pathos, logos
- Logical fallacies 101
- Addressing counterarguments
- Finding unstated assumptions

RECOGNIZING THE ELEMENTS OF ARGUMENT

In an argument text, the thesis statement puts forth a *claim*—the writer's opinion about a debatable issue. For a thesis statement to be a claim, it has to assert an arguable point. In contrast, the thesis statement of an information or evaluation essay may not be a claim.

Thesis statement that is not a claim: Laws about keeping wild animals as domestic pets vary across the United States. *This is a fact, not an arguable issue. An essay on this topic would present information about the laws in question.*

Thesis statement that is a claim: Keeping wild animals as domestic pets should be illegal. *This statement is an opinion; thus, it is a claim.*

As always, a thesis statement must be supported, and in an argument essay, the support usually consists of evidence in the form of reasons. **Reasons,** then, are the major supporting points of an argument essay. The supporting details for reasons consist of all the information, or **evidence,** a writer needs to back up, explain, illustrate, define, or otherwise defend the major supporting points.

An additional element in argument essays is a **counterargument,** the opposing argument. Writers will often include the opposing argument and then attempt to **refute** it, to show where it is weak and flawed.

STRUCTURING AN ARGUMENT

Imagine you are making the claim that parents should not use physical punishment to discipline their children. The following list shows one *reason* (a major supporting point) you might use to support your claim and the kinds of *evidence* (supporting details) you might use.

> **Claim (thesis statement):** Parents should not use physical punishment to discipline their children.
>
> **Reason (major supporting point):** Children who experience physical punishment act out in physical ways, such as by hitting or biting their peers.
>
> **Support (supporting details):**
>
> - Explain how children learn behaviors by imitating their parents.
> - Use a quote from the psychology textbook to support the point about how children learn.
> - Explain the results of a psychological study that showed physical punishment resulted in physically aggressive children.

Notice that the supporting details are very specific. In this case, the supporting details consist of an explanation, a quotation, and the results of a study, and they combine to make the reason believable. If we were to outline the rest of this essay, we would see additional reasons and the supporting details the writer would use to back them up.

Chapter 13 provides an integrated reading and writing project focused on analyzing and writing argument essays. The chapter includes additional information about using sources as evidence.

IDENTIFYING THREE TYPES OF APPEALS IN ARGUMENTS

Writers generally use three types of support for their claims: logical appeals, ethical appeals, and emotional appeals. An appeal is simply a type of reason.

To support an argument with **logical appeals,** a writer will use reasonable—logical—explanations. For example, if it is raining outside, it is reasonable to argue that your friend should take her umbrella with her when she leaves for work. Another example is to argue that people should avoid getting into debt because debt leads to decreased financial options in life. Logical appeals often make use of text patterns such as cause and effect and comparison-contrast.

In addition to logical appeals, writers also try to assure readers of their good intentions—that they are sincere, honest, and fair and that they have the readers' interests and concerns in mind. They use the testimony of knowledgeable experts to bolster their own credibility and to project self-confidence in their views. An **ethical appeal** consists of support that convinces us of the writer's trustworthiness, impartiality, expert knowledge, and goodwill.

A third type of support appeals to our emotions. Emotions are powerful; they can convince us to believe things and to take actions. For example, advertisements often tap into our emotions to sell products. A pair of name-brand, expensive athletic shoes may be the same quality as a pair of no-name sneakers, but wearing the expensive shoes gives us a *feeling* that the cheap shoes cannot provide. Appealing to our emotions can also mean appealing to our sense of shared values. In a written argument, we might tell the story of a child who is always hungry to make the claim that people should support a government supplemental food program because no child should have to suffer hunger. **Emotional appeals** can provide strong reasons for believing a claim or for taking an action.

PRACTICE Identifying the Elements of Argument

Match the term in the left column with the correct definition or example in the right column.

___g___ 1. argument

___d___ 2. reason

___c___ 3. ethical appeal

___a___ 4. emotional appeal

___f___ 5. logical appeal

___e___ 6. counterargument

___b___ 7. claim

a. If we don't get enough contributions, kittens like Sadie will be left to live a miserable, lonely life.

b. The thesis statement in an argument essay.

c. I have been a detective for twenty-five years, and I have never seen a defendant more guilty than Mr. Sellers.

d. A major supporting point for an argument essay's thesis statement.

e. The point of view of the opposing side.

f. You should buy the Chevrolet instead of the Ford because the Chevrolet gets better gas mileage.

g. An opinion supported by reasons.

RECOGNIZING ARGUMENTS BY ANALYZING TOPICS

One way to recognize an argument essay is to focus on the essay's topic. Some topics are arguable, and some are not. An arguable topic is one that can be stated as a question whose answer is *debatable*—that is, it can be considered from multiple perspectives. Here are some topic questions whose answers are *not* arguable.

Question: What is the H1N1 flu?

Arguable or not? This question is not arguable because the answer is universally agreed on. Medical professionals know what H1N1 flu is. Thus, a paper that answers this question will simply inform, not argue.

Question: What kinds of college financial aid are available for veterans?

Arguable or not? The answer to this question requires some research, but the answer is easily found and is clear-cut. We do not have to argue about the kinds of financial aid available for veterans because there is an authoritative answer to this question. A paper on this topic will inform, not argue.

Although the questions above are not arguable as they are stated, we can refocus them as arguable issues. To do so, we simply ask, "With what aspects of this topic might people disagree?" Notice how refocusing can result in arguable issues:

Refocus: Should the United States require people to be vaccinated against the H1N1 flu?

Arguable or not? The issue is now arguable. People will disagree on whether the vaccine should be required by law.

Refocus: Should veterans be given more financial aid opportunities than nonveterans?

Arguable or not? Now the issue is arguable. Some people will think the answer is *yes*, and others will disagree.

PRACTICE ● Recognizing Arguable Issues

Below, you will find a table that lists questions on different topics. If a topic question is arguable, write "arguable" in the right column next to the question. If it is not arguable, then find an issue related to the question that would be arguable. Write the new, arguable question in the right column next to the question. Two examples are given.

Question	Your Response
Example: Should public schools continue to offer summer vacations, or should schooling be year-round?	Arguable
Example: What is text messaging?	Not arguable. Change to this: Why should text messaging while driving be illegal?
1. Should the first two years of college be free?	Arguable
2. What does it mean to "drink responsibly"?	Arguable
3. Who was Thomas Jefferson?	Not arguable. Possible refocus: Could Thomas Jefferson have done more to abolish slavery in the US Constitution?
4. What is the history of tattooing?	Not arguable. Possible refocus: Should parents be allowed to get tattoos for their children under the age of eighteen?

RECOGNIZING ARGUMENT TEXTS BY THEIR CHARACTERISTICS AND KEY WORDS

In addition to recognizing argument texts by analyzing their topics, you can also use the characteristics of argument texts and the key words associated with argument as clues.

CHARACTERISTICS OF ARGUMENT TEXTS

- Texts that argue have persuasion as their purpose.
- The subject of argument texts is an arguable issue.
- Arguments present the writer's opinion on the issue.
- Arguments present reasons and supporting details to back up the writer's opinion.
- Arguments often use research and analysis as support.

Teaching Resources: See the handout "Annotating Arguments."

Consider starting class by analyzing a short editorial each day you teach the elements of argument.

Key Words of Argument Texts			
according to	argues	because	claims
counters	evidence	furthermore	illogical
in fact	logic	reasons	refutes
since	supports	therefore	thus

READING AND ANNOTATING AN ARGUMENT ESSAY

As you read the essay that starts on the next page—"Keep Guns off Campus" by Dennis Henigan—published in the *Huffington Post*, notice the elements of argument as they are pointed out.

Keep Guns Off Campus

by Dennis Henigan

Lexile: 1480L

In the wake of the Tucson shooting, Arizona's legislature is considering various bills addressing guns and violence. The legislation with the best chance of passage has nothing to do with strengthening the state's laws to prevent dangerous individuals from easily acquiring the firepower that enabled Jared Loughner to shoot 19 people in about 16 seconds, killing six of them. Incredibly, the bill with the most momentum would force Arizona colleges and universities to allow the concealed carry of guns on campus.

The Arizona bill is one of many similar bills being pushed in states across the nation, as the gun lobby seeks to overcome the collective judgment of college administrators, faculty and students that allowing guns on campus is a recipe for disaster. Up until now, sanity has prevailed, as such bills have failed 43 times in 23 states in recent years. But the forces of "guns everywhere" are back, and pitched battles are underway, not only in Arizona, but in Texas and elsewhere.

It all started with the Virginia Tech mass shooting of almost four years ago, which prompted "gun rights" proponents to argue that the shooting could have been stopped if one of the students in the targeted classrooms had been carrying a gun and could have returned fire. It is revealing that none of the students and teachers who actually were under fire that day have become proponents of concealed carry on campus. Indeed, Colin Goddard, who was shot four times in his French class, has become a crusader for stronger gun laws, as poignantly depicted in the documentary *Living for 32,* now being shown on college campuses coast-to-coast. . . .

The argument supporting guns on campus is based on a bizarre assessment of relative risks. Its proponents seek to create the remote possibility that a legal gun carrier will be in the right place at the right time when a killer attacks, and will act effectively to stop the attacker, *when the attack itself, particularly a mass attack, is itself a remote possibility.* In order to create the unlikely chance of this "good guy shoots attacker" scenario becoming reality, the proponents of campus concealed carry seek to ensure a proliferation of guns in classrooms, dorm rooms, dining halls, sports stadiums—anywhere where a violent attack may occur.

This necessarily means introducing a broad new array of obvious risks into everyday life on college campuses. Those risks seem anything but remote: that an argument between a professor and a disgruntled student will erupt in gunfire; that an intoxicated student will accidentally discharge his gun while showing it off at a Friday afternoon keg party; that a student's momentary despair over a romantic break-up will turn lethal as he finds a gun and turns it on himself.

The pro-gun crowd assails "gun-free zones" that allegedly invite the violent to attack the unarmed, but the reality is that currently gun-free college campuses are far safer than the gun-saturated communities that surround them. Justice Department figures show that college students aged 18 to 24 experience violence at a 20% lower rate than non-students in the same age group. In addition, 93% of the violence against students occurs off campus.

Sidebar annotations:

Background: In February 2011, at a political gathering in Tucson, Arizona, Congresswoman Gabrielle Giffords and several others were shot by a lone gunman. Giffords survived, but six others, including a nine-year-old girl, did not.

Additional background: Expands the essay's scope to show that this is an issue for everyone—not just Arizonans.

Major supporting point: The argument that having a gun would have stopped the shooter is flawed.

Counterargument: provided by writer

Refutation of counterargument starts.

Refutation of counterargument continues.

Supporting point for refutation: Allowing guns on campuses actually creates more problems.

Hypothetical examples

Major supporting point (a counterargument): The argument that gun-free zones attract violence is flawed.

Refutation of counterargument

Examples: statistics from an authoritative source, the Justice Department

---

(continued)

Given that in most states gun owners must be 21 to carry concealed weapons, the "guns on campus" activists question why law-abiding adults licensed to carry in other locations should be barred from doing so on college campuses. Several obvious responses come to mind.

First, the experience of states in making it easier to carry concealed weapons hardly recommends extending concealed carry to college campuses. The evidence is mounting that very dangerous people are being given concealed carry licenses, that they are committing egregious violence with guns, and that liberalized concealed carry is associated with more violent crime, not less. Why should we subject our largely peaceful college campuses to a policy that has led to greater danger outside those campuses? After all, Jared Loughner was a legal concealed carrier under Arizona law until he shot 19 people.

Second, college campuses are particularly hazardous environments for widespread gun possession and carrying. They are populated largely by individuals aged 18 to 24, a highly volatile time of life and the age group with the highest incidence of such behaviors as binge drinking and drug use. Moreover, those young people live in dormitories, group houses and other high-density situations in which it is difficult to ensure that a gun always will be in the possession of the person licensed to carry it.

The pressures of college life itself add to the risk, particularly the risk of suicide. Chancellor Francisco Cigarroa of the University of Texas, in an eloquent letter to Governor Rick Perry opposing concealed carry on campus, cited the concerns of "campus health professionals, who know and deal with the reality of the emotional and psychological pressures of academic life, separation from family, relationships—all pressures that contribute to the harsh reality that suicide is the second leading cause of death among college students."

Finally, don't believe for a minute that the "gun rights" crowd is content to limit campus concealed carry to 21-year-old seniors and grad students. At the same time the gun lobby is pressing the Texas legislature to force Texas universities to allow concealed carry, the NRA is pursuing a lawsuit to strike down, as a violation of the Second Amendment, the Texas law setting 21 as the minimum age to carry concealed. If the NRA gets its way, it will be freshmen and all other students who will be eligible to carry loaded guns on campus.

Students are standing with their professors and administrators in resisting laws forcing campuses to accept guns. The student government at the University of Texas has come out foursquare against such laws. Just this week, 57% of the Texas A&M student body voted against guns on campus. These are young people who have grown up around guns, yet understand they have no place on a college campus.

Ultimately, this is not just a campus safety issue. It also is an issue involving the core values served by institutions of higher education. It is difficult to imagine anything more destructive to an environment of academic freedom—in which controversial issues can be passionately debated free of fear and intimidation—than students or professors "strapped" as they participate in those debates.

Students, faculty and administrators get it. Do our lawmakers?

Annotations (right margin):

Major supporting point: The argument that people who can carry guns should be able to carry them on campus is flawed.

Counterargument

Refutation—reason 1: Concealed carry licenses result in more violence, not less.

Refutation—reason 2: College campuses are more hazardous environments for carrying guns.

Refutation—reason 3: Suicide, in particular, might become more prevalent on college campuses.

Refutation—reason 4: Allowing this action will lead to even more extreme gun laws.

Major supporting point: Students agree that guns on campus won't solve the problem.

Major supporting point: This is an education issue, not a gun rights issue.

Conclusion

PRACTICE ● Analyzing an Argument Text

Using a separate sheet, answer the following questions about "Keep Guns Off Campus" by Dennis Henigan.

1. Is this essay's thesis statement (the writer's claim) stated or implied? If it is stated, write out the sentence, and if it is implied, write it in your own words.

2. Henigan devotes a significant portion of his essay to the opposing argument—that guns should be allowed on campus. Why? Explain your answer.

3. Henigan's major supporting points consist of refutations of the counterargument and his own supporting reasons. Which type of support—refuting the counterarguments or providing his own reasons—do you find most effective? Why?

4. Henigan's conclusion paragraph is extremely short. Do you think it was an effective way to conclude his essay? Why or why not?

Connect IRW Power of Process Assignment: See the IM for a list of readings in PoP students can use to analyze argument texts. The Connect IRW *Common Places* Master Course contains pre-loaded PoP assignments that require students to analyze argument essays.

1. The thesis statement is implied, but the title states it: We should keep guns off campus.

2. Part of making his case is showing how the ideas proposed by the opposition are wrong.

3. Answers will vary.

4. Answers will vary.

USING ARGUMENT IN YOUR WRITING

When you have an assignment to write a persuasive essay, you will need to use the argument text pattern. Follow these guidelines.

1. Make sure your topic is an arguable topic. The primary test is to state the topic in the form of a question and then ask whether the answer to that question is debatable. If the answer is debatable, your topic is probably suitable for an essay employing the argument text pattern.

2. Prewrite to determine what your claim will be, and write a thesis statement. Once you have a thesis statement, you can come up with the best kind of support.

3. Analyze your audience before you construct reasons for your claim. Audience awareness is crucial in determining the kinds of arguments that are likely to persuade an audience and the kinds that are likely to fail. Use these principles to think through your audience's needs and expectations:

- **Write for a diverse audience.** Imagine your audience will contain people who hold a variety of viewpoints, some who agree with you and some who do not. Imagine your audience to be composed of people from various backgrounds, of various ages, of various ethnicities, and so on. For example, if you are trying to convince your audience that women should not serve in active military combat, you should keep in mind that approximately 50 percent of readers will be female. If your thesis is likely to make your audience defensive, it is especially important to word your thoughts carefully and respectfully. It is never appropriate to include profanity or remarks that are racist or sexist or that show disrespect for those who are older or who have disabilities. Showing respect to your audience is key. The technique used by some radio and television hosts of making provocative and biased statements in the guise of "argument" may earn them high entertainment ratings and income, but it is not appropriate or useful in academic argument or in any argument that seeks to find meaningful solutions to problems.

- **Think about the kinds of evidence your audience might find convincing.** Many types of evidence can be used in argument papers: statistics, stories, analogies, facts, studies, explanations of causes and effects, definitions, and predictions. If you are writing an essay for a history professor, it is probably important to use relevant facts, details, and maybe even stories. If you are writing for a general audience, use research that your audience can easily understand. Evidence such as studies, quotes from authorities in the field, and logical explanations of cause and effect can be effective in supporting your thesis. Remember that you will probably have a lot of evidence to choose from as you write your paper. Select only evidence that you think will be effective for your audience.

- **Always imagine that you are writing for a skeptical audience.** Imagine that as they study your paper, your readers are muttering, "Where's the evidence?" or "I disagree" or "Prove it!" Make sure you anticipate the audience's doubts and address them in your paper. Another way to be mindful of your audience's doubts is to be fully aware of the opposing position. If you are arguing for random drug testing in the workplace, for example, you should be fully aware of all the reasons against workplace drug testing. In your paper, you can address the reasons that opponents would offer and then refute them.
- **Keep in mind that your audience is interested in hearing your thesis and your evidence, but your audience also wants to think that you—as a writer—are credible and believable.** Your readers will be judging not only your argument but also *you*. To come across as knowledgeable and competent to a general audience, you must ensure that your paper is written in standard English, conforms to an acceptable format, and demonstrates that you have done the reading necessary to know what you are talking about. Additionally, your argument should show that you are fair to the opposing side. You can demonstrate this fairness by thoroughly understanding the opposing argument and by showing respect to those who advocate it.

4. Identify the reasons you will use to support your claim. List all the reasons you can think of, and analyze each one. Which ones will the opposing side easily refute? Which ones are the most logical? Which, if any, might elicit a positive emotional response from readers? Determine the best reasons and then work on finding support to explain and develop those reasons fully.

5. Analyze counterarguments, and plan how you will refute them. In many argument essays you will find a counterargument (the opposing viewpoint). To show you understand the argument of the other side, your essay can include the arguments of the opposing side and your objections to those arguments.

In professional essays, writers use counterarguments for a variety of reasons. First, by acknowledging the strengths of the opposing argument, they establish goodwill, the sense that they are fair-minded and are giving credit to the valid points of their opponents. Second, explaining a counterargument shows that a writer has carefully listened to the opposing viewpoint. An argument can be fair only when both parties actually listen to each other and consider each other's point of view. Third, knowing the best points of the counterargument enables writers to craft an argument that is effective because they know the points they need to refute. This strategy is similar to the way football coaches and players think. If you can anticipate the play the opposing team will make, you can construct a good counterstrategy.

One way to use argument successfully is to fully understand the *best* arguments of the opposing position. Suppose you strongly believe that gun control laws should be strengthened. When you feel strongly about an issue, it's easy to not really hear the opposing argument. But hearing the opposing argument is not only important; it's absolutely necessary. If you cannot address the opposing argument, point by point, and show why your position is superior, you will not be able to write a convincing essay.

6. Create a simple outline for your argument essay. Determine the order in which you will present each reason and the supporting details needed to develop each reason. If you plan to include counterarguments and refute them, use your outline to note where these elements will occur in your essay.

AVOIDING COMMON LOGICAL ERRORS

It is important to use logical reasons when you construct an argument, but it can be easy to make logical errors. Avoid the following logical errors in your writing.

Faulty Causes or Effects

You cannot say that X caused Y without having some proof. Imagine that your town recently elected a new mayor. In the two years she has been in office, the unemployment rate in your city has increased. It is illogical to claim that X (electing the new mayor) caused Y (the increase in unemployment). Maybe these two things were a coincidence. Unless you have additional information to prove that X caused Y, it is unfair and illogical to make that claim.

You cannot say that if we do action X, then Y will happen, unless you have good evidence. Some people create fear-inducing predictions to convince others of a point of view. For example, a parent who wants her son to go to college might say that if he does not go to college (X), he will end up jobless and homeless (Y). Does she have proof for that prediction? No. She says it to scare her son into believing her point that every successful person goes to college. Making a prediction without enough evidence to do so is a logical error.

Teaching Resources: See the PPT "Avoiding Logical Errors." See also the exercise "Logical Errors Worksheet."

Faulty Generalizations

A *generalization* is a statement made about an entire group or class, such as "All horses are animals." Generalizations based on evidence can be fair, but unsubstantiated generalizations are often faulty. For example, consider this statement: women are better chefs than men. Such a generalization is simply not logical. Some women may be better chefs than some men, but it does not follow that all women are better chefs than all men.

Almost any broad statement about a racial, ethnic, socioeconomic, or gender group will result in a generalization that is unfair. Generalizations are commonly used incorrectly in two specific ways: making a statement based on small samples and unfairly representing the opponent's viewpoint.

Generalizations Based on Small Samples

Assume that you had a BXC smartphone and that it performed very poorly. You cannot logically claim that BXC smartphones are low quality because you have only *one* piece of evidence—one phone. Your experience with one sample (one BXC smartphone) is too limited for you to draw conclusions about BXC phones. What if BXC produced two million smartphones and yours was the only one that had problems? Since you do not know the data about the larger group, it is illogical to make a generalization about BXC smartphones.

Unfair Representations of Your Opponent

Imagine reading an argument against gun control in which the writer says people who want guns to be more widely available do not care about human life and want to be able to kill people. This kind of error is unfair because it relies on a stereotype, rather than evidence, about gun rights proponents. It is also unfair because it misrepresents the argument of the group.

Faulty Analogies

One way that people often make a point is by making a comparison. In the study of argument, comparisons are called *analogies*. Here are some examples of analogies.

- Comparing marijuana to alcohol to support an argument that marijuana should be legal
- Comparing the leader of a country to Hitler to support an argument that war against the leader's country is a good idea

- Comparing a current situation—like a recession—to a situation in the past to support an argument that we need to take X or Y action

Analogies can often clarify ideas for readers. It is acceptable to use analogies as long as the two things being compared are similar enough to support the point being made. By definition, the two things being compared in an analogy are different. The critical question is, how different are they?

It would not be fair, for example, for a professor to expect her freshmen writing students to write like students in a senior-level advanced writing course. The analogy between those two groups would be illogical. Neither is it fair to make a comparison like this: young people can serve in the military at age 18, so they should be able to drink at age 18. The assumption is that serving in the military is similar to drinking alcohol. Is it? In what ways are those two things similar? In the military, 18-year-olds are heavily supervised and trained. They can serve in the military because of this training. Are 18-year-olds who want to drink going to be supervised as they drink and trained in the safety and health principles that govern responsible drinking? Probably not. Thus, the comparison of these two things is not logical.

PRACTICE ● Using Argument in Your Writing

1. Consider the following list of topics for an essay using the argument text pattern. For each one, decide whether it is an arguable issue. If it is not an arguable issue, refocus the topic so that it becomes arguable.

   a. The need to make adoptions more affordable

   b. Why people should be organ donors

   c. What diabetes is and how it is treated

   d. Why a missile defense program is a bad idea for the United States

   e. The history of yoga

   f. How we can improve driver's education programs

2. Choose one of the following questions, and use it as the basis for an essay using the argument text pattern.

   a. Do Americans value entertainment more than education?

   b. What are the principles of socialism? Once you learn what they are, judge for yourself: Is socialism an undesirable form of government? Make an argument to prove your point.

   c. Do group projects constitute an effective method for teaching students? Do they really help students learn?

   d. Should all children be required to learn to read music?

   e. Should airline pilots be allowed to carry guns?

   f. Should public school teachers be allowed to carry guns?

   g. Should parents enter their children in beauty pageants?

Connect IRW Writing Assignment: Set up the Practice assignments in Connect IRW to give students access to peer review tools. When you set up the assignment, you can create a rubric for easier grading. These assignments are pre-loaded in the Connect IRW *Common Places* Master Course.

See the IM for additional source-based essay argument assignments.

1 a. Arguable issue.

   b. Arguable issue.

   c. Possible refocus: Are current treatment strategies for diabetes the best treatments available?

   d. Arguable issue.

   e. Possible refocus: Can yoga reduce anxiety as effectively as anti-anxiety medication can?

   f. Possible refocus: Do driver's education programs need to be improved? If so, how can we improve them?

2. Answers will vary.

GRAMMAR FOCUS — Passive and Active Voice

Consider this: If you were a prosecutor making the case that a defendant is guilty, which of these sentences would best serve your argument?

A. The defendant <u>threw</u> the woman to the ground and <u>grabbed</u> her purse.

B. The woman <u>was thrown</u> to the ground, and her purse <u>was grabbed</u>.

Sentence A is a direct statement that assigns blame, and it clearly tells us that a particular person (the defendant) did the crime. Sentence B describes the same situation, but it does not tell us *who* did the throwing and grabbing. It does not assign responsibility for the action. Most readers would find sentence A, which is in the active voice, more persuasive than sentence B, which is in the passive voice.

Voice is one way to describe verbs in a sentence. If a verb is in the **active voice,** the verb's subject (underlined in the following example) *performs* the action.

Example: <u>Tasha</u> threw the javelin.

Tasha—the subject of the sentence—is clearly the doer of the action; she was the one who did the throwing.

If a verb is in the **passive voice,** its subject (underlined below) *receives* the action.

Example: The <u>javelin</u> was thrown by Tasha.

The subject, *javelin,* is not doing the action; rather the javelin is being acted upon. It is the recipient of the action. The sentence includes *by Tasha,* so we know who threw the javelin. However, because the doer of the action is not the subject, the sentence has less impact.

Generally, the active voice is best for most writing. Sentences in the active voice are usually more straightforward and lively than those in the passive voice.

There are times, however, when you may want to use passive instead of active voice.

1. USE PASSIVE OR ACTIVE VOICE FOR EMPHASIS

The subject of a sentence is usually the focus of the reader's attention. So, if you want to emphasize a particular element, make that element the subject.

Passive voice: Evidence that hunter-gatherers lived in Texas as far back as 15,500 years ago was recently unearthed by anthropologists.

Emphasizes the newly discovered evidence about prehistory in Texas.

Active voice: Anthropologists recently unearthed evidence that hunter-gatherers lived in Texas as far back as 15,500 years ago.

Emphasizes who discovered the new evidence about prehistory in Texas.

To decide where to put the emphasis in a sentence, imagine that your sentence is answering a question.

Passive voice: Evidence that hunter-gatherers lived in Texas as far back as 15,500 years ago was recently unearthed by anthropologists.

Answers this question: What was recently discovered about prehistory in Texas?

Active voice: Anthropologists recently unearthed evidence that hunter-gatherers lived in Texas as far back as 15,500 years ago.

Answers this question: Who recently discovered new evidence about prehistory in Texas?

(continued)

2. USE PASSIVE OR ACTIVE VOICE TO EVADE OR INDICATE RESPONSIBILITY

The passive voice can conceal or deemphasize responsibility for an action. For that reason, it is sometimes used in controversial or politically sensitive writing.

Passive voice: During those decades, many Indian children were forcibly removed from their families.

Active voice: During those decades, the federal government forcibly removed many Indian children from their families.

3. USE THE PASSIVE VOICE WHEN THE DOER IS UNKNOWN OR ASSUMED

When readers will presumably know who the doer is, the passive voice allows you to write a more concise sentence.

Passive voice: The new song was written, arranged, recorded, and produced in a matter of months.

Active voice: In a matter of months, the songwriter wrote the new song, the arranger arranged it, the singer recorded it, and the recording studio produced it.

Because it is not necessary to spell out all the doers of various actions, as in the active voice sentence, the passive voice allows the writer to create a more concise sentence.

A RELATED ISSUE: STARTING SENTENCES WITH *There is/was* AND *It is/was*

When writers are composing a first draft, they often resort to using *There is/was* and *It is/was* to begin sentences. Sometimes using these expressions makes it easy to get thoughts down in sentence form. But with few exceptions, these expressions can diminish the quality of the writing. The revision stage is a good time to rewrite these sentences for greater impact. Consider these examples.

Acceptable: There is evidence that high-quality early childhood programs can have a positive effect on the health of adults years later.

Better: Evidence shows that high-quality early childhood programs can have a positive effect on the health of adults years later.

Better: High-quality early childhood programs can have a positive effect on the health of adults years later, according to some evidence.

When you see a sentence in your writing that begins with *There is/are* or *It is/was,* ask yourself, "What is important in this sentence? What do I want to emphasize?"

Sentences beginning with *There is/are* or *It is/was* are grammatically correct, but they are weak. With some effort they can be transformed into sentences that can more effectively communicate your ideas to readers.

SENTENCE COMBINING

In the example that follows, notice how the short sentences are combined into longer sentences that employ active voice.

Ideas to combine:

- That the design was flawed was well known by the company.

- Documentation of the flaw was made before the car seats were manufactured.

- Negligence is what caused the car seats to be manufactured in such a way.

Encourage students to search for *There is/are* and *It is/was* in their writing and see if each occurrence can be reworded.

(continued)

Combined using active voice: The company was negligent when it manufactured the car seats. Even though it knew the design was flawed, the company manufactured the car seats anyway.

EXERCISES

Combine each set of sentences into longer, smoother sentences, and use active voice when appropriate.

Answers will vary. Sample answers are provided.

1. Ideas to combine:

- The old house was inspected by the landlord.

- It was inspected by him after the flood.

- The flooring had been warped by the floodwaters.

- However, the frame of the house had been spared.

- The house was still in good condition.

   Answer: The landlord inspected the old house after the flood. Although the floodwaters had warped the flooring, they had spared the house's frame. The house was still in good condition.

2. Ideas to combine:

- Children should be taught problem-solving skills.

- Critical thinking skills can be developed by the teaching of problem solving.

- There is a true sense of accomplishment that can be felt by children who can solve problems.

   Answer: Learning to solve problems helps children develop critical thinking skills and feel a true sense of accomplishment.

3. Ideas to combine:

- One serious disease is diabetes.

- An increased risk of heart disease can be a result of diabetes.

- An increase in the risk of stroke can be caused by diabetes.

- Eye problems can be caused by diabetes.

- It is known that nerve damage can occur.

- Foot or leg amputations can be caused by complications of diabetes.

   Answer: Diabetes is a serious disease that can result in an increased risk of heart attack and stroke. Additionally, diabetes can cause eye problems and nerve damage. Complications of diabetes can result in foot or leg amputations.

Skill at organizing documents can transfer directly to the skill of organizing the tasks, events, and materials required in a wide range of careers and is essential in fields such as paralegal work.

Organizing, Drafting, and Summarizing

Have you ever watched a movie that presents plot events in a jumbled order? For example, a movie may start with a dramatic scene—such as a standoff between good guys and bad guys—and then loop back in time to provide the backstory, the information that helps viewers understand the standoff. Or perhaps you have seen a movie that *seems* to be taking place in the present, but at the end of the film you learn that the actions were only a dream. Film-makers make very intentional choices about the order in which they present scenes, and these choices can have dramatic effects on viewers.

Writers also carefully select the order in which they present information. Becoming more aware of the ordering strategies other writers use will help you comprehend the texts you read and will enable you to experiment with these strategies when you write your own essays.

A careful reading of a text can also help you record the writer's ideas in a detailed outline or a graphic organizer, which you can use to write an accurate summary. Many students find that a crucial study skill is to write outlines and summaries of the texts they study. A related skill—writing a paraphrase—also requires a careful, close reading of a text. In this chapter you will have the opportunity to hone these skills.

CHAPTER OBJECTIVES

After completing this chapter, students will be able to do the following:

- **Identify common strategies for ordering information.**
- **Use information-ordering strategies in writing.**
- **Use outlines and graphic organizers to analyze a text's organization.**
- **Use outlines to draft essays.**
- **Use outlines to write detailed and brief summaries.**
- **Write paraphrases.**

Connect IRW LearnSmart Achieve: Assign the topics "Recognizing and Applying Organizational Structures" for adaptive learning to accompany the chapter.

Teaching Resources: See the Chapter Quiz.

IDENTIFYING COMMON STRATEGIES FOR ORDERING INFORMATION

As you analyze texts, notice the choices writers make about the order in which they present information. In general, when we talk about the order of information, we are referring to where writers place the thesis statement and the major supporting points. Three common strategies for ordering information are to use order of importance, chronological order, and spatial order.

Order of Importance

Writers use **order of importance** to organize reasons, concepts, and general information. They consider the effect on readers when deciding whether to place the most important item first or last. Presenting the most important major supporting point first immediately alerts readers to the point's significance for the thesis statement. Placing the most important major supporting point last can also be effective because this point will be fresh in the minds of readers as they finish the text.

In the following example, the writer places the most important major supporting point last to emphasize its value. Note also that placing a major supporting point last in the thesis statement gives it more emphasis than the other points.

Order of Importance Organization in an Essay

INTRODUCTION

Introduction paragraph

Thesis statement: Sibling rivalry is good for children because it promotes better listening skills, better social skills, increased problem-solving skills, and increased self-control.

BODY

Topic sentence for major supporting point 1: One good thing about sibling rivalry is that it promotes better listening skills.

Topic sentence for major supporting point 2: Children who fight with siblings also have better social skills than children who do not.

Topic sentence for major supporting point 3: Even more significantly, sibling rivalry helps children develop problem-solving skills.

Topic sentence for major supporting point 4: Most importantly, children who fight with siblings have greater self-control than children who do not.

CONCLUSION

Conclusion paragraph

Writers also use order of importance to determine where to place information in mixed-pattern essays. The main objective of ordering is to present the information in such a way that readers can more easily follow it. For example, if you are writing an informative essay to help readers understand what a tsunami is and what it can do, starting with a definition of *tsunami* will be helpful. Readers might gain a clearer understanding if you compare tsunamis with other types of destructive natural events, such as hurricanes, tornadoes, and avalanches. This information could be followed by a discussion of the causes and effects of tsunamis, and you might end the essay with the most important supporting point—the most destructive effects of tsunamis—as the simple outline about tsunamis on the next page shows.

Connect IRW Power of Process Assignment: See the Instructor's Manual (IM) for a list of readings in Power of Process that use these three ordering strategies. Students can analyze and annotate the strategies using the Power of Process wheel.

See pre-loaded PoP assignments that require students to analyze ordering strategies in the Connect IRW *Common Places* Master Course.

Order of Importance Organization in a Mixed-Pattern Essay

INTRODUCTION

Introduction paragraph

Thesis statement: Tsunamis are among the most destructive natural events in the world.

BODY

Paragraph 2: Definition of *tsunami*

Paragraph 3: Comparison of tsunamis with other destructive natural events (use examples)

Paragraph 4: What causes tsunamis

Paragraph 5: Some effects of tsunamis

Paragraph 6: Most destructive effects of tsunamis

CONCLUSION

Conclusion paragraph: Better warning systems are being developed.

Chronological Order

Chronological order uses time or sequence to organize ideas. Events are usually presented in chronological order; steps in a process are presented sequentially. Notice that in the following simple outline, the stages of training for medical doctors are discussed in the order in which they occur—that is, chronologically.

Chronological Order Organization in an Essay

INTRODUCTION

Introduction paragraph

Thesis statement: The three stages of training for medical doctors are medical school, internship, and residency.

BODY

Paragraph 2: Medical school

Paragraph 3: Internship

Paragraph 4: Residency

CONCLUSION

Conclusion paragraph

Spatial Order

Spatial order uses the physical position of objects to organize ideas. Many descriptive passages use spatial organization, as the example on the next page shows. Notice how prepositional phrases (underlined) guide the reader around the cabin's interior.

Spatial Order Organization in a Descriptive Paragraph

The cabin that would be my home for three months needed repair. I walked <u>through the doorway</u>, and <u>to my left</u> I saw an ancient black cookstove. It seemed to be in better condition than anything else in the cabin. <u>Directly above the stove</u> was a hole in the roof about the size of a truck tire. Light streamed in and pooled on the rotted floorboards that had fallen victim to rain, snow, and ice. <u>On the left side</u> of the cabin was an old aluminum cot, its canvas clearly suffering from dry rot. A knee-high pile of trash was heaped <u>in the back corner underneath three shelves next to</u> the only window in the cabin. It would be a long winter.

Transitional Terms for Information-Ordering Strategies

The transitions in the boxes that follow are helpful additions that you can use to identify the order of information in a particular text. You can also use these in your own writing.

TRANSITIONS FOR ORDER OF IMPORTANCE	TRANSITIONS FOR CHRONOLOGICAL ORDER	TRANSITIONS FOR SPATIAL ORDER
first, second, third, significantly, more significantly, most significantly, importantly, more importantly, most importantly, above all, of less significance, of less importance	first, second, third, before, to begin, to continue, during, next, while, until, when, afterward, finally, to conclude	to the right, to the left, above, below, inside, outside, under, beneath, behind, around, beside, next to, adjacent, joining, continuing around, in front of, in back of

By being aware of the ordering strategy a writer uses, you can more effectively understand a passage, the text pattern or patterns being used, and the organization of the content.

PRACTICE ① Identifying Ordering Strategies

On the basis of the transitions and content in each passage below, identify the order of arrangement the author has used. Use *OI* for order of importance, *CO* for chronological order, and *SO* for spatial order.

CO **1.** In April 1952, my father lost his job. He became depressed, and the entire summer, he sat on the front porch smoking cigarettes and barely talking. Mother could do little to console him, for he snapped at anyone who dared conversation. In August of that year, I turned six years old.

OI **2.** Perhaps the most significant cause of the war was famine and starvation. The people had reached a point of desperation. There was not even enough food to steal from the wealthy. Disenchantment with the priest's advice—while not as significant as the incessant hunger—was prevalent. The priest's assurances of better days to come were hollow utterances in a world of deprivation and despair.

SO **3.** The top floor of the building was full of windows overlooking the bay. The view was splendid. To the left was the Golden Gate Bridge, resplendent in the morning sun. In the distance was Mount Tamalpais's peak.

USING INFORMATION-ORDERING STRATEGIES IN YOUR WRITING

Making intentional decisions about the order in which you present ideas will help you write more clearly and effectively. To select an appropriate ordering strategy for the type of information you are providing, keep the following factors in mind.

Uses for Organizing Strategies

ORDER OF IMPORTANCE	CHRONOLOGICAL ORDER	SPATIAL ORDER
• Reasons • Classifications (types) • Comparison-contrast information • Causes and effects	• Historical information • Narratives • Processes • Stages or steps • Causes and effects	• Descriptions

In your essay, be sure to present your points in the same order in which they occur in your thesis statement. For example, earlier in the chapter, an example of chronological order contained this thesis statement:

> The three stages of training for medical doctors are medical school, internship, and residency.

In the body paragraphs, the writer should discuss these stages in the order in which they appear in the thesis statement.

PRACTICE ② Using Order of Importance, Chronological Order, and Spatial Order

Complete the following paragraph-writing activities.

1. Order of importance: Write a paragraph in which you present the three most important priorities in your life. Put the most important priority last. Use appropriate transitions.

2. Chronological order: Write a paragraph in which you describe an event, such as what happened during a recent family celebration, or a process that follows a particular sequence, such as how to change a flat tire.

3. Spatial order: Write a paragraph in which you describe your kitchen. Use appropriate transitions.

Answers will vary.

An effective learning activity is to have pairs of students trade their spatial descriptions with each other. Tell students to read their partner's paper and, based on the details, draw the kitchen that is described. Each student should then evaluate the accuracy of the partner's drawing and reassess his or her own description.

USING OUTLINES AND GRAPHIC ORGANIZERS TO ANALYZE A TEXT'S ORGANIZATION

An outline can be helpful to you as a reader and as a writer. As a reader, an outline helps you understand the organization of a text and the relationships among ideas in the text. It equips you with everything you need to write a good summary of the reading. As a writer, an outline helps you determine where to place support and how to organize your ideas.

Creating Outlines to Analyze Organization

There is no one-size-fits-all pattern of organization that works for every text. However, most texts do have three components: an introduction, a body, and a conclusion. The number of paragraphs in these three components can vary. Some writers even offer three or four paragraphs of introductory material before getting to the main idea. When you outline a text, be aware that writers do not always place information in the order you expect.

To write an outline for a text you are reading, you need to find the writer's main idea and determine the major supporting points. Sometimes the writer provides clues, such as headings and subheadings. When you see them, notice the differences in size, style, and color. For example, in a textbook on business management and **entrepreneurialism**, chapter titles are large and always appear at the top of a page, main headings appear in green, subheadings are smaller than main headings and appear in blue, and sub-subheadings are in black. As you study the example below, think about what information each section of the text might present.

Teaching Resources: See the IM for a list of Power of Process readings that demonstrate the diverse ways writers organize introductions, body paragraphs, and conclusions. See the Connect IRW *Common Places* Master Course for pre-loaded assignments to analyze PoP readings with diverse organizational strategies.

Vocabulary Collection Word:
entrepreneur

Your in-context definition:

_____

_____

A dictionary definition:

_____

_____

CHAPTER 4

Starting a Business

Entrepreneurialism

PERSONAL TRAITS OF ENTREPRENEURS

Entrepreneurs Are Visionary
Entrepreneurs Are Personable
Entrepreneurs Are Highly Motivated
Entrepreneurs Are Researchers

In a text that does not contain headings and subheadings, you can still distinguish the elements of importance and determine their relationship to one another. The annotations in the following essay identify the elements a reader would use to construct an outline.

How Delaying Gratification Predicts Future Success
by Kari Gardner

"I want what I want, and I want it *now.*" We live in a world in which instant gratification is not merely desired: it's expected. If Internet access is delayed for even a few seconds, we are frustrated. If our fast food is not fast enough, we are miffed, and so it goes.

What is required in these circumstances is *delayed gratification*, the ability to postpone the fulfillment of an immediate desire in order to obtain a more substantial reward in the future. To put it more informally, delayed gratification means putting off having something now so you can get something better later on.

Introduction: examples of how people have trouble delaying gratification

Definition

(continued)

Educators and psychologists alike say that being able to tolerate delayed gratification is an extremely valuable skill. People who can put off immediate gratification are more likely to have what it takes to be successful in the important things in life. And there is research to support that opinion.

In the late 1960s and early 1970s, psychologists at Stanford University (led by Walter Mischel) performed a series of studies that came to be known as the Marshmallow Experiment. Young children (from four to six years old) were given a large, fluffy marshmallow and were told they could eat the marshmallow now, or they could wait fifteen minutes and get a second marshmallow.

Many of the kids who were able to delay gratification distracted themselves from the marshmallow by covering their eyes with their hands, turning their backs to the treat, kicking the table, and so forth. Other children who successfully delayed eating the marshmallow used their imaginations to reframe the treat as something else. For example, by thinking about the marshmallow as a cloud or by thinking the marshmallow was just a picture of a marshmallow, children were able to resist eating it immediately.

Of course, a significant number of children simply could not wait. Some nibbled on the marshmallow and eventually popped the whole thing into their mouths, and some ate it almost immediately.

In follow-up studies years later, the psychologists determined that the children who were able to wait longer—to postpone their gratification—tended to do substantially better as adults than those children who were less patient. The psychologists based their assessment on the analysis of the test subjects' levels of behavioral problems, drug and alcohol addiction, educational achievement, SAT scores, and other measures. Although recent studies have suggested that the fundamental issue is more complex than simple self-control, the basic point still stands: it is important to learn to tolerate delayed gratification.

Psychological tests are not the only way to demonstrate the importance of delayed gratification. Proof that it pays to put off pleasure is all around us. People who have the patience and willpower to regularly invest even small amounts of money can easily become very wealthy—if they are willing to wait long enough for their money to multiply. Students who seek college degrees earn them by putting off pleasure today for the reward of a degree tomorrow. And athletes who make it to the top know very well the importance of working hard today so that they can perform well tomorrow.

It will always be easier to eat the marshmallow right away, but doing so may not always be the best choice.

Thesis statement

Major supporting point 1 (implied): The Marshmallow Experiment shows that delayed gratification skills lead to more success in life.

Details: focus on how the experiment was set up (process analysis)

Details: focus on what happened in the experiment (cause and effect)

Details: the conclusion drawn from the experiment (explanation)

Major supporting point 2

Details: people who delay gratification to pursue success (examples)

To outline a text, list the main idea (whether stated in a thesis statement, as in this case, or implied), the major supporting points, and the supporting details that follow the major supporting points. When writing an outline, always use quotation marks if you use actual phrases and sentences from the text, as shown in the outline on the next page. Doing so enables you to remember which words are yours and which came from the source.

Simple Outline of "How Delaying Gratification Predicts Future Success" by Kari Gardner

Thesis statement: "People who can put off immediate gratification are more likely to have what it takes to be successful in the important things in life."

Major supporting point 1 (implied): The Marshmallow Experiment shows that delayed gratification skills lead to more success in life.

> **Supporting details:**
> - How the experiment was set up
> - What happened in the experiment
> - The conclusion drawn from the experiment

Major supporting point 2: "Proof that it pays to put off pleasure is all around us."

> **Supporting details:**
> - People who invest
> - Students who graduate
> - Athletes who train

The preceding outline of "How Delaying Gratification Predicts Future Success" is a simple outline. It includes just the minimum amount of information necessary to map the essay. If you need to remember more of the details than a basic outline allows, you can construct an **enhanced** outline by including additional important information, as this example demonstrates (the added information is in *italics*):

Enhanced Outline of "How Delaying Gratification Predicts Future Success" by Kari Gardner

Introduction: Provides examples of how people have trouble tolerating delayed gratification. **Definition** *of delayed gratification: "the ability to postpone the fulfillment of an immediate desire in order to obtain a more substantial reward in the future."*

Thesis statement: "People who can put off immediate gratification are more likely to have what it takes to be successful in the important things in life."

Major supporting point 1 (implied): The Marshmallow Experiment shows that delayed gratification skills lead to more success in life.

> **Supporting details:**
> - How the experiment was set up: *Children were given the option of one marshmallow now or two later.*
> - What happened in the experiment: *Some children waited to eat the marshmallow, and some did not.*
> - The conclusion drawn from the experiment: *Children who waited had more success as adults.*
>   - *Assessment based on behavioral problems, drug and alcohol addiction, educational achievement, SAT scores*

Major supporting point 2: "Proof that it pays to put off pleasure is all around us."

> **Supporting details:**
> - People who invest *(end up wealthy if they wait)*
> - Students who graduate *(put off pleasure today for reward tomorrow)*
> - Athletes who train *(practice today for performance rewards tomorrow)*

Vocabulary Collection Word:
enhanced

Your in-context definition:

_____

_____

A dictionary definition:

_____

_____

Teaching Resources: Several partially completed outlines that go with particular Power of Process readings are available as reproducible exercises. Consider having students fill in the remaining parts of these outlines as a way to kick-start the process of learning to outline.

The enhanced outline has more information than the basic outline, particularly in the supporting details. Practice your outlining skills by completing the following assignment.

Teaching Resources: See Power-Point Presentation (PPT) "How to Write an Enhanced Outline."

PRACTICE 3 Outlining a Brief Reading

Read the following passage, and annotate the thesis statement, major supporting points, and supporting details. Then, on a separate sheet, create a simple outline for the reading.

Achieving Optimum Fitness

YOUR ANNOTATIONS

Physical activities play an important role in fitness. Many people participate in endurance exercises, such as walking, running, and swimming, but optimum fitness requires more than endurance activities. Strength training and flexibility development are also important. Maximum fitness can be achieved by performing these three types of exercises regularly.

Thesis statement

Exercises such as brisk walking, jogging, and swimming help athletes develop endurance. Endurance training is accomplished by participating in aerobic activities for an extended period of time. Biking, dancing, and yard work (for example, pushing a lawnmower or raking leaves) also qualify as endurance training. These activities involve relatively low-intensity actions performed for extended periods of time. Twenty minutes of continuous activity is typically considered the minimum length of time necessary for significant improvement in endurance. The intensity should be between 60 and 85 percent of maximum heart rate.

Major supporting point 1

Supporting details

Generally speaking, endurance exercises require repeated movement of the large muscles in the arms, legs, or hips. These movements are required to get one's heart pumping rapidly. The principal positive effects of endurance exercise are to the cardiovascular system. (That's why endurance training is also referred to as *cardio*.) Endurance exercise keeps the heart, lungs, and circulatory system healthy and improves overall fitness. As a result, doing cardio helps delay or prevent many diseases that are common in older adults, such as diabetes and heart disease. In addition, building endurance makes it easier to carry out many everyday activities, such as climbing stairs. A bonus of moderate to intense endurance exercise is that the body releases endorphins, natural painkillers that promote an increased sense of well-being.

More supporting details

Strength training is another important activity for fitness. Sometimes called *resistance training*, strength training involves using muscles against a resistant force. The muscles are said to be "under load." Most often the resistance is the function of gravity and weights, although other methods are available (for example, strong elastic bands, and pneumatic/hydraulic cylinders). "Free weights" include barbells and dumbbells with heavy disks attached. Weight machines operate on the same property of gravity.

Major supporting point 2

Supporting details

Lifting weights actually causes microdamage to muscles, which become stronger when they rebuild themselves. At least one day of rest between exercising any particular muscle group is recommended. When properly performed, strength training provides significant benefits in addition to an increase in muscle strength and mass. The connective tissues of the musculoskeletal system—tendons and ligaments—are also strengthened. That is very significant for joint stability, particularly as people age. Weight training also increases bone strength and density, which is very important in

More supporting details

(continued)

the prevention of osteoporosis. An increase in HDL ("good") cholesterol has been linked to resistance training. Increased muscle mass leads to a higher metabolic rate; that means that a person with a muscular body is burning more calories while resting than a person with less muscle mass.

<u>The aspect of fitness people are less likely to consider is flexibility.</u> **Nonetheless**, flexibility is very important for daily life as well as for professional competition. Flexibility exercises stretch the muscles, ligaments, and tendons. The result is that the body becomes more limber. Being flexible gives a person more freedom of movement for other exercises as well as for everyday activities. Stretching exercises, when done properly, assist with posture by balancing the tension placed across the joint by the muscles that cross it. Proper posture minimizes stress and maximizes the strength of all joint movements. Many cases of chronic lower back pain are actually a function of a lack of limberness in the upper legs and in the lower back.

Perhaps the form of exercise most specifically focused on flexibility is yoga. In addition to yoga's obvious contribution to limberness, many practitioners find that it has a positive psychological effect. (Of course, that can be said for the first two types of exercise as well!) Those who regularly practice yoga report that they experience a reduction in anxiety, stress, depression, chronic pain, and sleep difficulties. Put positively, they report a higher general sense of well-being.

A person who engages regularly in endurance exercises, strength training, and flexibility development will become fit. Adding a healthy diet, adequate water intake, and sound sleeping patterns to these three physical activities will result in an optimum level of health and fitness.

Major supporting point 3

Vocabulary Collection Word:
nonetheless

Your in-context definition:
_____
_____

A dictionary definition:
_____
_____

Supporting details

More supporting details

CREATING GRAPHIC ORGANIZERS TO ANALYZE ORGANIZATION

A **graphic organizer** is a visual map that displays much of the same information as an outline. Graphic organizers are designed to show relationships among ideas. Some people find that working with graphic organizers is easier than working with outlines.

Many word-processing programs have a feature, like SmartArt in *Microsoft Word*, that offers templates for graphic organizers. However, you can also draw a graphic organizer by hand.

To create a graphic organizer, begin by drawing a box at the top of the page. The box should be as wide as your sheet of paper because it will form the canopy for all the boxes that follow. As you reread your text, find what you think is the main idea or thesis statement, and write it inside the box. Remember to use quotation marks if you are using a direct quote.

Consider suggesting that students use different colors to distinguish the "levels" of the boxes in a graphic organizer.

> "People who can put off immediate gratification are more likely to have what it takes to be successful in the important things in life."

Next, look for a major supporting point—an idea that directly proves the main point. Draw a narrower box with this information in it, and connect it to the main box, as shown on the next page.

"People who can put off immediate gratification are more likely to have what it takes to be successful in the important things in life."

The Marshmallow Experiment shows that delayed gratification skills lead to more success in life.

As you come across details, add more boxes, connecting the new boxes to the ideas that they support. When you find new major supporting points that directly prove the main idea, add boxes for those too. Step back and look at the graphic organizer. Does the arrangement of boxes seem logical to you, with lesser ideas supporting greater ideas? If not, rearrange the boxes so that they better reflect a logical organization. As a final step, you might find it helpful to label the boxes that contain the thesis statement and the major supporting point.

Consider explaining to students that their first draft of a graphic organizer will likely contain cross-outs, arrows, and other editing marks because it is a work in progress.

Thesis statement: "People who can put off immediate gratification are more likely to have what it takes to be successful in the important things in life."

Major supporting point 1: The Marshmallow Experiment shows that delayed gratification skills lead to more success in life.

Major supporting point 2: "Proof that it pays to put off pleasure is all around us."

How it was set up

What happened

Conclusion drawn

People who invest

Students who graduate

Athletes who train

Teaching Resources: See the available, reproducible graphic organizer exercises.

Outlines and graphic organizers illustrate the *logic* of a text. Sometimes, though, a writer will jump around in presenting ideas and information. For example, to arouse readers' interest in what lies ahead, a writer may start an essay with a detail for a point that will come later on in the text. In your graphic organizer, be sure to attach the detail to the point that it supports even if the detail appears out of order in the text.

USING OUTLINES TO DRAFT ESSAYS

In addition to serving as a tool to help you understand readings, outlines also make drafting your essay easier. The best kind of outline to use for writing is an enhanced outline. It should contain your thesis statement, your main supporting points, and the supporting details you will use to develop each main supporting point. We will follow the process of Ian, a writing student, as he uses an enhanced outline to draft his essay.

Ian is writing an essay to convince his classmates that investing at an early age is wise. He has already used prewriting to generate ideas, has written a thesis statement, has determined his major supporting points, and has developed the supporting details he will use to develop his ideas. Here is the enhanced outline Ian has created for his essay. Notice that he has indicated the source for each quote he uses—an article entitled "Six Misconceptions about Investing Young" by Jean Folger (www.investopedia.com) and a personal communication from Sean Williams, an investment banker he contacted.

Ian's Enhanced Outline

Title: Start with a Penny

Introduction: I'll tell the story of my grandparents, who came to the United States with nothing and ended up having over a million dollars, simply because they have made small deposits into their investment account each week since they were young.

Thesis statement: One of the most important preparations college students can make for the future is to start investing immediately.

Major supporting point 1: Accruing wealth comes from making small investments over a long period of time.

    Support: Explanation of mathematics

- "A person who starts at age 20 and invests $100 per month until age 65 (a total contribution of $54,000) will have more than $200,000 when he or she reaches age 65 assuming a 5% return" (Folger).
- Example of my grandparents (actual amount they invested)

Major supporting point 2: Almost anyone, even college students, can find small amounts of money to invest.

    Support: Definition—"Discretionary income includes money spent on luxury items, vacations and non-essential goods and services" (Folger).

- How to find discretionary income
- How discretionary income adds up (provide explanation)
- Provide examples

Major supporting point 3: Additionally, investing is easy, and starting to invest at a young age will help you get into the habit of investing.

    Support: Explanation about how easy it is to invest

- Example of setting up an investment account
- Example of buying bonds
- Quote from investment company: "Many people have the idea that investing requires a lot of technical knowledge, but it doesn't. All you need to do is come in and talk with an adviser. The process is similar to setting up a savings account" (Williams).

Major supporting point 4: Finally, college students should start investing because they will most likely need the money.

    Support: Social security and retirement plans may not work.

- Quote: "It is difficult to predict where social security will be in future years, and many investors learned the hard way in the last decade that employee-sponsored retirement plans don't always work out" (Folger).
- As you age, expenses increase.
- Examples of expenses

Conclusion: End by telling readers about the relaxing life my grandparents now enjoy (their travels, nice home, etc.) because of their investments.

Because Ian has a wealth of information in his outline—including quotes, stories, and examples—he can start drafting the body paragraphs by writing sentences for each item on his outline. Using an outline to guide you will make the drafting process easier, but you may still find that your outline is incomplete. Once you start drafting, you may think of additional ideas that would make your essay better. You can always add these ideas to your outline and make sure they fit.

The two columns below demonstrate how Ian uses his outline to draft the sentences in the first body paragraph. Ian had planned to devote only one paragraph for each major supporting point. However, as he began writing, he realized that the explanation of how the math of investing works was requiring a lot of space. Thus, he decided to create a new paragraph for the remaining support he wished to discuss.

Ian's First Draft

Accruing wealth comes from making small investments over a long period of time. My grandfather explained the process so that it was very easy to understand. He told me to imagine loaning a friend $10. Because you loaned him the money, he gives you a 10 percent fee ($1) when he repays the loan. Now you have $11 to loan. Your friend borrows the $11, again paying a 10 percent fee. This time the fee is $1.10. When your friend repays the money, you have $12.10. You haven't done anything but loan money to earn the extra $2.10! Now, imagine you keep doing this until you have $200. When you loan out the $200, you get 10 percent, which is $20. You then have $220 to loan. When you loan it out, you earn $22. The amount of interest goes up as the amount of money you have to loan increases.

The reason to invest at a young age is that if you keep reinvesting your profits, you can accumulate a great deal of wealth over a long time. In fact, "a person who starts at age 20 and invests $100 per month until age 65 (a total contribution of $54,000) will have more than $200,000 when he or she reaches age 65 assuming a 5% return" (Folger). As in Folger's example, my grandparents started by investing $20 a month. They probably never thought they would be millionaires in retirement!

Ian's Enhanced Outline

Major supporting point 1: Accruing wealth comes from making small investments over a long period of time.

Support: Explanation of mathematics

[Explanation of mathematics continues]

- "A person who starts at age 20 and invests $100 per month until age 65 (a total contribution of $54,000) will have more than $200,000 when he or she reaches age 65 assuming a 5% return" (Folger).

- Example of my grandparents (actual amount they invested)

As Ian continues to write body paragraphs, he will make decisions like the one he made regarding creating a new paragraph. Good writers constantly review, revise, and rethink their outlines during the drafting process. Don't be afraid to make changes when you believe those changes would make your essay better. Consider the checklist that follows as you draft your own essays:

- Am I using enough support to fully develop the idea?
- Should I break paragraphs (or combine paragraphs)?
- Should I change the order in which I present information?
- When I reread my essay from the beginning, are there places where the ideas seem not to fit together?
- Are there places where I repeat ideas?

These are only some of the considerations to keep in mind during the drafting process. You will analyze your paper in even more depth as you revise it.

PRACTICE 4 Drafting Body Paragraphs from an Outline

Ian's second major supporting point is that college students can find discretionary income—extra money—to invest. Using Ian's prewriting and outline (both below), draft a paragraph or more for this major supporting point. Use a separate sheet for your draft.

IAN'S PREWRITING

Where college students can find extra money:

- Part-time work
- Not having a cell phone (or having only a basic cell phone)
- Not buying cable TV
- Avoiding debt
- Donating plasma
- Using a portion of birthday gifts to invest

IAN'S ENHANCED OUTLINE

Major supporting point 2: Almost anyone, even college students, can find small amounts of money to invest.

Support: Definition—"Discretionary income includes money spent on luxury items, vacations and non-essential goods and services" (Folger).

- How to find discretionary income
- How discretionary income adds up (provide explanation)
- Provide examples

Answers will vary.

Consider having students use discussion as a prewriting method to come up with additional ways of finding extra money to invest.

USING OUTLINES TO WRITE DETAILED AND BRIEF SUMMARIES

In addition to being a tool for understanding texts and for drafting, outlining assists in writing summaries. In both workplace and academic writing, summarizing is an important skill. As an employee, you may be called on to read a work-related report and summarize it for your boss or coworkers. Or you may be given a thick booklet of guidelines and be expected to follow them. Being able to summarize the booklet and extract the most important information will help you follow the guidelines. In college, you will often summarize textbook chapters and other materials.

The Purpose of a Summary

A **summary** is a shortened version of a source. In a summary, you present the main idea and major supporting points of the source in your own words. A summary must be accurate, appropriately focused, and objective. To ensure the accuracy of your summary, you must correctly understand the text you are summarizing. Thus, it is vital that you read, annotate, analyze, and reread the source until you feel confident you understand it.

To give your summary an appropriate focus, you must carefully choose the points from the original source that you wish to emphasize. Specifically, you need to focus on the main idea (or thesis), the major supporting points for the main idea, and any other important ideas presented after—or in conjunction with—the central idea. If you focus on supporting details and neglect the main idea or the major supporting points, then your summary will not give readers an accurate understanding of the source. One way to choose the most important points to focus on is to write an enhanced outline of the source. An enhanced outline will provide the exact content you will need for a summary.

Finally, summaries must be **objective**. Being objective means that you do not express an opinion on the text you are summarizing. Whether you agree or disagree with the source does not matter in a summary: your goal is to simply present the source's ideas in a brief way.

Steps for Writing Summaries

The ten steps listed here will help you write an effective summary. You may occasionally quote directly from the text, but most of the summary should be in your own words.

Step 1: Read and annotate the source.

Spend sufficient time reading and annotating the source material. As always, mark the main idea and major supporting details. Look for the information that supports the major supporting details.

Step 2: Create an enhanced outline.

By creating an enhanced outline, such as the one presented earlier in this chapter on "How Delaying Gratification Predicts Future Success," you will have most of the information you will need to write a summary.

Step 3: Start with bibliographic information.

A helpful way to start a summary is to provide bibliographic information about the source. Bibliographic information includes the following:

- Author's name and credentials, if available
- Title of the source (use quotation marks for an article title; italics for a book title)
- Type of publication (specify *book* or *journal*; use italics for a journal title)
- Publisher and place of publication for a book
- Date of publication (add volume and issue numbers for a journal, if available)

We will follow the process that Jason, a college student, follows to write a summary based on the enhanced outline for "How Delaying Gratification Predicts Future Success" on page 229.

> In 2005, *Prescott Journal of Ideas* published a brief essay called "How Delaying Gratification Predicts Future Success" by Kari Gardner, a professor of education at Hinton University's Graduate School of Education.
>
> The bibliographic information includes the date, the name of the journal (in italics), the title of the article (in quotation marks), and the author's name and credentials.

We could have worded the bibliographic information differently. Following are two alternative opening statements:

In 2005, Kari Gardner, a professor of education at Hinton University's Graduate School of Education, published a brief essay, "How Delaying Gratification Predicts Future Success," in *Prescott Journal of Ideas*.

"How Delaying Gratification Predicts Future Success," by Kari Gardner, a professor of education at Hinton University's Graduate School of Education, was published in *Prescott Journal of Ideas* in 2005.

Vocabulary Collection Word:
objective

Your in-context definition:
_____
_____

A dictionary definition:
_____
_____

Step 4: Write a sentence that tells the reader the topic of the source.

After you read the source, you should have a clear idea of the topic being addressed. Express this topic in one sentence, as Jason did here.

Gardner's essay concerns the issue of delayed gratification.	Source's topic

Step 5: Tell the reader the main idea of the text.

If the thesis statement is explicitly stated in the source, you can quote it directly. If you quote the author's words from the original published source, be sure to note the page on which the words appear. For a source you obtained electronically—such as through your library's online **databases**—you will usually need only the writer's name. Do not use page numbers from a printout of a source, unless the printout shows an exact replica of the article's pages.

    If the writer's thesis statement is implied—not stated directly—you will need to write a sentence that accurately reflects the thesis statement. In her essay, Gardner includes a thesis statement, so Jason quoted the statement directly.

Vocabulary Collection Word:
database

Your in-context definition:
_____
_____

A dictionary definition:
_____
_____

The essay's thesis statement is clear: "People who can put off immediate gratification are more likely to have what it takes to be successful in the important things in life" (Gardner).	Source's thesis. The author's name is included in parentheses after the quote. Notice where the punctuation is placed.

Step 6: Use the writer's major supporting points and supporting details to summarize the body of the text.

This section will probably be the lengthiest part of your summary. Put all of these ideas in your own words. Here is the main part of Jason's summary.

Gardner proves that people who can delay gratification seem to be more successful in life. She discusses the Marshmallow Experiment in which children were given the option of eating one marshmallow immediately or waiting fifteen minutes and getting a second marshmallow. The children who waited for the second marshmallow ended up becoming more successful adults.	Topic sentence Source's first major supporting point Summary of supporting details
Another point Gardner makes about delaying gratification is that people who are able to wait sometimes end up getting benefits. For example, people who invest and are patient can become wealthy. Students who work hard in college can graduate, and athletes who train hard can succeed in their sports.	Source's second major supporting point Summary of supporting details

Step 7: If any of the points need more explanation, add a sentence or two to provide it.

If your reader might not understand a particular supporting point without an explanation, then you must provide it. Read your summary as if you had never read the original source. Are there places where the supporting details need to be explained in more depth? Keep in mind that a summary should be short, so provide explanations only if they are really needed. Jason added information (shown on the next page) to one of the paragraphs in his summary to explain points that might be unclear to the reader.

> She discusses the Marshmallow Experiment in which children were given the option of eating one marshmallow immediately or waiting fifteen minutes and getting a second marshmallow. The children who waited for the second marshmallow ended up becoming more successful adults. They had fewer behavioral problems, less drug and alcohol addiction, greater educational success, and higher SAT scores.

Additional information

Step 8: Discuss any other important points the author makes.

Sometimes sources will include important points that fall outside the main idea and the major supporting points for the main idea. For example, some sources begin by discussing the background of the issue being discussed. Writers sometimes include definitions, alternative points of view, or additional considerations about the topic. If the additional points in a source are important to readers' understanding to the text, include them. In her essay, Gardner provides a definition of *delayed gratification*. Jason decided to include this definition in his summary since understanding this concept is important to the meaning of the text.

> Gardner defines *delayed gratification* as "the ability to postpone the fulfillment of an immediate desire in order to obtain a more substantial reward in the future."

Additional information needed for understanding

Step 9: Tell the reader how the source ends.

A simple but effective way to end a summary is to briefly tell the reader how the writer ends his or her article. Here is the end of Jason's summary.

> Gardner ends her essay with some advice. "It will always be easier to eat the marshmallow right away, but doing so may not always be the best choice."

End of summary

Step 10: Once you have determined the content of your summary, you are ready to write a draft.

Read Jason's completed **detailed summary** on the next page. Notice not only the content but also the formatting. The summary follows MLA style guidelines.

Example of a Detailed Summary

Teaching Resources: See the IM for the APA version of this sample summary.

Alameda 1

Jason Alameda

Dr. Hall

ENGL 1301.33

12 October 2014

A Summary of "How Delaying Gratification Predicts Future Success"

In 2005, *Prescott Journal of Ideas* published a brief essay called "How Delaying Gratification Predicts Future Success" by Kari Gardner, a professor of education at Hinton University's Graduate School of Education.

Gardner's essay concerns the issue of delayed gratification. The essay's thesis statement is clear: "People who can put off immediate gratification are more likely to have what it takes to be successful in the important things in life" (Gardner).

Gardner proves that people who can delay gratification seem to be more successful in life. She discusses the Marshmallow Experiment in which children were given the option of eating one marshmallow immediately or waiting fifteen minutes and getting a second marshmallow. The children who waited for the second marshmallow ended up becoming more successful adults. They had fewer behavioral problems, less drug and alcohol addiction, greater educational success, and higher SAT scores.

Another point Gardner makes about delaying gratification is that people who are able to wait sometimes end up getting benefits. For example, people who invest and are patient can become wealthy.

MLA-style heading

Title, centered

Bibliographic information

Source's topic and thesis

Source's first major supporting point and supporting details

Source's second major supporting point and supporting details

Alameda 2

Students who work hard in college can graduate, and athletes who train hard can succeed in their sports.

Gardner defines *delayed gratification* as "the ability to postpone the fulfillment of an immediate desire in order to obtain a more substantial reward in the future."

Additional background information: definition

Gardner ends her essay with some advice. "It will always be easier to eat the marshmallow right away, but doing so may not always be the best choice."

End of summary

Jason's detailed summary above is about half the length of the original text. Sometimes you will want to write summaries that are much shorter. For example, if you need only a brief reference to Gardner's essay in a paper you are writing, you might want only a few lines of summary. In such cases, it is sufficient to include brief bibliographic data and the writer's main point. Here is an example of a **brief summary.**

Example of a Brief Summary

In her essay entitled "How Delaying Gratification Predicts Future Success," Kari Gardner shows that people who can delay gratification end up more successful than those who cannot.

Whether you write a detailed summary or a brief one, your most important task is to provide an accurate representation of the ideas in the text you are summarizing. Try your hand at writing summaries by completing the following exercise.

PRACTICE 5 Writing Detailed and Brief Summaries

In Practice 3, you created an outline for "Achieving Optimum Fitness." Use your outline to write a detailed summary for the reading. When you are finished with the detailed summary, write a brief summary.

Answers will vary.

WRITING PARAPHRASES

A **paraphrase** is a rewording of a *portion* of a text in your own words to make the meaning of the original text more clear. Paraphrases help you integrate a source's ideas smoothly into your own writing without overusing direct quotations.

While summaries pull out the main ideas and major supporting points from texts, paraphrases focus on clarifying and rewording a particular idea in a text. Another difference between a summary and a paraphrase is that a summary condenses the most important information in a text into a shorter version. A paraphrase, on the other hand, rewords each sentence to help clarify its meaning; thus, a paraphrase will often be as long as the original text.

A paraphrase is similar to a summary in that both must be written in your own words; any wording from the original source must be enclosed in quotation marks and integrated into your own writing. Also, just like a summary, a paraphrase must properly reference the original source.

To write a paraphrase, read the original carefully, and then put it aside. Write what you understand about the original material in your own words. Then check your paraphrase to make sure that it reflects the meaning of the original and that you have not inadvertently used the language of the original without quotation marks. Notice how, in the following paraphrase, the student writer puts into her own words the ideas in the original text, an excerpt from *Selecting a Career in Mental Health*.

ORIGINAL FROM *SELECTING A CAREER IN MENTAL HEALTH* BY CAMILLE ROBERTS	STUDENT'S PARAPHRASE
Psychology is both a science and a profession. As a science, psychology is the study of how people perceive, think, feel, and act; as a profession, it is concerned with predicting how people will act, helping people modify their behavior, and helping organizations, communities, and societies change. Some psychologists focus on research. These professionals conduct experiments and observe human behavior to add to our knowledge about how the mind works. Other psychologists focus on helping people and institutions change their behavior, structure, or functions. They spend time working with individuals and groups of people by analyzing their behaviors and helping them learn to modify their behaviors.	Roberts points out that psychology is a science as well as a profession. The science of psychology covers "how people perceive, think, feel, and act," and it includes research to discover new insights about these elements. Two kinds of psychologists can be identified. First, some psychologists are researchers who spend their time doing experiments and observing people. These psychologists help create information and add to what we already know about how the mind works. The other type of psychologist works directly with people to help them change behaviors that are not working well. This type of psychologist may also work with groups of people to help them change their behaviors.

Remember that you cannot use paraphrased ideas without citing the source. Additionally, if you use any of the source's original language in your paraphrase, you must treat the language as a direct quote and use quotation marks. For example, in the preceding paraphrase, notice that the student includes a direct quotation from the source—in quotation marks—in her second sentence.

PRACTICE 6 Writing a Paraphrase

The following reading about antibiotic resistance is from the Centers for Disease Control and Prevention. Write a paraphrase of this reading.

Antibiotic resistance is a quickly growing, extremely dangerous problem. World health leaders have described antibiotic-resistant bacteria as "nightmare bacteria" that "pose a catastrophic threat" to people in every country in the world. Each year in the United States, at least 2 million people become infected with bacteria that are resistant to antibiotics, and at least 23,000 people die each year as a direct result of these infections. Many more people die from other conditions that were complicated by an antibiotic-resistant infection.

Answers will vary. Here is one possible paraphrase:

The Centers for Disease Control and Prevention warn that antibiotic-resistant bacteria are becoming a major health threat for people around the world. Millions of people succumb to infections that are not easily cured by antibiotics, and many die from the infections or from infection-related causes.

CHAPTER ACTIVITIES

READING AND ANNOTATING

The following passage is from *Mirror for Humanity*, an anthropology textbook by Conrad Phillip Kottak published in 2014. Read and annotate the passage. In particular, identify the thesis statement, the major supporting points, the supporting details, and any other information that would be suitable for an outline, graphic organizer, or summary. If the thesis statement is implied rather than explicit, write it in your own words. When you are finished, answer the questions that follow.

Experiencing Culture: Personal Space and Displays of Affection

by Conrad Phillip Kottak

A few years ago I created and taught a course called Experiencing Culture to American college students in Italy. Students wrote biweekly journals reflecting on the cultural differences they observed between Europeans and Americans. One thing that really struck them was the greater frequency and intensity of PDAs—public displays of affection—between romantic couples in Italy, compared with the United States.

The world's nations and cultures have strikingly different notions about displays of affection and personal space. Cocktail parties in international meeting places such as the United Nations can resemble an elaborate insect mating ritual as diplomats from different countries advance, withdraw, and sidestep. When Americans talk, walk, and dance, they maintain a certain distance from others. Italians or Brazilians, who need less personal space, may interpret such "standoffishness" as a sign of coldness. In conversational pairs, the Italian or Brazilian typically moves in, while the American "instinctively" retreats from a "close talker." Such bodily movements illustrate not instinct, but culture—behavior programmed by years of exposure to a particular cultural tradition.

To what extent are you a product of your particular culture? How much does, and should, your cultural background influence your actions and decisions? Americans may not fully appreciate the power of culture because of the value their culture places on the individual. We have seen that individualism is a distinctive shared value, a feature of American culture, transmitted constantly in our daily lives. In the media, count how many stories focus on individuals versus groups. . . . Certainly we have distinctive features because we are individuals, but we have other distinct attributes because we belong to cultural groups.

To return to the cultural contrast that so impressed my American students in Italy, there are striking contrasts between a national culture (American) that tends to be reserved about displays of physical affection and national cultures in which the opposite is true. Brazilians approach, touch, and kiss one another much more frequently than North Americans do. Middle-class Brazilians teach their kids—both boys and girls—to kiss (on the cheek, two or three times, coming and going) every adult relative they ever see. Given the size of Brazilian extended families, this can mean hundreds of people. Women continue kissing all those people throughout their lives. Until they are adolescents, boys kiss all adult relatives. Men typically continue to kiss female relatives and friends, as well as their fathers and uncles throughout their lives.

Do you kiss your father? Your uncle? Your grandfather? How about your mother, aunt, or grandmother? The answer to these questions may differ between men and

YOUR ANNOTATIONS

Lexile: 1170L

Vocabulary Collection Word:
attribute

Your in-context definition:
_____
_____

A dictionary definition:
_____
_____

women, and for male and female relatives. Culture can help us to make sense of these differences. In America, a cultural homophobia (fear of homosexuality) may prevent American men from engaging in displays of affection with other men. Similarly, American girls typically are encouraged to show affection; this is less true for boys.

However, culture is not static. Sarah Kershaw (2009) describes a recent surge of teenage hugging behavior in American schools. Concerned about potential sexual harassment issues, parents and school officials remain suspicious of such PDAs, even if the younger generation is more tolerant. Even American boys appear to be more likely nowadays to share nonromantic hugs, as such expressions as "bromance" and "man crush" enter our vocabulary. Hugging also has migrated online, where Facebook applications allowing friends to send hugs have tens of thousands of fans.

It's important to note that cultural traits exist because they are learned, not because they are natural or **inherently** right. Ethnocentrism is the error of viewing one's own culture as superior and applying one's own cultural values in judging people from other cultures. How easy is it for you to see beyond the ethnocentric blinders of your own experience? Do you have an ethnocentric position regarding displays of affection?

Vocabulary Collection Word:
inherently

Your in-context definition:

_____

_____

A dictionary definition:

_____

_____

Questions for Consideration

1. What is the author's thesis statement? If the author expresses it in a sentence, copy the sentence. If not, put the thesis statement in your own words.
2. What are the chief differences between displays of public affection in the United States and Brazil?
3. What does the author identify as some reasons for American attitudes about public affection?
4. Does the author present this information in an unbiased way, or does he present his own opinion?
5. What is ethnocentrism?

USING MODELS TO PRACTICE COMPOSING

Earlier in this chapter, you studied a detailed summary of "How Delaying Gratification Predicts Future Success," which you will use as a model for writing your own summary of Conrad Phillip Kottak's "Experiencing Culture: Personal Space and Displays of Affection."

1. On a separate sheet, construct an enhanced outline or graphic organizer of Kottak's text.
2. Follow your outline and the steps below to write a detailed summary of "Experiencing Culture." Use the detailed summary of "How Delaying Gratification Predicts Future Success" on page 239 as a model.
   - Write a title for your summary.
   - Write an introduction paragraph that provides bibliographic information for the reading. Start with the date, the publication, and the title.
   - Write a paragraph in which you provide the topic and the writer's main idea.
   - Write a paragraph about the first major supporting point the writer uses. Include information about the support used to back up this major supporting point.
   - Write a paragraph for each additional major supporting point the writer uses. Include information about the support used to back up each major supporting point.

Questions for Consideration

1. "It's important to note that cultural traits exist because they are learned, not because they are natural or inherently right."
2. In the United States, PDAs are frowned upon and make people uncomfortable. In Brazil, they are expected and accepted.
3. The author's reasons include American individualism, years of cultural conditioning, and homophobia.
4. The author reports on what his students said and observed and presents information about cultural differences. The tone is objective.
5. Ethnocentrism is the belief that your culture's traditions and practices are correct and should be practiced by other people.

- Provide any additional information needed to understand the reading.
- Write a brief ending for your summary by telling readers how the writer ended the text.

A READING AND WRITING ASSIGNMENT

Conrad Phillip Kottak writes about the cultural preferences of most North Americans regarding displays of affection. As Kottak notes, cultural preferences change over time. Write an essay in which you discuss three or four cultural preferences, rules, or traditions that have changed over time. For example, at the beginning of the twentieth century, most middle-class American women did not work outside the home. However, this tradition has changed, and now a majority of women work outside the home. What other preferences, rules, or traditions can you think of that have changed? Here are some areas to consider:

- Child care and child rearing
- Roles of fathers, mothers, grandparents, children
- Rules of etiquette, such as table manners, greetings, rules of politeness
- Traditional activities, such as those involving holiday customs, family meals, birthday parties

Use the Quick Start Guide to Integrated Reading and Writing Assignments to help you with this process.

THINKING FROM AN INSTRUCTOR'S POINT OF VIEW

Imagine that you have enrolled in a college program that will enable you to become a construction manager. The required book for your first class is thick, and the chapters are long. Your instructor announces that the first major exam will be in two weeks, and it will cover three chapters. When a classmate asks whether the instructor will be handing out a review sheet, he replies that he will not. Your classmate is unhappy and does not understand why the instructor would be so seemingly coldhearted. He asks you to explain the situation to him.

The best way to help your classmate understand the situation is to consider it from the instructor's point of view. Write two or three paragraphs in which you explain the instructor's decision to the best of your ability.

ADDING TO YOUR VOCABULARY

This chapter's vocabulary words appear below.

entrepreneur	attribute	enhanced	inherently
nonetheless	objective	database	

Choose five of the vocabulary words from this chapter that you would like to add to your vocabulary, and think about how you can use them this week. For example, one of this chapter's words is *nonetheless*. You can often substitute *nonetheless* for *but*, as in the example that follows.

Example: I put bread on my shopping list, *but* I forgot to buy it at the store.

I put bread on my shopping list. *Nonetheless,* I forgot to buy it at the store.

List each of the five words you plan to use this week, and make note of a context in which you could use each word.

Example: *Nonetheless.* I can use this in ordinary conversation with my spouse.

Teaching Resources: See the IM for a variation of this essay assignment in which students use excerpts from Emily Post's 1922 book, *Etiquette in Society, in Business, in Politics and at Home* to write a comparative essay.

Connect IRW Writing Assignment: The peer review tools in Connect IRW allow students to anonymously comment on each other's papers. You can set up the assignment so that students cannot go on to write a second draft until they have received peer review comments. This assignment has been preloaded into the Connect IRW *Common Places* Master Course.

Teaching Resources: See the IM for additional vocabulary activities.

See the Connect IRW *Common Places* Master Course for vocabulary study practices that accompany this chapter, as well as a chapter vocabulary quiz.

ADDITIONAL ASSIGNMENTS

1. Earlier in this chapter you read about how children in the Marshmallow Experiment who were able to delay gratification turned out to have more successes in life than the children who could not resist temptation. Write three or four paragraphs about times in your life when you decided to either delay gratification or not. What were the circumstances? As you look back, do you think you made the right choice? Explain these situations and reflect on them in your writing.

2. Create a graphic organizer for the essay you wrote in response to "Experiencing Culture: Personal Space and Displays of Affection."

3. Do an Internet search to find information about one of the cultures to which you belong. For example, if you are a horse lover, search for information about equestrian (horse) culture. List some of the cultural beliefs, behaviors, or attributes you find online. Make sure you reference the Web site on which you find the information. Write an essay in which you respond to these attributes by either agreeing that they are part of your culture or disputing them. Explain your reasoning.

4. *Ethnocentrism* results in our believing that our cultural practices are the best ones. What is the problem with ethnocentric thinking? Explain. Think of an example in history when ethnocentrism led to tragedy. Write a paragraph about the tragedy and how it resulted from ethnocentrism.

1. Answers will vary.
2. Answers will vary.
3. Answers will vary.
4. Answers will vary, but students might write about colonial expansion, the extermination of Native Americans, or the Holocaust, for example.

EMOTIONAL INTELLIGENCE

An important part of emotional intelligence is the ability to understand and deal with your feelings. To be able to do that, you must be able to *name* your feelings.

Sounds easy, right? It's surprisingly difficult sometimes. For example, many people experience periods of unhappiness but cannot quite name what they are feeling. They may feel sad, angry, hopeless, helpless, fearful, or any number of other emotions. By being able to accurately name what you are feeling, you can then find ways to deal with your emotions.

Think of a time you felt very upset. What was the emotion that caused you to be upset? For example, if you have ever come close to being in a car accident caused by another driver, you have probably experienced anger. Underneath that anger, however, would be fear. Write a paragraph about a time you were very upset. What were the emotions responsible for your condition? Work on naming your emotions, and consider writing about your emotions when you experience upsetting (or even joyous) occasions.

Answers will vary.

CULTURAL LITERACY

As a college student, you will often hear terms associated with higher education. Improve your cultural literacy by learning these terms. Read through the list of words and phrases on the following page. Write definitions for all of them, guessing about the ones that are unfamiliar. Next, compare your answers with a classmate's. Finally, use the Internet or a dictionary to determine what the terms mean. Work on learning the terms you do not know by trying to include them in your daily conversation.

Answers will vary.

- Higher education
- Associate's degree
- Bachelor's degree
- Master's degree
- Doctorate
- Postsecondary
- Learning objectives
- GPA
- Graduate school
- Undergraduate
- Online courses
- Standardized tests
- Transfer student
- Certificate program
- Syllabus
- Core curriculum
- Matriculation
- College catalog

As an alternative, consider having students brainstorm aloud to come up with a list of terms they have heard in college and would like to have definitions for. Have students collaborate to define the words.

Are there other words you have heard associated with college that you want to understand? If so, add them to this list.

CRITICAL THINKING

Most of us make predictions every day. If we are stuck in traffic, we predict how late we may be for our appointments. If we are struggling to find the motivation to do an unpleasant task, we predict what will happen if we put the task off or avoid it altogether.

Answers will vary.

Since predicting is such a common human experience, we should predict as accurately as we can. To predict accurately, we must consider *every* possibility and then choose the most likely one. Failure to think about every possibility can lead to disaster.

Hone your prediction skills by making a list of at least ten possible outcomes for the following scenario: You just took a job as a stocker in a warehouse. The company requires you to work forty hours per week, and you were lucky enough to find a college schedule that enables you to take two courses, requiring six hours per week on campus. In the middle of the semester, you will be moving into your first apartment. How might the semester turn out?

After you make your list of possibilities, determine which possibility is most likely. Next, list actions you could take to minimize any negative consequences you have predicted.

When you finish, answer this question in a paragraph: how can making accurate predictions help you as a student, as an employee, and as a person?

METACOGNITION

Look back at the last few years of your life and assess the major decisions you made. Now, consider your ability to make good predictions. Think about times when you made predictions that turned out to be accurate. Perhaps you predicted you would really like a particular job, so you took the position and you did, indeed, really like the job. Why do you think you made a good prediction in that scenario? Explain.

Answers will vary.

Now think about a time when you made a bad prediction. Perhaps you were in a failed relationship or did not prepare well enough for a test or assignment. Why do you think you made a poor prediction in that scenario?

On the whole, have you been good at making accurate predictions? Think through your past experiences and reflect on them. How can you make better predictions in the future?

The beginning of a path should be inviting, and the end should make the journey worthwhile. In the same way, as readers we expect texts to invite us in and then end agreeably. In addition, as writers we need to focus on composing engaging introductions and satisfactory conclusions.

Titles, Introductions, and Conclusions

Have you ever picked up a magazine, perhaps while waiting in line at the grocery store, because something on the cover caught your eye? Sometimes a photo gets us curious, or perhaps a title or a description on the cover arouses our interest. Magazine editors depend on intriguing titles and introductions to sell their products. In the same way, good writers create titles and introductions that entice readers.

Titles, introductions, and conclusions frame a text and help readers understand its structure and content. The title is the first clue about a text's content. The introduction often provides background information or uses another method to invite readers to continue reading. The conclusion serves an important function, too. It provides **closure** for readers—the sense that the essay has reached its end.

Mastering the creation of effective titles, introductions, and conclusions is part of writing well. One way to achieve this mastery is to use your reading and analysis skills to determine how successful writers construct these elements.

CHAPTER OBJECTIVES

After completing this chapter, students will be able to do the following:

- **Analyze and create titles.**
- **Read, analyze, and create introductions.**
- **Read, analyze, and create conclusions.**

Connect IRW LearnSmart Achieve: Assign the topics "Analyzing and Writing in Response to a Writing Prompt" for adaptive learning to accompany the chapter.

Teaching Resources: See the Chapter Quiz.

ANALYZING AND CREATING TITLES

The primary purpose of a title is to give readers an idea about the contents of the essay or to make readers curious about it. Many essays have straightforward titles, as the examples on the next page show.

Essay Content	Straightforward Title
An essay explaining ikebana—the Japanese art of flower arranging	"What Is Ikebana?"
An essay comparing and contrasting nuclear energy and geothermal energy	"A Comparison of Nuclear and Geothermal Energy"
An essay arguing that medicinal marijuana should be legal	"Why Medicinal Marijuana Should Be Legal"

Titles should be short—ideally, just a few words—although there are no set rules about how many words a title should have. Here are some examples of titles that are unnecessarily long.

- "A Brief Explanation of Ikebana, the Japanese Art of Flower Arranging"
- "A Comparison and Contrast Essay Concerning the Differences between Nuclear Energy and Geothermal Energy"
- "The Debate about Medicinal Marijuana: Why Marijuana Should Be Legal for Medicinal Purposes"

Some titles are creative; they provide more than a straightforward glimpse into the text's content. Consider these titles.

Consider giving students titles from an online database and asking them to analyze those that arouse their interest.

Essay Content	Creative Title
An essay explaining ikebana—the Japanese art of flower arranging	"Ikebana: It's Not Just for Japanese Florists"
An essay comparing and contrasting nuclear energy and geothermal energy	"Geothermal: An Alternative to the Nuclear Option"
An essay arguing that medicinal marijuana should be legal	"Marijuana Is Good Medicine"

These titles do not explicitly announce what the essay is about. Rather, they give the reader an idea of the topic.

Another feature of two of these titles is the colon (:). Colons introduce lists or explanations. In the case of the examples given above, the colon separates a word (the main part of the title) from a brief phrase that provides more information (the subtitle). In the title "Ikebana: It's Not Just for Japanese Florists," the phrase after the colon explains a bit about the topic, ikebana. The same occurs with this title: "Geothermal: An Alternative to the Nuclear Option." In titles, a colon generally introduces an explanation.

Teaching Resources: See the "Critiquing and Creating Titles" exercise.

Titles that are not straightforward generally require more creativity to compose. Consider documentary film titles, for instance. Like a written essay, a documentary film has a point to make. A film may have a political message, or it may seek to explain important concepts, such as nuclear proliferation or the health-care crisis, or it may simply document historical events.

Think about some of the documentary films you have seen lately. Did their titles entice you? The documentary film about former Vice President Al Gore's attempts to educate Americans about destructive global climate change is called *An Inconvenient Truth*. The title does not announce the film's subject but rather calls attention to the importance of the film's content. On the other hand, the title of Ken Burns's documentary *The National Parks: America's Best Idea* reveals not only the film's subject but also the filmmaker's view of the subject.

Be aware of titles as you encounter them. Think about how well they accomplish the tasks of indicating the content of the work and making you want to read (or view) it.

PRACTICE ① Analyzing Titles

Read each of the titles that follow, and indicate whether it is a straightforward title or a creative title. Then make a prediction about the text's content.

Title	Straightforward or Creative?	Predicted Content of Text
1. Keys to Passing Algebra	Straightforward	Information on studying for a course in algebra
2. Waking Up: Overcoming Depression and Anxiety	Straightforward	Presentation of strategies for overcoming depression and anxiety
3. Old McDonald Had a Heart Attack: Fast-Food Perils	Straightforward and creative	Arguments about how fast food can be bad for a person's heart
4. How to Reform Immigration Laws	Straightforward	Arguments in favor of a particular immigration policy

PRACTICE ② Choosing Titles

Each item below describes an essay. Choose an appropriate title for each essay, and label the title as either "straightforward" or "creative." Construct at least two creative titles.

Answers will vary. Sample answers are provided.

1. In this essay, the writer argues that race should not be a factor in adoptions.

   Title: Love Comes in All Colors

   Type of title: Creative

2. This personal essay, by a journalist who survived Hurricane Katrina in New Orleans, concerns his struggle with depression afterward.

   Title: The Storm after the Storm

   Type of title: Creative

3. The writer of this essay argues that migrant farmworkers live in terrible conditions.

   Title: The Sad Plight of Migrant Workers

   Type of title: Straightforward

4. In this essay, the writer explains how scientists develop flu vaccines.

   Title: Creating a Flu Vaccine

   Type of title: Straightforward

READING, ANALYZING, AND CREATING INTRODUCTIONS

An introduction serves two functions: it attempts to engage readers, and it offers hints about what the text will concern. Most readers expect an introduction to give them a sense of where the essay will go and what they will learn or experience by reading it. Good readers use the introduction of an essay to develop a set of expectations about what the text will concern.

How Introductions Function

An introduction can consist of one paragraph, or it can have several paragraphs. In the introduction paragraphs, we will often find the essay's thesis statement, but not always. Writers decide where to place the thesis statement based on the content of the essay and on the audience.

Like a first impression at a job interview, an introductory paragraph carries a great deal of weight. It may not be fair to judge an essay by its introduction, but as readers, we all do. The time and effort spent crafting a carefully written, engaging introduction will be worthwhile.

Strategies for Introductions

Writers often use one of these seven strategies to compose introduction paragraphs. The strategies are summarized in the following table and discussed below.

Strategies for Introductions	
Starting with a question	Ask one or more questions that you answer later on in the essay.
Starting with a story	Tell one or more anecdotes, or start a story that you finish later on in the essay.
Starting with background information	Give information about the topic that readers might need—for example, history or definitions.
Starting with a surprise	Begin with one point of view on the topic, and then switch unexpectedly.
Starting with data	Provide relevant statistics on the topic.
Starting with a quotation or adage	Offer a quotation, perhaps from an expert, or an appropriate saying.
Starting with an objective overview	Give both sides of an argument in neutral language before proceeding to focus on a particular point of view.

■ "Once upon a time . . ." is a famous introduction. What does it tell the reader? How do beginnings help us anticipate the content to come?

Teaching Resources: See the *PowerPoint* presentation (PPT) "The Power of Introductions."

Each of these strategies is described in more detail below and is illustrated by a professional selection. In addition, an example shows how each strategy could be used to introduce an essay about the benefits of walking. As you study the examples, pay attention to the hints that the introduction paragraphs give regarding the essay content. Also, think about how you can use these strategies in your own writing.

Starting with a Question

Sometimes writers use a question or a set of questions to introduce a topic. The question often presents the topic and leads to the writer's main point. Notice how starting with questions works in the following example.

Introduction from "Campus Diversity and Student Self-Segregation: Separating Myths from Facts" by Debra Humphreys

When students went off to college this fall, they entered more diverse campuses than ever before. For many students, in fact, their college community is the most diverse they have ever encountered. Most students entering college today come from high schools that are predominantly or exclusively one racial or ethnic group. Given this reality, how are students interacting with one another educationally and socially in college? How socially segregated are college campuses? Is campus diversity leading to educational benefits for today's college students or are students too separated into enclaves on campus to benefit from campus diversity?

Three questions introduce the topic. The writer answers these questions later in the text.

Humphreys does not immediately answer the questions she raises in the introduction paragraph. Rather, she uses the questions to focus attention on the issue of self-segregation in colleges. Later in her essay, she answers the questions in her thesis statement.

When you come across texts that start with a question, the *answer* to the question is often the main idea of the reading. Sometimes, though, a question is used simply to get the audience to think about the topic rather than to introduce a specific thesis statement.

Using This Strategy in Your Writing.   One way to use this strategy is to make the first sentence of your introduction paragraph a question. If you create a question whose answer will be your thesis statement, you can discuss **conceivable** answers to this question but save *your* answer for last. Your answer to the question will be your thesis statement.

(Make sure to check your instructor's preferences before using the second-person pronoun *you*. While the use of second person is appropriate for *informal* writing, it is generally not acceptable in formal, academic writing.)

Here is an example of an introduction that uses a question at the beginning of the paragraph.

Vocabulary Collection Word:
conceivable

Your in-context definition:

_____

_____

A dictionary definition:

_____

_____

Example: Starting with a Question

Is walking really a legitimate form of exercise? Many people think walking is not strenuous enough to have health benefits. They think that to get in good shape, people must run, do aerobics, kickbox, or participate in another high-intensity exercise. While all of those are good exercises, the reality is that strenuous exercise is not the only way to work out productively. Millions of people who walk for exercise can attest to the power of walking. The truth is simple: walking for exercise results in a variety of health benefits.

A question suggests that the topic is walking for exercise. The question is followed by possible answers.

The writer transitions away from what others think.

The writer ends with a thesis statement that answers the opening question.

PRACTICE ③ Writing an Introduction That Uses a Question

Imagine you are writing an essay in which you discuss qualities needed in a successful manager. You have decided to use this thesis statement:

Successful managers must be able to work well with others, solve problems, and manage their time wisely.

On a separate sheet, write an introduction paragraph using this thesis statement. Use the strategy of *starting with a question*.

Connect IRW Discussion Board (DB) Assignment: Create DB threads for students to use to post the introductions they write for Practices 3–8. Consider having students comment on each other's introductions. See the Instructor's Manual (IM) for suggestions.

Starting with a Story

Writers know that everyone likes a good story. One way to create interest is to begin a text with a story. If a writer knows of an anecdote that fits the topic and her point, she may use that story as a starting point. Sometimes writers use **hypothetical stories**—stories that are made up but are realistic enough to be **credible** and likely. A hypothetical story will work only if it relates to your point and comes across as believable to a reasonable audience.

Look at the beginning paragraph of "Life with Asperger's Syndrome." The writer starts by telling a short story about Paul, a child with Asperger's syndrome. Notice that the anecdote is very brief, and it helps the writer introduce the topic. The writer does not present her thesis statement in the first paragraph; she waits until the second paragraph to provide background information on Asperger's syndrome and to state her main idea.

Vocabulary Collection Word:
credible

Your in-context definition:

_____

_____

A dictionary definition:

_____

_____

Introduction from "Life with Asperger's Syndrome"

Eleven-year-old Paul paced nervously back and forth at the bus stop. His school bus is supposed to arrive every morning at 7:04. Usually Paul could see the bus coming down the street at 7:03, but this morning, at 7:03, there was no bus. A feeling of panic washed over him. When his watch said 7:04, tears began to stream down his face. The bus was not on time. By 7:05, he could not stand it any longer and ran home. If Paul had not been diagnosed with Asperger's syndrome, his mother would probably have been puzzled by this behavior, but she was not shocked. Because he has Asperger's syndrome, Paul is not like other children.

Asperger's syndrome is a type of autism. Many people have heard of autism before, but not many know about Asperger's syndrome. Autism comes in many forms, some very severe and some quite mild. People who have Asperger's are considered to be on the mild "high functioning" side of the autism range. People with classic autism are often unable to talk and do not like being touched, while many of those with Asperger's can function fairly normally in these areas. However, there are some challenges for those who have Asperger's syndrome, and some of these challenges are significant.

A short anecdote about Paul begins.

Transition from the story to the topic: Asperger's syndrome

Background information

Thesis statement

The story about Paul is much more interesting than a fact about Asperger's syndrome and might encourage the audience to keep reading.

Be aware as a reader that while some texts *are* primarily about a story, others will simply use stories to make a point or to begin the text, as "Life with Asperger's Syndrome" does. When you read a text that begins with a story, first determine whether the story is what the entire essay will be about. If it is not, ask yourself, "What point is the writer making with this story?"

Using This Strategy in Your Writing.   Most people like reading a good story, so they will tune in right away. The key is finding a story that is appropriate for your point. For example, if you want to make the point that insomnia is a disorder that affects the quality of life for those who suffer from it, then including a story about a person's experience with insomnia might be a good way to start an introduction. The example that follows shows how you can use a story to introduce an essay.

Vocabulary Collection Word:
autism

Your in-context definition:

_____

_____

A dictionary definition:

_____

_____

Vocabulary Collection Word:
therapeutic

Your in-context definition:

_____

_____

A dictionary definition:

_____

_____

Example: Starting with a Story

In 2007, Felicity Martinez was twenty-four, and she was dying. She had been diagnosed with melanoma not long after she found a suspicious-looking mole on her right shoulder. Felicity got depressed. She knew that depression would not help her put up the strongest fight she could against cancer. Her doctor prescribed a variety of treatments for depression, and they worked. Felicity believes that one of the treatments that especially helped her take control of her life and feel empowered was a therapeutic walking routine. Walking helped her become more centered and more determined as she fought and eventually beat the disease. As Felicity's story shows, walking for exercise can result in a variety of positive effects.

The writer starts with a story (narrative) about Felicity Martinez.

The writer uses a transition to move from the specifics of the story to the thesis statement about walking.

Notice that the writer did not abruptly stop Felicity's story. Instead, after giving Felicity's thoughts about her experience, the writer used a transition ("As Felicity's story shows") to gracefully move to the thesis statement.

When you use a story in an introduction, make sure the story is *entirely* related to your point. In the example above, if Felicity had survived cancer and then incidentally became a walker, her story would not really show that walking can be a life-changing activity.

PRACTICE 4 Writing an Introduction That Uses a Story

Imagine you are writing an essay in which you discuss qualities needed in a successful manager. You have decided to use this thesis statement:

> Successful managers must be able to work well with others, solve problems, and manage their time wisely.

On a separate sheet, write an introduction paragraph using this thesis statement. Use the strategy of *starting with a story.* Consider telling a story about a work experience you had with a good or bad manager.

Starting with Background Information

Some topics are complex enough that audiences need background information. Thus, using background information to lead up to the main point is one way to write an introduction. Notice the annotations in the following example, "Using Media to Make a Difference," from *Introduction to Mass Communication: Media Literacy and Culture* by Stanley J. Baran.

Introduction from "Using Media to Make a Difference: Social Media and the Middle East Democracy Movement" by Stanley J. Baran

Tens of thousands of Iranians from all walks of life took to the streets in the summer of 2009 to protest what they saw as the illegitimate reelection of President Mahmoud Ahmadinejad. The government, already skilled at slowing the Internet and shutting down opposition websites, immediately expelled or placed under house arrest all foreign journalists, closed opposition newspapers, and used its own state-run radio and television stations to first ignore the protests and then blame them on outside Western agitators hostile to Iran. The protesters responded by using the Internet and social media to make a difference for their Green Revolution and democracy.

Topic: using social media for political change

The entire introduction paragraph consists of background information about the protest in 2009.

The writer reveals his thesis statement in the first paragraph.

As a reader, be careful not to confuse background information with the writer's main idea. As you read an introduction paragraph, ask yourself, "Will the information being presented help me understand this concept or issue more clearly?" When introductory paragraphs provide *a summary of an event* that happened or *a definition of a concept*, that information may be background material.

Using This Strategy in Your Writing.   Sometimes, providing background information in the introduction paragraph can help readers more fully understand the context of your thesis statement. Present the background information logically so that it leads to the thesis statement.

Example: Starting with Background Information

Americans have a problem with obesity. According to the Centers for Disease Control and Prevention, to be obese means having a body mass index (BMI) of 30 or higher. Another category of weight management is *morbid obesity.* People who are morbidly obese are at high risk for breathing and walking problems, as well as death. We are a nation that has a high obesity rate, and our children are included in the problem. However, there is something we can do to start making changes: we can walk. If we all began to walk every day, obesity rates in our country would drop dramatically.

> The writer starts with background information about obesity.
>
> The sentence forms a transition from the background information to the thesis statement.

In the example above, the background information defines obesity and gives some of its consequences. The writer ends the paragraph with the thesis statement—a solution to the problem.

Be aware that any background information you provide must be true and accurate. Never make up data or statistics. If your instructor allows you to use source material for an assignment, be sure to credit the source properly and provide complete bibliographic information.

PRACTICE ⑤ Writing an Introduction That Uses Background Information

Imagine you are writing an essay in which you discuss qualities needed in a successful manager. You have decided to use this thesis statement:

> Successful managers must be able to work well with others, solve problems, and manage their time wisely.

On a separate sheet, write an introduction paragraph using this thesis statement. Use the strategy of *starting with background information.*

Several practices in this chapter ask students to write introductions and conclusions. Consider having students post their paragraphs on the Connect IRW Discussion Board. They can learn from reading the work of their peers.

Starting with a Surprise

Startling a reader with a shocking statement or by using irony can be an effective technique in an introduction. One way irony works is for a person to say the opposite of what she means. For example, if a ballpoint pen were to explode in your book bag, you might say "Lovely!" Of course, you don't really think the explosion was lovely, and your tone of voice will certainly convey that.

Irony also can be situational. If a police officer gets a ticket for speeding, we would call the situation ironic. If you get into an accident that wrecks your car the day after you pay off your car loan, the situation would be ironic. The use of irony is one type of surprise that can introduce an essay. Notice how an element of surprise is used in the following example, "Love as a Story," from the textbook *Understanding Human Sexuality* by Janet Shibley Hyde and John D. DeLamater.

Vocabulary Collection Word:
irony

Your in-context definition:

_____

_____

A dictionary definition:

_____

_____

Introduction from "Love as a Story" by Janet Shibley Hyde and John D. DeLamater

When we think of love, our thoughts often turn to the great love stories: Romeo and Juliet, Cinderella and the Prince (Julia Roberts and Richard Gere), King Edward VIII and Wallis Simpson, and *Pygmalion/My Fair Lady.* According to Sternberg, these stories are much more than entertainment. They shape our beliefs about love and relationships, and our beliefs in turn influence our behavior.

> The writers explain the effects of love stories.

(continued)

Zach and Tammy have been married 28 years. Their friends have been predicting divorce since the day they were married. They fight almost constantly. Tammy threatens to leave Zach; he tells her that nothing would make him happier. They lived happily ever after.

Valerie and Leonard had a perfect marriage. They told each other and all of their friends that they did. Their children say they never fought. Leonard met someone at his office, and left Valerie. They are divorced.

Wait a minute! Aren't those endings reversed? Zach and Tammy should be divorced, and Valerie and Leonard should be living happily ever after. If love is merely the interaction between two people, how they communicate and behave, you're right—the stories have the wrong endings. But there is more to love than interaction. What matters is how each partner interprets the interaction. To make sense out of what happens in our relationships, we rely on our love stories. A love story is a story about what love should be like, and it has characters, a plot, and a theme.

> The writers give examples of two love stories that are ironic.

> The text makes a transition from the surprise of the stories to the writers' thesis statement.

> The thesis statement appears at the end.

Notice that the writers of this selection use the ironic stories to introduce their thesis statement. The stories clearly serve a function. Sometimes, writers will use facts that are surprising or will make shocking statements as a way to catch the attention of their readers.

Using This Strategy in Your Writing.   One way to use surprise is to employ irony, as the writers of "Love as a Story" do. Another way is to start by offering commonly believed information and to then show that this information is wrong.

Imagine you are writing an essay to argue that homework is *not* a good learning tool for school children. You might begin your essay with all of the common assumptions about homework: that it helps kids learn, that doing homework shows independent thinking, that it fosters discipline, and so on. Close to the end of the paragraph, however, you could tell your readers that this **conventional** wisdom is actually *wrong*. By making readers think they know what you are going to say, you provide a mild shock when you actually say the opposite. As a result, you may make readers want to know more about your unexpected thesis statement.

This method is tricky to master, but it can be an effective introduction for some essays. Notice how it works in the following example.

Vocabulary Collection Word:
conventional

Your in-context definition:

_____

_____

A dictionary definition:

_____

Example: Starting with a Surprise

Walking is a ridiculous form of exercise. How can people who take leisurely strolls around town call themselves exercise enthusiasts—as if walking counts as a legitimate exercise? We all walk, every day, all the time, yet a large percentage of Americans are still overweight. If people really want to exercise, they need to get serious and train like professional athletes. Does this kind of thinking sound familiar? Anyone who believes such foolish ideas has never tried walking for exercise. People who do walk for exercise tell a different story about walking. They talk about how walking has changed their health, has sharpened their thinking, and has helped them sleep better at night, among other benefits. Anyone who walks regularly knows that walking for exercise results in a variety of positive effects.

> The first sentences present misconceptions about walking. The sentences are italicized to represent overheard speech.

> The question serves as a transition. Then the writer contradicts the italicized ideas.

> The thesis statement makes the *opposite* case from the earlier italicized point of view.

As a reader, notice the important shift from the italicized thoughts to the nonitalicized writer's voice. This is the place where the writer leads to her thesis statement. Not all writers will use italics in this way, but there will likely be a transition between the initial ideas presented and the writer's opposite ideas.

Surprise introductions can be difficult to write. Readers need to "get" the surprise. If you use irony, for instance, readers must be able to identify the irony. If you find surprise introductions too difficult to write well, then choose a more straightforward method.

PRACTICE 6 Writing an Introduction That Uses a Surprise

Imagine you are writing an essay in which you discuss qualities needed in a successful manager. You have decided to use this thesis statement:

> Successful managers must be able to work well with others, solve problems, and manage their time wisely.

On a separate sheet, write an introduction paragraph using this thesis statement. Use the strategy of *starting with a surprise.*

Starting with Data

Data—statistics, percentages, studies, and other types of information—can be incredibly powerful, but this kind of information can also be mind-numbing. Before you consider using data, be sure to check with your instructor about whether source materials can be used for your assignment. Data always come from a source, and you will always need to cite the source if you use data.

Notice the annotations in the following introduction to "Driven to Distraction: Our Wired Generation" by Larry Rosen.

Introduction from "Driven to Distraction: Our Wired Generation" by Larry Rosen

A recent Pew Internet & American Life Project report surveyed 2,462 middle school and high school advanced placement and national writing project teachers and concluded that: "Overwhelming majorities agree with the assertions that today's digital technologies are creating an easily distracted generation with short attention spans and today's students are too 'plugged in' and need more time away from their digital technologies." Two-thirds of the respondents agree with the notion that today's digital technologies do more to distract students than to help them academically.

The source of the data is given, together with details.

A quotation is followed by more data.

In this example, the writer does not place his thesis statement in the first paragraph. Rather, the first paragraph gives us data to get us thinking about the effects of digital technologies on students.

Using This Strategy in Your Writing.   If you find data that are truly interesting and perhaps even surprising, presenting some of that information can be an effective way to introduce your topic. Keep in mind that using data from a reputable source is crucial, as is making readers aware of the source. Also, remember to ask your instructor whether using a source is acceptable for the assignment. The following example shows how you might use data as a way to introduce a topic.

Example: Starting with Data

According to an article by professional tennis player Martina Navratilova, "Walking 150 minutes a week can reduce the risk of developing diabetes by nearly 60 percent." The benefits of walking also extend to weight loss, she says. She points to a study showing that regular walking resulted in weight loss—primarily in the abdominal area—for the study's participants. Far from being a useless activity, walking for exercise results in a variety of positive effects.	The introduction starts with the source of the data, as well as a quotation. Additional data are given. The thesis statement is a logical conclusion of the data presented earlier.

Notice that statistical information is always used to support a point. The information itself is rarely, if ever, the main point of a text.

PRACTICE ⑦ Writing an Introduction That Uses Data

Imagine you are writing an essay in which you argue that the minimum wage should be raised. You have decided to use this thesis statement:

> The minimum wage in the United States should be raised so that every worker has a chance to escape poverty.

On a separate sheet, write an introduction paragraph using this thesis statement. Use the strategy of *starting with data.* Choose from the data given below to write your introduction.

> Quotation: "Today, the real value of the minimum wage has fallen by nearly one-third since its peak in 1968. And right now, a full-time minimum wage worker makes $14,500 a year, which leaves too many families struggling to make ends meet."
>
> *Source:* The White House Web site at www.whitehouse.gov.

> Quotation: "President Obama took action to lift more workers' wages by requiring that federal contractors pay their employees a fair wage of at least $10.10 an hour."
>
> *Source:* The White House Web site at www.whitehouse.gov.

Starting with a Quotation or Adage

Sometimes, as a writer, you think of the *perfect* quotation or adage (a common saying that states something most people believe to be true). Using a quotation or an adage to start an introduction can be effective.

Since a quotation or adage is likely to be a single sentence, using this method of introduction requires writers to either add an explanation or additional information. In the introduction that follows, Tait Trussell combines an adage with a story to begin his essay "Healing Humor." The adage Trussell uses is actually the main idea he will make in his essay; thus, in this case, the adage is also the thesis statement. Most of the time, a quotation or adage will simply introduce the topic rather than serve as the thesis statement.

Introduction from "Healing Humor" by Tait Trussell

Research is showing that laughter is good medicine. It was a remarkable case, a generation or so ago. Norman Cousins, the editor and researcher, found laughter to be a cure for a serious disease he had contracted. Cousins was editor of the *Saturday Review of Literature*. He was diagnosed in 1964 with spondylitis, an acute inflammation of the spine. He was given only a few months to live. Cousins was sure that negative thoughts can cause illness. So, he reasoned that positive thoughts could have the opposite effect. He left the hospital and checked into a hotel where he watched humorous movies and shows. He found that 10 minutes of hearty laughter resulted in at least two hours of pain-free sleep. He continued this "treatment" until he recovered. He wrote a widely read book about his amazing recovery.	An adaptation of "laughter is the best medicine," a common adage, this sentence serves as the thesis statement.

An adage like the one Trussell uses is effective because most readers have heard it before but may not have believed it was true.

Using This Strategy in Your Writing.   If you find a striking quotation, saying, short song lyric, poem, or any other such item, you can use it to start your introduction paragraph. You must be sure that the item you are using fits the topic *exactly*. If you choose a quote that "kind of" fits, your reader will simply think the introduction paragraph is odd. Notice that the writer of the example below did not have a perfect adage for her thesis. Instead, she chose to adapt a well-known adage.

Example: Starting with a Quotation or Adage

We all know that an apple a day is supposed to keep the doctor away, but eating apples will not necessarily make you fit. A healthier version of the old adage might be "A walk every day keeps illness away." While diet is important for health, it is not the only way to stay healthy. A daily walk for exercise results in a variety of positive effects.	The writer starts with a well-known adage and then critiques it. The writer suggests a new adage that acts as a transition to the thesis statement. The thesis statement appears at the end.

As a reader, any time you see an adage, ask yourself, "What is the general truth the adage presents?" Use the answer to gain understanding about the writer's point.

PRACTICE ⑧ Writing an Introduction That Uses a Quotation or Adage

Imagine you are writing an essay in which you discuss qualities needed in a successful manager. You have decided to use this thesis statement:

Successful managers must be able to work well with others, solve problems, and manage their time wisely.

On a separate sheet, write an introduction paragraph using this thesis statement. Use the strategy of *starting with a quote or adage*.

Starting with an Objective Overview

Some essays begin with a simple overview of the issue being discussed. If the issue is controversial, an objective overview requires both sides of the issue to be presented. An objective overview can be used to introduce an informative article about the issue, or it can be used at the beginning of a persuasive essay to show that the writer is aware of both sides of the issue.

The following paragraph is an example of an objective overview used as an introduction to an informative article, "Wal-Mart and the Local Economy," by Mitch Renkow.

Introduction from "Wal-Mart and the Local Economy" by Mitch Renkow

With total revenues in excess of $250 billion per year and more than 1.3 million employees worldwide, Wal-Mart Stores, Inc., is the largest corporation in the world. Wal-Mart's staggering—and continuing—growth traces directly to its pioneering of an innovative business model that features sophisticated supply chain management and aggressive cost-cutting. That model, as revolutionary as was that of the Sears & Roebuck Co. in the late 1800s, has profoundly altered patterns of local retail and wholesale trade, as well as the logistics of the transportation and distribution of goods. Wal-Mart sells a wide array of products at lower prices than competing retail outlets. It also hires large numbers of local workers, as well as generating substantial property tax and sales tax revenues for local communities. Nonetheless, Wal-Mart is a frequent target of hostile sentiment, and announcements of plans to build a new Wal-Mart in a given community are often met with considerable protest. Much of the antagonism toward Wal-Mart is rooted in the perceived dislocating effects that new Wal-Mart stores have on competing "mom-and-pop" retail stores.

> **Pro position:** The writer starts with positive info about Wal-Mart and its successes.
>
> The writer goes on to give historical info about Wal-Mart's business practices.
>
> **Con position:** The writer gives "the other side": hostility toward Wal-Mart.

In this article, the writer will not take a position on whether Wal-Mart is good for society or the economy. Rather, as the introduction indicates, he will discuss both sides. The objective overview in the introduction paragraph forecasts the discussion to come.

Not much information is provided about either side of the issue in Renkow's introduction paragraph. He will provide more details in the article itself. This is one way to present a very basic overview of the two sides of an issue. Another way is to write one paragraph presenting one viewpoint and a second paragraph for the opposite viewpoint. In the third paragraph, the writer presents the thesis statement.

Vocabulary Collection Word:
advocate

Your in-context definition:

_____

_____

A dictionary definition:

_____

_____

Using This Strategy in Your Writing.   To use this strategy in your own writing, be sure that you clearly understand both sides of the issue. Provide an overview of both sides, and then present your thesis statement. If you are writing an argument essay, be sure to word your introduction and thesis statement in such a way that readers understand which point of view you are **advocating**.

Example: Starting with an Objective Overview

Although we know that exercise is important, very few Americans participate in regular exercise. Realizing this, several national companies have begun to offer their employees 20 minutes per day—in addition to regular breaks and lunch time—to simply take a walk. These employers argue that their companies save money by encouraging daily walks since

> Pro argument in favor of time off for exercise at work

(continued)

walkers have lower health-care expenses and higher morale. Some executives, however, say their companies will lose valuable productive time by providing time for daily walks. They believe their employees already have enough time—through scheduled breaks and lunch—to exercise if they really want to. Although both sides make valuable points, companies who have implemented walking programs are beginning to see real benefits from them. A close examination of this issue will show that the potential benefits of giving employees time to walk each day far outweigh any negative consequences.

Con argument against time off for exercise at work

Transition moves from the two points of view to the writer's thesis statement

Thesis statement

Notice that even though both sides of the issue are briefly mentioned, the writer ends with a thesis statement that shows the position he supports.

PRACTICE 9 Reading, Annotating, and Analyzing Introductions

The introductions from two essays follow. Read and annotate each introduction, and then answer the analysis questions that follow each one.

PASSAGE A: Introduction from "Probing Question: Is 'Just Say No' an Effective Anti-Drug Approach?" by Tom Fitzgerald

YOUR ANNOTATIONS

Many people remember the famous anti-drug slogan coined by former first lady Nancy Reagan: "Just Say No." Critiqued by some for reducing a complex issue to a catch phrase, Reagan's campaign is generally considered to have been unsuccessful, and the phrase "just say no" has become a pop-culture joke.

Quote of a commonly used phrase (and widely known program)

1. What strategy did the writer use to write this introduction paragraph?

   Use of a quote or adage

2. What do you predict the essay will be about, based on the introduction and the title?

   The effectiveness of the "Just Say No" campaign

PASSAGE B: Introduction from "Mark Lepper: Intrinsic Motivation, Extrinsic Motivation and the Process of Learning" by Christine Vandevelde

YOUR ANNOTATIONS

Some years ago, after a lecture, Professor Mark Lepper was approached by a couple who told him about a system of rewards they had set up for their son, which had produced much improved behavior at the dinner table. "He sits up straight and eats his peas and the Brussels sprouts and he is really very well behaved," they reported. Until, that is, the first time the family dined at a nice restaurant. The child looked around, picked up a crystal glass from the table and asked, "How many points not to drop this?" A fine example, says Dr. Lepper, of the detrimental effects of over-reliance on rewards to shape children's behavior.

Starts with a story

1. What strategy did the writer use to write this introduction paragraph?

   Use of a story

2. Did the writer include his thesis statement in this paragraph?

   No

3. What do you predict the essay will be about, based on the introduction and the title?

   Types of motivation and how we learn

PRACTICE ⑩ Choosing Introduction Strategies

Below are three thesis statements. If you were writing an essay for the following thesis statements, which type of introduction paragraph might you use for each one? Why? Explain in one or two sentences.

1. Thesis statement: We need to take action to save our beaches.

   Answers will vary, but using statistics about beach degradation might be an effective way to start this essay.

2. Thesis statement: Instead of punishing students who use smartphones in class, instructors should integrate smartphone technology into their teaching.

   Answers will vary, but this essay might benefit from the use of a story about how students want to use smartphones in class for everything.

3. Thesis statement: If you believe a person is having a stroke, there are four actions you can and must take.

   Answers will vary, but this essay might be introduced with a question such as "Would you know what to do if someone near you were having a stroke?"

Connect IRW Power of Process Assignment: For more practice, consider having students analyze the introduction methods of three readings in PoP. See the IM for a list of suggested readings. See the Connect IRW *Common Places* Master Course for pre-loaded PoP assignments that require students to analyze the introductions of select readings.

READING, ANALYZING, AND CREATING CONCLUSIONS

We have all seen movies that end poorly, leaving us with a sense that the movie should not have ended just yet or should have had a different ending. Texts can also suffer from poor endings. The examples that follow will help you understand the function of conclusions and learn how to craft effective endings for your own writing.

Vocabulary Collection Word:
impart

Your in-context definition:

_____

_____

A dictionary definition:

_____

_____

How Conclusions Function

The main purpose of a conclusion is to help the reader gain a sense of *closure*—a feeling that it is the right time to bring the writing to an end—and a sense that something has been accomplished, a point has been made, or an idea has been shared.

To **impart** closure, conclusions often re-emphasize the purpose of the essay. Conclusions may also make predictions, emphasize the importance of the issue being discussed, or provide the end of a story that was started in the introduction paragraph.

By analyzing a conclusion, you can sometimes tell whether you fully understand the writer's main point. For example, if the essay is intended to persuade, then the conclusion can serve as a last attempt to get readers to do or believe what the writer is advocating. If the essay presents an analysis and draws a conclusion, the conclusion paragraph is a good place to reiterate the results or findings. While conclusions do not always restate the main point, the content in them should be consistent with the main idea of the essay.

Strategies for Conclusions

Four strategies, summarized in the table on the next page and illustrated in the examples that follow, are commonly used to conclude essays. Keep in mind that regardless of the conclusion strategy employed, an essay can also end with a **proposal**—a suggestion that readers take particular actions in response to what the writer is saying in the essay.

As you read each example, think about whether the conclusion produces a sense of closure. You may notice that conclusion paragraphs often make use of more than one strategy, as the annotations will show. Notice also that the writers do not use "in conclusion" or "to conclude." A good conclusion does not have to announce itself.

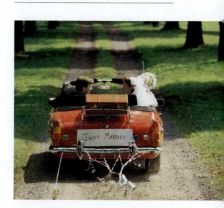

■ In a fairy tale, "happily ever after" tells us the story has come to an end. What do you think readers expect from a satisfactory conclusion?

Strategies for Conclusion Paragraphs	
Concluding by restating and summarizing	Emphasize the thesis or the key points in the essay by restating them in different words.
Concluding by answering an earlier question	Answer a question you asked in the introduction to the essay.
Concluding by finishing a story	Tell the end of a story that you began in the introduction to the essay.
Concluding by speculating	Explain some results, events, or other consequences that *might* occur.

Concluding by Restating and Summarizing

A common method of concluding an essay is to emphasize the thesis statement by restating it. You have read the introduction paragraph Mitch Renkow uses to start his informative essay on Wal-Mart. Now read the conclusion paragraph, and notice how he sums up his informative essay.

Conclusion from "Wal-Mart and the Local Economy" by Mitch Renkow

As is commonly the case with any large shock to the economic system, the coming of a new Wal-Mart to a given community is accompanied by a multitude of different impacts on different individuals and on the local government. Some of these impacts are unambiguously positive for certain groups—lower prices for consumers being an example. Some are unambiguously negative for other groups, such as the loss of business experienced by competing retail outlets. And still others will vary on a case-by-case basis, such as the impacts on local employment and the local government's budget. To a very large extent, whether a new Wal-Mart is a "good" or "bad" thing for an individual depends on which of these varied impacts are most strongly relevant to that individual.

The writer summarizes positive effects.

The writer summarizes negative effects.

The writer restates the thesis statement.

As a reader, pay particular attention to the conclusion paragraphs. Often, if the writer reiterates a point in the conclusion, that point will be the text's thesis statement. You can sometimes check your knowledge of the thesis statement by studying the writer's closing words.

Using This Strategy in Your Writing. When you use this method for concluding your writing, be sure to continue composing *new* sentences. It may be tempting to simply insert the thesis statement word for word, but avoid doing so. In the following example, notice that the last sentence adds emphasis to the writer's thesis statement by calling walking "the perfect exercise." Make sure your final sentence wraps up the essay and gives readers a sense of closure.

Connect IRW Discussion Board (DB) Assignment: Create DB threads for students to use to post the conclusions they write for Practices 11–14. Consider having students comment on each other's conclusions. See the IM for suggestions.

Example: Concluding by Restating and Summarizing

Walking is clearly an effective form of exercise. Anyone can walk, and very little special gear is needed to participate in a walking program. It is an economical way to exercise, and it pays off in both mental and physical benefits. Walking may just be the perfect exercise.

The thesis statement is reworded.

The support is briefly summarized.

The short final sentence provides a simple ending for the essay.

PRACTICE ⑪ Writing a Conclusion by Restating and Summarizing

Read the following student essay on the topic of divorce. Then, on a separate sheet, write a conclusion paragraph for it that uses the strategy of *restating or summarizing.* You will use this essay again for Practices 12 and 14.

Answers will vary.

What Causes Divorce?

Most people enter marriage with the thought that they will never divorce. Since about half of all marriages *do* end in divorce, it is important to understand just what causes marriages to fall apart. Just what goes wrong? Why do so many marriages end in divorce? While no two marriages are alike, three causes seem to be at the root of many divorces: lack of faithfulness, lack of respect, and lack of communication.

One of the most common reasons for divorce is infidelity. For many people, an affair means the end of their marriage. The reason an affair often causes divorce is that it makes one partner lose trust in the other. The only way to be really open and truthful with one's spouse is to be able to trust him or her. Without trust, the closeness and unity that should be in a marriage disappear. For example, after Meredith's husband had an affair, she found herself constantly worrying about whether her husband was lying to her. This worry caused their marriage to erode further. Meredith began to confide to her friends when she needed someone to lean on, and she felt that her marriage was a failure. Once a partner has an affair, it may be impossible to regain the spouse's trust. This can be the death knell for a marriage.

Another cause of divorce is having a lack of respect for one's partner. Most people start their relationships with respect for their partners. Over time, however, couples begin to notice each other's flaws. If they are not careful, these flaws can lead to disrespect. One partner may begin to think negative thoughts about the other. The marriage will begin to suffer when the spouses begin to point out each other's flaws. Also, if one partner shows disrespect for the ideas or opinions of the other, the couple will begin to feel divided, not unified. For example, it would be difficult for a Democrat to be married to a Republican if each of the partners showed disrespect for the other's viewpoints. This kind of disrespect is not only damaging; it can be very hurtful. Everyone wants to be loved and respected, and if one's spouse is not respectful, it is difficult to stay married.

Good communication is another requirement for a happy marriage. Not having good communication is another reason for divorce. All couples will have occasional problems. Talking is really the only way to bring resolution to these problems. Couples who bury their feelings or who do not want to fight because they think fighting is a destructive thing can end up with communication problems. No one likes to fight, but sometimes people have honest disagreements. When people are not allowed to voice their anger, that anger can intensify. It can cause one partner to make false assumptions about the other, and it can result in a miserable situation. If this misery lasts for very long, the couple will consider divorce as a way to ease their pain.

Concluding by Answering an Earlier Question

Essays that begin with questions can neatly conclude by going back to the question and reminding readers of its answer. Review Debra Humphreys's introduction, which appears earlier in this chapter. She began her essay by asking questions, and she ends it with a summary of the answers. She uses two paragraphs to bring her essay to a conclusion.

Conclusion from "Campus Diversity and Student Self-Segregation: Separating Myths from Facts" by Debra Humphreys

There is little cause for alarm, some cause for celebration and much hope for what lies ahead. The reality is that while there is still a long way to go before American higher education will truly reflect the full diversity of American society, college campuses are becoming much more diverse and their diverse campus environments are having a significant positive effect on this generation of students.

College campuses are not dominated by widespread racial/ethnic segregation and the racial/ethnic clustering that does occur isn't impeding intergroup contact. In fact, the existence of racial/ethnic groups and activities, along with other comprehensive campus diversity initiatives, is contributing to the success of today's college students and preparing them to help build a healthier multicultural America for the future.

> The essay answers some of the questions posed in the introduction paragraph, and the conclusion sums up the answers.
>
> Answer to "How socially segregated are college campuses?"
>
> Answer to "Is diversity leading to educational benefits?"

Using This Strategy in Your Writing. To use this strategy, find new words to repeat the question asked in the introduction. In the example of writing introductions with questions earlier in the chapter, we asked, "Is walking really a legitimate form of exercise?" While the thesis statement provides an answer to the question, the writer can emphasize the answer by repeating the question-and-answer strategy in the conclusion, as shown in the following example.

Notice also that the last sentence is a lighthearted imitation of a television infomercial. This kind of encouragement can be a pleasing way to end an informal essay that advocates an action.

Example: Concluding by Answering an Earlier Question

Is something as simple as taking a daily walk really going to improve your health? The answer is a resounding "Yes!" Not only will walking improve your health and your mood, but it will also make your commitment to an exercise program easier since it requires so little and costs next to nothing. So lace up your sneakers and start your no-risk free trial today!

> The introduction question is reworded here.
>
> The answer repeats the reasoning used in the essay.
>
> The last sentence is a proposal—a call to action for readers.

Notice that both the question and the answer have been reworded for the conclusion paragraph. Never repeat an idea without rewording it.

PRACTICE 12 Writing a Conclusion Paragraph by Answering an Earlier Question

Reread the essay "What Causes Divorce?" in Practice 11. The writer uses these questions in the introduction:

- Just what goes wrong?
- Why do so many marriages end in divorce?

On a separate sheet, write a conclusion paragraph for the essay that uses the strategy of *answering an earlier question*.

Concluding by Finishing a Story

Like returning to an earlier question, another method of concluding is to return to an earlier story. When using stories to introduce essays, writers will sometimes give only a portion of the story and save the story's ending to wrap up the essay. Earlier in this chapter, you read the introduction to "Life with Asperger's Syndrome," an essay that began with a short anecdote about Paul, a child with Asperger's. The writer discusses Asperger's syndrome in the body paragraphs. When she is ready to conclude, she goes back to Paul's story and continues it:

Conclusion from "Life with Asperger's Syndrome"

Paul did not get to school on time on the day he walked home from the bus stop. After his mother talked with him about the need to be flexible regarding time, Paul was able to calm down and eventually go to school. With time and maturity, Paul will learn how to deal with such situations. While life with Asperger's will present challenges, many of those who have it have proven that these challenges will not keep them from living happy, productive lives.	The writer finishes the story begun in the introduction.

Using This Strategy in Your Writing.   To use this method of concluding, make sure your introduction presents a story. If you have already given readers the ending, you can provide an "update" that bring the readers' attention back to the story.

The example below provides an ending to the story of Felicity Martinez, which was used earlier in this text to start an essay about walking. Notice how the ending provides an update of Felicity's situation.

Example: Concluding by Finishing a Story

Felicity Martinez credits walking with transforming her life during her battle with cancer, but her story does not end there. Today, Felicity is a fitness and wellness instructor at Lombardy Health Institute. She specializes in exercise therapy for cancer recovery and prevention. Felicity believes, as do many others, that the benefits of a simple activity like walking are not easily grasped, and she is determined to give to others what walking gave to her.	The writer returns to the story begun in the introduction. The writer gives an update or provides the ending of the story. The writer uses the end of the story to emphasize the thesis statement.

Going back to Felicity's story helps readers feel that not only has the writer made her point, but also that Felicity's story has been thoroughly told.

PRACTICE ⑬ Writing a Conclusion Paragraph by Finishing a Story

For Practice 4, you used a story to write an introduction to an essay. Return to that introduction. On a separate sheet, write a conclusion paragraph for the same essay that uses the strategy of *finishing a story*.

Concluding by Speculating

After thinking about an issue, we often speculate about what that issue means to us personally or to the larger world. To *speculate* is to wonder. For example, when we consider how easy it is to take a walk every day and the healthful effects of walking, we may wonder why more people do not do this. We may, in addition, speculate about what life would be like if everyone began to walk more. This speculation might lead to a prediction. Perhaps if more people walked regularly, our health insurance costs would go down. Or perhaps cities would begin to develop more pedestrian-friendly transit routes.

Speculations that predict or that ask "what if" can also be used to forecast dire consequences so that readers will understand the seriousness of an issue or will take action. In "Homo Sapiens RIP," Andrew Gumbel writes about how some people see artificial intelligence used in robots as a serious threat. Notice how Gumbel uses speculation to conclude his essay. (Note: In his conclusion, Gumbel quotes Bill Joy, a computer expert.)

Conclusion from "Homo Sapiens RIP" by Andrew Gumbel

"We have yet to come to terms with the fact that the most compelling 21st-century technologies . . . pose a different threat than the technologies that have come before," Joy writes. "Specifically, robots, engineered organisms, and nanobots share a dangerous amplifying factor: they can self-replicate. A bomb is blown up only once—but one bot can become many, and quickly get out of control. . . .

"I think it is no exaggeration to say we are on the cusp of the further perfection of extreme evil, an evil whose possibility spreads well beyond that which weapons of mass destruction bequeathed to the nation-states, on to a surprising and terrible empowerment of extreme individuals."

> The writer repeats the problem by quoting Bill Joy, an expert.

> The writer ends by quoting Joy's speculations about the future.

Using This Strategy in Your Writing. Carefully consider your thesis statement. If your thesis statement and essay lead you to make speculations and predictions, consider using this strategy. Be careful that these predictions tie directly into your thesis statement's point. Word your predictions in such a way so that your audience understands these things *might* occur, not that they *will* occur.

The following example shows how we might conclude the essay on the benefits of walking with an ending that uses speculation.

Example: Concluding by Speculating

If more people began to walk for exercise, we might see significant changes in the health of our country. These changes might result in lower costs for health insurance, longer lives, and happier people. Cities might begin to accommodate walkers by creating pedestrian-friendly transit routes, thus reducing traffic. The benefits of walking are worth giving it a try.

> The first three sentences speculate about how walking could change the future.

> The final sentence proposes an action ("giving it a try").

Note that these predictions or speculations are not part of the writer's support for his thesis statement. They are merely encouragements inserted at the end to motivate readers to try walking. The writer is careful to use the word *might* to avoid saying or implying that these results will definitely occur.

Connect IRW Power of Process Assignment: For more practice consider having students analyze the conclusion methods of three readings in PoP. See the IM for a list of suggested readings.

PRACTICE ⑭ Writing a Conclusion Paragraph by Speculating

Reread the essay "What Causes Divorce?" in Practice 11. On a separate sheet, write a conclusion paragraph for the essay that uses the strategy of *concluding by speculating*.

See the Connect IRW *Common Places* Master Course for pre-loaded PoP assignments that require students to analyze the conclusions of select readings.

CHAPTER ACTIVITIES

READING AND ANNOTATING

The following selection is from *Experience Sociology*, a textbook written by David Croteau and William Hoynes. Read and annotate the selection. Before you read, study the three definitions Corteau and Hoynes provide in their text:

- *Deviance* is "behavior that does not conform to basic cultural norms and expectations."
- *Social control* consists of "the incentives and punishments that promote conformity in social life."
- *Agents of social control* are "the authorities and social institutions that enforce norms and rules, attempt to prevent rule violations, and identify and punish rule violators."

(Note: The selection contains parenthetical references to sources the authors have used. Full information about these sources, listed in the authors' text, is not given here.)

Deviance as a Marketable Product

by David Croteau and William Hoynes

YOUR ANNOTATIONS

Lexile: 1370L

As society changes, definitions of deviance change as well, bringing about new mechanisms of social control. One area of interest to sociologists in recent years has been the commercialization of deviance, the process by which nonconformist activities or styles turn into commercial products. These new products often create dilemmas for agents of social control.

In many cultures, specific periods of time are set aside as occasions when otherwise deviant behavior is accepted and even encouraged. Brazil's Carnival and New Orleans's Mardi Gras celebrations, for example, can involve excessive public drinking, dancing in the streets, and public nudity. Recently these occasions have taken on a decidedly commercial tone. Mardi Gras and Carnival are tourist attractions more than religious festivals. Another example, familiar to many college students, is spring break, which can offer the promise of unbridled partying while bringing much-needed dollars into local economies.

Practicing deviance for fun in special times and places has become a form of tourism, a short vacation from the routines of everyday life. This idea of a vacation from norms and rules is captured in the advertising slogan "What happens in Vegas, stays in Vegas."

One sociologist refers to these activities as "playful deviance": people "travel to symbolic spaces of leisure to participate in temporary forms of transgressions that they will not perform in places where they live" (Redmon 2003, 27). Playful deviance takes place apart from everyday life and is generally a short-term activity. People experience playful deviance as both exciting and liberating, an opportunity to act like someone else for a short time.

The marketing of vacations as opportunities for "playful deviance" is just one form of the marketing of deviance. Businesses also increasingly look to deviant subcultures for new opportunities, as in the cases of tattoos and body piercing. Skateboarding also used to be part of a deviant subculture, involving young people who didn't play traditional sports, didn't wear traditional clothes or hairstyles, and often had a defiant attitude toward authorities. Skateboarding and other extreme sports were outsider activities in the 1970s and 1980s, but today they are increasingly popular and mainstream: top skateboarders have corporate sponsors, skateboard styles are available in suburban malls, and X Games broadcasts are among the most popular programs on ESPN.

The world of indie music provides many similar examples, as alternative bands become popular on radio stations, MTV, and in the major-label music business. Punk, rap, and grunge music all began in deviant subcultures, and all three became commercial genres of music and fashion. The irony is that alternative music—and youth subcultures, more generally—become commercially successful because they have their roots in nonconformity. Deviance sells because it represents authenticity in a society full of mass-produced images (Moore 2005). Commercial success is a double-edged sword, however. As deviant activities and styles are marketed widely, they gain visibility and popularity that may undermine their initial authentic image. Once youth subcultures are absorbed into the mainstream corporate culture, these expressions of nonconformity often lose credibility. Historian Thomas Frank (1997) refers to "the conquest of cool" to describe the process through which hipster style morphed from its association with alienated youth to the centerpiece of corporate advertising in the 1970s.

Businesses have learned that deviance can be packaged and sold. The advertising campaigns and new product lines directed at the global youth market are saturated with images associated with individuality, authenticity, and rebellion. Advertisers and market researchers actively seek out deviant youth subcultures, trying to anticipate upcoming trends. In a type of street research known as "cool hunting," businesses search for groups of kids—often connected to deviant subcultures—who are perceived to be a window on what's likely to be popular in the near future (Gladwell 1997). In the world of the cool hunt, deviance is a potentially valuable commodity.

Many types of nonconformist behavior are not obviously harmful, even though some people consider them offensive. In some cases—such as sporting a dramatically unconventional hairstyle or cross dressing at school or work—the potential stigma associated with deviance may become a kind of badge of honor, one that people wear proudly to proclaim their independence from stifling forms of convention. It would be a mistake, however, to conclude that the growth of deviance as a leisure activity or commercial product is a sign that social control has weakened substantially. Instead, embracing deviance and transforming nonconformity into a leisure activity are becoming new mechanisms of social control. Considered in this way, deviance-as-leisure is a kind of safety valve, allowing us to blow off steam from the pressure of social conformity without threatening basic social norms. In the age of tell-all reality television, YouTube videos, and online role-playing games, we are fast becoming a society in which both performing and consuming deviance are popular forms of entertainment that may largely reinforce existing norms and social structures.

Questions for Consideration

1. What point about deviance do the writers want readers to understand?
2. Give an example of a deviant activity or behavior that has been commercialized. Explain how it became commercialized.

Questions for Consideration

1. Deviance can be packaged as a product and sold so that people can safely and temporarily experience it.
2. In Western culture, tattoos used to indicate special rebel status or perhaps military affiliation. Now everyone gets tattoos, and the tattoo industry exists commercially.

3. The writers say that deviance helps musicians and other artists separate themselves from the crowd. However, they warn, "commercial success is a double-edged sword." What do they mean by this warning?

4. Explain the concept of "playful deviance."

USING MODELS TO PRACTICE COMPOSING

Reggie is a student in an English class and has been given a reading and writing assignment. Here are Reggie's annotations of his assignment.

Reggie's Annotated Assignment

Read, annotate, and analyze "Deviance as a Marketable Product." Make sure you understand the definitions of *deviance, social control, agents of social control, commercialization,* and *playful deviance.* You will need to use these key words in the essay you will write.

Write an essay in which you discuss a deviant behavior that has become commercialized or that has become a type of playful deviance. Start your project by using prewriting to select a deviant behavior. Plan your essay so that it includes the following elements: an explanation of the deviant behavior, a discussion of how it was commercialized or became playful deviance, and a discussion of how "agents of social control" regard the commercialized behavior. End your essay by speculating on the future of the deviant behavior you selected. Will the behavior cease to be deviant, in your opinion? You may use examples—both real-life and hypothetical—to discuss the deviant behavior.

Give credit to the authors of the reading when you use concepts from their text.

Margin annotations:

3. As soon as a deviant musician is accepted, he or she becomes normalized. The deviance that was at one time new and dangerous becomes common. The appeal of the new musician or artist may then decrease.

4. Playful deviance is a mild departure from accepted behavior, usually taking place away from home and for a short time.

Read, annotate, and analyze the text

Understand definitions (will use them in the essay)

Write an essay

Select a deviant behavior that has been commercialized (bought and sold)

Do 3 things: explain behavior, discuss its commercialization/playful status, discuss how "agents" regard it

End by speculating on future of deviant behavior

May use examples

Give credit when necessary

Reggie starts by using simple listing to prewrite about behaviors that are deviant, and he then figures out which ones have been commercialized.

Deviant behaviors:
- Tattoos—have been commercialized
- Piercings—have been commercialized
- Riding a motorcycle—has been commercialized
- Gambling—has been commercialized
- Prostitution—still deviant
- Cheating on a spouse—still deviant
- Using marijuana—is becoming commercialized
- Dropping out of high school—still deviant
- Having an unusual hair color—has been commercialized
- Nude beaches—still deviant?

Next, Reggie decides on a behavior to discuss in his essay, and he uses another prewriting activity—freewriting—to generate ideas about the topic. Notice that Reggie uses some of the assignment requirements to guide his prewriting.

Going to Nude Beaches

Explanation of behavior—being nude in public has always been a deviant behavior, is illegal, is considered immoral by some, still taboo.

Discussion of its commercialization /playful deviance—Nude beaches created to give people a way to be deviant without breaking laws. Maybe going to nude beaches is playful deviance? Unsure . . . nude beaches are advertised as providing a unique experience. People might go to a nude beach occasionally but then go back to where they live and not appear nude in public, temporary deviance.

Discussion of how "agents" regard it—Not a lot of talk about it, but probably still frowned upon by most people (by my parents and grandparents for sure!). Since nude beaches are legal, some "agents" aren't outraged. The nudity is controlled and contained in particular areas of a beach. So maybe the deviant behavior won't "infect" others . . . maybe that's why agents are OK with it.

Future of deviant behavior—Can't see nude beaches ever becoming normal, but who knows? Nudity in the US is a real taboo.

Reggie is now ready to create an outline for his essay on his computer.

Reggie's Outline

Title: Nude Beaches in the United States

Introduction ideas: Start with a hypothetical example (Barbara and Fred)

Thesis statement: Nude beaches in the United States offer a type of playful deviance.

Major supporting point 1: Public nudity in the United States is always considered deviant behavior.

- Laws are against it.
- People have moral objections to it.
- Give examples of how people react to nudity.

Major supporting point 2: Nude beaches allow people to participate in "playful deviance."

- Give definition of "playful deviance."
- Explain how nude beaches make it OK temporarily.
- Explain why Barbara and Fred like playful deviance.

Major supporting point 3: Since public nudity is rare and occurs only among consenting adults, our society seems to tolerate the existence of nude beaches.

- Give reasons why agents are OK with this:
  - It is temporary.
  - It is restricted to certain locations and certain people.
- It's still illegal.

Conclusion/speculation: Public nudity will probably never be accepted in the US.

Now that Reggie has an outline, he uses the remaining steps in the writing process to draft his essay, revise it, and edit it. What follows is Reggie's final draft. Annotate Reggie's draft for thesis statement, major supporting points, and other important elements. Also, determine the introduction and conclusion strategies Reggie uses.

Chambers 1

YOUR ANNOTATIONS

Reggie Chambers

Mr. Roberts

ENGL 0402

24 October 2014

— MLA heading

Nude Beaches: Playful Deviance in the United States

Barbara and Fred wake up to a beautiful Saturday in July and pack some lunches in a cooler. Barbara is especially looking forward to this day of relaxation on the beach because her engineering job has been stressful lately. Fred is also in need of a break. As a commercial pilot, he often flies over beautiful beaches but rarely gets to enjoy them. Arriving at the beach, Barbara and Fred set up some chairs, take out some sunscreen, and then take off all their clothes. These two ordinary and upstanding people occasionally visit a nude beach. Like many people who go to nude beaches, Barbara and Fred enjoy the temporary break from societal norms. For them and for many others, nude beaches in the United States offer a type of playful deviance.

— Introduction strategy: starting with a story

— Surprise twist in narrative

— Thesis statement

Public nudity in the United States is always considered deviant behavior. Most cities have laws against public nudity. One of the virtues children are taught is modesty. It is true that teens have begun to dress less modestly over the years, but in general, people are expected to cover up their private parts in public. Going against social rules about nudity is a type of defiance. Unlike some other types of defiance, such

— Major supporting point 1 (topic sentence)

Chambers 2

as tattoos and piercings, nudity is still prohibited, and the only way to practice it is to carefully select a place where nudity is OK.

Nude beaches allow people to participate in "playful deviance." According to David Croteau and William Hoynes, "Playful deviance takes place apart from everyday life and is generally a short-term activity. People experience playful deviance as both exciting and liberating, an opportunity to act like someone else for a short time." Going to a nude beach fits this definition. While Barbara and Fred would never appear nude in their own community, they can go to a nude beach and deviate from the norm. This type of deviation is relaxing to people like Barbara and Fred or may be a type of fun.

So how do people get away with having nude beaches since public nudity is considered deviant? Most of the time, deviant behavior is not tolerated by "agents of social control," the people who enforce cultural norms, according to Croteau and Hoynes. In the case of nude beaches, agents of social control are tolerant because they know that nudity is still being controlled. Only on certain beaches is public nudity allowed. It is restricted to adults, and it is not common. If every beach became a nude beach, the agents of social control would probably not tolerate it. But since public nudity is rare and occurs only among consenting adults, our society seems to tolerate the existence of nude beaches.

If things stay the way they are, it is likely that nude beaches will continue to be tolerated. It is unlikely that the deviant behavior (nudity in public) will increase, and it is unlikely that nude beaches will totally go away. Because nude beaches offer a type of playful deviance that is restricted by age and by place, Barbara and Fred will probably be able to continue their occasional Saturday expeditions.

YOUR ANNOTATIONS

Transition to next point

Major supporting point 2 (topic sentence)

Quotation integrated into text

Rhetorical device—asking a question

Major supporting point 3 (topic sentence—at end of paragraph)

Conclusion strategies: speculating and finishing a story

A READING AND WRITING ASSIGNMENT

Now that you have analyzed Reggie's process for completing his essay assignment, write an essay of your own in response to the same assignment. (See "Reggie's Annotated Assignment" on page 269.) Use the Quick Start Guide to Integrated Reading and Writing Assignments to assist you in the writing process.

THINKING FROM AN INSTRUCTOR'S POINT OF VIEW

Just as a creative title and an interesting introduction can entice you to read an article, you can create titles and introductions that make your instructor look forward to reading your work. Many students are content to write titles and introductions that are "good enough." For instance, a writing instructor assigned a paper on homelessness—what it is, why it exists, and how we should respond to it as a society. Here are the titles from eleven papers she received:

1. Homelessness
2. Homelessness in the United States
3. Homelessness
4. [no title]
5. Why Is There Homelessness?
6. We Are Responsible for Homelessness
7. The Homelessness Cure
8. Homelessness in Society
9. Being Homeless Sucks
10. Why Homelessness Matters
11. Homes for All

Clearly, some of these titles are better than others.

Students do not always view their instructors as the audience for their writing. Keeping in mind that your instructors *are* your primary audience will help you design an essay with a title that they may find interesting.

The same is true for introductions and conclusions. The typical introduction paragraph for the students' homelessness essays went something like this:

> Homelessness is a big problem in this day and age. Almost every city in the United States has homeless people in it. However, we can fix the problem of homelessness by talking about what it is and understanding what causes it.

The typical conclusion paragraph went something like this:

> In conclusion, homelessness is a problem that must be fixed. If society used some of the strategies in this essay, no one would have to be homeless anymore.

Not only are the introduction and conclusion paragraphs boring, but they are also inaccurate. The introduction says that we can fix the issue of homelessness by talking about it and understanding it. These are great things to do, but they will not fix homelessness. The conclusion is much too optimistic. Very few solutions are ever universally effective.

Students sometimes write these types of titles, introductions, and conclusions because they do not take the time to think creatively and to consider the needs of their audience. As you construct titles, introductions, and conclusions, work on standing apart from the crowd. Make sure you take the time to be creative. Use strategies in this chapter to your advantage.

Consider guiding students as they select topics. See the IM for a discussion of how to guide this assignment and for additional writing assignments that meet the learning objectives of this chapter.

Students may find it interesting to read a list of the essay titles you receive from students in your other classes. Seeing how their peers title their work may give them ideas about how they can title their own.

Thinking Creatively

1. Which of the titles do you think the instructor found most interesting and impressive? Why? Write a paragraph explaining your choice.

2. Without using any of the titles from the previous list, create a new title for the essay assignment on homelessness.

3. Write a creative introduction for this thesis statement: *Homelessness is a serious problem, but there are some actions we can take to start solving it.*

4. Imagine you have written an essay about steps we can take to solve homelessness. Write a creative conclusion paragraph to end your essay.

⊙ ADDING TO YOUR VOCABULARY

This chapter's vocabulary words appear below.

See the IM for additional vocabulary activities. See the Connect IRW *Common Places* Master Course for vocabulary study practices that accompany this chapter, as well as a chapter vocabulary quiz.

conceivable	credible	autism	advocate
irony	conventional	therapeutic	

Choose five of the vocabulary words from this chapter that you would like to add to your vocabulary, and think about how you can use them this week. For example, one of this chapter's words is *advocate*. You can often easily substitute *advocate* for *suggest* or sometimes *say*, as in the example that follows.

Example: I am *saying* that you should obey speed limit laws.

I am *advocating* that you obey speed limit laws.

List each of the five words you plan to use this week, and make note of a context in which you could use each word.

Example: *Advocating*. I can use this word when I give advice to a family member.

⊙ ADDITIONAL ASSIGNMENTS

1. Imagine you are writing an essay with this thesis statement: *Six steps can help you be a more organized person.* The six steps you will discuss are these:

   Answers will vary.

   - Make and use lists.
   - Keep a neat desk.
   - Organize paperwork effectively and daily.
   - Use your smartphone's organizational tools.
   - Identify the obstacles that keep you from being organized, and make a plan to deal with them.
   - Hire help when it is necessary.

   Write an introduction paragraph, a conclusion paragraph, and a title for this essay.

2. Find an essay in this textbook that could benefit from a new introduction paragraph or conclusion paragraph, and write the paragraph.

3. **a.** Scan magazines, textbooks, or other texts. Choose a text with an interesting title. Explain in a paragraph what makes the title interesting.

   b. Do the same for an introduction: find a text that contains a well-written introduction. Write a paragraph explaining why you find the introduction well written.

   c. Follow this same procedure for a conclusion paragraph. Be sure to write down the name of the essay (or textbook chapter) in which you found the interesting or well-written introduction and conclusion.

4. Take out an essay you wrote for this course or for another course. Rewrite the title, introduction, and conclusion using strategies from this chapter. Work on improving the interest and quality of all three elements.

EMOTIONAL INTELLIGENCE

Two types of motivation exist. First, there is *extrinsic motivation.* Something that motivates us extrinsically is something that is outside of us. For example, if a person stands over me with a stun gun and commands me to move rocks, I will move the rocks—not because I want to move rocks, but because I am being forced to move them. *Intrinsic motivation* is motivation that comes from inside. If I am building an outdoor fire pit with rocks, I will move the rocks because I want to build the fire pit.

Studies show that students who do work because they are intrinsically motivated to succeed in college *always* do better work than students who do work because they are being forced to. Think of a time when you did a college assignment that you *wanted* to do, not because you were forced to. Now think of an assignment you did because you had to. What was the difference in the quality of those assignments? Explain your answer in a paragraph.

Think about how you can be intrinsically motivated to do college assignments in which you are not personally interested. How can you transform extrinsic motivation to intrinsic motivation—even when the assignments are not ones you long to do? Write a paragraph explaining your ideas.

Answers will vary, but students should talk about ways they can make an assignment personally relevant.

CULTURAL LITERACY

History is full of books that have been highly influential. From the list below, choose five works that you have not studied, and do an Internet search for each one. Determine why the work is famous. Summarize the work—most are books—in one or two sentences.

Answers will vary.

The Diary of Anne Frank
The King James Version Bible
The Iliad and *The Odyssey*
Invisible Man (Ellison)
The Koran

The Origin of Species
The Water Margin
Romeo and Juliet
Aesop's fables
Uncle Tom's Cabin

CRITICAL THINKING

Ethnocentrism means using your own cultural perspective to evaluate the beliefs and conventions of people from other cultures. For example, a person who lives in the United States may think in an ethnocentric way if he thinks *like an American* and cannot imagine an issue from the perspective of someone who lives in another country.

If you ask many Americans to list the most important documents in the world, they will probably choose works central to American life, such as the U.S. Constitution and the Declaration of Independence. If you ask a Chinese person to list the most important documents, that person is likely to list Chinese books.

Thinking critically requires us to be aware of our tendency to think in ethnocentric ways and to try to think from a broader perspective. Here are some examples of customs and beliefs that have their basis in ethnocentrism:

- Many Muslim women wear head scarves for religious or cultural reasons. Think of an item that people from other religions and cultures might wear. Why do you think people wear these items? What do these items tell others about the wearer's identity and beliefs?

- One delicacy of French cuisine is snails, called *escargot* (pronounced es-car-GO)—a dish that has not gained wide popularity in the United States. Think of other cultural food preferences that you have encountered or read about. Are you

Answers will vary. Ethnocentric beliefs that students might choose to write about include these:
- *Arranged marriage is ridiculous.*
- *Cleanliness is next to godliness.*
- *Horse meat should not be eaten.*
- *It is wrong to kill whales.*
- *People should work forty hours per week.*

adventurous about trying other foods? Or do you prefer to stay with foods you find familiar? Do you think our reactions to people's culinary preferences affect how we feel about their culture or society? Why or why not?

- China, which has a culture of honoring and respecting the elderly, recently passed an "Elderly Rights Law" that makes it illegal for adults to "snub" or "neglect" their elderly parents. What cultural obligations do Americans feel toward their parents? Is there a consistent cultural attitude, or do the expectations vary by region, economic class, or ethnic group? How do cultures respond when changes in society make it difficult to honor long-standing expectations?

Choose one of these topics, and write a paragraph answering the questions given. Alternatively, write a paragraph about your own observations about ethnocentric beliefs.

METACOGNITION

Metacognitive ability means you can see yourself from the outside. Answer the following questions from a metacognitive point of view. Are you an ethnocentric thinker? (An ethnocentric thinker is unable to see things from a different cultural perspective.) Is this something you can change? Explain.

Answers will vary.

An inference is an educated guess. By examining the details of this photo, what inferences can you make? Readers and writers work with inferences in texts as well as in illustrations.

Inferences and Tone

An inference is a conclusion a person draws based on evidence. When we read, we **infer** by examining the information the writer provides. On the other hand, when we speak or write, we can **imply** meanings without stating them outright. For instance, when we need to finish a conversation, we might say something such as "It's getting late." Our words *imply* a deeper meaning— "We need to end this conversation"—and we hope our listeners will *infer* this meaning from what they hear us say.

As readers and observers, we make inferences every day. We might see a restaurant with a paint-worn and disheveled appearance and infer that the food must not be good. Or perhaps we find ourselves in stop-and-go traffic and infer that the freeway will be clogged for a long time, so we take an exit and find an alternative route.

Sometimes our inferences are correct, and sometimes they are totally mistaken. We may learn that the "rundown" restaurant is a fabulous eatery that has been featured on a televised food program, or we may learn that the freeway was not clogged: debris from a tire blowout had simply slowed down traffic temporarily. Being able to make accurate inferences is crucial for good communication.

CHAPTER OBJECTIVES

After completing this chapter, students will be able to do the following:

- **Use details in images and texts to draw accurate inferences.**

- **Analyze the assumptions that influence inferences.**

- **Analyze assumptions to control implications in writing.**

- **Analyze tone in texts.**

- **Recognize first, second, and third person in readings, and make appropriate writing choices concerning person.**

- **Choose an appropriate tone for writing assignments.**

- **Analyze figurative language to make accurate inferences.**

- **Use figurative language in writing.**

- **Draw accurate inferences from graphics.**

Connect IRW LearnSmart Achieve: Assign the topic "Reading to Infer/Writing to Imply" for adaptive learning to accompany this chapter.

USING DETAILS IN IMAGES AND TEXTS TO DRAW ACCURATE INFERENCES

One way to make accurate inferences is to consider details. The details in an image or a text give us information on which we can base our inferences.

Details in an Image

When we observe an image such as a photograph, the details in the photo help us draw inferences. Study the picture shown here. What inferences can you draw from the details in the photo?

Teaching Resources: See the Chapter Quiz.

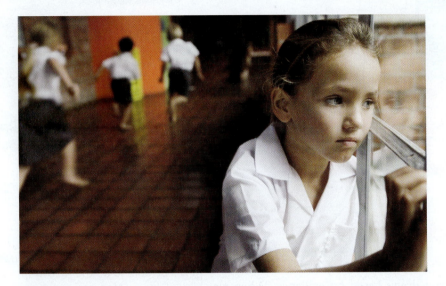

Teaching Resources: See the *PowerPoint* (PPT) "Making Visual Inferences" as an enjoyable and interesting way to start this chapter.

Perhaps you noticed the girl in the forefront and the three children in the background. The girl gazing out the window does not have a smile on her face, and her eyebrow is slightly raised. Her intense gaze suggests worry. The children in the background, meanwhile, are running barefoot. All the children have on similar clothing. We might infer that these children are in school because they seem to be wearing school uniforms. We might also infer that the girl looking out the window is not part of the group or that she is not in a playful mood. We may infer that she is lonely or worried or that she wants to be somewhere other than school. These are **sound** inferences because we can support them with the details in the photo.

What would you say to a person who looks at the photo and thinks the girl is nervous and unhappy because she is a new student at the school and misses her old friends? We can see that she is unhappy, but we really cannot see why. The fact that she is not playing with the other children does not give us enough information on which to base the inference that the school is new to her and that she misses her friends. While it would be easy to imagine many different reasons for the girl's posture and facial expression, we can use only the reasons that are supported by evidence to draw correct inferences.

Vocabulary Collection Word:
sound

Your in-context definition:

_____

_____

A dictionary definition:

_____

_____

Details in a Text

To be sound, an inference must be based on the actual information in a text. Read the following passage, and notice the details that are underlined.

> As I walked to my trigonometry class on the first day of the semester, I felt full of hope. Math had never been an easy subject for me, but I knew that with determination, I could do anything. I really believed that.

(continued)

I found a seat in the middle of the classroom and glanced at the people around me. Most looked nonchalant, as if taking a class in trig were not a big deal. No one spoke.

Five minutes after the class was supposed to begin, a man who looked too young to be a professor walked into the class, slung his gray, worn backpack on the professor's table, and started writing an equation on the board. He muttered something about page 33, so I fumbled through my textbook to find the page. Nothing on the page looked remotely like what the professor had written on the board.

He kept explaining. Something.

"You understand?" he asked the class, turning back to the board before anyone could answer.

I felt that sinking feeling in my stomach that I have felt in so many math classes before. It would be a long semester after all.

We can use the details to make some inferences. We can safely infer that the instructor is young, based on the narrator's description. Some people might be tempted to say the instructor is a teaching assistant, not a professor, but we do not have enough details to make that inference.

Can we infer that the other students are more advanced in mathematics than the narrator? The narrator describes the other students as *nonchalant* (calm, not anxious), but we would need more information to know whether the students are really better at math than the narrator.

Would we be right to infer that, by the end of the passage, the narrator is not optimistic about his ability to do well in the class? Yes, we can make this inference because the last sentence tells us the narrator feels the same way he did in previous math classes, and we know from a detail earlier in the passage that math had never been an easy subject for him.

While we can infer that the narrator has a negative feeling about the class, we *cannot* accurately infer that he will fail. We simply do not have enough information to make that inference. The instructor may turn out to be a wonderful teacher, and even if the instructor is not wonderful, the student may still pass the class.

Base your inferences on the actual details of the passage. Do not add your own assumptions.

Now we will look at a text that is a bit more complex and use it to judge inferences. Read and carefully annotate the following selection from *A First Look at Communication Theory* by Em Griffin. Pay special attention to the details it offers.

Connect IRW Power of Process Assignment: Students can practice their skills in drawing accurate inferences by using readings in PoP. See the Instructor's Manual (IM) for suggested readings and ideas for setting up the assignments.

See the Connect IRW *Common Places* Master Course for pre-loaded assignments that require students to analyze the inferences in select readings.

What We Can Learn from the *Challenger* Disaster

by Em Griffin

YOUR ANNOTATIONS

[1]On the morning of January 28, 1986, the space shuttle *Challenger* blasted off from the Kennedy Space Center in Florida. [2]Seventy-three seconds later, millions of adults and school children watched on television as the rocket disintegrated in a fiery explosion, and the capsule plunged into the Atlantic Ocean. [3]The death of all seven crew members, and particularly teacher Christa McAuliffe, shocked the nation. [4]For many Americans, the *Challenger* disaster marked the end of a love affair with space. [5]As they learned in the months that followed, the tragedy could have been—should have been—avoided.

(continued)

[6]President Reagan immediately appointed a select commission to determine the probable cause(s) of the accident. [7]The panel heard four months of testimony from NASA officials, rocket engineers, astronauts, and anyone else who might have knowledge about the failed mission. [8]In a five-volume published report, the presidential commission identified the primary cause of the accident as a failure in the joint between two stages of the rocket that allowed hot gases to escape during the "burn." [9]Volatile rocket fuel spewed out when a rubber O-ring failed to seal the joint.

[10]The average citizen could understand the mechanics of the commission's finding. [11]After all, everyone knows what happens when you pour gasoline on an open flame. [12]What people found difficult to fathom was why NASA had launched the *Challenger* when there was good reason to believe the conditions weren't safe. [13]In addition to the defective seal, the commission also concluded that a highly flawed decision process was an important contributing cause of the disaster. [14]Communication, as well as combustion, was responsible for the tragedy.

The details in the passage suggest that the following inferences are sound:

- **The *Challenger* tragedy was thoroughly investigated.** We expect a thorough investigation to include a number of different people who represent different agencies and have different viewpoints. We also expect a thorough investigation to take a significant amount of time. Further, a thorough investigation should be meaningful. The details in the passage show that the investigation met all of these expectations. Thus, we can infer that it was a thorough investigation.

- **After the disaster, teachers and school children discussed the tragedy.** While the writer does not say this explicitly, he does provide details that allow us to make this inference. First, he tells us that "millions of adults and school children watched on television as the rocket disintegrated in a fiery explosion" (sentence 2). It is reasonable to think that children who watched the disaster on television would have been upset by it. Further, since many of these children were watching the disaster from their schools, it is reasonable to infer that their teachers would have discussed the tragedy with them.

One pitfall when drawing inferences is to allow your own personal beliefs, ideas, or biases to influence the inferences you draw. The following inferences are *not* sound. Read each explanation to understand why.

- **The *Challenger* tragedy demonstrated that Americans should not support the space program.** This incorrect inference may be caused by not reading the passage carefully enough, or it may be prompted by the reader's own opinion about the space program. In the passage, we read, "For many Americans, the *Challenger* disaster marked the end of a love affair with space" (sentence 4). Just because many Americans stopped loving space exploration, that does not mean they necessarily wished to end the space program. This inference goes beyond what the details of the text tell us. To make this incorrect inference, the reader has to *add to* the information of the text.

- **NASA engineers did not know how to design flawless O-rings.** This inference is not sound because there are no details in the passage to support it. What we learn in the passage is that the O-ring failed and that communication contributed to this failure. There is no suggestion anywhere that the engineers lacked knowledge. Further, in sentence 5, we read that "the tragedy could have been—should have been—avoided." This suggests that the engineers were perfectly capable of making flawless O-rings but that other factors contributed to the disaster.

As you look for inferences in texts, make sure you use the actual details that the text supplies, not ideas you bring to the text. Be sure you can point to the details that make your inferences accurate.

PRACTICE (1) Drawing Inferences Based on a Text's Details

Use the passage from *A First Look at Communication Theory* to determine whether the inferences that follow are sound. Write *S* for inferences that are sound and *NS* for those that are not sound. Write a sentence explaining your reasoning for each answer.

_S_   **1.** The president at the time was Ronald Reagan.

> Since Ronald Reagan commissioned the investigation, we can infer that he was in power at the time.

_NS_   **2.** The writer believes that school children should not be allowed to watch rocket launches.

> The writer merely reports that children watched the event; he does not suggest that children should not be allowed to watch launches.

_S_   **3.** Some people at NASA were probably worried about something going wrong with the launch.

> The writer asks why NASA launched the rocket when "there was good reason to believe the conditions weren't safe." If there was good reason to believe this, someone probably did believe it.

_NS_   **4.** The panel investigating may not have been qualified to make the investigation.

> There is no evidence in the article to support this inference.

_NS_   **5.** Some people involved in the launch knew the shuttle was going to blow up during liftoff.

> There is no evidence in the article to support this inference.

_S_   **6.** Even the most minor details of space flight must be considered for the flight to be safe.

> The fact that the small o-ring's failure contributed to the tragedy supports this inference.

ANALYZING THE ASSUMPTIONS THAT INFLUENCE INFERENCES

As we interpret the clues in a photo or a text to make inferences, another factor often comes into play: our assumptions. An **assumption** is a belief you hold to be true. For example, because of your experiences, you may have made the assumption that you live in a safe town. You may infer, based on this assumption, that it is safe to leave your doors unlocked at night. Of course, your assumption can be wrong; if it is, your inference—that you can safely leave your doors unlocked—will also be wrong.

It is not always easy to examine our assumptions because sometimes we do not even recognize them. For example, as children, we believed the rest of the world was just like the world in which we grew up. As we matured, we learned this assumption is wrong: other people think very differently and live very differently than we do. Some children grow up with the assumption that they will go to college. Others grow up assuming they

Teaching Resources: Learning to analyze assumptions can help students in personal—as well as academic—ways. See the IM for more assignments to support this learning objective.

will not finish high school. Assumptions like these shape our lives. One of the goals of an education is to help students examine the assumptions they hold and to change those beliefs when it is necessary or helpful to do so.

Assumptions That Affect Our Inferences about Events

Demetria is in her first semester in college. For the first major exam in her history class, she spends thirty minutes before class looking over her textbook. This is the method of studying she used in high school, and she usually passed her tests. When she gets the graded test back, she is astonished to see that she earned a 40. Demetria had incorrectly assumed that college tests would be like high school tests.

Let's imagine that you work for a company that conducts fire drills ten times a year. You are at work and finishing an overdue report. The fire alarm bell rings, and you look around. People are walking toward the exits, chitchatting about the day's events. No one is running out of the building, you don't see smoke, and you don't hear shouting. Your assumption is that a real fire emergency will look different than a fire drill; thus, you infer that there is no danger at hand. Consequently, you continue writing your report—until black smoke starts filling the office.

What went wrong? There were signs that should have guided you to the correct inference. You heard the fire alarm bell, and you knew that it is used to signal fires and warn employees to evacuate. You saw coworkers exiting the building. But your assumption—that a real fire emergency would seem different than a fire drill—led you to make the wrong inference.

Assumptions That Affect Our Inferences about Texts

Readers can make incorrect inferences about texts because their assumptions are faulty. Read the following example to see how assumptions can influence the inferences we make.

Teaching Resources: See the PPT "Dangerous Assumptions."

> **Text:** I sat in the den glaring at the TV, dumbfounded by what was taking place on the football field. The Colts' quarterback was sacked again—the third time in the game. In disgust, I guzzled the last of the beer in the can and sank down into the dilapidated, old couch.
>
> **Inference 1:** The speaker is a Colts fan.
>
> **Inference 2:** He is unhappy with the Colts' performance.

The speaker's actions clearly show unhappiness with the events in the Colts' football game, so the idea that the speaker is a Colts fan is a sound inference. Part of the second inference—that the speaker is unhappy with the Colts' performance—is a sound inference. The word *disgust* gives us some proof for the speaker's feelings. However, the pronoun *he* is a problem! Is there any evidence in the paragraph that the speaker is male? Reread the paragraph to see.

In fact, the speaker could be male or female. However, many readers will make the false assumption that the football fan is male, and the stereotype about beer-drinking male football fans adds to this assumption. In this case, we are incorrect to assume the football fan is a male. The only basis we have for that inference is a stereotype about football fans.

Let's consider another example. Read the text below, and analyze the assumptions used to make the inferences.

> **Text:** Positive psychology is, as Dorothy Foltz-Gray defines it, "a discipline that aims not just to relieve suffering but also to increase happiness." The focus of psychology for many years has been to determine what psychological disorders

are and how we can treat them. Positive psychology, a discipline that has gained popularity in the last twenty years, asks different questions. Rather than focusing on disorders, positive psychology seeks to determine what makes us psychologically *well*. What are the stabilizing factors that cause some people to live happy, productive lives? Positive psychology seeks to answer that question.

Inference 1: Dorothy Foltz-Gray is a psychologist.

Inference 2: Psychologists now value positive psychology more than traditional psychology.

Did you infer that Dorothy Foltz-Gray is a psychologist? What assumption might lead a person to make that inference? (See if you can answer this question before reading on to find the answer!)

A reader might also infer that psychologists now value positive psychology more than traditional psychology. Can you figure out the assumption on which that inference might be based?

The first inference—that Dorothy Foltz-Gray is a psychologist—rests on the assumption that a person who defines a term or writes about an issue must be an expert in the field from which that term comes. And sometimes that assumption is true. Textbooks, for example, offer plenty of definitions, and they are always written by professionals in the field. But we might also read articles written by journalists in which we find definitions. Journalists write about a broad range of topics: they are not necessarily experts in a field other than journalism. What's more, students often offer definitions in informative essays, and they are not experts either. Thus, we cannot assume that just because someone proffers a definition or writes about a subject, he or she is an expert in a field.

The second inference—that psychologists now value positive psychology more than traditional psychology—is also based on a false assumption. The assumption is that if something is gaining popularity, it must be better or more valuable than its competitors. In science, however, this assumption is not true. In fact, scientists are often cautious of new theories and are usually slow to change their beliefs. Because the assumption is false, the inference that positive psychology is now valued more than traditional psychology is also false.

As you make inferences, ask yourself, "What assumptions am I making?" While it is very difficult to identify your assumptions, doing so is the first step to thinking more critically and making more accurate judgments.

PRACTICE ❷ Analyzing Assumptions to Make Sound Inferences

Make an inference about each of the situations described below. Determine the assumption on which you based your inference. Finally, evaluate your inference and assumption. Is the assumption reasonable? Is the inference sound? Write a sentence explaining your evaluation.

Answers will vary. Sample responses are provided.

1. My history class will be an online class.

Inference: I won't need to spend nearly as much time on my history class as I will need to spend on my on-campus sociology class.

Assumption: Online classes require less time.

Evaluation: Incorrect.

(continued)

2. Kendra enjoys doing her taxes and volunteers to calculate taxes for her friends and family. She wants to be an accountant.

    Inference: Kendra is good at math.

    Assumption: People who enjoy mathematical work and want jobs in fields that require math skills are likely to be good at math.

    Evaluation: Correct.

3. Tom lives in a city known for high crime rates. In fact, Tom's next-door neighbor's apartment was burglarized last week. After buying groceries one evening, Tom arrives home to see his door ajar. Standing quietly at the door, Tom hears shuffling noises inside the apartment.

    Inference: Someone is robbing Tom's apartment.

    Assumption: The only possible explanation is that Tom's apartment is being robbed.

    Evaluation: Incorrect.

4. Kaylea had always been shy and bookish, and her hard work paid off when she learned she was the valedictorian of her high school.

    Inference: Kaylea is the most likely student to succeed in life.

    Assumption: Kaylea's high school experience will accurately allow us to predict her post–high school success.

    Evaluation: Incorrect.

ANALYZING ASSUMPTIONS TO CONTROL NEGATIVE IMPLICATIONS IN YOUR WRITING

An important part of writing is considering how a reader will understand your text. One way readers understand texts is by drawing inferences. Thus, good writers think about the potential inferential meanings readers may draw from their writing.

Anticipating Negative Implications in Your Writing

Consider this example. Imelda is writing an essay on why stevia—a very low calorie plant-based sweetener—is better than all the other very low calorie sweeteners on the market. Imelda truly believes in stevia, for she has read reports about its superiority to other sweeteners. It just so happens that Imelda's family owns a stevia production company. Imelda knows that if she mentions her family's business, readers may infer that she believes in stevia only because her family owns a company that produces it. Her awareness of this potential inference will help Imelda make choices about the content to include in her essay and how to word her ideas.

Here is another example. Dawn knows she will miss her English class to study for a biology test, so she writes her English instructor the e-mail message shown here.

From this note, the instructor may infer that Dawn thinks her biology class is more important than the English class. The rewritten e-mail message that follows is an improvement.

The revised e-mail is not deceptive. It accomplishes the same task—informing the instructor that Dawn will be absent—without implying that another class is more important.

The most effective writers compose their texts with their readers in mind. Anticipating the negative inferences readers might make enables writers to make wording choices that control—to the extent possible—the inferences readers draw from their texts.

PRACTICE 3 Composing Carefully to Support Correct Inferences

The following paragraph has been worded in such a way that readers can draw incorrect inferences. Think about the inferences listed below, and then revise the details in the paragraph so that readers cannot draw the incorrect inferences.

Teaching Resources: See the mini-quiz, "Making Accurate Inferences."

> A requirement of acceptance into the nursing program at Farrell College is volunteerism. Acceptable candidates have completed twenty hours of health-care related volunteer work. A way to meet this requirement is to work in a nursing home as a volunteer aide. Doing so meets the requirement and gives candidates the requisite experience in caring for elderly people.

Incorrect inferences:

- From the paragraph, readers might infer that if candidates have twenty hours of volunteer work, they will be accepted into the nursing program. However, volunteer work is only one of the acceptance requirements, so this inference is incorrect.

- The wording of the paragraph might lead some readers to infer that to meet the volunteerism requirement, potential candidates must volunteer in a nursing home. However, volunteering in a nursing home is only one way to meet the requirement, so this inference is incorrect.

Write your own version of the paragraph so that readers cannot make the two incorrect inferences listed above.

Answers will vary. A possible revision is provided.

> One of the requirements of acceptance into the nursing program at Farrell College is volunteerism. To meet this requirement, candidates must have completed twenty hours of health-care related volunteer work. While there are many ways to meet this requirement, one way is to work in a nursing home as a volunteer aide.

Analyzing Assumptions in Your Writing

To be a good communicator, you have to analyze the assumptions in your writing. If you are writing for a general audience, analyze your assumptions about what the audience knows. While you can expect the audience to have general knowledge, such as understanding the major differences between the games of basketball and football, you cannot expect a general audience to know the exact rules of each game. It's important to write in such a way that you explain ideas that a general audience would need to have clarified.

In addition to making assumptions about an audience's knowledge, we are all guilty sometimes of making assumptions based on stereotypes. Many people hold unconscious assumptions about other people related to race or ethnicity, religion, gender, sexual orientation, disability, age, profession or employment, socioeconomic status, political affiliation, or the place where they live or come from. Since it can be hard to recognize our unconscious assumptions, asking ourselves questions about what we have written can help us identify problematic assumptions:

- **Have I avoided making sweeping generalizations about groups of people?**

   Not appropriate: We all know that lawyers cannot be trusted to tell the truth about this issue.

   Appropriate: That attorney has misled the public on a key legal point.

- **Have I referred to a person's gender, race, or other attributes only when doing so was essential to the point I was making?**

   Not appropriate: A woman judge heard the case and rendered the verdict.

Appropriate: Sandra Day O'Connor was the first woman to serve as a justice on the U.S. Supreme Court.

- **Have I avoided ascribing stereotypical characteristics to people, even when the characteristics seem "positive"?**

  Not appropriate: Like most gay men, he has a great fashion sense, which has helped him succeed in costume design.

  Appropriate: Smith's extraordinary fashion sense has helped him succeed in costume design.

- **Have I avoided implying that the "average" person or reader belongs to a specific race, religion, gender, or other group?**

  Not appropriate: Today, the average person looking for a wife may not hesitate to consult an online dating site.

  Appropriate: Today, the average person looking for a spouse may have little reluctance in consulting an online dating site.

- **Have I been as specific as possible in referring to groups of people?**

  Not specific: American Indians served as coded message senders during World Wars I and II because they could communicate in a language that was not known to America's enemies.

  Specific: Soldiers from the Cherokee, Choctaw, Lakota, Comanche, and Navajo tribes served as coded message senders during World Wars I and II because they could communicate in Native American languages that were not known to America's enemies.

PRACTICE ④ Analyzing Assumptions in Your Writing

A college student has been asked by his former high school to talk to students about his experience in applying to colleges. The paragraph that follows is from the talk he is preparing. Find two problematic assumptions the student is making. Explain why these assumptions are problematic. How do you think the student's listeners will react to this paragraph?

> When I got a rejection letter from Monroe Tech, I was pretty upset at first. But when I heard that my classmate John had gotten in, I became really angry. I could see the college taking Lee ahead of me. Everyone knows Asian kids are super smart at math. But John? His major after-school activity was playing for the school's football team. How could he be a better student than I am?

The problematic assumptions are (1) that all Asian students are smart, especially at math, and (2) that football players are not good students. Listeners might react negatively, thinking the student's unfair assumptions had gotten in the way of an objective view of the situation.

Connect IRW Power of Process Assignment: Have students analyze tone in PoP readings. See the IM for a list of appropriate readings.

See the Connect IRW *Common Places* Master Course for pre-loaded assignments requiring students to analyze tone in selected readings.

ANALYZING TONE IN TEXTS

If you have children or have spent time around children, you know a disrespectful tone when you hear one. To such a tone, a parent may reply, "Don't take that tone with me!" So, what exactly is tone?

Tone is the attitude with which a message is conveyed. We might use a tone of respect when we speak, or we might use a tone that reveals frustration, anger, or impatience.

Both voice and body language help us discern tone in face-to-face communication. In texts, however, we depend on textual clues to help us identify tone.

Have you ever noticed how difficult it is to determine the tone of a text message or an e-mail? Read the e-mail message that follows. What is its tone?

Connect IRW Writing Assignment: See paragraphs that need to be revised for tone in the IM. You can set these up as Connect IRW writing assignments or use the pre-loaded assignments in the Connect IRW *Common Places* Master Course.

Help Choosing a major - Message (HTML)

FILE MESSAGE INSERT OPTIONS FORMAT TEXT REVIEW

To... Sherrie.Student@CBD.edu

Subject: Help Choosing a Major

Sherrie,

You asked for some help in choosing a major. How can I possibly help you with that?

—Dr. Zimmerman

As you read the e-mail message, did you hear a helpful tone in the last sentence, or did you hear a sarcastic tone? Because readers could infer a sarcastic tone, it would be better to write a reply that leaves no room to wonder about the writer's attitude. Compare the following message. Notice how adding a few extra details and making intentional choices about wording help the writer convey a tone that is decidedly positive. Writers must carefully select their words to help readers understand the tone they hope to establish.

Help Choosing a major - Message (HTML)

FILE MESSAGE INSERT OPTIONS FORMAT TEXT REVIEW

To... Sherrie.Student@CBD.edu

Subject: Help Choosing a Major

Sherrie,

You asked for some help in choosing a major. I'd be glad to help you if you think I can truly be of assistance.

I will be in my office tomorrow at 1:00. Drop by if you can. If another time would work better, just send me a list of dates and times that would work for you, and I'll see if I can find one that works for me, too.

Take care.

—Dr. Zimmerman

Objective Tone

One way to understand tone is to consider two types: objective and subjective. When a writer attempts to write a text *without* tone or with a neutral tone, we say that the writer uses an **objective tone.** Imagine a news anchor reading the evening news. The anchor's job is to minimize the tone in her voice so that she presents the news in a nonbiased, or objective, manner. The anchor is speaking as a reader, not as an individual. Thus, we are not supposed to focus on the anchor and her particular views. Read the following text for an example of objective tone.

Example of Objective Tone

> People who are regularly late for meetings or other appointments can eventually develop a reputation for being less dependable than others. Coworkers and acquaintances rarely know or understand the situations that cause a person to be habitually late, and even if they are aware of such circumstances, they may still come to view the late person as unreliable. In turn, having a reputation as an unreliable person makes it more difficult to receive promotions or be entrusted with high-level tasks.

A few characteristics will help you identify an objective tone.

- **An objective tone is established by avoiding emotionally charged terms.** For example, the passage above refers to a habitually late person as being seen as "an unreliable person," a term that is far less emotionally charged than "a loser" or "a slacker."

- **An objective tone is also established by using impartial, unbiased language.** The passage about habitually late people does not say such people are "poor employees." The writer does not make a judgment; she merely explains a potential effect from being consistently late to appointments.

- **An objective tone is most often associated with formal writing**—writing for professional or academic purposes. For example, if a writer uses slang (such as the word *loser*) to describe a habitually late person, not only does such a word convey an emotional and biased tone, but it also makes the text informal.

When a writer uses an objective tone, we are more likely to infer that the information is reliable. We may not be correct, of course, but we expect reliable information to be delivered in an impersonal, objective way. Thus, when we see the use of an objective tone, we can use it as a clue for making inferences. For example, in the paragraph about people who are habitually late, it would be wrong to make the inference that the writer has **disdain** for such people. The writer does not reveal her own attitude toward the subject. We would also be wrong to infer that the writer is never late for her own appointments. She reveals nothing about her behaviors or her attitudes. For all we know, the writer might be a habitually late person herself! Thus, when you identify an objective tone, you cannot make inferences about the writer's attitude toward the topic.

Subjective Tone

A **subjective tone** is used when a writer is not trying to present information in a neutral way. We have shown how news anchors attempt to use an objective tone so that they do not reveal their personal biases about issues. Political commentators, on the other hand, discuss news events but do so in a subjective, biased way. They are paid to offer their opinions on current events, so using a subjective tone is appropriate. A few characteristics will help you identify a subjective tone.

Students benefit from learning about how difficult it is to present a topic objectively—even when objectivity is the goal. Consider having students analyze the choices of news stories featured on various online newspapers to determine the paper's objectivity. See the IM for more information.

Consider bringing in junk mail to be analyzed for its tone. Advertisers who make their mail look as if it came from the U.S. government or from another legitimate source are masters at attempting to create objective-looking documents for subjective purposes.

Vocabulary Collection Word:
disdain

Your in-context definition:

_____

_____

A dictionary definition:

_____

_____

- **A subjective tone makes use of emotional clues.** Sometimes writers use a subjective tone to convey anger or to convey delight; or they may use a subjective tone to write sarcastically, to express surprise, or to convey warmth and friendship.
- **A subjective tone can express bias**—a person's preferences or particular point of view. If a person is biased, that simply means the person has an opinion about a subject.
- **Unlike objective writing, subjective writing is often informal.** That is, writers may use everyday language, slang, contractions, and a conversational tone, as if they were having a chat with their readers.

Sometimes we hear the term *biased* and think it means "unfair." However, a person who is biased about a subject is not necessarily unfair. When you write an essay on a controversial topic, such as immigration reform, and submit it for grading, you can expect that your instructor will be biased about the issue, but he or she can still grade your paper fairly.

We see bias in texts when writers reveal their personal opinions or points of view. Writers seeking to be objective try to present a topic in a neutral manner. The use of a subjective tone is appropriate when writers want to present their personal views or reveal information about themselves. A subjective tone will often allow readers to infer the writer's bias or attitudes toward a subject. It can also reveal the writer's emotions about the subject.

The use of a subjective tone is intentional: writers hope readers will come to share the same emotions or opinions as they do. Read the following example to become familiar with subjective tone in texts and the inferences we can draw from such texts.

Example of Subjective Tone

I work with a poor colleague who is always late. He's not only late to meetings, but he's late to work every single day. The variety of excuses he uses when he stumbles through the door each morning is always amusing. He cannot help but utter some lame excuse. "I was caught in traffic. Darn freeway!" or "I can't believe my alarm clock failed me again!" It would be so much better—and so much more appropriate—for him to creep over to his office and slink into his chair like the clueless **buffoon** he is.

Vocabulary Collection Word:
buffoon

Your in-context definition:

_____

_____

A dictionary definition:

_____

_____

In the example, the writer uses *I* (first person), as well as contractions, both of which are characteristics of informal writing. The writer does not attempt to hide his own attitude about his coworker. Indeed, he calls his colleague a "clueless buffoon," just in case readers did not pick up on his **contempt**.

If we carefully examine the writer's word choices, we can get a better idea of his tone and his attitude.

- "Poor colleague." The term *poor* reveals the writer's disdain or contempt.
- "Stumbles through the door." A person who stumbles through a door is clumsy, a detail that is consistent with the name used in the last sentence, *buffoon.*
- "Some lame excuse." The adjective *lame* suggests that the coworker cannot even think of a good reason for his tardiness. And *excuse* suggests that the reason is not legitimate.
- "Creep over to his office and slink into his chair." The verbs *creep* and *slink* are generally used to describe how animals move; such words **dehumanize** the coworker and add to the tone of disdain.
- "Clueless buffoon." Any time a writer engages in name-calling, you can be sure the tone is not objective. Besides adding to the subjective tone, this detail adds an element of condescension and meanness to the writer's tone.

Vocabulary Collection Word:
contempt

Your in-context definition:

_____

_____

A dictionary definition:

_____

_____

Vocabulary Collection Word:
dehumanize

Your in-context definition:

_____

_____

A dictionary definition:

_____

_____

Because a subjective tone reveals a great deal about the writer's thoughts and attitude, you can create accurate inferences by analyzing the tone. Notice how the inferences that follow are based on the writer's subjective, **condescending** tone.

Accurate inference: The writer has contempt for his colleague.

Accurate inference: The writer does not think his colleague's reasons for being late are legitimate.

Accurate inference: The writer feels superior to his colleague.

Complete the following exercise to try your hand at distinguishing between objective and subjective tones, and then use your analysis of tone to make accurate inferences.

PRACTICE 5 Identifying Tone to Make Accurate Inferences

Read each of the following passages, and answer the corresponding questions.

PASSAGE A: Excerpt from *Business Now* by Amit Shah

An entrepreneur has several potential sources of capital: personal savings, relatives, former employers, banks, finance companies, venture capitalists (a person or investment company that loans money to businesses), and government agencies such as the SBA [Small Business Administration], the Farmers Home Administration, and the Economic Development Authority. Isabella Capital, LLC, is a venture capital firm that focuses on woman-owned businesses.

There are also angel investors, usually wealthy people who invest their own money in a business in return for a share of the company. Angel investors are different from venture capitalists, in that venture capitalists usually invest other people's money, while angel investors invest their own funds. The Angel Capital Association operates in North America and works to bring together angel investors and entrepreneurs.

1. What is the tone of this passage?

    Objective

2. On the basis of the tone, is it accurate to infer that the writer approves more highly of angel investors than the other kinds of investors mentioned in the paragraph? Explain your answer.

    It is not accurate to infer that the writer approves more highly of angel investors. He presents each type of investor with the same nonemotional language. The reader may come to believe angel investors are best, but the writer does not imply that.

PASSAGE B

So-called authorities urge everyone, every year, to get the flu shot. Almost all the people I know seem to go for the hype and rush to the local clinic or local drugstore, stand in line, and pay for this vaccination. What they don't realize is that they're paying for a mixture of vaccine and toxic chemicals—such as mercury and thimerosal—that is not even guaranteed to work. In fact, when my neighbor got a flu shot, she became so ill with a flu-like sickness that she could barely get out of bed. When ignorance meets fear, people make extremely bad decisions. You won't see me in line for a flu shot, and I've never had the flu yet!

(continued)

Vocabulary Collection Word:
condescending

Your in-context definition:

_____

_____

A dictionary definition:

_____

_____

1. What is the tone of this passage?

Subjective

2. On the basis of the tone, is it accurate to infer that the writer thinks she is smarter than people who get flu shots? Explain your answer.

The writer does imply that people who get flu shots are ignorant and that she is smarter than they are. She actually states, "When ignorance meets fear, people make extremely bad decisions." Since she is not one of the ignorant ones making the "bad decisions," we can infer that she thinks she is smarter than they are.

Formal Writing

The kind of writing you will do for college assignments is formal writing. Business reports, letters, legal documents, and many other professional texts consist of formal writing. The characteristics of formal writing include the following:

- Use of third person (*one*); avoidance of first person (*I*) and second person (*you*)
- Avoidance of slang
- Avoidance of contractions
- Use of proper grammar
- Use of higher-level sentence structure (more complex sentences) and vocabulary

Save informal writing for correspondence—such as e-mail and text messages—between friends and for other informal occasions. Do not use it in your academic writing. Even though many people think of e-mail as an informal mode of expression, it is better to use formal rather than informal writing for e-mail messages to employers and professors. Above all, do not use the informal language of text messaging in academic or job-related e-mail messages.

GRAMMAR FOCUS   Point of View

Writers have the choice of using first-, second-, or third-person point of view. The point of view is conveyed by the pronouns a writer uses.

First-person pronouns: I, me, my, mine, myself; we, us, our, ours, ourselves

Second-person pronouns: you, your, yours, yourself

Third-person pronouns: he, him, his, himself; she, her, hers, herself; they, them, their, theirs, themselves; it, its, itself; one, oneself

The point of view a writer uses contributes to establishing a subjective or objective tone. The key is to choose the correct point of view for your writing purpose.

1. USE FIRST-PERSON POINT OF VIEW FOR A SUBJECTIVE TONE

First-person point of view is the writer's voice, so it draws attention to the writer and conveys a more intimate and subjective tone than second- or third-person point of view. Sometimes such a tone is desirable, as in a narrative essay, autobiography, or personal letter. At other times, using first person may detract from the authority of your voice. Consider the difference in these two statements.

(continued)

Uses first person: In my opinion, using physical punishment to teach children lessons is not wise.

Does *not* use first person: Using physical punishment to teach children lessons is not wise.

The example using first person (*In my opinion*) weakens the impact of the idea that is presented by implying that it is simply a matter of the writer's belief. While the second example is still an assertion of a belief, it is more confident and objective and therefore seems to be universally true.

Teaching Resources: See the exercise, "Writing in Third Person," to help students learn to revise point of view.

2. USE SECOND-PERSON POINT OF VIEW TO GIVE INSTRUCTIONS

Second-person point of view addresses readers directly, so it can convey a personal tone. However, statements in second person can sound demanding. At its worst, the use of second person can result in writing that is the equivalent of wagging one's forefinger, as these examples show.

Uses second person: You need to stop playing on your cell phone and start listening in class.

Does *not* use second person: Students need to stop playing on their cell phones and start listening in class.

Notice how the first example (*You . . . your*) sounds like a personal scolding. The second example gets across the same idea without scolding the reader.

Second-person writing can be used effectively in business letters, in instructions and how-to or process texts, and in speeches. For example, in a how-to text, a writer may use second person to personalize instructions, as follows.

Uses second person: When you calculate your income taxes, you will need your W-2 forms from the previous year, as well as any other forms that show the income you earned during the tax year.

Remember also that command statements are implicitly in second person.

Uses a command: To calculate your income taxes, use your W-2 forms from the previous year, as well as any other forms that show the income you earned during the tax year.

The word *you* is implied as the subject of *use* (*To calculate your income taxes,* [*you*] *use* . . .). Notice how terse a command can be; because of their no-nonsense tone, commands are best employed sparingly.

3. USE THIRD-PERSON POINT OF VIEW FOR ACADEMIC WORK AND OTHER FORMAL WRITING

Third person helps create an objective tone. The writing sounds more authoritative because the information in the text is not tied to the writer's voice. Note the following example.

Uses third person: Several educators have studied issues associated with higher education. They believe that the most significant problem in higher education is affordability.

(continued)

Compare this with the following example, which uses first person.

Uses first person: I believe that the most significant problem in higher education is affordability.

Using third person—and avoiding *I think* or *I believe*—de-emphasizes the writer and puts the focus on the idea, which is presented as a significant view that can be supported by evidence, and not just as the writer's personal opinion.

As a general rule, use third person for all academic writing. Formal business writing and government reports also require third-person point of view.

SENTENCE COMBINING

The examples that follow show how to take ideas expressed in one point of view, combine them, and change them into third-person point of view.

Ideas to combine and express in third person:

- I believe we should allow casino gambling in Texas.
- It should be legal.
- You may think casinos create addictions to gambling.
- That is simply not true.
- I have not gotten addicted even though I've gambled for years.

Combined sentences using third person: Casino gambling should be legal in Texas. Although some people believe casinos create gambling addictions, that is simply not the truth. People can gamble for years without becoming addicted to it.

Try your hand at converting first and second person into third-person texts.

EXERCISES

You will find three sets of sentences below. Combine the sentences to make smoother, longer ones, and change all first- and second-person pronouns into third person. You may change the wording as much as you like as long as you communicate the same ideas.

Answers will vary. Sample responses are given.

1. Ideas to combine and express in third person:

   - You should use three guidelines to control credit card spending.
   - You will avoid getting into financial difficulty if you do.
   - You should not charge more than you can afford.
   - You should always pay more than the minimum amount due each month.
   - You should use cash for luxury items.
   - Luxury items are things like iPads, expensive purses, and car stereos.

   Answer: By using three guidelines to control credit card spending, consumers can avoid getting into financial difficulty. Consumers should not charge more than they can afford, should always pay more than the minimum amount due each month, and should use cash for luxury items such as iPads, expensive purses, and car stereos.

2. Ideas to combine and express in third person:

   - One education law is called the No Child Left Behind Act.
   - Under this act, you have more options for your children's education.

(continued)

- You can choose a public school other than the one in your district.
- You can do this if the school in your area is not performing well.
- You can do this if your local school is unsafe.

Answer: Under the No Child Left Behind Act, families have more options for their children's education. Parents can choose a school other than the one in their district if their local school is not performing well or is unsafe.

3. Ideas to combine and express in third person:

- The flu and the common cold have symptoms.
- These symptoms are similar.
- I can tell you that the flu is worse than the common cold.
- You have symptoms such as fever, body aches, tiredness, and cough.
- Your flu symptoms are more intense than your cold symptoms.

Answer: The flu and the common cold have similar symptoms, but the flu is worse than the common cold. Flu symptoms, such as fever, body aches, tiredness, and cough, are more intense than cold symptoms.

CHOOSING AN APPROPRIATE TONE FOR YOUR WRITING ASSIGNMENTS

If your purpose in writing is to inform, you should strive to create an objective tone. Doing so will help readers understand that you are writing to inform them, not persuade them. To create an objective tone, write on a formal level by avoiding contractions, slang, and conversational-style language. Avoid emotional language and bias, also. Notice the differences between the two examples that follow:

Subjective tone: People who make the mistake of getting the flu shot aren't the sharpest tools in the shed.

cliché used in conversational-style language

contraction

Objective tone: People who choose to get the flu shot may not be properly informed about the dangers and **efficacy** of the vaccine.

When you are writing a text in which you want to reveal your own opinion or set a particular tone, be sure to choose language carefully to reveal the *type* of subjective tone you wish to communicate. For example, a text written with a subjective tone can be worded in such a way as to communicate different feelings.

- **Subjective tone communicating anger:** People who avoid the flu shot are ignorant fools. They are so selfish that they don't care that their choice might result in a major flu epidemic.

    Potential inference: The writer is angry and feels threatened by those who resist the flu shot.

- **Subjective tone communicating compassion:** People who avoid the flu shot are simply unaware of the tragic results that can follow their decision. They want the

Vocabulary Collection Word:
efficacy

Your in-context definition:

_____

_____

A dictionary definition:

_____

_____

best for their families, but their lack of information leads them to make choices that, sadly, may result in more harm than good.

> **Potential inference:** The writer feels sorry for people who resist the flu shot and thinks they are simply misinformed.

If you choose an appropriate tone for your writing, your potential readers will be more likely to make correct inferences about the content you are communicating.

PRACTICE ⑥ Writing to Convey a Particular Tone

Write three paragraphs, each with a different tone. In each paragraph, explain the same content. Specifically, write about one reason why some people make the decision to drive when they are legally intoxicated. In the first paragraph, convey your idea using an objective tone. In the second, use a subjective tone that communicates anger. For the third paragraph, use a subjective tone that communicates compassion.

Answers will vary.

Practice 6 can be challenging for students. Consider using a collaborative writing process.

ANALYZING FIGURATIVE LANGUAGE TO MAKE ACCURATE INFERENCES

Figurative language is language that creatively suggests meanings beyond the literal meanings of the words. A word's **literal** meaning is its *actual* meaning. For example, the literal meaning of the word *star* is a celestial body made of gases. However, we also use the word *star* in a figurative way to suggest a person who is a celebrity. Similarly, we frequently use adjectives in nonliteral ways: a *sweet* car is not one made of sugar; a *crabby* customer does not have an exoskeleton and pincers; and a *chilling* reminder does not change a room's temperature. These adjectives are used figuratively: they convey meanings that are not literal.

One way figurative language works is by tapping into the connotations of words. Words have both connotations and denotations. The **denotation** of *rock*, for instance, is a mass of solid material from the earth. A husband who says that his wife is "his rock" does not mean she is a mass of solid material. He is using the qualities of a rock to describe his wife: she is unchanging, dependable, and solid. These positive qualities are **connotations:** they are ideas that go beyond the word's denotation to suggest additional meanings.

Recognizing when a word is used in a nonliteral way can help you make correct inferences. For example, consider the following passage, from sports reporter Tom Orsborn's blog on the Web site of the *San Antonio Express-News*. Note especially the figurative language, some of which is underlined.

Consider having students practice using figurative language by writing descriptions of everyday things such as the bagel they had for breakfast, their experience renewing a driver's license, or their first car (or bicycle, apartment, etc.).

> Nicknamed "The Brick Layer" by defensive line coach Rod Marinelli, Dallas Cowboys end George Selvie is ready to do some heavy lifting with Anthony Spencer out for the year.
>
> "It's just going out there and working hard every day, just laying bricks," Selvie said, when asked about his moniker. "That's what we say, 'Brick layer, go lay some bricks today.' I just go out there and do my job and, hopefully, a couple of times I get thrown a bone and get a sack."

You probably figured out that George Selvie is a football player, not a brick layer. Calling him a "brick layer," however, adds meaning to Selvie's role on the team. Laying bricks, in this context, is an ordinary kind of job that takes a particular skill. Readers can infer that Selvie is not playing a flashy role in his position. They can also infer that being a brick layer is a positive thing. The coach's instruction to "go lay some bricks today" is matter-of-fact and reveals that this activity is a necessary element for team success.

We can find additional figurative expressions in the passage. For example, Selvie says he will occasionally get "thrown a bone." Obviously, no one really throws bones at him, but just as getting a bone is a treat for a dog, getting "a sack" is a treat for Selvie. "Sacking" a quarterback does not mean putting the guy in a big bag; it means tackling him to prevent a pass or a play. The passage contains one more figurative expression. If you examine the paragraph closely, you will find it. Metaphors and similes are commonly used types of figurative language. A **metaphor** is the use of a word in a nonliteral way to suggest a comparison. Calling Selvie a "brick layer" is using a metaphor. The metaphor works because we attribute to Selvie the characteristics of brick layers. Here are some additional examples of metaphors:

- "Our copy machine is a *fossil* that, surprisingly, still functions." This metaphor works by transferring a characteristic of a fossil—its old age—to the copy machine. We can infer that the copy machine is old.

- "I found a *gem* at the garage sale—a signed photograph of Martin Luther King, Jr." A photograph is not a gem, but in the same way that a gem is rare and valuable, the signed photograph is also. We can infer that the signed photograph may be worth significant money.

Similes function the same way metaphors do, but they draw attention to themselves as figurative language because they are used in conjunction with the words *like* or *as*. Here are a few examples of similes:

- "When I opened the dishwasher door, water gushed out *like a tidal wave*." By comparing the water to a tidal wave, the writer leads readers to infer that a large quantity of water quickly rushed out of the dishwasher.

- "The policy was *as clear as mud*." Since mud is not clear, we can infer that the policy was not clear either.

A third type of figurative language is **personification,** the use of human (and sometimes animal) qualities to describe an inanimate object. Notice how personification works by studying the examples that follow:

- "The table *groaned* with the weight of years of unopened mail, packed boxes, and old office supplies." A table cannot groan, but a human or an animal can. Using the term *groan* to describe the table helps readers think of the table as a person under too much stress.

- "My old iPod *drew its last breath* yesterday. I will be shopping for another one today." The personification of the iPod as a kind of living creature is a creative way to imply that the iPod is irreparably broken.

Carefully analyzing the figurative language in readings can help you gain a better understanding of the writer's point, the writer's attitude toward that point, and the inferences you can draw from the text.

Connect IRW Power of Process Assignment: Have students analyze particular readings in Power of Process and annotate figurative language. A list of appropriate readings is in the IM.

See the Connect IRW *Common Places* Master Course for preloaded PoP assignments that require students to analyze figurative language in select readings.

PRACTICE ⑦ Drawing Inferences from Figurative Language

Analyze the following passage. Underline each of the figurative words or phrases you find, and answer the questions that follow.

> Alaska is a land of extremes. There is no other way to say it. It's extreme in temperature—from 50° below zero to close to 100°F within a single year. It's extreme in landscape—from valleys so wide that you can't see across them to mountains that reach to the sky. It's extreme in population density—from Anchorage with its bustling 300,000 people to the hundreds (or perhaps thousands) of people who live alone in cabins as isolated as desert islands. It's extreme in the amount of sunlight it receives. Above the Arctic Circle, the sun hides in winter, peeking out only occasionally. But in the summer, the sun is a constant companion, sometimes brightening the sky for twenty-four hours at a time. Regardless of these extremes—or perhaps because of them—Alaska is irresistible to many.

1. Where is personification used in this paragraph?

    The writer compares the sun to a companion who hides and peeks out. Mountains are said to reach, suggesting that they have arms.

2. Based on the figurative language in this passage, what can you infer about Alaska?

    Alaska is unusual and beautiful. People who live in Alaska (or visit it) are more aware of the sun's effects.

USING FIGURATIVE LANGUAGE IN YOUR WRITING

One of the functions of figurative language is to suggest meanings by the use of comparisons. Metaphors and similes suggest that one thing is like another, and personification takes the qualities of something that is alive and attributes them to something that is inanimate. By suggesting meanings, figurative language adds to how readers understand texts. For example, a writer could describe a restaurant in a literal way.

> **Literal description:** My Bánh Mì is a Vietnamese restaurant that features freshly baked bread and traditional bánh mì sandwiches.

But the use of figurative language to describe the restaurant helps readers infer what makes the restaurant special.

> **Figurative description:** Stepping into My Bánh Mì *is like* stepping into a bakery tucked away on a side street in Saigon.

While both sentences are well written, the use of figurative language in the second sentence suggests that the restaurant has a certain ambience; the first sentence does not make the same suggestion.

In the following sentences, notice how the figurative description suggests meanings that the literal description does not.

> **Literal description:** The neglected lodge had old carpeting and smoke-stained wallpaper. It was not a good location for the reception.

> **Figurative description:** The neglected lodge looked *like* a smokers' lounge from the 1960s. The *walls barely held on* to their *tired* and peeling wallpaper, and the thick shag carpet under our feet *seemed to crawl* with bugs. It was no place for a reception.

While the literal description may be accurate, it does not provide the reader with the details needed to really visualize the lodge. The figurative description, on the other hand, helps the reader more clearly understand what the lodge was like in its state of disrepair. The second description allows the reader to make accurate inferences.

When possible, use figurative language to suggest meanings. Instead of *telling* readers what things are like, use figurative language so that readers will have a more active role in imagining and making correct inferences. When you use figurative language, readers may find your writing more enjoyable and richer in meaning than they would otherwise.

Be careful about overusing figurative language. A text with too many metaphors or too much personification may end up sounding silly. Also, be careful about mixing metaphors. A **mixed metaphor** is a sentence or set of sentences that makes use of more than one metaphor and, as a consequence, results in confusion (or laughter), as these examples show:

> I'm grasping at the last straw. (*Grasping at straws* is combined with *the last straw*.)
>
> I was out on a limb without a leg to stand on. (*Out on a limb* and *without a leg to stand on* are both metaphors, but they don't belong together.)
>
> We'll burn that bridge when we come to it. (Combines *Don't burn your bridges* and *We'll cross that bridge when we come to it*.)

PRACTICE ⑧ Experimenting with Figurative Language to Suggest Meanings

Use figurative language—metaphors, similes, and personification—to complete each writing task. When you finish writing each description, reread your writing and ask yourself, "What inference could a person make from this writing?"

Answers will vary.

1. Write two or three sentences in which you use figurative language to describe a dog that looks vicious.

2. Write two or three sentences in which you use figurative language to describe a memorable meal.

3. Write two or three sentences in which you use figurative language to describe a particular quality of a boss, a friend, a coworker, or a family member. For example, you could describe a friend's constantly positive attitude.

DRAWING ACCURATE INFERENCES FROM GRAPHICS

Many texts are accompanied by visuals, such as charts, graphs, artwork, cartoons, and photos. Often visuals are not explained: they are simply presented alongside other information. Thus, readers must infer their meanings.

General Guidelines for Reading Graphics

At the beginning of this chapter, you saw how readers can make inferences based on the details in an image. When photos are not accompanied by a caption, readers must infer their meaning. Just as the details of a photo can help you make inferences, the same is true for the details of graphics—graphs, charts, and illustrations. You can make accurate inferences from graphics by following these guidelines.

Teaching Resources: See the PPT "Analyzing Graphics."

Step 1: Read the graphic's title.

Because charts, graphs, and illustrations contain so few words, it is crucial to start by reading the title. From the title you can often determine the type of information offered. In the graphic below, for example, the title helps us understand the three elements that make up the graph: unemployment, weekly earnings, and education.

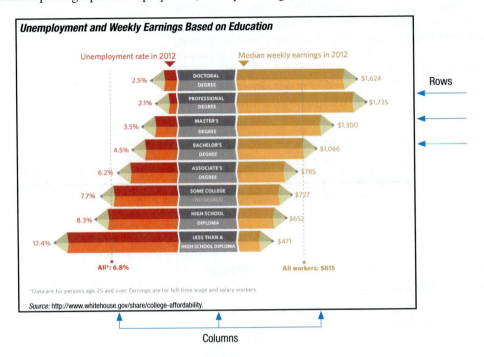

Step 2: Read the descriptions in the graphic.

Often, graphics use colors to code particular pieces of information. In the graph shown above, red depicts the unemployment rate in 2012. Gray presents education level, and yellow depicts median weekly earnings in 2012. Like tables, graphs often present information in columns and rows. Rows are always horizontal, and columns are vertical.

Step 3: Write sentences based on a graph's details.

By putting graphic information into your own words, you can more easily understand the meaning of the information. For example, start with the bottom row of information. It tells us that in 2012, the people who had less than a high school diploma (gray) experienced an unemployment rate of 12.4 percent (red) and made approximately $471 a week (yellow). We can write sentences expressing the data for each row in the graph. Here are two of the sentences we can construct.

- People who had a bachelor's degree had an unemployment rate of 4.5 percent and earned approximately $1,066 a week.
- People who had a doctoral degree had an unemployment rate of 2.5 percent and earned approximately $1,624 a week.

Step 4: Draw inferences from your sentences.

What conclusions can you draw from the content of your sentences? In the case of the graph, we can analyze the sentences listed above. From these sentences, we can infer the following.

Inference: In general, the more education a person has, the less likely he or she is to be unemployed and the more money per week the person will make.

Note that there is one exception. People with doctoral degrees had slightly more unemployment and made slightly less money per week than people with professional degrees. Notice how the inference contains the phrase *in general*. When wording inferences, be careful to use qualifiers such as *most, some, on the whole,* and *usually*.

PRACTICE ⑨ Drawing Inferences from Graphics

The graphic entitled "Conditions Treated by Most Commonly Used Drugs" is from the Food and Drug Administration. Use the four-step process to analyze the graphic. After completing your analysis, make two inferences.

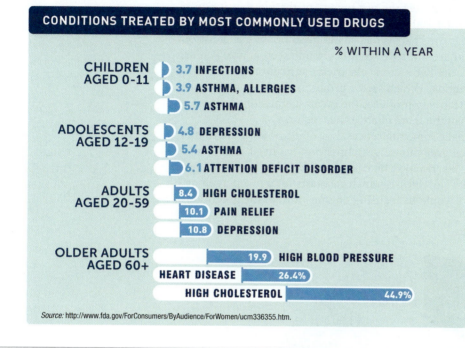

CONDITIONS TREATED BY MOST COMMONLY USED DRUGS

% WITHIN A YEAR

CHILDREN AGED 0-11
- 3.7 INFECTIONS
- 3.9 ASTHMA, ALLERGIES
- 5.7 ASTHMA

ADOLESCENTS AGED 12-19
- 4.8 DEPRESSION
- 5.4 ASTHMA
- 6.1 ATTENTION DEFICIT DISORDER

ADULTS AGED 20-59
- 8.4 HIGH CHOLESTEROL
- 10.1 PAIN RELIEF
- 10.8 DEPRESSION

OLDER ADULTS AGED 60+
- 19.9 HIGH BLOOD PRESSURE
- HEART DISEASE 26.4%
- HIGH CHOLESTEROL 44.9%

Source: http://www.fda.gov/ForConsumers/ByAudience/ForWomen/ucm336355.htm.

Another way to help students learn to make inferences from graphics is to have them create graphics themselves. See the IM for assignments that have students create graphics to convey information and inferences.

Special Considerations for Reading Line Graphs, Pie Charts, and Maps

A **line graph** shows relationships between data by plotting points. You may be familiar with line graphs from math courses. A line graph has a vertical axis and a horizontal axis. Each axis represents different values—such as years, amounts, and so on. In the example that follows, the horizontal axis indicates years, and the vertical axis indicates the percentage of increase. The graph measures two things: the increase in the miles people travel and the increase in population. The legend indicates what the different-colored lines represent.

Growth in Population & Vehicle Miles Traveled, 1970-2000
Pacific Southwest Region

Percent increase since 1970

— Miles Traveled
— Population Growth

Sources: U.S. Census Bureau, Bureau of Transportation Statistics (Federal Highway Administration)

■ Line graph.

Notice that the distance traveled (depicted by the purple line) increases at a faster rate than the population (green line). One inference we can make from this data is that people are traveling more than they used to.

In addition to line graphs, you will encounter graphs that are round—often called **pie charts.** These graphs divide data into groups, and each group is represented by a "slice" of the pie chart. The size of each slice indicates the percentage of the pie that it constitutes. Added together, they generally total 100 percent. The title, given in the middle of the pie chart shown here, indicates that the chart is displaying greenhouse gas emissions categorized by economic sector. If you are not sure what economic sectors are, you can look at the pie pieces and see that there are five sectors: electricity, agriculture, commercial and residential, industry, and transportation. Which sector produces the most greenhouse gas emissions? The chart shows that electricity produces the greatest emissions because its share of the pie is 33 percent, larger than the share of any other sector.

By analyzing this chart, you can make some inferences. For one, it is accurate to infer that if we want to substantially reduce greenhouse gas emissions, we need to put more emphasis on transforming sectors like electricity, which accounts for a high percentage of total emissions, rather than sectors like agriculture, which accounts for a low percentage. By addressing electricity emissions, we would be focusing on one-third of the greenhouse gas emissions in the country.

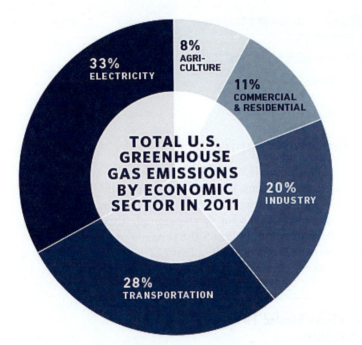

Source: http://www.whitehouse.gov/share/climate-action-plan.

■ Pie chart.

Maps are another way to present information. The map of the United States on the next page depicts the hours per week a person would need to work at minimum wage to afford an apartment in each state. Notice how the graphic uses color to depict data.

From this map, we can infer that the least expensive states to live in are in the southern and middle United States. Living on the East Coast is expensive, as is living in California, Florida, Alaska, and Hawaii. What other inferences can you draw from this graphic?

Another thing to remember about interpreting graphics is that most of the time, graphics are comparative. That is, they provide data that allow readers to make comparisons and to create inferences from those comparisons. For example, the map enables readers to compare the affordability of living in particular states. The comparison of data makes the graphic meaningful because it allows readers to use the data to make inferences and decisions.

2014 HOURS AT MINIMUM WAGE NEEDED TO AFFORD RENT

In no state can minimum wage workers afford a two-bedroom rental unit at Fair Market Rent, working a standard 40-hour work week, without paying more than 30% of their income.

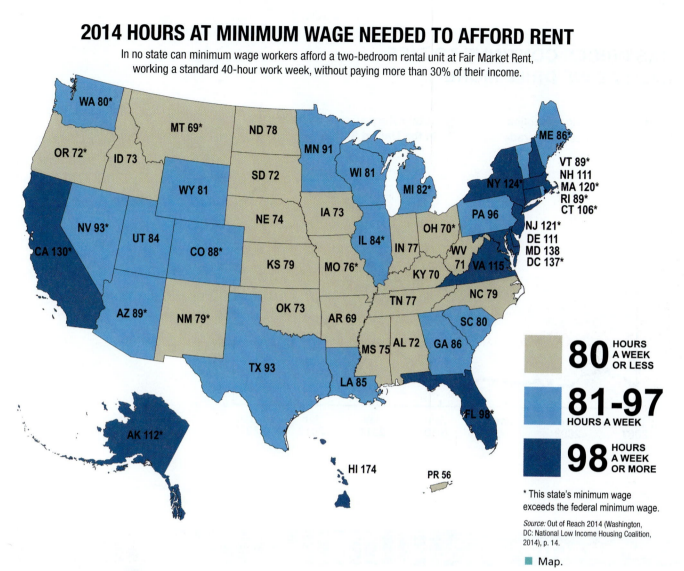

WA 80*
MT 69*
ND 78
MN 91
ME 86*
OR 72*
ID 73
VT 89*
NH 111
WI 81
SD 72
NY 124*
MA 120*
RI 89*
CT 106*
WY 81
MI 82*
PA 96
NV 93*
UT 84
IA 73
NE 74
OH 70*
NJ 121*
DE 111
MD 138
DC 137*
CA 130*
CO 88*
IL 84*
IN 77
WV 71
VA 115
KS 79
MO 76*
KY 70
AZ 89*
NM 79*
OK 73
AR 69
TN 77
NC 79
SC 80
MS 75
AL 72
GA 86
TX 93
LA 85
FL 98*
AK 112*
HI 174
PR 56

80 HOURS A WEEK OR LESS

81-97 HOURS A WEEK

98 HOURS A WEEK OR MORE

* This state's minimum wage exceeds the federal minimum wage.

Source: Out of Reach 2014 (Washington, DC: National Low Income Housing Coalition, 2014), p. 14.

■ Map.

PRACTICE ⑩ Analyzing Inferences Drawn from Graphics

These numbered statements are followed by a line graph, on the next page. Study the line graph, and then determine whether the statements and inferences are accurate.

Accurate or inaccurate?

Accurate 1. Statement: In January 2008, fewer than three hundred rigs were operating in the United States, and the price of gas was a little more than $1.00.

Accurate 2. Statement: In 2011, gas prices reached their highest point.

Inaccurate 3. Statement: Every time the number of rigs operating is increased, gas prices increase.

Accurate 4. Inference: For the most part, gas prices have increased over time, even though the number of oil rigs has generally increased during the same period.

Inaccurate 5. Inference: A dramatic increase in the number of oil rigs will result in a dramatic decrease in the cost of gasoline. ("Inaccurate" should be the answer.)

Accurate 6. Inference: Factors other than the amount of drilling we do in the United States affect the cost of gasoline.

(continued)

GAS PRICES CONTINUE TO RISE
EVEN AS WE DRILL MORE

Monthly average gasoline retail price - regular grade

Total rotary oil rigs operating in the United States

CHAPTER ACTIVITIES

READING AND ANNOTATING

The following explanation of unwarranted assumptions is excerpted from a critical thinking textbook, *Beyond Feelings: A Guide to Critical Thinking*, 9th edition, by Vincent Ruggiero. Read and annotate the text, and then answer the questions that follow.

Unwarranted Assumptions

by Vincent Ruggiero

Assumptions are ideas that are merely taken for granted rather than produced by conscious thought. Making assumptions is natural enough, and many assumptions are not only harmless but helpful. When you get up in the morning and head out for class, you assume your watch is working, the car will start, and the professor will be there to teach. You may occasionally encounter a surprise—a broken watch, a dead car battery—but that won't invalidate the assumption or diminish the time it saves you. (You wouldn't get much accomplished if you had to ponder every move you made each day.)

Lexile: 1080L

YOUR ANNOTATIONS

Definition

Some assumptions are helpful.

When are assumptions unwarranted? Whenever you take too much for granted—that is, more than is justified by your experience or the particular circumstance. Smokers who assume that because the habit hasn't caused them noticeable physical harm already it never will are making an unwarranted assumption. So are sunbathers who assume that their skin is impervious to solar radiation and investors who assume a stock tip they found on an Internet bulletin board is reliable.

Assumptions are unwarranted when you take too much for granted.

Many people who hold a pro-choice position on abortion assume that the right to an abortion is expressed in the U.S. Constitution, that the *Roe v. Wade* Supreme Court decision is logically unassailable, and that the pro-life position is held only by conservative Christians. All three assumptions are unwarranted. Justice Byron White, in his *Roe v. Wade* dissent, rejected any constitutional basis for the majority decision, terming it an "exercise of raw judicial power." The argument that life begins when the genetic "blueprint" is established at conception and that a human being is present from that moment on, though unfashionable, is not illogical. And abortion is opposed not only by conservative Christians but also, for example, by Mennonites, Muslims, Buddhists, and Hindus. Although Jews remain divided on the issue, many oppose abortion. . . . Nonreligious groups opposing abortion include the Atheist and Agnostic Pro-Life League, Pagans for Life, Libertarians for Life, Feminists for Life, and the Pro-Life Alliance of Gays and Lesbians. (All of these groups have Web sites.)

Examples: wrong assumptions regarding the pro-choice argument

The most common unwarranted assumptions include the following:

List of the most common unwarranted assumptions (UA):

The assumption that people's senses are always trustworthy. The fact is that beliefs and desires can distort perception, causing people to see and hear selectively or inaccurately.

UA: Our senses are trustworthy.

The assumption that if an idea is widely reported, it must be true. Fiction can be disseminated as far and as widely as truth.

UA: A widely reported idea is true.

The assumption that having reasons proves that we have reasoned logically. Reasons may be borrowed uncritically from others, and even if they have been thought out, they may still be illogical.

UA: Having reasons = logical argument.

The assumption that familiar ideas are more valid than unfamiliar ones. Familiarity merely indicates having heard or read the idea before; it provides no guarantee that what we have heard or read is correct.

UA: Familiar ideas are more valid than less familiar ones.

The assumption that if one event follows another in time, it must have been caused by the other. The order of and closeness in time between two events could have been accidental.

UA: Chronological occurrence = causality.

The assumption that every event or phenomenon has a single cause. Some events have multiple causes. For example, in medicine it is well known that numerous risk factors may contribute to a person's contracting a disease.

UA: Every event has a single cause.

The assumption that the majority view is the correct view. Majorities have been wrong—for example, in supporting the execution of witches and in condoning slavery.

UA: The majority is right.

The assumption that the way things are is the way they should be. Humans are imperfect, and their inventions, including ideas, always allow room for improvement.

UA: Things are best as they are.

The assumption that change is always for the better. In some cases, change improves matters; in others, it makes matters worse. For example, when the government has sought to gain revenue by increasing tax rates, the net effect usually has

UA: Change is always for the better.

been a decline in revenue. (For numerous examples of the error of this assumption, do a Google search using the search term "unintended consequences.")

The assumption that appearances are trustworthy. Appearances can be mistaken. For example, American novelist Sinclair Lewis was traveling on an ocean liner to England. As he and a friend were walking on the deck, he noticed a woman sitting on a deck chair reading one of his novels. Filled with pride, he remarked to his friend what a good feeling it was to see someone so absorbed in his work. At that very moment, the woman threw the book overboard.

UA: You can trust what you see.

The assumption that if an idea is in our mind it is our own idea and deserves to be defended. Some, ideally most, ideas in our mind are the result of our careful analysis. Others, in some cases an embarrassingly large number, are uncritically absorbed from other people and therefore are not "our own" in any meaningful sense.

UA: Any idea you have thought of is worthy of defending.

The assumption that the stronger our conviction about an idea, the more valid the idea. An idea's validity is determined by the amount and quality of the evidence that supports it. The strength of our conviction is irrelevant. In other words, it is possible to be absolutely convinced and still be wrong.

UA: A strong conviction = a valid idea.

The assumption that if we find an error in someone's argument, we have disproved the argument. An argument can contain minor flaws yet be sound. For example, one or two items of evidence may be flawed, yet the remaining evidence may be sufficient to support the argument. Simply said, it takes more than nitpicking to disprove an argument.

UA: An error in an argument makes the argument invalid.

Remember that assumptions are usually implied rather than expressed directly, much like the hidden premises in arguments. To identify them, develop the habit of reading (and listening) between the lines for ideas that are unexpressed but nevertheless clearly implied. Once you have identified an assumption, evaluate it and decide whether it is warranted.

Read/listen between the lines for assumptions; evaluate assumptions.

Questions for Consideration

1. What is the difference between a warranted assumption and an unwarranted assumption? Offer examples of each, and explain in a paragraph.
2. The writer includes a long paragraph about the abortion controversy. What is the writer's main point about abortion opinions? In other words, in what way does the abortion controversy help the writer make his point about assumptions? Explain in a paragraph or two.
3. Is the paragraph about abortion written with an objective or subjective tone? Explain your answer in a paragraph.
4. Choose one of the assumptions the writer discusses, and provide an example of a time when you held that assumption and learned that it was wrong. How did you come to understand that the assumption you held was wrong?
5. Imagine that a friend or family member tells you, "I would never live near a nuclear power plant." What assumption is the speaker making? Is the assumption warranted or unwarranted? Explain.

Questions for Consideration

1. A warranted assumption is "justified by your experience or the particular circumstance." Warranted assumption: if you hear thunder, rain is likely. Unwarranted assumption: if you hear thunder, a flash flood is likely.
2. The abortion debate is fraught with assumptions. Even commonly believed ideas can be based on unwarranted assumptions.
3. It is written in an objective tone. The writer is not taking a position on the issue.
4. Answers will vary.
5. Answers will vary.

USING MODELS TO PRACTICE COMPOSING

Leticia is a student in a writing class. She has been given a writing assignment, which she has annotated. Read through the assignment instructions Leticia's professor provided, and note how Leticia annotated the assignment. Did she neglect to annotate a key point? If so, add your own annotation.

Leticia's Annotated Assignment

Essay assignment: Read and annotate "Unwarranted Assumptions," paying particular attention to the various types of assumption errors people commonly make. Select three or four assumptions that can have disastrous results in the context of college. For example, consider the effects of believing this assumption: *If an idea is widely reported, it must be true.* Perhaps you have heard from several students that to pass Dr. B's essay exam, all you have to do is find a way to talk about global warming in each of the essay questions. These students explain that because Dr. B is passionate about global warming, she gives high grades to students who discuss it. You are tempted to believe these students because *so many* students have told you the same thing. Believing them, however, could be a disastrous decision.

(margin notes) Read and annotate article

Select 3 or 4 assumptions

Example

After you select three or four assumptions to analyze, use a method of prewriting to think about how using the assumptions to make decisions in college can have tragic consequences. Write an essay in which you present each of these assumptions and the examples you have found or created. (You may use hypothetical examples.) Use your examples to show how the assumption is not true. Be sure to discuss the potential negative effects of using the assumption to make college-related decisions. Your essay should be written in formal language and have an objective tone.

(margin notes left) Prewrite

In essay, present assumptions, use examples to show assumptions aren't true, and present the negative effects of making these assumptions.

(margin notes right) Figure out how using the assumption = tragic consequences

Formal language, objective tone

After annotating her assignment, Leticia was ready for prewriting. She started by selecting several assumptions and uses freewriting—writing without stopping for 15 minutes—to think about how each assumption might lead to disastrous results in college. Here's Leticia's freewriting—done on a computer—on one of the assumptions.

Assumption 1: The stronger our conviction about an idea, the more valid the idea.

OK, let's say I really, really believe algebra is stupid. I don't even question my belief because I believe it so strongly. So I may not study hard for algebra, or I may have a bad attitude in the class or be angry about having to take it. That might result in failing the class or being miserable. OK, another thing I might believe . . . So let's say I'm in a class and we're talking about something controversial, like abortion, and I have my strong beliefs about it. Just because my beliefs are really strong, I might not think any other person's ideas are valid. So I'd be closed off to learning about what other people think, and that might mean I wouldn't learn much. I'd be stuck with my own views and not learn or grow.

After freewriting about several assumptions, Leticia chose three assumptions as the topic to be discussed in her essay. She created a thesis statement and a simple outline.

Leticia's Simple Outline

INTRODUCTION PARAGRAPH

Thesis statement: In college, making decisions based on false assumptions can have disastrous effects.

Body paragraph 1: One assumption that can have negative effects in college is believing that our senses are always trustworthy.

Body paragraph 2: Another assumption that can get college students into trouble is the belief that if an idea is widely believed, it must be true.

Body paragraph 3: Finally, negative effects can result from believing that because we have reasons for a position, we have reasoned logically.

CONCLUSION PARAGRAPH

At this point, Leticia started drafting her essay. What follows is one of the body paragraphs from her essay. Read and annotate the paragraph to identify the assumption she is discussing and the negative effects she identifies. Annotate passages that help you identify the tone Leticia is using.

Leticia's Paragraph

One assumption that can have negative effects in college is believing that our senses are always trustworthy. For example, many students rely on only one sense—such as hearing—to learn material. They assume that they can trust their hearing to prepare them for tests and to help them learn. However, no one hears everything. It is impossible to listen to every single thing an instructor says, even if the instructor speaks loudly and clearly. In addition, people can hear things differently. One student may say that the professor said the homework is due on Tuesday, and another may say the professor said the homework is due on Thursday. These kinds of disagreements are common because our senses really are not perfect. Depending on one sense—hearing, for example—can cause a student to get the facts wrong and to not understand course information. It would be much better to assume our senses are flawed and to use more than one sense to understand course material. Listening to a lecture is fine, but because our senses can be wrong, it is wise to also read the course material.

YOUR ANNOTATIONS

Assumption: Senses are trustworthy.

Example: hearing

Why hearing is not trustworthy:

- It's impossible to listen to every single thing.
- People hear things differently.

Negative effect of depending on one sense

A READING AND WRITING ASSIGNMENT

Now it is your turn to write an essay about assumptions in response to the assignment Leticia's instructor gave her (page 307). Follow these steps, using Leticia's work as a model.

1. Reread Leticia's assignment and any additional annotations you made.
2. Use freewriting to think about how different assumptions can have negative effects when used to make decisions in college.
3. Choose three assumptions; if you need to, use additional prewriting to develop more ideas about the negative consequences of the assumptions.
4. Write a thesis statement.

Connect IRW Writing Assignment: Use Connect IRW to create this writing assignment and make available peer review tools.

This writing assignment has been pre-loaded into the Connect IRW *Common Places* Master Course.

Teaching Resources: See the IM for additional writing assignments that require students to analyze assumptions, including additional source-based writing tasks.

5. Create a simple outline that contains your thesis statement and topic sentences for your body paragraphs. Write as many body paragraphs as you need to support your thesis statement.

6. Using your outline, draft the introduction, body paragraphs, and conclusion for your essay.

7. As you revise and edit your writing, look for words and phrases that express the tone of your essay. Make any necessary changes to achieve an objective tone.

Use the Quick Start Guide to Integrated Reading and Writing Assignments for assistance.

THINKING FROM AN INSTRUCTOR'S POINT OF VIEW

Do you ever make inferences about your instructors? You might think some are brilliant, some are just putting in their time, and so on. To make such inferences, you probably made mental notes about your instructors' strengths and weaknesses, not intentionally, but unconsciously. These judgments contributed to an overall impression, and on the basis of that impression you made inferences.

Instructors sometimes make inferences about students, and employers may make inferences about their employees. Imagine you are an instructor. Consider the scenarios that follow. What inference would you make about each student? Write your inferences on a sheet of paper.

1. Reynaldo is ten minutes early to every class meeting.

2. Melissa texts under her desk most days in class.

3. Rachel works in the tutoring lab with tutors almost every day after class.

4. Jonathan often borrows a pen and paper from his classmates.

5. Carolyn does not show up on the first day, even though she has registered for the course.

6. Li helps other students in class when she is finished with her work.

7. Donnie puts his head down and sleeps most days in class.

8. Ahzab greets his instructor most days by asking, "How are you doing?"

1. Reynaldo is a conscientious student.
2. Melissa is naive about her ability to pass class without listening, or Melissa thinks she knows the content already.
3. Rachel really cares about her work and her grades.
4. Jonathan is unorganized or does not take school seriously.
5. Carolyn may be confused, or she may think the first day of class is useless.
6. Li is mature and is probably going to be a good student.
7. Maybe Donnie works nights, or maybe he spends too many hours out late partying or playing video games.
8. Ahzab is a very considerate student.

ADDING TO YOUR VOCABULARY

This chapter's vocabulary words appear below.

sound	contempt	efficacy	condescending
buffoon	dehumanize	disdain	

Teaching Resources: See the IM for additional vocabulary activities.

See the Connect IRW *Common Places* Master Course for vocabulary study practices that accompany this chapter, as well as a chapter vocabulary quiz.

Choose five of the vocabulary words from this chapter that you would like to add to your vocabulary, and think about how you can use them this week. For example, one of this chapter's words is *buffoon*. You can often substitute *buffoon* for *clown* or *joker*, as in the example that follows.

Example: Some *joker* thought it would be funny to push all of the buttons on the elevator.

Some *buffoon* thought it would be funny to push all of the buttons on the elevator.

List each of the five words you plan to use this week, and make note of a context in which you could use each word.

Example: *Buffoon.* When one of my children is acting silly at an inappropriate time, I can call him a buffoon.

○ ADDITIONAL ASSIGNMENTS

1. Write an essay in which you analyze how social cues lead us to form inferences. For example, if you are in a conversation with someone and the person starts looking away, nodding, and saying "uh-huh" but is obviously not listening to you, you are likely to infer that the person is not interested in talking to you. In your essay, discuss four or five inferences we can make from social cues.

2. Write a paragraph in which you explain how people use assumptions to draw inferences.

3. Write a list of inferences you can draw from the following infographic, "Save Water in the Yard This Summer," which appears on the Environmental Protection Agency's Web site.

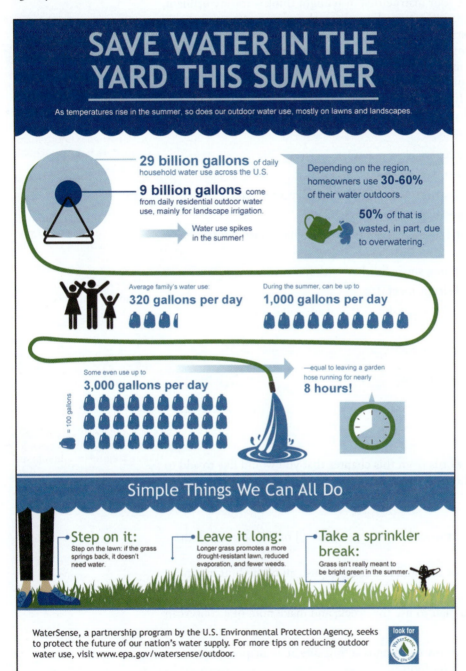

1. Answers will vary.
2. Answers will vary.
3. Some possible inferences:
   - Many people don't know that they waste water.
   - People don't realize they are overwatering.

Some students will need guidance identifying social cues and their significance. This assignment is a good opportunity to talk about social cues and to use some of the insights from emotional intelligence pedagogy. See the IM for ideas about how to present this topic and use it as a writing prompt. Also, the IM presents a list of readings you may wish to use with students to give them background information.

4. Write an essay in which you discuss a time when you used an unwarranted assumption and made a serious mistake. Explain why you held the assumption, why you did not question it, the decision you made, and why the decision was a mistake. Explain the consequences of this mistake and what you could have done to prevent it.

4. Answers will vary.

EMOTIONAL INTELLIGENCE

Good emotional intelligence requires that we make sound inferences about other people and about social situations. Have you ever misinterpreted another person's actions? If so, you have made an incorrect *social* inference. For example, we might infer that a quiet person is a snob. After getting to know the person, however, we may discover the person is not a snob at all but is shy. Think of a time when you made an incorrect social inference. What caused you to make this mistake? What can you learn from the experience? Explain in a paragraph.

Answers will vary.

CULTURAL LITERACY

Cultural assumptions are beliefs held by a specific culture. For example, in some cultures, it is assumed that parents know what's best for their children and that they have the right and responsibility to secure spouses for them. Identify an assumption in American culture or in another culture to which you belong. Explain what the assumption is and how it influences your behavior. Next, explain how other cultures might view your cultural assumption. Might other cultures think your assumption is strange or unwarranted? Write one or two paragraphs to explain.

Answers will vary.

CRITICAL THINKING

The following dialogue demonstrates how using an unwarranted assumption can result in an incorrect inference. Study the dialogue and determine the assumption that was used to draw the incorrect inference.

Mac: I'm taking an online course, and I've written my professor three times in the last two days, but he hasn't responded! I think he's ignoring my concerns. The college should fire him.

Casey: Oh, you didn't know that the college's e-mail system has been down for the last two days?

Write a paragraph explaining your analysis.

Answers will vary.

METACOGNITION

One way to have more metacognitive awareness is to think about *how your thinking* is affected by your assumptions. To do this, spend a moment considering how your life would be different if you held each of the assumptions below. Write a sentence or two explaining how your thoughts and actions might change if you really believed each assumption.

Answers will vary.

- Everyone you meet will like you and will treat you kindly.
- Your instructors really care about you and your success.
- Most of the people in your city are criminals.
- You will someday have a college degree and a great job.

10

Making a clay pot involves a series of modifications. Sometimes the potter even has to start anew. Writing is a similar craft: successful essays require thoughtful reshaping and revising.

Revising and Editing

Have you ever painted a room in your house or apartment? If so, you know that while painting can start out as an enjoyable project, it quickly becomes hard work. As you get closer and closer to finishing the painting job, you begin to long for the moment when you can stand back and look at what you have accomplished. What happens if you stand back, sighing in relief, only to notice that one half of the room needs another coat, and paint dripped onto the baseboard, and you see a spot on the ceiling? Even worse, what happens if you realize that the color is just not right?

If you really want the room to look perfect, you will have to make some revisions. Some revisions will be major, such as changing the color of the paint. Other revisions may be less difficult, such as adding another coat or cleaning up areas where the paint went out of bounds. In writing, too, you will find that you must make revisions even after you thought you were done. How well you focus on making minor as well as major changes will determine the quality of your finished work.

The purpose of revising is to make sure your writing communicates its message as well as it can. For a text to communicate successfully, it must be well organized and unified, well developed, and clearly presented. Additionally, writing should be edited so that it is free from grammatical and mechanical errors.

CHAPTER OBJECTIVES

After completing this chapter, students will be able to do the following:

- **Revise for better organization and unity.**
- **Revise for better development.**
- **Revise for better clarity.**
- **Connect pronouns to unambiguous antecedents.**
- **Make revisions during drafting.**
- **Revise with an audience in mind.**
- **Edit and format an essay.**
- **Create agreement between subjects and verbs.**

Connect IRW LearnSmart Achieve: Assign the topics "Writing Process" for adaptive learning to accompany the chapter.

REVISING FOR ORGANIZATION AND UNITY

If you use a well-planned outline, you will be able to create texts that follow a logical plan of presentation. One hallmark of an organized paper is **unity**. A text has unity if the paragraphs are appropriately related to the main idea.

Teaching Resources: See the Chapter Quiz.

Paragraphs have unity when the sentences within them are related to the paragraph's topic sentence. No random thoughts or "stray" ideas occur in unified writing.

One way to revise with unity in mind is to analyze the organization of your essay. Ask yourself whether each body paragraph clearly supports the thesis statement. Then examine the sentences in each paragraph. Do the sentences support the paragraph's topic sentence? Every sentence in your essay should be related to the ideas around it. If you see a sentence with information that is unrelated to the main idea of the paragraph, either revise it so that it supports the information in the paragraph or omit the sentence altogether.

Another task in revision is to determine whether changing the organization of the ideas will make your writing easier to follow. The following example, featuring a paragraph from an article on opening a bakery, demonstrates how changing the organization of sentences can result in much better writing. Here is the original paragraph, which discusses one major supporting point of the article.

Teaching Resources: See the *PowerPoint* presentation (PPT) "Revising for Unity and Organization." Also see the worksheet "Exercises in Revising for Unity and Organization."

> [1]One of the most demanding parts of owning a bakery is cleaning up. [2]Most bakeries are small operations, and their owners cannot afford to hire custodial staff. [3]Thus, the bakers themselves are responsible for cleanup duties. [4]Whenever flour, sugar, cocoa, and other powdery foods are used in a kitchen, there will be a mess, regardless of how careful kitchen staff are. [5]Cleaning up requires a great deal of time, and the process is physically demanding. [6]Potential bakery owners should be aware of the time and effort that must be expended to simply keep the kitchen clean. [7]Perhaps the most important part of cleanup is keeping the floor clean. [8]Oils are always involved in the baking process and present a true hazard if they end up on the floor. [9]And because oil is an expensive ingredient, bakers should be especially careful with it.

Sentence 1: major supporting point (topic sentence)

Sentence 4: examples of foods that make a mess

Sentences 5 and 6: details about time and effort needed for cleaning up

Sentences 7 and 8: details about keeping floors clean and hazards of oil

Sentence 9: detail about cost of oil

Only one sentence is truly out of place. Can you tell which one? Most of the sentences support the topic sentence, sentence 1. They give examples of messy foods, discuss the time and effort needed for cleaning up, and point out the particular importance of dealing with spilled oil.

Sentence 9, however, does not belong in the paragraph. Although the sentence deals with oil, which is discussed in the paragraph, the information it gives—the high cost of oil—has nothing to do with the task of cleaning up a bakery kitchen. We can see why the writer included the sentence while drafting the paragraph; it seems to be linked to the discussion of oil. But if the writer takes the time to revise, she will see that the cost of oil is not really important to the point she is making in the topic sentence.

The writer had planned to end her paragraph with the most **precarious** aspect of a messy kitchen—the floor. However, by ending her paragraph with a discussion of the hazards of oil, she has separated the mess caused by oil from the messes caused by powdery foods. It would be more logical to put the specific *causes* of a messy kitchen together. Thus, the paragraph would be improved if sentences 7 and 8 were nearer to the sentences about powdery foods. Here is the revised paragraph.

Vocabulary Collection Word:
precarious

Your in-context definition:
_____
_____

A dictionary definition:
_____
_____

> One of the most demanding parts of owning a bakery is cleaning up. Most bakeries are small operations, and their owners cannot afford to hire custodial staff. Thus, the bakers themselves are responsible for cleanup duties. Whenever flour, sugar, cocoa, and other powdery foods are used in a kitchen, there will be a mess, regardless of how careful kitchen staff are. Perhaps the most important part of cleanup is keeping the floor clean. Oils are always involved in the baking process and present a true hazard if they end up on the floor. Cleaning up requires a great deal of time, and the process is physically demanding. Potential bakery owners should be aware of the time and effort that must be expended to simply keep the kitchen clean.

Major supporting point (topic sentence)

Cause: powdery foods

Cause: oils

Complete the practice exercise that follows to improve the organization and unity of a paragraph.

PRACTICE ① Improving the Organization and Unity of a Paragraph

Read the paragraph that follows, annotating it to determine how its organization can be improved. Using sentence numbers, note the order in which you would place the sentences. If any sentences detract from the paragraph's unity, reword or delete them. Next revise the paragraph on a separate sheet. Reword sentences, if necessary, to write a clearer, more organized paragraph.

YOUR ANNOTATIONS

[1]While a wide variety of majors and minors exist for college degrees, four primary types of degrees are common. [2]The associate's degree requires roughly sixty hours of college credit, approximately two years of full-time college course work. [3]The doctorate requires approximately four years of course work beyond the master's degree. [4]Not many people wish to be in college long enough to earn doctorate degrees. [5]A master's degree requires two years of course work beyond a bachelor's degree, approximately six years of course work from the start of college. [6]The time spent on a master's degree usually pays off. [7]A bachelor's degree requires approximately four years of college: two years to earn an associate's degree plus two more years to obtain the bachelor's degree.

Suggested order: 1, 2, 7, 5, 3. Omit sentences 4 and 6.

REVISING FOR BETTER DEVELOPMENT

Development refers to the quantity and the quality of supporting details you use to back up your ideas. To judge the development of your writing, first think about the main idea you are communicating. Without looking at your draft, make a list of the questions your audience would need to have answered in order to fully understand or accept your main idea. Next, read your paper. Have you included enough information for readers to understand or accept the main idea? Is the information the *right kind* of information?

In the following paragraph, the writer's main idea is to explain one method for financial decision making. Read the annotations to see the kind of development this paragraph needs.

Teaching Resources: See the PPT "Revising for Better Development." Also see the worksheet "Exercises in Revising for Better Development."

[1]One way to make smart fiscal decisions is to use the Internet for research. [2]Almost any topic can be thoroughly researched with an Internet search. [3]Many consumers have questions about their finances. [4]Using Internet sources can help consumers make smarter decisions.

Sentence 1 is the topic sentence.

Sentences 2 and 3 provide no new information.

Sentence 4 repeats the information in the topic sentence.

A reader interested in learning how to use the Internet for financial research will need more specific information than the writer offers. Notice that sentences 2 and 3 do not contribute new information to develop the idea of using an Internet search. Also, sentence 4 simply repeats the information in the topic sentence. Repeated information detracts from a paragraph's development and takes up space that should be given to useful information.

By thinking of some of the questions readers may have, the writer can revise the paragraph to make it much more detailed and helpful. Here are some questions the writer could answer:

- *For what kinds of financial decision making is the Internet helpful?* The Internet provides advice for getting a mortgage, figuring out the most economical transportation options, and finding the credit cards with the lowest interest rates, as well as information on many other financial topics.

- *Can you give me an example of how a financial Web site might help me?* For example, www.bestccsaround.com offers information to help consumers find credit cards with low interest rates.

- *How can I put the knowledge I gain from such Web sites to use?* Many of the Web sites even contain links that will take consumers to sites where they can apply for low-interest financial products. For example, www.creditcarddreams.com links consumers to credit cards that fit their needs.

Thinking through readers' potential questions allows the writer to revise the paragraph so that it is much more fully developed. Notice how the writer has used the answers to these questions to revise the paragraph, providing major supporting points and details that improve its development.

One way to make smart fiscal decisions is to use the Internet for research. Web sites	Topic sentence
provide advice for getting a mortgage, figuring out the most economical transportation	
options, and finding the credit cards with the lowest interest rates, as well as information	Major supporting point 1
on many other financial topics. For example, *Best Credit Cards Around* (www.bestccsa	
round.com) offers information on the interest rates of loans and credit cards available	Supporting details
to consumers. Many of the Web sites even contain links that will take consumers to	
sites where they can apply for low-interest financial products. For example, Credit Card	Major supporting point 2
Dreams (www.creditcarddreams.com) links consumers to credit cards that fit their needs.	Supporting details

Complete the practice exercise that follows to improve the development of a paragraph. As you complete the exercise, try to think like a reader. What information would a fully developed paragraph give readers?

PRACTICE ② Improving the Development of a Paragraph

The following paragraph's main idea needs better development. List questions readers might ask, and use the answers to make changes to the paragraph. Rewrite the paragraph on a separate sheet.

> Some people opt to purchase smartphones instead of laptop computers because the apps on smartphones can do almost everything one expects from a computer. While reading the screen may be a bit more difficult with a smartphone, the computer capabilities are quite amazing.

Readers' questions:

Answers will vary, but a sample response is given.

1. What are smartphones?

2. What are apps?

3. Can you name something I can do with an app?

4. What are some of the computer capabilities of a smartphone?

5. How do the prices of smartphones and laptop computers compare?

6. Can you do word processing on a smartphone?

Sample revision: Some people opt to purchase smartphones instead of laptop computers. Smartphones are far easier to transport than laptops, and they generally cost less, too. Plus, the apps (computer applications) on smartphones can do almost everything one expects from a computer. For example, a smartphone app can enable users to browse the Web and even read a document written in *Word* or saved as a PDF file. Moreover, Web apps that enable users to compose documents are also available for smartphones. While reading is a bit more difficult on a smartphone screen, the computer capabilities are quite amazing.

REVISING FOR BETTER CLARITY

Writing clearly starts at the level of word selection. It is important to choose the very best word to communicate a thought. The suggestions in this section will help you express your ideas clearly.

Look for Awkward or Vague Expressions

In an essay about whether college education should be free, a student, Sandra, wrote this sentence:

> Some teens have immaturity and may turn to certain illegal things to gain what they could have from college.

Can you spot places where the student's expression could be clearer? Think about these points:

- The expression "teens have immaturity" is awkward. The more standard expression is to say "teens are immature."
- "Turn to" is not exactly what the writer means. Perhaps she is trying to say that some teens may *resort to* certain illegal things.
- The phrase "certain illegal things" is vague. Why not be concrete and specific? This unclear wording leaves readers wondering what those *certain illegal things* might be. Her sentence would be improved if she substituted "selling drugs or engaging in crime" for "certain illegal things."
- Finally, she says teens might turn to crime to "gain what they could have from college." Being more specific helps clear up any **ambiguity**, so a better sentence ending would be "have the kind of money a college education would have provided."

Here is Sandra's sentence revised for clarity:

> Some teens are immature and may resort to selling drugs or engaging in crime to have the kind of money a college education would have provided.

Restate Complicated Ideas Out Loud

Later in her paper, Sandra wrote this passage:

> Everyone deserves the **incentive** to go to college free, so to make Americans fine with using taxes on college, you can put in certain rules such as making a certain amount of tries at one class before you have to pay and things like that to push them even more would be in place.

Sometimes when students write sentences like these, if an instructor asks them to explain their ideas aloud in their own words, they will construct much clearer sentences. Consider this exchange.

INSTRUCTOR: Sandra, you wrote, "You can put in certain rules such as making a certain amount of tries at one class before you have to pay and things like that to push them even more would be in place." What did you mean by that?

SANDRA: Oh, I just meant that we could put certain rules in place. For example, students would have a specific number of attempts to pass a class. Once they reached the maximum attempts, they would have to pay for the class themselves.

INSTRUCTOR: Beautiful! Now write down what you just said, and you will have a very clear explanation of your point!

Speaking your ideas out loud can help you revise sentences in more easily understood language.

Teaching Resources: See the PPT "Revising for Better Clarity" and the worksheet "Exercises in Revising for Better Clarity."

Vocabulary Collection Word:
ambiguity

Your in-context definition:

_____

_____

A dictionary definition:

_____

_____

Vocabulary Collection Word:
incentive

Your in-context definition:

_____

_____

A dictionary definition:

_____

_____

Write Complete Sentences for Every Idea

Another tip is to revise a long passage by writing complete sentences for every idea. First, break the passage into parts that reflect different ideas. Then write at least one full sentence for each idea that you have identified. In the following example, each idea from Sandra's original statement (in the left column) is rephrased as at least one sentence (in the right column).

INSTEAD OF . . .	TRY . . .
Everyone deserves the incentive to go to college	Everyone deserves an incentive to go to college.
free,	One incentive would be to make college free.
so to make Americans fine with using taxes on college,	Americans may not want their tax money to pay for free college education. They may be afraid students will abuse the new system.
you can put in certain rules	To help Americans accept the idea of free college, we could make rules.
such as making a certain amount of tries at one class	One rule could be to limit the number of times students can take a class.
before you have to pay and things like that to push them even more would be in place.	We could say that students could take a class only so many times before they would have to pay for it themselves.

Imagine a Younger Audience

Finally, you can improve the clarity of your sentences sometimes by imagining you are writing for a younger audience. Writers often tend to explain things more clearly to young people. For example, Sandra wrote the following sentence:

> The way to education for most individuals in our society is unknown.

The sentence is vague and uninformative. To understand how to improve it, Sandra imagined a child asking for clarification.

CHILD: What does *that* mean?

SANDRA: Most people don't know how they are going to pay for college.

Sandra's simpler and clearer rewording would greatly improve the quality of her writing. Contrary to what some students think, a long and complex sentence that is difficult to understand is *not* good writing. Aim for clear sentences, even if that means making them very simple.

PRACTICE ③ Revising for Clarity

The following paragraph is from a student's essay. First, annotate the passage, identifying any words, phrases, or sentences that could be expressed more clearly. Next, use one of the methods described above to revise each unclear item. Write your revised paragraph on a separate sheet. At least four items need to be revised.

Gambling would not damage the state of Texas in any way but would actually see development through it. Once Texas decided to make gambling legal, that in itself would be a general improvement because a casino and other gambling essentials would make for great tourist arenas, and those attractions could cause more hotels, restaurants, and even other attractions to be built along the state. People would definitely want to move here, so our state would be expanded that much more.

Consider having students look at their previous papers to find sentences marked "awkward" or "unclear" and to revise.

Teaching Resources: See the worksheet "Disentangling Ideas" to help students see how many different ideas can be extracted from awkwardly worded sentences.

YOUR ANNOTATIONS

Sections that would benefit from revision have been underlined. Students' revised paragraphs will vary.

GRAMMAR FOCUS   **Clarity in Pronoun Reference and Agreement**

Connect IRW Assignment: See "Pronouns: Reference, Agreement, and Case" in the Grammar section for additional assignments.

Using pronouns correctly can help you write more clearly. Pronouns are words that take the place of nouns, and they include words such as *he, she, it, they, that, one,* and *everyone.* Writers use pronouns to avoid unnecessary repetition and to keep sentences short. Note the unnecessary, and uninteresting, repetition in the following example.

Noun repeated:

The water shortage caught citizens by surprise, but the city was prepared for
　　noun phrase
the water shortage.
　　noun phrase

To use a pronoun effectively, readers must be able to identify the pronoun's **antecedent,** the noun or noun phrase to which the pronoun refers. In the following example, the pronoun *it* replaces *the water shortage.*

Clear antecedent:

The water shortage caught citizens by surprise, but the city was prepared for it.
　　antecedent　　　　　　　　　　　　　　　　　　　　　　　　　　　　　　pronoun

　　Using a pronoun instead of repeating the noun phrase makes the sentence more concise without sacrificing clarity. You can follow these guidelines to use pronouns and antecedents correctly.

1. USE SINGULAR PRONOUNS FOR SINGULAR ANTECEDENTS AND PLURAL PRONOUNS FOR PLURAL ANTECEDENTS

Most antecedents are clearly either singular or plural. Make sure the pronoun matches, or agrees with, its antecedent.

　　Faulty: The city council was prepared for the water shortage. They had made sure adequate supplies were on hand.

In the preceding example, the pronoun *they* is plural, but the antecedent (*the city council*) is singular. Consequently, the pronoun and the antecedent do not agree. We can correct the sentence by making the antecedent and the pronoun both plural.

　　Corrected: The city council members were prepared for the water shortage. They had made sure adequate supplies were on hand.

　　When a pronoun takes the place of another, different pronoun, make sure the two pronouns are both either plural or singular.

　　Faulty: Everyone in the city tried to conserve water. For example, they watered their lawns less frequently than usual.

The pronouns *they* and *their* are plural, but the antecedent *everyone* is singular. One way to correct the sentence is to replace *everyone* with a plural antecedent.

　　Corrected: Residents in the city tried to conserve water. For example, they watered their lawns less frequently than usual.

(continued)

Writers need to pay special attention to words like *anyone, everyone, no one,* and *someone* when they are used as antecedents. Pronouns that refer to these words must be singular.

2. MAKE SURE THE PRONOUN CAN REFER TO ONLY ONE ANTECEDENT

Sometimes a pronoun reference is vague or unclear. If the pronoun can refer to more than one antecedent, readers will be confused.

Unclear antecedent: The drought and water shortage caught citizens by surprise, but the city was prepared for it.

Is *drought* the antecedent, or is *water shortage* the antecedent? What happens if we change *it* to *them*?

Unclear antecedent: The drought and water shortage caught citizens by surprise, but the city was prepared for them.

This sentence is also confusing! What does the word *them* refer to—*the drought and water shortage* or *citizens*? Notice how the corrected version of the sentence clears up any potential confusion.

Corrected: The drought and water shortage caught citizens by surprise, but the city was prepared for both events.

In the final version, the writer chooses to use a synonym (*both events*) rather than a pronoun because using a pronoun would cause confusion.

3. PLACE PRONOUNS CLOSE TO THEIR ANTECEDENTS

Sometimes in paragraphs the pronoun gets separated too far from the antecedent, and the separation can result in confusion. The reader may forget what antecedent the pronoun is referring to.

Faulty: Citizens had hoped the water shortage in July would last only briefly. They began to water their lawns less frequently than usual, conserve water in their homes, and comply with the city's additional conservation guidelines. But it did not.

The pronoun *it* is so far away from the antecedent, *the water shortage,* that readers may experience confusion.

Corrected: Citizens had hoped the water shortage in July would last only briefly. They began to water their lawns less frequently than usual, conserve water in their homes, and comply with the city's additional conservation guidelines. But the water shortage did not last briefly. It continued for another six weeks.

Use a pronoun only if the antecedent is nearby. Notice that the last sentence uses *it,* but because *the water shortage* is nearby, the reference for *it* is easily identified.

4. PROVIDE ANY MISSING ANTECEDENTS

Sometimes an antecedent is missing altogether. In some cases, the writer may believe he has provided an antecedent but actually has not.

(continued)

Faulty: The citizens conserved water in a number of ways. They saw it as a serious responsibility.

This passage has a pronoun—*it.* But what noun or noun phrase is the antecedent for the pronoun? The writer may mean to say that "conserving water" was seen as a serious responsibility. Notice, however, that the phrase *conserving water* does not appear in the first sentence. Thus, there is no antecedent for the pronoun.

Corrected: The citizens conserved water in a number of ways. They saw conserving water as a serious responsibility.

In the corrected sentence *it* is replaced with *conserving water.*

SENTENCE COMBINING

The following example achieves clarity while using pronouns. Notice that the sentences to combine use the same nouns repeatedly. In the revision, the short sentences are combined and some nouns are replaced with pronouns, but the antecedents are always nearby and easily identifiable.

Ideas to combine:

- There is a Northern Rio Grande National Heritage Area in New Mexico.

- Different cultures coexist in the Northern Rio Grande National Heritage Area.

- The cultures' languages, crafts, and architecture coexist.

- The Northern Rio Grande National Heritage Area includes impressive natural resources.

- The Northern Rio Grande National Heritage Area includes breathtaking scenery.

- The Northern Rio Grande National Heritage Area includes abundant recreational resources.

Revised using pronouns and antecedents: The Northern Rio Grande National Heritage Area in New Mexico is a place where different cultures—with their languages, crafts, and architecture—coexist. It includes impressive natural resources, breathtaking scenery, and abundant recreational resources.

Try your hand at using pronouns clearly by completing the following exercises.

EXERCISES

You will find three sets of sentences below. Combine the sentences to make smoother, longer ones, and use at least two pronouns to avoid repeating nouns excessively. Make sure you use pronouns in such a way that their antecedents are clearly identifiable.

Answers will vary. Sample answers are provided.

1. Ideas to combine:

- One highly contagious disease is chicken pox (varicella).

- The most usual symptoms are rash, fever, headache, sore throat, and cough.

(continued)

- Chicken pox can also lead to very serious complications for vulnerable people.
- The best protection against chicken pox is the chicken pox vaccine.
- The chicken pox vaccine has been used widely in the United States since 1995.

Answer: One highly contagious disease is chicken pox (varicella). Its most usual symptoms are rash, fever, headache, sore throat, and cough, but chicken pox can also lead to very serious complications for vulnerable people. The best protection against the disease is the chicken pox vaccine, which has been used widely in the United States since 1995.

2. Ideas to combine:

- Older people may have more difficulty falling asleep.
- People may have insomnia or awaken more often.
- People may awaken three or more times a night.
- Medical conditions may interfere with peaceful sleep.
- Older people get about the same number of hours of sleep.
- Older people may spend more time awake in bed than they used to.

Answer: Older people may have more difficulty falling asleep or have insomnia. They may awaken more often—three or more times a night. Medical conditions may interfere with peaceful sleep. Even though older people get the same number of hours of sleep, they may spend more time awake in bed than they used to.

3. Ideas to combine:

- The Florissant Valley lies thirty-five miles west of Colorado Springs.
- Visitors can see the Rocky Mountains.
- The Rocky Mountains are to the north.
- The Rocky Mountains are to the east.
- The meadows in the Florissant Valley are filled with native grasses and wildflowers.
- The native grasses and wildflowers wave in the breeze.
- The meadows are a beautiful sight.

Answer: Florissant Valley lies thirty-five miles west of Colorado Springs. To the north and east, visitors can see the Rocky Mountains. The meadows in the Florissant Valley are a beautiful sight. They are filled with native grasses and wildflowers that wave in the breeze.

Teaching Resources: See the mini-quiz "Using Pronouns Correctly."

MAKING REVISIONS DURING DRAFTING

You are ready to begin drafting after you have selected and narrowed your topic, used prewriting to generate ideas, written a thesis statement and topic sentences, and constructed an outline. At this point, you have already accomplished much of the hard work of writing. Drafting is simply putting into words all of the ideas you have generated.

As you draft your paper, plan on using a writing process that is recursive. Something is recursive if it occurs again and again. In writing, a recursive process involves moving forward in the following way:

- Writing sentences and paragraphs
- Stopping occasionally to reread everything you have written
- Revising what you have written before moving forward

Many good writers use a recursive writing process.

Some student writers hesitate to use a recursive process because it takes more time than just plodding ahead without revising. While this method does take more time, it also results in *much* better writing!

Another tip is to read your work out loud when you are rereading your draft. Sometimes you will hear passages that need to be worded more clearly, paragraphs that lack unity, or sentences that need to be combined or separated.

Try using this recursive writing process by completing the following exercise.

PRACTICE ④ Using the Recursive Writing Process

Write a paragraph on one reason why the minimum wage should or should not be raised. First, use a prewriting activity to generate ideas for the paragraphs, then write a topic sentence and outline for the paragraph, and finally use the recursive writing process to compose the paragraph. Specifically, after each sentence you write, go back to the beginning of the paragraph and read it again, making any changes you feel are needed.

MAKING REVISIONS AFTER DRAFTING

To revise well requires a heightened awareness of the audience. Because you are usually not near readers when they read your text, you cannot clear up confusion, add missing information, or explain the tone of the message. Your readers must infer your meaning from only one thing: the words you have chosen to use.

For college writing assignments, your audience is usually your instructor but can sometimes include your peers, depending on the purpose of the assignment. Keeping in mind your audience's values, expectations, needs, assumptions, and abilities will help you write a paper that communicates your ideas clearly to that audience. If you revise with a reader in mind, you will almost always find opportunities to make changes.

Using the questions in the chart on the next page will help you find the parts of your writing that need to be revised.

Revision Questions	
Organization and unity	• Are my ideas organized in a logical and convincing way? • Does my writing have a successful introduction and conclusion?
Clarity	• Is my main idea clearly stated or implied? • Have I made the relationship between the support and my main idea clear?
Development	• Have I provided enough support (definitions, examples, comparisons, causes, effects, and so on) for the main idea? • Have I answered readers' potential questions?
Tone	• Is the tone of my paper appropriate?
Assignment requirements	• Does the paper meet assignment requirements?

Student Example of Preparing to Revise a Draft

To demonstrate the essay revision process, we will observe the revision process used by Maria, a student in a college reading and writing class. Maria has drafted an essay for her English class. To begin the revision process, she reviews the assignment instructions, which she had annotated at the start of the assignment.

Maria's Annotated Assignment

Write an essay to be published in our college newspaper. (You do not really have to publish your essay, but imagine that your audience will be the student body and anyone else who reads our newspaper.) Your topic is this: Should instructors assign group projects? Some students dislike group projects because not everyone in the group does the work, so these projects unfairly reward slackers. Other students love group projects because they learn from their peers and enjoy working with them. What is your point of view on this topic? Select one of these views:

- Group projects are good assignments.
- Group projects are good assignments only if they include certain conditions.
- Group projects should not be assigned.

Discuss at least three reasons for your position.

Annotations:
- Write a college newspaper essay.
- Audience = student body
- Topic
- Provide my opinion
- Looks good! Use this.
- Need 3 reasons.

After rereading the assignment instructions, Maria thinks about each particular assignment element:

- Write for a student audience.
- Choose one point of view.
- Give three reasons.

Maria also figures out her instructor's unstated expectations:

- Write a thesis statement.
- Write an introduction, body, and conclusion.
- Make sure the paper is developed enough.
- Use correct grammar and spelling.

I have to tell her what I think about group projects. *I did that—I think. Will check and make sure.*

Correct grammar and spelling. *I need to look over grammar and run a spell-checker, and then I need to read it myself to check for misspellings and other obvious errors.*

She told me that my last paper was not "developed" enough. *I need to make sure that the body paragraphs are as full as I can make them so that she is convinced of my thesis.*

I need a thesis statement. *I have that.*

I have to provide three reasons to back up my point of view. *OK, I did that.*

I know that I am supposed to have an introduction paragraph, a body, and a conclusion. *I do have those, but some of them are not very good.*

Write for a particular audience: the student body. *I did not really think about how different students might react to my essay.*

Student Example of a Draft Annotated for Revision

Now that Maria has reviewed the assignment, she can start the revision process. She begins by printing out a copy of her draft. Having a paper copy to write on is the best way to revise. It is easier to skip over mistakes when you read a computer screen, so revise with a pen in your hand.

To begin, Maria consciously shifts her thinking so that she is reading her paper not as herself but as her readers—the student body and others who read the newspaper. As she reads, she makes notes about what her readers might think. She looks for places where organization and unity, clarity, and tone can be improved.

Maria's Annotated Draft

Intro is too short.	I do not understand why every instructor at Marquez College seems to love group projects. Group projects are truly a waste of time, to be honest.
I didn't state my thesis: Group projects should not be assigned.	Sounds rude.
	I clearly remember my speech class here at Marquez College. The most difficult assignment I ever did in my life was in that class, and it was a group assignment in which we had to choose a controversial issue, find the best research we could on that issue, and use that research to make an argument for or against the issue. It was a horrible experience.
I didn't explain why it was so horrible. Need more details.	This sentence is too long!!! This para is all negative. Need a more positive tone.

(continued)

A bit rude. Need to say how great that prof's lectures actually were!

Readers may not get what I mean by "terrible decisions." Needs more explanation. Seems random—cut.

Grammar? Revise.

Maybe profs could tell us how to get to know one another quickly and then move on to the assignment.

Give more details about the slacker. Use term "slacker"?

Unrelated—delete.

Sounds so snobby!

In my speech class, our professor sat at her desk and read a book while we struggled to make sense of the assignment in groups. Instead of reading, she could have been really teaching us. I want to learn from my professor, not my classmates.

In another class, the professor assigned the group project and made some terrible decisions about due dates and announcements. Most of the groups were scrambling at the last minute to throw something together for a grade. ~~The topic was global warming.~~

Another reason to not assign group work is the issue of time. Groups spend so much time just figuring out how to work together that little time is available for the project. It is usually impossible for all group members to meet at the same time, so there are lots of e-mails and texts we have to send. And even wasted time in personal meetings make group projects unpleasant. People feel awkward, so we end up talking about our lives and getting to know each other. Getting to know my classmates is fine, but it's not why I enrolled in the course.

The way group projects are graded is simply unfair. For example, I did most of the work in my group, but the other group members got the same grade I did. A slacker got the very same grade I got. ~~He was actually a jerk I knew from high school.~~ What did he learn from this project? He learned that he can get away with being a slacker.

I can tolerate working with students, but do not base my grade on that work. Instructors can assign group projects, but they should also teach students how to work in groups.

Reorganize this para so it doesn't start with the example.

But not all instructors handle group projects in this way. I should say that.

An instructor might say the purpose of a group project is to teach time management. If they would give some guidelines or ideas about time management, maybe group projects wouldn't be so horrible.

Maybe this is a rude tone.

Sounds whiny.

Maybe give an idea about how projects could be graded more fairly?

Last sentence doesn't fit thesis statement. Do I want to say group projects are OK if instructors do certain things, or do I want to stick with idea that group projects should never be assigned? Revise.

Student Example of a Revised Draft

Maria has come up with a variety of ideas for improving her paper when she revises. What follows is Maria's revised essay. Notice that Maria changed her point of view from the one she initially highlighted in the assignment. So she changed her thesis statement to reflect her new point of view. As you read it, annotate the areas where you see other changes. Do you see any other places where Maria could make more improvements?

Maria Colonio

Prof. Liu

English 110

4 April 2014

Professors: Just Say "No" to Group Projects

Group projects are popular assignments at Marquez College and probably at many other colleges. I understand why teachers use group projects. They want students to learn to work together, and they want us to help one another in the learning process. However, I do not think these goals are met very well by group projects as most instructors assign them. For group projects to really work, professors need to include specific information about how the groups should function and how individual student grades will be determined.

I clearly remember my speech class here at Marquez College. The most difficult assignment I ever did in my life was in that class. It was a group assignment. We had to choose a controversial issue, find the best research we could on that issue, and use that research to make an argument for or against the issue. It was not a good experience. My group was dysfunctional. As a student concerned about grades, I was the one who did the calling and e-mailing to beg group members to contribute to the project. In the end, I alone did the work. I learned quite a bit, but it simply was not fair that the other group members received the same grade of "A" that I did.

One reason to not assign group work is the issue of time. Groups spend so much time just figuring out how to work together that little time is available for the project. It is usually impossible for all

Colonio 2

group members to meet at the same time, so there are lots of e-mails and texts we have to send. This could be time we spent on the task, not on coordinating meetings with our fellow students. And even meetings include a lot of wasted time. People feel awkward, so we end up talking about our lives and getting to know one another. That is fun, but it is not exactly the kind of learning I want to be doing in college. If instructors would give groups instructions to spend five minutes on introductions, five minutes to exchange information, and so on, groups would function better.

The second reason group projects should not be assigned is that the way they are graded is sometimes seen as unfair by students. I am sure my professors all try to be fair, but group projects sometimes make it impossible. For example, I did most of the work in my group, but the other group members got the same grade I did. I researched the issue along with another student, while three of our classmates sat in the library and talked. One guy never attended the group meetings, and he only did a small portion of what he was assigned to do. He turned in a paragraph the day before our paper was due, but he got the very same grade I got. What did he learn from this project? He learned that he can get away with being a slacker. That is not the kind of message professors are trying to send to their students. A better way to grade group projects would be to give students individual grades based on the quality of the project and the participation level of the student. That way, even if the project is an "F," the student who worked the hardest has a chance to pass.

Another reason why I dislike group projects and think they should not be assigned is that I want to learn from my professor, not my fellow

Colonio 3

students. No offense, fellow students, but you guys do not have the master's degree or doctorate that our professors have. I get much more out of a good discussion or lecture than a group project. Teachers have lots of knowledge and expertise. Finding a way to share this knowledge would be much more valuable than assigning a group project.

I know that some professors value group projects because of the cooperation required to do them. I do not mind working with my fellow students, but please do not base my grade on the classmates in my group. If Marquez College faculty use group projects, I hope they will consider helping the groups function better and assigning individual grades to individual students. These steps will make group work something students can really use for learning.

Maria's essay changed dramatically through the revision process. Examine the important changes Maria made by completing the following exercise.

Connect IRW Writing Assignment: Use the peer editing tools in Connect IRW to have students revise one another's essays.

PRACTICE 5   Determining a Student's Revision

List three changes Maria made in her revised draft on pages 326–328, and explain the effect the change might have on the reader.

Answers will vary. Some possible answers are provided.

Determining a Student's Revisions

1. Maria added a title. Readers will expect a title, and Maria's title is witty and appropriate. By adding a title, Maria is meeting readers' expectations.

2. Maria took out this sentence: *He was actually a jerk I knew from high school.* By taking out this sentence, Maria is unifying her essay. Readers won't be confused by reading unnecessary information.

3. Maria improved the tone of her essay in places, such as this one: *Another reason why I dislike group projects and think they should not be assigned is that I want to learn from my professor, not my fellow students. No offense, fellow students, but you guys do not have the master's degree or doctorate that our professors have.* This reasonable tone will help readers think Maria is giving constructive criticism, not just complaining.

REVISING WITH AN AUDIENCE IN MIND

As Maria revised her essay, she tried to see her writing as the college newspaper readers would see it. Keeping an audience in mind as you revise is crucial. More important, however, is understanding what particular audiences need and expect from your texts.

Let's consider an essay directed at a different audience. Pauline works at a **marketing** company, Imperial KRC Brands, as a receptionist. She has learned that her company offers a "Back to College" incentive plan. This plan allows employees six hours off work per week to attend college classes. Additionally, the plan pays for any college expenses that management has approved. The company awards only two such scholarships per department, and other employees in Pauline's department are also applying. Applicants must each write an essay to make their case. Here are the essay instructions that Pauline's company has issued.

Vocabulary Collection Word:
marketing

Your in-context definition:

_____

_____

A dictionary definition:

_____

Back to College Incentive Plan

Applying for College Tuition Payment: As part of Imperial KRC Brands' interest in professional development, we have set aside funds to pay for college tuition for select employees. Because these funds are limited, employees need to request these funds and fully explain why such funds should be granted to them. To apply, please follow these instructions:

1. Write an essay of no more than 500 words in which you discuss the following:

   - Your employment history with Imperial KRC Brands
   - The college program or degree you are pursuing
   - The reason you are pursuing this program or degree
   - How this program or degree will help you be a better employee at Imperial KRC Brands
   - Where you are in your studies or graduation plan
   - Specific details regarding the amount of funding you will need for the academic year

2. Submit this essay to your supervisor by the deadline: April 12.

Example of an Essay Draft Written for an Employer

Pauline is nervous about writing this essay. She has written essays for college instructors, but she has never written any major documents for work purposes. Nonetheless, she has produced a draft of her essay, and she now needs help revising it for her particular audience. Here is Pauline's draft. As you read it, annotate any places you believe need revision.

Pauline's Draft

I have worked here at Imperial KRC Brands for four years as a receptionist, it has been a great career for me so far. I want to go back to college to get my degree. You cannot make that much as a receptionist, I know that I could get more secretarial skills, but my real goal is to get a bachelor's degree in accounting.

I think accounting would be a good career choice for me because I am good with numbers and I love math and I am extremely organized. All important for accountants. I know this because my brother is an accountant and I have helped him on the weekends. I have also talked with Stacy McMann in the Accounting Department, she thinks my aptitude for accounting is strong.

YOUR ANNOTATIONS

(continued)

I would like Imperial KRC Brands to cover my tuition expenses because if I get my accounting degree, I will continue to work for Imperial. I will give back to the company.

I want to start back in the fall semester, approximately on August 27th. I would need to leave early two days a week in order to make it in time for class. I can train someone to take my place during the times I would be gone.

Thank you.

YOUR ANNOTATIONS

We are now going to compare Pauline's draft with the instructions she received.

FROM THE INSTRUCTIONS	WHAT PAULINE WROTE	HOW PAULINE MIGHT REVISE FOR IMPROVEMENT
"Write an essay of no more than 500 words."	Pauline's essay is 211 words, so it is well below the maximum of 500.	Pauline meets this requirement but misses an opportunity. She could add almost 300 words to strengthen her case.
Discuss "your employment history with Imperial KRC Brands."	Pauline offers only one sentence about her employment history: "I have worked here at Imperial KRC Brands for four years as a receptionist, it has been a great career for me so far."	Pauline does not fully meet this requirement. When a person is asked to "discuss" something, we usually expect more than one sentence. Pauline could have talked about how she has mastered new tasks on this job, how she has advanced (if she has), how she has made positive contributions to the company, and so on. Additionally, this passage contains a comma splice, an error she should correct when editing.
Discuss "the college program or degree you are pursuing."	Pauline writes, "My real goal is to get a bachelor's degree in accounting. I think accounting would be a good career choice for me because I am good with numbers and I love math and I am extremely organized. All important for accountants. I know this because my brother is an accountant and I have helped him on the weekends. I have also talked with Stacy McMann in the Accounting Department, she thinks my aptitude for accounting is strong."	Pauline did a much better job here but could still improve. She could have elaborated more on her organizational abilities as a receptionist. It was a good idea to include the work she has done for her brother because it shows she has an idea what accounting will entail. Also, she uses the endorsement of a coworker, Stacy McMann. If Stacy has a good reputation, this endorsement will be helpful. In the editing process, Pauline should correct the grammatical errors in these sentences.
Discuss "the reason you are pursuing this program or degree."	Pauline makes it clear that financial concerns are part of her decision.	This passage meets the requirement but could be improved. While it is true that a paycheck is important, a letter requesting college funding may not be the place to talk about salary. We like to think that people get college degrees because they are cut out for a particular line of work, not just because they want more money.
Discuss "how this program or degree will help you be a better employee at Imperial KRC Brands."	Pauline writes, "If I get my accounting degree, I will continue to work for Imperial. I will give back to the company."	Pauline does not fully meet this requirement. One thing she needs to reconsider is the word *if*. Pauline's essay would be much stronger if she used the word *when* instead of *if*. Also, Pauline did not give her audience many reasons to invest in her.
Discuss "where you are in your studies or graduation plan."	Pauline does not answer this question at all. Perhaps she simply overlooked it.	Pauline needs to address the issue of her status in college.
Include "specific details regarding the amount of funding you will need for the academic year."	Pauline writes, "I want to start back in the fall semester, approximately on August 27th. I would need to leave early two days a week in order to make it in time for class. I can train someone to take my place during the times I would be gone."	Pauline does not fully meet this requirement. It is helpful that she provides the start date and has a plan for the days she will be gone, but she must include the amount of funding she needs since the assignment clearly asks for that information.

Example of a Revised Draft Written for an Employer

By comparing Pauline's writing to the assignment instructions, we found a number of places where her essay could be improved. In the next box you will see how Pauline revised her essay. Her revisions are underlined and appear in blue ink. As you read her revised essay, annotate the areas of improvement. In your annotations, explain why you think the particular passage shows improvement.

Pauline's Revision

I have worked here at Imperial KRC Brands for four years as a receptionist. It has been a great career for me so far. When I began here four years ago, I did not know much about clerical work. My experiences as a receptionist have taught me many things, such as how to use software programs like *Excel* and *Microsoft Word*, how to keep an organized calendar of appointments, and how to assist management in a variety of tasks, including phone work and file organization. I have also become more aware of my own interests in life. I am writing because one of my interests is accounting, and I am asking Imperial to help me achieve my goal of a B.S. in Accounting.

I think accounting would be a good career choice for me. I am good with numbers, and I love math. Additionally, I am extremely organized. All of these qualities are important for accountants. I have had some experience with accounting work. My brother is an accountant, and I have helped him update records on the weekends. I have also talked with Stacy McMann in the Accounting Department. She has commented on my organizational abilities, and she thinks my aptitude for accounting is strong.

I am asking Imperial KRC Brands to cover my tuition expenses. Specifically, I will need $9,250.00 for the 2014–2015 academic year. I plan to continue to work for Imperial even after I finish college. This has been a wonderful work environment for me, and I want to give back to the company.

I have about 62 hours in college credit at this point, making me almost a junior. I want to start back in the fall semester, which begins on August 27. I would need to leave early two days a week in order to make it in time for class. I can train someone to take my place during the times I would be gone, if that would be helpful.

Finally, I want to thank Imperial KRC Brands for caring so much about its employees. The opportunity to go back to college is an opportunity I will not squander.

YOUR ANNOTATIONS

One way to make reading and writing skills more relevant for students is to show them how their skills can be used in their careers. See the IM for work-related IRW assignments.

Pauline's essay changed dramatically during the revision stage. It is now 357 words compared with the original 210, and it is better developed. Furthermore, she addresses each of the requirements listed in the essay instructions. Her audience will read a polished, carefully revised essay, and Pauline's chances for getting the tuition scholarship are now much greater.

EDITING AND FORMATTING AN ESSAY

The best way to distinguish editing from revising is to think of revising as re-visioning ideas, and editing as finding mistakes in specific grammatical and stylistic details. Editing helps you prepare your revised text for submission.

People who are employed as editors are trained to find *every* error in a text. The range of errors one could look for is very wide. When you edit, it is important to focus on the most common areas of difficulty that you have in writing. If you know that you have particular trouble with a certain grammatical concept, such as subject-verb agreement, make sure that you take extra time during the editing stage to check the agreement of each subject and verb.

Using SMART TRACS to Edit Your Essay

In addition to checking for the specific errors you tend to make, use the **acronym** SMART TRACS to remember ten issues to check for in your paper.

Vocabulary Collection Word:
acronym

Your in-context definition:

_____

_____

A dictionary definition:

_____

_____

Teaching Resources: See the IM for resources students can use to help them master grammatical and mechanical errors. Also, see "Editing and Revising Practice," available only in Create™, for exercises.

SMART TRACS Editing Plan

Use the SMART TRACS editing plan to check your work for common writing errors.

S = Spelling
M = Missing words
A = Accurate punctuation
R = Repeated words
T = Terminal punctuation
T = Tense consistency
R = Rhythm
A = Active voice
C = Confusing words
S = Sources

S = Spelling. The good news is that the spelling of many words can be checked with the spell-checker in your word-processing program. However, words that sound the same but are spelled differently need special consideration. A spell-checker will not catch the incorrect use of *their* for *there,* for example. If you are writing by hand and come to a word you are unsure about, take a guess at its spelling, and then look up the word in a dictionary. Do not yield to the temptation to skip over it and hope you have spelled it correctly. Keeping a list of words you often misspell will help you learn to spell them properly.

M = Missing words. Have you ever read a with a missing word? (Read that again: did you see that it should have included the word *sentence?*) We sometimes leave out words because we think more quickly than we write. Additionally, our brains can compensate for left-out words. For example, you were probably able to understand the first sentence in this paragraph because your brain uses context clues to think about what the word likely is. We can even figure out words with missing letters. See whether you can understand this sentence: *I wld lke to hve a stk for dinnr.* Our minds are able to add in the missing letters, missing words, and misspellings. Thus, it is important that you read your paper very carefully when looking for missing words. Read each sentence aloud very slowly. Better yet, have a friend read your paper aloud to you.

A = Accurate punctuation. Inaccurate punctuation, especially involving commas and semicolons, can result in major sentence errors, such as these:

Run-ons (sentences joined without any punctuation)

Comma splices (sentences joined with only a comma)

Fragments (sentences lacking a subject, verb, or both)

(continued)

Check all commas to make sure you are using them correctly. Check semicolons to be sure that you are using them only to separate two related, complete sentences.

R = **Repeated words.** It is very easy to use the same word repeatedly. Read this paragraph for an example of repeating the same word repeatedly. If you repeatedly use the word *repeat,* for example, readers may not take your writing seriously. You may need to repeat a writing assignment if you repeatedly repeat the same word. One way to avoid repetition is to use synonyms. Additionally, read your paper out loud and listen. You are sometimes more likely to *hear* repeated words than to see them.

T = **Terminal punctuation.** Have you ever written a question and ended it with a period instead of a question mark. (We just did!) Be sure to check all of the sentences in your paper to make sure you use the appropriate *terminal* (ending) punctuation. Use a period—the most common terminal punctuation mark—only with a complete sentence. Use a semicolon only at the end of one complete sentence and the beginning of another. A comma is *not* a terminal punctuation mark. Do not use it to join two complete sentences. By analyzing each punctuation mark in your writing, you will be better able to spot sentence fragments and run-ons. To find comma splices, read sentences aloud to determine where they should end. Use appropriate punctuation between two complete sentences.

T = **Tense consistency.** In general, if you start your essay or paragraph in past tense, stay in past tense. If you start in present tense, stay in present tense. There will be times when you will need to shift tense, such as when you refer to something in the past. Be very mindful of verb tenses during the revision process. Circle each verb, and check to make sure you have chosen the appropriate tense.

R = **Rhythm.** If you read your paper out loud, you will be able to hear the rhythm of your sentences. Good writing usually consists of sentences of different lengths and different types. Read the two passages below out loud to hear the differences in their rhythms:

> **Passage A:** The ceremony started. We recited the Pledge of Allegiance. We sang the national anthem. The guest speaker talked. She delivered a speech. The speech was about giving back to society. The graduates stood up to be recognized. Their names were called. The graduates walked up to the stage. They received their diplomas. They walked back to their seats.

> **Passage B:** The ceremony started with the Pledge of Allegiance and the national anthem. Next, a guest speaker delivered a speech to the graduates about giving back to society. Soon, the graduates stood up to be recognized. As their names were called, they walked to the stage, received their diplomas, and walked back to their seats.

Use variety in sentence length and sentence type to create writing that is more rhythmically appealing.

A = **Active voice.** To use active voice, structure the sentence so that the agent (subject) doing the action (verb) is presented in the proper place. Start by

(continued)

analyzing the main verb of the sentence. In the example below, *broke* is the main verb. To write the sentence in active voice, put the agent—the person who did the breaking—first, as the example shows:

Active voice: John broke the window.

Passive voice: The window was broken by John.

Sentences written in passive voice are often wordier and more complicated than they would be if they were written in active voice. In addition, many writing instructors characterize sentences in active voice as being "stronger" than those in passive voice. Thus, from a stylistic perspective, using active voice is often (though not always) preferable.

C = Confusing words. A large number of words in the English language are commonly misused. Examples include *their, they're, there; its, it's; two, too, to; affect, effect; loose, lose;* and *desert, dessert.* To improve this aspect of your writing, start by reading through a list of the most commonly confused words. Mark those that you have trouble with. Make note cards for those words, and include their meanings and rules for use. As you read and write, refer to your note cards so that you learn the correct usage of the problem words. When you revise, look for the specific words on your note cards by using your word processor's "Find" function. Check each of the words to make sure you have used it correctly, and make changes where necessary.

S = Sources. If your writing contains sources, make sure that you have (a) integrated the source material grammatically; (b) used a proper attribution convention; (c) created a works cited or references list; and (d) correctly formatted your paper.

In the exercise that follows, you will use the SMART TRACS editing plan to make changes to the first two paragraphs of a student's essay.

PRACTICE 6 Editing a Text

Read the two paragraphs that follow from a student's essay on how to raise healthier children. Use SMART TRACS to look for specific types of errors. When you find errors, annotate them. When you finish, rewrite the student's paragraphs on a separate sheet to correct the errors.

Parents do want the best for their children. To have a good education, strong morals, respectful to others, and to grow up to be strong and healthy. So parents always thinking of ways to protect the future of their kids and to do that is making sure they're healthy.

First, parents need to consider the healthy foods they will feed their children. When their toddlers parents shouldn't give up them alot of sweets try to balance it out by giving them plenty of healthy fruits and vegetables. For instance healthy foods like carrots, apples, grapes, sweet peppers, and oranges should be given to the children. These healthy foods are much healthier than the junkfood most children crave. Even though its hard to get kids to eat healthy vegtables. The best kinds of vegtables are

(continued)

Teaching Resources: For a sample of these paragraphs with edits and suggested revisions included, see the IM.

You may wish to use this sentence as an opportunity to discuss the appropriateness of starting sentences with *so, and, well, but,* and similar words. In some cases, these words function as *discourse markers.* The problem with starting sentences with *so* and *and* is the tendency of the novice writer to create fragments.

the healthy leafy green vegtables like collard greens, spinach, and green beans These are the foods that have positive health affects. As far as healthy snacks for them I would give them gram crackers, yogurt and popcorn but not soda, you could switch that out with a healthier drink such as natural juice, milk or some water.

Subject-Verb Agreement

A common and significant error is a lack of agreement between a subject and its verb. If you know that you are prone to make this error, focus on it while editing, and take a moment to review the basics of subject-verb agreement.

A singular subject must be matched with a singular verb, and a plural subject must be paired with a plural verb. In the following examples, the sentence's subject is in italics, and the sentence's verb is underlined.

Examples: An *animal* releases hormones as a response to stress.

Animals release hormones as a response to stress.

You may notice that nouns ending in -*s* (plural nouns) often agree with verbs that *do not* end in -*s*. While there are exceptions, it can be helpful to check subject nouns and verbs for their -*s* endings and to make sure the subject and verb agree.

Examples: hawk flies (singular)   hawks fly (plural)

psychologist listens (singular)   psychologists listen (plural)

she is   they are

As the last example above shows, even irregular verbs (*is*) have an -*s* ending in the singular.

The guidelines that follow show how to think about particular subject-verb agreement situations that can be confusing.

1. IF A SUBJECT CONTAINS TWO OR MORE NOUNS OR PRONOUNS JOINED BY *AND*, USE A PLURAL VERB

Often a subject contains two or more nouns or pronouns joined together. If *and* is used to connect the parts of the subject, then the verb should usually be plural.

Example: An *evaluation* and **an** *analysis* **are** included in the report.

A rare exception occurs when the two nouns are typically thought of as a single unit.

Example: *Steak and eggs* is my favorite breakfast.

2. IF A SUBJECT CONTAINS *OR* OR *NOR*, MAKE THE VERB AGREE WITH THE PART OF THE SUBJECT CLOSEST TO THE VERB

If two nouns or pronouns in a subject are joined by *or* or *nor*, the subject is not necessarily plural. The part of the subject that is nearest to the verb determines

Often students who struggle with subject-verb agreement do not have English as their primary language, or they use cultural English variants that employ nonstandard subject-verb constructions. It can be helpful to identify students who have difficulty with subject-verb agreement from diagnostic writing samples early in the semester. Once they are identified, you can direct these students to individualized study programs (in Connect IRW or in tutoring programs) that can help them develop subject-verb agreement skills.

The review here is designed to present the general concept of subject-verb agreement and to help students handle tricky situations. Students who struggle with subject-verb agreement should work on the skill in more depth.

Teaching Resources: See the IM for additional suggestions and ESL instruction tips.

(continued)

whether the verb is singular or plural. When a singular subject noun is connected by *or* or *nor* to a plural subject noun, place the plural noun closer to the verb, and use a plural verb, as in the following examples.

Examples: The *awl* [singular noun] **or** the *bits* [plural noun] belong in the bin.

Do the *bits* **or** the *awl* belong in the bin?

In the question example above, the helping verb (*do*) shows that the verb is plural.

3. WATCH OUT FOR WORDS THAT COME BETWEEN THE SUBJECT AND THE VERB

Sometimes a phrase or a clause that comes between the subject and the verb can cause confusion about subject-verb agreement. Remember that the verb should agree with the subject, not with a noun or pronoun in the phrase or clause.

Examples: The *computers* **in the new lab** are easy to use.

The *diagram* **that came with the instructions** identifies the parts.

To determine the right agreement, mentally strike through intervening words to identify the correct subject.

4. DETERMINE WHETHER SUBJECTS INDICATING QUANTITIES ARE SINGULAR OR PLURAL

Words such as *fraction, majority, part,* and *percent* are typically followed by a prepositional phrase. In those cases, the **object of the preposition** determines whether you should use a singular or plural verb. If the object of the preposition is singular, use a singular verb. Likewise, if the object of the preposition is plural, use a plural verb.

Examples: *Forty percent* **of the hay** has been distributed.

Forty percent **of the bales** have been distributed.

5. FOR NOUNS THAT CAN BE PLURAL OR SINGULAR, USE THE VERB FORM THAT REFLECTS THE MEANING OF THE SENTENCE

Many nouns that refer to groups of people can be either singular or plural. Some examples are *audience, board, committee, council, family, group, set,* and *team.* In a sentence describing the action of the entire group, a singular verb is needed. In a sentence describing the actions of individuals in a group, a plural verb is logical.

Example: The *committee* has voted in favor of the proposal.

The *committee* have different views on the proposal.

If a plural verb sounds awkward, try inserting a plural noun into the subject, as follows.

Example: The *committee members* have different views on the proposal.

6. DETERMINE WHETHER PRONOUN SUBJECTS ARE SINGULAR OR PLURAL

Pronouns that include the word *one* or *body* are singular and need singular verbs. Some pronouns—for example, *both, few, many,* and *several*—are plural and need

(continued)

plural verbs. A few pronouns—*all, any, more, most, some*—can be singular or plural depending on the meaning of the sentence. As with nouns indicating quantities, a prepositional phrase may determine whether the pronoun is singular or plural.

Examples: *More* is known today about effective urban planning strategies.

More [strategies] are used by planners to resolve overcrowding issues.

All of the study **participants** have been paid a nominal fee.

All of the study's **cost** has been covered by a grant.

7. USE SINGULAR VERBS FOR MONEY, TIME, AND TITLES

A sum of money, a period of time, or a title of a work is thought of as a single unit and so takes a singular verb.

Examples: *Twenty years* is a long time to spend in college.

Seventy-five dollars is the price of the ticket.

Bury My Heart at Wounded Knee is the assigned reading.

SENTENCE COMBINING

The examples that follow show how to combine sentences and select the appropriate verb to create subject-verb agreement.

Ideas to combine using correct subject-verb agreement:

- Nearly half the electricity created in the United States results from burning coal.

- Soot is a by-product of burning coal.

- Toxic air emissions are a by-product of burning coal.

- There are other by-products of burning coal.

- These by-products include acid rain.

- They include smog.

Combined sentences with subject-verb agreement: Nearly half the electricity created in the United States results from burning coal. Soot and toxic air emissions are by-products of burning coal. Other by-products include acid rain and smog.

Try your hand at combining sentences and selecting the appropriate verbs to create subject-verb agreement.

EXERCISES

You will find three sets of sentences below. Combine the sentences to make smoother, longer ones, and make sure subjects and verbs agree.

1. Ideas to combine:

- Genes probably influence the development of autism spectrum disorders.

- The environment seems to influence the development of autism spectrum disorders.

Answers will vary, but sample responses are provided.

(continued)

- The disorders are usually diagnosed in children rather than adults.
- The cause is being researched.
- Methods for treating autism spectrum disorders are being researched.

Answer: Genes and the environment probably influence the development of autism spectrum disorders. Autism spectrum disorders are usually diagnosed in children rather than adults. The cause and methods for treating autism disorders are being researched.

2. Ideas to combine:

- Contracts are signed by people.
- The people who sign them are called "parties" to the contract.
- One party signs the contract.
- Another party signs the contract.
- The agreement is between both parties.

Answer: Contracts are signed by people who are called "parties" to the contract. Both parties sign the contract, and the agreement in the contract is between both parties.

3. Ideas to combine:

- Nanoscience is a relatively new scientific interest.
- Nanoscience is the study of very small things, such as atoms.
- Nanoscience involves using small things for inventions.
- Agricultural practices are affected by nanoscience.
- Computer technology is affected by nanoscience.
- Certain fields of study use nanoscience.
- One field is chemistry.
- Another field is physics.

Answer: Nanoscience is the study of very small things, such as atoms, and it is a relatively new scientific interest. Nanoscience involves using small things for inventions. Both computer technology and agricultural practices are affected by nanoscience. Certain fields of study, such as chemistry and physics, use nanoscience.

Formatting Your Essay

In addition to being revised and edited, the final draft of your paper should meet the formatting requirements specified by your instructor. If your instructor has not given you specific information about how to format your paper, use the formatting specifications from the Modern Language Association. See the Quick Start Guide to Integrated Reading and Writing Assignments for basic information about MLA style.

Important formatting considerations include these:

- Setting the correct margins and tabs
- Using a correct header and page number system
- Using an appropriate heading
- Knowing whether to use a cover sheet, binder, staple, or paper clip for submitting your paper

Teaching Resources: If you do not teach APA or MLA at this course level, see the IM for suggestions for handling citations.

Teaching Resources: See the IM for handouts and a *Power-Point* presentation on setting up *Microsoft Word* to produce a correctly formatted paper in MLA or APA style.

- Using appropriate line spacing
- Using the appropriate font and font size
- Using the appropriate method for documenting sources

Using the correct format for setting up and submitting your paper is one of the easiest parts of writing. Make sure you get credit for this easy task by following instructions perfectly.

CHAPTER ACTIVITIES

READING AND ANNOTATING

The following essay is about revising. The writer, Benjamin Percy, teaches creative writing at Iowa State University and has published novels and short stories. As you read and annotate Percy's essay, think about the comparisons he is making.

Home Improvement

by Benjamin Percy

The Realtor said, "It's got good bones." That's what people say about ugly houses—and this was an ugly house. No one had done a thing to it since 1965, the year it was built. Every inch of the place was plastered with flocked or floral-patterned wallpaper, even the insides of the cabinets. All the light fixtures were white orbs collared by thin brass rings. The outside of the oven grew as hot as the inside. The master bedroom had curtains that matched its shaggy carpet that resembled in its color nothing so much as a mint green urinal puck. The roof was rotten and sagging. The furnace and gutters were rusted out.

But my wife and I walked through the backyard, a quarter acre of rich grass bordered by shade plants and mature ash trees whose branches came together overhead like a cathedral's roof. And we stood before the river-rock fireplaces and sat on the three-season porch and laid our hands flat along the walls and smiled as you would when rubbing a belly ripe with pregnancy. And bought the place.

This was April 2008, and we were shoving books into boxes, packing up the moving truck, when the phone rang with good news: I had sold my novel, *The Wilding*. My editor at Graywolf Press, Fiona McCrae, told me how excited she was about the manuscript, but wondered if I might be **amenable** to some changes. Of course, I said. What did she have in mind? "How about let's start with the point of view?" she said. "Might we shift it from first to third? And in doing so, with the freedom afforded to the characters, perhaps we could add five interlocking plotlines all coming to a head at once?" The book had good bones, in other words, but it needed some renovation.

Fiona has a British accent and somehow this makes everything she says sound reasonable. So I said, "Sure, no problem." And I meant it. I recognized the narrative as less of a novel and more of an extended short story, a shnovel. Here was the architectural solution, a new blueprint delivered from the contractor to the carpenter. I felt fired up, ready to flip open my toolbox and get to work. It wasn't until later, when I printed the manuscript and began to riffle through its pages, that I shuddered at the job ahead of me.

I'm no stranger to starting over. I wrote three failed novels before selling *The Wilding*. They were not a waste of time, not at all. I learned from them the humility that comes from watching something you've spent years working on turn to dust in your hands.

YOUR ANNOTATIONS

Lexile: 1070L

Vocabulary Collection Word:
amenable

Your in-context definition:

_____

_____

A dictionary definition:

_____

_____

And I discovered—by dissecting their cold carcasses—the many ways I might rob their organs and bones, their images and characters and settings and metaphors, and rearrange them, reimagine them, as short stories.

"Refresh, Refresh" is a good example. For my graduate thesis I wrote a (wretched) novel called "King of the Wild Frontier" (panned by students, faculty, agents, and editors alike). The fight scenes that appear in "Refresh, Refresh" are almost directly lifted from it, though their context couldn't be more different. Neither could the early and late drafts of the short story. Originally "Refresh, Refresh" was supernatural—my agent helped me transform it into scorched-earth realism. Originally it was forty pages—the Paris Review helped me winnow it down to eighteen. Originally the grandfather played a much larger role, and his subplot involved an amputated foot preserved in a bucket of formaldehyde—he ended up getting his own story, "The Killing" (which also recycles a number of scenes from "King of the Wild Frontier"). I could go on about the axed weight-lifting scenes, the three boys who became two, the brain-damaged vet, Floyd, who every night set up his karaoke machine outside the Dairy Queen and served as a kind of Greek chorus. Gone.

So much of revision, I've discovered, is about coming to terms with that word: gone. Letting things go. When revising, the beginning writer spends hours consulting the thesaurus, replacing a period with a semicolon, cutting adjectives, adding a few descriptive sentences—whereas the professional writer mercilessly lops off limbs, rips out innards like party streamers, drains away gallons of blood, and then calls down the lightning to bring the body back to life.

Revision doesn't come easy. That's why I used to resist it. When I received comments on my work, my eyes skimmed over the criticism and homed in on the compliments. That's no way to be. You've got to write every day as if you were clocking in for a job. Or if not every day, then damn near it. If you're not disciplined in your production—if you're writing only when the mood strikes or when a deadline looms—then naturally you'll be more protective of your work so that when it comes time to cut, your saw will tremble with hesitation. But if you're producing reams of pages you'll be less resistant to revision, because you know it won't be long before another load of timber comes down the road.

I discovered this in grad school, when writing became a full-time job and when critiques became sharp toothed, long nailed. One time a professor handed me back a manuscript with every single page slashed through with an enormous black X. There were no comments except a single word scrawled over the title: Don't.

When I later spoke to the professor, I pushed him further, asking what he meant, exactly. Don't what? Don't bother? Was the story no good? No, he said. That wasn't it. He liked the story—"Just don't write it that way." His advice served as an eraser. I pretended the original document no longer existed, and when I began another draft, it filled up a clean white screen unchained from the rusted-out sentences written previously.

I have thrown away thousands of pages—and sometimes you need to do that—sometimes you have to start over. But sometimes you don't. Sometimes your story needs some serious renovation—the walls are full of mold, the roof is leaking—and sometimes it simply needs some cosmetic work, a little paint splashed on the walls.

I've learned that revision is far less intense and traumatic when I begin a story with its end in mind. I used to be an organic writer, who had no game plan, who followed tooth-and-claw instinct, who considered writing an act of discovery. I let the garden grow and returned to it later to trim back the tangles, rip out the weeds.

Vocabulary Collection Word:
organic

Your in-context definition:

_____

_____

A dictionary definition:

_____

_____

Dan Chaon—the author of such dynamite collections as *Among the Missing*—is such a writer. For every fifteen-page short story, he produces more than a hundred pages. His stories "Big Me" and "The Bees" went through so many drafts that he "would have probably been better off writing a novel," he says. Sometimes he lays the pages down on the floor and wanders among them, rearranging them, isolating some scenes, crumpling up others and tossing them aside, until finally he decides what the story is about and returns to his desk to realize the piece in a shorter form.

On the other end of the spectrum is the Lego-block writer. He has his design in mind and snaps each piece into place and takes pleasure in how tidily everything comes together. I've tried this, too, and though it might work for some, for me it made the act of writing feel lifeless, boring.

I now fall somewhere between these two categories. I know my ending—maybe not everything about it, but generally where things will end up, what will happen—and I know one or two scenes that occur in the middle. In aiming toward them, I take far fewer wrong turns.

I used to consider editing something you did once a story was completed. I now begin each day by reading what I have already written. If it's a short story, I mean from the first line forward. If a novel, I mean from the start of the chapter I'm working on. I sometimes spend hours editing before I shift to an imaginative mode and begin to punch out new material. So I'm essentially in a constant state of revision, and by the time I finish the story, I might have edited it two dozen times, turning it over and over in my hands, sanding it until it's free of slivers.

Faulkner said, "Kill your darlings," and in that tradition I created a cemetery folder. In it I have files—tombstones, I call them—with titles like "Images" or "Metaphors" or "Characters" or "Dialogue." Into these I dump and bury anything excised from a story. For some reason, having a cemetery makes it easier to cut, to kill. Perhaps it's because I know the writing isn't lost—it has a place—and I can always return to the freshly shoveled grave and perform a voodoo ceremony.

It took me a year to rewrite *The Wilding,* to move from first to third person, to free up those characters and braid together their stories. And when I handed it in to Fiona in March 2009, she said—again, with a British accent—"Fantastic. Exactly what we wanted. Now would you mind cutting several of these subplots? And maybe we could add another in a female perspective? And while we're at it, how about let's rethink the ending?" And, and, and.

And then I got back to work.

I was hammering at the keyboard all week, and hammering at my house all weekend. I ripped out the carpeting and wrenched out the thousands of tacks and staples, to reveal gleaming hardwood. I scored the wallpaper and sprayed it with hot, soapy water and scraped—and scraped—and scraped away damp bits of paper, leaving the drywall beneath pitted. So I mudded and sanded and textured and painted. I tossed out the oven. I tossed out the curtains. I unscrewed the cracked, yellowing outlets and light switches and replaced them with white plates and once shocked myself so badly that my thumbnail bled and turned black. I pulled out the brass and shoved in wrought-iron light fixtures. We had a new roof thrown on, new gutters hung.

Not long ago, our Realtor stopped by to check on us. He shook my hand—a hand yellowed with calluses and crosshatched with scrapes, colored with bruises. He hardly recognized the house just as I hardly recognize the novel as it has moved from first to final draft. "You've been working hard," he said, and I said, "Yes."

Questions for Consideration

1. In his essay, Percy compares revising to several other activities. List the comparisons he uses.

_____

_____

2. What is his attitude toward revising his work?

_____

_____

3. What advice would Percy likely give college freshmen about academic writing?

_____

_____

4. Percy mentions several of his writing projects that were not good. For example, he writes, "One time a professor handed me back a manuscript with every single page slashed through with an enormous black X. There were no comments except a single word scrawled over the title: Don't." He does not seem to be embarrassed by these "failures." Why do you think he lacks embarrassment? Why do you think he shares these events from his past?

_____

_____

5. What process have you used to revise your writing in the past? Has your process been effective? What have you learned from Percy's essay about an effective revision process?

_____

_____

USING MODELS TO PRACTICE REVISING AND EDITING

Below you will find a list of specific revision and editing strategies, followed by a student paragraph, "Tattoos on Children," on the next page. As you read the paragraph, look for opportunities to make the changes listed, and then revise or edit as appropriate.

Revision and Editing Strategies

1. Find two short sentences, and combine them to make a longer sentence.

   Sentences 2 and 3 could be combined. Also, sentences 8 and 9 could be combined.

2. Find a sentence that could be followed with an example. Write a sentence providing the example.

   Sentence 4 could be followed by an example.

3. Consider how the order of the sentences could be improved. List the sentence numbers in the order in which you would place them.

   A better order for sentences is 1, 2, 3, 5, 4, 6, 7, 8, 9.

4. Find an error in word choice by considering commonly confused words. Change the misused word to the appropriate one.

   In sentence 4, *affects* should be *effects*.

5. Find a phrase that is vague. Revise it so that its meaning is clear by using more specific, concrete terms.

   In sentence 4, *various affects* [*sic*] is a vague phrase.

Questions for Consideration

1. Sample answers:

- Renovating a house
- Following a new blueprint
- Dissecting old carcasses
- Creating a monster? "Lops off limbs, rips out innards like party streamers, drains away gallons of blood, and then calls down the lightning to bring the body back to life."
- Gardening
- Using cosmetics
- Building with Legos
- Sanding something
- Killing, dumping, and burying

2. When he began writing, he disliked revising. Over time, however, he came to realize its importance and its power. He now regards revising as part of a writer's work.

3. He would probably encourage freshmen to care about their writing and to embrace the hard work it entails. He would probably tell them that creating a first draft is only a minor part of the writing process; revision is a major part.

4. He knows that no one can produce really good writing without revision, so he is not embarrassed by a first draft that fails. He knows he will do significant work on the draft, as all good writers do. Additionally, he may have the confidence to believe that he will eventually be able to revise a poor rough draft into something good (or he can always throw it away).

5. Answers will vary.

Answers will vary, but sample answers are provided.

Tattoos on Children

[1]Should parents be allowed to get their children tattooed? [2]What if a parent of a two-year-old child decides to put a "tramp stamp" on the child's back? [3]Should this be legal? [4]Modifying a child's body can have various affects. [5]These are some of the questions state legislators have to consider in this new era of body art. [6]The argument against allowing parents to tattoo their children is the fact that tattoos are permanent. [7]The interesting counterargument is that we have not questioned other practices that modify a child's body. [8]Circumcision, for example, is perfectly legal. [9]It significantly changes a child's body.

Teaching Resources: For a reproducible copy of Jalyn's essay to use in class for revising and editing, see the IM.

Connect IRW Writing Assignment: Use Connect IRW to set up this assignment for drafting and/or peer review. This assignment has been pre-loaded into the Connect IRW *Common Places* Master Course. See the IM for alternative writing assignments to meet this chapter's objectives.

A READING AND WRITING ASSIGNMENT

Below, you will find an essay assignment and a rough draft written by Jalyn Martin, a student in an English class. First, read and annotate the assignment, and then read through Jalyn's rough draft. Revise his rough draft, and use SMART TRACS to edit it. Produce a final copy of Jalyn's paper in a correctly formatted document.

Essay Assignment for English 1301

Write an essay in which you provide a single change or a variety of changes parents can make to help their children be healthier. Imagine you are writing to have your essay published in a parenting magazine. Be sure to take the audience into consideration as you write. In addition, follow these instructions:

- Offer at least three reasons for your position.
- Include topic sentences for each of the body paragraphs.
- Make sure that each body paragraph is well supported.
- Use standard English grammar, correct spelling, and appropriate punctuation.
- Do not include the use of any sources.
- Format your essay using MLA style.

YOUR ANNOTATIONS

Jalyn's Draft

An old saying is *the work of a child is to play*. This adage is absolutely true, but it does not specify the type of play children need. More and more, children are abandoning the good, wholesome play that occurs in backyards and on sidewalks. Play is becoming an inside activity, and it is becoming solitary. Is sitting in front of a video game really the kind of play that should be *children's work*? There is nothing wrong with inside play, but children need more outside play than they get. Parents can help their children be healthier by making them play outside.

YOUR ANNOTATIONS

(continued)

First, Children need sunshine. Playing outside means children will get the Vitamin D they need. Our bodies need vitamin D. You may know that vitamin D comes from milk, but it also comes from being in the sun. Without it, children are more susceptible to diseases. Additionally, being in the sun seems to have an affect on your mood. Who can be sad or grumpy on a beautiful sunny day?

Second, Video games make our kids lazy, so people need to send their kids outside. People debate whether violent video games make children more violent. Too much staring into a tv screen can't be a good habit. Besides, when you are playing video games, they are sitting down all day. Everybody needs to play some video games, but playing too much can turn you into a couch potato.

Third, There are things kids can do outdoors that they can never do indoors. Exploring nature, building forts, doing mischievous things like graffiti, getting to know the kids that live around them. Outdoor play makes kids be more creative. They have to come up with their own games. They can also get to know the children who live around them. They can ride bikes. They can explore parts of their neighborhood they would never see if they were in front of a tv all day.

Parents who care about their children's health need to consider sending their kids outside, a healthy kid is a kid who comes in totally wiped out and filthy from a wonderful day playing cowboys and Indians or hiking through the woods with their buddies. If we want our children to not be overweight and to get the vitamins they need, we should encourage them to play outside. The way we all did when we were children.

◉ THINKING FROM AN INSTRUCTOR'S POINT OF VIEW

Carol Sweedler-Brown, an English professor, wondered whether handwriting ability has an effect on the grades students receive. Samuel Miller, another researcher, explains in the following passage what Sweedler-Brown did to answer this question.

> One example of the research is Sweedler-Brown's 1992 study in which 27 original essays were graded in three graphic modes: typed, nicely handwritten, and poorly handwritten. Nicely handwritten copies of the essays received significantly higher scores than the poorly handwritten or typed versions. There was no difference in the scores between the typed and poorly written versions, revealing a strong grader bias toward good handwriting.

As Sweedler-Brown's research shows, handwriting *does* have an effect on one's grade. While it may not be fair that handwriting matters, it does.

As a student, it is important to know that every assignment you submit produces an impression. What factors other than handwriting can you think of that can help you make a good impression when turning in assignments? List at least three ways to submit work that produces a favorable impression. Is there anything that might prevent you from putting into practice the items on your list? Write a paragraph explaining your answer.

Teaching Resources: See the IM for additional vocabulary activities. See the Connect IRW *Common Places* Master Course for vocabulary study practices that accompany this chapter, as well as a chapter vocabulary quiz.

⊙ ADDING TO YOUR VOCABULARY

This chapter's vocabulary words appear below.

precarious	acronym	incentive	organic
marketing	ambiguity	amenable	

Choose five of the vocabulary words from this chapter that you would like to add to your vocabulary, and think about how you can use them this week. For example, one of this chapter's words is *amenable*. You can often substitute *amenable* for *open to* or *OK with*, as in the example that follows.

Example: Marcus is *OK with* having the party at his house.

Marcus is *amenable to* having the party at his house.

List each of the five words you plan to use this week, and make note of a context in which you could use each word.

Example: *Amenable*. I can use this with my kids when they propose going somewhere or doing something.

⊙ ADDITIONAL ASSIGNMENTS

1. Revising and editing enable you to improve your writing. People who restore automobiles or houses participate in a kind of revision process. Even cooking makes use of revision. Chefs, for example, might alter a recipe five or six times before they consider it perfect. Write an essay in which you compare the process of revising a text to the revision process of some other creative activity. In what ways are the processes similar?

2. Write an essay about a time when you "revised" a product or a process repeatedly. Describe the process you used. Explain what motivated you to keep revising until the product was nearly perfect.

3. One of the most common writing errors is to use particular words incorrectly. Many writers struggle with commonly confused words such as *affect* and *effect*. One way to master confusing words is to intentionally study them and use them. Make a list of ten words you commonly confuse. Write an essay, story, letter, or e-mail in which you use each of these ten words correctly. When you are finished, use the revising and editing process to refine your work.

4. The word *revision* includes two word parts with which you are familiar: *re* (again) and *visi* (to see or view). *Revision*, then, means "to see again." At right are two photographs. Choose one photograph. Imagine you are an artist and a client has asked you to revise her house or her old truck. Envision what the house or truck *could* look like. What particular features would you change to make it more beautiful or more appealing? Explain your vision in one or two paragraphs. Revise and edit your paragraphs when you are finished.

5. Find an essay you wrote for this writing class or for another college course, and print out a copy. Read your paper out loud, imagining yourself reading it for the first time. Use the processes in this chapter to revise and edit your paper. When you are finished with your revision, repeat this entire process. See if revising the paper a second time makes a difference in the quality (and quantity) of your writing.

EMOTIONAL INTELLIGENCE

What is *netiquette*? If you are unsure, do an Internet search, and read about the topic. Write two or three paragraphs in which you define *netiquette* and explain some common netiquette guidelines. Be sure to give credit to any sources you use.

Answers will vary, but students might mention common netiquette rules such as the following:

- In e-mails, use an appropriate subject line.
- Avoid profanity and coarse language.
- Do not use all caps when typing.
- Use emoticons appropriately.

CULTURAL LITERACY

Every culture has its artifacts—songs, art, literature, activities, traditions—that are meaningful in a special way. Spend a moment and think about artifacts from your culture that are important to you. Perhaps you and your family are very patriotic and celebrate July 4th by raising the flag. Perhaps making tamales at Christmas or on other occasions is a cultural tradition that your family cherishes. Find three artifacts from your culture and explain in a few paragraphs what they mean to you.

Answers will vary.

CRITICAL THINKING

One element of critical thinking is being imaginative and creative enough to think about options. Often, the more options you consider, the better your decision. Practice thinking creatively by considering career choices. First, make a list of three things you want in a career. Here is an example of such a list:

Answers will vary.

1. A salary of at least $15 an hour
2. The ability to work during the day (no night shifts!)
3. A career that involves the use of a computer

Using your list, think creatively about the various careers that meet these criteria. See if you can come up with twenty potential careers. Push yourself and think hard. If you cannot come up with twenty potential careers, ask your friends and classmates to help you. Once you make your list, circle the careers on it that you had not thought of before. Do any interest you? Write a paragraph in which you discuss a few of the new ideas you thought of.

METACOGNITION

Think back to a group project in which you participated. Imagine that you can see yourself—and all of the other group members—from the outside. Evaluate your role in the group. Did you contribute in a positive way? Were you the leader? How important a role did you play? If you were an instructor, how would you evaluate the role you played in the group project? Explain in one or two paragraphs.

Answers will vary.

PART 3

Integrated Reading and Writing Projects

The use of social media has brought about changes in the way we live our lives. What are the effects of these changes on our individual lives and relationships?

Project 1: Working with Informative Texts

Social Media—For Better or Worse

Many of the texts you will encounter in college and in your career will be informative texts: they will provide important information about a subject or a task. As with all types of writing, to get the most from informative texts, you need to exercise critical reading skills. As a writer, you will sometimes be called on to create informative texts, and what you know from your critical reading of informative sources will help you with that task.

For this project, you will examine four readings that present issues related to social media. Most people have used *Facebook*, *Twitter*, *Flickr*, or another type of social media. Our culture has so quickly embraced social media that users have not had time to think through the potential dangers of these forms of communication. Policy makers are scrambling to write privacy laws to protect the public, and advertisers are rushing to take advantage of the marketing opportunities afforded by *Facebook*, *YouTube*, and the like. Average users, meanwhile, are experimenting with these new communication technologies in a variety of ways—from finding people to date to sparking political protests—and quickly discovering new and innovative uses for them.

CHAPTER OBJECTIVES
After completing this chapter, students will be able to do the following:

- **Examine an informative reading and writing assignment and identify a purpose.**

- **Use a critical reading process to examine four readings and use them as sources.**

- **Use an effective writing process to compose an informative essay.**

- **Revise and edit an informative essay, and use MLA or APA style to format the essay.**

Connect IRW LearnSmart Achieve: Assign the topics "Writing in Response to Reading," "Evaluating, Synthesizing, and Documenting Sources," and "Analyzing and Writing in Response to a Writing Prompt" for adaptive learning to accompany the chapter.

As you read the selections in this chapter, you will be prompted to learn about the positive and negative aspects of social media. Some of the issues you will read about may be new to you; others may be familiar. As you read, concentrate on gaining a broad understanding of why social media issues are worthy of our attention. After you have read the sources, you will have the opportunity to focus on a social media issue in an essay of your own. To start this process, we will focus on your work as a reader.

GETTING STARTED

The readings that follow present some of the benefits of using social media and some of the problems associated with their use. As you read each one, follow these steps, which will guide you through the process of completing this assignment.

Analyze Your Assignment

As you begin a reading and writing assignment, the first step is to read the assignment instructions carefully. Analyze the assignment by highlighting the verbs and making notes in the margin. The assignment for this chapter appears in the box below. Notice the annotations.

Connect IRW Writing Assignment: Use the Connect IRW writing tools to set up this writing assignment. You can create a rubric to use for grading, assign drafts, assign peer review activities, and have students submit their essays through Connect IRW. See the Instructor's Manual (IM) for more information. Alternatively, use the pre-loaded version of this assignment in the Connect IRW *Common Places* Master Course.

Informative Reading and Writing Assignment

The primary purpose of <mark>informative writing</mark> is to provide readers with information in a clear and organized way. Your assignment is to <u>find an aspect of social media about which readers need more information</u> and to <u>write an informative essay on that aspect</u>. As you read through sources, you will learn about a variety of issues: how social media has been used to foster political movements, which privacy concerns related to social media issues can affect people the most, how social media use differs among user populations, how social media can affect academic success, and so on.

Informative focus

Find an aspect of social media readers need to know more about.

Write informative essay.

You will select an issue you wish to communicate to readers. Keep in mind that the <mark>purpose of your essay is not to make any persuasively oriented claims</mark>. In other words, you will not be writing your own argument about why we should take privacy more seriously, for example. Rather, your <mark>essay will simply present the major points readers should consider</mark>. Your essay will provide the information necessary for readers <mark>to know what the issue concerns</mark> and, if applicable, <mark>what some writers have suggested be done about it</mark>.

Purpose is not to persuade.
Present major points.

Present
—what the issue concerns
—what some writers suggest be done

Since you know you will be writing an essay on social media topics, take a moment to jot down some social media issues that come to mind. Thinking about potential topics beforehand will help you make better connections to the selections you will read.

Identify Your Purpose

Once you have read the assignment, you can clarify your purpose for reading the selections that follow. The selections will provide you with the information you need to learn about the social media issues that are important. Because part of the assignment is to select an issue to present to readers, one purpose for reading the selections is to find a topic to use for your own essay. When you write your own essay, you will be presenting the "information necessary for readers to know what the issue concerns" and "what some writers have suggested be done about it." Thus, as you read, your purpose will be to locate such information. Keeping your purpose in mind will help you read in a more focused way.

WORKING WITH READINGS

Before you start reading, you will need a game plan for understanding the selections and getting the most out of the reading process. Follow these steps.

Preview the Reading and Think about the Topic

A good way to start previewing is to analyze the reading's contextual information. Where was it published? What does the publication information suggest about the reading? Who wrote it? What are the author's qualifications? Can you predict any biases based on the author's background or the publication information?

You can use your analysis of the context in two ways: first, it will help you understand the source; second, by making a note of the bibliographic information, you will have all of the data you'll need to cite the reading later if you use it as a source in your own writing. Make notes about the context by finding and recording the following bibliographic information about the reading:

- Author
- Title
- Name and type of publication (example: *Houston Chronicle*, newspaper)
- Date of publication
- Your notes about what the context tells you

Next, preview the text and identify the topic. Knowing the topic will help you anticipate what the writer may say about it. As you preview the text, jot down what you think the text may be about. For example, the first selection you will read is "Driven to Distraction: Our Wired Generation" by Larry Rosen. Just by reading the title, you can guess that the writer may be interested in how technology can be a distraction to people. You will not know whether the writer thinks we should unplug our technology or use it more often until you read the selection more closely, but you can already begin thinking about distraction as an issue. Does your use of technology distract you from important things? Is this an issue you have considered before? By thinking about the issue a bit before reading Rosen's article, you can compare what Rosen says with what you think. Doing this will help you remember what the article says because you will have existing ideas to which you can tie the new information from Rosen's article. Also, if you can find a way to relate the information to your own life, you will be much more likely to find the article interesting and to understand it.

Read and Annotate the Text

As you read each selection, focus your annotations on finding the writer's main idea and major supporting points. Usually, these elements will present the most important information in the text. Also be on the lookout for details that support these points. Annotate any information that is either (a) part of the main idea and major supporting details or (b) significant to your understanding of the writer's point.

Teaching Resources: See the *PowerPoint* (PPT) "Social Media Issues."

Connect IRW Power of Process Assignment: Each reading can be set up in Power of Process so that students go through a reading process that matches the steps in this chapter. See the IM for more information. These PoP assignments are pre-loaded into the Connect IRW *Common Places* Master Course.

In addition to annotating these elements, mark any ideas that grab your attention. Make additional annotations about content that you find especially thought-provoking. When you read in a focused, interested way, you engage in a kind of dialogue with the text. A text may present a new idea, and you may think, "That's interesting" or "I didn't know that," or you may think of a question. Those thoughts that come to mind are like gold nuggets in their value to you as a writer, for they are the places where you may be able to join the conversation with your own ideas later in your own essay. Any time you like something you read, question something you read, or read something again because it is interesting, stop to highlight the text or add a sticky note and write down your thoughts on the passage.

As you read about particular issues regarding social media use, look for key words associated with the issues. For example, Rosen's article concerns the issue of how technology can distract us from important things. He uses these key words: *anxiety, attention span, device, distract, distraction, environment, performance, technology, texting.* If you can identify the key words, you can use them later when you write your own essay.

Finally, be on the lookout for passages that might make good quotations for your own essay. If you find an explicitly stated thesis statement, mark it with a star or check mark to indicate it might be a useful quote. Do the same for any other passages where the writer presents insights effectively or includes data or evidence you would like to quote in your own essay. Of course, you will not know for certain whether the quotation will work until you plan your paper, but marking at least three quotes gives you some options from which to choose.

Outline and Summarize Each Reading

While looking for "nuggets" is important, nothing is more important than understanding the writer's main idea and the support he uses for it. Recently, a friend confided that she had to read a chapter *seven* times (yes, seven!) before she understood it—and it was a four-page chapter. If one reading of a selection leaves you stumped about its meaning, read it again. The second time, though, do something different. Move to a less comfortable location (so that you can be more alert), drink some coffee, read the passage out loud, read it with a classmate, or make another small change. If you still have trouble understanding the reading, take it to your campus's academic support center and work with a lab instructor, or work with your professor or a tutor.

Once you understand the reading, write a simple outline that includes the writer's thesis statement and the major supporting points. Include any supporting details you found particularly important or think you may want to use in your own writing. Next, write a brief summary of two to three sentences in which you explain the writer's main idea and major supporting points in your own words.

Prepare an Information Sheet for Each Reading

You have probably taken notes on sources before, perhaps using note cards or writing out pages of notes. An information sheet provides some of the same information as note cards or note pages, but it includes a few additional items.

The best way to create an information sheet is to type your information into a computer file. That way, when you write your paper, you will be able to simply copy and paste the information you need into your essay.

To create an information sheet, do the following:

- Start by listing the reading's title, writer, and publication information.
- Make a few bulleted notes about how you might use the source and how the source compares with other sources. Note any other information you might find useful later. Assume that you will not remember anything about the reading and will need the notes to help you recall your most important ideas.
- Include the brief outline and brief summary you have composed.

Connect IRW Discussion Board (DB) Assignment: Create DB threads that help students articulate their comprehension of the articles, and create threads that help students read the articles critically. See the IM for particular DB thread prompts, or use the pre-loaded DB prompts in the Connect IRW *Common Places* Master Course.

- List the issues addressed in the reading. For example, if the selection addresses privacy issues on *Facebook*, make a note of that. If the writer includes a related issue—such as privacy issues on *Twitter*, make a note of that issue, also. Some readings will discuss a central issue but will reference other issues along the way.

- For each issue you identify, make a list of the key words the writer uses to discuss the issue. You can later use these key words in your own writing about the issue.

- As you read the selection, you identified at least three passages you believed would make good quotes. Copy these quotes into your information sheet. Make sure you copy them word for word, including punctuation. Put quotation marks around them on your information sheet so that you will know the words came directly from the text. Follow each quote with the writer's name, and if you are using a print source (not a computer-based text), write down the page number. Here's an example:

"More than half of the people surveyed in the IHH study reported that they did not take extra precautions to keep their Facebook data private" (Wilson 33).

By copying these quotes into your information sheet, you will have them at the ready to be used in any essay you write.

READINGS FOR AN INFORMATIVE ESSAY

As you read the first source for this project, keep in mind your goal: to learn about social media issues so you can write an informative essay about one of those issues. Read with an eye to finding definitions, explanations, data, and any other kind of information that will help you—and potentially the readers of your essay—understand the issue. Annotate the information you believe is most important. Of course, also annotate the other important elements discussed above.

SOURCE 1	"DRIVEN TO DISTRACTION: OUR WIRED GENERATION"

"Driven to Distraction" was published in the *St. Paul Pioneer Press*, a newspaper in St. Paul, Minnesota. As you read this source, you will notice it begins with a description of the writer. For the first source, we have provided annotations that can serve as a model for the kind of annotating you should do for the remaining three selections.

ABOUT THE AUTHOR

Larry Rosen is a professor of psychology at California State University and the author of five books on the "psychology of technology." He wrote *TechnoStress: Coping with Technology @WORK @HOME @PLAY* (1998); *Me, MySpace, and I: Parenting the Net Generation* (2007); and *The Mental Health Technology Bible* (1997).

If your students have access to computers (or smartphones) in class, consider having them do an Internet search for Larry Rosen to see what additional information they can learn. With some prompting, students can usually make predictions about what the text will include based on the author's biographical information.

Driven to Distraction: Our Wired Generation
by Larry Rosen

A recent Pew Internet & American Life Project report surveyed 2,462 middle school and high school advanced placement and national writing project teachers and concluded that: "Overwhelming majorities agree with the assertions that today's digital technologies are creating an easily distracted generation with short attention spans and today's students are too 'plugged in' and need more time away from their digital technologies." Two-thirds of the respondents agree with the notion that today's digital technologies do more to distract students than to help them academically.

Lexile: 1450L

Students can use a graphic organizer to determine whether each sentence presents data, an explanation of data, or a conclusion drawn from data—all of which are generally used as support.

Background: The writer begins with findings from a Pew report.

Mind you, we are talking about teachers who typically teach . . . students . . . we would generally think of as [not] highly distractible.

Recently my research team observed 263 middle school, high school and university students studying for a mere 15 minutes in their homes. We were interested in whether students could maintain focus and, if not, what might be distracting them. Every minute we noted exactly what they were doing, whether they were studying, if they were texting or listening to music or watching television in the background, and if they had a computer screen in front of them and what websites were being visited.

The results were startling considering that the students knew we were watching them and most likely assumed we were observing how well they were able to study. First, these students were only able to stay on task for an average of three to five minutes before losing their focus. Universally, their distractions came from technology, including: (1) having more devices available in their studying environment such as iPods, laptops and smartphones; (2) texting; and (3) accessing Facebook.

Other researchers have found similar attention spans among computer programmers and medical students, and in those studies technology provided the major sources of distraction.

We also looked at whether these distractors might predict who was a better student in general. Not surprisingly those who stayed on task longer and had well-developed study strategies were better students. The worst students were those who consumed more media each day and had a preference for switching back and forth between several tasks at the same time.

One additional result stunned us: If the students checked Facebook just once during the 15-minute study period, they had a lower grade-point average. It didn't matter how many times they looked at Facebook; once was enough. Not only did social media negatively impact their temporary focus and attention, but it ultimately impacted their entire school performance.

So, what was going on with these students? We have asked thousands of students this exact question and they tell us that when alerted by a beep, a vibration, or a flashing image they feel compelled or drawn to attend to that stimulus. However, they also tell us that even without the sensory intrusions they are constantly being distracted internally by thoughts such as, "I wonder if anyone commented on my Facebook post" or "I wonder if my friend responded to the text message I sent five minutes ago" or even "I wonder what interesting new YouTube videos my friends have liked." Three-fourths of teens and young adults check their devices every 15 minutes or less and if not allowed to do so get highly anxious. And anxiety inhibits learning.

I am convinced that learning to live with both internal and external distractions is all about teaching the concept of focus. In psychology we refer to the ability to understand when you need to focus and when it is not necessary to do so as "metacognition," or knowing how your brain functions. In one recent study we found a perfect demonstration of metacognition, albeit totally by accident. In this study we showed a video in several psychology courses, which was followed by a graded test.

Students were told that we might be texting them during the videotape and to answer our text messages. In fact, one-third did not get a text message, one-third got four texts during the 30-minute video, and the other third got eight texts, enough, we guessed, to distract them and make them unable to concentrate on the video. One other wrinkle was that we timed the text messages to occur when important material was being shown on the videotape that was going to be tested later.

*Side notes (right column):*

Background: The writer begins discussing his own research.

Support for major supporting point (MSP) 1

Key word: *focus*

Major supporting point 1 (implied): Technology is an external distraction to students.

More support for MSP 1

Major supporting point 2 (implied): Poor performance is related to multitasking with technology.

Support for MSP 2

Potential quote

Major supporting point 3

Teaching Resources: See the IM for teaching suggestions and a graphic organizer students can use to analyze this essay.

Support for MSP 3

Potential quote

Major supporting point 4

Key words: *internal and external distractions, metacognition*

Support for MSP 4

Additional support for MSP 4

We were right that the students who got eight texts did worse—they averaged a "D" on the test—but the students who received four texts and the students who did not receive a text message during the video got a "C" on our test. However, a mistake in our instructions told us more about what was going on inside the students' heads when the text arrived. We told students to reply to our text messages, but we did not tell them when to reply. Those students who manifested a knee-jerk reaction to their vibrating phone and answered our texts immediately were the ones who got the lower test grades. Those few students who opted to wait a few minutes to respond got the highest scores in the class.

Additional support for MSP 4

After the study, when asked why they did not respond immediately they told us that they were waiting for a time when the videotape material seemed less important and not likely to be on the test. Those students were using their metacognitive skills to decide when was a good time to be distracted and when it was important to focus.

Additional support for MSP 4

How do we teach focus in a world that is constantly drawing our attention elsewhere? One strategy that we are using in classrooms around the world is called "technology breaks." Here's how it works: In many classrooms students are allowed to use their smartphones, tablets, or laptops as tools to search the Web, access social media, or perform other activities that promote learning. In such classrooms teachers often report that in between times that students are using their devices for schoolwork, they are checking their email and text messages, tweeting, or accessing social media.

Major supporting point 5

Key word: technology breaks

Support for MSP 5

A tech break starts with the teacher asking all students to check their texts, the Web, Facebook, whatever, for a minute and then turn the device on silent and place it upside down on the desk in plain sight and "focus" on classroom work for 15 minutes. The upside down device prohibits external distractions from vibrations and flashing alerts and provides a signal to the brain that there is no need to be internally distracted since an opportunity to "check in" will be coming soon.

More support for MSP 5

At the end of the 15-minute focus time the teacher declares a tech break and the students take another minute to check in with their virtual worlds followed by more focus times and more tech breaks. The trick is to gradually lengthen the time between tech breaks to teach students how to focus for longer periods of time without being distracted. I have teachers using this in classrooms, parents using it at the dinner table or at a restaurant, and bosses using tech breaks during meetings with great success. So far, though, the best we can get is about 30 minutes of focus thanks to Steve Jobs (and others) for making such alluring, distracting technologies.

MSP 5 support continues

Technology is not going to disappear from our world and, in fact, it is only going to get more appealing as screens become sharper, video becomes clearer, and touch screens become the norm, all of which attract our sensory system and beckon us to pay attention to them rather than schoolwork or the people in front of us.

Conclusion begins.

With more electronic social connections in our lives internal distractors are also increasing and tech breaks can be used to train the brain to focus without the worry and anxiety about what we might be missing in our virtual social world.

Thesis statement
Key words: tech breaks, anxiety
Good quote

SOURCE INFORMATION
Author: Larry Rosen
Title: "Driven to Distraction: Our Wired Generation"
Publication: *St. Paul Pioneer Press* (newspaper), accessed on Web
Date: 12 November 2012

After you have read and annotated the article, you are ready to write a simple outline and summary. Then you can create an information sheet that provides all the essential information about the source, including your outline and summary. What follows is an example of an information sheet for Rosen's article. Notice how it is constructed. You can use it as a model for your own information sheets.

Information Sheet: "Driven to Distraction: Our Wired Generation"

GENERAL NOTES

- Author: Larry Rosen, a professor of psychology
- Was published in *St. Paul Pioneer Press,* a newspaper
- Nov. 12, 2012
- Good source for research studies
- Focuses on multitasking, technology breaks, teaching students to focus
- Note to self: if I use this topic, talk about internal distractions being a problem

SIMPLE OUTLINE

Thesis statement: "With more electronic social connections in our lives internal distractors are also increasing and tech breaks can be used to train the brain to focus without the worry and anxiety about what we might be missing in our virtual social world" (Rosen).

Major supporting point 1 (implied): Technology is an external distraction to students (Rosen).

Major supporting point 2 (implied): Poor performance is related to multitasking with technology (Rosen).

Major supporting point 3: "Not only did social media negatively impact [students'] temporary focus and attention, but it ultimately impacted their entire school performance" (Rosen).

Major supporting point 4: "I am convinced that learning to live with both internal and external distractions is all about teaching the concept of focus" (Rosen).

Major supporting point 5: "One strategy that we are using in classrooms around the world is called 'technology breaks'" (Rosen).

BRIEF SUMMARY

Larry Rosen uses research studies to show that students suffer from external distractions when using technology as well as internal distractions associated with thinking about technology. The studies showed that better students did less multitasking, according to Rosen. He explains that lack of focus is associated with an overall decrease in academic performance. His main point is that using technology breaks can help students overcome some of these problems and focus better on schoolwork.

ISSUES AND KEY WORDS

- Issue: Does social media use result in distraction?
  Key words: *focus, internal and external distractions*
- Issue: How does social media distraction affect students?
  Keywords: *metacognition, internal and external distractions*

Students may not know anything about the reputation of the Pew Research Center. Consider having them do an Internet search to learn about it. The following description comes from http://www.pewresearch.org/about: "Pew Research Center is a nonpartisan fact tank that informs the public about the issues, attitudes and trends shaping America and the world. It conducts public opinion polling, demographic research, media content analysis and other empirical social science research. Pew Research does not take policy positions. It is a subsidiary of The Pew Charitable Trusts."

(continued)

- Issue: Can classroom technology breaks help students focus?
  Keywords: *anxiety, tech breaks, focus*

POTENTIAL QUOTES

- "If the students checked Facebook just once during the 15-minute study period they had a lower grade-point average. It didn't matter how many times they looked at Facebook; once was enough" (Rosen).
- "Three-fourths of teens and young adults check their devices every 15 minutes or less and if not allowed to do so get highly anxious. And anxiety inhibits learning" (Rosen).
- "[T]ech breaks can be used to train the brain to focus without the worry and anxiety about what we might be missing in our virtual social world" (Rosen).

Now that you have observed the practice of reading, annotating, and analyzing an article as a source, complete the following practice exercise to synthesize your understanding of the process.

PRACTICE 1 Reading, Annotating, and Analyzing Sources

On a separate sheet of paper, answer the questions below about "Driven to Distraction: Our Wired Generation."

1. Rosen cites research in his article. Why? What role does it play in the article?

2. Based on your reading of the article, who is the intended audience? What does Rosen want the intended audience to do after they read the article?

3. Read the summary on the information sheet. Does the writer of the summary use Rosen's words or her own words?

4. Look at how the quoted material on the information sheet is formatted. Imagine you are teaching students how to give credit to quotes or ideas from sources. Use the formatting on the information sheet to write a rule. Include information on when to use parentheses, what to put in them, and where to put punctuation, such as quotation marks and periods.

1. The research helps Rosen prove the points he is making. By using the research, Rosen can prove that technology distracts students and that technology breaks help students focus.

2. The intended audience is teachers, and Rosen would like them to use technology breaks to help their students focus on classwork and become better students.

3. The summary writer uses her own words.

4. Use quotation marks around direct quotes. At the end of the quote, enclose the writer's name in parentheses, and end with a period. Use the same method to give credit to the source's ideas, but do not use quotation marks.

The following exercise asks you to reflect on Rosen's article and consider how you might use his ideas in an essay of your own.

PRACTICE 2 Reflecting on the Article

On a separate sheet of paper, answer the following questions about "Driven to Distraction."

1. Have you ever been in a class with a teacher who provided technology breaks? If so, were they effective in helping you focus? If you are unfamiliar with technology breaks, do you think they would help students focus?

2. How important is this topic for general readers? How important is it for college students? Do you think people know enough about the effect of technology use on students? Explain your answer.

Answers will vary. For question 5, students should note that multitasking prevents students from focusing.

(continued)

3. Do most students already know what the writer has explained in this essay, or do you believe this would be new information for them? Explain your answer.

4. Rosen points out that students who do well academically use technology, but they do some things differently than their peers. What actions or behaviors separate the students who do well in school from those who do not?

5. What does the writer imply about multitasking—doing more than one thing at the same time? Have you found the writer's point about multitasking to be true in your own life? Explain.

SOURCE 2	**"OPENING STATEMENT ON THE SENATE SUBCOMMITTEE HEARING 'WHAT FACIAL RECOGNITION TECHNOLOGY MEANS FOR PRIVACY AND CIVIL LIBERTIES'"**

On July 18, 2012, the Senate Judiciary Subcommittee on Privacy, Technology and the Law held a hearing on facial recognition technology and privacy, "What Facial Recognition Technology Means for Privacy and Civil Liberties." The subcommittee chair, Senator Al Franken, gave the following opening statement, which appears on the senator's official Web site.

Follow the steps presented in this chapter as you read the selection, and keep your assignment and purpose in mind.

- Preview the reading and think about the topic.
- Read and annotate the text.

ABOUT THE AUTHOR

Al Franken is a US senator from Minnesota. He serves as chair of the Senate Judiciary Subcommittee on Privacy, Technology and the Law.

Opening Statement on the Senate Subcommittee Hearing "What Facial Recognition Technology Means for Privacy and Civil Liberties"

by Senator Al Franken

This hearing will be called to order. Welcome to the fourth hearing of the Subcommittee on Privacy, Technology and the Law. Today's hearing will examine the use of facial recognition technology by the government and the private sector—and what that means for our privacy and civil liberties.

I want to be clear: there is nothing inherently right or wrong with facial recognition technology. Just like any other new and powerful technology, it is a tool that can be used for great good. But if we do not stop and carefully consider the way we use this technology, it may also be abused in ways that may threaten basic aspects of our privacy and civil liberties. I called this hearing so we can start that conversation.

The dimensions of our faces are unique to each of us—just like our fingerprints. And just like fingerprint analysis, facial recognition technology allows others to identify you with what's called a "faceprint," a unique file describing your face.

I believe that we have a fundamental right to control our private information— and biometric information is already among the most sensitive of our private information, mainly because it is both unique and permanent. You can change your password.

YOUR ANNOTATIONS

Lexile: 1220L

An understanding of the importance of this issue depends on students' knowledge of the importance of civil liberties. You may want to have this discussion before students begin reading the article.

You can get a new credit card. But you can't change your fingerprint, and you can't change your face. Unless you go to a lot of trouble.

But facial recognition creates acute privacy concerns that fingerprints do not. Once someone has your fingerprint, they can dust your house or your surroundings to figure out what you've touched. Once someone has your faceprint, they can get your name, they can find your social networking account and they can find and track you in the street, in the stores you visit, the government buildings you enter, and the photos your friends post online.

Your face is a conduit to an incredible amount of information about you. And facial recognition technology can allow others to access all of that information from a distance, without your knowledge and in about as much time as it takes to snap a photo.

People think of facial recognition as something out of a science fiction movie. In reality, facial recognition technology is in broad use today. If you have a drivers' license, if you have a passport, if you are a member of a social network, chances are good that you are part of a facial recognition database.

There are countless uses of this technology, and many of them are innovative and quite useful. The State Department uses facial recognition technology to identify and stop passport fraud—preventing people from getting multiple passports under different names. Using facial recognition technology, Sheriff Larry Amerson of Alabama, who is with us here today, can make sure that a prisoner being released from the Calhoun County jail is actually the same prisoner that is supposed to be released.

But there are uses of this technology that should give us pause.

In 2010, Facebook, the world's largest social network, began signing up all of its then-800 million users in a program called Tag Suggestions. Tag Suggestions made it easier to tag close friends in photos. That's a good thing.

But the feature did this by creating a unique faceprint for every one of those friends. And in doing so, Facebook may have created the world's largest privately-held database of faceprints—without the explicit consent of its users. To date, Tag Suggestions is an opt-out program. Unless you have taken the time to turn it off, it may have already been used to generate your faceprint.

Separately, last year, the FBI rolled out a facial recognition pilot program in Maryland, Michigan and Hawaii that will soon expand to three more states. This pilot lets officers in the field take a photo of someone and compare it to a federal database of criminal mugshots. The pilot can also help ID a suspect in a photo from an actual crime. Already, several other states are setting up their own facial recognition systems independently of the FBI. These efforts will catch criminals: they already have.

Now many of you may be thinking that that's an excellent thing. I agree with you. But unless law enforcement facial recognition programs are deployed in a very careful manner, I fear that these gains could eventually come at a high cost to our civil liberties.

I fear that the FBI pilot could be abused to not only identify protesters at political events and rallies, but to target them for selective jailing and prosecution, stifling their First Amendment rights. Curiously enough, a lot of the presentations on this technology by the Department of Justice show it being used on people attending political events or other public gatherings.

I also fear that without further protections, facial recognition technology could be used on unsuspecting civilians innocent of any crime—invading their privacy and exposing them to potential false identifications.

This paragraph and the paragraphs that precede it provide a good example of acknowledging the merits of the opposing argument before making one's own argument.

Since 2010, the National Institute of Justice, which is a part of DOJ, has spent $1.4 million to develop facial recognition-enhanced binoculars that can be used to identify people at a distance and in crowds. It seems easy to envision facial recognition technology being used on innocent civilians when all an officer has to do is look at them through his binoculars.

YOUR ANNOTATIONS

DOJ: Department of Justice.

But facial recognition technology has reached a point where it is not limited to law enforcement and multi-billion dollar companies: it can also be used by private citizens. Last year, Professor Alessandro Acquisti of Carnegie Mellon University used a consumer-grade digital camera and off-the-shelf facial recognition software to identify one out of three students walking across a campus.

I called this hearing to raise awareness about the fact that facial recognition already exists right here, today, and we need to think about what that means for our society. I also called this hearing to call attention to the fact that our federal privacy laws are almost totally unprepared to deal with this technology.

Unlike what we have in place for wiretaps and other surveillance devices, there is no law regulating law enforcement use of facial recognition technology. And current Fourth Amendment case law generally says that we have no reasonable expectation of privacy in what we voluntarily expose to the public—yet we can hardly leave our houses in the morning without exposing our faces to the public. So you don't need a warrant to use this technology on someone. You might not even need to have a reasonable suspicion that they're involved in a crime.

The situation for the private sector is similar. Federal law provides some protection against true bad actors that promise one thing yet do another. But that's pretty much as far as the law goes. If a store wants to take a photo of your face when you walk in and generate a faceprint—without your permission—they can do that. They might even be able to sell it to third parties.

Thankfully, we have a little time to do better. While this technology will in a matter of time be at a place where it can be used to quickly and reliably identify a stranger, it isn't there just yet. And so I have called the FBI and Facebook here today to challenge them to use their position as leaders in their fields to set an example for others—before this technology is used pervasively.

The FBI already has some privacy safeguards in place. But I still think that they could do more to prevent this technology from being used to identify and target people engaging in political protests or other free speech. I think the FBI could do more to make sure that officers use this technology only when they have good reason to think that someone is involved in a crime. I also think that if the FBI did these things, law enforcement agencies around the country would follow.

For their part, Facebook allows people to use Tag Suggestions only on their close friends. But I think Facebook could still do more to explain to its users how it uses facial recognition—and to give them better choices about whether or not to participate in Tag Suggestions. I think that they could make clear to their users just how much data they have—and how they will and will not use their large and growing database of faceprints. And I think that if Facebook did these things, they would establish a best practice against which other social networks would be measured.

My understanding is that for the past few months, Facebook Tag Suggestions has been temporarily disabled to allow for some technical maintenance. It seems to me that Facebook has the perfect opportunity to make changes to its facial recognition program when it brings Tag Suggestions back online.

I'm also calling the Federal Trade Commission to testify because they are in the process of actually writing best practices for the use of this technology in industry. I urge the Commission to use this as an opportunity to guarantee consumers the information and choices they need to make informed decisions about their privacy.

In the end, though, I also think that Congress may need to act—and it wouldn't be the first time it did. In the era of J. Edgar Hoover, wiretaps were used freely with little regard to privacy. Under some Supreme Court precedents of that era, as long as the wiretapping device did not actually penetrate the person's home or property, it was deemed constitutionally sound—even without a warrant. And so in 1968, Congress passed the Wiretap Act. Thanks to that law, wiretaps are still used to stop violent and serious crimes. But police need a warrant before they get a wiretap. And you can't wiretap someone just because they're a few days late on their taxes—wiretaps can be used only for certain categories of serious crimes.

I think that we need to ask ourselves whether Congress is in a similar position today as it was 50 or 60 years ago—before passage of the Wiretap Act. I hope the witnesses today will help us consider this and all of the different questions raised by this technology.

SOURCE INFORMATION

Author: Al Franken

Title: "Opening Statement on the Senate Subcommittee Hearing 'What Facial Recognition Technology Means for Privacy and Civil Liberties'"

Publication: Al Franken's official Senate Web site http://www.franken.senate.gov/?p=news&id=2144

Date: 18 July 2012

When you have finished reading and annotating the selection, complete the exercise below to create notes for this source.

PRACTICE ③ Creating an Information Sheet for "Opening Statement on the Senate Subcommittee Hearing 'What Facial Recognition Technology Means for Privacy and Civil Liberties'"

Using your annotations and the sample information sheet from "Driven to Distraction," create an information sheet for this selection that includes the following:

- General notes
- Simple outline
- Brief summary
- Issues and key words
- Potential quotes

Teaching Resources: Grading each information sheet each student submits is an onerous task. Consider (1) giving all of the information sheets one grade, (2) *deducting* points from students' essay grades if information sheets are not submitted or are not of high quality, or (3) awarding extra points for high-quality information sheets. See the IM for a discussion of strategies for grading the IRW projects in chapters 11–13.

| SOURCE 3 | "THE BAD, THE UGLY, AND THE GOOD OF KIDS' USE OF SOCIAL MEDIA" |

The following article appeared on May 28, 2013, in *The Power of Prime,* a blog written by Jim Taylor, on *Psychology Today*'s Web site.

Follow the steps presented in this chapter as you read the selection, and keep your assignment and purpose in mind.

- Preview the reading and think about the topic.
- Read and annotate the text.

ABOUT THE AUTHOR

Jim Taylor holds a PhD in psychology and is an adjunct professor at University of San Francisco. He has published twelve books and more than seven hundred articles and has appeared on NBC's *Today Show* and ABC's *World News This Weekend,* as well as on the Fox News Channel and a number of radio shows. His specialty is the psychology of business, sports, and parenting.

The Bad, the Ugly, and the Good of Kids' Use of Social Media

by Jim Taylor

YOUR ANNOTATIONS

Lexile: 1410L

Whether we like it or not, the Internet, social media, and all of the related technology are here to stay. As evidenced every day in so many ways, this new technological landscape brings many wonderful benefits to our family's lives and relationships. At the same time, as with any new innovations, this impact has a dark side.

Though the study of the effects of social media on children is still relatively new, there is a growing body of evidence demonstrating what I will call the bad, the ugly, and the good (because I prefer to conclude this post on a positive note). I will describe some recent findings that are worth considering as you increasingly expose your children to different types of technology.

The Bad: Facebook Depression

There's no doubt that Facebook is one of the most powerful forms of media for communication today. More than a billion users chat, share photos, and keep their friends and family up to date on their lives regularly. Yet, there is a dark side to its use, along with other forms of social media, that has been labeled Facebook Depression, though this phenomenon also includes anxiety, other psychiatric disorders, and a range of unhealthy behaviors.

Perhaps the most comprehensive study to date found that Facebook overuse among teens was significantly correlated with narcissism. Among young adults, Facebook overuse was also associated with Histrionic Personality Disorder, Antisocial Personality Disorder, Bipolar Disorder, and Sadistic, Passive-Aggressive, Borderline, Paranoid, and Somatoform Personality Disorders. This study also explored the strength of Facebook use as a predictor of these psychiatric disorders and found that, even when demographics, such as age, gender, median income, ethnicity, and education were controlled, Facebook use was one of the three strongest predictors.

For more information about personality disorders, including definitions for each of the disorders listed here, visit PubMed Health at the US National Library of Medicine: http://www.ncbi.nlm.nih.gov /pubmedhealth/PMH0001935.

An analysis of 15 studies found that increased media exposure, including television, movies, video games, and the Internet, was associated with violent behavior and isolation. It reported that children who watched violent shows were not only more likely to be more aggressive, but also to have fewer friends and to be more secluded socially. The researchers concluded that children who are aggressive will have fewer friends and be more likely to be bullies (because they are more aggressive) or victims of bullying (because they are isolated).

Another study of adolescent girls found that the more they used texting, instant messaging and other social media to discuss their problems, particularly romantic difficulties, the more depressive symptoms they presented. The researchers argued that the ease and frequency that technology affords children to communicate allows them to "co-ruminate," that is, dwell on their problems without providing any solutions.

The Ugly: Internet Addiction

Addiction was the most widely used descriptor of the one-day moratorium on technology in the research I just described in a recent post. Internet addiction is commonly characterized as excessive use of the Internet that interferes with daily functioning and that can lead to distress or harm.

A review of research from the past decade has found that adolescents who demonstrated Internet addiction scored higher for obsessive–compulsive behavior, depression, generalized and social anxiety, attention deficit hyperactivity disorder, introversion, and other maladaptive behaviors. This research also revealed an interesting pattern of parental involvement. Those youth who were judged to have an Internet addiction rated their parents as lacking in love and nurturance, being overinvested, unresponsive, angry, and severe disciplinarians.

There is considerable debate within the mental-health field about whether dependence on technology is a true addiction, like alcohol, drugs, or gambling. In fact, the American Psychiatric Association, which produces the Diagnostic and Statistical Manual (think shrinks' bible), decided not to include Internet Addiction in their latest revision. Some experts in the field argue that the unhealthy dependence on technology may be a symptom of some more fundamental pathology, such as depression or anxiety, and that so-called Internet addicts use technology to self-medicate and relieve their symptoms. Plus, unlike alcohol and drugs, Internet use doesn't cause any direct physiological or psychological harm.

Despite this uncertainty in the psychological community, the students in the survey I wrote about in my last post made it clear that they believe Internet addiction is very real. It certainly passes the "duck test" (if it looks like a duck and sounds like a duck, it's probably a duck). Not only did the students miss the functions that the technology offered, for example, texting, surfing the Web, and listening to music, but they actually craved the devices themselves. Said an English student, "Media is my drug; without it I was lost. I am an addict. How could I survive 24 hours without it?" Added an American student, "After experiencing this dreadful 24-hours, I realized that our obsession with media is almost scary. I could not even begin to imagine the world if it was media-free."

So what specifically does Internet use provide to people such that it gets to the point of unhealthy behavior often associated with addiction? One study examined the types of gratification that people gain from the Internet and found that four specific forms of gratification were, cumulatively, most predictive of the tendency toward Internet addiction: virtual community (feeling connected to a group), monetary compensation (money they earned through various Web-based activities), diversion (distraction from their lives), and personal status (the feeling of individual standing they gained from Internet use). These types of gratification are normal for children, yet there is something about the Internet that morphs them into unhealthy needs that appear to become addicting.

This so-called addiction appears to go deeper than just psychological dependence. There is emerging evidence indicating that, for example, our interaction with technology produces the same neurochemical reaction—a burst of dopamine—as that found with alcohol, drug, sex, and gambling addictions. Persistent exposure to technology-related cues, such as the vibration from a smartphone announcing the arrival of a new text message or the ping of an incoming tweet, can cause people to get caught in a vicious cycle of dopamine stimulation and deprivation. Moreover, the brevity of technology, for example, 140-character text messages, lends itself to this vicious cycle because the information received isn't completely satisfying, so people are driven to seek out more information for their next shot of dopamine. Imagine your children growing up with this relationship with technology and the strength of its grip on them if they are allowed ungoverned and unguided use of technology.

The Good: Social Media Can Help

Certainly, the research I've just described doesn't paint a very rosy picture of the influence of technology on children. It's not all bad though. Studies have shown that more time spent with social media is related to increased "virtual empathy," meaning that expressed through technology, and "real-world empathy" (considered a related, but separate factor). The best predictor of virtual empathy was the time spent on Facebook and the use of instant messaging. More of both forms of empathy means more social support, always a good thing for children.

Social media can also help those young people who experience shyness or social anxiety. Introverted young people can gain comfort and confidence in social interactions in several ways. Shy children can use social media to overcome what is perhaps their most difficult challenge, namely, initiating new relationships, in a low-risk environment. They can avoid awkwardness that is endemic to making friends by allowing them to gain familiarity with others and build friendships online. Introverted children can also practice social skills with the relative distance and safety afforded by social media.

Technology may improve family relationships and encourage feelings of connectedness. First, technology can be used as a point of entry into children's lives and create opportunities for sharing. Second, they enable families to have quality time and pursue activities of shared interest.

Social media can have educational benefits for children as well. They are learning practical skills that are necessary for success in today's wired world. Specifically, children are learning how to use and become proficient with technology, developing their creative abilities, appreciating new and different perspectives, and enhancing their communication skills.

One study indicated that prosocial video games encourage helping behavior. The researchers found that young people were more likely to help others after playing a prosocial as compared to a neutral video game. In a related study, they observed a similar effect when given the opportunity to protect a stranger who was being harassed.

Technology may even help children to better cope with stress in their lives. Technology can potentially mitigate stress in a number of ways. First, technology provides children with more outlets through which to express their feelings of stress, thus allowing a cathartic effect. Second, social media can provide children with social support

YOUR ANNOTATIONS

Neurochemical reaction: a temporary change in brain chemistry.

Dopamine: a chemical in the brain associated with addiction and motivation.

which can act as a buffer against stressors. Technology, including Facebook postings and instant messaging, enables children to receive more, immediate, and diverse support from a wider range of people. Third, technology can allow children to find useful information that may help them to reduce their stress. Finally, technology may act as a distraction and a means of distancing children from the stressors, providing a respite from the stress and giving them the time and perspective to deal with the stress more effectively.

What Does This All Mean?

As I have often argued, technology is neither good nor bad, but, at the same time, it isn't neutral either. The impact that technology has on your children depends not on the technology itself, but rather on how you educate them about it and the experiences they have with it. It is your responsibility to become informed about the potential benefits and costs of this new digital age and then make deliberate decisions about the type and quantity of technology you expose your children to.

SOURCE INFORMATION
Author: Jim Taylor
Title: "The Bad, the Ugly, and the Good of Kids' Use of Social Media"
Publication: *Psychology Today* Web site
Date: 28 May 2013

PRACTICE ④ Creating an Information Sheet for "The Bad, the Ugly, and the Good of Kids' Use of Social Media"

Using your annotations, create an information sheet that includes the following:

- General notes
- Simple outline
- Brief summary
- Issues and key words
- Potential quotes

| SOURCE 4 | **"USING MEDIA TO MAKE A DIFFERENCE: SOCIAL MEDIA AND THE MIDDLE EAST DEMOCRACY MOVEMENT"** |

The following reading is a selection from the textbook *Introduction to Mass Communication: Media Literacy and Culture,* 8th ed., by Stanley J. Baran.

Follow the steps presented in this chapter as you read the selection, and keep your assignment and purpose in mind.

- Preview the reading and think about the topic.
- Read and annotate the text.

ABOUT THE AUTHOR
Stanley J. Baran has a PhD in communication research. He taught at University of Texas, where he led the Radio-TV-Film graduate program. Subsequently, he served as chair of the Department of Theatre Arts at San Jose State University. He has published seven books and many articles.

Students may benefit from a very brief overview of the Arab Spring movements, as well as a look at a map to see where the events took place. *The Guardian* presents an excellent interactive timeline of the events and the countries involved. See "Arab Spring: An Interactive Timeline of Middle East Protests" at www.theguardian .com/world/interactive/2011 /mar/22/middle-east-protest -interactive-timeline.

Using Media to Make a Difference: Social Media and the Middle East Democracy Movement

by Stanley J. Baran

YOUR ANNOTATIONS

Lexile: 1570L

Tens of thousands of Iranians from all walks of life took to the streets in the summer of 2009 to protest what they saw as the illegitimate reelection of President Mahmoud Ahmadinejad. The government, already skilled at slowing the Internet and shutting down opposition websites, immediately expelled or placed under house arrest all foreign journalists, closed opposition newspapers, and used its own state-run radio and television stations to first ignore the protests and then blame them on outside Western agitators hostile to Iran. The protesters responded by using the Internet and social media to make a difference for their Green Revolution and democracy.

Only a few decades before, the Polish Solidarity movement's communication tools were pamphlets, newspapers, and loudspeaker trucks. But in 2009, Iran's police and army, as they had ever since the 1979 Islamic revolution, easily silenced these outlets. However, rather than stop the insurrection in a country where a third of the population is linked to the Internet and 60% have cell phones, this crushing of dissent pushed the protesters to those very same media where they made dramatically effective use of Twitter and YouTube. Protest organizers used cell phones to direct people to Twitter, where thousands of dissidents could be instantly mobilized into hundreds of daily demonstrations and nightly rooftop protests, shouting "Alaho Akbar" (God is Great) in defiance of the government. Hours of violent and bloody cell phone video were uploaded onto YouTube, none more famous than the image of Neda Aga Soltan's death, migrating from there to media outlets across the world.

Did the Green Revolution's use of social media make a difference? After all, Ahmadinejad's repressive regime remained in power despite weeks of violent protest. Evidence that it did was to come soon, as satellite and Web video of the revolt fueled democratic hopes across the region.

On December 17, 2010, Tunisian street vendor Mohamed Bouazizi set himself afire to protest mistreatment by corrupt government police. Demonstrations erupted immediately, and protesters uploaded cell phone video of their rallies to Facebook, YouTube, and local broadcasters. These images of defiance sped electronically around the country, and the revolution swept into all parts of Tunisian society. Twenty-eight days after Bouazizi's sacrifice, Tunisia's dictator of 23 years, Zine el-Abidine Ben Ali, fled into exile in Saudi Arabia.

Those images also made their way to Egypt, where anger at the brutal June 6, 2010 beating of Khaled Said at the hands of corrupt Alexandria police had been simmering for months. Said's crime was that he had used his blog to post video of cops sharing the loot from a drug bust. Within five days of the 24-year-old businessman's death, demonstrators created a Facebook page, We Are All Khaled Said, to galvanize anger against the authoritarian government of Hosni Mubarak. Within a week, the page had 130,000 friends; by year's end, in a country of 5 million Facebook users, it had 473,000.

By March 2011 these images of oppressed people fighting for freedom and dignity in Iraq, Tunisia, and Egypt had spawned an "Arab Spring"—democracy movements in Yemen, Libya, Bahrain, Algeria, Morocco, Jordan, Oman, Iraq, Syria, and Saudi Arabia. Some, for example in Libya and Bahrain, were met with government brutality, but others produced "voluntary" reform on the part of once-powerful rulers who saw that new media were a growing, uncontrollable check on their authority. "While it is almost impossible to isolate the impact of social media tools from the general swirl of events that set off the popular uprisings across the Middle East," wrote the *New York Times*'s Jennifer Preston, "there is little doubt that they provided a new means for ordinary people to connect with human rights advocates trying to amass support against police abuse, torture and . . . permanent emergency laws allowing people to be jailed without charges. Facebook and YouTube also offered a way for the discontented to organize and mobilize. . . . Far more decentralized than political parties, the strength and agility of the networks clearly caught [Middle Eastern] authorities . . . by surprise, even as [these governments] quickly attempted to shut them down."

Cell phone video of the murder of Neda Aga Soltan, seen worldwide on the Internet, not only galvanized Iran's Green Revolutionaries, but earned them global support.

SOURCE INFORMATION
Author: Stanley J. Baran
Title: "Using Media to Make a Difference: Social Media and the Middle East Democracy Movement"
Publication: *Introduction to Mass Communication: Media Literacy and Culture,* 8th ed.
Publisher: McGraw-Hill
City: New York
Date: 2014
Page: 394

PRACTICE 5 Creating an Information Sheet for "Using Media to Make a Difference: Social Media and the Middle East Democracy Movement"

Using your annotations, create an information sheet that includes the following:

- General notes
- Simple outline
- Brief summary
- Issues and key words
- Potential quotes

DEVELOPING YOUR ESSAY

Now that you are familiar with some of the issues involving the use of social media, you are ready to write your own essay on a social media topic. The following steps will guide you through the process of using the sources you have read and analyzed to compose an informative essay.

Synthesize Your Sources

As you begin thinking about writing an informative essay on social media, first consider the topics addressed by the sources you have read. Make an **issues chart**—a chart on which you list all the issues raised in the sources you read. Issues are generally phrased as questions and may be more specific than topics. For instance, in Larry Rosen's article, the

Connect IRW Writing Assignment: The peer review tools in Connect IRW allow students to comment anonymously on others' essays. You can set up the assignment so that students cannot write a second draft until they have received peer review comments.

topic is social media use and distraction. He focuses on three issues: Does social media use result in distraction? How does social media distraction affect students? Can classroom technology breaks help students focus?

By making a chart that shows all the issues from every source you read, you will have a good number of issues from which to choose your own topic. Here is an example of such a chart with the topic and issues listed for two of the sources in this chapter. Fill in the topic and issues for the other sources.

Teaching Resources: Consider having your students save their documents to a free cloud storage site. Doing so allows students instant access to their work and eliminates the problem of lost flash drives. For more information about free, student-friendly cloud Web sites, see the IM.

Issues Chart

SOURCE	TOPIC	ISSUES
"Driven to Distraction: Our Wired Generation" by Larry Rosen	Social media use and distraction	• Does social media use result in distraction? • How does social media distraction affect students? • Can classroom technology breaks help students focus?
"Opening Statement on the Senate Subcommittee Hearing 'What Facial Recognition Technology Means for Privacy and Civil Liberties'"	Dangers of facial recognition technology	• Is facial recognition technology an invasion of privacy? • What are the potential abuses of the technology? • What laws about the technology should be created?
"The Bad, the Ugly, and the Good of Kids' Use of Social Media" by Jim Taylor	How social media affects kids	• Does *Facebook* contribute to depression? • What are the mental health effects of using social media? • Is Internet use addictive? • What are the healthy uses and benefits of social media?
"Using Media to Make a Difference: Social Media and the Middle East Democracy Movement" by Stanley J. Baran	Social media and political movements	• Do the political benefits of social media use outweigh its negative aspect? • Is uncensored Internet access a human rights issue?

Once you have identified the topics and the issues of the sources you read, you can begin the process of selecting a topic for your own essay.

Prewrite to Develop Your Ideas

Review the Assignment

One way to make sure your essay meets assignment requirements is to turn your annotated assignment into a grading sheet. Simply take each statement that provides a specific requirement and turn it into a question. The first three questions have been provided in the sample below. Fill in the remaining requirement questions.

Informative Reading and Writing Assignment

The primary purpose of <u>informative writing</u> is to provide readers with information in a clear and organized way. Your assignment is to find an aspect of social media about which readers need more information and to write an informative essay on that aspect. For example, as you read through sources, you will learn about a variety of issues: how social media has been used to foster political movements, which privacy concerns related to social media issues can affect people the most, how social media use differs among user populations, how social media can affect academic success, and so on.

Grading Sheet

Is the information presented in a clear and organized way?

Has the student written on an aspect of social media about which readers need more information?

Is the purpose of the student's essay to be informative?

(continued)

You will select an issue you wish to communicate to readers. Keep in mind that the purpose of your essay is not to make any persuasively oriented claims. In other words, you won't be writing your own argument about why we should take privacy more seriously, for example. Rather, your essay will simply present the major points readers should consider. Your essay will provide the information necessary for readers to know what the issue concerns and, if applicable, what some writers have suggested be done about it.

> Does the essay avoid making persuasively oriented claims?
>
> Does the essay present the major points readers should consider?
>
> Does the essay include what the issue concerns and what some writers suggest be done about it?

Select a Topic

Review the issues chart you created, and review your information sheets for each source in this chapter. Select an aspect of social media that readers should know more about. Choose a topic that allows you to *inform* readers. Avoid topics that would require you to prove your point, such as why social media is good for society or why people should require stronger privacy protections.

Use a Prewriting Method to Generate Ideas

Once you have selected a topic, use one of these prewriting strategies to jot down as many ideas about the topic as you can:

- **Discussion.** Go over your ideas with other students, your instructor, a tutor, or a family member.
- **Simple listing.** Write down ideas in list form.
- **Clustering (or *mapping*).** Create a graphic illustration with your topic in a center circle and ideas in other circles linked to it.
- **Journalistic questions.** Ask and answer the questions *Who? What? Where? When? Why?* and *How?*
- **Freewriting.** Write down everything that comes to mind about your topic for a limited period of time, such as three minutes.
- **Freetalking.** Talk aloud or into a recorder about your topic for two to three minutes.

You may jot down definitions, causes, effects, comparisons, or process steps; you may think of examples, explanations, descriptions, and related ideas. Without censoring your thoughts, write down as many ideas as you can.

After you have generated ideas, determine what your main idea will be. What is the main point you wish to communicate to your readers? If you have trouble working with a particular topic, go back to the issues chart you created and prewrite for a different topic. Choose an essay topic for which you can find a variety of information.

Construct a Thesis Statement

Once you know what your main point is, compose a thesis statement. Make sure your thesis statement is a complete sentence and that this sentence will help readers accurately predict the content of your essay. Check that your thesis statement is not too broad, is not just a statement of fact, and is not simply an announcement.

Too broad: The Internet is dangerous in many ways.

Statement of fact: Families have sued school districts over unsupervised Internet use by students.

Announcement: This essay will look at how dangerous the Internet can be for children.

Teaching Resources: Consider setting aside a day for students to work on these early writing process steps in class. Students who find the assignment overwhelming will feel more confident about writing their essays on their own after having completed the early steps in class. See the IM for additional ideas about teaching the projects in chapters 11–13.

For this assignment, also check to make sure your thesis statement does not signal a persuasive essay—that is, make sure it does not express your opinion or propose a course of action. If it does, reword the statement so that it is appropriate for an informative essay.

Persuasively focused thesis statement: Parents should not allow their children to use the Internet unsupervised because of the many dangers to which children are exposed.

Informative thesis statement: Children's unsupervised use of the Internet can be dangerous in a variety of ways.

Develop Support for Your Thesis Statement

Next, determine the *major supporting points* you will use to structure your essay. What are the major details readers will need to know to understand your main idea? Review your information sheets and your prewriting. Make a list of these details. You may find that you've already discovered these details in your prewriting. You may have points of your own you wish to add to those you found in the sources, and you may find that more than one source addresses the issue you are presenting.

Once you determine the major supporting details, figure out what *text patterns* might work to communicate the information. Notice how text patterns might be used for the details in an essay with the following thesis statement: *Children's unsupervised use of the Internet can be dangerous in a variety of ways.*

TEXT PATTERN	EXAMPLE
Narration	Anecdote about a high school friend who read nasty comments about herself on *Facebook*
Definition	Definition of social media
Illustration	Examples of hurtful tweets
Classification	Classification of interactive online activities into supervised (monitored forums) and unsupervised (*Instagram*) types
Comparison-contrast	Comparison of social media interactions with face-to-face interactions in moderating hurtful messages
Cause and effect	Effect of negative social media posts on children's self-esteem
Process analysis	Analysis of how negative social media messaging can spiral out of control

Once you have identified and examined your major supporting details, write a complete sentence for each one. These sentences will be the topic sentences you will use for your essay's body paragraphs.

Think about Your Audience's Needs to Create Minor Supporting Details

What kind of information will your audience need to fully understand each major supporting detail? One way you can determine this is to write a list of questions readers may have about your topic sentence. Once you have created a list of questions, decide how you can answer them. Which of the following kinds of details would be most helpful to readers?

- **Analogy:** An example that explains something unfamiliar by comparing it with something more familiar.
- **Concrete example:** Specific information that helps the reader understand the writer's point.
- **Description:** Sensory information that helps the reader understand a thing or concept.
- **Explanation:** A description of how something is constructed, how a task is performed, or how something works.
- **Fact:** A statement that is verifiably true.
- **Figurative language:** Language that expresses ideas in an indirect way, such as metaphors, similes, personification, and hyperbole.
- **Hypothetical example:** An example that asks the reader to imagine something that is not currently true.
- **Rhetorical question:** A question that the writer asks to make a point but does not expect the reader to answer. The answer may be provided in the text, or it may be self-evident.
- **Testimony:** A person's firsthand account of something.
- **Visual aid:** A photo, diagram, chart, cartoon, or any other graphic representation of content.

List the types of information you will use to support each topic sentence.

Determine How You Will Use Information from Your Sources

Some of the information you present to readers will come from your sources and the information sheets you created. You can use source information in a few ways.

- **Summaries.** If summarizing a source is an appropriate way to support one of your ideas, you can use the brief source summaries you wrote.
- **Quotations.** Take a look at the quotes you copied onto your information sheets. If these quotes are not the best ones to use, go back to the sources and look at your annotations. You will likely find source material easily if you have made good annotations. Be sure to follow the rules for integrating quoted material. You can find these rules in the Quick Start Guide to Integrated Reading and Writing Assignments.
- **Paraphrased ideas.** You can use ideas from sources rewritten in your own words. Any time you use an idea from a source, be sure to give credit to the source's author. Follow the rules discussed later in this chapter for giving credit to sources.

Create an Outline to Organize Your Essay

Once you have figured out the types of information you will use in body paragraphs, make a *simple outline*. Your simple outline should list the most important parts of your essay: the thesis statement and the major supporting points. Make sure you use complete sentences for all of these elements. Before you list your ideas on the outline, determine the order in which you will present them.

- **Order of importance.** Will you present the most important major supporting point first—or last?
- **Chronological or sequential order.** Will you use what happened first, second, and so on as a method to order your information?
- **Spatial order.** For example, will you start with one location, say, the home, and move to locations that are farther away—the neighborhood, the school, the city?

Make intentional decisions about the order of information you use. Place your ideas on the outline in the order they will appear in your essay.

Add Source Materials to Your Outline

Now you can use all of your notes, including your sources and prewriting, to create an *enhanced outline*—an outline on which you list the exact information you will use in your essay.

Use the following outline as an example for your own essay. Your outline will differ in the number of paragraphs, details, types of details, and so on, but the model below will give you an idea of what to include in your enhanced outline.

Teaching Resources: A handout of this enhanced outline is available. The handout does not include the specific source examples shown here.

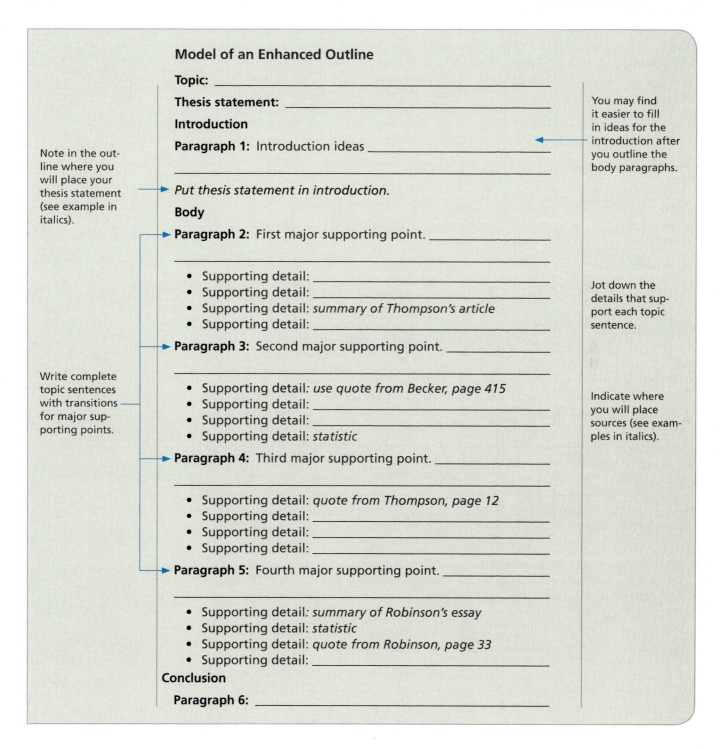

Model of an Enhanced Outline

Topic: _____

Thesis statement: _____

Introduction

Paragraph 1: Introduction ideas _____
_____

Put thesis statement in introduction.

Body

Paragraph 2: First major supporting point. _____
_____

- Supporting detail: _____
- Supporting detail: _____
- Supporting detail: *summary of Thompson's article*
- Supporting detail: _____

Paragraph 3: Second major supporting point. _____
_____

- Supporting detail*: use quote from Becker, page 415*
- Supporting detail: _____
- Supporting detail: _____
- Supporting detail: *statistic*

Paragraph 4: Third major supporting point. _____
_____

- Supporting detail: *quote from Thompson, page 12*
- Supporting detail: _____
- Supporting detail: _____
- Supporting detail: _____

Paragraph 5: Fourth major supporting point. _____
_____

- Supporting detail*: summary of Robinson's essay*
- Supporting detail: *statistic*
- Supporting detail: *quote from Robinson, page 33*
- Supporting detail: _____

Conclusion

Paragraph 6: _____

Note in the outline where you will place your thesis statement (see example in italics).

Write complete topic sentences with transitions for major supporting points.

You may find it easier to fill in ideas for the introduction after you outline the body paragraphs.

Jot down the details that support each topic sentence.

Indicate where you will place sources (see examples in italics).

Write a Complete Draft of Your Essay

Once you have made it to this point in the writing process, you have done a substantial amount of work. Now you are ready to follow these steps to draft your actual essay.

Keep an Audience in Mind

The best tool to use when drafting is your imagination: imagine having a conversation with a smart person who disagrees with your point. Word your essay in such a way that you would be able to convince this smart reader that your claim is correct.

Write an Introduction Paragraph

Many students find it comfortable to use a single paragraph to introduce the topic and to present the thesis statement. This method is fine, and in fact many professors prefer that you organize your essay in this way. If your instructor does not require you to put your thesis statement in the introduction paragraph, consider the options you have as a writer. You may want to start your essay with a brief story that takes up its own paragraph, or you may wish to reserve your thesis statement for your last paragraph. Think about your audience and the information you are presenting in order to make this decision.

You may wish to start your introduction with any of the following:

- A question
- A story
- Background information
- A surprise, such as a statement that goes against conventional wisdom
- Data (statistical information)
- A quotation or adage
- An objective overview of the issue

Choose an introduction method, and write the first paragraph. If you feel stuck at this stage, go ahead and write your body paragraphs first. Sometimes it is easier to write the introduction after you have already composed the body of your essay.

Write Body Paragraphs according to Your Outline

You have already planned the details you will be including in your essay. Now your task is to write them—in carefully constructed sentences. Be flexible with your outline. You may have planned to use only one sentence to present an explanation, for example, but suppose you begin writing the explanation and find that it would be easier for readers to understand if you used two sentences? Then, by all means, use two sentences. You may need to adjust your outline once you start the actual writing process.

Keep in mind this rule: A sentence should present one idea clearly. Sometimes you can write a sentence that presents two ideas clearly, but focus on clarity. If an explanation is complex, for example, it is probably better to write two shorter, clear sentences than a single long one, as in the following example.

Too complex for one sentence: Most adults realize that children who use the Internet unsupervised can fall victim to sexual predators who are experts at creating convincing schemes to obtain information from unsuspecting children.

Better: Most adults realize that children who use the Internet unsupervised can fall victim to sexual predators. These predators are experts at creating convincing schemes to obtain information from unsuspecting children.

As you draft, when you finish a paragraph or reach a spot where the ideas stop flowing, return to the beginning of your essay or to a previous paragraph and reread what you have written. You should constantly reread your writing, not always from the very beginning, but at least from the last paragraph you wrote. You will find many opportunities to revise by doing this, and you will also find grammatical and mechanical mistakes to fix along the way.

Write the Conclusion Paragraph

Once you have finished drafting, you are ready to write a conclusion paragraph. In an informative essay, one function of the conclusion paragraph can be to emphasize the importance of the information presented. Reread your entire essay before drafting the conclusion paragraph. You might want to use one of the following strategies in your conclusion:

- Restate and summarize your main point.
- Answer a question that you posed earlier in the essay.
- Finish a story that you started earlier in the essay.
- Speculate on a future outcome.

Make sure the conclusion paragraph gives readers a sense of closure. Then choose a short, descriptive title for your essay.

Teaching Resources: Chapter 14 gives in-depth information on how to integrate source materials ethically and correctly. A condensed list of instructions is in the handout "Integrating Sources."

Integrate Ideas and Quotes from Sources Correctly

If you have taken careful notes, you should be able to easily distinguish your ideas from the ideas you found in sources. To use sources ethically, write in such a way that readers know which information came from you and which came from source materials. The following paragraph, from a student essay, illustrates the guidelines for correctly integrating ideas from sources.

The first two sentences are the student's words and ideas.

Most adults realize that children who use the Internet unsupervised can fall victim to sexual predators. These predators are experts at creating convincing schemes to obtain information from unsuspecting children. For example, in Indiana, a forty-four-year-old man posing as a thirteen-year-old developed an online relationship with Leila, a twelve-year-old girl, as reported by privacy researcher John Marsh. After developing an online relationship with the man, Leila gave him her address and planned to meet him one night after her parents had gone to bed. Fortunately for Leila, "detectives conducted a sting operation that landed the man in custody, and the meeting never happened," as Marsh reports. Leila and her parents were told about her supposed boyfriend's real identity, and her parents have since taken measures to ensure that Leila uses the Internet only under strict supervision (Marsh).

When the student uses a direct quote, she gives credit to the source (Marsh).

The example comes from a source. The student puts the example in her own words, so she does not use quotation marks. However, she does give credit to the source at the end of the sentence.

Since this sentence clearly continues to summarize the story Marsh reported, readers know the information is from the source.

The last piece of information also came from Marsh, so the student uses a parenthetical reference to give credit.

If you are unsure whether to reference a source, go ahead and give credit. Your instructor can guide you through making some of the more complicated decisions about when and how to credit sources.

FINISHING YOUR ASSIGNMENT

If you have allowed yourself enough time for this project, you may find you have a day or two to set your essay aside and let it rest (and let yourself rest!). After forgetting your essay for a day or two, you can pick it up and read it more like an audience might read your paper. You may find ideas that need revision or grammatical errors that have to be corrected. To complete the revising and editing process, follow these steps.

Check That You Have Met Assignment Requirements

Review your assignment and your annotations of the assignment. Next, print a copy of your essay. Many writers find that reading and marking a paper copy of their essays helps them spot errors or identify places that need to be revised.

Before you do anything else, take out your assignment and check to make sure it meets every requirement. If necessary, revise it to meet the requirements.

Revise for Organization and Unity

If the organization strategy in your outline is sound, and if you have followed your outline to write your draft, your essay should be well organized. Sometimes in the process of writing a draft, however, you will realize that the elements should be rearranged. Use the revision process to read through your essay, noting how and where your essay may need organizational changes. Make sure each part of your essay is in its proper place.

A unified essay is one whose ideas all fit together to support the thesis statement. Ask yourself these questions:

- Do my major supporting points support my thesis statement?
- Are my ideas organized in a logical and convincing way?
- Have I used transitions to show relationships between ideas?
- Does my writing have a successful introduction and conclusion?

Read over your essay to see if adding transitions or rearranging paragraphs will help you create more unity in your writing and more effective organization of your ideas.

Revise for Development

Revise your paper with a reader in mind. Make sure your essay includes all of the information your reader needs to fully understand your ideas. Imagine the reader has no experience with the ideas you are presenting. Ask yourself these questions:

- Have I answered my reader's potential questions?
- Have I provided enough support (definitions, examples, comparisons, causes, effects, and so on) for the main idea?
- Are there places were I could add more support?
- Do I make unwarranted assumptions about what the reader knows? That is, have I defined and explained unfamiliar concepts and terms?

For example, if you reference *Flickr* in your paper, you may think your reader knows what *Flickr* is, but not everyone does. Provide a brief explanation so that the reader is not confused.

Example:　The use of *Flickr*, a Web site for uploading and sharing photos, can lead to some unintended consequences.

Consider having students use the assignment to create a check-off list of requirements that they submit as a cover sheet. See IM for ideas about grading strategies that give students incentive to use correct formatting.

Ask a classmate, lab instructor, tutor, or family member to read your paper and to write questions in the margin when he or she needs more information. Revise your paper to answer the questions that you deem important.

Revise for Clarity

Often, sentences are unclear because writers do not fully figure out what they are trying to say before they write. One way to revise is to read each sentence out loud. As you read it, listen. Does the sentence communicate your idea effectively? Is the tone appropriate? Would you normally use the particular words you're using to communicate this idea? If you were explaining the idea to a friend, how would you say it? The goal is not to include slang or informal language, but rather to speak clearly and simply. If you can think and speak clearly and simply, you can write sentences that are easily understood.

Additionally, you can create more clarity when you break out the ideas in a long, complex sentence. Once you know the ideas you wish to express, you can decide whether to use a single sentence for each idea or to use a variety of sentence types.

> **Unclear:** Internet advertising is on some *Google* searches making them hard to understand what's the advertisement and what's the real link.

The ideas being expressed:

- Advertisements appear on *Google*.
- When a person searches, these ads come up.
- It can be hard to understand the search results because of these ads.
- It is difficult to separate the actual search results from the advertisements.

Once you have figured out the ideas you wish to express, you can combine sentences in an intentional way so that your idea is stated clearly.

> **Clear:** When a person does a search on *Google*, Internet ads appear. Distinguishing the ads from the actual search results can be difficult.

Remember that your first duty as a writer is to communicate clearly. If a short sentence with simple words helps you communicate an idea clearly, use it! Do not make sentences overly complex or include words from a thesaurus to impress your reader. Unless you are very careful, these tactics can lead to less impressive writing than you might have accomplished with simple words and structures.

Create a Works Cited or References List

Go through your paper and list all the sources you used. Create a works cited list if you are writing a paper in MLA (Modern Language Association) format, or create a list of references if you are using APA (American Psychological Association) format. Follow the detailed instructions provided by your instructor for creating these lists.

Check for Plagiarism

You are aware that every time you use an idea from someone else—whether you put the idea into your own words or quote directly—you must give credit to the source, both in the text of your essay and in a works cited or references list. If you do not give credit properly, your paper will be considered plagiarized. Double-check your paper to make sure you have avoided plagiarism. Print a copy of your essay and follow these steps to check whether you have integrated and credited sources correctly:

1. Highlight each idea in your paper that came from a source, whether you put the idea in your own words or quoted it.
2. Check to see that you have given credit to the source, either by mentioning the source in the sentence or by using a parenthetical reference.

Connect IRW Writing Assignment: Consider using peer review to have students comment on unity, development, and clarity. By assessing others' essays, students may become more attentive to the same elements in their own writing.

Teaching Resources: If your course objectives do not include learning to create MLA or APA works cited or references lists, see the IM for ideas about how to handle documentation.

See chapter 14 for complete guidelines for creating in-text references and works cited pages or references lists as well as sample MLA-style and APA-style papers students can use as models for formatting their essays.

3. Check that each source appears as a properly formatted entry in your works cited or references list.

4. Make sure that each time you used a quote or an attribution tag (for example, ". . . said Wilson"), you did so in a way that is grammatically correct. If you do not integrate quotes correctly, you can end up with comma splices, run-on sentences, or sentence fragments.

Edit Your Essay Using SMART TRACS

Editing consists of checking your paper for grammatical and mechanical errors. Always use the spell-checker on your word processor or computer, but consider also using a grammar-checker. Be aware that both grammar-checkers and spell-checkers do have their limitations; you are ultimately responsible for the correctness of your paper.

Most students know their grammatical and mechanical strengths and weaknesses. If you know you tend to confuse *affect* and *effect*, take the time to go back through your paper and check each usage of those words. If you have a tendency to make subject-verb agreement errors, check each and every subject-verb relationship and make changes where necessary. If you are not sure whether your paper is grammatically and mechanically sound, spend time with a lab instructor or tutor. While this person may not show you every error in your paper, he or she can tell you whether your paper needs significant editing and can help you identify the types of errors you are making. You can also improve your paper by consulting with lab instructors, using grammar-checkers, and asking classmates to read your paper and offer feedback. Taking the time to enlist the help of others can make a difference in the grade you earn.

Use the SMART TRACS guidelines to edit your paper. SMART TRACS stands for the following: **S**pelling, **M**issing words, **A**ccurate punctuation, **R**epeated words, **T**erminal punctuation, **T**ense consistency, **R**hythm, **A**ctive voice, and **C**onfusing words. If you have questions as you edit, work with a tutor or writing center instructor.

Chapter 10 provides a detailed explanation of SMART TRACS.

Put Your Essay in the Proper Format

Your instructor may want you to follow MLA or APA publication style for your essay. Make sure your paper layout, heading, header, font type and size, and spacing all conform to your instructor's requirements. If you are not sure about those requirements, ask. Do not use a binder for your paper unless your instructor tells you to do so. Specifically, check these formatting issues before submitting your paper:

Teaching Resources: See the PPT "Simple Overview of MLA Documentation" or the PPT "Simple Overview of APA Documentation."

- Heading
- Header (and page numbers)
- Spacing
- Margins
- Title
- Font type and size
- Formatting of quotations
- Formatting of the works cited or references

You have likely been saving your work throughout this process, but as you finish your work, be certain to save a digital copy of your corrected paper. Use a file name you will recognize if you need to search for your paper. One of the most secure ways to save an electronic file is to use a free "cloud" account from a site such as *Dropbox* or *Google*. You can save your paper to your account and access it from anywhere. Always keep both a saved electronic copy and a hard copy (printout) of your work.

ADDITIONAL ASSIGNMENTS

1. Evaluate the quality of the sources in this chapter. For each source, write a paragraph in which you answer these questions:

    -   How much information did the writer manage to pack into the source?

    -   How clearly did the writer explain the information?

    -   Were there any passages that could have been explained more clearly? Cite an example, and tell how it could be improved.

2. One of the readings in this chapter discusses the political uses of social media in the Middle East. Think about how social media serve political functions in the United States. Write an essay in which you present your ideas. Provide examples for each political use you discuss. For instance, the election campaigns of President Barack Obama used social media effectively to connect with current and potential supporters.

3. Create a short video, a *PowerPoint* presentation, or an infographic in which you present information about a social media topic. For instance, you might create a *PowerPoint* presentation in which you show how facial recognition works.

4. Write an essay for a parenting magazine in which you offer guidelines parents should follow to monitor their children's Internet usage. Explain the importance of each guideline, and provide an example of what could happen if parents do not follow it.

Overpopulation, the increasing scarcity of fresh water, the loss of species biodiversity, and the declining health of the oceans are environmental concerns that have a direct impact on our future and the future of the planet. While we must address all these concerns, which problem should be our highest priority?

Project 2: Working with Analysis and Evaluation Texts

Our Vulnerable Planet

Any time you examine an idea, event, or object in depth, you are analyzing it. **Analysis** consists of examining the individual components of a subject. For example, you might analyze an engine by inspecting its parts and learning about them. **Evaluation** consists of making a judgment about something you have analyzed. After analyzing an engine, you might conclude that it is flawless, or you might conclude that a cylinder or some other part is not working properly, based on your analysis. We use analysis and evaluation in college and in the workplace to make judgments and to reach decisions. In this chapter, you will use your critical reading and writing skills to analyze sources and to create your own analysis and evaluation essay.

Most people have heard that climate change is a serious threat to our world. Because climate change poses so many challenges, other environmental issues may not seem as important. However, a variety of issues—some of them related to climate change, and some not—threaten the world we live in. Four of those issues are addressed in the reading selections in this chapter.

Some experts draw our attention to the water crisis. The amount of available freshwater for drinking is decreasing while the world's need for water is increasing. A number of factors are to blame for this situation, including some that we cannot control, such as drought.

CHAPTER OBJECTIVES

After completing this chapter, students will be able to do the following:

- **Examine an analysis and evaluation reading and writing assignment and identify a purpose.**

- **Use a critical reading process to examine four readings and use them as sources.**

- **Use an effective writing process to compose an analysis and evaluation essay.**

- **Revise and edit an analysis and evaluation essay, and use MLA or APA style to format the essay.**

Connect IRW LearnSmart Achieve: Assign the topics "Writing in Response to Reading," "Evaluating, Synthesizing, and Documenting Sources," and "Analyzing and Writing in Response to a Writing Prompt" for adaptive learning to accompany the chapter.

Another environmental issue of concern is a decrease in biodiversity and the extinction of species. This issue may not be on the news every other night, but scientists warn that losing species can affect the health of ecosystems and the health of humans.

While water shortages and biodiversity are serious issues, some experts believe that overpopulation is the most serious environmental issue we are facing. Far more people are being born than are dying. Eventually, experts on overpopulation contend, this increase will become a serious issue as natural resources are stretched thin.

A final area of concern presented in this chapter is the health of the oceans. *Acidification*—the process of becoming more acidic—is making our ocean water unhealthy, and sometimes toxic, for sea animals. Ongoing pollution poses a real threat to the future health of our oceans, as does overfishing.

All of these environmental issues are serious, but which one is most pressing? How should we determine which issue deserves more of our attention and energy? For this project, you will make that judgment. You will analyze these environmental issues by reading about them in the four sources in this chapter. Using a set of criteria, you will then determine which of these issues is the most urgent, and you will write an essay in which you present your analysis and evaluation. The steps that follow will guide you through this reading and writing project.

Connect IRW Discussion Board (DB) Assignment: Create DB threads that help students articulate their comprehension of the articles, and create threads that help students read the articles critically. See the IM for particular DB thread prompts.

GETTING STARTED

Before you begin, we will examine the steps you should take to help you prepare for reading and annotating the sources with an eye toward your assignment.

Analyze Your Assignment

When you are presented with sources to read in preparation for a writing assignment, the first task is to determine *how* to read them. Beyond reading to understand the writers' ideas, what should you focus on? Analyzing the writing assignment will help you define your focus while reading. Notice how the annotations for this chapter's writing assignment, shown here, bring out particularly important elements to focus on when reading the sources.

Connect IRW Writing Assignment: Use the Connect IRW writing tools to set up this writing assignment. You can create a rubric to use for grading, assign drafts, assign peer review activities, and have students submit their essays through Connect IRW. See the Instructor's Manual for more information. Alternatively, use the pre-loaded version of this assignment in the Connect IRW *Common Places* Master Course.

Analysis and Evaluation Reading and Writing Assignment

You will read four selections that present serious environmental threats. Your task is to read, annotate, and analyze each source. Next, you will create a list of criteria to help you determine which environmental threat is the most serious, the one that deserves our attention first. You will then use these criteria to evaluate the environmental threats and make a judgment about the one we should prioritize.

Once you have analyzed the sources and used criteria to make an evaluative judgment, you will write an essay in which you present your analysis, criteria, and evaluation. You will need to use evidence from the sources to support your point, giving credit to those sources by using the method of documentation approved by your instructor.

*Annotations (left):*
- Create a list of criteria to determine the most serious threat.
- Make a judgment.
- Use evidence from the sources.
- Give credit to the sources using an approved method.

*Annotations (right):*
- Read, annotate, and analyze four selections about environmental issues.
- Use the criteria to evaluate the environmental threats.
- Write an essay to present your analysis, criteria, evaluation.

As you read about these serious environmental issues, you will need to find a way to judge which of them is the most serious. The way to do this is to establish criteria. **Criteria** are measurements or standards we develop to help us make decisions. For example, to decide on an apartment, you might consider criteria such as the monthly rent, the apartment's size, its location, and the shopping or dining establishments nearby. By using these criteria, you can make a judgment about which apartment best fits your needs.

You will use criteria in the same way to judge which environmental issue is most in need of our attention. As you read, be aware not only of what the writers say about the issues, but also of potential criteria you can use to measure the seriousness of the issues. For example, one criterion you can consider is how many people will be affected by the environmental threat. If only a small region is affected, the threat is less significant than a threat that affects entire continents. You will discover a number of criteria you can use in your evaluation as you read and analyze the sources.

Identify Your Purpose

The best place to start any assignment is with a clear understanding of your purpose. One purpose for your reading is to get information about the environmental threats discussed in the sources. You will also be reading to observe how professional writers analyze and evaluate these environmental issues so that you can write an essay in which you do the same thing. Since the purpose of your reading is to help you write an essay, you will need to read critically—examining content and identifying writing strategies.

Connect IRW Power of Process Assignment: Each readings can be set up in Power of Process so that students go through a reading process that matches the steps in this chapter. See the IM for more information. These PoP assignments are pre-loaded into the Connect IRW *Common Places* Master Course.

WORKING WITH READINGS

Using a strategic reading process to get all of the information you need from each source will help you focus and plan your essay as you go. The steps that follow will guide your reading process.

Preview the Reading and Think about the Topic

Start by analyzing the source's context. Who wrote it? Is the writer an expert? How might the writer's expertise or affiliation affect his or her point of view? For example, a writer for the National Oceanic and Atmospheric Administration (NOAA), a US federal agency, might have a slightly different point of view from that of Greenpeace, an independent environmental advocacy group based in the Netherlands. While some information is provided about the authors of the readings in this chapter, you can find out more by doing your own Internet searches.

Next, determine the topic of the source by previewing the reading. Analyze the title, and then scan the headings and subheadings, any photos, and finally the entire reading. Make a few predictions about what you believe the writer will discuss. Think about the topic. What do you already know about it? If water scarcity is the issue, for example, think through what you already know about water scarcity. Has water ever been rationed in your city? What have you heard about water availability in cities across the United States? As you read new information, try to connect it to what you already know about the subject.

Teaching Resources: See the *PowerPoint* (PPT) "Our Vulnerable Planet."

Here are two ways to encourage students to get additional bibliographic information:

- If you have access to a computer classroom, have students do the searches in class, either individually or in groups.

- Use a discussion board thread for students to post the information they find in their searches.

Read and Annotate the Text

Focus your first reading of the text on understanding the writer's *thesis statement* (the main idea of the reading) and the text's *major supporting points* (the ideas that provide evidence for the thesis statement). In longer readings, you may find several important ideas that seem like main ideas. Annotate each of these important ideas. You might simply write "imp. idea" in the margin. When you finish reading, look over each annotation. Which of your annotations identify major supporting points? Mark them with an abbreviation such as "msp." Which of your annotations refer to details that explain the major supporting points? You might use an abbreviation such as "sup" to indicate these details.

Once you have determined the major supporting details, you can use them to figure out the *broader* point they support. This broader point is likely to be the writer's thesis statement. Start by writing out the thesis statement in your own words, and then look for a sentence that matches yours. If you cannot find such a sentence, the thesis statement may be implied.

Be willing to change any incorrect annotations you have made. For example, at the beginning of a reading, you may believe a certain idea is a major supporting point, but after you finish the reading, you may realize the point is simply a detail. People who have extremely good reading skills make these kinds of mistakes all the time. Sometimes it is not possible to fully understand the relationships among ideas in a text until you read the text through more than once.

Focus your next reading of the selection on determining the criteria the writer is using to show the importance of the environmental issue. For example, if an entire portion of an article on water scarcity focuses on how manufacturing will be affected, the criterion being considered is "effect on manufacturing." If an article on water scarcity is written for farmers, the focus may be on how water shortages will hurt crops. Another writer may consider the issue of water scarcity in terms of how it will affect people who live in the Southwest.

As you notice issues and criteria, note them. Note also the key words used to discuss each criterion. The table that follows provides an example of two criteria with associated key words.

Issue: Water Scarcity

CRITERIA	KEY WORDS
Effects on crops	agriculture agricultural yields irrigation
Effects on major cities	rationing relocation of manufacturing and industry job losses relocation of residents

You do not yet have to choose the criteria you will use to judge which issue is the most serious. Simply be aware of the criteria that the writers use, and annotate the criteria when you see them.

Notice ideas that are unusual or interesting to you, and annotate them. When you chance upon "gold nuggets"—information that you find particularly noteworthy or that you think might be good to use in your own essay—be sure to make a note. Sometimes an interesting passage will make you ponder or will leave you with a question. Annotate passages like this, and jot down your thoughts. If you think of a question as you read a passage, write it down. If a passage reminds you of something, or if you can draw a connection to something in your life, make an annotation. If you find a startling or interesting fact or example, annotate it.

Teaching Resources: Determining the main idea of a long essay can be particularly challenging for students since many of the major supporting points are discussed in depth. For a handout on this topic, see "Understanding Long Readings."

Connect IRW Discussion Board (DB) Assignment: Create DB threads that help students articulate their comprehension of the articles, and create threads that help students read the articles critically. See the IM for particular DB thread prompts, or use the pre-loaded DB prompts in the Connect IRW *Common Places* Master Course.

To help students understand the way criteria are used to make judgments, consider asking them to debate their favorite Mexican (or Italian or Chinese) food restaurant in town. Discussion will help them figure out the criteria they think are most important for judging a restaurant's quality.

Make sure you find at least three passages that would be suitable as quotes, and put a star or check mark by each. Always read with an eye open for kernels of information that might be useful to you later when you are writing your own essay on the same or a related topic.

Outline and Summarize Each Reading

After you have read the source enough to feel that you fully understand it, write a simple outline for it. Include the writer's main idea, all of the major supporting points, and any supporting details you find important. From your simple outline, write a brief summary. When you refer back to your notes, the summary will help you remember the source's content. Additionally, you may find it helpful to include in your essay a brief summary of a source you have read.

Prepare an Information Sheet for Each Reading

With your outline and summary done, you can combine the other notes you took during the reading process to construct an information sheet. This page should include the source's bibliographic information, any general notes you took or ideas you had about the source, your outline, a brief summary, a list of the issues and key words in the essay, and potential quotes. Type the quotes into your information sheet word for word, and include the writer's name in parentheses after each quote. Later when you write your essay, you can simply copy and paste quotes into it.

Connect IRW Power of Process Assignment: Each reading can be set up in Power of Process so that students go through a reading process that matches the steps in this chapter. See the IM for more information.

Teaching Resources: If your course objectives do not include learning to create MLA or APA works cited or reference lists, see the IM for ideas about how to handle documentation.

READINGS FOR AN ANALYSIS AND EVALUATION ESSAY

Now we will put these steps into practice by using them to read, annotate, and analyze the first source. After we work through this process for the first reading, you will be prompted to use these steps on your own for the remaining three sources.

SOURCE 1 **"GLOBAL WATER CHALLENGE"**

The following selection is from *Environmental Science: A Study of Interrelationships*, 13th edition, a science textbook written by Eldon D. Enger and Bradley F. Smith and published in 2013.

To begin the reading process, we will preview the reading and think about the topic. The title gives us a clue about the topic: water as a global environmental issue. If you look over the selection, you will see that it covers water scarcity, water's uniqueness, and the need for clean drinking water. What do you already know about these issues? Are any of these issues particularly relevant to the area where you live? For example, many parts of the United States endure drought periodically, and some cities ration water during dry periods. By thinking about your existing knowledge, you can fit the new information into what you already know.

Next, notice the information about where this selection was published, and read the authors' biographies below. You will notice that the selection is from an environmental science textbook and that the authors are both professors and environmental scientists. Based on this information, you can expect the reading to be credible and the writers to be knowledgeable. Once you have previewed the reading and learned about its authors and context, you are ready to read and annotate the text itself.

ABOUT THE AUTHORS

Eldon D. Enger is an emeritus professor of biology at Delta College near Saginaw, Michigan. He received the Bergstein Award for Teaching Excellence and the Scholarly Achievement Award from Delta College and was selected as a Fulbright Exchange Teacher twice—to Australia and Scotland. He has made numerous contributions to environmental and humanitarian causes.

Bradley F. Smith is the dean of Huxley College of the Environment at Western Washington University in Bellingham, Washington. He was the first director of the Office of Environmental Education for the US Environmental Protection Agency from 1991 to 1994. He has a PhD from the School of Natural Resources and the Environment at the University of Michigan.

If your students have access to computers (or smartphones) in class, consider having them do an Internet search for the authors' names to see what additional information is available. With some prompting, students can usually make predictions about what the text will include based on the authors' biographical information.

Global Water Challenge

by Eldon D. Enger and Bradley F. Smith

In New Delhi, India, citizens wake in the morning to the sound of a megaphone announcing that freshwater will be available only for the next one hour. People then rush to fill the bathtub and other receptacles with water to last the day. New Delhi's endemic shortfalls of water occur largely because water managers decided several years ago to divert large amounts from upstream rivers and reservoirs to irrigate crops.

In arid Phoenix, Arizona, citizens often wake to the sounds of sprinklers watering suburban lawns and golf courses. Although Phoenix sits amid the Sonoran Desert, it enjoys a virtually unlimited water supply. Politicians there have allowed irrigation water to be shifted away from farming operations to cities and suburbs, while permitting recycled wastewater to be employed for landscaping and other nonpotable applications.

In China, almost a quarter of all surface water remains so polluted that it is unfit even for industrial use, while less than half of total supplies are drinkable. Despite tougher regulations over the last decade, China has struggled to rein in the thousands of small paper mills, cement factories, and chemical plants discharging industrial waste directly into the country's waterways. These three stories provide a look at some of the critical water challenges we are facing in the world today.

Global freshwater resources are threatened by rising demands from many areas. Growing populations need more water for drinking, hygiene, sanitation, food production, and industry. Climate change, meanwhile, is expected to contribute to more droughts. Policymakers must figure out how to supply water without degrading the natural ecosystems that provide it. Existing low-tech approaches can help reduce scarcity, as can ways to increase supplies, such as improved methods to desalinate water. Governments at all levels must start setting policies and making investments in infrastructure for water conservation. And, finally, individuals need to know how much water they use and how that amount used can be reduced. It has been said that we will find substitute forms of energy that are not fossil-fuel based, but we will never find a substitute for water.

Water in its liquid form is the material that makes life possible on Earth. All living organisms are composed of cells that contain at least 60 percent water. Furthermore, their metabolic activities take place in a water solution. Organisms can exist only where they have access to adequate supplies of water. Water is also unique because it has remarkable physical properties. Water molecules are polar; that is, one part of the molecule is slightly positive and the other is slightly negative. Because of this, the water

---

Lexile: 1300L

Writers use three examples to introduce the topic and lead up to the implied thesis statement.

Key word: *freshwater*

Example: Water is scarce for New Delhi's people.

Example: Water is scarce for farming operations in Arizona.

Key words: *wastewater, nonpotable* (not drinkable)

Example: Some water is so polluted in China that even industries cannot use it.

Thesis statement (implied): Water challenges today are critical, and governments must take action to solve these challenges.

Major supporting point (MSP) 1 (implied): Water scarcity is an issue that must and can be addressed.

Support for MSP 1

Key words: *freshwater resources, scarcity, desalinate, infrastructure, conservation*

Excellent quote. This may be one way in which the water issue is the most serious.

Major supporting point 2 (implied): Water is unique because it makes life possible, has remarkable physical properties, and is valuable for societal and industrial activities.

molecules tend to stick together, and they also have a great ability to separate other molecules from each other. Water's ability to act as a solvent and its capacity to store heat are a direct consequence of its polar nature. These abilities make water extremely valuable for societal and industrial activities. Water dissolves and carries substances ranging from nutrients to industrial and domestic wastes. A glance at any urban sewer will quickly point out the importance of water in dissolving and transporting wastes. Because water heats and cools more slowly than most substances, it is used in large quantities for cooling in electric power generation plants and in other industrial processes. Water's ability to retain heat also modifies local climatic conditions in areas near large bodies of water. These areas do not have the wide temperature-change characteristic of other areas.

For most human as well as some commercial and industrial uses, the quality of the water is as important as its quantity. Water must be substantially free of dissolved salts, plant and animal waste, and bacterial contamination to be suitable for human consumption. The oceans, which cover approximately 70 percent of the Earth's surface, contain over 97 percent of its water. However, saltwater cannot be consumed by humans or used for many industrial processes. Freshwater is free of the salt found in ocean waters. Of the freshwater found on Earth, only a tiny fraction is available for use. (See figure 1 on the next page.) Unpolluted freshwater that is suitable for drinking is known as potable water. Early human migration routes and settlement sites were influenced by the availability of drinking water. At one time, clean freshwater supplies were considered inexhaustible. Today, despite advances in drilling, irrigation, and purification, the location, quality, quantity, ownership, and control of potable waters remain important concerns.

To understand how water can become scarce, consider that the human population numbered under 2 billion in 1900, surpassed 6 billion by 2000, and is surging toward 9 billion by 2050. And we're not the only living organisms on this planet that need freshwater to survive.

The global water supply, by comparison, is finite. Whether it's in the form of ice, vapor, steam, or liquid, the amount of water on Earth today is about the same as the water that slaked the planet's thirst a million years ago. Only a very thin slice of that supply is the liquid freshwater that we depend upon for drinking, washing, irrigation, manufacturing, energy, and more.

The world's total water supply is estimated at about 1.38 billion cubic kilometers (333 million cubic miles). Of this, about 97.5 percent is saltwater and about 2.5 percent is freshwater. Most of the freshwater (78 percent) is locked up in glaciers and ice caps, about 21 percent is groundwater in deep sediments or soil, and less than 1 percent is surface water. About 87 percent of surface freshwater is in lakes, 11 percent in wetlands, and 2 percent in rivers.

Some areas of the world have abundant freshwater resources, while others have few. In addition, demand is increasing for freshwater for industrial, agricultural, and personal needs. Shortages of potable freshwater throughout the world can also be directly attributed to human abuse in the form of pollution. Water pollution has negatively affected water supplies throughout the world. In many parts of the developing world, people do not have access to safe drinking water. The World Health Organization estimates that about 25 percent of the world's people do not have access to safe

---

Support for MSP 2

Criterion: effects on health and life

Criterion: effects on industry

Criterion: effects on our lifestyles (water affects sewer system, electricity generation, local environments)

Major supporting point 3 (implied): Water quality must be addressed.

Support for MSP 3

Key words: *quality, irrigation, purification*

Criterion: relative scarcity of resource

Criterion: relative urgency

Major supporting point 4 (implied): Several factors result in water scarcity.

Support for MSP 4

Potential quote

Criterion: difficulty of finding a solution

Key words: *groundwater, demand*

Criterion: extensiveness of problem

Support for MSP 4

Potential quote

Oceans 97.57%

Total water

Ice and glaciers 1.90%
Groundwater 0.50%
Rivers and lakes 0.02%
Soil 0.01%

Freshwater

Ice and glaciers 78.19%

Groundwater 20.58%

Rivers and lakes
0.82%

Soil 0.41%

FIGURE 1 **Freshwater Resources**
Although water covers about 70 percent of the Earth's surface, over 97 percent is saltwater. Of the less than 3 percent that is freshwater, only a tiny fraction is available for human use.

drinking water. Even in the economically advanced regions of the world, water quality is a major issue. According to the United Nations Environment Program, 5 million to 10 million deaths occur each year from water-related diseases. The illnesses include cholera, malaria, dengue fever, and dysentery. The United Nations also reports that these illnesses have been increasing over the past decade and that without large economic investments in safe drinking-water supplies, the rate of increase will continue.

Unfortunately, the outlook for the world's freshwater supply is not very promising. According to studies by the United Nations and the International Joint Commission (a joint U.S.-Canadian organization that studies common water bodies between the two nations), many sections of the world are currently experiencing a shortage of freshwater, and the problem will only intensify.

Potential quote

Key word: *water-related diseases*

Criterion: health effects

Major supporting point 5

Water, used by households, agriculture, and industry, is clearly the most important good provided by freshwater systems. Humans now withdraw about one-fifth of the world's rivers' base flow (the dry-weather flow or the amount of available water in rivers most of the time), but in river basins in arid or populous regions the proportion can be much higher. This has implications for the species living in or dependent on these systems, as well as for human water supplies. Between 1900 and 2010, withdrawals increased by a factor of more than six, which is greater than twice the rate of population growth.

Water supplies are distributed unevenly around the world, with some areas containing abundant water and others a much more limited supply. In water basins with high water demand relative to the available runoff, water scarcity is a growing problem. Many experts, governments, and international organizations are predicting that water availability will be one of the major challenges facing human society in the twenty-first century and that the lack of water will be one of the key factors limiting development.

. . . Water experts define areas where per capita water supply drops below 1,700 m^3/year [about 449,000 gallons] as experiencing water stress—a situation in which disruptive water shortages can frequently occur. . . . [B]y 2025, assuming current consumption patterns continue, at least 3.5 billion people—or 43 percent of the world's projected population—will live in water-stressed river basins. Of these, 2.4 billion will live under high water stress conditions. This per capita water supply calculation, however, does not take into account the coping capabilities of different countries to deal with water shortages. For example, high-income countries that are water scarce may be able to cope to some degree with water shortages by investing in desalination or reclaimed wastewater.

Several river basins, including the Volta in Ghana, Nile in Sudan and Egypt, Tigris and Euphrates in the Middle East, Narmada in India, and the Colorado River basin in the United States, will go from having more than 1,700 m^3 to less than 1,700 m^3 of water per capita per year. Another 29 basins will descend further into scarcity by 2025, including the Indus in Pakistan, Huang He in China, Seine in France, Balsas in Mexico, and Rio Grande in the United States.

Increasing scarcity, competition, and arguments over water in the first quarter of the twenty-first century could dramatically change the way we value and use water and the way we mobilize and manage water resources. Furthermore, changes in the amount of rain from year to year result in periodic droughts for some areas and devastating floods for others. However, rainfall is needed to regenerate freshwater and, therefore, is an important link in the cycling of water.

SOURCE INFORMATION

Authors: Eldon D. Enger and Bradley F. Smith

Title: "Global Water Challenge"

Publication: *Environmental Science: A Study of Interrelationships,* 13th ed.

Publisher: McGraw-Hill

City: New York

Date: 2013

Pages: 333–34

**Side notes:**

Support for MSP 5

Criterion: economic effects

Key words: *base flow, river basins, withdrawals*

Support for MSP 5

Potential quote

Key words: *per capita water supply, consumption patterns, water stress, desalination*

Support for MSP 5

Potential quote: effects in the US

Support for MSP 5

Once you believe you correctly understand the reading, create an information sheet. The example that follows includes enough information to help you remember the main points of the reading so that you can use the source for your own writing later on.

Information Sheet: "Global Water Challenge"

GENERAL NOTES

- Authors: Eldon D. Enger and Bradley F. Smith
- Was published in a textbook (*Environmental Science: A Study of Interrelationships*)
- Presents reasons why the issue of water is so important

SIMPLE OUTLINE

Thesis statement (implied): Water challenges today are critical, and governments must take action to solve these challenges.

Major supporting point 1 (implied): Water scarcity is an issue that must and can be addressed.

Major supporting point 2 (implied): Water is unique because it makes life possible, has remarkable physical properties, and is valuable for societal and industrial activities.

Major supporting point 3 (implied): Water quality must be addressed.

Major supporting point 4 (implied): Several factors result in water scarcity.

Major supporting point 5: "Unfortunately, the outlook for the world's freshwater supply is not very promising" (Enger and Smith).

BRIEF SUMMARY

In "Global Water Challenge," Eldon D. Enger and Bradley F. Smith discuss the issue of water and its importance now and for the future. They point out that water challenges today are critical and governments must take action to solve these challenges. One challenge they discuss is water scarcity. Because water is unequally distributed throughout the world, scarcity affects regions differently. Scarcity is increasing because of droughts and overpopulation. Another challenge they discuss is water purity. Freshwater is required not only for human drinking but for most industrial uses, and freshwater supplies are dwindling. The authors discuss the uniqueness of water and show that nothing can take its place. The future will hold greater water challenges, according to the authors. For all of these reasons, governments must take the global water crisis seriously.

CRITERIA

- Effects on health and life
- Effects on industry
- Effects on our lifestyles (water affects sewer system, electricity generation, local environments)
- Relative scarcity of resource
- Relative urgency
- Difficulty of finding a solution
- Extensiveness of problem
- Health effects
- Economic effects

(continued)

KEY WORDS

freshwater	conservation	base flow
wastewater	quality	river basins
nonpotable	irrigation	withdrawals
freshwater resources	purification	per capita water supply
scarcity	groundwater	consumption patterns
desalinate	demand	water stress
infrastructure	water-related diseases	desalination

POTENTIAL QUOTES

- "It has been said that we will find substitute forms of energy that are not fossil-fuel based, but we will never find a substitute for water" (Enger and Smith).
- "[T]he amount of water on Earth today is about the same as the water that slaked the planet's thirst a million years ago" (Enger and Smith).
- "The World Health Organization estimates that about 25 percent of the world's people do not have access to safe drinking water" (Enger and Smith).
- "According to the United Nations Environment Program, 5 million to 10 million deaths occur each year from water-related diseases. The illnesses include cholera, malaria, dengue fever, and dysentery" (Enger and Smith).
- "[W]ater stress [is] a situation in which disruptive water shortages can frequently occur. . . . [B]y 2025, assuming current consumption patterns continue, at least 3.5 billion people—or 43 percent of the world's projected population—will live in water-stressed river basins. Of these, 2.4 billion will live under high water stress conditions" (Enger and Smith).
- "Several river basins, including the Volta in Ghana, Nile in Sudan and Egypt, Tigris and Euphrates in the Middle East, Narmada in India, and the Colorado River basin in the United States, will go from having more than 1,700 m^3 to less than 1,700 m^3 of water per capita per year" (Enger and Smith).

Complete the following exercise to bring together your knowledge of how to work with a source to produce meaningful information for a writing project.

PRACTICE ① Reflecting on the Selection

On a separate sheet, answer the following questions about "Global Water Challenge."

1. What is the purpose of this selection: To inform? To analyze? To evaluate? To persuade? Explain your answer in a paragraph or two.

2. List at least three reasons why the issue of water is important.

3. Which of the criteria used to discuss the seriousness of this issue do you find most important? (See the information sheet above.) For example, one criterion the writers use to judge the issue of water is the effect on human health. Which three criteria do you think are the most important? Explain your answer.

4. Choose one of the passages identified as a "good" or "possible" quotation, and explain when it would be appropriate to quote the passage in a paper you are writing.

Sample answers for Practice 1 follow.
1. The primary purpose is to inform, but the writers would also like readers to believe that something needs to be done about this problem.
2. Water is vital for life; we need water for industry; poor water quality results in disease.
3. Answers will vary.
4. The quotes would be appropriate as follows:
- "It has been said. . . . "—to stress the importance of the water issue.
- "[T]he amount of water on Earth. . . ."—to emphasize the point that water supply does not increase.
- "The World Health Organization. . . ."—to support the claim that we must do something to make safe water available to everyone.
- "According to the United Nations. . . ."—to shock people into seeing why they should do something about providing clean water for everyone.
- "[W]ater stress [is] a situation. . . "—to show that the water issue is urgent.
- "Several river basins. . . ."—to show the issue affects the United States as well as the rest of the world.

This selection includes information from the Web site of the World Wildlife Fund. The organization explains its goals simply: "We seek to save a planet, a world of life. Reconciling the needs of human beings and the needs of others that share the Earth, we seek to practice conservation that is humane in the broadest sense."

Follow the steps presented in this chapter as you read the selection, and keep your assignment and purpose in mind.

- Preview the reading and think about the topic.
- Read and annotate the text.

ABOUT THE AUTHOR
The material in this selection came from the Web site of the World Wildlife Fund.

The Loss of Biodiversity

Our planet is amazing. Viewed by someone not from our world, it could be seen as one big, finely tuned, and ultimately incredible machine with lots of cogs, pulleys, and wheels (animals, plants, and environments) working together. What we do not always see so clearly is how the cogs, pulleys, and wheels depend on one another to create the healthy world we enjoy. Perhaps more importantly, we do not always remember that our food, fuel, medicine, and other essentials come from the intricate workings of our planet. Fortunately, this complex and incredible machine can take some knocks and bruises. It can bounce back, stretch, adapt, and mend.

However, we are beginning to pull and stretch it further than it has ever been stretched before. We are entering unknown territory, where some of the extinctions we are causing may have deep and profound effects on how we live our lives. In the grand time scale of our planet, these effects may be currently seen as the equivalent of storm clouds gathering on the horizon. But rest assured, the storm is coming unless we begin to value and protect our planet.

A critical part of preserving our planet's ability to provide us with a livable environment is to protect biodiversity. Biodiversity refers to the existence of many millions of distinct biological species, the product of four billion years of evolution.

The word *biodiversity* itself is actually quite new. *Biodiversity* was coined as a contraction of "biological diversity" in 1985. A symposium in 1986, and the follow-up book *BioDiversity,* edited by biologist E. O. Wilson, paved the way for common acceptance of the word and concept.

Discussions about biodiversity have increased recently as the world has begun to lose species and habitats at an ever-increasing and alarming rate. One of the primary questions raised in these discussions is *Why is biodiversity decreasing?* Almost always, the answer is *Us.*

Another important question is *Just how many species are we losing?* This is a question that is difficult to answer. To begin with, we do not truly know what we have. Ours is a complex world, and we discover species new to science all the time.

Scientists were startled in 1980 by the discovery of a tremendous diversity of insects in tropical forests. In one study of just 19 trees in Panama, 80% of the 1,200 beetle species discovered were previously unknown to science. Surprisingly, scientists have a better understanding of how many stars there are in the galaxy than how many species there are on Earth (World Resources Institute).

YOUR ANNOTATIONS

Lexile: 1180L

Thus, if we don't know how much there is to begin with, we don't know exactly how much we are losing. But we do have research that indicates the news is not good. Just to illustrate the degree of biodiversity loss we are facing, consider this scientific analysis.

The rapid loss of species we are seeing today is estimated by experts to be between 1,000 and 10,000 times higher than the natural extinction rate. These experts calculate that between 0.01 and 0.1% of all species will become extinct each year. If the low estimate of the number of species out there is true—i.e., that there are around 2 million different species on our planet—then that means between 200 and 2,000 extinctions occur every year. But if the upper estimate of species numbers is true—that there are 100 million different species coexisting with us on our planet—then between 10,000 and 100,000 species are becoming extinct each year.

Unlike the mass extinction events of geological history, the current extinction challenge is one for which a single species—ours—appears to be almost wholly responsible. This is often referred to as the Sixth Extinction, so named because there have been five previous extinction waves in geological history. (The fifth crisis was the one that resulted in the extinction of the dinosaurs and nearly all large animal species living at that time.) The sixth may be the most catastrophic of all. It is estimated that half of all plant, animal, and bird species on the planet will become extinct before 2100.

So without arguing about who is right or wrong or what the exact numbers are, there is little debate that the crisis of biodiversity loss is very serious.

Biodiversity has declined by more than a quarter in the last thirty-five years. The Living Planet Index (LPI), which tracks nearly four thousand populations of wildlife, shows an overall decrease in wildlife populations of 27% between 1970 and 2005. In other words, the number of vertebrate animals in our world is decreasing. That is not good news.

In general terms, human population growth and our consumption habits are the reasons for this enormous loss. Specifically, habitat destruction and wildlife trade are the major causes of population decline in species. We have picked, logged, plucked, and hunted the flowers, trees, animals, and fish for medicine, souvenirs, status symbols, building materials, and food. And this overexploitation (hunting, fishing, bycatch) is not sustainable.

Bycatch: animals accidentally caught by nets used in commercial fishing.

Globally, we now require the equivalent of 1.4 planets to support our lifestyles. This is humanity's current ecological footprint—the demand people place on the natural world. In 2009, we used 40% more resources than nature can regenerate in a year. This problem—using resources faster than they can regenerate and creating waste such as CO_2 faster than it can be absorbed—is called *ecological overshoot.*

We currently maintain this overshoot by liquidating the planet's natural resources. We can cut trees faster than they regrow and catch fish at a rate faster than they repopulate. While this can be done for a short while, overshoot ultimately leads to the depletion of the resources on which our economy depends.

Adding to the problem is climate change. The full effects and impact on biodiversity and how life may (or may not) adapt is still very much an unknown quantity. What we do know, however, is that the next thirty years are critical. We also know that humans and human behavior have changed the Earth's ecosystems more rapidly and extensively in the past fifty years than in any other period of human history. Because biodiversity underpins the health of the planet, it has a direct impact on all our lives.

The Earth's natural assets are made up of plants, animals, land, water, the atmosphere, *and* humans. Together we all form part of the planet's ecosystems; thus, if there is a biodiversity crisis, our health and livelihoods are at risk too. Species, habitats, and local communities are under pressure or direct threat, such as the loss of access to fresh water.

Put simply, reduced biodiversity means millions of people face a future where food supplies are more vulnerable to pests and disease and where freshwater is in irregular or short supply. Human health is strongly linked to the health of ecosystems that meet many of our most critical needs. Understood in this way, the loss of biodiversity is, arguably, the greatest threat to world stability and security today.

One way decreases in biodiversity threaten the way we live is that such a decrease results in a reduction of ecosystem services. The term *ecosystem services* refers to the services we get from the natural world. Included under this umbrella designation are water, soil formation and protection, pollution breakdown and absorption, climate stability, and recovery from natural disasters.

How much are ecosystem services worth globally? According to IUCN, the World Conservation Union, the monetary value of goods and services provided by ecosystems is estimated to amount to some $33 trillion per year, a number that looks like this: $33,000,000,000,000.

Besides losing ecological services as biodiversity decreases, we will also see changes in our own cultural diversity. Cultural diversity and biodiversity are intimately related to each other. Humans have adapted to life according to the particular environment they have found themselves in. At the same time, they have had to draw on those resources to sustain themselves—whether that was in the icy tundra or tropical forests. This knowledge has been passed from generation to generation via language and practical teachings. It has shaped ways of life and worldviews and has served material as well as psychological and spiritual needs.

Cultural diversity has also led to the development of a strong "sense of place." If we lose our place, do we in effect lose ourselves?

Unquestionably, biodiversity decline and loss of ecosystem services pose a major global threat to future generations of humanity and even to the future of our planet. The good news is that there are things you can do to help reduce the threats to biodiversity. Here are some ways you can make a difference:

- Do not buy products made from the skin, fur, bone, shell, beak, or hooves of an endangered species. Buy wood and wood products that come from a sustainable source. Some analysts estimate the international trade of illegally logged products at around $5 billion per year. By questioning where your garden furniture or wooden flooring comes from, you can support those suppliers who are using sustainable logging practices. Look for the Forest Stewardship Council (FSC) label to be sure you are buying sustainably produced wood.

- Reduce paper consumption. Paper makes up 28% of municipal solid waste in the United States, more than any other material Americans throw away. Recycling can really make a difference. Using 100% recycled paper saves twenty-four trees per ton of paper. Americans recycled nearly 66% of the paper they used in 2011, but more can be done. Recycling reduces greenhouse gas emissions, conserves natural resources, and saves landfill space. Buy sustainable seafood. The diversity

YOUR ANNOTATIONS

The FSC promotes the care, management, and conservation of the world's forests.

of marine life is being systematically eroded by overfishing. Seventy-five percent of the world's fisheries are fully or overexploited. However, being intentional in shopping for seafood can help keep our oceans alive. Choose fish that are sustainable, avoiding endangered species like bluefin tuna or North Sea cod and selecting instead seafood labeled with the blue Marine Stewardship Council (MSC) logo.

The MSC promotes the responsible and sustainable production of seafood.

While most people probably cannot name a single recently extinct species, biodiversity does matter. Biodiversity contributes to the Earth's ability to provide clean water, nutritiously varied and abundant foods, oxygen, climate stability, and cultural diversity. If we fail to appreciate the importance of biodiversity, we may be ensuring not only the destruction of most species on Earth, but also our very own demise.

SOURCE INFORMATION
Title: "The Loss of Biodiversity"
Publication: World Wildlife Fund
(http://wwf.panda.org/about_our_earth/biodiversity)

Once you have finished reading and annotating the selection, create an information sheet for it.

PRACTICE ② Creating an Information Sheet for "The Loss of Biodiversity"

Using your annotations, create an information sheet that includes the following:

- General notes
- Simple outline
- Brief summary
- Criteria and key words
- Potential quotes

Answers will vary.

SOURCE 3   "POPULATION GROWTH"

The reading that follows, "Population Growth," is an excerpt from the 13th edition of *Environmental Science,* a textbook coauthored by William P. Cunningham and Mary Ann Cunningham.

Follow the steps presented in this chapter as you read the selection, and keep your assignment and purpose in mind.

- Preview the reading and think about the topic.
- Read and annotate the text.

ABOUT THE AUTHORS

Dr. William P. Cunningham is an emeritus professor at the University of Minnesota. In his thirty-eight-year career at the university, he taught a variety of biology courses, including Environmental Science, Conservation Biology, Environmental Health, Environmental Ethics, Plant Physiology, General Biology, and Cell Biology.

Dr. Mary Ann Cunningham is an associate professor of geography at Vassar College. She is interested in the structure and function of landscapes and in how changing landscapes influence habitat availability, especially for birds. She also studies how landscape change influences environmental quality and water quality.

Teaching Resources: Grading each information sheet each student submits is an onerous task. Consider (1) giving the information sheets one grade, (2) *deducting* points from students' essay grades if information sheets are not submitted or are not of high quality, or (3) awarding extra points for high-quality information sheets. See the IM for a discussion of strategies for grading the IRW projects in chapters 11–13.

Population Growth

by William P. Cunningham and Mary Ann Cunningham

YOUR ANNOTATIONS
Lexile: 1320L

Every second, on average, four or five children are born somewhere on the earth. In that same second, two other people die. This difference between births and deaths means a net gain of roughly 2.5 more humans per second in the world's population. In 2013 the total world population was at least 7.2 billion people and was growing at 1.13 percent per year. This means we are now adding nearly 80 million more people per year, and if this rate persists, our global population will double in about 62 years. Humans are now probably the most numerous vertebrate species on the earth. We also are more widely distributed and manifestly have a greater global environmental impact than any other species. For the families to whom these children are born, this may well be a joyous and long-awaited event. But is a continuing increase in humans good for the planet in the long run?

Many people worry that overpopulation will cause—or perhaps already is causing—resource depletion and environmental degradation that threaten the ecological life-support systems on which we all depend. These fears often lead to demands for immediate, worldwide birth control programs to reduce fertility rates and to eventually stabilize or even shrink the total number of humans.

Others believe that human ingenuity, technology, and enterprise can extend the world carrying capacity and allow us to overcome any problems we encounter. From this perspective, more people may be beneficial rather than disastrous. A larger population means a larger workforce, more geniuses, more ideas about what to do. Along with every new mouth comes a pair of hands. Proponents of this worldview—many of whom happen to be economists—argue that continued economic and technological growth can both feed the world's billions and enrich everyone enough to end the population explosion voluntarily. Not so, counter many ecologists. Growth is the problem; we must stop both population and economic growth.

Yet another perspective on this subject derives from social justice concerns. In this worldview, there are sufficient resources for everyone. Current shortages are only signs of greed, waste, and oppression. The root cause of environmental degradation, in this view, is inequitable distribution of wealth and power rather than population size. Fostering democracy, empowering women and minorities, and improving the standard of living of the world's poorest people are what are really needed. A narrow focus on population growth only fosters racism and an attitude that blames the poor for their problems while ignoring the deeper social and economic forces at work.

Whether human populations will continue to grow at present rates and what that growth would imply for environmental quality and human life are among the most central and pressing questions in environmental science. We will look at some causes of population growth as well as how populations are measured and described. Family planning and birth control are essential for stabilizing populations. The number of children a couple decides to have and the methods they use to regulate fertility, however, are strongly influenced by culture, religion, politics, and economics, as well as basic biological and medical considerations. We will examine how some of these factors influence human demographics.

Human Populations Grew Slowly Until Relatively Recently

For most of our history, humans have not been very numerous compared to other species. Studies of hunting and gathering societies suggest that the total world population was probably only a few million people before the invention of agriculture and the domestication of animals around 10,000 years ago. The larger and more secure food supply made available by the agricultural revolution allowed the human population to grow, reaching perhaps 50 million people by 5000 B.C.E. For thousands of years, the number of humans increased very slowly. Archaeological evidence and historical descriptions suggest that only about 300 million people were living at the time of Christ.

Until the Middle Ages, human populations were held in check by diseases, famines, and wars that made life short and uncertain for most people. Furthermore, there is evidence that many early societies regulated their population size through cultural taboos and practices such as abstinence and infanticide. Among the most destructive of natural population controls were bubonic plagues (or Black Death) that periodically swept across Europe between 1348 and 1650. It has been estimated that during the worst plague years (1348–1350) at least one-third of the European population perished. Notice, however, that this didn't retard population growth for very long. In 1650, at the end of the last great plague, there were about 600 million people in the world.

. . . Human populations began to increase rapidly after 1600 C.E. Many factors contributed to this rapid growth. Increased sailing and navigating skills stimulated commerce and communication between nations. Agricultural developments, better sources of power, and better health care and hygiene also played a role. We are now in an exponential or J curve pattern of growth.

It took all of human history to reach 1 billion people in 1804, but little more than 150 years to reach 3 billion in 1960. To go from 5 to 6 billion took only 12 years. Another way to look at population growth is that the number of humans tripled during the twentieth century. Will it do so again in the twenty-first century? If it does, will we overshoot the carrying capacity of our environment and experience a catastrophic dieback? There is evidence that population growth already is slowing, but whether we will reach equilibrium soon enough and at a size that can be sustained over the long term remains a difficult but important question.

Perspectives on Population Growth

As with many topics in environmental science, people have widely differing opinions about population and resources. Some believe that population growth is the ultimate cause of poverty and environmental degradation. Others argue that poverty, environmental degradation, and overpopulation are all merely symptoms of deeper social and political factors. The worldview we choose to believe will profoundly affect our approach to population issues. In this section we will examine some of the major figures and their arguments in this debate.

Does Environment or Culture Control Human Populations?

Since the time of the Industrial Revolution, when the world population began growing rapidly, individuals have argued about the causes and consequences of population growth. In 1798 Thomas Malthus (1766–1834) wrote "An Essay on the Principle of Population," changing the way European leaders thought about population growth. Malthus marshaled evidence to show that populations tended to increase at an exponential, or compound, rate while food production either remained stable or increased only slowly. Eventually human populations would outstrip their food supply and collapse into starvation, crime, and misery. He converted most economists of the day from believing that high fertility increased gross domestic output to believing that per capita output actually fell with rapidly increasing population.

In Malthusian terms, growing human populations stop growing when disease or famine kills many, or when constraining social conditions—late marriage, insufficient resources, celibacy, and "moral restraint"—compel others to reduce their birth rates. Several decades later, the economist Karl Marx (1818–1883) presented an opposing view, that population growth resulted from poverty, resource depletion, pollution, and other social ills. Slowing population growth, said Marx, required that people be treated justly, and that exploitation and oppression be eliminated from social arrangements.

Marx and Malthus developed their theories about human population growth when views about the world, technology, and society were much different than they are today. But these different views of human population growth still inform competing approaches to family planning today. On the one hand, some believe that we are approaching, or may have surpassed, the earth's carrying capacity. Joel Cohen, a mathematical biologist at Rockefeller University, reviewed published estimates of the maximum human population size the planet can sustain. The estimates, spanning 300 years of thinking, converged on a median value of 10–12 billion. We are more than 7 billion strong today, and growing, an alarming prospect for some. Cornell University entomologist David Pimental, for example, has said: "By 2100, if current trends continue, twelve billion miserable humans will suffer a difficult life on Earth." In this view, birth control should be our top priority.

On the other hand, many scholars agree with Marx that improved social conditions and educational levels can stabilize populations humanely. In this perspective, the earth is bountiful in its resource base, but poverty and high birth rates result from oppressive social relationships that unevenly distribute wealth and resources. Consequently, this position believes, technological development, education, and just social conditions are the means of achieving population control. Mohandas Gandhi stated it succinctly: "There is enough for everyone's need, but not enough for anyone's greed."

Technology Can Increase Carrying Capacity for Humans

Optimists argue that Malthus was wrong 200 years ago in his predictions of famine and disaster because he failed to account for scientific and technical progress. In fact, food supplies have increased faster than population growth since Malthus's time. For example, according to the UN FAO Statistics Division, the average per capita daily food consumption across the whole world provided 2,435 calories per day in 1970, while in 2000 the average caloric intake reached 2,807 calories. Even poorer, developing countries saw a rise, from an average of 2,135 calories per day in 1970 to 2,679 in 2000. In that same period the world population went from 3.7 to more than 6 billion people. Certainly terrible famines have stricken different locations in the past 200 years, but they were caused more by politics and economics than by lack of resources or population size. Whether the world can continue to feed its growing population remains to be seen, but technological advances have vastly increased human carrying capacity so far.

Entomologist: a scientist who studies insects.

Mohandas Gandhi (1869–1948) used nonviolent protests to help India gain independence from Great Britain. His methods for demanding civil rights inspired many other civil rights leaders.

UN FAO: United Nations Food and Agriculture Organization.

The burst of world population growth that began 200 years ago was stimulated by scientific and industrial revolutions. Progress in agricultural productivity, engineering, information technology, commerce, medicine, sanitation, and other achievements of modern life have made it possible to support thousands of times as many people per unit area as was possible 10,000 years ago. Economist Stephen Moore of the Cato Institute in Washington, D.C., regards this achievement as "a real tribute to human ingenuity and our ability to innovate." There is no reason, he argues, to think that our ability to find technological solutions to our problems will diminish in the future.

Much of our growth and rising standard of living in the past 200 years, however, has been based on easily acquired natural resources, especially cheap, abundant fossil fuels. Whether rising prices of fossil fuels will constrain that production and result in a crisis in food production and distribution, or in some other critical factor in human society, concerns many people. However, technology can be a double-edged sword. Our environmental effects aren't just a matter of sheer population size; they also depend on what kinds of resources we use and how we use them. This concept is summarized as the I = **PAT** formula. It says that our environmental impacts (I) are the product of our population size (P) times affluence (A) and the technology (T) used to produce the goods and services we consume.

While increased standards of living in Brazil, for example, have helped stabilize population, they also bring about higher technological impacts. A family living an affluent lifestyle that depends on high levels of energy and material consumption, and that produces excessive amounts of pollution, could cause greater environmental damage than a whole village of hunters and gatherers or subsistence farmers.

Put another way, if the billions of people in Asia, Africa, and Latin America were to reach the levels of consumption now enjoyed by rich people in North America or Europe, using the same technology that provides that lifestyle today, the environmental effects will undoubtedly be disastrous. Growing wealth in China—its middle class is now estimated at about 300 million, or nearly the entire population of the United States—is already stressing world resources, for example, and has made China the largest emitter of CO_2. There are now more millionaires in China than in all of Europe, and China has passed the United States in annual automobile production.

But China has also become the global leader in renewable energy, and is now promoting electric vehicles. Ideally, all of us will begin to use nonpolluting, renewable energy and material sources. Better yet, we'll extend the benefits of environmentally friendly technology to the poorer people of the world so everyone can enjoy the benefits of a better standard of living without degrading our shared environment.

Population Growth Could Bring Benefits

Think of the gigantic economic engines that large countries, such as the United States and China, represent. More people mean larger markets, more workers, and efficiencies of scale in mass production of goods. Moreover, adding people boosts human ingenuity and intelligence that will create new resources by finding new materials and discovering new ways of doing things. Economist Julian Simon (1932–1998), a champion of this rosy view of human history, believed that people are the "ultimate resource" and that no evidence suggests that pollution, crime, unemployment, crowding, the loss of species, or any other resource limitations will worsen with population growth. In a famous bet in 1980, Simon challenged Paul Ehrlich, author of

The Population Bomb, to pick five commodities that would become more expensive by the end of the decade. Ehrlich chose metals, which actually became cheaper, and he lost the bet. Leaders of many developing countries insist that, instead of being obsessed with population growth, we should focus on the inordinate consumption of the world's resources by people in richer countries.

SOURCE INFORMATION

Authors: William P. Cunningham and Mary Ann Cunningham
Title: "Population Growth"
Publication: *Environmental Science,* 13th ed.
Publisher: McGraw-Hill
City: New York
Date: 2015
Pages: 135–39

When you have finished reading and annotating the selection, complete the exercise below to create notes for this source.

PRACTICE ③ Creating an Information Sheet for "Population Growth"

Using your annotations, create an information sheet that includes the following:

- General notes
- Simple outline
- Brief summary
- Criteria and key words
- Potential quotes

Answers will vary.

SOURCE 4   **"SEA CHANGE: FOOD FOR MILLIONS AT RISK"**

The article that follows was published in *The Seattle Times,* Seattle's major newspaper, in 2013.
    Follow the steps presented in this chapter as you read the selection, and keep your assignment and purpose in mind.

- Preview the reading and think about the topic.
- Read and annotate the text.

ABOUT THE AUTHOR

Craig Welch has been writing about the environment and natural resources for *The Seattle Times* for more than thirteen years. He is a two-time winner of the Society of Environmental Journalists' top prize for beat reporting and is a former Nieman Fellow at Harvard University. This article appeared in the December 21, 2013, issue of *The Seattle Times.*

This article is part of a series of stories about ocean degradation made possible by a grant from the Pulitzer Foundation. The article appears in full, along with many other stories by the authors, on the *Seattle Times* Web site at http://apps.seattletimes.com/reports/sea-change/2013/dec/21/food-for-millions-at-risk. The accompanying photography is remarkable and may pique student interest.

Sea Change: Food for Millions at Risk

by Craig Welch

Tadi had just returned in his dugout canoe from scanning crevices in a nearby reef for octopus. He and his neighbors spend every day this way—scouring the ocean for something to eat or sell. Fishing, here, is about survival.

Their stilt village has no industry, no land, no running water. They dive without oxygen, wearing hand-carved wooden goggles, and carry spear guns hacked from logs with their machetes. They eat what they catch and sell the rest, using the money to buy everything else they need: boat fuel, root vegetables, rice, wood.

Without fishing, "how would I feed my family?" asked Tadi, who like many Indonesians has only one name.

Now Tadi's community, like countless others across the globe, is on a collision course with the industrialized world's fossil-fuel emissions.

Hundreds of millions of people around the world rely on marine life susceptible to warming temperatures and ocean acidification, the souring of seas from carbon dioxide emitted by burning coal, oil and natural gas. That includes Northwest oyster growers and crabbers in the frigid Bering Sea, who now face great uncertainty from shifts in marine chemistry.

But from Africa to Alaska, many coastal communities face a substantially greater risk. These cultures are so thoroughly dependent on marine life threatened by CO_2 that a growing body of research suggests their children or grandchildren could struggle to find enough food.

The science of deciphering precisely who might see seafood shortages remains embryonic.

But with many of the most at-risk coastal communities already facing poverty, marine pollution, overfishing and rising seas, the potential for calamity is high.

"I can't tell you how many people will be affected," said Sarah Cooley, at Woods Hole Oceanographic Institution in Massachusetts, who studies links between acidification and food security. "But it's going to be a very big number."

Said Andreas Andersson, an acidification and coral reef expert with the Scripps Institution of Oceanography in San Diego: "These people are literally going to be fighting for their lives."

Among the most vulnerable to changing ocean conditions are people like Tadi and his 1,600 fellow villagers—even if they don't quite view it that way yet.

Culture Built on Sea

From his elevated perch sheltered from the midday sun, Tadi could see huts with wispy thatch roofs connected by the rickety planks of his village boardwalk. Everything stood a dozen feet above emerald waters.

Like many in his village, he's uncertain of his age. But for as long as he can remember, Tadi has netted, trapped, hooked or speared grouper, snapper, wrasses and parrotfish. Sometimes the men in his village disappear to the open sea for days to chase small tuna.

Women swarm the tide flats gathering clams, sea cucumbers, urchins and sea grass. They then paddle to a fish market on nearby Kaledupa Island, where even meaty catches fetch just a few dollars.

Among his peers, Tadi is considered one of the best spear fishermen. And no wonder: He said he stabbed his first fish when he was barely older than a toddler.

That childhood in the ocean left an impression. Every animal seemed huge. Sea life teemed wherever he looked.

"I could choose with my spear whatever fish I want," Tadi said through a translator. "I never caught any small fish."

Tadi taught his son, Laoda, to fish this way. Laoda has since taught his son, Adi.

The Sama people, or Bajau, are known as sea gypsies or sea nomads because they once lived mostly on boats. They roamed Southeast Asia between Malaysia, the Philippines and Indonesia, living off the sea, until governments began encouraging them to settle. Tadi's offshore village was built in the late 1950s.

Today, up to a million sea nomads are sprinkled throughout the Coral Triangle. Their lives are a blend of old ways and new.

Some divers in Tadi's village ruptured their eardrums as kids to make equalizing easier. Women dab their faces with rice paste for sunscreen. Villagers stack dead coral for support around the poles that hold their homes. Even fishing weights are sometimes homemade, forged by melting lead in aluminum cans over small open fires and pouring it into wooden molds.

Diesel generators provide electricity a few hours each night, and some residents use it to power televisions. Some fishermen wear expensive dive watches. On a mound of coral rubble beneath one hut is a surprisingly well-maintained billiard table.

After centuries of traveling far and wide, the Bajau's relocation concentrated their human waste and limited the range of their fishing. This happened just as some in their village adopted the destructive practices of Asia's worst fishing fleets. A few here fish with coral-destroying bombs or cyanide. Some from the village and nearby islands gather colorful reef fish for sale to the aquarium trade. Commercial trawlers from elsewhere cause more damage. It all takes a toll.

Trawler: a fishing boat that uses a net to catch fish.

"There's been a pretty substantial decrease in their catches per amount of effort since the 1990s," said Paul Simonin, a Cornell University graduate student who has tracked Bajau fishing data.

Tadi's neighbors and nearby island communities still land plenty of fish, but their reefs have seen better days. Everyone works a bit harder to find food.

And a coming storm from CO_2 will only make things worse.

Troubled Reefs

Scientists are still navigating the complex ways carbon dioxide can alter the marine world. But some impacts are clear.

Rising temperatures already wreak havoc on corals. Warming waters can cause corals to eject the algae that give them their vibrant color, weakening or killing reefs and turning them white. This process is known as bleaching. Without reductions in global emissions, 90 percent of reefs by midcentury are projected to see severe bleaching episodes every year.

Ocean acidification will just compound the problem.

A quarter of the CO_2 spewed by cars and power plants winds up in the ocean. That lowers the pH, makes waters more corrosive and reduces carbonate ions, which then makes it harder for marine creatures to build their shells and skeletons.

Acidification can directly harm animals throughout the food web, from microscopic plankton to some fish. It endangers corals, weakening their skeletons, inhibiting growth, and increasing the likelihood of bleaching. In fact, acidification even accelerates the dissolution and breakdown of the reef.

Together, souring seas and warming can be worse than the sum of their parts.

"Temperature has zapped a lot of reefs so far, but longer-term effects are likely to come from acidification," said Charles Sheppard, a professor at England's University of Warwick who studies climate-change impacts on coral reefs.

These ocean changes may not directly hit the octopus and fish Tadi catches, but will almost certainly rearrange the foods available for those creatures to eat. And loss of coral, by itself, usually translates to fewer fish and marine creatures—often substantially fewer.

Earlier this month, researchers working on reefs naturally bathed in CO_2 in Papua New Guinea reported finding half as many small invertebrates—crabs, shrimp, sand dollars, marine worms—as on healthy corals.

"Think about a coral reef as a city, a lot of buildings and houses," Andersson said. "Without the houses, you have no inhabitants."

Scientists are still learning how much—or how little—marine life might adapt. Some corals appear more resilient than others, and bleaching doesn't always ruin healthy reefs, said David Kline, a coral and climate change scientist at Scripps.

But reefs across Southeast Asia, in particular, already are a fraction of what they once were, according to a 2007 analysis. And reefs taxed by pollution or overfishing are more susceptible to mat-forming algae. In the worst cases, after bleaching, this weedy slime can smother corals for good.

Sheppard has seen how bad things can get. A few years after a 1998 bleaching off Qatar, he went diving on a nearby reef.

Except for weeds, "I didn't see one other living thing," he said. "No fish, urchins, starfish, mollusks. Nothing. For acres and acres, it was all dead."

He likened the stress many reefs face to a person suffering multiple illnesses.

"A bit of temperature rise. A bit of acidification. A bit of overfishing. These things add up," he said. "If someone has measles and influenza and chickenpox and malaria all at the same time, they're probably going to die."

Millions Face the Threat

In the grassy shallows a few hundred yards from Tadi's hut, his neighbor Mbilia sat curled in her canoe, plucking sea urchins from the water and halving them with her machete.

She could not even contemplate a reef with almost no fish. The prospect, to her, seemed amusing.

"I am an old woman," Mbilia said. "I'm not thinking a lot about that."

Tadi and Laoda usually don't think about it much, either. But there are days when fishing is so slow it's a possibility they just can't ignore.

"Sometimes we eat everything in one day," Laoda said. "But if we can't find anything, we don't eat."

Some Bajau don't believe humans can alter the marine world. Even harder to grasp is the possibility that actions now could cause future decay. For some here, successful fishing is dictated by the whims of testy sea gods.

"They do not see a cause-and-effect relationship the way we do," said Julian Clifton, a University of Western Australia professor who has studied Tadi's village. "The Bajau get characterized as backward because they don't get this idea. But their relationship with time is different from ours. They live in a sort of constant present."

It's in part why villagers don't know their own ages.

If fishing worsens dramatically for Tadi, options appear limited. Fishermen could keep pushing out into the ocean, or the village could fold up and move away, or turn to fish farming. The first might be possible. The second two are much harder.

The Bajau are short on money and clout. They remain among the region's poorest coastal residents, an ethnic minority often disparaged by others. And by the time they could face real trouble, others around the world may have similar problems, straining resources that otherwise might help.

At least 6 million people in 99 countries fish coral reefs, according to research published in the journal *PLOS One* in June. Another 400 million or more are tied indirectly to coral. Indonesia alone is home to nearly 1,000 inhabited islands, many of which are filled with people who depend on reefs.

"In the 15 or 16 countries we've surveyed, 50 to 90 percent of their protein comes from fish," said Johann Bell, a fish expert helping Pacific Island nations deal with threats to seafood. "It's a huge problem. There are going to be many who just fall below the radar."

Some places, like the South Pacific's Cook Islands, import much of their food, including chicken, mussels, beef, pork and shrimp, with income generated by industries at risk from CO_2—reef fishing, pearl oyster growing, reef tourism.

In one village in Tanzania in East Africa, three-quarters of households fish or make their living off troubled reefs, with no other jobs nearby. And most villagers migrated from places with even less work and poorer food options.

"Getting another job would mean starting a farm or setting up a bodega, both of which take a huge upfront investment they don't have," said Joshua Cinner, a research fellow with James Cook University in Australia.

Poor vanilla farmers in Madagascar already work several other jobs—yet fish reefs for food and income. In Haiti and Senegal, residents already struggling with malnutrition eat large volumes of wild shellfish, which are particularly threatened by acidification.

Even in southeast Alaska, a few coastal communities are so isolated that subsistence gathering of at-risk clams and crab is essential.

Subsistence gathering: the process of gathering food one needs to survive.

"There may be a grocery store but food is tremendously expensive," said Cooley, at Woods Hole. "Not everyone has $10 for a can of Spam."

"It Chills Me"

Thirty feet below the sea surface, Tadi's son, Laoda, inched toward a hefty perchlike reef fish called a sweetlips. He squeezed the spear gun's trigger. A metal shaft pierced the fish's scales. Laoda floated up and grabbed a breath.

Some young men in their village already escape to Malaysia to work on ships. Others dream of their children working on land.

Scientists hope growth in fish farming could help remote villages keep hunger at bay. Bell and others are helping subsistence fishermen boost their luck catching tuna and other open-ocean species. A few Bajau villages now farm seaweed for income.

But without CO_2 reductions, many see rough seas ahead. Carol Turley, at the United Kingdom's Plymouth Marine Lab, was among the first to suggest that some coastal people will face starvation risks as a result of warming and acidification. Even now, she said, "it chills me."

"I keep, keep hoping that I'm wrong about all this, but I don't think I am," she said.

For now Tadi and Laoda will keep fishing—and continue not thinking much about the future. That is how Tadi was raised. It's how he raised Laoda.

Laoda would like his son, Adi, to get an education, so he could try something new if he wishes. But Laoda and Tadi also said it would be OK if Adi stayed a fisherman.

Adi already has shown his grandfather's talent with a spear gun.

SOURCE INFORMATION

Author: Craig Welch

Title: "Sea Change: Food for Millions at Risk"

Publication: *The Seattle Times*

Date: 21 December 2013

When you have finished reading and annotating the article, complete the exercise below to create notes for this source.

PRACTICE 4 Creating an Information Sheet for "Sea Change: Food for Millions at Risk"

Using your annotations, create an information sheet that includes the following: *Answers will vary.*

- General notes
- Simple outline
- Brief summary
- Criteria and key words
- Potential quotes

DEVELOPING YOUR ESSAY

The readings in this chapter have given you information about four of the serious environmental issues we face today. As you analyze these sources and evaluate the most important environmental issue, the following steps will lead you through the process of writing your essay on this topic.

Synthesize Your Sources

At this point, you have read about a variety of environmental issues, and you have been introduced to various criteria writers use to analyze those issues. Using a chart like the one we began earlier in this chapter, write down each environmental issue, the criteria used to analyze the issue, and the key words associated with each criterion. Some of the criteria will be the same for the different issues. For example, one writer may discuss the health effects of the shortage of sanitary drinking water, and another may discuss the health effects of polluting the oceans.

Prewrite to Develop Your Ideas

Review the Assignment

When you have a complex assignment like this one, it is helpful to break the task into steps. Start by rereading the assignment, paying particular attention to the highlighted verbs.

Teaching Resources: Consider having your students save their documents to a free cloud storage site. Doing so allows students instant access to their work and eliminates the problem of lost flash drives. For more information about free, student-friendly cloud Web sites, see the IM.

Analysis and Evaluation Reading and Writing Assignment

You will read four selections that present serious environmental threats. Your task is to read, annotate, and analyze each source. Next, you will create a list of criteria to help you determine which environmental threat is the most serious, the one that deserves our attention first. You will then use these criteria to evaluate environmental threats and make a judgment about the one we should prioritize.

Once you have analyzed the sources and used criteria to make an evaluative judgment, you will write an essay in which you present your analysis, criteria, and evaluation. You will need to use evidence from the sources to support your point, giving credit to those sources by using the method of documentation approved by your instructor.

*Annotations (left):*
- Create a list of criteria to determine the most serious threat.
- Make a judgment.
- Use evidence from the sources.
- Give credit to the sources using an approved method.

*Annotations (right):*
- Read, annotate, and analyze four selections about environmental issues.
- Use the criteria to evaluate the environmental threats.
- Write an essay to present your analysis, criteria, and evaluation.

Select an Issue to Write About

Make a list of the things you need to do—based on the highlighted verbs—and put your list in a logical order. Determine which one you need to do first, which one second, and so on.

1. Create a list of criteria to determine the most serious threat.
2. Use the criteria to evaluate the environmental threats.
3. Make a judgment about which environmental issue should be considered most serious.
4. Write an essay to present your analysis, criteria, and evaluation.
5. Use evidence from the sources.
6. Give credit to the sources using an approved method.

Create a List of Criteria to Determine the Most Serious Threats

You have already noted the criteria you found in the sources you read. List all of the criteria you found, and if you wish, you may add your own criteria to the list. The box that follows provides a few examples of the kinds of criteria to list.

Criteria for Evaluating the Seriousness of Environmental Issues

- Effects on health
- Effects on jobs
- Potential of the issue to cause loss of human life
- Potential of the issue to damage wildlife

Use the Criteria to Evaluate Environmental Threats

Once you have generated a list of criteria, choose three or four from your list to use for your evaluation. Next, create a chart to help you analyze the issues. Examine each issue as it relates to each criterion you have chosen. If you are unsure about how a particular issue relates, just jot down "unsure." In the chart on the next page, two criteria have been analyzed for you as examples.

Margin notes (right, in red):

Teaching Resources: To help students understand how to establish and use criteria, see the PPT "Using Criteria for Evaluations." Also, see the exercise "Using Criteria."

Teaching Resources: Consider setting aside a day for students to work on these early writing process steps in class. Students who find the assignment overwhelming will feel more confident about writing their essays on their own after having completed the early steps in class. See the IM for additional ideas about teaching the project in chapters 11–13.

	WATER CRISIS	BIODIVERSITY	OVERPOPULATION	OCEANS
Effects on health	• Causes illness and death all over the world	• Loss of plant species can affect the creation of drugs • Changing ecosystems can have health effects (example: more mosquitos, more malaria)	• Potential starvation and malnutrition	• Affects health of sea animals • Mercury in fish affects human health • Can result in hunger/scarcity (overfishing)
Effects on jobs	• Increase in unemployment	• Unsure	• Unemployment will probably increase	• Loss of jobs in fish-related industry • Loss of lifestyle/home for many people

Decide Which Environmental Issue Should Be Considered Most Serious

As you examine your completed chart, use the information to identify the issue you believe is most important. To make this decision, you may have to rank the criteria you have chosen. For example, if you use "effects on jobs" and "effects on health" as criteria, you should determine which of these criteria is most important.

Once you have evaluated each issue by using the criteria, you are ready to decide which issue you believe should be prioritized. The issue you select will become the topic of your essay.

Construct a Thesis Statement

Once you have selected a topic, you are ready to write a thesis statement. Since you have already used criteria to determine which issue is most important, you can use those criteria to support your thesis statement. You can write an open thesis statement (your point of view without listing your reasons) or a closed thesis statement (your point of view with a shortened list of reasons).

Open thesis statement: The environmental issue that must be prioritized is the global water crisis.

Closed thesis statement: The environmental issue that must be prioritized is the global water crisis because of the effects water has on the economy, our lifestyles, and our health.

Develop Support for Your Thesis Statement

To develop support, work with each criterion individually. You may want to do additional prewriting by listing ideas about the criterion's relationship to the issue, like this:

The Water Crisis—Effects on Economy

- Industries would lay off workers or close.
- People would move from locations that have water shortages; domino effect—businesses in those areas would close, cities absorbing the new people might face water shortages themselves.
- The world economy might be affected; countries without enough water may go broke; imports from those countries may cease, causing a domino effect.

Create an Outline to Organize Your Essay

Once you have figured out the analysis and evaluation, you can create an outline to organize your thoughts. Sometimes students believe their essays must consist of only five paragraphs, but as you will see in the outline on the next page, the number of paragraphs in an essay depends on the content. For instance, the economic effects of a water short-age would be experienced on both a local level and an international level. Because the writer would have enough information to discuss these effects separately, she can create an outline for her essay that includes two body paragraphs on the economic effects of water shortages. She will develop the next two criteria—effects on lifestyle and effects on health—in a single paragraph each.

Simple Outline

Title: Why We Must Solve the Water Problem

INTRODUCTION

Paragraph 1: Start with an overview of the problems mentioned in this chapter. Work up to the most serious problem: water.

Thesis statement: The environmental issue that must be prioritized is water scarcity and quality because of the effects water has on the economy, our life-styles, and our health.

BODY

Paragraph 2: A water shortage will have serious effects on the economies of many cities in the United States.

Paragraph 3: In addition to affected local economies, a water shortage will affect the world's economies.

Paragraph 4: A shortage of water will also affect the lifestyles of most people.

Paragraph 5: Most importantly, a shortage of potable water will result in serious health effects for people around the globe.

CONCLUSION

Paragraph 6: Brief discussion of how water shortages are related to most of the other environmental problems.

Add Source Materials to Your Outline

Now that you have a basic outline, you can add source materials to it. Decide where you will use ideas from your sources, and make notes on your outline. If you plan to use par-ticular quotes, copy and paste the quotes into your outline, making sure to include the writer's name in parentheses. If you are using APA style, you should also note the date of the source and the page number, if available, like this: (Williams, 2006, p. 15). The example below shows how the writer added source material to a section of her outline and included MLA-style citations.

Paragraph 2: A shortage of potable water will have serious effects on the economies of many cities in the United States.

- Each city affected differently, especially those that depend on river basins:
  - "Several river basins, including . . . the Colorado River basin in the United States, will go from having more than 1,700 m^3 to less than 1,700 m^3 of water per capita per year" (Enger).
- Explanation of quote from Enger.
- Water shortages in major cities will decrease industry.

(continued)

- Industry will move.
- People will lose jobs, so people will move.
  - Hypothetical example showing domino effect in a US city
- Economy will be affected by loss of jobs, loss of consumers/customers in areas.

Notice that some of the information comes from a source, but the explanation, discussion, and hypothetical example come from the writer. In this kind of essay, you will need to think about what the effects might be. The sources you use will give you basic information, but you can imagine scenarios that will help your reader understand the importance of the environmental issue. For example, the source tells us that cities that depend on river basins for their water will be vulnerable to water scarcity. You can use this information to imagine what might happen in such cities, creating a hypothetical scenario:

Hypothetical Example

Suppose a city depends on a river basin for its water supply. If the river basin dries up, the city will face severe problems. Water could be imported from other areas, but the cost would be high. Industries that depend on water might go bankrupt or might pack up and leave town. Workers from those industries would be left jobless. They, too, might have to move to find jobs. When people start moving out of a city, the local economy crashes. Restaurants, shops, and other businesses that depend on consumers are affected, and without those consumers, businesses will close. Soon, an entire city will be devastated because of one primary cause: a water shortage.

Consider spending some time in class helping students learn to write good hypothetical examples. Knowing how to write a reasonable and convincing hypothetical example will help students with many writing tasks, as such examples are appropriate for a variety of writing purposes.

Write a Complete Draft of Your Essay

At this point, you have completed your analysis and evaluation, and you have constructed an outline. You can now start drafting your essay. As you draft, follow these steps.

Keep an Audience in Mind

The best tool to use when drafting is your imagination: imagine having a conversation with a smart person who disagrees with your point. Word your essay in such a way that you would be able to convince this critical reader that your claim is correct.

Write an Introduction Paragraph, and Consider Where You Will Place Your Thesis Statement

The introduction can be a great place to provide background information. For this topic, you have compared a number of environmental issues to determine the one that is most pressing. To introduce your essay, you could comment on the importance of each issue and lead up to your thesis statement.

Write Body Paragraphs according to Your Outline

Use your detailed outline to draft your essay. Any time you refer to the sources or to your notes, keep in mind you will need to cite those sources. In other words, if you look back to a source for an idea, that idea came from the source; thus, include a simple reference to the source when you refer to it in your paper. For more information about how to correctly integrate material and credit your sources, see the Quick Start Guide to Integrated Reading and Writing Assignments.

End with an Effective Conclusion

One method for concluding an essay about the potential effects of something is to make a prediction. What will happen if we do not address water issues now? Make sure the prediction you use is reasonable. For example, it would be unreasonable to say that if your city does not take action immediately, it will shut down in five years. It would be reasonable, however, to say that if we don't start solving this problem now, we will be facing a crisis situation later. Using a prediction to reiterate the importance of the issue may encourage readers to act on the issue.

Integrate Ideas and Quotes from Sources Correctly

When you use source materials, integrate them grammatically so that they work with your words to form complete sentences. The improper integration of quotations can result in a comma splice or a run-on sentence.

Comma splice error: Mark Miller explains that the struggle to find clean water will be the issue that defines the next twenty years, "We are focused on energy production, but water will be the issue on which our lives will depend."

Correct: Mark Miller explains that the struggle to find clean water will be the issue that defines the next twenty years: "We are focused on energy production, but water will be the issue on which our lives will depend."

Correct: Mark Miller explains that the struggle to find clean water will be the issue that defines the next twenty years, claiming, "We are focused on energy production, but water will be the issue on which our lives will depend."

Run-on error: Mark Miller explains that the struggle to find clean water will be the issue that defines the next twenty years "We are focused on energy production, but water will be the issue on which our lives will depend."

Correct: Mark Miller explains that the struggle to find clean water will be the issue that defines the next twenty years: "We are focused on energy production, but water will be the issue on which our lives will depend."

In addition to avoiding comma splice and run-on errors, avoid using a quotation without providing information about its origin. Use short attributive tags to show where the quote came from.

Quotation without an introduction: It is dangerous for people to merely hope the water problem will go away. "Not everyone is ready to face the issue" (Miller).

Better: It is dangerous for people to merely hope the water problem will go away, but as Miller notes, "Not everyone is ready to face the issue."

To introduce quotations and the ideas of others, use key words such as these:

argues	explains	points out	says	suggests
contends	notes	replies	states	writes

As always, make sure you give credit to any idea or quote you have used from a source.

Teaching Resources: Chapter 14 provides in-depth information on how to integrate source materials ethically and correctly. A condensed list of instructions is available in the handout "Integrating Sources."

FINISHING YOUR ASSIGNMENT

The revision process is not the moment to slack off. It is actually the best time to convert mediocre writing into excellent writing. The entire text is before you, and you can now leisurely read it, assess it, and revise it to turn it into a polished, finished paper. The following steps will help you do just that.

Check That You Have Met Assignment Requirements

The assignment is to write an analysis and evaluation essay. Make sure your essay meets the requirements of the assignment:

- Create a list of criteria to determine the most serious threat.
- Use the criteria to evaluate the environmental threats.
- Make a judgment about which environmental issue should be considered most serious.
- Write an essay to present your analysis, criteria, and evaluation.
- Use evidence from the sources.
- Give credit to the sources using an approved method.

Consider having students use the assignment to create a check-off list of requirements. You can ask students to submit this check-off list as a cover sheet. See the IM for ideas about grading strategies that give students incentive to use correct formatting.

Revise for Organization and Unity

An organized essay uses a logical sequence of ideas. To check your paper's organization, read and annotate it just as you would read and annotate another writer's work. For each body paragraph, write a short phrase that summarizes the content. Next, look at all of the short phrases you have written. Do they match your outline? Do the body paragraphs appear in the right order? Should the order be changed to present the information more logically? Are there any missing points you should make?

Check your paper for unity in addition to organization. A unified paper includes in it only information that is relevant and that supports the point you are making. In a paper like the one you are writing, the body paragraphs should focus on the serious effects of the issue you are discussing. Avoid rambling into discussions of other topics.

Revise for Development

To revise for development, focus on the body paragraphs. Ask, "Did I include enough support to answer readers' questions about my topic sentence?" For example, if you are writing about the health effects of the water crisis, name particular health effects and provide information about them. In "Global Water Concerns," the authors provide examples, statistics, and other information you can use to help readers understand your point. Just be sure to give credit to the source.

As you write body paragraphs, do not assume readers will know what you mean. Provide examples, and follow them with explanations. For example, if you are talking about a river basin, readers may need to know what a river basin is. Readers will not necessarily know the point you are making with the examples you use. By thinking like a reader, you can more easily identify the places that need more development.

As you revise for development, be willing to make substantive changes. Imagine, for instance, that a section in which you discussed a health effect is weak for some reason. Perhaps you could not find enough information or you just did not have much to say about it. Consider taking that section out and writing a new passage about a different effect. These kinds of substantive changes are part of the revision process. Revision takes just as long as—and sometimes longer than—drafting. Keep in mind that it is at this stage of the writing process that you can turn your ideas into a polished piece of writing.

Connect IRW Writing Assignment: Consider using peer review to have students comment on unity, development, and clarity. By assessing others' essays, students may become more attentive to the same elements in their own writing.

Revise for Clarity

Since you have read four selections about the topic and have done your own analysis, you are entrenched in the subject. Remember, however, that your readers have not just done research. Thus, you need to include details in your essay for readers who are unfamiliar with the environmental issue you are discussing.

To make your writing clear, first explain what the issue is. For example, regarding water, the issue involves two things: water quality and water availability. The earth is full of water, but very little of it is suitable for drinking. Readers will need to understand that fact, so your paper should explain it. Water quality is another issue readers may not understand. Just because we have freshwater available, that does not mean it is potable. Unless you explain this information, readers may not take the water issue seriously, believing that we have plenty of water on earth. If you write your essay for the least informed reader, you will be more likely to include the material all readers need to clearly understand your point.

When revising for clarity, spend time looking at each individual sentence. If you even suspect a sentence may not be clear, revise it. Read each sentence out loud. If the sentence sounds even a bit "off" to you, reword it. Sometimes you will need to reword a sentence over and over before you find the perfect combination of words to communicate your thoughts.

Create a Works Cited or References List

Include each source you used in your paper in a works cited or references list, depending on your instructor's preferences. Do not include in the list any sources you have not actually used in your essay.

Check for Plagiarism

You are aware that every time you use an idea from a source—whether you put the idea into your own words or quote directly—you must give credit to the source, both in the text of your essay and in a works cited or references list. If you do not give credit properly, your paper will be considered plagiarized. Double-check your paper to make sure you have integrated source material and credited sources correctly. Print a copy of your essay, and follow these steps:

1. Highlight each idea in your paper that came from a source, whether you put the idea in your own words or quoted it.
2. Check to see that you have given credit to the source, either by mentioning the source in the sentence or by using a parenthetical reference.
3. Check that each source appears as a properly formatted entry in your works cited or references list.
4. Make sure that each time you used a quote or an attribution tag, you did so in a way that is grammatically correct. Remember, if you do not integrate quotes correctly, you can end up with comma splices, run-on sentences, or sentence fragments.

Edit Your Essay Using SMART TRACS

Once you have revised your paper, print out another copy to use for editing.

One strategy you can try is to improve on the grammatical weaknesses of previous writing assignments. To do this, take out any graded writing assignments that you have. Make a list of the errors. Which errors did you make most often? Once you find your most common errors, read about them in this textbook or online. A simple Internet search for "comma splices" will lead you to some excellent resources to use for study. Learn how to avoid them and how to replace them with correct grammatical structures.

Next, read the paper you have just completed, looking for the particular errors you have just studied. Make corrections as needed. Be sure to use the other resources available to you, such as a spell-checker and grammar-checker. Keep in mind that grammar-checkers do not always offer sound advice. For instance, sometimes a grammar-checker will tell you that a complete sentence is a fragment. Always use your own grammatical knowledge to check the grammar-checker!

Another idea for editing is to try something new. If you have not done so before, take your paper to your college's writing center or support lab. Ask an instructor or tutor to go over the paper with you. Alternatively, if you have access to an online tutorial tool, submit your paper and get suggestions from the online tutors. Explore any resources your college offers, and select one to use. Your instructor will have information about the tools at your disposal.

Teaching Resources: Helping students craft clear sentences is one of the greatest challenges writing instructors have. Students are sometimes reluctant to work on the "picky" details of choosing the best words for their thoughts, but you can use a variety of in-class teaching tools to help students engage in this process. See the IM for more information and for exercises on revising sentences.

See chapter 14 for complete guidelines for creating in-text references and works cited pages or references lists, as well as sample MLA-style and APA-style papers students can use as models for formatting their essays.

Teaching Resources: See the PPT "Simple Overview of MLA Documentation" or the PPT "Simple Overview of APA Documentation."

Finally, use the SMART TRACS guidelines to edit your paper. SMART TRACS stands for the following: **S**pelling, **M**issing words, **A**ccurate punctuation, **R**epeated words, **T**erminal punctuation, **T**ense consistency, **R**hythm, **A**ctive voice, and **C**onfusing words. If you have questions as you edit, work with a tutor or writing center instructor.

Chapter 10 provides a detailed explanation of SMART TRACS.

Put Your Essay in the Proper Format

Keeping your instructor's directions in mind, review your paper's formatting. Check the margins, heading, header, font, and font size. Check spacing. Make sure you have a title. If you are required to use MLA- or APA-style formatting, make sure you consult the appropriate instructions.

Congratulations! If you have reached this point, you have likely finished your project! Make sure to save a copy in two different places. For example, if you save your paper on a flash drive, also save it to a cloud site. (Clouds are virtual file cabinets that you access through the Internet. You can set up an account and save your documents in the cloud. Examples of cloud services are *Microsoft Live*, *Google Cloud*, *Dropbox*, and *Mozy*. Many offer free accounts.)

Always make sure you print two copies of your paper: one to keep and one to submit. Having two copies will ensure that if one copy ends up under a leaking cup of coffee, you will still have a clean copy to submit for grading.

⊙ ADDITIONAL ASSIGNMENTS

1. Write a short essay in which you evaluate the effectiveness of each reading selection in the chapter. Who is the selection's target audience? Is the selection credible? Is its thesis fully supported? Is it well organized and clearly written? Does it achieve its purpose? Devote one paragraph to each selection.

2. For this assignment, you evaluated four environmental issues and selected the most serious one. How did the other issues compare to the issue you selected? Which issue was second in importance? Third? Explain your ranking.

3. If you could propose only one solution to the environmental issue you discussed, what would it be? Explain your answer.

4. Create a short video, *PowerPoint* presentation, poster display, piece of art, or song in which you try to convince a general audience to take seriously the issue you discussed in your paper.

13

As one of the world's largest retail chains, Wal-Mart has stimulated a considerable amount of debate on key economic and societal issues. What impact should its critics and defenders have on how Wal-Mart does business?

Project 3: Working with Argument Texts
The Impact of Wal-Mart

An argument essay presents a *claim*—a person's opinion on a topic—and reasons and evidence to support the claim. Because argument essays are generally complex, readers need strong critical reading skills to analyze them. Similarly, writers need strong critical thinking skills to write an argument that is sound, that resonates with readers, and that presents the very best support available for a claim. In this chapter, you will use your critical reading and writing skills to analyze sources and to create your own argument essay.

If you are not familiar with the controversies surrounding Wal-Mart, you may be surprised to learn that many people debate whether Wal-Mart, a huge retailer with stores all over the world, has been good for society. Some people believe the retailer's enormous power has hurt jobs for workers in the United States, that it treats employees unfairly, and that Wal-Mart's business practices are unethical. Other writers, however, point out that Wal-Mart is a perfect example of a successful business. They acknowledge that some of Wal-Mart's business strategies may seem harsh but say that the company has managed to sell products for prices that would not otherwise be available to consumers.

The readings in this chapter present several viewpoints on Wal-Mart. As you read these selections, you will be prompted to think critically about the content with an eye toward understanding the concerns raised in each one. You will also be asked to create reading notes that will eventually help you

CHAPTER OBJECTIVES
After completing this chapter, students will be able to do the following:

- Examine an argument reading and writing assignment and identify a purpose.

- Use a critical reading process to examine four readings and use them as sources.

- Use an effective writing process to compose an argument essay.

- Revise and edit an argument essay, and use MLA or APA style to format the essay.

Connect IRW LearnSmart Achieve: Assign the topics "Writing in Response to Reading," "Evaluating and Supporting Arguments," "Evaluating, Synthesizing, and Documenting Sources," and "Analyzing and Writing in Response to a Writing Prompt" for adaptive learning to accompany the chapter.

write your own argument essay. The sources you read will stimulate your thinking about the issues, and they will provide you with key words and potential quotations to help you enter into the dialogue about Wal-Mart. After you finish the four readings, you will be prompted to think about the concepts that unify them. Finally, you will use your knowledge, notes, and creative ideas to write your own argument essay. To start this process, we will focus on your work as a reader.

GETTING STARTED

The readings that follow present different viewpoints about Wal-Mart. Some express explicit arguments; that is, the writers' opinions are clearly stated. Others do not explicitly state the writer's point of view. Some of the readings are informative pieces that will provide you with information rather than offer arguments. As a reader, you must determine each source's thesis statement and major supporting points. If the thesis statement is a claim, you will need to find the reasons used to support the claim. The steps that follow will guide you through this process.

Analyze Your Assignment

The best way to read sources is to have a clear idea of the purposes for which you are reading. You can do this by thoroughly analyzing the reading and writing assignment. What follows is the writing assignment that you will complete later in this chapter. It has been annotated to identify the most important elements.

Connect IRW Writing Assignment: Use the Connect IRW writing tools to set up this writing assignment. You can create a rubric to use for grading, assign drafts, assign peer review activities, and have students submit their essays through Connect IRW. See the Instructor's Manual (IM) for more information. Alternatively, use the pre-loaded version of this assignment in the Connect IRW *Common Places* Master Course.

Argument Reading and Writing Assignment

The sources in this chapter present a variety of debated issues involving Wal-Mart. Select one of these issues, and write an essay in which you argue your viewpoint. You will need to clearly define the issue, explain both sides of the issue, write a claim stating your opinion, and write supporting paragraphs in which you provide sound evidence to back up your claim. Use information from the sources in this chapter as one way to support your claim.

Select an issue.

Purpose: Argue my viewpoint on the issue.

Define the issue.

Explain both sides of the issue.

Write a claim.

Write supporting paragraphs.

Use sources to support claim.

Identify Your Purpose

A close reading of the assignment reveals that your purpose for reading is to familiarize yourself with the issues so you can choose one issue for your essay. Further, you will have to understand the issue well enough to be able to explain both sides of it. Thus, as you read, you will need to figure out each writer's point of view. Eventually, you will use the readings as sources for your own writing, so you should read them actively by annotating them and taking notes.

WORKING WITH READINGS

The strategies you will use to read the sources for your essay are much the same as those used for other reading tasks, but they also include some additional, argument-specific activities. Follow these steps to read the source materials carefully and critically.

Wal-Mart Is Good f[...]

by John Semmens

To some, Wal-Mart is a '[...]
that Wal-Mart's fortune[...]
accused the company of [...]
becoming the largest b[...]
Wal-Mart has more reve[...]

To get this big, '[...]
"poverty wages" and [...]
"squeezes" vendors, fo[...]
foreign "sweatshops."[...]
Wal-Mart disregards th[...]
passions of competitors[...]
unsuccessful in organizi[...]
free market, they are w[...]

The nature of comp[...]
expected to bemoan the[...]
The strategy and tactic[...]
warranted, imitated. Cc[...]
market is continuous, tc[...]
political opposition to V[...]

Unions in America[...]
members. Under regula[...]
can convert businesses [...]
bargains on behalf of a[...]
even be compelled to p[...]
rules governing electior[...]
in favor of the union's [...]
certainly within their rig[...]

Ideologues who rar[...]
economy, success goes tc[...]
needs. Businesses must i[...]
chandise. Customers are [...]
business, Wal-Mart inclu[...]

We all know that c[...]
considered savvy shoppi[...]
can be. This focus has er[...]

Low prices benefit I[...]
winning strategy for W[...]
him or her to buy othei[...]
when prices are lower t[...]
further at lower prices, i[...]
nesses making and sellir[...]

The sheer size of W[...]
to the economy. Growir[...]
accurately interpreting [...]

Preview Readings and Think about the Topic

Before reading any source, start by previewing the headings and subheadings, as well as any photos, captions, and tables, so that you can make predictions about the content and the writer's point of view. Read the author's biography, if the information is supplied, or do a quick Internet search on the author. Based on the author's education, qualifications, and prior publications, can you guess the author's point of view on the subject? Making a guess before you read will help you be attentive to details that will confirm or deny your hunch.

Take note of the type of source you are reading and its original publication information. If, for instance, you are reading an editorial—a short, opinionated essay—published in *Harvard Business Review*, the writer is likely to have a pro-business point of view. Take note of the date of publication, as the date can provide useful information about the writer's point of view. For example, articles about racial profiling written before the terrorist attacks of 9/11 may have a slightly different focus from articles written after the attacks.

As you preview the reading, try to determine the topic. The title may give you a clue about the topic, but scanning for repeated words and analyzing subheadings can also provide clues. Once you determine the topic, consider what you already know about the issue. For example, if the topic is discriminatory hiring practices, think about any personal experiences you have had at Wal-Mart. What information do you already know about Wal-Mart's hiring practices? Do you know anyone who has worked at Wal-Mart? Have you read anything about the issues surrounding Wal-Mart's hiring practices? If you have no ideas at this point, that is OK. If you do have some ideas, see how the information in the reading fits with the information you already have.

Whether you have significant prior knowledge or none at all, it is crucial to keep an open mind. Avoid forming a rigid opinion about any of the issues related to the topic until after you have read a number of sources. Allow the research to convince you. Become thoroughly familiar with the best arguments on both sides of the issue. If you wait to develop an *informed* opinion, you will be a more confident writer and will write a more convincing argument.

Read and Annotate the Text

After you read a selection, you should be able to write out the author's *thesis statement* (whether it is implied or explicit) and the *major supporting points*. As you read the selections for this assignment, keep in mind you will use them to help you write an argument paper. Some of these readings will be arguments themselves. They will present the writers' claims—their opinions—and the reasons that support those claims.

Not all readings in this chapter are arguments. Some present an overview of the issues that frame Wal-Mart discussions. In these readings, you will find information that will help you understand the arguments of both sides: those defending Wal-Mart's practices and those critiquing Wal-Mart's practices. To correctly identify the thesis statement of a source, you will need to know whether the writer is presenting a personal argument or providing an overview of the arguments of others.

Once you determine a reading's thesis statement, annotate the major supporting points. Keep in mind that some of the material will consist of *supporting details*, information that explains the major supporting points in more depth.

In addition to annotating the thesis statement and major supporting points, annotate key words used in the debate. Each debatable issue will have certain key words that writers use repeatedly. For example, writers who claim Wal-Mart does not pay its employees enough will often use the term *living wage*. Annotate these kinds of terms. When you write your own essay, you can use these terms to enter into the conversation knowledgeably.

Finally, mark at least three passages you believe are significant. It is always good to identify the writer's thesis statement as a potential passage to quote. You can also quote particular supporting details you find to be especially effective or convincing. Another idea is to mark quotations that are particularly colorful or expressive. Select these

Teaching Resources: Students' confusion about why they should be able to explain both sides of an issue can result in writing with an unclear point of view. It may help to emphasize that being able to articulate another point of view does not mean agreeing with it. See the IM for further discussion and teaching ideas.

Teaching Resources: See the *PowerPoint* (PPT) "The Wal-Mart Debate."

Connect IRW Discussion Board (DB) Assignment: Create DB threads that help students articulate their comprehension of the articles, and create threads that help students read the articles critically. See the IM for particular DB thread prompts, or use the pre-loaded DB prompts in the Connect IRW *Common Places* Master Course.

For a review of the elements of argument, refer students to chapter 6, or use the PPT "The Elements of Argument."

compete to see who can
trols such a large marke
to carry their product. Th
has most others finding
which promoted a "Buy
for the loss of uncoun
to outsource their proc
targets. Finally, the lab
and Saipan have all bee
clothing produced for V

SOURCE INFORMATION

Author: Joseph DesJardins
Title: "Discussion Case: Wa
Publication: *An Introductic*
Publisher: McGraw-Hill
City: New York
Date: 2014
Pages: 49–52

PRACTICE 3

Using your annotation

- General notes
- Simple outline
- Brief summary
- Issues and key word
- Potential quotes

SOURCE 4 "W.

The following article a
from the Foundation t
Wal-Mart by focusing
   Follow the steps p
your assignment and p
own opinion on the to

- Preview the readin
- Read and annotate

ABOUT THE AUTHOR
John Semmens is a rese
a libertarian/conservative
a contributing author to
edited by Gabriel Roth.

what we want businesses to do. This is what the free market encourages them to do. It is estimated that Wal-Mart's impact on prices accounted for 12 percent of the economy's productivity gains in the 1990s. This also helped reduce the effect of the Federal Reserve's inflation of the money supply.

But what about the methods Wal-Mart uses to achieve its goal of low prices? What about its exploitation of labor? The free market requires that transactions be carried out voluntarily between the parties. No one is forced to work for Wal-Mart. The wages it pays must be adequate to secure the services of its employees. Would Wal-Mart's employees like to be paid more? Sure, everyone wants higher pay. If its employees could get higher pay elsewhere, Wal-Mart would lose its best workers to the businesses paying those higher wages.

The same goes for the alleged uncompensated overtime. Wal-Mart can't force its employees to work overtime without compensation. Employees are not chained to their stations. They are free to leave and take other jobs if the pay or working conditions at Wal-Mart are less than satisfactory.

Neither can Wal-Mart "squeeze" vendors, compelling them to accept deals that they would prefer to refuse. Of course, sellers would like to get as high a price for their wares as they can. Likewise, buyers would like to get as low a price as they can. Both have to settle on a price that is mutually agreeable. Wal-Mart has a reputation for keeping its word and paying promptly. This enables its suppliers to plan their production and provides a reliable cash flow to help fund operations.

If some of Wal-Mart's suppliers choose to manufacture their products overseas, that is because doing so lowers their costs. Sure, the costs may be lower because the wages demanded by foreign workers in places like Bangladesh are low and the workplaces may be "sweatshops" compared to conditions in U.S. factories. But this is hardly the cruel exploitation that Wal-Mart's critics describe. The relevant comparison is not to the working conditions Americans have become accustomed to after two centuries of industrial progress and wealth beyond the wildest dreams of inhabitants of the less-developed countries. The relevant comparison is to the alternatives available in these less-developed economies.

Companies that employ people in factories in less developed economies must offer a compensation package sufficient to lure them from alternative occupations. So as bad as these "sweatshop" wages and working conditions may appear to Americans who have a fabulous array of lucrative employment opportunities, they are obviously superior to the alternatives that inhabitants of less-developed economies are offered. If the "sweatshop" jobs weren't superior, people wouldn't take them.

Wal-Mart and Small Communities

The claim that Wal-Mart "disregards the concerns of small communities" is also contradicted by the evidence. If Wal-Mart's stores were not in tune with the concerns of shoppers in small communities, the stores wouldn't make a profit and would eventually shut down. If Wal-Mart's stores were not in tune with the concerns of job seekers in those communities, the stores wouldn't be able to staff their operations. The concerns that Wal-Mart rightly disregards are those of local businesses that would prefer not to have to deal with new competition. The absence of rigorous competition leads to high prices in many small communities. While this may be good for the profit margins of established businesses, it is not necessarily a condition to be preferred over the benefits for the majority of the inhabitants of the community that result from robust competition.

Wal-Mart runs the largest corporate cash-giving foundation in America. In 2004 Wal-Mart donated over $170 million. More than 90 percent of these donations went to charities in the communities served by Wal-Mart stores.

From an economic perspective, when all the claims are dispassionately evaluated it looks like Wal-Mart promotes prosperity. The company is helping consumers get more for their money. It is providing jobs for willing employees. It is stimulating its suppliers to achieve greater economies in manufacturing. It is encouraging trade with less-developed economies, helping the inhabitants of Third World nations to improve their standards of living. Far from "disregarding the concerns of small communities," Wal-Mart offers an appealing place to shop and work.

Wal-Mart is doing all these good things and making a profit of around $9 billion a year. This is a profit margin of less than 4 percent. That's mighty efficient. To call Wal-Mart a "corporate criminal" is slander. Wal-Mart is a model of how successful capitalism is supposed to work. It is a company that should be emulated, not reviled.

YOUR ANNOTATIONS

SOURCE INFORMATION
Author: John Semmens
Title: "Wal-Mart Is Good for the Economy"
Publication: *The Freeman*
Date: 1 October 2005
Volume: 55
Number: 8
Pages: 8–10

PRACTICE ④ Creating an Information Sheet for "Wal-Mart Is Good for the Economy"

Using your annotations, create an information sheet that includes the following: *Answers will vary.*

- General notes
- Simple outline
- Brief summary
- Issues and key words
- Potential quotes

DEVELOPING YOUR ESSAY

Now that you have read the sources and constructed information sheets for each one, you can start the process of writing your own essay on an issue in the Wal-Mart debate. The following steps will guide you through the process.

Synthesize Your Sources

Once you have read each selection in the chapter, you need a method to put together the information each source provides.

First, start by making a chart that provides a master list of each issue you discovered in the selections you read. Do this by creating a chart with two columns. Use the column on the left to list the issues; in the column on the right, express each issue as a question. Write down as many issues as you can. Use your information sheets and the annotated readings to help you remember each issue. The sample chart below lists two issues to get you started.

ISSUE	ISSUE EXPRESSED AS A QUESTION
Wages	Should Wal-Mart pay its employees higher wages?
American jobs	Does Wal-Mart cause a decrease in American jobs?

Teaching Resources: Blank graphic organizers are available for all of these synthesizing activities.

Once you have listed the issues and turned them into questions, select two or three issues in which you are interested and create a **pro-con chart**—a chart that lists arguments for each side of an issue, both *for* (pro) and *against* (con). For example, one of the issues in the Wal-Mart debate is whether Wal-Mart should pay its employees higher wages. Reasons for and against are listed in the sample chart that follows. Notice that each reason includes the author's name.

Pro-Con Chart
Issue: Wages
Issue as a question: Should Wal-Mart pay its employees higher wages?

PRO	CON
Wal-Mart should raise pay. • Wal-Mart's profits are exorbitant (author's name). • Wal-Mart does not pay a living wage (author's name).	Wal-Mart should not raise pay. • Companies are in business to make the greatest profit possible (author's name). • Keeping wages low results in lower prices on goods (author's name).

Another graphic organizer you can create is a **source comparison table**, a chart that helps you compare several sources according to their ideas about particular issues. On the left side of the table, list *all* the issues raised in the sources you have read. Add one column for each source. In the boxes within the column, write what the source says about the issue. If a source does not address a particular issue, leave the box blank. The example below shows how three fictional sources might deal with three real issues.

ISSUE	WILLIAMS ARTICLE	BENTON ARTICLE	CHAVEZ ARTICLE
Should Wal-Mart offer better benefits to employees?	Yes. Wal-Mart can afford to do so and has an ethical obligation to provide better health-care and sick leave benefits.		Maybe, depending on whether an employee is full-time or part-time.
Is it ethical for Wal-Mart to demand such low prices from suppliers that American manufacturers cannot compete with international manufacturers?	No. Wal-Mart is ruining American jobs.	Yes. Wal-Mart's primary responsibility is to make money, not guarantee American jobs.	Yes. Wal-Mart is right to use global resources to lower prices for customers.
Is Wal-Mart guilty of age discrimination in its hiring practices?	Yes. Williams refers to three court cases.		No evidence exists to support the idea that Wal-Mart is guilty of age discrimination.

After creating a source comparison table or pro-con chart, you will be able to visualize the topics addressed by your sources more easily, and you can make better selections about the sources to use for your essay.

Prewrite to Develop Your Ideas

Review the Assignment

Although you have already read through and annotated the assignment, review it again before starting the writing process. Use the assignment to guide your topic selection.

Argument Reading and Writing Assignment

The sources in this chapter present a variety of debated issues involving Wal-Mart. Select one of these issues, and write an essay in which you argue your viewpoint. You will need to clearly define the issue, explain both sides of the issue, write a claim stating your own opinion, and write supporting paragraphs in which you provide sound evidence to back up your claim. Use information from the sources in this chapter as one way to support your claim.

Select an issue.

Purpose: Argue my viewpoint on the issue.

Define the issue.

Explain both sides of the issue.

Write a claim.

Write supporting paragraphs.

Use sources to support claim.

Select an Issue to Write About

As you synthesized sources, you created graphic organizers to analyze the issues. Select one of these issues. Double-check to make sure your choice is an arguable issue. An arguable issue is one that can be stated as a question whose answer is debatable; that is, the issue can be considered from multiple perspectives. Here is a topic that is *not* arguable.

TOPIC	WHY IT IS *NOT* ARGUABLE
Wal-Mart's size	This topic requires some research, but the information is easily found and is clear-cut. We do not have to argue about a topic that can be answered by facts.

We can turn Wal-Mart's size into an arguable issue by finding a related issue about which people have differing opinions. Consider the following example.

ISSUE STATED AS A QUESTION	WHY IT IS ARGUABLE
Does the size of Wal-Mart stores have negative effects on communities?	People will have varying opinions on this issue.

Use a Prewriting Method to Generate Ideas

Once you have selected an issue, spend some time jotting down ideas by using a prewriting method. Write down your opinion on the issue, and list potential reasons you could use to support your opinion, or use another method to think about the support you might construct. If you have a difficult time coming up with ideas, try prewriting on a different issue. Use your source information pages and your graphic organizers to help you as you prewrite. After you feel confident about the issue you have chosen and believe you can generate enough support to back up your opinion, you are ready to move to the next step.

Construct a Thesis Statement

If you haven't already done so, change the issue you will write about into a question. Now, using ideas from your sources, write a statement in which you answer the topic question. This answer will be your thesis statement. It should be the claim you hope to persuade readers to believe. Make sure your thesis statement is worded carefully and that it states exactly what you are attempting to prove. For instance, notice how the second thesis statement below is better than the first because it is more specific.

Vague:	Wal-Mart is bad for communities.
Specific:	Wal-Mart negatively affects communities by driving out competition, keeping wages low, reducing the number of jobs available, and limiting consumers' product choices.

Develop Support for Your Thesis Statement

Determine the very best reasons you can use to support your claim. Start by following these suggestions.

Make a List of Supporting Reasons

Examine the reasons listed on the pro-con chart you created. List all the possible reasons you could use to support your claim. If you have ideas that are not on the pro-con list, include them. Do not censor potential reasons; simply list them at this point.

Narrow Your List of Reasons

One way to narrow a list of reasons is to combine some of them. For example, in your list, you may have written these reasons:

- Wal-Mart causes people to lose jobs.
- Wal-Mart causes small businesses to close.
- Wal-Mart increases unemployment.

These reasons are all related. When small businesses close, people lose jobs, and when people lose jobs, unemployment increases. Thus, you can talk about all of these reasons in a single paragraph. Look through your list of reasons and group together the ones that are logically connected. When you finish, make sure you have at least three or more reasons to use in support of your claim.

Review the Logic of Your Reasons

Make sure none of your reasons are based on faulty logic. Avoid generalizations; avoid predictions that have no logical foundation; avoid misrepresenting the opposing side. Be careful about the cause and effect relationships you assert. If you are uncertain about whether your reasons are logical, discuss them with your professor, a tutor, or a lab instructor.

Create an Outline to Organize Your Essay

Once you have a claim and supporting reasons, you can create an outline. As you create the outline, turn your supporting reasons into complete sentences. At this point, your outline should include the following elements: title, topic question, thesis statement, and your reasons (major supporting points) expressed as topic sentences.

Each reason needs to be supported by evidence. Think about the types of evidence your audience might find convincing. Many types of evidence can be used in

Teaching Resources: Consider setting aside a day for students to work on these early writing process steps in class. Students who find the assignment overwhelming will feel more confident about writing their essays on their own after having completed the early steps in class. See the IM for additional ideas about teaching the projects in chapters 11–13.

Teaching Resources: See the IM for more information about helping students avoid logical errors.

argument essays: statistics, stories, analogies, facts, studies, explanations of causes and effects, definitions, contrasts, and so on.

One way to select evidence is to imagine that you are writing for a skeptical audience. Imagine that as people read your paper, they are muttering "Where's the evidence?" "I disagree." "Prove it!" Make sure you anticipate your readers' doubts and address them in your paper. Jot down the kind of support you will use to back up each reason.

Add Source Materials to Your Outline

First, look through your outline to determine where you have already used ideas you have found in sources. For example, perhaps one of the reasons you have put on your outline came from an essay written by an expert named Williams. Put the author's name next to that reason so that you will remember to give credit to Williams when you write your draft.

Second, add source material to your outline where it can be used effectively. To determine where to use quoted material or statistics, find the locations in your outline where having information from authoritative sources will help you make your point. For example, to prove that Wal-Mart causes unemployment to go up, you could use statistics from a source. This kind of evidence is not only impressive; it is mandatory. A reader might say, "How do you know?" Present your evidence to answer that question.

Always remember, though, that the paper you are writing is *your* argument. While you should use some support from other writers, do not overuse your sources. Provide your own explanations. Think about the issue yourself, and use your own words and ideas when you can. Here is a portion of the kind of outline you will create.

Topic: Wal-Mart's effects on communities

Question: When a Wal-Mart store is built in a small or medium-size city, does Wal-Mart have a negative effect on the community?

Thesis statement: Wal-Mart negatively affects communities in small and medium-size cities by driving out competition, keeping wages low, reducing the number of jobs available, and limiting consumers' product choices.

Major supporting details (reasons) stated as topic sentences

1. First, Wal-Mart affects communities negatively by driving out competitors.

   Minor supporting details:
   - **Explain** why smaller stores cannot compete with Wal-Mart's prices.
   - **Use quote:** "By purchasing such large quantities of product, Wal-Mart can negotiate prices with suppliers that are much lower than the prices mom-and-pop stores pay for the same products" (Williams).
   - **Give an example:** Explain what happened to David's Grocery when Wal-Mart moved into my hometown.

Write a Complete Draft of Your Essay

At this point, you have finished the prewriting process and are ready to start drafting. Use your outline to structure your thoughts as you draft your essay.

Keep an Audience in Mind

The best tool to use when drafting is your imagination: imagine having a conversation with a smart person who disagrees with your point. Word your essay in such a way that you would be able to convince this smart reader that your claim is correct.

Consider Presenting Background Information in Your Introduction

A common way of introducing an argument essay is to provide the background of the issue. Sometimes writers include both sides of the issue in the introduction paragraph and then present their position in the thesis statement. If you have trouble starting with the introduction, write the body paragraphs first. Sometimes you can write a stronger introduction after you've completed the entire essay.

Write the Body Paragraphs

If you have written a complete outline, you should be able to simply turn your outline into sentences to form body paragraphs. Keep in mind that each reason will start a new paragraph. Reasons can sometimes be expressed and explained in single paragraphs, but there is no reason to limit such explanations to only one paragraph. You may be familiar with the five-paragraph essay format, in which each body paragraph presents a single reason for the writer's position. Instead of limiting your writing to five paragraphs, ask yourself, *How many paragraphs do I need to fully support this reason?* Let the answer to that question dictate the number of body paragraphs you use.

End with an Effective Conclusion

Concluding an essay can be approached in several different ways. Some conclusion paragraphs point out how important the issue is. Some make predictions or reiterate the writer's claim, and some recommend a course of action. Make sure the conclusion you write provides readers with a sense of closure—the feeling that the essay is over and should come to an end.

Integrate Ideas and Quotes from Sources Correctly

As you write body paragraphs, be sure to integrate source material carefully and correctly. Use attributive tags, correct punctuation, and parenthetical references. Do not wait until later to add attributive tags and to give credit to your sources. If you wait, you may forget which passages came from sources, an error that will result in a plagiarized paper.

Remember that you must give credit not only for direct quotations but also for ideas that you summarize from a source. Avoid plagiarism and a failing grade by being vigilant about referring to your sources. If you need help integrating source materials, talk with your instructor.

FINISHING YOUR ASSIGNMENT

The revision process is not the moment to slack off. It is actually the best time to convert mediocre writing into excellent writing. The entire text is before you, and—if you have allowed yourself enough time—you can now leisurely read it, assess it, and revise it to turn it into a polished, finished paper. The following steps will help you do just that.

Check That You Have Met Assignment Requirements

To start the revising and editing process, review your assignment and your annotations of the assignment. Then print a copy of your paper. Check to make sure your essay meets every requirement of the assignment. If necessary, revise it to meet the requirements.

Revise for Organization and Unity

When you draft an essay, you are working with individual words and sentences; you are not looking at the *whole* essay. Revision is your opportunity to read what you have written and determine whether your ideas are presented in an organized way. Perhaps when you reread your paper, it will become clear to you that you should present a particular idea earlier in the essay. You have the opportunity to make that change now during the revision process.

To help students think about how to write introductions, use the readings in this chapter to analyze the writers' introduction methods.

Teaching Resources: Chapter 14 gives in-depth information on how to integrate source materials ethically and correctly. A condensed list of instructions is in the handout "Integrating Sources."

Consider having students use the assignment to create a check-off list of requirements. You can ask students to submit this check-off list as a cover sheet.

Additionally, consider how unified your essay is. Do all the ideas in the essay reinforce the major supporting points? One way to show that the ideas in your essay are unified is to use transitions. During the revision process, weed out ideas and details that clearly do not belong, and add transitions to show the relationships among the ideas that remain. If you need to, add explanations to show how the ideas are connected. Unify the content so that readers can see how each sentence and paragraph belongs where it is placed.

Connect IRW Writing Assignment: Consider using peer review to have students comment on unity, development, and clarity. By assessing others' essays, students may become more attentive to the same elements in their own writing.

Revise for Development

One of the most important parts of writing a convincing argument essay is using convincing support. Use the revision process to read your paper as a skeptical reader would. Jot down questions a reader might ask, such as "Where's the proof for this?" Any time you can jot down a question in the margin of your draft, revise your paper to make sure you provide an answer to that question. Ideally, you should provide readers with enough support so that they don't have to ask, "How do you know?"

Revise for Clarity

The best writing is clear writing. It is better to write a short, simple sentence that is clear than to write a long, complex sentence that leaves readers wondering about your point. Read each sentence out loud. If you have any doubt whether a sentence is clearly written, ask yourself, "How would I reword this sentence if I were speaking to a friend?" If your reworded sentence is clearer, revise the original sentence.

One way to determine clarity is to share your paper with others. Ask them to read it and locate unclear sentences, and then ask them to tell you what they thought your paper meant. If readers do not understand your point, determine where your ideas were not clearly expressed. Sometimes writers make clarity mistakes because they leave out information. Make sure your essay includes every bit of necessary information. Having others read your paper can be an excellent way to learn whether information is missing.

Create a Works Cited or References List

Each source you use in your paper—whether for quotations or ideas—must appear in a works cited list or list of references. Be sure to include the list when you submit the final paper.

Teaching Resources: See the PPT "Simple Overview of MLA Documentation" or the PPT "Simple Overview of APA Documentation."

Check for Plagiarism

You already know how important it is to give credit to any sources you use. Even so, take this opportunity to read over your paper again. Highlight any idea that came from a source other than your own mind. Make sure each of these sources is marked with a parenthetical reference.

Edit Your Essay Using SMART TRACS

Editing starts with running spell-checkers and grammar-checkers. Keep in mind that these tools are not fail-proof. In fact, grammar-checkers can make suggestions that are actually *wrong*! As a writer, you are responsible for making sure your paper is correct. Use the SMART TRACS guidelines to edit your paper. SMART TRACS stands for the following: **S**pelling, **M**issing words, **A**ccurate punctuation, **R**epeated words, **T**erminal punctuation, **T**ense consistency, **R**hythm, **A**ctive voice, and **C**onfusing words.

If you still have questions, take your paper to a writing center for help. If you usually have points taken off for grammatical errors, be proactive. Check for the specific errors you tend to make. Consider working with a lab instructor or tutor before handing in your paper.

Put Your Essay in the Proper Format

It is common to be weary by this point in the writing process. After all, you have just written a research-based paper! And if you have followed every step carefully, you have put a lot of work into your essay and have created something you can be proud of. Before you submit your paper, however, make sure to check one of the simplest things: your paper's format. Your instructor will have given you formatting instructions. Specifically, check these formatting issues before submitting your paper:

- Heading
- Header (and page numbers)
- Spacing
- Margins
- Title
- Font type and size
- Formatting of quotations
- Formatting of the works cited or references list

As you put the final touches on your essay, remember that the paper you submit reflects not only your reading and writing processes, but also your ability to follow instructions and produce quality work. Make sure you use this assignment as an opportunity to show your instructor you have mastered all three abilities.

⊙ ADDITIONAL ASSIGNMENTS

1. Write a short essay in which you evaluate the effectiveness of each reading selection in the chapter. Who is the selection's target audience? Is the selection credible? Is its thesis fully supported? Is it clearly written and well organized? Does it achieve its purpose? Devote one paragraph to each selection.

2. Write an essay in which you take the opposite point of view from one of the readings in this chapter. Use the Quick Start Guide for Integrated Reading and Writing Assignments for help.

3. Write an essay in which you propose a solution or course of action for a Wal-Mart problem identified in one of the readings. You may have to do additional research to find possible ideas.

4. Use the essay you have written to create a *PowerPoint* presentation or a video in which you present your claim and your reasons. Which of your creations—your essay or your *PowerPoint* or video—do you think would most effectively present your argument to your classmates? Write a paragraph to explain your answer.

PART 4

Additional Skills

14 Using Sources

AVAILABLE ONLY IN create™

Strategies for Reading and Writing Exams

Professionals know that for the best outcome, they must use good sources and position their materials with care, whether they are building a house, catering a party, or writing an essay.

Using Sources

Many—if not most—of the writing assignments you will do in college and at work will include the use of source materials. What should be the connection between a source's ideas and your own ideas? When should you refer to sources in your writing? How do you use sources without plagiarizing? How do you integrate quotes and source references smoothly? These are a few of the questions we will consider in this chapter to help you use sources accurately, ethically, and effectively.

CHAPTER OBJECTIVES

After completing this chapter, students will be able to do the following:

- **Prepare to use source materials.**
- **Work with readings for a source-based essay.**
- **Develop a source-based essay.**
- **Create in-text references in MLA and APA styles.**
- **Format an MLA paper and prepare a works cited list.**
- **Format an APA paper and prepare a references list.**
- **Check an essay for plagiarism.**

GETTING STARTED: PREPARING TO USE SOURCE MATERIALS

The best way to start any reading and writing task is to analyze and annotate the assignment itself. In the simple example that follows, the student's annotations point out the significant verbs that will help him determine exactly what to focus on when reading the sources.

Teaching Resources: See the Chapter Quiz.

Connect IRW LearnSmart Achieve: Assign the topics "Writing in Response to Reading," and "Evaluating, Synthesizing, and Documenting Sources" for adaptive learning to accompany the chapter.

English 0301 Reading and Writing Project

Most cities have recycling programs of some sort. In the essays that follow, you will learn about the cities with the best recycling programs in the United States. As you read about these cities, determine the factors that help them rank high in their recycling initiatives. Once you have determined these factors, think about the recycling program in your own city. How does it compare with the cities you have read about? Write an essay in which you use the factors you have identified to compare your city's recycling program to those you have read about. Evaluate how good a job your city is doing with its recycling program, and provide your evaluation in your essay. Your essay should have two parts: an analysis of your city's recycling program based on the factors you have read about, and an evaluation of the quality of your city's recycling program.

Read sources.

Determine factors used to judge recycling programs.

Compare my city's recycling program with the programs of cities in the articles.

Write an essay and use the factors for the comparison.

Evaluate my city's program.

Essay should have an analysis and an evaluation.

By annotating the assignment, the student has identified the tasks he must focus on when he reads the source material. He is clear about his purpose: to figure out what makes the recycling programs of particular cities good. He must also figure out the factors that are used to judge the recycling programs (such as percentage of waste recycled, public awareness and participation, and so on). With these things in mind, the student can read in a more focused way.

WORKING WITH READINGS

When you are ready to start reading the sources, use a previewing process to guide your work. Start by considering who wrote the source, for whom it was written, and when and where it was published. After previewing, read and annotate the sources. Next, create an outline, a summary, and an information sheet for each source. As you work with sources, keep in mind the information that follows.

Examining Authors for Bias and Credibility

One way to assess the credibility of a source is to evaluate the author: her position, her reputation, and the subjects she often writes about. A quick Internet search will help you obtain this information. Knowing the writer's background will help you understand her authority on the subject—as well as her biases. For example, if a writer has a reputation as an advocate of prison reform, you can expect her article to reflect that point of view. If she teaches criminology at a university or is a prison warden, her position lends credibility to her writing. Researching the writer's background will enable you to refer to her credentials later when you draft your essay. Doing so will tell your readers that the source you are using is credible.

Reputable Web sites go to some trouble to be transparent about who runs them and who writes for them. If you cannot find information about the source of the information on a Web site, be wary about using it for research. If you learn only that an article on a site is authored by Millard Wentworth, for example, you have not really learned anything (unless the name Millard Wentworth is meaningful to you!). If author biographies are provided, you have a bit more information and can rank the site a bit higher in terms of credibility. To determine more about a site's author or sponsoring organization, conduct a search using *Google* or another search engine.

Examining Audience

Examining the potential audience for a source will add to your understanding. Consider an article about diabetes that appears in a journal for doctors. The writer has made certain assumptions about the medical knowledge of the audience. When you read the

Traditionally, many developmental writing instructors have not taught source-based writing. However, most integrated reading and writing programs do require source-based writing. Institutions (and programs) vary in the depth of coverage with which they present MLA or APA styles. See the Instructor's Manual (IM) for ideas about how to teach the basic principles of documentation without going into as much depth as this chapter does.

article, you may need to consult dictionaries or other sources to understand it. An article that appears on the Web site of People for the Ethical Treatment of Animals (PETA) will be written for an audience that, for the most part, shares PETA's views. Knowing the beliefs of the audience will help you more accurately understand the writer's point.

Examining Date and Historical Context

Another aspect of the source to consider is when it was published. If the source is not current, consider its historical context. Suppose you are reading an article about the oil industry, and you notice that it was written in 1976. If you know that the United States experienced an energy crisis in the mid-1970s, you will better understand the issues discussed in the article. If you notice that an article about preparing for disaster was written in 1999 and you know that some people were anxious about entering the next millennium, you will have additional insight into the piece. The historical context can affect your understanding of a piece of writing. In general, unless a source is important or ground-breaking in its field (for example, a work on psychology by Sigmund Freud), use sources written within the last five years.

Examining the Source for Bias and Credibility

A source is *biased* if it advocates or promotes a particular view on an issue. For example, suppose you want to determine whether high-fructose corn syrup is good for you. If you look at the Web site of a company that produces high-fructose corn syrup, you would expect to find information that is biased in favor of the product and the many ways it improves foods and beverages. Likewise, it is unlikely that you would find arguments against the product. Therefore, you would be unwise to base your determination solely on the evidence of that biased Web site.

At times, reading biased sources might suit your writing task. For instance, in a persuasive essay, you might want to present the viewpoint of the corn syrup company as well as the viewpoint of those opposed to the wide use of corn syrup as a sweetener (a viewpoint that will also be biased). Comparing these two biased sources may be helpful in such a paper. Often, however, writers are best served by looking for sources that are neutral and do not have an interest in promoting a particular point of view.

Teaching Resources: See worksheet "Examining Sources."

Examining the Source for Bias

Sources may come from general magazines, scholarly journals, Web sites, and a variety of other publications. Knowing a source's origin will help you predict potential biases. Some journals and magazines directly reveal their biases. For example, just the name of *The American Conservative* gives you a clue about the magazine's political orientation. If you go to the magazine's Web site, you will find a definitive statement of the magazine's biases. The magazine says, "To solve the country's seemingly intractable—and, in the long-term, lethal—strategic, economic, and socio-cultural problems requires a rediscovery of traditional conservatism. That's the mission of *The American Conservative*." Similarly, if you do an Internet search on book publishers, you also may be able to detect biases. Ignatius Press, for example, describes itself as the "primary publisher in U.S. of Pope Benedict XVI's books." We can expect books from Ignatius Press to have a Roman Catholic bias.

Determining the bias of Web sites can be a bit trickier. One way to do so is to examine its **domain name**—the last part of its Web address. Common domain names are *.com*, *.gov*, *.edu*, and *.org*. If a Web site address ends in *.com*, it is a commercial Web site, and you should suspect it will contain biases in favor of the product or service it is selling. Web sites whose domain is *.org* (meaning that it represents an organization) may be less biased, but *.org* sites often promote ideas. For example, PETA has this on its home page (www.peta.org): "Animals are *not* ours to eat, wear, experiment on, use for entertainment, or abuse in any other way." The bias of PETA's organizational Web site is clearly stated. Note that having a bias does not mean a source is disreputable; it simply tells you the source is not neutral.

Web sites sponsored by federal, state, and local governments have the domain *.gov*. Much of the information on government Web sites—in particular, statistical information—is simply factual. However, the Web site of a particular agency or department (for example, the US Environmental Protection Agency) may advocate for activities such as conservation and more regulation, which other organizations (for example, energy companies) do not favor. Additionally, individual senators and congressional representatives have Web sites that end in *.gov*. These sites will be biased because they will present the senator's or representative's point of view.

Web sites that end in *.edu* are educational—that is, associated with colleges, universities, and other recognized educational institutions. While these sites are likely to be less biased than *.com* sites, it is important to remember that professors and even students often have personal Web sites sponsored by their institution. Those personal Web sites often present points of view about issues. Thus, these sites will also present bias.

In the end, you—as a consumer of information—must always be the one to make a careful choice about the bias of a particular Web site or source. Bias is not necessarily a bad thing, but as a researcher, you must know whether your sources are biased or take a neutral point of view.

Examining the Source for Credibility

In general, you can determine the **credibility** of a source—its trustworthiness—by examining its origin. For example, we expect articles in *The New York Times* to be written ethically and credibly. Similarly, we expect articles that appear in **peer-reviewed** journals (journals that have a stringent process for selecting what they publish) to be credible. On the other end of the credibility spectrum are tabloids that present celebrity gossip and news items that are often unverifiable—ranging from accounts of alien landings to reports of six-headed babies. You can often do an Internet search of a source's name to learn more about its reputation and credibility.

To assess a source that comes from a Web site, you must assess the Web site itself. Study the Web site shown below and the clues that are pointed out as you review the following factors. First, a professional Web site will be well edited and will not contain

Teaching Resources: See the PPT "How Believable Is That Web Site?"

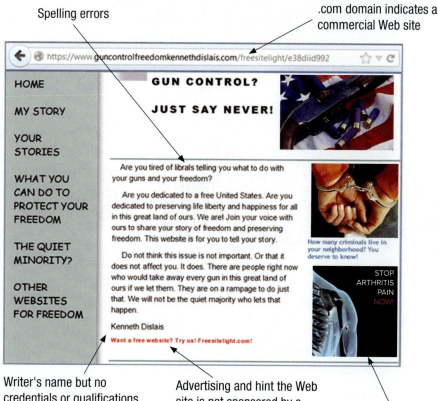

Spelling errors

.com domain indicates a commercial Web site

Writer's name but no credentials or qualifications

Advertising and hint the Web site is not sponsored by a notable organization

Advertising

■ A Web site that is biased and is *not* credible.

errors in spelling or grammar. Ideally, it should not carry advertising. Some credible Web sites do allow advertising, but as a rule, look for those that do not. Advertising is a sign that the owner of the Web site wants to make money by luring people to the site; thus, the owner may decide to post the content that draws in the most people, which may not necessarily be the most authoritative content on a subject. Additionally, a credible Web site will offer support for the information it posts. For example, some Web sites provide bibliographies to show the sources the authors consulted, a practice that allows readers to evaluate the credibility of the information.

Clearly, the Web site shown on the previous page is biased, but its bias is not the problem. The real question is whether we should regard its writer, Kenneth Dislais, as a credible or qualified source for information about gun control. He offers no biographical information about himself; in fact, we have no information about the sponsors of the Web site either. The only information we have is that it was created by means of a free Web site generator. Why should we believe that Kenneth Dislais knows *anything* about the issue of gun control? We do know one thing: he did not use a spell-checker to proofread his Web site! Further, the site includes advertisements that are not related to the content. In summary, when you encounter sites like this one, question the value of the information. Can you verify that it is anything other than a mouthpiece for one unknown individual? If not, the site lacks credibility and is a poor source.

Now, take a look at another Web site for an organization that opposes gun control. Notice that this site, sponsored by Citizens for Responsible Gun Ownership, is biased but credible.

.org – suggests that the site may be biased

Physical address enhances credibility

Contact information enhances credibility

Describes the group's mission

---

www.crgo.org

Citizens for Responsible Gun OwnershipCRGO.org

33822 Pasadena Blvd.
Chicago, IL 60106

Our Mission   Education   Ownership   Press   About Us

Citizens for Responsible Gun Ownership is an advocacy group that believes it is possible to retain Second Amendment rights *and* reduce gun violence and accidental shootings.

Our response to gun control advocates is that we must educate people, inform them, and ensure that anyone who owns a firearm knows how to do so safely. Our public awareness and education campaigns include presentations, television advertisements, and free literature.

Join us and help spread the word that gun ownership and a safe living environment can go hand in hand.

Martin Dreitz
President and Founder

Last updated April 1, 2014

Questions? Contact us at 800-555-3993 or e-mail us: inquire@crgo.org

CRGO Board Members (click on names provides information about supporters (board members) for biographical information)

Rene Caritas, Chair

Donovan M. Kemp, Executive Director

Carol C. Pringle, Director of Development

John Lauhaus, Director of Public Relations

Janice Nylinger, Secretary

■ A Web site that is biased but is also credible.

The Web site goes to some trouble to let viewers know who sponsors it, where the organization is located (its physical address), and the group's philosophy and mission. Also, the clear identification of the site's founder and president and easy availability of information about its supporters (board members) lend it credibility. Moreover, the site provides ways for the sponsoring organization to be contacted, which suggests that the group is well-established. While we know that the site will be biased because it exists to promote the rights of gun owners, we can have some confidence that it may ultimately prove to have trustworthy information.

Finally, let's examine a Web site that is credible but is not biased on the issue of gun ownership. Notice the characteristics of this objectively oriented site, Yes-or-No.org.

.org site—may be biased   Probably depends on donations   Nonprofit

Provides info about the organization

Provides sources and bibliography

Presents the issue

Presents both sides of the issue

■ A Web site that is *not* biased and is credible.

Yes-or-No.org provides numerous clues that it is credible and seeks to be objective. Its name suggests that we will learn about both sides of issues. The site confirms this idea by providing a neutral introduction to the issue of carrying concealed guns and then offering both sides of the argument. Also, the Web site enhances its credibility by giving resources and bibliographies. We can see that Yes-or-No.org is a nonprofit educational organization that depends on donations and is not funded by people on a particular side of an issue. These facts help establish the site as both credible and objective.

PRACTICE ① Examining Sources

Bibliographic information is given below for two textual sources and a Web site. All of these sources concern the effects of aspartame, the artificial sweetener used in many products, including NutraSweet. Using this information and an Internet search engine to look up information about the publication and the writers, answer the questions that follow each source.

1. Author: Joe and Teresa Graedon

Title: "How Safe Is Aspartame?"

Source: *The Buffalo News*

Date: 4 January 2006

a. How credible are these writers?

Very credible. Joe Graedon is a pharmacologist, a best-selling author, and an adjunct professor at the University of North Carolina. Teresa Graedon, PhD, is a medical anthropologist.

b. Does anything about the publication (*The Buffalo News*) suggest bias?

No. The Buffalo News is the daily paper for western New York, published both in print and online. It appears to uphold traditional standards for journalism.

2. Author: John Briffa

Title: "Aspartame and Its Effects on Health: Independently Funded Studies Have Found Potential for Adverse Effects"

Journal: *BMJ* (*British Medical Journal*), vol. 330, no. 7486, pp. 309–10

(continued)

Publisher: BMJ Publishing Group

Date: February 2005

   a. How credible is this writer?

     Very credible. John Briffa is an MD who has written many books on health.

   b. Does anything about the publication (*British Medical Journal*) suggest bias?

     No. In fact, it is peer reviewed, so it's less likely to be biased than magazines or news articles.

   c. For what audience was this written?

     Doctors, researchers, and other health professionals.

3. http://www.aspartame.org

   a. How credible is this Web site?

     Only somewhat.

   b. Does anything about this Web site suggest bias?

     Yes. It focuses only on benefits and refers to any potential drawbacks as "myths." Also, the focus is weight loss and calorie control rather than overall health.

   c. What did you learn about the authors of this Web site?

     Very little; no specific people are named.

Since Web sites are constantly changing, see the IM for a list of other sites that can be analyzed if the particular site in Question 3 is inaccessible.

Reading and Annotating Sources

The best way to work with sources is to print them out and have a pen, pencil, and highlighter ready. Read the source, using a pencil to annotate the ideas that seem to be important. It is difficult to recognize the most important ideas in a text the first time you read it, so using a pencil will enable you to go back and make changes.

Read the source a second time, this time using your pen and highlighter to annotate the text. Mark the major supporting points, the thesis statement, nuggets of information you find interesting or useful, potential quotes, and any passages about which you have questions. Write questions and comments in the margin. If you are reading more than one source, annotate any connections you notice between the sources.

If, after you have read the source several times, you are confused or unsure about its meaning, read it again. There is nothing wrong with reading a source several times; in fact, doing so is quite common and always useful. Another idea to help with your comprehension is to write down the topic on a piece of paper. Next, write down the main point the writer is making about the topic. Put this information into a sentence. What you have written *should* be the writer's thesis statement. Work with your course instructor or a lab instructor if you need additional help comprehending a text.

As you search for potential quotes, think about the assignment. If you keep in mind the kind of paper you will be writing, you are more likely to select appropriate quotes. You cannot be totally certain about which parts of your sources you will actually use in your paper until you create an outline and work on a draft. To select quotes you think you may use, look over your annotations. You should have noted the main idea, major supporting points, and particularly interesting minor supporting details. These are potentially useful passages to use as quotations. It is vitally important to copy these passages *word-for-word*. A quote must include the exact words you find in the original source.

Outlining, Summarizing, and Preparing Information Sheets for Sources

Once you have read and understood a source, prepare a brief outline and a brief summary. Create an *information sheet* that includes the outline and summary and enough information to render the source useful as a reference as you write your essay. Under the heading "General Notes," write all the bibliographic information you have (author, title, publication, date of publication, city of publication, pages) and comment on any points of interest to you. For example, you could note an essay idea that the source suggests to you. Here's a sample format for an information sheet.

Model for an Information Sheet

INFORMATION SHEET :

GENERAL NOTES
- Authors:
- Publication:
- Date:
- [Interesting points]

SIMPLE OUTLINE
  Thesis statement:
  Major supporting point 1:
  Major supporting point 2:
  Major supporting point 3:

BRIEF SUMMARY

ISSUES AND KEY WORDS

POTENTIAL QUOTES

When you have created an information sheet for each source, you are ready to start the next phase of the integrated reading and writing process: developing your essay.

PRACTICE ② Selecting Information to Use from Sources

What follows is one of the articles referred to in Practice 1.
- Read and annotate the article.
- On a separate sheet, use the format shown above to prepare a page of notes. Include bibliographic information, a simple outline, a brief summary, and three quotes.

How Safe Is Aspartame?

by Joe Graedon and Teresa Graedon

People love to hate artificial sweeteners. Starting with saccharin in the late 1950s, some have enthusiastically embraced the idea of sweets without calories. Others have warned that saccharin, cyclamate and aspartame are too dangerous for human consumption.

The debate is often intensely emotional. Cyclamate was removed from the market in 1969 when animal studies showed an excess of tumors in rats exposed to the sweetener. This remained controversial for the next 20 years, but the Food and Drug Administration did not reverse itself.

The FDA proposed pulling saccharin off the market in the mid-1970s, also on the suspicion that it might cause cancer. The agency let those plans drop due to public outcry and congressional outrage.

(continued)

General notes:

- Authors: Joe Graedon and Teresa Graedon
- Publication: *The Buffalo News,* accessed on Web
- Date: 4 January 2006

YOUR ANNOTATIONS

Lexile: 1110L

Saccharin is the sweetener most often sold in pink packages. A common brand is Sweet'n Low. Cyclamate is approved for use in many countries but is banned in the United States. Aspartame, most often sold in blue packages, was initially marketed as NutraSweet. Its health effects are widely debated.

The most popular noncaloric sweetener for the past few decades has been aspartame. This artificial sweetener was introduced with great fanfare in 1981 as one of the safest alternatives to sugar ever created. The FDA announced when it approved aspartame, "Few compounds have withstood such detailed testing and repeated, close scrutiny, and the process through which aspartame has gone should provide the public with additional confidence of its safety."

That's their story, and they're sticking to it. Through the years, though, frightening tales of aspartame toxicity have circulated on the Internet.

One reader wrote: "I know from firsthand experience that there are very serious problems with aspartame. In 1996 I was diagnosed with epilepsy. At that time I was trying to lose weight and eating a lot of products with aspartame.

"I became suspicious and stopped eating aspartame-laced products. Even though my neurologist was skeptical, I was able to discontinue my seizure medicine and have not had further seizures."

Others have blamed aspartame for a wide variety of health problems including headaches, dizziness, confusion, memory loss, depression, blindness, ADD, ALS, lupus and multiple sclerosis.

With dozens of symptoms attributed to aspartame, it is easy to discount the diatribes. We were skeptical about the more exaggerated claims, especially regarding links to cancer.

Recent research by a European foundation has forced us to look at aspartame in a new light, however. A study published online in the journal *Environmental Health Perspectives* (Nov. 17, 2005) involved 1,800 rats and six dosage levels of aspartame in their chow.

The rats in this study were not sacrificed but lived out their natural lives and were examined upon death. The authors report an excess of leukemias, lymphomas and malignant tumors among rats fed aspartame at several dosage levels.

Critics charge that the researchers did not follow standard protocols for this type of study. The investigators respond that "the findings speak for themselves."

Source Information

Author: Joe Graedon and Teresa Graedon

Title: "How Safe Is Aspartame?"

Publication: *The Buffalo News,* accessed on Web

Date: 4 January 2006

Simple outline:

Thesis statement: The debate about the safety of artificial sweeteners is ongoing.

Major supporting point 1: Cyclamate was banned due to concerns about its safety.

Major supporting point 2 : Saccharin was approved, banned briefly, and later approved again by the FDA.

Major supporting point 3: The FDA says the legal sweetener aspartame is safe, but others disagree.

Brief summary: The authors note that the debate over the safety of artificial sweeteners has gone on since the 1950s. An early sweetener, cyclamate, is still banned by the FDA, even though it is legal in other countries. Saccharin was legal, and then it was banned, only to be brought back to markets by the FDA. The FDA has tested aspartame, a legal sweetener introduced in 1981, and has found it to be a safe alternative to sugar. The FDA also notes that aspartame has undergone rigorous testing. Still, many do not trust the findings, and stories of toxicity continue to circulate. In a 2005 study, one European research foundation found significant cancers and tumors in rats that were exposed to the substance. Thus, the debate and the questions continue.

Quotes will vary.

DEVELOPING YOUR SOURCE-BASED ESSAY

Once you have read, annotated, analyzed, and prepared information sheets for all your sources, you are ready to start thinking about your own essay. It is wise to go back to the assignment and reread it before going on. You should look frequently at the assignment during the reading and writing process to stay on track. After you have reviewed the assignment, follow these steps to start developing your essay.

Synthesizing Sources

Begin by categorizing your sources according to focus or point of view. For example, assume you are reading about the changing definition of the family in the United States. Some of your sources discuss types of families (such as single-parent families and multi-generational families). Others discuss why our definitions of the family are changing. You could categorize your sources into "types" and "explanations."

Or imagine you are reading about a controversial topic, such as the effects of violent video games. Some sources claim that such games enhance problem-solving skills and hand-eye coordination. Others claim that these games have little to no effect on participants. Still others claim that there is a direct relationship between playing violent video games and being violent in real life. You might put these sources into the groups "pro," "con," and "neutral/other." Once you have a clear picture of the points of view of your sources, you can choose the best categories. If you categorize your sources, you will more easily be able to locate the source you need to support a particular point while writing.

Another way to synthesize your sources is to create a table that is designed specifically for your assignment. For instance, if you were working on the recycling assignment, you would need to know details about the various recycling programs from each city. You would also need to know which factors the writers analyzed to judge the effectiveness of the programs. Thus, you could make a table like the one that follows to synthesize your information.

	SOURCE 1: MATTAVILLE, WASHINGTON	SOURCE 2: WESTERSON, FLORIDA	SOURCE 3: RIO TERRA, CALIFORNIA
Percentage of community that participates in recycling program	81	88	84
Percentage of trash recycled	78	82	82
Recycling of glass?	Yes	No	Yes
Recycling of paper and plastic?	Yes	Yes	Yes
Recycling of furniture?	Yes	No	No
Recycling of wood?	Yes	Yes	Yes

This kind of table will help you see how each recycling program compares to the others, and it will help you determine the criteria (in the left column) you can use in your analysis of your own city's recycling program. Of course, the content of the chart you create will depend on the content of the sources you are analyzing.

Prewriting to Develop Your Ideas

As you read your sources, make notes, and synthesize the source material, you will start to have an idea of what you want to communicate in your thesis statement. Use a prewriting method to generate ideas about the topic. One way to start is to prewrite about each of the elements you need to include in your paper. For example, in the assignment we analyzed earlier, these are the required elements:

- Factors used to judge recycling programs
- Comparison of my city's recycling program with the programs of cities in the articles
- Analysis of my city's program using factors for comparison
- Evaluation of my city's program

Use prewriting to generate ideas for each of the elements that will be in your essay.

Constructing a Thesis Statement and Support

Once you believe you understand the issues well enough to know what point you would like to make, construct a thesis statement. Make sure your thesis statement is grammatically correct and that it communicates the main message you want to express in your paper.

After writing a thesis statement, you will choose your major supporting points. Let's take the example of Krystal, a student who is writing an essay about the dangers of concussions from playing football. She has read a number of sources on the topic, and her prewriting has led her to compose this thesis statement.

> The effects of concussions sustained while playing football are so serious that players should demand changes or refuse to play the game.

On the basis of her reading and thesis statement, Krystal lists the information she needs to support her position. What will her readers need to know? As she determines her readers' needs, she jots them down in the left column. Then she writes a complete sentence for each need in the right column, making sure the sentence supports her thesis statement.

Thesis statement: The effects of concussions sustained while playing football are so serious that players should demand changes or refuse to play the game.

TO SUPPORT MY THESIS STATEMENT, I WILL NEED TO . . .	MAJOR SUPPORTING POINTS
Explain the effects of concussions	Scientists have learned that concussions have serious long-term effects on the brain. [List effects.]
Suggest changes that can decrease these negative effects	Players and those who care about them should demand changes. • The first thing that can be done is to reduce the number of concussions by changing some of the rules in football. • A second solution is to require the use of a new type of helmet. • Third, football coaches, trainers, physicians, players, and the families of players must be trained to identify concussions and consult the appropriate health-care professionals so that concussions are treated correctly.
Convince players to not play if such changes are not made	Players must educate themselves about the realities and then stand up for themselves—if necessary, by refusing to play—for the sake of their long-term health and for those who care about them.

Notice how the major supporting points in the second column are directly related to both the thesis statement and to the readers' needs.

Creating an Outline

Krystal is now ready to create an outline. An outline does not have to be formal to be effective, but it does need to be written with care. The thesis statement and the major supporting points must be included in the form of well-written, complete sentences. Ideally, Krystal should be able to simply copy those sentences from her outline and put them directly into her paper.

As Krystal creates her outline, she determines how many body paragraphs she will need for each major supporting point. Some major supporting points can be expressed in a single paragraph, but others may need more than one body paragraph. Krystal's outline, which follows, demonstrates this idea.

Outline for a Source-Based Essay

Topic: Concussions in football

Thesis statement: The effects of concussions sustained while playing football are so serious that players should demand changes or refuse to play the game.

INTRODUCTION

Paragraph 1: Explain why so many people are talking about this issue these days. Start with the story of Dave Duerson. End with thesis statement.

BODY

Paragraph 2 (major supporting point 1—effects): Scientists have learned that concussions have serious long-term effects on the brain.

Paragraph 3 (major supporting point 2—changes): Players and those who care about them should demand changes. The first thing that can be done is to reduce the number of concussions by changing some of the rules in football.

Paragraph 4 (major supporting point 3—changes): A second solution is to require the use of a new type of helmet.

Paragraph 5 (major supporting point 4—changes): Third, football coaches, trainers, physicians, players, and the families of players must be trained to identify concussions and consult the appropriate health-care professionals so that concussions are treated correctly.

Paragraph 6 (major supporting point 5—refuse to play): Players must educate themselves about the realities and then stand up for themselves—if necessary, by refusing to play—for the sake of their long-term health and for those who care about them.

CONCLUSION

Paragraph 7: Explain how this issue affects not only NFL players but also kids across the country. Urge a solution.

Consider explaining to students how this outline's organization is different from the five-paragraph essay format many of them have been taught. Rather than starting with a set structure (a five-paragraph outline), the writer started by determining what readers will need to know. She then organized her outline so that she answered readers' potential questions. Helping students think about an audience's needs promotes critical thinking during the planning and writing process.

Adding Source Material and Details to Your Outline

Teaching Resources: See the handout/exercise "Using Audience Analysis to Plan Your Essay."

Now that she has an outline, Krystal can start adding minor supporting details, including source materials. She has to consider carefully when and where to use quotes from her sources. She will not want to overuse her research by including too many quotes or by merely summarizing a variety of sources. The result would be a paper that jumps from quote to quote or from summary to summary without tying the information together in a way that represents her perspective and insights. Professors want to see *your* writing. So remember that quotes are best used sparingly and only when they truly support the point you are making.

Remember that when you use specific ideas from *any* source, even if you put them into your own words, you *must* give credit to the author of those ideas. Many students wonder whether they need to cite sources for well-known ideas, or **common knowledge**. Krystal may write, for instance, that football is a dangerous sport. Because many others have said the same, she does not have to cite other people who have made this general statement. In contrast, a statistic on the number of head injuries in football *would* need to come from a cited source because a statistic is not common knowledge. In her paper, Krystal will include specific information about the effects of concussions and solutions to the concussion problem that she learned about from her sources, and she will cite these sources when she uses them.

As Krystal considers how best to support her thesis statement, she selects several sources that will be advantageous and adds them to her outline. She uses the last name of the writer to refer to the source materials she will incorporate in her essay.

Essay Outline Annotated to Include Sources

Topic: Concussions in football

Thesis statement: The effects of concussions sustained while playing football are so serious that players should demand changes or refuse to play the game.

INTRODUCTION

Paragraph 1: Explain why so many people are talking about this issue these days. Start with the story of Dave Duerson. End with thesis statement. Use Jackson source for Duerson's story.

BODY

Paragraph 2 (major supporting point 1—effects): Scientists have learned that concussions have serious long-term effects on the brain. Use Monroe source and CDC source for quotes and statistics.

Paragraph 3 (major supporting point 2—changes): Players and those who care about them should demand changes. The first thing that can be done is to reduce the number of concussions by changing some of the rules in football. Use Davidson source to explain possible rule changes.

Paragraph 4 (major supporting point 3—changes): A second solution is to require the use of a new type of helmet. Use Jackson source and Monroe source for new helmet innovation information.

Paragraph 5 (major supporting point 4—changes): Third, football coaches, trainers, physicians, players, and the families of players must be trained to identify concussions and consult the appropriate health-care professionals so that concussions are treated correctly. Use quotes from CDC source.

Paragraph 6 (major supporting point 5—refuse to play): Players must educate themselves about the realities and then stand up for themselves—if necessary, by refusing to play—for the sake of their long-term health and for those who care about them. Use the story of the Melville City League as an example—Monroe source.

CONCLUSION

Paragraph 7: Explain how this issue affects not only NFL players but also youth football players across the country. Urge that a solution be found.

PRACTICE 3 Choosing Source Materials

The following paragraphs about anger management are from "Controlling Anger before It Controls You," which appears on the Web site of the American Psychological Association. Following the paragraphs you will see an outline for a student's essay on anger management. Read the source paragraphs and the outline. Choose two passages that provide helpful information and would make good quotes for the essay. Underline each quote, and note where you would put it in the outline.

Source Paragraphs

According to Jerry Deffenbacher, PhD, a psychologist who specializes in anger management, some people really are more "hotheaded" than others are; they get angry more easily and more intensely than the average person does. There are also those who don't show their anger in loud spectacular ways but are chronically

YOUR ANNOTATIONS

(continued)

irritable and grumpy. Easily angered people don't always curse and throw things; sometimes they withdraw socially, sulk, or get physically ill.

People who are easily angered generally have what some psychologists call a low tolerance for frustration, meaning simply that they feel that they should not have to be subjected to frustration, inconvenience, or annoyance. They can't take things in stride, and they're particularly infuriated if the situation seems somehow unjust: for example, being corrected for a minor mistake.

What makes these people this way? A number of things. One cause may be genetic or physiological: There is evidence that some children are born irritable, touchy, and easily angered, and that these signs are present from a very early age. Another may be sociocultural. Anger is often regarded as negative; we're taught that it's all right to express anxiety, depression, or other emotions but not to express anger. As a result, we don't learn how to handle it or channel it constructively.

Source: © 2005 by the American Psychological Association.

Outline for a Student's Essay

Introduction

    Thesis statement: People who have trouble controlling their anger can learn techniques to manage it.

Body

    Major supporting point 1: What are anger disorders?

    Major supporting point 2: What causes anger disorders?

    Major supporting point 3: How is anger management disorder diagnosed?

    Major supporting point 4: How is anger management disorder treated?

    Major supporting point 5: What is the outlook for people who go through anger management programs?

Conclusion

> Answers will vary. Sample answers follow. (1) "People who are easily angered generally have what some psychologists call a low tolerance for frustration, meaning simply that they feel that they should not have to be subjected to frustration, inconvenience, or annoyance." Use for MSP 1. (2) "There is evidence that some children are born irritable, touchy, and easily angered, and that these signs are present from a very early age." Use for MSP 2.

Writing a Complete Draft of Your Essay

Once you have an outline ready, you can use it to compose a first draft. Keep in mind that an outline is a plan, and as such it is changeable. If you write a body paragraph and find that you have not planned for enough support, change your outline by adding more examples or perhaps an anecdote or a comparison.

Use a recursive process when you draft. To *recur* means "to happen again." Recursive drafting means that you go back and reread what you have written, make changes, and resume drafting. After completing each paragraph, read your essay from the beginning. You will find areas that need more development, are unclear, and so on. Make changes as you draft.

Integrating Ideas and Quotes from Sources Correctly

As you draft your paper, integrate source material carefully. The key to using quotes effectively is knowing *when* to use them and *how* to integrate them. During the process of reading source materials, you annotated your sources and identified significant passages. You also wrote down possible quotations on your information sheets. Keep in mind that because you wrote your notes before you knew exactly what you would be saying in your paper, the quotes you chose may not be the best ones to support your points. Be willing to go back to the source to choose the most appropriate quotes for your purpose.

A **quotation** consists of the exact words of a source. Even if the writer of the source made a grammatical error, you must reproduce the source exactly, errors included. You

> The Quick Start Guide to Integrated Reading and Writing Assignments presents each step in a graphic for easy reference.

must acknowledge the source in the body of the text as well as in a list of references or works cited, which you will learn about later in this chapter.

Determining When to Use Quotations

Using quotations carefully can help you write an impressive, well-researched paper. However, if you use quotes like seasoning salt—sprinkling them here and there at random—you will have a paper that makes little sense. Use quotations only in the following situations.

- **You need to support your point of view with authoritative information.** The most common reason for using a quote is to back up your own ideas by citing professionals or experts who agree with you.

  Example: Some serious psychological disorders show up during the early adult years. Ian Christopher points out that "schizophrenia, generalized anxiety disorders, and bipolar disorder commonly manifest in early adulthood."

- **You wish to provide complex or technical explanations.** Sometimes only experts can explain complex phenomena. Carefully select quotes when an expert can offer a better explanation than you can.

  Example: According to the Center for Genetic Origination, mutation consists of "the moment when a nucleotide sequence of the genome of an organism or related being undergoes change."

- **Using your own wording of a concept or idea would not be as effective as quoting the source's wording.** When you find a source that words an idea perfectly, it is fine to quote that source as long as you give credit.

  Example: George Orwell writes, "Doublethink means the power of holding two contradictory beliefs in one's mind simultaneously, and accepting both of them."

- **The source has used a particularly important phrase, and you do not want to change the wording of that phrase.** In the following example, the last name of the source's writer is provided in parentheses.

  Example: The detective refers to himself as "the lone ranger of the casino industry" (Cavanaugh).

Let's consider Krystal's project and her decision to quote from experts. Krystal is arguing that football players must demand changes to the game because the effects of concussions are so serious. Since she is not a doctor or a medical researcher, she needs support from experts to prove that concussions are truly as bad as she says. She has chosen a source written by a doctor who is an authority, but now she must choose the actual quote to use. Here is the source, along with Krystal's reasoning process.

Commentary: Concussions in Football
by Michael Craig Miller

Lexile: 1180L

Consider what happens to the brain on impact. It accelerates very quickly, then decelerates just as quickly as it bangs into the skull. Nerve cells get stretched, connections between nerve cells get disrupted or sheared. Neurologists dispute the definition of a concussion, but terminology aside, all of this causes a short-term disturbance in brain function. It's no wonder that victims feel dazed, assuming they remain conscious.

But there is growing evidence that professional football players are prone to the kind of brain damage common in boxers, a condition that used to be called

Have this in my notes, but I need more detail.

Good information, but doesn't show how serious concussions are.

(continued)

dementia pugilistica, but is now referred to as chronic traumatic encephalopathy (CTE). Postmortem analyses of the brains of players who died relatively young have revealed signs of neurodegeneration similar to that found in Alzheimer's disease.

More recently, researchers have focused attention on the effect of *repetitive* impacts, which are common in football. One concern is that of "second-impact syndrome." If two head injuries occur in relatively rapid succession, such as within the course of one game, the outcome can be catastrophic, with brain swelling and death. So players are at great risk if they return to the field too soon.

Excerpted from the *Harvard Mental Health Letter*. © 2010, Harvard University. Note: Harvard Health Publications does not endorse any products or medical procedures.

Source Information
Author: Michael Craig Miller
Title: "Commentary: Concussions in Football"
Publication: *Harvard Mental Health Letter*
Date: January 2010
ISSN: 1057–5022
Volume: 26
Issue: 7
Page: 8

Excellent information because it shows how serious the damage is and refers to "evidence." Clearly written from medical perspective; don't want to use this whole passage, though. I've underlined best parts.

Can show how concussions can be even more serious by using this passage.

After thinking carefully, Krystal decides the quote will work best if it reveals the source's authority on the subject *and* supports the point that concussion effects are serious. Krystal decides against using a quote she had previously identified in order to find one that perfectly fits her ideas.

Effective writers are selective about using quotations. The following guidelines will help you make decisions about when and what to quote.

- **Do not use a quote just to use a quote.** Always have a good reason for quoting a source.

- **Avoid using quotes too often.** If you pepper your essay with too many quotes, your voice will be lost, and you will not communicate your message effectively.

- **Use a lengthy quote only when you have a very good reason to do so.** Quotations—especially those that are more than two or three sentences long—take up a lot of space. You may be tempted to fill your paper with long quotations (and thus more easily reach a required word count), but do not yield to this temptation.

- **Avoid starting a paragraph with a quote.** Take ownership of the paragraphs in your paper by starting them with your own words. Use quotes very selectively to supplement your voice and your ideas; *your* voice should be the dominant voice heard in an essay.

- **Avoid using dialogue-style quotations.** Instead of repeating the dialogue as you might in a story, use a single quotation or your own words, as in the following example.

Dialogue:	Colleen said, "You're always making irresponsible choices."
	"Maybe you're right," I replied.
Better:	Colleen told me I am always making irresponsible choices. Maybe she was right.

PRACTICE ④ Determining When to Use Quotations

The following paragraphs are from a student's essay about the positive effects of learning to play an instrument. Rihanna has used research to support her ideas. Each direct quote is shown in bold and numbered. Read through these paragraphs, and determine when her use of research is appropriate and when it is not appropriate. Use the guidelines in this chapter to help you decide.

Rihanna's Paragraphs

[1]**"Learning piano taught me persistence," claims Benjamin Briggs.** Briggs is a classical pianist living in Chicago. Many musicians who have achieved an impressive level of mastery find that their practicing habits have influenced their ability to persist in other tasks. Some musicians become adept at other skills, such as cooking, painting, or writing poetry. For Briggs, the persistence skills he gained as a musician have affected other parts of his life:

> [2]**I have used the same persistence techniques in other areas of my life. When I began running, I didn't even think about giving up after that first, awful day of heavy breathing and sweating. I simply got up the next morning and did the same thing: ran three miles that nearly killed me. I think my persistence at piano kind of taught me not to give up in anything. I am always surprised when my children give up so easily after a failed attempt at something. I remember my first time working through a Rachmaninoff piece. It was futile, I thought. But some months later, I was playing the piece decently, and by the end of a few more months, I got it.**

Not all musicians begin their musical careers enjoying practice time. Jan-Lin Chu has also benefited from the persistence required to master her instrument, the cello, but she did not always enjoy the process. Chu says that her hours of practice each day at first made her feel trapped, but she had little control over her time: her mother strictly required three hours of practice daily (Chu 15). [3]**Chu eventually became "a happy little prisoner," as she says in her journal, when she made peace with her practice responsibilities and grew to even enjoy the time (15).** She credits her persistence in practicing cello with her recent mastery of Spanish, a language she had hoped to learn for a long time. [4]**Learning Spanish, says Chu, "is much like learning pieces for cello. It requires persistence, daily work, patience, and practice" (17).**

Assess Rihanna's use of quotes. Which quotes should she leave in? Which should she take out? Explain your answers.

1. Quote 1: <u>This is a good quote, but it would be better for Rihanna to start the paragraph with her own words.</u>

2. Quote 2: <u>This quote is too long. Perhaps Rihanna could use one or two sentences but not the whole thing.</u>

3. Quote 3: <u>The use of "happy little prisoner" is effective, as it is a special phrase that captures a lot of feeling.</u>

4. Quote 4: <u>Rihanna could eliminate this quote. It repeats the idea from the previous sentence without adding anything new.</u>

Determining How to Use Quotations

As you might have gathered by now, good writing requires authors to integrate quotes smoothly. You can quote in two ways. The first is to use the actual words from a source. The second is to put the source's ideas into your own words.

Whether you use a **direct quotation** (the exact words from a source enclosed in quotation marks) or an **indirect quotation** (the ideas of a source put into your own words), you must follow these guidelines.

Teaching Resources: See the PPT "Effectively Integrating Quotations" and the exercise "Integrating Quotations."

Represent the Source Fairly

When you quote, you are providing readers with another person's ideas, and you must do so accurately. Be thoroughly familiar with the entire source—the main idea, major supporting points, minor supporting details, examples, and so on—so that you do not misrepresent the writer's ideas.

Present the Source Accurately

When you use the ideas of a source in a direct quote, you must restate the words *exactly as they appear* in the original source. Check and double-check to make sure your transcription is accurate.

Even if the author has made a spelling or grammatical error in the words you are quoting, you must include it in your quote. You can indicate that the error was in the original source by using the Latin adverb *sic*, which means "that's how it was written."

Example: Trenton Wiley writes that coaches still "fail to take concushins [sic] seriously enough."

Use Attributive Tags

An **attributive tag** gives credit to the author of the quote you are using in your essay. These tags can be used to introduce a quote, to interrupt a quote, or at the end of a quote. In addition to giving credit to the author, attributive tags can provide information about the source or about the author's credibility or viewpoint, as the examples in the table show.

Attributive Tags for Quotations

LOCATION OF ATTRIBUTIVE TAG	EXAMPLE	EXPLANATION
Before the quote: According to	According to Michael Craig Miller, MD, editor in chief of the *Harvard Mental Health Letter*, "Postmortem analyses of the brains of players who died relatively young have revealed signs of neurodegeneration similar to that found in Alzheimer's disease."	The attributive tag goes before the name, and the name is followed by a comma. The writer's degree (MD) and his position or affiliation are also included to lend credibility to his words. Since the quote is a complete sentence, the first word is capitalized. The period at the end of the sentence goes inside the quotation marks.
Before the quote: As . . . writes, As . . . says, As . . . notes, As . . . claims, As . . . states, As . . . remarks, As . . . shows, As . . . contends,	As Michael Craig Miller, MD, writes in the *Harvard Mental Health Letter*, "Postmortem analyses of the brains of players who died relatively young have revealed signs of neurodegeneration similar to that found in Alzheimer's disease."	This attributive tag emphasizes where the doctor's writing was published.
After the quote: —claims . . . —according to . . . —as . . . writes	"Postmortem analyses of the brains of players who died relatively young have revealed signs of neurodegeneration similar to that found in Alzheimer's disease," claims Michael Craig Miller, MD, an advocate of stronger safety guidelines for football.	The sentence begins with the quote. At the end of the quote, a comma and then quotation marks are used. These are followed by the attributive tag (*claims*) and the writer's credentials. Notice that the attributive tag is followed with a comment about the doctor's viewpoint, which further helps the reader understand Dr. Miller's position.

Use Indirect Quotes Correctly

When you want to briefly summarize a source or refer to an idea from a source, you can create an indirect quote by using your own words. When you put ideas in your own words, you do not use quotation marks. However, you still have to give credit to the source. One way to create an indirect quote is to use attributive tags.

Example: According to Samara Johnston, those who voyaged to the Americas had to learn methods for dealing with illness and death.

Another way is to state the idea and follow it with a reference in parentheses.

Example: Those who voyaged to the Americas had to learn methods for dealing with illness and death (Johnston).

Note that the period goes *after* the parenthetical reference. Later in the chapter, you will find an explanation of when and how to use parenthetical references in your writing.

Avoid Run-on Sentences and Sentence Fragments When Using Quotes

You know that run-on sentences and sentence fragments are all errors. But did you know that if you use quotes incorrectly, you can create these kinds of errors?

For example, this quote is a complete sentence: "Postmortem analyses of the brains of players who died relatively young have revealed signs of neurodegeneration similar to that found in Alzheimer's disease." If you joined this quotation to another complete sentence without appropriate punctuation, you would create a type of run-on sentence known as a *comma splice*. To avoid run-ons and sentence fragments when using quotes, follow these guidelines.

Teaching Resources: See the mini-quiz "Quoting Grammatically."

- **When the quote is a complete sentence, do not add it to another complete sentence. Use correct punctuation to separate the two complete sentences.**

    Incorrect, with comma splice: Michael Craig Miller, MD, would like to see stronger regulations in place to prevent concussions in football, "Postmortem analyses of the brains of players who died relatively young have revealed signs of neurodegeneration similar to that found in Alzheimer's disease."

    Corrected by creating two complete sentences: Michael Craig Miller, MD, would like to see stronger regulations in place to prevent concussions in football. According to Miller, "Postmortem analyses of the brains of players who died relatively young have revealed signs of neurodegeneration similar to that found in Alzheimer's disease."

    Note: When you quote complete sentences, capitalize the first word of the quoted sentence.

- **When a quote is *not* a complete sentence, it cannot stand on its own, even with an attributive tag. Add your own words to the fragment to make it into a complete sentence. Clearly identify the source's words by using quotation marks around the quote.**

    Incorrect, with fragment: Michael Craig Miller, MD, cites evidence of serious damage from concussions. "Neurodegeneration similar to that found in Alzheimer's disease."

    Corrected by adding words to make a complete sentence: In the brains of people who have suffered concussions, researchers have found "neurodegeneration similar to that found in Alzheimer's disease," according to Michael Craig Miller, MD.

    Note: Do not capitalize fragments that you quote.

- **You can interrupt a quote with an attributive tag, but you cannot put a complete sentence on one side of the attributive tag and a complete sentence on the other side.**

    Incorrect, with a comma splice: "If two head injuries occur in relatively rapid succession, such as within the course of one game, the outcome can be catastrophic, with brain swelling and death," states Dr. Michael Craig Miller, "So players are at great risk if they return to the field too soon."

Corrected by inserting attributive tags: "If two head injuries occur in relatively rapid succession, such as within the course of one game, the outcome can be catastrophic, with brain swelling and death," states Dr. Michael Craig Miller. "So players are at great risk if they return to the field too soon," Miller explains.

Apply Correct Punctuation Rules for Quotations

Most of the time, punctuation goes inside the quotation marks.

Example: A more effective form of punishment, writes Dr. Brennan, "is intentional exclusion."

If a question mark is part of the quotation, put it inside the quotation marks.

Example: She asked, "Why should we bother to learn this?"

When you have a quote within a quote, use single quotation marks for the internal quote, and double quotation marks for the outer one.

Example: According to Marilyn Jackson, "County officials called the new ordinance 'a necessary evil.'"

Learn to Use Ellipses

An ellipsis is a mark made up of three spaced dots (. . .) that indicates the omission of words from quoted material. Study the list that follows to see how to use ellipses correctly. If you have additional questions about the use of ellipses, refer to a style manual such as the *MLA Handbook for Writers of Research Papers* or the *Publication Manual of the American Psychological Association*.

Teaching Resources: See the exercise "Using Ellipses Correctly."

- **Original source:** On the voyage to the Americas, illness was a common cause of death.

  Material to omit from the middle of the sentence: On the voyage ~~to the Americas,~~ illness was a common cause of death.

  Use an ellipsis to show omission: "On the voyage . . . illness was a common cause of death."

- **Original source:** With little to no medicine available, not much could be done for those who became ill.

  Material to omit from the end of the sentence: With little to no medicine available, not much could be done ~~for those who became ill.~~

  Use an ellipsis to show omission: "With little to no medicine available, not much could be done. . . ."

  Note: The ellipsis follows the period at the end of the sentence.

- **Original source:** On the voyage to the Americas, illness was a common cause of death. With little to no medicine available, not much could be done for those who became ill. Consequently, mariners had to solve the problem of disposing of the dead.

  Entire sentence to be omitted: On the voyage to the Americas, illness was a common cause of death. ~~With little to no medicine available, not much could be done for those who became ill.~~ Consequently, mariners had to solve the problem of disposing of the dead.

  Use an ellipsis to show omission: "On the voyage to the Americas, illness was a common cause of death. . . . Consequently, mariners had to solve the problem of disposing of the dead."

Give Credit to the Source to Avoid Plagiarism

As you learned earlier, *plagiarism* is using someone else's words or ideas without giving that source proper credit. To avoid plagiarism, you must make sure every source you use in your essay is credited both in the text itself and in a list of sources at the end of the essay. Neglecting to properly credit sources is plagiarism, even if you do not intend to plagiarize.

Just as with quotations, every time you use a writer's idea—even when you put it into your own words—you must give the writer credit by using an attributive tag or by putting the writer's name in parentheses after the idea.

Example: Christa Brennan writes that children who have to earn video gaming privileges are better equipped for hard work later in life.

Example: It may be true that children who have to earn video gaming privileges are better equipped for hard work later in life (Brennan).

If you continue to use information from the same source, make sure that you consistently give credit to the source. Do not move between your own ideas and the source's ideas without making it clear where the source's ideas start and end. Here is an example.

UNCLEAR	CLEAR
Christa Brennan writes that children who have to earn video gaming privileges are better equipped for hard work later in life. Children who earn those privileges begin to associate leisure time with work. By making this connection, children come to expect that they will have to earn certain recreational privileges. As a result, these children have a less difficult time accepting the hard work that is required in college and in the workplace. Parents should consider having children earn privileges such as video gaming by completing some kind of work or chore.	Christa Brennan writes that children who have to earn video gaming privileges are better equipped for hard work later in life. According to Brennan, children who earn those privileges begin to associate leisure time with work. By making this connection, children come to expect that they will have to earn certain recreational privileges; as a result, these children have a less difficult time accepting the hard work that is required in college and in the workplace (Brennan). Clearly, parents should consider having children earn privileges such as video gaming by completing some kind of work or chore.

PRACTICE 5 Constructing Accurate and Effective Quotations

Below are four paragraphs about anger management from an article, "Controlling Anger before It Controls You," on the American Psychological Association's Web site. The paragraphs discuss one method for managing anger called *cognitive restructuring*. After the source, you will see a student's paragraph about cognitive restructuring. Unfortunately, the student has not credited any sources in his paragraph. He needs to do so, not only to show where he learned about cognitive restructuring, but also to improve his writing. On a separate sheet, rewrite the student's paragraph and use at least two quotes (direct or indirect) to improve the writing and to show where the student's ideas came from.

Source Paragraphs

Cognitive Restructuring

Simply put, this means changing the way you think. Angry people tend to curse, swear, or speak in highly colorful terms that reflect their inner thoughts. When you're angry, your thinking can get very exaggerated and overly dramatic. Try replacing these thoughts with more rational ones. For instance, instead of telling yourself, "oh, it's awful, it's terrible, everything's ruined," tell yourself, "it's frustrating, and it's understandable that I'm upset about it, but it's not the end of the world and getting angry is not going to fix it anyhow."

(continued)

Answers will vary. Sample answer follows. According to the American Psychological Association, one way to master anger is to use a technique called "cognitive restructuring." In an article on the association's Web site, the authors explain that the key to doing this is recognizing the negative ways our minds think when we are angry and replacing negativity with logical thoughts. Sometimes, the article points out, by changing the words we use to describe events to ourselves, we can become calmer and more rational. ~~Certain terms are not only unhelpful to think of, but they are also illogical. An example of cognitive restructuring is to reword a negative event.~~ For example,

Be careful of words like "never" or "always" when talking about yourself or someone else. "This !&*%@ machine never works," or "you're always forgetting things" are not just inaccurate; they also serve to make you feel that your anger is justified and that there's no way to solve the problem. They also alienate and humiliate people who might otherwise be willing to work with you on a solution.

Remind yourself that getting angry is not going to fix anything, that it won't make you feel better (and may actually make you feel worse).

Logic defeats anger, because anger, even when it's justified, can quickly become irrational. So use cold hard logic on yourself. Remind yourself that the world is "not out to get you," you're just experiencing some of the rough spots of daily life. Do this each time you feel anger getting the best of you, and it'll help you get a more balanced perspective. Angry people tend to demand things: fairness, appreciation, agreement, willingness to do things their way. Everyone wants these things, and we are all hurt and disappointed when we don't get them, but angry people demand them, and when their demands aren't met, their disappointment becomes anger. As part of their cognitive restructuring, angry people need to become aware of their demanding nature and translate their expectations into desires. In other words, saying, "I would like" something is healthier than saying, "I demand" or "I must have" something. When you're unable to get what you want, you will experience the normal reactions—frustration, disappointment, hurt—but not anger. Some angry people use this anger as a way to avoid feeling hurt, but that doesn't mean the hurt goes away.

Source: © 2005 by the American Psychological Association.

Student's Paragraph

One way to master anger is to use cognitive restructuring. The key to doing this is recognizing the negative ways our minds think when we are angry and replacing negativity with logical thoughts. Sometimes by changing the words we use to describe events to ourselves, we can become calmer and more rational. Certain terms are not only unhelpful to think of, but they are also illogical. An example of cognitive restructuring is to reword a negative event. For example, if you get cut off in traffic, instead of calling the act *unfair* or *unjust,* think of it as *an unfortunate incident.* You can even make up hypothetical reasons for the event. Tell yourself the person may be going to the hospital to meet a loved one who was in an accident. This kind of restructuring can make frustrating events more tolerable.

[Margin annotation:] if you get cut off in traffic, instead of calling the act *unfair* or *unjust,* think of it as *an unfortunate incident.* You can even make up hypothetical reasons for the event. Tell yourself the person may be going to the hospital to meet a loved one who was in an accident. This kind of restructuring can make frustrating events more tolerable.

CREATING IN-TEXT REFERENCES IN MLA AND APA STYLES

Giving proper credit for sources involves (1) creating in-text references at the places in your essay where you use sources and (2) supplying complete information about each source in a list at the end of the essay. Both the Modern Language Association (MLA) and the American Psychological Association (APA) have published guidebooks with instructions on how to properly credit sources—the *MLA Handbook for Writers of Research Papers* and the *Publication Manual of the American Psychological Association,* respectively. Your instructor will very likely have you use one of these style guides. Following are basic guidelines for creating in-text references.

Using MLA Style for In-Text References

Parenthetical documentation is the term given to the MLA's method for giving in-text credit to sources. The parenthetical reference (information in parentheses) gives the reader enough information to locate full bibliographic information for the source in the list of works cited at the end of the essay.

Let's say that one of your sources is an article by Jeanette LeFarve titled "Understanding Anorexia." Because you found this article in a magazine in the library (not in a computer database), you can see the article's original page numbers. You wish to quote this passage from page 15 of the article: "Anorexia is actually a mental disorder that manifests in physical symptoms." To use this quote, you would find an attributive tag that fits into your sentence. The first time you use a source, you should give the writer's first and last name in the attribution. If you use the source again, you can use only the last name, since readers have already been introduced to the source. Here is an example.

MLA Style for an In-Text Reference (When Author's Name Is in the Sentence)

> According to Jeanette LeFarve, "Anorexia is actually a mental disorder that manifests in physical symptoms" (15).

Notice that the end quotation marks appear *before* the parenthetical reference and that the period follows the parenthetical reference. Notice also that LeFarve's name does not appear in the parentheses because it is used in the attributive tag. Thus, readers will understand that the quote comes from LeFarve and that it appears on page 15 in the source. If readers want to find the original source, they can look at the list of works cited at the end of your essay, find Jeanette LeFarve's name, and use the bibliographic information to look up the article.

If you refer to LeFarve's article without using her name in an attributive tag, you will need to put her name in the parenthetical reference. Here is an example.

MLA Style for an In-Text Reference (When Author's Name Is Not in the Sentence)

> "Anorexia is actually a mental disorder that manifests in physical symptoms" (LeFarve 15).

Notice that the parenthetical reference follows the end quotation mark and is followed by a period. Notice also that there is no comma between the writer's name and the page number.

Sources obtained from a Web site or from an online database often do not include the original page numbers, so when using those sources, you will not be able to include page numbers in your in-text reference. Do not use the page numbers from a printout of an article from the Web; they are not the original page numbers. If you use a source that does not have page numbers, you can either include just the writer's name in a parenthetical reference or simply use an attributive tag to credit the writer. When readers do not see a page number, they will know that the source you used did not contain page numbers, as in the following examples.

MLA Style for an In-Text Reference to a Source without Page Numbers

> One scientist claims that anorexia can be cured by behavioral therapy (Mallin).

or

> Mallin claims that anorexia can be cured by behavioral therapy.

Remember that you should not use quotation marks when you are putting an idea into your own words. Notice that at the end of the first example, the period follows the parenthetical reference.

If you use an article that has no author listed, use the full title of the work, if brief, in quotation marks, in place of the author's name. If the title is long, use the first few significant title words. For example, for a quote on page 25 of an anonymous article entitled "Fighting Anorexia," you would refer to the source as in the following example.

MLA Style for an In-Text Reference to a Source with No Author

"The clinics that specialize in anorexia often treat the disorder with a variety of treatment modalities" ("Fighting Anorexia" 25).

Finally, you will sometimes want to use a source that is quoted by another source. For instance, imagine that in Mallin's article about anorexia, she quotes this statistic from a treatment center: "approximately 1% of female teenagers have anorexia." If you would like to use this quote in your paper, you may do so, but you will need to add *qtd. in* (for "quoted in") to your parenthetical reference, as shown in the following example.

MLA Style for an In-Text Reference to a Source Quoted in Another Source

Few people realize that "approximately 1% of female teenagers have anorexia" (qtd. in Mallin).

In the list of works cited, you will include an entry for Mallin's article. Readers can then locate Mallin's article if they wish to find information about the original source.

For more information on MLA style for in-text references, consult the latest edition of the *MLA Handbook for Writers of Research Papers*.

A helpful exercise is to have students create a summary of the most important information in this section of the chapter. They can refer to their summaries when they are writing papers and need to remember the most importation citation and documentation rules.

Using APA Style for In-Text References

When you cite sources in APA style, two pieces of information are essential: the name of the author and the date of the source. As with MLA style, you use parentheses to show where quotes and ideas came from.

When you use a writer's idea and include the writer's name in the sentence, put the date of the source in parentheses; in another set of parentheses, include the page number where the information was found, as in the following example.

APA Style for an In-Text Reference (When Author's Name Is in the Sentence)

According to Heinmann (2004), the prevalence of anorexia nervosa among girls in grades 7 and 8 rose by 5% from 1998 to 2002 (p. 21).

Because the author of this essay is using her own words rather than quoting from Heinmann directly, she does not use quotation marks. The date of Heinmann's article (in this case, a year) follows his name in parentheses. The end of the sentence contains a parenthetical reference with the page number. Note that in APA style, you use the abbreviation *p.* for "page" (or *pp.* for "pages") and then insert the number. The sentence period follows.

If you do not mention the name of the writer in your text, include the writer's name in the parenthetical reference with the date and the page number, as in the following example.

APA Style for an In-Text Reference (When Author's Name Is Not in the Sentence)

The prevalence of anorexia nervosa among girls in grades 7 and 8 rose by 5% from 1998 to 2002 (Heinmann, 2004, p. 21).

Notice that the writer's name is followed by a comma, the date of publication, another comma, and the page number.

If no author is indicated in the source, cite the first significant word or words of the title instead, as shown below.

APA Style for an In-Text Reference to a Source with No Author

> Several girls reported feeling uneasy with their bodies ("Why Girls," 2006, pp. 31–32).

Notice that the abbreviated title is in quotation marks to indicate that the source is an article (or other short work) with no author indicated. The comma goes inside the end quotation mark, and the date and the page numbers follow.

Page numbers should be included only when you have the original page numbers from the source. If you are looking at a book, you can see the original page numbers. If you are looking at a journal article online, you will probably not see page numbers, so you cannot use them in your parenthetical references. For more information on APA style for in-text references, consult the latest edition of the *Publication Manual of the American Psychological Association*.

The differences between the MLA and APA citation systems may seem minor—whether you need a comma, whether you use *p.* before the page number, and so on. However, using these systems properly shows your instructor that you take your research seriously and that you are good at following instructions.

Setting Off a Long Quotation

Both MLA and APA give guidelines for setting off long quotations so that they stand out in the text of an essay.

In MLA style, set off a quotation of more than four lines by indenting it one inch from the left margin. Do not use quotation marks; follow the quote with a period and then the parenthetical reference, as in the following example.

MLA Style for a Long Quotation

> Educational researchers are calling for innovative ways to deal with misbehaving children in public schools:
>
> > There are alternatives to meting out punishment that treats our school children like criminals. Instead of sending students to the principal's office or worse—calling police into classrooms to deal with disorderly conduct—schools can equip their teachers with tools proven to create safe, supportive learning environments and defuse disruption. The very things that mitigate student stress and bad behavior make a school what it's supposed to be: a healthy and productive place to learn. (Cantor 341)

In APA style, set off a quotation of forty words or more by indenting it a half inch from the left margin (the same indentation required by a new paragraph). Omit the quotation marks, and after the period at the end of the quoted passage, insert a parenthetical reference that includes the writer's last name, the date, and any page numbers.

APA Style for a Long Quotation

> Educational researchers are calling for innovative ways to deal with misbehaving children in public schools:
>
> > There are alternatives to meting out punishment that treats our school children like criminals. Instead of sending students to the principal's office or worse—calling police into classrooms to deal with disorderly conduct—schools can equip their teachers with tools proven to create safe, supportive learning environments and defuse disruption. The very things that mitigate student stress and bad behavior make a school what it's supposed to be: a healthy and productive place to learn. (Cantor, 2013, p. 341)

MLA STYLE: FORMATTING A PAPER AND PREPARING A WORKS CITED LIST

For a source-based paper in an English class, most instructors require the use of MLA style. The following section covers a few of the basic MLA style requirements. For complete information about how to use MLA style, see the latest edition of the *MLA Handbook for Writers of Research Papers*. Your library or writing center is likely to have a copy.

Formatting a Paper in MLA Style

Most instructors who require MLA style can immediately tell whether a paper adheres to the MLA guidelines just by glancing at it. MLA style requires the following formatting elements:

- One-inch margins on all sides
- A header in the top margin area that includes the student's last name and the page number (with no *p.* abbreviation)
- A heading that includes the student's full name, instructor's name, course information, and date
- The date in this format: 12 February 2012
- A centered title—regular text font, not bold or underlined
- Double-spacing throughout, with no additional space between the heading, title, or body of the paper
- Left-justified text, with no end-of-line hyphenation
- Half-inch indentions to begin new paragraphs

If you are unfamiliar with word processing and think you may have trouble formatting your paper, ask for assistance from someone in your library or writing center. A staff member there should be able to help you learn how to format your paper using word-processing software. See also the student paper later in this chapter for an example of MLA formatting.

The second and following pages of a source-based essay in MLA format must also conform to MLA requirements. These pages should (a) have the same header as the first page (your last name and page number), (b) have the same one-inch margins on all sides, and (c) be double-spaced. Only the first page of an essay should have the heading and title.

In general, do not use folders, plastic binders, or any sort of cover for source-based essays. A source-based essay should not have a title page unless your instructor directs you otherwise. Use black ink and a simple 12-point font such as Times New Roman. If your instructor has not given you specific directions regarding how to bind your paper, use a staple or a paper clip. And always keep a copy of your paper.

Creating Entries for an MLA Works Cited List

For each source you refer to in your essay, full bibliographic data must appear in a works cited list. Only sources you used within your paper for ideas or quotes should be included. If you read a source but did not refer to it in your paper, do not add it to your works cited list.

The sources on your works cited list are called *entries*. If you have referred to five sources in your paper, you will have five entries on your works cited list. Each type of source has its own format. The following sections present a few of the most common formats for entries. If you use other types of sources than those listed here, consult the latest edition of the *MLA Handbook for Writers of Research Papers* for guidance.

An Article in a Scholarly Journal

Last name, first name. "Title of article." *Title of publication* volume.issue (year of publication): page numbers. Medium.

While students are often familiar with using computers for Web browsing, a surprising number of students need to learn how to set up their papers to use the correct formatting. Consider requiring students to learn how to use Microsoft Word by giving them an assignment to be completed outside of class. See the handout/exercise "Using Microsoft Word for Academic Writing in MLA Style" or "Using Microsoft Word for Academic Writing in APA Style"

Martin, Louise. "The Nature of Anorexia." *Journal of Disease Therapies* 255.3 (2005): 13–21. Print.

Note: The specific punctuation *counts*! Do not forget the period after the writer's name, the period after the article's title, the period between the volume number and the issue number, the parentheses around the date, the colon after the date, and the final period. In addition, pay attention to which words are capitalized. In MLA style, the first and last words of titles are capitalized, as are all principal words.

An Article in a Newspaper

Last name, first name. "Title of article." *Name of newspaper* [city] day month year: pages. Medium.

Hernandez, Simon. "What You Need to Know about Your Teenage Daughter." *Daily News* [Marysville] 13 June 2007: D1+. Print.

Note: If the newspaper title includes the city's name (for instance, *The New York Times*), there is no need to supply the city in the works cited entry. Also, if a newspaper article extends beyond one page, use a plus sign (+) to indicate this fact. Finally, if you obtained the newspaper in print, finish the entry with "Print." If you obtained the newspaper from the Web, use "Web" instead of "Print," and add the date you accessed the online article, like this:

Hernandez, Simon. "What You Need to Know about Your Teenage Daughter." *Daily News* [Marysville] 13 June 2007: Web. 11 Nov. 2008.

An Article in a Magazine

Last name, first name. "Title of article." *Name of magazine* month year: pages. Medium.

Washington, Misa. "Not Eating?" *Good Housekeeping* Dec. 2007: 35–37. Print.

Note: Abbreviate all months except for May, June, and July. A magazine differs from a journal in that magazines usually publish less scholarly items and appear more frequently than journals.

One idea for helping students learn the basics of MLA or APA documentation is to have students collaboratively set up a works cited or references page for an essay. See the handout/exercise, "Creating a Bibliography."

A Book

Last name, first name. *Title of book*. City of publication: name of publisher, year. Medium.

Durmond, William. *Clinical Studies of Anorexia*. New York: Tranham P, 2006. Print.

Note that if the publisher's name includes the word *Press*, abbreviate that word as *P* (with no period).

If there are two or three authors, include all authors' names in the order in which they appear on the title page. For all authors after the first one, give the first name and then the last name, as shown below.

Durmond, William, and Martina McDaniel. *Clinical Studies of Anorexia*. New York: Tranham P, 2006. Print.

A Work in an Anthology

Last name, first name. "Title of the specific work." *Title of the anthology*. Ed. editor's name. City of publication: name of publisher, year. Pages of the specific work. Medium.

Capps, Li. "Brooklyn's Story." *Stories of Girls in Crisis*. Ed. Ann-Marie Tillich. Chicago: Chicago Media Publishers, 2000. 90–95. Print.

Note: An anthology is a collection of writings.

An Article in a Reference Book

"Title of article." *Title of reference book*. Number of edition. Year of publication. Medium.

"Anorexia Nervosa." *Talbot's Medical Dictionary*. 5th ed. 2007. Print.

A Work Found Only on the Web

Information from Web sites can be difficult to document, especially if the item is not from an online newspaper, journal, or database. For these other kinds of items, provide as much of the following information as you can:

1. Name of the author or editor of the work
2. Title of the work (if the work's title is the same as the title of the Web page, skip this step)
3. If the work is a Web page, title of the Web page (italicized)
4. Version or edition used (if you can find this information)
5. Publisher or sponsor of the site; if none is available, use *n.p.*
6. Date of publication (day, month, and year); if unavailable, use *n.d.*
7. Medium of publication; use the word *Web*
8. Date of access (the date you retrieved the work)

Here is an example of an article from the Cleveland Clinic's Web site:

"Anorexia Nervosa." *Cleveland Clinic*. Cleveland Clinic Medical Advisory Board. n.d. Web. 14 Feb. 2010.

A Periodical in an Online Database

Use the same format you would use for an article obtained in print, except conclude the entry with the following information:

1. Title of the database (italicized)
2. Medium of publication consulted (Web)
3. Date of access (day, month, and year)

Here is a source you saw previously (for an article in a print magazine). It has been converted to the format used for an online database:

Washington, Misa. "Not Eating?" *Good Housekeeping* Dec. 2007: 35–37. *Academic Search Premier*. Web. 25 Mar. 2008.

A Sample Paper in MLA Style

What follows is a source-based essay that uses MLA style written by a student, Meg Almond. You can use this model to format your own papers in MLA style. Note that your works cited list should start on a new page and should be the last item in your paper. It should include the same header as the rest of the paper (your last name and the page number). The list should be double-spaced and alphabetized. The first line of each entry should start at the left margin, and subsequent lines in the entry should be indented one-half inch.

1"

½"

Almond 1

Meg Almond

Dr. Hoeffner

English 0301

26 May 2014

Causes of Anorexia Nervosa

In a land with an overabundance of food, some people starve themselves to death. These people are victims of anorexia nervosa, defined by the Mayo Clinic as "an eating disorder that causes people to obsess about their weight and the food they eat." Anorexia, as it is often called, is usually seen as a mental disorder that affects the body. People who have it tend to "equate thinness with self-worth" (Mayo Clinic). While the Mayo Clinic's description is correct, it is not complete. The causes of anorexia are more complex than most people realize.

To begin, some researchers think there might be a medical basis for anorexia. Swedish researchers have learned some interesting things from studying people with anorexia. According to Thea Jourdan of the *Daily Mail*, a London newspaper, "The Swedish research showed that sufferers of anorexia and bulimia have unusually high levels of certain antibodies in their blood. These antibodies are produced by their own immune system in response to infections." Jourdan goes on to explain that the antibodies have an effect on brain chemicals, and a by-product is that one's appetite is affected. Jourdan points

Double-spacing throughout; 1-inch margins; 1/2-inch paragraph indent

Title centered

Introduction

Quotation as part of a sentence

Parenthetical reference to a Web source without page numbers

Thesis statement

Transition ("To begin") to major supporting point 1

Attributive tag giving author and source

Quotations as evidence

Almond 2

out that it may be wise to reclassify anorexia "as an auto-immune disease (a bit like rheumatoid arthritis)." If anorexia is found to be caused by a virus or if it is classified as an autoimmune response, the treatment of sufferers would change dramatically.

Another possible cause for anorexia is genetics. A National Institutes of Health study called the Genetics of Anorexia Nervosa is designed to research the role genetics plays in anorexia ("Researcher"). The genetic theory is that certain people have a set of genes that work together to create a genetic tendency toward anorexia. These genes are often found in more than one person in a family, according to the genetic theory ("Researcher"). Craig Johnson directs the eating disorders unit at Laureate Psychiatric Hospital in Tulsa, Oklahoma. He claims that "if a person has a family member who has had anorexia nervosa, she or he is 12 times more at risk of developing the illness." In his words, "Genetics loads the gun. Environment pulls the trigger" (qtd. in "Researcher").

Understanding that researchers are not sure about the causes of anorexia is very important. When a person develops anorexia, she is often blamed for the disease. She is told "Just eat!" as if she had complete control over her destiny. Since people think anorexia is a disease that is only in the mind, they think anorexia sufferers must *want* to be sick, or they must want to be thin.

Reba Loftin, a friend from high school, has suffered from anorexia for three years and is desperate to get better. She has been

Major supporting point 2

Parenthetical reference to a source listed by title (no author name)

Quote integrated into a sentence with that

Major supporting point 3

Personal example as evidence

Almond 3

in and out of treatment for the disorder. "It's frustrating when people say things like 'She just wants attention.' They really don't know what it's like. I mean, if I eat two or three french fries, I feel guilty all day" (Loftin). At 5 feet 4 inches and 101 pounds, Reba is very thin, but she cannot look at herself without feeling disgusted. "I know it's not rational, but I can't control my feelings" (Loftin). People like Reba do not want attention. They simply cannot control the irrational thoughts that flood their minds.

Many disorders and conditions are caused by brain chemistry problems. People who are depressed take medicines to help the brain work right, and people who have other disorders such as autism or ADHD also have medicines to help change their brain chemicals. Maybe someday researchers will discover a medicine that will help change the brain chemicals responsible for anorexia. If people learn that the causes of anorexia are more complex than they realized, those who suffer from the condition, as well as their families, will have an easier time fighting it. As Robert Finn says, "Rethinking the purely psychoanalytic model has a number of implications. For one thing, parents can quit blaming themselves, family dysfunction, or careless comments for causing their children's anorexia." Research and science may someday give us the answer, but until we have it, blame is not the solution.

Conclusion

Ending with a quote and a speculation

Almond 3

Works Cited

Finn, Robert. "Fallacies about Anorexia Undermine

Treatment." *Clinical Psychiatry News* 33.8 (2005): 50.

Web. 11 Mar. 2014.

Jourdan, Thea. "Anorexia Is a Real Disease." *Daily Mail* 27 Sept.

2005. Web. 11 Mar. 2014.

Loftin, Reba. Personal interview. 3 Mar. 2014.

Mayo Clinic. "Diseases and Conditions: Anorexia Nervosa."

Mayo Clinic Patient Care and Health Info. Rochester,

MN: Mayo Clinic. 5 Jan. 2012. Web. 9 Mar. 2014.

"Researcher Says Anorexia May Be Genetic." *AP Online.* 21

Feb. 2007. *HighBeam Research.* Web. 11 Mar. 2014.

Annotations (right margin):

- Works cited list starting on a new page; title centered
- Entries alphabetical and flush left with subsequent lines indented 1/2 inch
- Article in a publication found online
- Article in a newspaper found online
- Personal interview
- Organization as author
- Listed by title (no author)

APA STYLE: FORMATTING A PAPER AND PREPARING A REFERENCES LIST

Professors of sociology, psychology, and other social science disciplines often prefer APA style to MLA style. As you saw earlier for in-text citations, the two styles are similar, but there are a few differences. We will look at the basic principles of APA style here. For a more comprehensive explanation, consult the latest edition of the *Publication Manual of the American Psychological Association*.

Formatting a Paper in APA Style

In APA style, source-based essays must conform to the following formatting guidelines:

- The paper starts with a separate title page that includes a running head, the page number, the complete title of the work, the writer's name, and the writer's affiliation (such as a university or a company), if any. See the sample paper later in this chapter for an example.

- A running head (the title in shortened form) appears at the top left of each page. On the first (title) page, the words *Running Head* and a colon precede the title. Subsequent pages have just the shortened title.

- A page number appears in the upper right corner on all pages, including the title page.

- An abstract appears on the second page. An abstract is a 150- to 250-word summary of your paper. It is often easiest to write this brief summary after you are finished writing the paper. Type "Abstract" on the top line of page 2. On the next line, without indenting, start writing the abstract.

- The body of the paper begins on the third page. It starts with the title centered on the top line of the page, followed by a double space.
- The paper must be double-spaced.
- All margins are one inch.
- Paragraphs are indented a half inch (except for the abstract, which is not indented).

Do not use folders, plastic binders, or any sort of cover for your source-based essay. Use a simple 12-point font such as Times New Roman, and print in black ink. If your instructor has not given you specific directions regarding how to bind your paper, use a staple or a paper clip. Remember always to keep a copy of your essay. See the sample APA paper later in this chapter for an example of APA formatting.

Creating Entries for an APA References List

A paper in APA style ends with a list of references, which are the sources you have used in the paper. A reader should be able to flip to the references page of your essay and easily find information for every source mentioned in your paper. The list of references should be organized alphabetically by author or, if the work has no author, by the first significant word of the title. If you used several works by the same author, they should be listed in chronological order of publication date.

The sources you include on your reference page must be formatted correctly. A few of the APA guidelines differ in significant ways from the MLA guidelines. In particular, in APA, the author's last name is spelled out, but initials are used for the first and middle names. Additionally, APA capitalization guidelines differ from those for MLA. For titles of journals, magazines, and newspapers in a references list, capitalize the main words, as usual. But for article and book titles, capitalize only the first word and any proper nouns. The titles of articles are not italicized and are not put in quotation marks, but the titles of books, journals, magazines, and newspapers are italicized.

The information below provides only a few of the many types of source formats specified by the APA. For complete information, consult the latest edition of the *Publication Manual of the American Psychological Association*.

An Article in a Scholarly Journal

> Last name, initial. (Date of publication). Title. *Periodical title, volume*(issue), page numbers.
>
> Martin, L. (2005). The nature of anorexia. *Journal of Disease Therapies, 255*(3), 13–21.

As in MLA style, the details *matter*! Use periods and commas correctly. Notice the rules regarding spacing—for example, there's no space between the volume and issue numbers. Also notice what is and is not italicized here and in the following examples.

An Article in a Newspaper

> Last name, initial. (Date). Title of article. *Name of newspaper*, page numbers.
>
> Hernandez, S. (2007, June 13). What you need to know about your teenage daughter. *New York Times*, pp. B11–12.

An Article in a Magazine

> Last name, initial. (Date). Title of article. *Name of magazine*, page numbers.
>
> Krantz, M. (2007, December). New solutions for daycare. *Good Housekeeping*, 35–37.

A Book by a Single Author

> Last name, initial. (Date). *Title of book*. City of publication, state abbreviation: name of publisher.
>
> Durmond, W. (2006). *Clinical studies of anorexia*. New York, NY: Tranham.

A Book with More Than One Author

List each additional author (up to seven total); use an ampersand (&) before the last author.

> Williams, W., O'Connell, T., & Rouch, M. (2006). *Environmental factors in eating disorders*. Chicago, IL: United Medical Publishers.

A Work in an Anthology

> Last name of article author, initial. (Date). Title of work. "In" editor of the anthology (Ed.), *title of the anthology* (page numbers). City of publication, state abbreviation: publisher.

> Kennedy, D. (2002). Sustaining thought in brain injury patients. In J. T. Crasch (Ed.), *The brain and regenerative transformation* (pp. 332–335). Washington, DC: Collman Brothers.

A Work Found Only on the Web

APA requires an entry to include retrieval information—either a Web page or, preferably, a DOI designation. A **DOI (digital object identifier)** is an alphanumeric code that identifies a specific online reference. Most articles in databases are assigned a DOI. If you can find the DOI of a source, follow the instructions here for referencing that source.

An Online Article with DOI

> Author's last name, initial. (Date of publication). Title of article. *Title of periodical, volume*(issue), page numbers. doi: unique identifier

> Martin, J. (2003). Toward a theory of consciousness. *Journal of Neuroscience, 112*, 313–321. doi: 10.1033/0005-022X.30.8.750

An Online Article without DOI

If an article retrieved from an online source does not have a DOI, use the URL for the site from which you retrieved the item:

> Braggar, B. (1997). A view from the top. *Journal of Progress, 31*, 244–247. Retrieved from http://jopd/archives/ava

Research from a Web Site

Start with the name of the Web site and the date the Web site was last updated—if available (and if not, use *n.d.*). Then give the name of the document and the URL, as in the following example.

> Brady Center to Prevent Gun Violence. (2008, November 30). *Brady background checks: Fifteen years of saving lives* [Report]. Retrieved from http://www.bradycampaign.org/sites/default/files/brady-law-15years.pdf

A Sample Paper in APA Style

The references page should include a running head and page number, and the title *References* should be centered at the top. Each of the entries should be double-spaced and formatted with hanging indentation, as seen in this sample paper in APA style.

Title Page

Running Head: CAUSES OF ANOREXIA NERVOSA   1

Causes of Anorexia Nervosa
Megan Almond
Marshall Community College North

— Title, writer's name, and institution centered top to bottom and left to right

Paper

— 1-inch margins all around; double-spacing throughout

CAUSES OF ANOREXIA NERVOSA   2

— Running head and page number

Causes of Anorexia Nervosa

— Title centered

In a land with an overabundance of food, some people starve themselves to death. These people are victims of anorexia nervosa, defined by the Mayo Clinic (2012, para. 1) as "an eating disorder that causes people to obsess about their weight and the food they eat." Anorexia, as it is often called, is usually seen as a mental disorder that affects the body. People who have it tend to "equate thinness with self-worth" (Mayo Clinic, 2012, para. 2). While the Mayo Clinic's description is correct, it is not complete. The causes of anorexia are more complex than most people realize.

— Paragraph number in a parenthetical reference for a source without page numbers

— Source, date, and paragraph number in a parenthetical reference after integrated quote

To begin, some researchers think there might be a medical basis for anorexia. Swedish researchers have learned some interesting things from studying people with anorexia. According to Thea Jourdan (2005) of the *Daily Mail*, a London newspaper, "The Swedish research showed that sufferers of anorexia and bulimia have unusually high levels of certain antibodies in their blood. These antibodies are produced by their own immune system in response to infections" (para. 6). Jourdan goes on to

— Date of publication after attributive tag

CAUSES OF ANOREXIA NERVOSA   3

explain that the antibodies have an effect on brain chemicals, and a
by-product is that one's appetite is affected (para. 7). Jourdan points
out that it may be wise to reclassify anorexia "as an auto-immune
disease (a bit like rheumatoid arthritis)" (para. 7). If anorexia is
found to be caused by a virus or if it is classified as an autoimmune
response, the treatment of sufferers would change dramatically.

Another possible cause for anorexia is genetics. A National
Institutes of Health study called the Genetics of Anorexia
Nervosa is designed to research the role genetics plays in anorexia
("Researcher," 2003, para. 2). The genetic theory is that certain
people have a set of genes that work together to create a genetic
tendency toward anorexia. These genes are often found in more
than one person in a family, according to the genetic theory
("Researcher," 2003, para. 4). Craig Johnson directs the eating
disorders unit at Laureate Psychiatric Hospital in Tulsa, Oklahoma.
He claims that "if a person has a family member who has had
anorexia nervosa, she or he is 12 times more at risk of developing
the illness." In his words, "Genetics loads the gun. Environment
pulls the trigger" (as cited in "Researcher," 2003, para. 4).

Understanding that researchers are not sure about the
causes of anorexia is very important. When a person develops
anorexia, she is often blamed for the disease. She is told "Just eat!"
as if she had complete control over her destiny. Since people think
anorexia is a disease that is only in the mind, they think anorexia
sufferers must *want* to be sick, or they must want to be thin.

Parenthetical
reference for a
source listed by title

CAUSES OF ANOREXIA NERVOSA   4

Reba Loftin, a friend from high school, has suffered from anorexia for three years and is desperate to get better. She has been in and out of treatment for the disorder. "It's frustrating when people say things like 'She just wants attention.' They really don't know what it's like. I mean, if I eat two or three french fries, I feel guilty all day" (personal interview, March 3, 2014). At 5 feet 4 inches and 101 pounds, Reba is very thin, but she cannot look at herself without feeling disgusted. "I know it's not rational, but I can't control my feelings" (personal interview, March 3, 2014). People like Reba do not want attention. They simply cannot control the irrational thoughts that flood their minds.

Many disorders and conditions are caused by brain chemistry problems. People who are depressed take medicines to help the brain work right, and people who have other disorders such as autism or ADHD also have medicines to help change their brain chemicals. Maybe someday researchers will discover a medicine that will help change the brain chemicals responsible for anorexia. If people learn that the causes of anorexia are more complex than they realized, those who suffer from the condition, as well as their families, will have an easier time fighting it. As Robert Finn (2005) says, "Rethinking the purely psychoanalytic model has a number of implications. For one thing, parents can quit blaming themselves, family dysfunction, or careless comments for causing their children's anorexia" (para. 16). Research and science may someday give us the answer, but until we have it, blame is not the solution.

Parenthetical reference for a personal communication (APA does not require an entry in the references list)

CAUSES OF ANOREXIA NERVOSA   5

References

Finn, R. (2005). Fallacies about anorexia undermine

    treatment. *Clinical Psychiatry News, 33*(8), 50.

    doi: 10.1016/S0270-6644(05)70609-3

Jourdan, T. (2005, September 27). Anorexia is a real

    disease. *Daily Mail.* Retrieved from www.highbeam

    .com /doc/1G1-136726656.html

Loftin, R. (2014, March 3). Personal interview.

Mayo Clinic. (2012, January 5). Diseases and conditions:

    Anorexia nervosa. *Mayo Clinic Patient Care and*

    Health Info. Retrieved from www.mayoclinic.org

    /diseasesconditions/anorexia /basics/definition

    /con-20033002

Researcher says anorexia may be genetic. (2007,

    February 21). *AP Online.* Retrieved from

    www.highbeam.com/doc/1Y1-103448899.html

Annotations (right margin):

- References list starting on a new page; title centered
- First line of entry at left margin with subsequent lines indented 1/2 inch
- Scholarly article with a DOI
- Newspaper article retrieved from a Web site
- Entry for a personal interview, if required by instructor
- Organization as author
- Article listed by title (no author given)

CHECKING YOUR ESSAY FOR PLAGIARISM

Plagiarism—using another person's words or ideas without giving proper credit—is a serious offense in academic writing. It can lead to a failing grade and even to dismissal from college. Certainly, submitting a paper you have not written and claiming it as your own work is plagiarism—and professors can recognize such intentional plagiarism right away. But plagiarism can also be unintentional; it can result from paying insufficient attention to how you credit your sources. To make sure you have properly credited your sources, use the following checklist.

Checklist for Documentation

1. Reread your entire paper. Underline each section where you used an idea or a quote from a source. Now, for each of these underlined sections, answer the following questions:
   - Have you provided the necessary attribution so that it is clear to readers where the quotation or idea came from?
   - Have you provided a parenthetical reference for the source that will enable readers to find the corresponding entry in your works cited or references list?
2. Compare the amount of source information to the amount of your own writing. What is the ratio? Aim to have no more than 30 percent of your paper come from source information.
3. Make a list of the sources you used in your paper. Is there an entry with complete information for each source on the works cited or references list?
4. Proofread each works cited or references entry. Do the entries conform to the appropriate style—MLA or APA?

Remember that if you have trouble understanding either MLA or APA style, you can seek assistance from tutors, learning center instructors, librarians, your instructor, and online resources.

PART 5

Well-Crafted Sentences

Combining sentences adds interest and variety to writing, just as combining different elements adds interest and variety to a visual display.

Sentence Combining: Phrases and Clauses

Have you ever been amazed at how eloquently some people write? Some people put together sentences in such a way that their writing is a rhythmic, flowing cascade of thoughts. These people have a wealth of tools at their fingertips when they write, and many of these tools include strategies for combining sentences. Combining sentences not only adds variety and clarity to writing but also helps guide the reader in following the writer's course of ideas.

Look at the following paragraph, which does not make use of any sentence-combining strategies.

Paragraph A: Our planet is composed of four different layers. These layers have varying physical and chemical properties. The outer layer is called the *crust*. It averages about fifty miles in thickness. It consists of about a dozen large, irregularly shaped sections. These sections are called *tectonic plates*. The plates slide over one another. They slide under one another. They slide past one another. These sliding events take place on top of a second layer of the Earth called the *mantle*.

The sentences in the paragraph above are complete sentences, and they express the writer's thoughts adequately. But they are boring! Notice how similar they are in length. Combining some of the sentences results in a much more eloquent (and more pleasing to read) version.

Paragraph B: Our planet is composed of four different layers that have varying physical and chemical properties. The outer layer, which is called the *crust*, averages about fifty miles in thickness, and it consists

UNIT OBJECTIVES

After completing this unit, students will be able to do the following:

- **Combine sentences using prepositional phrases (and punctuate correctly).**
- **Combine sentences using verbal phrases (and punctuate correctly).**
- **Combine sentences using coordinating conjunctions (and punctuate correctly).**
- **Combine sentences using dependent words (and punctuate correctly).**
- **Combine sentences using conjunctive adverbs (and punctuate correctly).**

Connect IRW LearnSmart Achieve: Assign the topics "Parts of Speech Review," "Coordination and Subordination," "Fragments, Run-Ons, and Comma Splices" and "Sentence Variety" for adaptive learning to accompany the chapter.

of about a dozen large, irregularly shaped sections. These sections, referred to as *tectonic plates*, slide over, under, and past one another on top of a second layer, known as the *mantle*, that lies beneath the crust.

Can you tell the difference between the two paragraphs? To write the second paragraph, the writer did three things.

- Combined short, choppy sentences into longer ones. Paragraph A has ten sentences; paragraph B has three.
- Changed wording so that fewer sentences start with *it* or *they* (words the author repeated too frequently).
- Created sentences of varying lengths. The first sentence in paragraph B is considerably shorter than the two that follow it.

These changes made the paragraph *much* easier to read and greatly improved the writing style.

The explanations and exercises in this unit present sentence-combining strategies that will help you learn new ways to create sentences. The goal of this section of the text is to give you additional tools to use as a writer. If you like a particular sentence-combining strategy, annotate it or put a sticky note on the page. Intentionally use the strategy in your next writing assignment. Experiment with these strategies. The more adept you become at combining sentences, the more impressive, eloquent, and effective your writing will become.

COMBINING PHRASES TO CREATE NEW SENTENCES

Phrases are sets of words that function as a group but do not include both a subject and a verb. Because phrases lack either a subject or a verb or both, they cannot stand alone as complete sentences. Two important types of phrases are prepositional phrases and verbal phrases.

Combining Sentences Using Prepositional Phrases

Prepositions are words that connect a noun or a pronoun to other elements in a sentence. A preposition is always a part of a *prepositional phrase*. In the following example, the prepositional phrase is underlined, and the preposition is in bold print.

In the textbook, a chart illustrates important terminology.

Prepositional phrases are useful because they enable writers to communicate more information in a sentence than would be possible otherwise. For example, consider the information presented by the following sentences:

- Many monarch butterflies spend each winter in the same particular location.
- They winter in Mexico.
- They live in huge colonies.
- They stay all winter in trees.
- These trees are located in the mountains.
- The mountains are in southern Mexico.

These sentences convey a great deal of information. The problem is that reading them is cumbersome. These choppy little sentences require the reader to start and stop repeatedly. What if all of these ideas could be combined into one single, smooth sentence? By taking the prepositional phrases (underlined) out of the short sentences and joining them together, the writer can produce a longer, smoother sentence that conveys the same ideas:

Monarch butterflies spend each winter in huge colonies in trees in the mountains of southern Mexico.

By combining prepositional phrases, we can create a much more compact, interesting sentence.

Common Prepositions

The chart below lists some of the most common prepositions. Notice that some prepositions are single words, and some are made up of two words.

Common Single-Word Prepositions					
about	as	by	in	on	to
after	at	during	into	out	under
against	before	for	like	over	with
around	between	from	of	through	without

Common Double-Word Prepositions			
according to	close to	inside of	out from
ahead of	due to	instead of	out of
aside from	except for	near to	outside of
because of	far from	next to	regardless of

A prepositional phrase contains *at least* a preposition and its **object,** which is a noun or pronoun. In the example that follows, you will see four prepositional phrases. The prepositions are in bold print, and the objects are underlined and identified.

Examples: **at** the dance, **over** the moon, **with** Timothy, **because of** the storm
                     object   object   object   object

Prepositional phrases function like adjectives and adverbs. They typically answer questions such as these: *What kind? Which one? When? Where? How?* Using prepositional phrases effectively makes writing more descriptive, more precise, and more interesting.

Examples of Prepositional Phrases

SENTENCE WITHOUT PREPOSITIONAL PHRASE	A READER'S QUESTION	ANSWER	EXPANDED SENTENCE USING PREPOSITIONAL PHRASE
My favorite reading materials are books.	What kind of books?	books about science	My favorite reading materials are books about science.
The truck is for sale.	Which truck?	the truck by the fence	The truck by the fence is for sale.
The shopping rush will end.	When?	after the holiday season	The shopping rush will end after the holiday season.
They need to show up on time.	Where?	at the worksite	They need to show up on time at the worksite.
She paid for the calculator.	How?	with cash	She paid for the calculator with cash.

How to Use Prepositional Phrases

First, use prepositional phrases to add interesting and pertinent details to your writing. Read the following paragraph, which has two prepositional phrases (underlined). As you read, can you think of details a reader might want to know that would make the passage more interesting and informative?

Paragraph A: We have all seen litter accumulate. It ends up as marine debris and is deposited ashore. Indeed, take a walk along any beach and you are likely to encounter ocean garbage.

Perhaps a reader would want to know exactly *where* litter accumulates and exactly *how* it gets deposited on the shore. We can add details such as these in individual sentences, as in paragraph B below. Notice that these added sentences have prepositional phrases (underlined).

Paragraph B: We have all seen litter accumulate. It accumulates in cities. It accumulates along roadways. Much of it collects together. It collects in storm drains. It collects in canals. It flows through streams. It flows through rivers. It flows into our oceans. It is driven by currents—sometimes thousands of miles from its origin. It ends up as marine debris and is deposited ashore. It is driven by wind and tide. Indeed, take a walk along any beach in the world and you are likely to encounter ocean garbage.

The additional sentences give the reader much more information. However, because all the new sentences are short and constructed in the same way, the writing is very choppy and repetitive. Glance back at all of the uses of *it*. The writer can use sentence-combining strategies to write less repetitive, choppy sentences. Notice how in paragraph C, the writer combines prepositional phrases to create an effective and detailed passage.

Paragraph C: We've all seen litter accumulate in cities and along roadways. Much of it collects in storm drains and canals and eventually flows through streams and rivers and into our oceans. Driven by currents—sometimes thousands of miles from its origin—some marine debris is deposited ashore by wind and tide. Indeed, take a walk along any beach in the world and you are likely to encounter ocean garbage.

The power of prepositional phrases lies in their ability to add meaningful descriptive information to passages.

PUNCTUATION TIP   **Prepositional Phrases**

Generally speaking, a prepositional phrase that begins a sentence should be followed by a comma, especially if the phrase contains three or more words.

Examples: Before the flood, our house was in beautiful condition.

Around the first of each year, tax preparers become busy.

Note that commas are *not* used when prepositional phrases appear in the body of sentences, even if one prepositional phrase follows another one.

Examples: The hands on the clock on the wall seemed to move incredibly slowly.

Monarch butterflies winter in huge colonies in trees in the mountains of southern Mexico.

PRACTICE ① Adding and Combining Prepositional Phrases

A. Add prepositional phrases to the simple sentences that follow. Add at least three prepositional phrases to each sentence. Underline each prepositional phrase.   *Answers will vary.*

Example: The chapter was short.

The chapter about podiatry in my medical textbook from 1972 was short.

1. Students eat.

_____

2. The class will travel.

_____

(continued)

3. Moving was difficult.

_____

4. Diana passed.

_____

5. Women can vote.

_____

B. Combine each group of sentences below into one sentence using prepositional phrases. Be sure to follow the punctuation guidelines. Underline each prepositional phrase.

Sample answers are provided.

Example:

- She found her wallet.
- It was in her jacket.
- Her jacket was on the washing machine.

She found her wallet in her jacket on the washing machine.

1. Some people enjoy hunting for coins.

They do their searching on weekends and holidays.

Hunting for coins is a hobby for these folks.

Some people enjoy hunting for coins as a hobby on weekends and holidays.

2. Caches of coins are sometimes buried in open fields or forests.

Usually, coins buried in such locations are hidden near landmarks.

Landmarks are features like tall trees or boulders.

Caches of coins are sometimes buried near landmarks like tall trees or boulders.

3. Coins are sometimes hidden underground but merely stashed unburied.

Treasure hunters have found hoards of coins in caves.

A deserted mine could be the location of a treasure trove.

Old, abandoned cellars have been known to be the spot where hidden coin stashes were located.

Coins are sometimes stashed underground in places like caves, deserted mines, and abandoned cellars.

4. Coin hoards have been found in old, unused sheds and barns.

Ghost towns are filled with buildings that would make good hiding places for a trove of coins.

Any structure can be a location for a hidden coin cache.

Coin hoards can be found in structures like old, unused sheds and barns or the buildings in ghost towns.

5. Even a house can potentially be a hiding place for hidden treasure.

Within a house, coins can be hidden in the walls.

They can be hidden under floorboards or in an attic.

Attics are full of nooks and crannies.

With coins potentially in walls, under floorboards, or in attic nooks and crannies, even a house can be a hiding place for hidden treasure.

(continued)

6. Metal detectors can facilitate locating hidden coins.

Treasure seekers use metal detectors in searching the ground in fields and forests.

Metal detectors are used when treasure hunters explore underground sites.

They are useful even within structures for scanning inside walls, floors, and attics.

Treasure seekers use metal detectors to locate hidden coins in fields and forests, in underground sites, and even within the walls, floors, and attics of structures.

Combining Sentences Using Verbal Phrases

A **verbal** is a verb form that functions in a sentence as a noun, adjective, or adverb. In a sense, a verbal is both a verb and some other part of speech. It may have its own modifiers and objects, and the verbal plus the words that accompany it together form a **verbal phrase.** Three types of verbal phrases occur in English:

- *to + verb* phrases
- *-ing* phrases
- *-ed/-en* phrases

Verbal phrases provide you with a tool for creating sentence variety, one of the characteristics of good writing. Learning to use the three types of verbal phrases will expand your sentence-writing ability. In addition, verbal phrases help you accomplish other writing goals.

to + verb Phrases

Form a *to + verb* (also known as an **infinitive**) by putting the word *to* in front of a verb stem.

    to + write = to write
    to + sleep = to sleep
    to + speak up = to speak up

A *to + verb* phrase is composed of the *to + verb* itself together with any accompanying words. In the following examples, the verbal is in bold print and the *to + verb* phrase is underlined.

To acquire the entire collection is a worthy goal.

He is the man **to call** about a job.

-ing Phrases

To form an *-ing* verbal, add *-ing* to the end of the verb. Sometimes the final *-e* of a verb must be deleted (as with the verb *leave* in the example below) or the final letter of a verb must be doubled (as with *plan* in the example below) before the *-ing* is added.

    find + ing = finding
    leave − e + ing = leaving
    plan + n + ing = planning

An *-ing* verbal phrase consists of the verbal together with its accompanying words. In these examples, the *-ing* verbal is in bold print and the verbal phrase is underlined.

Finding the lost keys made her day.

Planning efficiently, Luis was able to complete his work on time.

The hardest part of beginning college for some teenage students is **leaving** home.

The **winding** path disappeared into the woods.

-ed/-en Phrases

An *-ed/-en* phrase consists of the *-ed/-en* form of a verb together with the words that accompany it. (The *-ed* or *-en* form of a verb, sometimes called the **past participle**, appears in verbs such as *has written* and *will have talked*. Occasionally, the form is irregular; for example, *buy* becomes *bought* in *has bought* and *do* becomes *done* in *have done*.) In the following examples, the verbal is in bold print and the verbal phrase is underlined.

The young widow, **supported** lovingly by her family, worked through her grief.

A drain **clogged** with hair is one of a plumber's most common problems to solve.

Done with the assignment, the children were free to play outside.

She could work any sudoku puzzle **given** enough time.

How to Use Verbal Phrases

Verbals of all three types can be used for a variety of purposes. The explanations and exercises that follow will walk you through the process of identifying when to create verbal phrases to accomplish particular purposes.

Using Verbal Phrases to Add Information Verbal phrases can perform some of the same functions as prepositional phrases. The questions *what kind*, *which one*, and *how* are often addressed using verbals of the *-ing* and *-ed* varieties. For example, consider this sentence:

Chenille Café is an unusual restaurant.

It's a complete sentence; nothing is wrong with it. However, you may wish to say more about how the restaurant is unusual. You could add these sentences to do so.

- The restaurant offers specialty desserts.
- It has French toast cheesecake.
- It offers banana meringue cookies.
- It sells caramel pie.

Now the reader has more information, but the string of short sentences makes for choppy and crude writing. Using a verbal enables you to write one sentence combining all these ideas. Note how the underlined verbal phrase below incorporates the ideas into the sentence.

Offering specialty desserts such as French toast cheesecake, banana meringue cookies, and caramel pie, the Chenille Café is an unusual restaurant.

The following chart shows ways in which verbal phrases can answer questions.

SENTENCE WITHOUT VERBAL PHRASE	A READER'S QUESTION	ANSWER	EXPANDED SENTENCE USING VERBAL PHRASE
My favorite reading materials are books.	What kind of books?	books by athletes	My favorite reading materials are books **written** by athletes.
		books about investigations	My favorite reading materials are books **involving** investigations.
The truck is for sale.	Which truck?	the truck on the lot	The truck **sitting** on the lot is for sale.
		the truck our family once owned	The truck once **owned** by our family is for sale.
She paid for the calculator.	How?	with a credit card	She paid for the calculator **using** a credit card.

PRACTICE ❷ Using Verbal Phrases to Add Information

Combine each group of sentences below by creating a verbal phrase that answers *what kind, which one,* or *how.* An example has been provided.

Sample answers are provided.

Example:

- Margie was touched by the generosity of her coworkers.
- She could not speak without crying.

Margie, touched by the generosity of her coworkers, could not speak without crying.

1. Children of undocumented immigrants live in the United States.

   They need the chance for a college education.

   <u>Children of undocumented immigrants living in the United States need the chance for a college education.</u>

2. The children of undocumented immigrants are affected by their parents' legal status.

   The children often believe they cannot be admitted to a college in the United States.

   <u>The children of undocumented immigrants, affected by the legal status of their parents, often believe they cannot be admitted to a college in the United States.</u>

3. Undocumented students are not legally prohibited from enrolling in college.

   No such federal law exists.

   <u>No federal law prohibiting the admission of undocumented students exists.</u>

4. Colleges write their own policies about the admission of undocumented students.

   These policies vary from college to college.

   <u>Written by the colleges themselves, policies about the admission of undocumented workers vary from college to college.</u>

5. Many undocumented students hope to obtain a college education in the United States.

   Opportunities exist for them to do so.

   <u>Opportunities exist for undocumented students hoping to obtain a college education in the United States.</u>

Using Verbal Phrases to Express Purpose Verbal phrases allow you to explain a reason concisely. Consider these sentences:

- Building a new house takes time.
- It also requires a lot of planning.
- It is often more expensive than buying an existing house.
- It is wasteful.
- Buy an existing home rather than build a new one!

These sentences convey the writer's reasoning, but they take a lot of space, repeat words, and offer no sentence variety. A more effective alternative is to combine the sentences using verbal phrases (underlined below, with verbals in bold).

    <u>**To save** time and money and **to reduce** planning and waste</u>, potential homeowners should buy an existing home rather than build a new one.

    Notice that *to + verb* phrases are often used to express purpose or, as shown in the chart on the next page, to answer the question *why.*

SENTENCE WITHOUT VERBAL PHRASE	A READER'S QUESTION	ANSWER	EXPANDED SENTENCE USING VERBAL PHRASE
The deer scrambled up the embankment.	Why?	because of the rising floodwaters	The deer scrambled up the embankment **to escape** the rising floodwaters.
Lori locked the door.	Why?	for some peace and quiet	Lori locked the door **to get** some peace and quiet.
We went to the market.	Why?	We needed some fresh vegetables.	We went to the market **to buy** some fresh vegetables.

PRACTICE ③ Using *to + verb* Verbal Phrases to Express Purpose

Combine each group of sentences below by creating a *to + verb* phrase to answer the question *why.* An example has been provided.

Example:

- Searle-Gorley Industries will produce a new kind of radar.
- They will use space-related technology as the basis for this production.

To produce a new kind of radar, Searle-Gorley Industries will use space-related technology.

1. The Supplemental Nutrition Assistance Program (SNAP) was created by the federal government.
   It reduces hunger in America.
   The Supplemental Nutrition Assistance Program (SNAP) was created by the federal government to reduce hunger in America.

2. SNAP provides food resources for struggling Americans.
   It helps them while they are between jobs or unemployed.
   To help struggling Americans while they are between jobs or unemployed, SNAP provides food resources.

3. SNAP needs continued government funding.
   Approximately fifteen million children live in food-insecure households.
   To provide food for the fifteen million American children who live in food-insecure households, SNAP needs continued government funding.

4. The program expands and contracts.
   It responds to the ebb and flow of the economy.
   To respond to the ebb and flow of the economy, the program expands and contracts.

5. SNAP assists the food banks that so many people depend on.
   More people can be helped that way.
   To help more people, SNAP assists the food banks that so many people depend on.

Using Verbal Phrases to Name Activities Verbals can act as nouns to name activities or actions: *singing, hoping, lifting, thinking.* The verbals most commonly used as nouns are *-ing* and *to + verb* verbals. Notice how the *-ing* verbal (in bold print) acts as a noun in the following example.

Plowing is a basic task of most farmers.

Because *plowing* is a verbal and not an ordinary noun, an object (such as *field*) and other words can be included as a part of a verbal phrase, as in the sentence below.

Plowing <u>a field on a hot summer day</u> is an unpleasant task at best.

object

The following example shows that *to + verb* verbal phrases can also function well as nouns.

To plow <u>a field on a hot summer day</u> is an unpleasant task at best.

object

Verbals that function as nouns often answer the question *what.*

What is the greatest human endeavor?

To pursue <u>wisdom</u> is the greatest human endeavor.

The writer could just as well use an *-ing* verbal:

Pursuing <u>wisdom</u> is the greatest human endeavor.

PRACTICE ④ Using Verbal Phrases to Name Activities

Combine each group of sentences below by creating a verbal phrase that names an activity. Use either *-ing* or *to + verb* verbal phrases.

Sample answers are provided.

Example:

- People who counsel others must be sensitive.
- People who counsel others must have good listening skills.

To counsel others, a person must be sensitive and have good listening skills.

1. Veterans return from military service.
   They look for jobs.
   However, they find that landing a job is difficult.
   Returning from military service, veterans looking for jobs find that landing one is difficult.

2. In the civilian world, a veteran may not qualify for the same type of job she held in the military.
   That is the case when the veteran lacks the civilian certifications or licenses needed for employment in a given field.
   Lacking civilian certifications or licenses needed for employment in a given field, a veteran may not qualify for the same type of job she held in the military.

3. Veterans often must repeat education or training.
   Doing so provides them with the "piece of paper" needed for employment.
   Veterans often must repeat education or training to get the "piece of paper" needed for employment.

4. We should find a method for officially certifying veterans' skills in the civilian setting.
   We should make veterans' transition to civilian life as smooth as possible.
   To make veterans' transition to civilian life as smooth as possible, we should find a method for officially certifying their skills in the civilian setting.

5. We should show our appreciation to veterans for their service.
   One way to show our appreciation is to facilitate their re-entry into the workforce.
   To show our appreciation to veterans for their service, we can facilitate their re-entry into the workforce.

Using Verbal Phrases to Replace Unclear Pronouns Sometimes writers use words such as *it*, *that*, *this*, *these*, and *those* without making clear what these words refer to. Consider this example:

> The students planned to survey the freshman class. However, it would take time.

Readers are left confused. What would take time—the planning, the survey, or both? Replacing *it* with a verbal phrase (underlined) can eliminate this confusion. Note the differences in meaning in the following sentences.

> The students planned to survey the freshman class. However, **planning** the survey would take time.

> The students planned to survey the freshman class. However, **conducting** the survey would take time.

> The students planned to survey the freshman class. However, **planning** and **conducting** the survey would take time.

In all these sentences, the verbal phrase acts as a noun, replacing the pronoun *it* as the subject of the sentence.

Even when pronoun reference is not a problem, using verbal phrases to replace pronouns can make for clearer and more precise writing—a goal of every good writer. Look at the following example:

> Mika hopes to make it through the shift without incident. **That** is her only goal.

What is Mika's only goal? *To make it through the shift without incident.* The following sentence replaces the vague pronoun *that* with a verbal phrase.

> **To make** it through the shift without incident is Mika's only goal.

Combining the two sentences in this manner both clarifies and condenses.

PRACTICE ❺ Using Verbal Phrases to Clarify Pronoun Reference

Combine each group of sentences below. Use verbal phrases to replace the unclear pronouns. An example has been provided.

Sample answers are provided.

Example:

- Mark would rather read than mow the lawn.
- He sometimes neglects it for a long time.

Mark would rather read than mow, so he sometimes neglects mowing the lawn for a long time.

1. Many students put off selecting a major and starting a degree program.
   They say it is too stressful.

   Many students say they put off selecting a major and starting a degree program because making this decision is too stressful.

2. After a year or two of dabbling in different courses, students may feel comfortable about selecting a major.
   They are more confident about it.

   After a year or two of dabbling in different courses, students may feel comfortable enough to select a major since they are more confident about making the choice.

3. Of course, many students later change their majors.
   They should not feel bad about this.

   Of course, many students later change their majors, and they should not feel bad about making this change.

(continued)

4. College is a good time to consider career options.

It will affect a person's future happiness.

College is a good time to consider career options because choosing a career will affect a person's future happiness.

5. Fortunately, career exploration workshops can help in the process.

Attending them can help students make better decisions.

Fortunately, students can make better decisions by attending career exploration workshops.

Using Verbal Phrases to Create Variety in Sentence Structure Knowing how to use verbal phrases gives you a way to vary the structures of sentences but keep their meanings. We have seen in the preceding examples how verbal phrases can introduce variety into a series of short, simple sentences. In addition, verbal phrases can introduce variety into any paragraph dominated by one type of sentence structure. Consider these sentences:

- Jill, who had to be taken to the hospital against her wishes, was upset.
- Her car, which had been totaled in the wreck, had to be towed away.
- The emergency room doctor, who reassured Jill's family, quickly explained that Jill would be fine.
- Jill's father, who sat in the waiting room, chattered incessantly.
- Jill's mother, who was satisfied with the care her daughter was receiving, read the newspaper.

Notice that every sentence has the same basic structure. Listed in sequence, the sentences make for tedious reading. Using verbal phrases in some sentences makes the passage easier to read and more interesting. The verbal phrases are underlined in the following examples.

- Jill, who had to be taken to the hospital against her wishes, was upset.
- Her car, **totaled** in the wreck, had to be towed away.
- **To reassure** Jill's family, the emergency room doctor quickly explained that Jill would be fine.
- Jill's father sat in the waiting room, **chatting** incessantly.
- **Satisfied** with the care her daughter was receiving, Jill's mother read the newspaper.

PRACTICE ⑥ Using Verbal Phrases to Create Variety in Sentence Structure

Combine the sentences in each sentence group below using a verbal phrase to replace all or part of one of the sentences, as the example illustrates.   Sample answers are provided.

Example:

- ECON 101 was the course about which I knew the least.
- ECON 101 was required for graduation.

ECON 101, required for graduation, was the course about which I knew the least.

1. A ceremonial blessing of the fleet, which is given by a local Catholic priest, is a custom in Biloxi, Mississippi.

It marks the beginning of shrimp fishing season.

Given by a local Catholic priest, a ceremonial blessing of the fleet marks the beginning of shrimp fishing season in Biloxi, Mississippi.

(Continued)

2. The Blessing of the Fleet is a tradition that has its origins in Europe.

Its purpose was to transmit God's grace for a safe and bountiful fishing season.

Intended to transmit God's grace for a safe and bountiful fishing season, the Blessing of the Fleet is a tradition that has its origins in Europe.

3. Fishermen travel long distances to reach Biloxi.

They want to participate in the blessing.

To participate in the blessing, fishermen travel long distances to Biloxi.

4. A procession that passes by the anchored "Blessing Boat" begins.

More than thirty shrimp boats are in the procession.

Passing by the anchored "Blessing Boat," a procession of more than thirty shrimp boats begins.

5. The priest, who stands on the "Blessing Boat," sprinkles holy water.

He sprinkles it on each of the passing shrimp boats.

Standing on the "Blessing Boat," the priest sprinkles holy water on each of the passing shrimp boats.

PUNCTUATION TIP   **Misplaced Modifiers**

A modifying phrase should be located as close as possible to the word it describes. Descriptive phrases that are not properly positioned are called *misplaced modifiers* and can create confusion for the reader. This issue is of special concern with regard to verbal phrase modifiers. In the following examples, the verbal phrases are underlined and the words that the phrases modify are in bold print.

Correct:	Driving home, **Jim** saw the old tree swing.
Misplaced modifier:	**Jim** saw the old tree swing driving home. (The swing was not driving home.)
Correct:	Coming down the stairs for dinner, **Rita** smelled the oysters.
Misplaced modifier:	**Rita** smelled the oysters coming down the stairs for dinner. (The oysters were not coming down the stairs.)

Similarly, if the modified word is missing from the sentence, the result, called a *dangling modifier,* can create confusion and even misreading.

Dangling modifier:	Walking down the street, a car hit a bicyclist. (The car was not walking down the street.)
Correct:	Walking down the street, **they** saw a car hit a bicyclist.

COMBINING CLAUSES TO CREATE NEW SENTENCES

A **clause** is group of words containing a subject and a verb. Here are some examples:

- the engineer is drawing a blueprint
- that the intersection is busy
- when a coyote howled at the moon

Some clauses are also sentences. A **sentence** has at least one clause, starts with a capital letter, has end punctuation, and can stand alone as a complete thought.

Sentence with one clause: The engineer is drawing a blueprint.
                             capital letter   end punctuation

A sentence can have more than one clause. In the following example, the two clauses (underlined) are joined by a connecting word (*so*).

Sentence with two clauses: The intersection is busy, **so** traffic is moving slowly.
                              clause   connecting word   clause

Imagine an entire paragraph made up of single-clause sentences. What would the effect be? Read paragraph A, which is made up of single-clause sentences.

Paragraph A: Registered nurses spend much of the day walking and standing. They also bend and stretch quite a bit. They must often lift and move patients. They are vulnerable to back injuries. Registered nurses work closely with people. The people may have infectious diseases. Nurses often come in contact with hazardous drugs. They often come into contact with other dangerous substances. Registered nurses must follow strict, standardized guidelines.

Now read paragraph B, in which some single-clause sentences have been joined together. The connecting words are underlined.

Paragraph B: Registered nurses spend much of the day walking and standing, and they also bend and stretch quite a bit. They must often lift and move patients, so they are vulnerable to back injuries. Registered nurses work closely with people who may have infectious diseases. Because they often come in contact with hazardous drugs and other dangerous substances, registered nurses must follow strict, standardized guidelines.

The variety in sentence length and type make paragraph B more interesting to read. Also, the ways in which the sentences are connected give the reader more information. In paragraph A, the cause and effect relationships are only implied. The causes are listed separately and are not tied to their effects, as they are in paragraph B. In the revised paragraph, the second sentence uses *so* and the fourth sentence uses *because*. These words clarify the cause and effect relationships.

Paragraph A:

- Registered nurses spend much of the day walking and standing.
- They also bend and stretch quite a bit.
- They must often lift and move patients.

  In this paragraph, the causes are listed separately and not tried to the effect.

- They are vulnerable to back injuries.   }   Effect

Paragraph B:

- Registered nurses spend much of the day walking and standing, <u>and</u> they also bend and stretch quite a bit.
- They must often lift and move patients, <u>so</u> they are vulnerable to back injuries.

  The combined sentences do a better job at helping readers notice the causes and effect.

Additionally, combining the following two sentences with the word *who* emphasizes the fact that nurses work with certain types of people.

Paragraph A:

- Registered nurses work closely with people.
- The people may have infectious diseases.

Presenting these ideas separately makes the second sentence seem unimportant.

Paragraph B:

- Registered nurses work closely with people <u>who</u> may have infectious diseases.

Combining the sentences shows readers why the information is important: nurses work with such people.

By carefully selecting clauses to connect, writers can produce texts that are clearer and that convey meaning more effectively.

Combining Sentences Using Coordinating Conjunctions

One way to join two or more clauses to create a sentence is by using a **coordinating conjunction (CC).** You may already be familiar with the seven coordinating conjunctions. They are often referred to using the acronym FANBOYS: *for, and, nor, but, or, yet, so.*

Think of these seven coordinating conjunctions as sentence connectors. In the same way that physical tools such as hammers and crowbars have specific purposes, coordinating conjunctions do also. For example, *but* is used to join two clauses to show that the clauses (underlined below) mean opposite things, as this example shows:

<u>Some Americans believe extreme measures should be taken for airport security</u>, **but** <u>others believe the measures violate their privacy rights.</u>

The first clause (*Some Americans . . . security*) expresses agreement with the use of extreme measures. The second clause (*others believe . . . rights*) expresses disagreement with extreme measures. Using *but* enables the writer to alert readers to the contrasting information in the two clauses.

PUNCTUATION TIP   **Comma Splices and Run-ons**

When combining two complete sentences with a coordinating conjunction (CC), use a comma after the first clause, and then add the conjunction and the second clause.

Correct:

<u>Fossils are plentiful in central Texas</u>, so <u>paleontologists are drawn there.</u>
        complete sentence   , CC   complete sentence

<u>Mammoth fossils have been found</u>, and <u>a camel fossil was discovered there.</u>
        complete sentence   , CC   complete sentence

Joining two complete sentences using a comma alone, without a coordinating conjunction, results in a **comma splice error.**

Comma splices:

<u>Fossils are plentiful in central Texas</u>, <u>paleontologists are drawn there.</u>
        complete   [comma]   complete   =   error:
        sentence   sentence   comma
                                                            splice

---

(continued)

Mammoth fossils have been found, a camel fossil was discovered there.
complete   [comma]   complete _=_ **comma**
sentence   sentence   **splice**

Joining two complete sentences by running them together without punctuation and without a coordinating conjunction results in a **run-on sentence error.**

Run-on sentences:

Fossils are plentiful in central Texas paleontologists are drawn there.

no comma or CC = **run-on sentence**

Mammoth fossils have been found a camel fossil was discovered there.

no comma or CC = **run-on sentence**

What follows are explanations of when to use coordinating conjunctions and guidelines for using them, followed by practice opportunities.

Using *for*

When to Use *for:* When you want to provide an explanation.

Why to Use *for:* To make clear which sentence is being explained.

Example: Solar technology works well in Arizona, <u>for</u> Arizona has very few cloudy days.

For tells the reader *why* solar technology works well in Arizona. If the sentences are separated, readers might see them as two unrelated facts:

- Solar technology works well in Arizona.
- Arizona has very few cloudy days.

When the sentences are combined using *for,* readers can see that the second clause is an explanation of the first.

How to use *for:* Find sentences that are related because one sentence explains the other. Use *for* to join the sentences.

PRACTICE ⑦ Using *for* to Join Sentences

Read each pair of sentences. Does one sentence answer the question *why* about the other sentence? If so, use *for* to write a single sentence that combines the two sentences. If not, explain why combining the sentences would not be appropriate.

1. One hazard of a volcano is a lahar. A lahar is a mixture of volcanic ash, rock, debris, and water.

   Combining these sentences with *for* would not be appropriate. The second clause tells *what* a lahar is; it does not answer the question *why.*

2. A lahar can be incredibly destructive to people who live nearby. It occurs quickly and can travel down the slopes of a volcano.

   A lahar can be incredibly destructive to people who live nearby, **for** it occurs quickly and can travel down the slopes of a volcano.

(continued)

3. Lahars are generated when a high volume of hot or cold water mixes with ash and rock and starts downslope. When most people think of volcanoes, they envision a mountain with a lahar.

   Combining these sentences with *for* would not be appropriate. The second sentence provides a new idea, not an explanation of the first sentence.

4. Rainfall or melting snow can be hazardous during a volcanic eruption. The combination of water and the eruption produces a lahar.

   Rainfall or melting snow can be hazardous during a volcanic eruption, **for** the combination of water and the eruption produces a lahar.

5. When moving, a lahar looks like a mass of wet concrete. As a lahar rushes down the sides of a volcano, the speed at which it moves as well as the amount of water and rock debris it carries constantly change.

   Combining these sentences with *for* would not be appropriate. The second sentence adds information about a lahar but does not continue to explain what a lahar looks like.

6. The beginning surge of water and rock debris is forceful. It often erodes rocks and vegetation from the side of a volcano and along any river valley it enters.

   The beginning surge of water and rock debris is forceful, **for** it often erodes rocks and vegetation from the side of a volcano and along any river valley it enters.

7. If a lahar enters a river, the hazards will increase. The eroding rock debris and additional water can cause the lahar to grow to more than ten times its initial size.

   If a lahar enters a river, the hazards will increase, **for** the eroding rock debris and additional water can cause the lahar to grow to more than ten times its initial size.

8. As a lahar moves farther away from a volcano, it will eventually begin to lose its heavy load of sediment. It will also decrease in size.

   Combining these sentences with *for* would not be appropriate. The second sentence provides a new piece of information, not an explanation.

Using *and*

When to Use *and*: When you want to add information or to join two sentences that are related in meaning.

Why to Use *and*: To put together clauses that contain related information.

> **Example:**   Geothermal heat is a major source of energy in Iceland, <u>and</u> it is used there both to produce direct heat for homes and businesses and to generate electricity.

And allows us to combine two related facts: that geothermal heat is a major source of energy in Iceland and that it is used there both to produce direct heat for homes and businesses and to generate electricity.

Writing often requires us to provide related pieces of information. Technically, we could write complete sentences for each separate piece of information, but doing so would result in very choppy writing, such as this:

> Wind technology works well in western Texas. It has been used there extensively since 1975. In certain parts of western Texas, wind turbines are visible as far as the eye can see.

Combining information that is related in meaning reduces choppiness and shows that the elements joined together are related. We can revise the previous sentences as follows. (Notice that the last sentence was *not* added to the combined sentence because it is not closely enough related in meaning to the previous sentences.)

Wind technology works well in western Texas, and it has been used there extensively since 1975. In certain parts of western Texas, wind turbines are visible as far as the eye can see.

How to Use *and:* Find sentences that each provide related pieces of information about the same subject. Use *and* to combine them.

PRACTICE ⑧ Using *and* to Join Sentences

Read each pair of sentences. Does one sentence provide additional related information about the other sentence? If so, use *and* (preceded by a comma) to create a single sentence that combines the two sentences. If not, explain why combining the sentences would not be appropriate.

1. Africanized honeybees get part of their genetic code from European honeybees. They get another part from African honeybees.

   Africanized honeybees get part of their genetic code from European honeybees, **and** they get another part from African honeybees.

2. Many questions about Africanized bees remain a mystery. Researchers have learned about some of the traits of Africanized bees.

   Combining these sentences with *and* would not be appropriate. The sentences are not closely related.

3. Beekeepers are especially concerned about the traits of Africanized bees. Manageability of the bees is a necessary condition for the productivity of a hive.

   Combining these sentences with *and* would not be appropriate. The second sentence is not adding another concern of beekeepers. Rather, it leads the reader to a more specific concern.

4. Beekeepers want to know whether Africanized bees produce as much honey as European bees. They want to know whether Africanized bees require more care than European bees.

   Beekeepers want to know whether Africanized bees produce as much honey as European bees, **and** they want to know whether Africanized bees require more care than European bees.

5. Africanized bees have a combination of African and European traits. It appears that African traits are showing themselves to be the dominant ones.

   Africanized bees have a combination of African and European traits, **and** it appears that African traits are showing themselves to be the dominant ones.

6. Both types of bees share some characteristics. Six biological and behavioral factors set Africanized bees apart from European bees.

   Combining these sentences with *and* would not be appropriate. The two sentences are not closely enough related to combine them.

7. One of these factors is especially significant. European queen honeybees mate disproportionately with African drones.

   Combining these sentences with *and* would not be appropriate. The second sentence elaborates on the first rather than adding a new point.

8. Thus, more of the genes in the colony are from African honeybees. The genetic makeup of the entire bee population is slowly affected.

   Thus, more of the genes in the colony are from African honeybees, **and** the genetic makeup of the entire bee population is slowly affected.

Using *nor*

When to Use *nor*: When you want to connect negative statements in a series, or, in conjunction with *neither,* when you want to connect two equally negative possibilities.

Why to Use *nor*: To avoid stringing together clause after clause of similar—but negative—statements *and* to show that two or more alternatives are equally negative.

> **Example:**   The bureaucrat was not very kind, nor was he particularly helpful.

1. Use *nor* to link two negative statements. *Nor* functions like *and* except that the two statements being joined are both negative. In the example above, we have two negative statements:

- The bureaucrat was not very kind.
- The bureaucrat was not particularly helpful.

These statements are similar because they both point out things the bureaucrat was *not.* Thus, we can use *nor* to link them.

2. Use *nor* together with *neither,* as in the following example.

> **Example:**   The committee members will neither phone Mark, nor will they
> interview him.

The *neither/nor* combination negates two different options. In the case of the example, the options are phoning and interviewing. By joining these ideas together in one sentence, the writer emphasizes that each option is equally rejected.

How to Use *nor*: Find two or more negative statements in a series. Use *nor* to join the clauses. Also, find two options that are equally negative, and use *neither/nor* to join them.

PRACTICE ⑨ Using *nor* to Join Sentences

Read each pair of sentences. Are they both negative statements? If so, use *nor* or *neither/nor* to write a single sentence that combines the two sentences. If not, explain why combining the sentences would not be appropriate.

1. In democratic societies like the United States, the voting process is protected by federal laws. The Federal Bureau of Investigation (FBI) is responsible for analyzing all cases of suspected election crimes.

   Combining these sentences with *nor* would not be appropriate. Neither sentence is negative.

2. The FBI does not investigate all potential election crime cases. They investigate only cases involving potential violations of federal law.

   Combining these sentences with *nor* would not be appropriate. Only the first sentence is negative.

3. For example, an individual may not give more than $4,600 to a federal candidate. Committees and groups may not exceed the limits set by law when making donations to federal candidates.

   An individual may not give more than $4,600 to a federal candidate, **nor** may committees and groups exceed the limits set by law when making donations to federal candidates.

4. A donor may not ask a friend to give money to a federal candidate and then reimburse the friend. To do so is a federal election crime.

   Combining these sentences with *nor* would not be appropriate. Only the first sentence is negative.

(continued)

5. A voter may not intentionally give false information when registering to vote. A voter may not cast more than one ballot in a federal election.

   A voter may not intentionally give false information when registering to vote, **nor** may a voter cast more than one ballot in a federal election.

6. When civil rights are alleged to have been violated in an election, the incidents are investigated by the FBI. For example, a scheme designed to keep minorities from voting would be under FBI jurisdiction.

   Combining these sentences with *nor* would not be appropriate. Neither sentence is negative.

7. While many federal election offenses exist, some common actions are not against the law. For instance, giving voters a ride to the polls is not illegal. Encouraging friends, neighbors, and acquaintances to cast a ballot is not against the law.

   While many federal election offenses exist, giving voters a ride to the polls is not illegal, **nor** is it against the law to encourage friends, neighbors, and acquaintances to cast a ballot.

8. Offering stamps to voters does not violate any law. Giving voters time off from work is not illegal.

   Neither offering stamps to voters **nor** giving voters time off from work violates the law.

Using *but*

When to Use *but*: When you want to show a difference in two ideas; when you want to indicate a change of direction.

Why to Use *but*: To help readers understand that one sentence is different (and perhaps opposite) in meaning from another sentence.

> **Example:** Senators and representatives love the idea of a law to make college education free, but they will not vote for one.

But indicates a complete change in direction in this sentence. Readers see *but* and are notified that the meaning of the sentence is about to change direction. In the example, *but* functions to join two contradictory statements:

- Senators and representatives love the idea of a law to make college education free.
- They will not vote for a law to make college education free.

When *but* is used, readers can see that it is possible for two contradictory conditions to exist. Also, *but* leads readers to the more important point. The clause that follows *but* reflects the actual case, the truth of the matter.

How to Use *but*: Find two sentences that are related to each other because the idea in one *opposes* the idea in the other. Use *but* to show this opposition.

PRACTICE 10 Using *but* to Join Sentences

Read each pair of sentences. Are the ideas in these sentences related but opposed to each other? If so, use *but* to write a single sentence that combines the two sentences. If not, explain why combining the sentences would not be appropriate.

1. Most people in the United States live in cities. They depend on the agricultural production of the countryside.

   Most people in the United States live in cities, **but** they depend on the agricultural production of the countryside.

(continued)

2. Fifty percent of the United States, 907 million acres, is cropland, pastureland, or rangeland. This land is owned and managed by farmers and ranchers and their families.

   Combining these sentences with *but* would not be appropriate. The sentences are not opposed to each other.

3. This 50 percent of the United States is owned and managed by less than 2 percent of US citizens. We rely on them to produce the food on which the American consumer depends.

   Combining these sentences with *but* would not be appropriate. The sentences are not opposed to each other.

4. Most of the time, our agricultural systems work. Shortages do sometimes occur.

   Most of the time, our agricultural systems work, **but** shortages do sometimes occur.

5. California, for example, provides a steady supply of strawberries to the United States and beyond. Diseases such as Fusarium wilt threaten the strawberry supply.

   California, for example, provides a steady supply of strawberries to the United States and beyond, **but** diseases such as Fusarium wilt threaten the strawberry supply.

6. When diseases affect large areas of cropland, supplies become limited and prices go up. Chemists and biologists work diligently to determine the causes of crop diseases.

   Combining these sentences with *but* would not be appropriate. The sentences are not opposed to each other.

7. In general, crops are planted in areas where the climate is favorable to growth. In recent years, extreme weather changes have threatened crops and made shortages inevitable.

   In general, crops are planted in areas where the climate is favorable to growth, **but** in recent years, extreme weather changes have threatened crops and made shortages inevitable.

8. Many people around the world depend on the United States to meet their food demands. Farmers, ranchers, and food scientists are determined not to let these people down.

   Combining these sentences with *but* would not be appropriate. The sentences are not opposed to each other.

Using *or*

When to Use *or*: When you want to offer clear alternatives.

Why to Use *or*: To indicate to readers two or more options from which to choose.

> **Example:**   Geology students must participate in a field trip, <u>or</u> they must create a project.

Or reveals options to the reader. In the example, the use of *or* makes it clear that two alternatives are available: a field trip or a project.

The term *or* is very specific in its meaning. Read the menu item below carefully, noticing what *or* tells you about the entrée:

> The grilled salmon can be served on a bed of rice pilaf, <u>or</u> it can be served atop grilled asparagus.

The use of *or* means diners will have to choose between rice pilaf and grilled asparagus.

Sometimes the combination *either/or* is used to present the alternatives in a sentence:

> <u>Either</u> the law should be repealed, <u>or</u> it should be changed.

Either/or puts a stronger emphasis on the fact that only two choices exist.

How to Use *or* and *either/or:* Find two sentences with related content, each of which provides an alternative to the other. Use *or* to connect them, or use *either/or* to connect them.

PRACTICE 11 Using *or* or *either/or* to Join Sentences

Read each pair of sentences. Are these sentences related, and do they also provide different alternatives? If so, use *or* or *either/or* to write a single sentence that combines the two sentences. If not, explain why combining the sentences would not be appropriate.

1. One reason Congress created the Affordable Care Act was to make sure anyone who wants health care can get it. The Affordable Care Act improves existing insurance in a variety of ways.

    Combining these sentences with *or* would not be appropriate. No pair of alternatives is offered.

2. In the past, consumers could get affordable insurance if their employers offered it. If they did not have employer-sponsored insurance, they would have to purchase insurance on the open market if they were to be insured.

    In the past, consumers could get affordable insurance if their employers offered it, **or** if they did not have employer-sponsored insurance, they would have to purchase insurance on the open market if they were to be insured.

3. Under the Affordable Care Act, workers can continue to participate in their employer's plans. Alternatively, virtually all consumers can purchase affordable insurance plans on the open market.

    Under the Affordable Care Act, workers can continue to participate in their employer's plans, **or** virtually all consumers can purchase affordable insurance plans on the open market.

4. Before the Affordable Care Act became law, insurance companies could use consumers' premiums for administrative costs. They could use consumers' premiums to provide health-care services.

    Before the Affordable Care Act became law, insurance companies could use consumers' premiums for administrative costs, **or** they could use consumers' premiums to provide health-care services.

5. Now, insurance companies must use consumers' premiums exclusively to provide health-care services. They will be out of compliance with the new law if they do not.

    Combining these sentences with *or* would not be appropriate. No pair of alternatives is offered.

6. Preventive care is now covered at no cost to the consumer. In the past, consumers had to pay for portions of preventive care.

    Combining these sentences with *or* would not be appropriate. No pair of alternatives is offered.

7. The new plan allows consumers to choose their own doctors. Those who want a doctor to be assigned can request one.

    Under the new plan, consumers can choose their own doctors, **or** they can have doctors assigned to them.

8. Many old plans prohibited people from using emergency services out of their area health-care networks. Now, health-care plans cover the use of emergency services outside of network areas.

    Combining these sentences with *or* would not be appropriate. No pair of alternatives is offered.

Using *yet*

When to Use *yet:* When you want to strongly emphasize a contrast between two ideas.

Why to Use *yet:* To focus readers' attention on the contrast itself rather than the ideas being contrasted.

> **Example:**   Jared is a pilot, <u>yet</u> he is afraid of heights.

Yet emphasizes the irony of the contrast in this example. *Irony* means the use of words that mean the opposite of what a reader would ordinarily expect, typically for humorous or emphatic effect. Compare the sentence above with the sentences that follow:

- Jared is a pilot.
- He is afraid of heights.

While these two sentences communicate the same ideas as the single sentence that uses *yet*, the ideas do not seem as connected as they do when they are joined in a single sentence using the conjunction *yet*. Additionally, readers cannot see the intentional irony as easily when the construction used involves two sentences rather than one.

We could use *but* instead of *yet*. If we used *but*, the sentence would not emphasize the irony of the situation as clearly as if we used *yet:*

> Jared is a pilot, <u>but</u> he is afraid of heights.

Using *but* makes the sentence sound much more ordinary than using *yet*.

How to Use *yet:* When you can join two sentences with *but*, try using *yet*. Be aware that *yet* provides a special emphasis on how the sentences offer contrasting information. Save the use of *yet* for those occasions when you want to draw attention to that contrast.

PRACTICE **12** Using *yet* to Join Sentences

Read each pair of sentences. Does one sentence contrast with the other, and does the contrast emphasize irony? If so, use *yet* to write a single sentence that combines the two sentences. If not, explain why combining the sentences would not be appropriate.

1. Hackers are computer experts who are able to penetrate secure computer systems to get access to data. Some people who hack into computers use the information they find for illegal activities.

    Combining these sentences with *yet* would not be appropriate. No contrast between the sentences is suggested.

2. Most Americans know that hackers pose real threats to online activities. People continue to use the Internet for very important financial transactions.

    Most Americans know that hackers pose real threats to online activities, **yet** people continue to use the Internet for very important financial transactions.

3. Ironically, private companies and government institutions have spent billions of dollars trying to outsmart the hackers. The hackers continue to break into even the most secure systems.

    Ironically, private companies and government institutions have spent billions of dollars trying to outsmart the hackers, **yet** the hackers continue to break into even the most secure systems.

4. Some people classify hackers into two groups, crackers and hackers. Crackers are the bad guys, the ones who hack for personal gain, and hackers are those who hack for fun or to show where weaknesses in "the system" can be found.

    Combining these sentences with *yet* would not be appropriate. No contrast between the sentences is suggested.

(continued)

5. Hackers may think they do no harm. Their activities can result in serious damage.

   Hackers may think they do no harm, **yet** their activities can result in serious damage.

6. Suppose, for example, that a hacker is able to break into a particular bank's computer system. If word gets out that the bank's system is vulnerable, crackers may begin to hack into it immediately.

   Combining these sentences with *yet* would not be appropriate. No contrast between the sentences is suggested.

7. Hackers acknowledge this possibility. They typically say that the good they do by alerting companies to their security vulnerabilities outweighs any possible negative consequences.

   Hackers acknowledge this possibility, **yet** they typically say that the good they do by alerting companies to their security vulnerabilities outweighs any possible negative consequences.

8. Perhaps the best thing a hacker can do is to take a job with a company that needs rigorous computer security. Such a position would be the perfect opportunity for an expert hacker.

   Combining these sentences with *yet* would not be appropriate. No contrast between the sentences is suggested.

Using *so*

When to Use *so*: When you want to show a cause and effect relationship.

Why to Use *so*: To join two clauses that are directly related by cause and effect.

> **Example:** The cost of living increased this year, so employees are asking for a 2 percent raise.

So brings together a cause (the increase in the cost of living) and an effect (employees' request for a raise). Joining together the two clauses with *so* makes it clear that the first clause is a reason for the second.

Sometimes it is difficult to see the cause and effect relationship between sentences without joining the ones that are related, as this example shows.

- The new manufacturing facility was completed.
- The company held a grand opening ceremony.
- Factory workers marched in protest.

Was the grand opening related to the completion of the new facility? We cannot be sure. Did the workers protest the completion of the facility or the ceremony or something else? We have no way of knowing. When some of the sentences are linked together, we can more clearly see the cause and effect relationships.

- The new manufacturing facility was completed, so the company held a grand opening ceremony.
- Factory workers marched to protest the lavishness of the ceremony.

How to Use *so*: Find sentences in which one sentence expresses a cause and the other sentence expresses its effect. Use *so* to combine them.

PRACTICE 🔞 Using *so* to Join Sentences

Read each pair of sentences. Does one sentence express a cause and the other sentence express its effect? If so, use *so* to write a single sentence that combines the two sentences. If not, explain why combining the sentences would not be appropriate.

1. Child labor has been tolerated in every country on earth. It still exists in many countries.

   Combining these sentences with *so* would not be appropriate. No cause and effect relationship is expressed.

2. The United States has strict labor laws protecting children. All children have the opportunity to go to school.

   The United States has strict labor laws protecting children, **so** all children have the opportunity to go to school.

3. Companies cannot put children in jobs that involve conditions detrimental to a child's health and well-being. Teenagers younger than eighteen cannot be employed as coal miners or hazardous cargo handlers, for example.

   Companies cannot put children in jobs that involve conditions detrimental to a child's health and well-being, **so** teenagers younger than eighteen cannot be employed as coal miners or hazardous cargo handlers, for example.

4. In general, teens must be sixteen or older to engage in most nonfarm work. Minors aged fourteen and fifteen may work outside of school hours in certain occupations under certain conditions.

   Combining these sentences with *so* would not be appropriate. No cause and effect relationship is expressed.

5. Minors of any age may be employed in certain jobs. They may deliver newspapers; perform in radio, television, film, or theatrical productions; or work in nonhazardous, nonfarm businesses solely owned by their parents.

   Combining these sentences with *so* would not be appropriate. No cause and effect relationship is expressed.

6. The laws that govern agricultural work differ from those that cover nonfarm work. Teens who work on farms may have different rights than those who work in nonfarm jobs.

   The laws that govern agricultural work differ from those that cover nonfarm work, **so** teens who work on farms may have different rights than those who work in nonfarm jobs.

7. The federal government allows children over the age of fourteen to work on farms after school hours. Each state has particular laws governing farm work.

   Combining these sentences with *so* would not be appropriate. No cause and effect relationship is expressed.

8. Child labor laws protect children and teenagers. Teens who want to work can do so without exploitation.

   Child labor laws protect children and teenagers, **so** teens who want to work can do so without exploitation.

Now that you have used each coordinating conjunction individually, complete the exercise that follows to try your hand at joining clauses using a variety of coordinating conjunctions.

PRACTICE ⑭ Using Coordinating Conjunctions to Combine Sentences

Some of the following groups of sentences can be combined using a conjunction from the FANBOYS list (*for, and, nor, but, or, yet, so*). Combine the sentences you believe should be joined. Keep in mind the reasons for joining sentences: to show how one sentence relates to another sentence; to avoid lists of short, choppy sentences; and to emphasize some ideas over others. Not all sentences need to be combined. For each set of sentences you join, be prepared to explain why you chose to join them. Be sure to combine at least five sets of sentences, but join more if you believe doing so would be effective.

Sample answers are provided.

1. Like cigarette smoking, hookah smoking uses tobacco to deliver the addictive drug nicotine.

   Although not all scientists agree, hookah smoking may be as toxic as cigarette smoking.

   Like cigarette smoking, hookah smoking uses tobacco to deliver the addictive drug nicotine, **and** although not all scientists agree, hookah smoking may be as toxic as cigarette smoking.

2. Some hookah smokers believe that this practice is less harmful than smoking cigarettes.

   Hookah smoking actually carries many of the same health risks.

   Some hookah smokers believe that this practice is less harmful than smoking cigarettes, **but** hookah smoking actually carries many of the same health risks.

3. Smoking cigarettes is not a healthy practice.

   Hookah smoking is not beneficial to health.

   Neither cigarette smoking nor hookah smoking is a healthy practice. Smoking cigarettes is not a healthy practice, **nor** is hookah smoking.

4. Hookahs are water pipes that are used to smoke specially processed tobacco that is typically flavored.

   Hookahs are also referred to by a number of different names, including narghile, argileh, shisha, hubble-bubble, and goza.

   Do not combine.

5. Hookah smoking is frequently practiced in groups.

   It can properly be referred to as a social activity.

   Hookah smoking is frequently practiced in groups, **so** it can properly be referred to as a social activity.

6. Health organizations are beginning to pay more attention to the health effects of hookah use.

   Hookah use has been on the rise around the world in recent years.

   Health organizations are beginning to pay more attention to the health effects of hookah use, **for** it has been on the rise around the world in recent years.

7. A Monitoring the Future survey found that in 2011, 18.5 percent of twelfth-grade students in the United States had used hookahs in the past year.

   An even higher percentage of university students—from 22 to 40 percent—have used hookahs in the past year.

   A Monitoring the Future survey found that in 2011, 18.5 percent of twelfth-grade students in the United States had used hookahs in the past year, **and** an even higher percentage of university students—from 22 to 40 percent—have used hookahs in the past year.

(continued)

8. Hookah smoking has been associated with lung cancer, respiratory illness, low birth weight, and periodontal disease.

   It exposes the smoker to more smoke over a longer period of time as compared to typical cigarette usage.

   Do not combine.

9. Young people often believe hookah smoking is a healthy choice.

   Cigarette smoking may actually be *less* harmful.

   Young people often believe hookah smoking is a healthy choice, **yet** cigarette smoking may actually be less harmful.

10. An average cigarette lasts 20 puffs.

    A typical one-hour hookah-smoking session involves 200 puffs.

    An average cigarette lasts 20 puffs, **but** a typical one-hour hookah-smoking session involves 200 puffs.

11. We need to increase public education about the dangers of hookah smoking.

    Another generation may suffer the same fate as did their cigarette-smoking parents and grandparents.

    We need to increase public education about the dangers of hookah smoking, **or** another generation may suffer the same fate as did their cigarette-smoking parents and grandparents.

12. Do not use hookahs yourself.

    Spread the word to others about the dangers of hookah use.

    Do not use hookahs yourself, **and** spread the word to others about the dangers of hookah use.

Combining Sentences Using Dependent Words

The use of coordinating conjunctions (FANBOYS) is not the only way to join sentences. Another method is to use dependent words. Remember that a clause is a group of words containing a subject and a verb. A clause that can stand alone as a complete thought is sometimes called an **independent clause**. When an independent clause begins with a capital letter and has end punctuation, it is a sentence.

   Independent clause: Accounting majors must take several math classes.

We can weaken the ability of a clause to stand alone by adding a dependent word, such as *although*, to it.

   Dependent clause: <u>although</u> accounting majors must take several math classes

   dependent word

When we add a dependent word, the clause—now a **dependent clause**—can no longer stand alone because it is now an *incomplete* thought. After reading a dependent clause, we wonder about the writer's point; we need more information.

   Writers can use dependent clauses effectively by combining them with independent clauses. In the following example, the dependent clause is underlined and the dependent word is in bold print.

   <u>**Although** accounting majors must take several math classes</u>, they do not need many English classes.

   Dependent words have a variety of functions, as the following chart shows. (Be aware that many of these words can also function as prepositions or as other parts of speech.)

Functions of Dependent Words

TO REVEAL CAUSES AND EFFECTS	TO SHOW COMPARISONS	TO SHOW CONTRASTS	TO SHOW POSSIBILITIES	TO PROVIDE TIME INFORMATION	TO MODIFY A NOUN OR ACT AS A NOUN
because for in order to since so that	as in the same way just as like that	although even though in spite of the fact regardless of the fact that that though whereas	if in case in the event once unless until whether (or not)	after as as long as as soon as before now that once since until when whenever while	that what whatever which whichever who whoever whom whomever whose

Using Dependent Words to Show How Ideas Are Related

As the chart demonstrates, dependent words can help readers more accurately decipher the relationships between the ideas in sentences. Consider these sentences:

- Art history is interesting to Shawna.
- She enjoyed taking the art history class.

If we want to show that Shawna's interest in art history was the cause of her enjoyment in the class, we can use the dependent word *because* to combine the sentences. The word *because* signals readers to look for a cause and effect relationship.

> <u>**Because** art history is interesting to Shawna</u>, she enjoyed taking the art history class.
>
> dependent clause (cause)   independent clause (effect)

Notice that the dependent clause (*because art history is interesting to Shawna*) provides the *cause*, and the independent clause (*she enjoyed taking the art history class*) provides the *effect:* the fact that art history is interesting to Shawna *caused* her to enjoy the art history class.

You can use dependent words to combine sentences to show different relationships. In these examples, the dependent clauses are underlined and the dependent words are in bold print.

- **To show cause and effect**

  Candidates rarely spend campaign time at schools **since** <u>minors cannot vote</u>.

  effect   cause

- **To show comparison**

  <u>**Just as** college is expensive</u>, life without a college degree is also expensive.

  situation A   (compared to)   situation B

- **To show contrast**

  We prepared for war **although** <u>Congress had not authorized military engagement</u>.

  situation A   (contrasted with)   situation B

- **To show possibility**

  A student cannot graduate **unless** <u>he or she passes an English course</u>.

  possibility   (related to)   condition

- **To show time**

  When they are young, children are often afraid of monsters.

  time information   (related to)   situation or action

- **To modify a noun or act as a noun**

  The final exam, **which** was given yesterday, covered the semester's work.

  modifies *exam*

  Whoever leaves the room last should turn out the light.

  acts as a noun

PUNCTUATION TIP   **Nonessential and Essential Modifier Clauses and Phrases**

A dependent clause that modifies a noun can be either essential or nonessential. Use commas around nonessential clauses only.

Nonessential modifier clauses: A nonessential clause adds interesting, but not necessary, information about the noun it modifies and should be set off with commas. Clauses beginning with *which* are always nonessential. In the following example, the nonessential dependent clause (underlined) modifies the word *form*. Notice the commas around the clause.

> The personnel form, which is required for all applicants, can be completed online.

Essential modifier clauses: A clause is essential when it identifies the noun it modifies. If the meaning of the sentence would not be clear without the modifying clause, then the clause is essential and should *not* be set off with commas. Modifier clauses beginning with *that* are always essential. In the following example, the essential dependent clause (underlined) modifies the word *class.*

> The English class that is required for graduation is offered only in the spring.

Essential and nonessential phrases: Like clauses, phrases can also be essential and nonessential. In the following example, the underlined phrase is not set off by commas.

> **Example:**   The compass displayed in the glass case is the oldest one.

If a customer asks, "Which compass is the oldest?" the phrase *displayed in the glass case* tells the customer which compass is being discussed. Therefore the phrase is essential to the meaning of the sentence and is not set off by commas. Consider, however, the following sentence.

> **Example:** The compass, battered by years of use at sea, guided us home.

In describing the compass as *battered by years of use at sea,* the writer is not identifying this particular compass as compared with some other compasses. Rather the writer is just providing extra information. Notice the commas around the verbal phrase. If a phrase merely provides additional information, then it is nonessential and should be set off by commas.

When a proper noun is used, any phrase that describes the person or thing cannot be *identifying* because its identity has already been provided by its name. So, phrases modifying proper nouns are always nonessential and are thus set off by commas.

> **Examples:**   Abraham Lincoln, born in Kentucky and raised in Indiana, is claimed by both states as a "native son."
>
> Lincoln, hoping to avert war, modified the content of his first inaugural address.

Using Dependent Words to Emphasize Ideas

Besides showing relationships, dependent words are used to emphasize the relative importance of one idea as compared to another. The separate clauses that follow do not give readers any clues about whether one idea is more important than the other.

- Sue had never missed a day of training.
- She could not finish the marathon.

Notice how the meaning of the sentences changes when we use the dependent word *although* to join the clauses.

> **Although** Sue had never missed a day of training, she could not finish the marathon.
>
> dependent clause = less important   independent clause = more important

The most important point in the combined sentence is that Sue could not finish the marathon.

We can change the emphasis of the sentence and suggest a different meaning by making the second clause dependent.

> **Although** she could not finish the marathon, Sue had never missed a day of training.
>
> dependent clause = less important   independent clause = more important

The emphasis in this sentence is on the fact that Sue had never missed a day of training. The point we might infer is that Sue is to be commended for her faithfulness to her training schedule.

PUNCTUATION TIP   **Fragments**

A dependent clause that stands alone is a sentence fragment. A dependent clause must be combined with an independent clause.

> **Fragment: After** I began to use a graphing calculator.
>
> dependent clause

When you make one clause dependent, joint it to an independent clause.

> **Correct: After** I began to use a graphing calculator, I scored higher on math tests.
>
> dependent clause   independent clause

In general, if the *dependent* clause comes first, put a comma after it.

> **Correct: After** I began to use a graphing calculator, I scored higher on math tests.
>
> dependent clause   comma   independent clause

If the *independent* clause comes first, a comma is not necessary and usually should not be used.

> **Correct:** I scored higher on math tests after I began to use a graphing calculator.
>
> independent clause   (no comma)   dependent clause

When to Use Dependent Words to Combine Sentences

Making clauses dependent is a way for you, as a writer, to help your writing more clearly convey your thoughts. Use dependent word clause constructions in these cases:

- When showing the relationship between clauses will help readers better understand your ideas
- When two sentences are related and you wish to emphasize the importance of one over the other

PRACTICE 15 Using Dependent Words to Reveal Relationships

For each group of independent clauses, follow these steps to practice using dependent words to combine sentences.

A. Read each group of sentences.

B. Determine whether the sentences in a group share one of these relationships:

Cause and effect

Comparison

Contrast

Conditionality

Time

Noun or Noun Modifier

C. If the clauses do share a relationship, choose a dependent word that expresses that relationship. Refer to the Functions of Dependent Words chart for a list of dependent words.

D. Check the punctuation rules, and make sure your combined sentences follow them.

1. People today from all walks of life have tattoos.

   The general public might believe that tattoos are completely safe.

   Relationship: Cause and effect

   Combined sentence: **Since** people today from all walks of life have tattoos, the general public might believe that tattoos are completely safe.

2. Tattoo artists are, generally speaking, conscientious about their work.

   They take measures to make sure their practice is safe and hygienic.

   Relationship: Cause and effect

   Combined sentence: **Because** tattoo artists are, generally speaking, conscientious about their work, they take measures to make sure their practice is safe and hygienic.

3. Tattooists try to maintain a sanitized work environment.

   Not all risks can be eliminated.

   Relationship: Contrast

   Combined sentence: **Although** tattooists try to maintain a sanitized work environment, not all risks can be eliminated.

4. A particular type of bacteria has been found in hospitals and has caused infections in patients after catheterization and minor surgeries.

   The bacteria is named nontuberculous mycobacteria (NTM).

   Relationship: Noun Modifier

   Combined sentence: A particular type of bacteria, **which** is called nontuberculous mycobacteria (NTM), has been found in hospitals and has caused infections in patients after catheterization and minor surgeries.

5. NTM has been found in hospitals.

   NTM has been found in certain tattoo inks.

(continued)

Relationship: Comparison

Combined sentence: **Just as** NTM has been found in hospitals, it has also been found in certain tattoo inks.

6. Some of these contaminated inks caused serious infections in tattoo recipients in at least four states in late 2011 and early 2012.

   The FDA is reaching out to tattoo artists, ink and pigment manufacturers, and public health officials to warn them of the potential for infection.

   Relationship: Cause and effect

   Combined sentence: **Because** some of these contaminated inks caused serious infections in tattoo recipients in at least four states in late 2011 and early 2012, the FDA is reaching out to tattoo artists, ink and pigment manufacturers, and public health officials to warn them of the potential for infection.

7. Getting the word out to tattooists is particularly critical.

   They are on the front lines.

   Relationship: Cause and effect

   Combined sentence: Getting the word out to tattooists is particularly critical **because** they are on the front lines.

8. A tattoo artist may diligently follow hygienic practices.

   The tattooist may not be aware that an ink itself is contaminated.

   Relationship: Contrast

   Combined sentence: **Even though** a tattoo artist may diligently follow hygienic practices, the tattooist may not be aware that an ink itself is contaminated.

9. Tattoo artists can minimize the risk of infection.

   They can use inks that have been processed to ensure they are free from disease-causing bacteria.

   Relationship: Conditionality

   Combined sentence: **If** tattoo artists use inks that have been processed to ensure they are free from disease-causing bacteria, they can minimize the risk of infection.

10. Awareness of the problem involving tattoo inks becomes widespread among tattoo parlor operators.

    The problem of infection related to tattoos will be greatly reduced.

    Relationship: Time

    Combined sentence: **When** awareness of the problem involving tattoo inks becomes widespread among tattoo parlor operators, the problem of infection related to tattoos will be greatly reduced.

Now that you have practiced using dependent words to show relationships between sentences, try your hand at using dependent words for emphasis.

PRACTICE 16 Using Dependent Words to Emphasize the Importance of Ideas

Below are eight groups of sentences. Add dependent words to combine the sentences in each group if you believe emphasizing one of the clauses over the other is important. Here are the specific steps to follow:

A. Read each group of sentences.

B. Determine which sentence you would like to make the most important in the group, and circle it.

(continued)

C. Select an appropriate dependent word, and use it to combine the two sentences.

D. Check the punctuation rules, and make sure your combined sentences follow them.

1. European immigrants colonized North America. The forests were thick, game was abundant, the water teemed with life, and the air was pure and clean.

   When European immigrants colonized North America, the forests were thick, game was abundant, the water teemed with life, and the air was pure and clean.

2. The settlers had a pioneering spirit. The natural bounty of the land was what really invited them to push westward in the early eighteenth century.

   Although the settlers had a pioneering spirit, the natural bounty of the land was what really invited them to push westward in the early eighteenth century.

3. They explored and built cities in the Southwest. They built cities in the Ohio Valley and Great Lakes regions.

   No change (no emphasis desired), but answers may vary.

4. Railroads were built to create easy passage across the country. Cities in the West and Midwest grew.

   After railroads were built to create easy passage across the country, cities in the West and Midwest grew.

5. Forests were logged, and plains and prairies were devoted to grain production and livestock. The environment began to suffer.

   As forests were logged and plains and prairies were devoted to grain production and livestock, the environment began to suffer.

6. Freshwater resources were threatened. Large sewer systems were needed for the collection of wastewater.

   Freshwater resources were threatened **because** large sewer systems were needed as places to dump wastewater.

7. More and more coal was being burned. City skies were darkening.

   City skies were darkening **as** more and more coal was being burned.

8. People began to realize that the environment is fragile. It became less acceptable to continue to abuse the environment.

   Once people began to realize that the environment is fragile, it became less acceptable to continue to abuse the environment.

Combining Sentences Using Conjunctive Adverbs

Conjunctive adverbs (CA) are another type of sentence connector. Conjunctive adverbs are words such as *consequently, however,* and *finally.* In the examples that follow, the words in bold print are conjunctive adverbs. Notice the punctuation that sets off the conjunctive adverbs.

Separate clauses:

Robotics is a rapidly developing field. Job opportunities are increasing.

Combined using a conjunctive adverb:

Robotics is a rapidly developing field**;** **consequently,** job opportunities are increasing.
       clause   CA   clause

Separate clauses:

The flu vaccine is effective. Not everyone chooses to receive it.

Combined using a conjunctive adverb:

The flu vaccine is effective; **however,** not everyone chooses to receive it.

<u>clause</u>   CA   <u>clause</u>

The chart below lists the most common conjunctive adverbs for each of six different functions.

Functions of Conjunctive Adverbs

ADDITION	ALTERNATIVE	CAUSE AND EFFECT	CONDITIONALITY	CONTRAST	TIME
additionally also besides equally furthermore moreover similarly	alternatively instead otherwise	consequently hence therefore thus	otherwise	conversely however nevertheless nonetheless rather	afterward finally meanwhile previously subsequently

Like coordinating conjunctions and dependent words, conjunctive adverbs help you show the relationship between two clauses. They are also effective methods of combining short, choppy sentences so that a text flows more smoothly.

However, conjunctive adverbs often have one attribute that other methods of combining clauses do not have: they elevate the diction of a sentence. **Diction** refers to the level of formality a writer establishes through word choice. In the example that follows, notice how the diction is affected by the use of a conjunctive adverb (in bold print):

Slang: Some people don't recycle 'cause it's a pain in the neck.

Casual diction: Some people think recycling is too difficult, so they don't do it.

Formal diction: Some people perceive recycling as a burden; **consequently,** these people do not participate in recycling.

The use of the conjunctive adverb *consequently* helps raise the diction level of the sentence.

Conjunctive adverbs are used more frequently in texts written on a formal level, such as scholarly articles, research papers, and legal and medical documents. Academic writing is formal writing, so using conjunctive adverbs is a perfectly acceptable—and often desirable—strategy to use in writing for college courses.

PUNCTUATION TIP   **Conjunctive Adverbs**

When you use a conjunctive adverb to connect two clauses, you must also use a semicolon before the adverb and a comma after it.

Correct:

Green tea is full of antioxidants; **thus,** many people drink it for their health.

    <u>independent clause;</u>   CA,   <u>independent clause</u>

White tea also has health benefits; **however,** it is not used as commonly as green tea.

    <u>independent clause;</u>   CA,   <u>independent clause</u>

Commas alone may not be used with a conjunctive adverb to join two clauses. If a writer uses commas alone, the result is a comma splice.

Comma splice:

Green tea is full of antioxidants, **thus,** many people drink it for their health.

    <u>independent clause,</u>   CA,   <u>independent clause</u>

(continued)

A conjunctive adverb cannot join two sentences without any surrounding punctuation or with just a comma. The result is a run-on sentence.

Run-on error:

Green tea is full of antioxidants **thus** many people drink it for their health.
(missing punctuation)

Green tea is full of antioxidants **thus,** many people drink it for their health.
(insufficient punctuation)

Using conjunctive adverbs correctly:

1. Make sure you are joining two independent clauses (complete sentences).

   Children need protection. Parents must provide it.
   independent clause   independent clause

2. Select a conjunctive adverb appropriate for the meaning of the sentences.

   Children need protection. **therefore** Parents must provide it.

3. Insert the correct punctuation marks around the conjunctive adverb, and use appropriate capitalization.

   Children need protection. **; therefore,** pParents must provide it.

   Children need protection; therefore, parents must provide it.

When to Use Conjunctive Adverbs to Combine Sentences

As you know, combining sentences can help writers avoid using the same single-clause sentences over and over. Using conjunctive adverbs to combine sentences, when appropriate, contributes to sentence variety and more eloquent writing. When you see that you have written many simple sentences, consider using conjunctive adverbs to combine some of them.

In addition to providing sentence variety, conjunctive adverbs help you more clearly communicate meanings. A simple example is using a conjunctive adverb to help readers understand time relationships. Read the sentences that follow:

- Matthew was in an auto accident.
- Matthew was seen drinking beer.

The sentences may result in confusion about time order. Was Matthew drinking when he was in the auto accident? Was Matthew drinking before or after the auto accident? Using a conjunctive adverb can clarify the confusion:

Matthew was in an auto accident; **afterward**, he was seen drinking beer.

Matthew was in an auto accident; **previously**, he was seen drinking beer.

The use of either *afterward* or *previously* clears up the confusion about when Matthew had the accident in relation to when he was seen drinking.

As you practice using conjunctive adverbs, find sentences that could be confusing to readers. Determine whether a conjunctive adverb might help clarify the meaning of the sentences or even make the relationships between sentences clearer. Practice using conjunctive adverbs to link clauses together when appropriate.

Using Conjunctive Adverbs to Show How Ideas Are Related

As the Functions of Conjunctive Adverbs chart demonstrates, each conjunctive adverb indicates a particular relationship. The sentences that follow provide an example for each of the types of relationships conjunctive adverbs can demonstrate.

- **To add information**
  Videos can help explain concepts; **additionally,** online sites can be effective tools.
  <u>statement A</u>　　　<u>added to</u>　　　<u>statement B</u>

- **To reveal alternatives**
  Students can study in the library; **alternatively,** they can study at home.
  <u>option A</u>　　　<u>compared with</u>　　　<u>option B</u>

- **To indicate cause and effect**
  The sun emits radiation; **thus,** using sunblock provides important protection.
  <u>cause</u>　　　<u>effect</u>

- **To indicate conditionality**
  Children must be taught manners; **otherwise,** they will behave like animals.
  <u>condition</u>　　　<u>related to</u>　　　<u>result</u>

- **To show contrast**
  The flu shot is supposed to be effective; **however,** its effectiveness is never universal.
  <u>idea A</u>　　　<u>contrasted to</u>　　　<u>idea B</u>

- **To indicate a time relationship**
  The jurors filed out of the courtroom; **meanwhile,** the defendant sat anxiously.
  <u>time information showing simultaneous events</u>

PRACTICE (17) Using Conjunctive Adverbs

Read each of the following groups of sentences. Use conjunctive adverbs to join the sentences when doing so will clarify meanings, show relationships, or eliminate choppiness. Using the Functions of Conjunctive Adverbs chart, select the appropriate conjunctive adverb for each group. Remember to use correct punctuation for each sentence you compose.

1. Millions of Americans are looking for jobs online.
   The Internet has become fertile ground for phony business opportunity schemes.
   Millions of Americans are looking for jobs online; **consequently,** the Internet has become fertile ground for phony business opportunity schemes.

2. These schemes sound like excellent opportunities.
   The company names sound legitimate.
   These schemes sound like excellent opportunities; **moreover,** the company names sound legitimate.

3. The wages promised by some of the employers are too good to be true.
   Desperate job seekers hold out hope that the jobs are real.
   The wages promised by some of the employers are too good to be true; **however,** desperate job seekers hold out hope that the jobs are real.

4. Unfortunately, most of these jobs are not good opportunities at all.
   They are actually schemes to swindle, not help, job applicants.
   Unfortunately, most of these jobs are not good opportunities at all; **instead,** they are actually schemes to swindle, not help, job applicants.

(continued)

5. Often, to apply, one must provide a great deal of personal information.

   Applicants routinely give out their driver's license number or social security number.

   Often, to apply, one must provide a great deal of personal information; **therefore,** applicants routinely give out their driver's license number or social security number.

6. People who are "hired" by these companies receive a paycheck from a company outside the United States.

   The explanation is that the employer does not have any banking set up in the United States.

   No conjunctive adverb is appropriate.

7. The amount of the check is significantly more than the employee is owed for salary.

   The employee is instructed to deposit the check and wire the overpayment back to the employer's bank.

   The amount of the check is significantly more than the employee is owed for salary; **hence,** the employee is instructed to deposit the check and wire the overpayment back to the employer's bank.

8. The employee does as instructed.

   The employer's check is found to be fraudulent, and the swindled "employee" loses his or her money.

   The employee does as instructed; **afterward,** the employer's check is found to be fraudulent, and the swindled "employee" loses his or her money.

COMBINED PRACTICE ▸ 1

Use coordinating conjunctions, dependent words, and conjunctive adverbs to combine the sentences in at least ten of the following groups. Be prepared to explain why you decided to combine the sentences and why you chose the method and the particular combining word that you used.

1. Cybersecurity, phishing, worms, Trojan horses, hackers, and viruses seem to be in the news every day.

   Are these threats really serious?

   No combining necessary.

2. Internet experts say that these threats are serious.

   You should take steps to protect yourself from being a victim of online privacy theft.

   Internet experts say that these threats are serious, **so** you should take steps to protect yourself from being a victim of online privacy theft.

3. The first step in protecting yourself is to recognize the risks.

   Become familiar with some of the terminology associated with cybersecurity.

   No combining necessary.

4. Hackers are everywhere.

   The goal of most of them is to exploit weaknesses in software and computer systems for their own gain.

   Hackers, **whose** goal is to exploit weaknesses in software and computer systems for their own gain, are everywhere.

(continued)

5. Their intentions are sometimes fairly benign and motivated primarily by curiosity.

   Their actions are typically in violation of the intended use of the systems that they are exploiting.

   Their intentions, **while** sometimes fairly benign and motivated primarily by curiosity, are typically in violation of the intended use of the systems that they are exploiting.

6. Their meddling often creates problems for users.

   These problems can include the downloading of malicious code such as viruses, worms, and Trojan horses.

   No combining necessary.

7. Some people use the terms *viruses, worms,* and *Trojan horses* interchangeably.

   Each has unique characteristics.

   Some people use the terms *viruses, worms,* and *Trojan horses* interchangeably; **however,** each has unique characteristics.

8. A virus is a type of malicious code.

   A virus requires the user to actually do something before it infects a computer.

   A virus, **which** is a type of malicious code, requires the user to actually do something before it infects a computer.

9. One action that could activate a virus is opening an e-mail attachment.

   Going to a particular Web page is another action that could trigger the downloading of a virus.

   Opening an e-mail attachment is one action that could activate a virus, **and** going to a particular Web page is another.

10. A worm is similar to a virus by design and is considered to be a subclass of a virus.

    Unlike a virus, worms have the capability to spread without any human action.

    A worm is similar to a virus by design and is considered to be a subclass of a virus; **however,** unlike a virus, worms have the capability to spread without any human action.

11. The victim computer becomes infected.

    The worm will attempt to locate and infect other computers.

    The victim computer becomes infected; **then,** the worm will attempt to locate and infect other computers.

12. Worms can spread through your entire computer and others' computers.

    Viruses cannot spread from one computer to another.

    Worms can spread through your entire computer and others' computers; **however,** viruses cannot spread from one computer to another.

13. A Trojan horse program is software that appears to be legitimate and useful.

    It will actually do damage once installed or run on a computer.

    A Trojan horse program is software that appears to be legitimate and useful, **but** it will actually do damage once installed or run on a computer.

14. Users on the receiving end of a Trojan horse are frequently tricked into opening the program.

    They believe that they are receiving legitimate software or files from a legitimate source.

    Users on the receiving end of a Trojan horse are frequently tricked into opening the program **because** they believe that they are receiving legitimate software or files from a legitimate source.

15. For example, a program may claim to be speeding up your computer.

    It may actually be sending your confidential information to a data thief.

    For example, a program may claim to be speeding up your computer, **yet** it may actually be sending your confidential information to a data thief.

(continued)

16. Spyware is sneaky software.

It piggybacks on downloadable software like screen savers, games, and music files.

Spyware is sneaky software **that** piggybacks on downloadable software like screen savers, games, and music files.

17. Spyware sends information about what you are doing on the Internet to a third party.

The third party can then target you with pop-up ads and other pesky intrusions.

Spyware sends information about what you are doing on the Internet to a third party, **who** can then target you with pop-up ads and other pesky intrusions.

18. Browsers enable you to block pop-up ads.

You can also install anti-spyware programs to stop other threats to your privacy.

Browsers enable you to block pop-up ads; **moreover,** you can also install anti-spyware programs to stop other threats to your privacy.

19. Viruses, worms, and Trojan horses are collectively referred to as malware.

The word *malware* is derived from a combination of *malicious* and *software.*

Viruses, worms, and Trojan horses are collectively referred to as malware, **which** is a word derived from a combination of *malicious* and *software.*

20. Having effective antivirus and spyware-removal software on your computer is a good start to protecting yourself from these intruders.

A practical protective step to take is to stay away from disreputable and unknown sites.

Having effective antivirus and spyware-removal software on your computer is a good start to protecting yourself from these intruders; **additionally,** a practical protective step to take is to stay away from disreputable and unknown sites.

COMBINED PRACTICE ②

What follows is the first draft of an essay. It contains very choppy sentences, many repeated words, and very few sentence connectors. Improve the draft by doing the following:

- Use coordinating conjunctions, dependent words, and conjunctive adverbs to combine some of the sentences in the essay.
- Make additional wording changes to clarify ideas.
- Make additional wording changes to avoid repetition.
- Rearrange ideas, if necessary.
- Make any other changes that will produce more eloquent writing.

Be sure to make at least six combined sentences. Write the finished draft on a separate sheet of paper.

True College Prerequisites

College students know what prerequisites are. They are courses. Students must take prerequisite courses before certain other courses. For example, English Composition I is a prerequisite. It must be taken before English Composition II. Other types of prerequisites exist as well. These other types of prerequisites are abilities that students should have

(continued)

developed even before starting college. They include a strong work ethic. The ability to be goal-oriented is a prerequisite. The ability to be organized is a prerequisite.

Not all college students are used to studying. Some high schools are not academically demanding. Others are. Some students enter college with a strong work ethic. Other students do not. *Work ethic* refers to a student's willingness to work hard. Passing college classes requires a work ethic. The work ethic should be strong. For example, learning a foreign language requires daily work. Some students have never studied on an every day basis. This requirement will be a change for those students. The same requirement is true of other courses. Math requires daily study. Some fast-paced courses require daily study. Students will need a strong work ethic. It will be required of them each week. It may be required each day.

Another prerequisite for college is to be goal-oriented. Students who are goal-oriented are good at setting goals. They set goals that are attainable. They create strategies to reach their goals. They troubleshoot their strategies to make sure their plans are working. For instance, goal-oriented students often plan out their semester class schedule far in advance of the registration period. They like to see what is coming. They like to plan for the future. Keeping the future in mind helps them be more motivated with the daily difficulties of college.

The ability to be organized is a prerequisite that can really be helpful in college. Organization alone can help students pass classes. Not being organized can cause students to miss due dates. It can cause students to misplace important papers. It can cause students to fail to set aside enough time for studying. Not being an organized thinker can also cause problems. Some students cannot organize their notes. They cannot organize the information presented in class. They cannot organize the information they read. Being able to organize course materials is important. It helps students manage the materials. It helps students condense the materials. It makes the materials easier to think about. It makes the materials easier to memorize.

Yes, some skills are prerequisites for college success. Students need these skills to succeed. Starting college with a strong work ethic is indispensable. Staying goal-oriented is vitally important. Being able to organize one's life is essential. Being able to organize one's course materials is crucial. These prerequisite skills are vital. They may make the difference between success and failure.

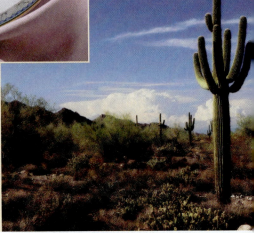

UNIT

2

> "The travelers were ready for the desert/dessert." Choosing the right word can make a difference in how well you communicate your ideas.

Spelling and Word Choice

Easy access to software and smartphone apps that check spelling as we write has made spelling a much less crucial skill than it once was. Even so, spelling remains significant. Indeed, the fact that technological tools have made correct spelling more commonplace makes it all the more important that writers get it right! Today's readers simply expect correct spelling.

In this unit we emphasize the aspects of spelling that computers cannot fix for us. First, we consider some broad strategies for improving spelling and look at a few spelling rules. Then, we present some specific words that are frequently confused. The unit concludes with a discussion of the use of clichés and slang.

UNIT OBJECTIVES

After completing this unit, students will be able to do the following:

- **Use four strategies for improving spelling.**
- **Apply four basic spelling rules.**
- **Use homophones and commonly confused words correctly.**
- **Avoid using clichés and slang in professional and academic writing.**

USING SPELLING STRATEGIES

Here are four useful strategies for improving your spelling.

- **Read.** Reading has a huge impact on spelling. If you see a word over and over, your mind grips that visual representation of the word.
- **Use a spell-checker.** Virtually all word-processing software packages include a spell-checker.

Connect IRW LearnSmart Achieve: Assign the topics "Spelling and Word Use" for adaptive learning to accompany the chapter.

- **Use a dictionary.** No longer do you need to lug around a twenty-pound dictionary. Free, excellent, and easy-to-use dictionaries are available online and as mobile apps. Three good online dictionaries are *Merriam-Webster*, *Oxford Dictionaries*, and the *American Heritage Dictionary*.

- **Make a list of words you commonly misspell.** You will be surprised how quickly you will remember the correct spelling of a word once you make a point of learning it.

APPLYING SPELLING RULES

The spelling of a great many words follows specific rules. These four basic spelling rules will help you improve your spelling.

The Order of *i* and *e*

You probably remember the little rhyme about spelling words that contain *-ie* or *-ei*:

Write *i* before *e*,

Except after *c*,

Or when it sounds like an *a*,

As in *neighbor* and *weigh*.

Examples: *i* before *e:* relief, believe, niece, chief

except after c: receive, ceiling, conceit, deceit

when it sounds like an a: vein, sleigh, weigh, neigh

Several exceptions to the rule do exist. The list below contains virtually all of the exceptions that you are likely to use in your writing.

ancient	deficient	glacier	science
atheism	efficient	height	seize
caffeine	either	heist	society
codeine	feisty	leisure	sovereign
conscience	foreign	neither	sufficient
counterfeit	forfeit	protein	weird

Teaching Resources: See the Instructor's Manual (IM) for Connect IRW assignments that support the objectives of this unit.

Teaching Resources: See the IM for tips for helping students remember exceptions to this rule.

Final -*e* and Suffixes

Drop the final *-e* before a suffix that begins with a vowel, but retain the final *-e* before a suffix that begins with a consonant.

Examples: arrive + ing = arriving   brave + ly = bravely

guide + ance = guidance   achieve + ment = achievement

date + ing = dating   like + ness = likeness

Final -*y* and Suffixes

Change a final *-y* that is preceded by a consonant to *-i* before a suffix (with one exception, as noted).

Examples: rely + -ance = reliance   study + -ed = studied

supply + -er = supplier   carry + -es = carries

beauty + -ful = beautiful   ugly + -est = ugliest

Exception: If the suffix begins with -*i* (as with -*ing*), then the final -*y* is retained:

rally + -ing = rallying   deny + -ing = denying

If the word ends in a -*y* that is preceded by a vowel, then add the suffix without making any change to the root word.

Examples: annoy + -ance = annoyance   destroy + -ed = destroyed

betray + -er = betrayer   monkey + -s = monkeys

joy + -ful = joyful   delay + -ing = delaying

Final Consonant and Suffixes

When adding a suffix that begins with a vowel, double a final single consonant if both of these criteria are met:

- A single vowel precedes the consonant.
- The word has only one syllable, or the last syllable is accented.

Examples in which both criteria are met:

grab + -ing = grabbing   submit + -ed = submitted   refer + -al = referral

Examples in which both criteria are *not* met:

pool + -ed = pooled (The final consonant is preceded by more than one vowel.)

mourn + -ful = mournful (The final consonant is preceded by another consonant.)

benefit + -ed = benefited (The last syllable is not accented.)

MASTERING COMMON USAGE ERRORS

Sometimes writing mistakes occur because a writer confuses one word for another; these kinds of missteps are called *usage errors.* Some spelling errors are usage errors; in other words, knowing which word is the proper one to use can often enable you to avoid a spelling mistake.

Frequently, the kind of confusion involved is a function of two words that sound the same (or almost the same) but are spelled differently (and are two entirely different words). Each of the words in such a pair is called a **homophone.** (We will include in this category "near homophones"—words that are not properly pronounced in an identical manner but are close enough to create usage problems.) However, not all usage mix-ups happen because words have similar pronunciations; we will address those other kinds of usage difficulties separately.

Homophones

Spell-checkers will, at best, detect only a few homophone errors. That is why learning common homophones is crucial.

accept/except

accept = (verb) to receive; to take in

except = (preposition) other than

Examples: I *accept* your apology.

I will buy everything on this table *except* the vase.

Quick Check   Fill in the blanks with the correct words.

Accept criticism! Doing so, while difficult, can pay huge dividends. If your boss tells you that everything in your performance is great _except_ your punctuality, take that as encouragement to be on time rather than as condemnation of the job you are doing.

advice/advise

advice = (noun) a recommendation as a guide to action; words of counsel
advise = (verb) to give advice; to counsel; to offer a suggestion

Examples: I strongly recommend that you take his _advice_.

The attorney will _advise_ you regarding this matter.

Quick Check   Fill in the blanks with the correct words.

How would you _advise_ me to proceed? What is your _advice_ ? No matter what your instructions are, I will follow your _advice_ .

affect/effect

affect = (verb) to influence or change
effect = (noun) result

Examples: The dark weather _affects_ my moods.

Sunshine has a positive _effect_ on me.

Quick Check   Fill in the blanks with the correct words.

The sun can _affect_ different people in different ways. One _effect_ that the sun has on some people is to contribute to their being in a good mood. Another _effect_ it can have is to cause sunburn.

allot/a lot

allot = (verb) to provide
a lot = (noun) a group of items; many

Note: _Alot_ is an incorrect spelling of _a lot_ and is not a word.

Examples: The professor will _allot_ the students one hour for the exam.

A lot of items are in the lost and found bin.

Quick Check   Fill in the blanks with the correct words.

The judge will allot each person six jars. The contest requires that we fill those jars

with as many pennies as we can. Without question, each of the jars will hold a lot

of pennies!

---

all ready/already

all ready = (adverbial phrase) entirely prepared; set to proceed

already = (adverb) has occurred previously

Examples: The kids were *all ready* for the trip. (Better: All of the kids were *ready* for the trip.)

I have *already* read this book.

Quick Check   Fill in the blank with the correct word.

We have already learned this material.

---

bare/bear

bare = (verb) to reveal

(adjective) to be in a revealed state

bear = (verb) to support or carry (both literally and figuratively)

(noun) a very large mammal with stocky legs, a long snout, and shaggy fur

Examples: My *bare* arms were cold in the auditorium.

The old *bear* is literally starving; I cannot *bear* to see it suffer so.

Quick Check   Fill in the blanks with the correct words.

The refrigerator is bare , but the pantry shelves are so loaded with dry goods that

I'm not sure that they can bear the weight. However, I simply cannot bear going

to the grocery store during the weekend, so we will just need to make do with

canned food for now.

---

brake/break

brake = (noun) the part of a vehicle that causes slowing and stopping

(verb) to slow or stop something, such as a vehicle

break = (noun) a recess period; a fracture (as in a bone)

(verb) to split into pieces; to interrupt; to take a recess

Examples: The *brakes* in his jalopy were dangerously worn.

When approaching a stop sign, you should *brake* smoothly.

We should probably take a fifteen-minute *break*.

The kids will *break* the glass figurines if they play with them.

Quick Check   Fill in the blanks with the correct words.

I was afraid that my car would _break_ down. I took it to the shop to have the _brakes_ checked. They said it would be an hour before anyone could look at the car because all of the mechanics were on _break_ . The shop boss said that before they do any work, they will drive the car and _brake_ hard to test the system.

---

breath/breathe

breath = (noun) a single inhalation and exhalation of air

breathe = (verb) to inhale and exhale air

Examples: She took a *breath* of air.

She needs to *breathe* the fresh air.

Quick Check   Fill in the blanks with the correct words.

The bus was so hot that it was hard to _breathe_ . I felt as though I could not take even a single _breath_ .

---

cite/sight/site

cite = (verb) to make reference to; to create a *citation*

sight = (noun) the faculty of vision; something seen

(verb) to see something; to adjust the aiming apparatus (as of a gun)

site = (noun) a location; a piece of land

Examples: You should always *cite* the sources used in an academic paper; in addition, you need to use the proper form for all of your *citations*.

The Christmas tree with all of its ornaments and lights was quite a *sight*.

The home is located at a very convenient *site*—near a bank, a pharmacy, and a grocery store. (The house is in a convenient *situation*.)

Quick Check   Fill in the blanks with the correct words.

The _site_ where the mammoths were found is a riverbed. It was quite a _sight_ to see so many people working to uncover the fossilized bones. The articles that the paleontologists write about the work being done there will no doubt frequently be _cited_ (past tense) in scholarly journals in the future.

clothes/cloths

clothes = (plural noun) attire, apparel, garments

cloths = (noun, plural of *cloth*) pieces of fabric, such as those used for cleaning

Examples: Back-to-school time means that we get to shop for *clothes*!

Cloths work far better than paper towels for some tasks.

Quick Check   Fill in the blanks with the correct words.

When I am ready to clean the house, I put on some old _clothes_, find some _cloths_ to dust with, get out the vacuum cleaner, and line up all of my cleaning products on the table.

coarse/course

coarse = (adjective) rough; vulgar; unsophisticated (as in *coarse* humor)

course = (noun) route; sequence; an academic class

(verb) to run through (as in blood coursing through a person's veins)

Examples: The *coarse* sandpaper was perfect for the job.

Which *course* of action should we take?

I am taking a *course* at the local community college.

The river *courses* through the lush valley.

Quick Check   Fill in the blanks with the correct words.

In one of my nursing _courses_, I learned something that pertained to my own health! I will need a _course_ of antibiotics to get rid of a persistent rash. The rash dries out my skin and makes it feel _coarse_.

complement/compliment

complement = (noun) something that completes or makes perfect

(verb) to provide an addition that fits well or is appropriate *compliment* = (noun) an expression of approval, esteem, or acknowledgment

(verb) to offer praise, admiration, or respect

Examples: Some people think milk is a perfect *complement* to cookies in the same way that ice cream exquisitely *complements* apple pie.

I never expected to receive a *compliment* from my boss, so I was shocked when she said to me in front of the entire work group, "I'd really like to *compliment* you on your performance this quarter."

Quick Check   Fill in the blanks with the correct words.

I couldn't wait to __compliment__ the host on the reception, which was such a nice

__complement__ to the lecture. I was delighted to receive several __compliments__ for the

dip and crackers I brought to the reception. Raspberry preserves are a wonderful

__complement__ to cream cheese in a dip.

conscience/conscious

conscience = (noun) a person's intuitive sense of right and wrong

conscious = (adjective) awake; intentional

Examples: My *conscience* tells me that I really should donate blood.

The hockey player was *conscious* after his fall.

I made a *conscious* decision to contribute more to charity this year.

Quick Check   Fill in the blanks with the correct words.

The defendant was __conscious__ of the crowd of angry people behind him. Even so, his

__conscience__ did not prompt him to confess.

decent/descent/dissent

decent = (adjective) proper; appropriate; satisfactory

descent = (noun) downward movement; downward slope

dissent = (verb) to disagree; to differ in opinion

(noun) the expression of an opposing view

Examples: The dress code required everyone to wear *decent* clothing.

The airplane began its *descent* into Chicago.

The senator expressed her *dissent* regarding the proposed bill.

Quick Check   Fill in the blanks with the correct words.

The used book of mythology that I bought recently is in _decent_ condition. It
includes my favorite myth—the story of Hercules's _descent_ into the underworld.
Although almost all of the reviews were glowing, I did read a couple that expressed
dissent as to its being a great collection of stories.

desert/dessert

desert = (noun) a dry, arid area, typically with a very warm climate

dessert = (noun) a sweet treat, usually the last course in a meal

Examples: Many types of cactus thrive in the *desert*.

          I'd like strawberry cheesecake for *dessert*.

Quick Check   Fill in the blanks with the correct words.

A restaurant in the _desert_ would probably earn more revenue from selling cold
drinks than from serving coffee and _dessert_ .

fair/fare

fair = (adjective) impartial or just; not cloudy (with reference to weather)

     (noun) an exhibition or exposition, such as a county *fair*

fare = (noun) a fee

     (verb) to experience good or bad fortune or treatment

Examples: Professor Hendricks is tough but *fair*.

          The children want to go to the state *fair* because they love the rides.

          I have money enough for train *fare*, but I don't have enough for an
airline ticket.

          Amy did not win a medal, but she did not *fare* too badly at the
tournament.

Quick Check   Fill in the blanks with the correct words.

Having the _fair_ occur right after school starts in the fall is not _fair_ ! School kids
want to be able to attend. Moreover, for the city to raise the standard bus _fare_
during this time of the year is also not _fair_ .

farther/further

farther = (adjective, adverb) to a greater length or distance (literally)

further = (adjective, adverb) to a greater degree (figuratively)

Examples: Soldier: "We marched *farther* today than you told us we would."

Sergeant: "If you complain *further*, I'll make you do it again!"

Quick Check   Fill in the blanks with the correct words.

I had to drive _farther_ to get to the college library than to the public library.

However, going to the library on campus will enable me to go much _further_ with

my research than I could have gone at the public library.

forth/fourth

forth = (adverb) onward; forward

fourth = (adjective) something that is number four in a series

Examples: She stretched *forth* her hands as she offered a blessing on the couple's marriage.

The sprinter did not receive a medal because he finished *fourth*.

Quick Check   Fill in the blanks with the correct words.

Although this campaign would represent their _fourth_ attempt, the emperor

exhorted his army: "Go _forth_ and conquer the enemy!"

hear/here

hear = (verb) to perceive sound

here = (adverb) in or at this place

Examples: Her ability to *hear* was compromised by ear infections.

We will have the trial *here* in our city.

Quick Check   Fill in the blanks with the correct words.

The rafting guide said, "Look, someone drowns _here_ every summer. So, it's vitally

important that you let me know if you can't _hear_ the instructions I'm giving."

hole/whole

hole = (noun) gap; opening

whole = (adjective) entire; complete

Examples: Some people like to wear jeans with *holes* in them.

We have to read the *whole* book for this class.

Quick Check   Fill in the blanks with the correct words.

The _whole_ house needed repair. The walls needed painting. The plumbing leaked.

The roof even had a huge _hole_ in it.

its/it's

its = (adjective) possessive form of *it*

it's = (contraction) *it is*

Examples: The tree dropped *its* (possessive) leaves in a matter of a few days.

The grass is suffering from the drought; *it's* (*it is*) turning brown.

Quick Check   Fill in the blanks with the correct words.

The house for sale looked promising, but _its_ roof was in bad shape. I thought,

"I don't know if _it's_ the house for us."

lead/led

The usage of these two words is especially complicated, so we will lay out the variations in a chart.

Word	Part of Speech	Rhymes with	Definition
lead	verb, present tense	bead, deed, feed	to guide, especially by going in advance
lead	noun	head, dead, red	a type of metal; a pencil's marking substance
led	verb, past tense	head, dead, red	past tense of the verb *lead*

Examples: You can *lead* a horse to water.

The pencil required for standardized tests is one with a No. 2 *lead*.

They *led* the donkeys to the feed trough.

Quick Check   Fill in the blanks with the correct words.

The art teacher said, "Watch as I _lead_ you through this exercise. Sketch lightly so

you don't break your pencil's _lead_. After I have _led_ you through it once, you will

be able to do it on your own."

loose/lose

loose = (adjective) not tight

lose = (verb) to not retain; to fail to win

Examples: The *loose* shoestring caused Andrea to trip.

We did *lose* the game, but we enjoyed ourselves anyway.

Quick Check   Fill in the blanks with the correct words.

Some school districts are making rules prohibiting the wearing of clothing that is too

loose . Students who violate these rules will _lose_ privileges.

passed/past

passed = (verb, past tense) proceeded; happened; exceeded

past = (adjective) a time ago

(noun) a time before the present

Examples: The runner who leads the marathon *passed* the halfway point minutes ago.

The old man told delightful stories taken from his colorful *past*.

Quick Check   Fill in the blanks with the correct words.

Once the deadline had _passed_ ,   it was too late to apply for the grant. I'd like to

put that lost opportunity out of mind and leave it entirely in the _past_ .

peace/piece

peace = (noun) tranquility; a sense of calm

piece = (noun) a part of something

Examples: Spreading *peace* throughout the world is a noble goal.

A *piece* of the jigsaw puzzle was missing.

Quick Check   Fill in the blanks with the correct words.

Those kids made so much noise that no one had any _peace_ all night. I'd sure like to

give them a _piece_ of my mind!

plain/plane

plain = (adjective) simple; unadorned

(noun) a vast area of mostly level land

plane = (noun) a flat surface; an airplane; a woodworking tool

(verb) to smooth or shape a wood surface by using a *plane*

Examples: While *plain*, Shaker furniture is nonetheless beautiful.

The open *plain* before us stretched as far as the eye could see.

In geometry, circles, squares, and triangles are figures that exist in a *plane*.

A carpenter can *plane* the uneven edge of a door.

Quick Check   Fill in the blanks with the correct words.

From up in the _plane_ I could see the _plain_ below us. The landscape was _plain_ yet beautiful. The countryside was so flat that I was reminded of a _plane_ in my geometry textbook.

---

principal/principle

principal = (adjective) first; most important; highest in rank or degree

(noun) leader of an elementary or secondary school; headmaster

principle = (noun) a law, rule, truth, or guideline

Examples: The *principal* reason I stayed home was my broken leg.

Ms. Williams is the new *principal* of the high school.

There are five *principles* of good citizenship.

Quick Check   Fill in the blanks with the correct words.

This morning, the high school _principal_ discussed the _principle_ of civility, which she said should govern the way students treat one another.

---

quiet/quit/quite

quiet = (adjective) noiseless

quit = (verb) to stop

quite = (adverb) completely; wholly

Examples: A *quiet* evening was just what I needed after my stressful day.

I plan to *quit* eating sweets after New Year's Day.

The dinner was *quite* wonderful.

Quick Check   Fill in the blanks with the correct words.

The woman is _quite_ a conversationalist. She wouldn't _quit_ talking long enough for anyone else to say anything. The rest of us were _quiet_ all night while we just listened to her.

right/rite/write

right = (adjective) correct; opposite of *left*

   (noun) a just claim (as in civil rights or human rights)

rite = (noun) a ritual

write = (verb) to put words and ideas into a visual form

Examples: Maria wants to do the *right* thing about her mistakes.

   One *rite* our culture observes is the celebration of birthdays.

   Anyone can learn to *write* with practice and diligence.

Quick Check   Fill in the blanks with the correct words.

The rite of fasting is part of many religions. Some believers like to write poetry

to express their experience and understanding of God. Each person chooses a way

to honor God that he or she believes is right .

sale/sell

sale = (noun) an event where items are offered for purchase

sell = (verb) to offer for purchase

Examples: The electronics store is having a huge *sale*.

   Rachel is going to *sell* her condo.

Quick Check   Fill in the blanks with the correct words.

I need to post a sign that says, "Tomatoes for sale ." We have so many tomatoes this

summer that if we don't sell some soon, I'm afraid that they will rot.

set/sit

set = (verb) to place something down; to fix or arrange something

sit = (verb) to rest the body on the buttocks

Examples: The grandfather *set* the groceries on the counter.

   The children will *sit* together at a separate table at the party.

Quick Check   Fill in the blanks with the correct words.

We will set the food on the counter and put all of the drinks in the refrigerator.

After we eat, we can all sit around and talk.

tail/tale/tell

tail = (noun) the often elongated appendage attached to the rear portion of an animal's body; something that resembles an animal's tail

(verb) to follow for surveillance purposes

tale = (noun) a story or fable (typically, a fictional story)

tell = (verb) to make known by speech or writing; to express (as a story, a lie, and so on)

Examples: Unfortunately, the car ran over our dog's *tail*.

FBI agents have been known to *tail* suspects for months.

Before beginning the fairy *tale*, the teacher will *tell* students about its historical background.

Quick Check   Fill in the blanks with the correct words.

I want to tell you one of Aesop's fables. It's the tale about the fox that lost its tail in

a trap.

their/there/they're

their = (adjectival pronoun) possessive form of *they*

there = (adverb) in or at that place (as opposed to *here*)

they're = (contraction) *they are*

Examples: *Their* insurance policy covered the cost of the wrecked car.

She drove the car *there* and then walked back here.

The children are hoping that *they're* (*they are*) going to the zoo today.

Quick Check   Fill in the blanks with the correct words.

My parents are visiting Colorado this month. They drove in their motor home, and

they are planning to stay there for several weeks. However, they're definitely

planning on leaving before the snow starts to fall.

threw/through

threw = (verb) past tense of *throw*

through = (preposition) in one side and out the other side of something

Examples: The pitcher *threw* the ball over 100 miles per hour.

We took the subway *through* the tunnel under the San Francisco Bay.

Quick Check   Fill in the blanks with the correct words.

Through his mask, the umpire clearly saw that the pitcher _threw_ the ball with the intention of hitting the batter.

---

to/too/two

_to_ = (preposition) indicates movement toward something

too = (adverb) also; in addition to

two = (noun, adjective) the number 2

Examples: I decided to go _to_ the mall.

Maria wanted to go _too_, so she rode with me.

Two eagles circled overhead.

Quick Check   Fill in the blanks with the correct words.

The man was _too_ tired to continue hiking. He walked over _to_ a tree, where he slumped down, took out all the food he had left—just _two_ cupcakes—and slowly ate them.

---

want/won't

want = (verb) to desire

won't = (contraction) _will not_

Examples: We all _want_ to see the film.

We _won't_ (_will not_) pay $20 per movie ticket.

Quick Check   Fill in the blanks with the correct words.

I know you don't _want_ to wait for the supervisor, but if you _want_ to take your luggage with you, you must wait. We _won't_ allow your luggage on the plane otherwise.

---

wares/wear/where

wares = (plural noun) things that are being sold by someone

wear = (verb) to use a particular garment as clothing

where = (adverb) at; in what location (_Where_ can also be used as an interrogative, a word used to ask a question, in the same manner as _who_, _what_, and _why_.)

Examples: The peddler showed his *wares* to the crowd.

She will *wear* that coat until the sleeves fall off!

The restaurant *where* the crime occurred is close to our neighborhood.

Where can we find another coat like it?

Quick Check   Fill in the blanks with the correct words.

" _Where_ can I find something special to _wear_ to the party?" I wondered. At that moment, an advertisement popped up on my computer screen.

"Take a look at our _wares_ !" the retailer's ad said just as I was struggling with the question as to _where_ I could find a unique dress for the reception. It seems that everyone _wears_ the same traditional designs.

---

weak/week

weak = (adjective) not strong

week = (noun) a period of seven days

Examples: He felt *weak* after skipping both breakfast and lunch.

Next *week* is going to be a very busy time at work.

Quick Check   Fill in the blanks with the correct words.

She felt _weak_ after having been sick in bed for a full _week_ .

---

weather/whether

weather = (noun) the condition of the atmosphere during some period of time
    (verb) to endure (as in *to weather a storm*)

whether = (conjunction) function word that introduces two alternatives

Examples: The bad *weather* meant we had to delay the shopping trip.

I didn't know *whether* (or not) you wanted cream in your coffee.

Quick Check   Fill in the blanks with the correct words.

It doesn't matter _whether_ the _weather_ is nice. The postal service always delivers the mail.

---

we're/were

we're = (contraction) *we are*

were = (verb) a past tense form of the verb *to be*

Examples: I hope *we're* (*we are*) going to get coffee after the play.

The children *were* glad to go outside to play.

Quick Check   Fill in the blanks with the correct words.

_We're_ going to the movies. We had planned to go yesterday, but we _were_ held up

by the traffic.

who's/whose

who's = (contraction) *who is*

whose = (adjective) indicates possession (*Whose* can also be used as an interrogative, a word used to ask a question, in the same manner as *who*, *what*, and *why*.)

Examples: I live near Mr. Carter, *who's* (*who is*) my dad's best friend.

The donor, *whose* name will not be announced, deserves credit nonetheless.

Whose scarf was left in the break room?

Quick Check   Fill in the blanks with the correct words.

She is the woman _whose_ husband won the raffle. She's the same woman _who's_

going to be in charge of the fund-raiser.

your/you're

your = (adjective) indicates possession

you're = (contraction) *you are*

Examples: I'd like to borrow *your* car.

If *you're* going to sleep over, we will need to locate a cot.

Quick Check   Fill in the blanks with the correct words.

I'm sorry that _you're_ not feeling well. Would you like me to pick _your_ children up

from school?

Other Commonly Confused Words

Sometimes as writers we face word choice challenges that are not related to the matter of homophones. We will address several cases in this section.

among/between

among = (preposition) used when referring to a group of three or more

between = (preposition) used when referring to a group of two

Examples: The workers began to talk *among* themselves.

Between you and me, I think Macy is the best candidate.

Quick Check   Fill in the blanks with the correct words.

The class members discussed the ideas _among_ themselves. Meanwhile, Gabriella and I devised a plan _between_ the two of us.

amount/number

amount = (noun) the quantity of something that *cannot* be counted

number = (noun) the quantity of something that *can* be counted

Examples: We received a large *amount* of rain over the weekend.

A large *number* of suggestions were submitted to the management staff.

Quick Check   Fill in the blanks with the correct words.

We saw a great _number_ of floats in the parade. The _amount_ of beer that people drank that day was astounding.

believe/feel

believe = (verb) to be convinced by logic or reason

feel = (verb) to experience an emotion; to touch

Examples: I *believe* that the defendant is guilty.

I *feel* sad for the victim's family.

Quick Check   Fill in the blanks with the correct words.

My view of the accident causes me to _believe_ that the driver of the green car was at fault. I _feel_ a great deal of concern for all those who were injured.

can/may

can = (verb) to be able to doing something

may = (verb) to be permitted to do something

Examples: Coach, you know that I *can* run the entire distance without hurting myself, so *may* I please enter the marathon?

Quick Check   Fill in the blanks with the correct words.

May I swim in your pool? I _can_ swim like a fish. I _can_ dive well, too!

casual/causal

casual = (adjective) informal

causal = (adjective) responsible for causing

Examples: *Casual* dress will be appropriate for the meeting.

A *causal* factor in the fire was the use of a space heater.

Quick Check   Fill in the blanks with the correct words.

Her attitude toward the interview was far too _casual_ .   In fact, her attitude was a

causal element in the company's decision to decline to offer her the job.

fewer/less

fewer = (adjective) not so many; smaller in number

less = (adjective) not so much; smaller in amount

Examples: *Fewer* shoppers made major purchases this season than last season.

The tank actually has *less* gasoline in it than the gauge indicates.

Quick Check   Fill in the blanks with the correct words.

If we can make the vaccine readily available, the result will be _less_ disease, _fewer_

deaths, and consequently a much happier society.

lay/lie

Determining how to use these two words is particularly complicated, so we will lay out the variations in a chart.

Word	Part of Speech	Definition	Past Tense
lay	verb	to set something down	laid
lie	verb	to recline	lay

Examples: I *lay* the logs on the back porch every autumn.

I *laid* the logs on the back porch last year but not this year. (past tense of *lay*)

The cat *lies* on the rug every afternoon.

The cat *lay* on the rug for an hour, but then it got up. (past tense of *lie*)

Quick Check   Fill in the blanks with the correct words:

I need you to _lie_ down in your bed and rest. Children who are ill must _lay_ aside

other activities until they are healthy. I know that yesterday you _lay_ down most of

the day, and I know that you _laid_ aside all of the things you wanted to do, but you

still must _lie_ in bed and rest today.

AVOIDING CLICHÉS AND SLANG

Most of us use clichés and slang in everyday speech. Thus, it is easy for these expressions to slide into our writing. Avoiding clichés and slang in your writing will make your writing more professional and will keep it in line with the standards of academic writing.

Clichés

A **cliché** is a phrase or sentence that is commonly used and often overused. For example, "better safe than sorry" is a common cliché, as is "peace of mind." There is nothing wrong with using clichés in casual conversation; we all do it. The primary complaint against clichés is that using them does not require us to think critically about language choices. Sometimes we reach for a cliché simply because it is handy, not because it fits our purpose better than other phrases. Thus, the writer who depends on clichés may be seen as lazy and considered less creative than the writer who does not.

Even worse than using a cliché is *misusing* a cliché. Here are just a few examples of how clichés are misused—and consequently do not make sense!

Standard Cliché	Confused Form of Cliché
It's not rocket science. (It's not brain surgery.)	It's not rocket surgery.
tough row to hoe	a tough road to hoe
dog-eat-dog world	doggy-dog world

You can avoid making mistakes with clichés simply by avoiding their use. Instead of using a cliché, create your own unique phrase. A common type of cliché is a simile—a comparison using *as* or *like*. By creating your own original expressions, you will avoid making embarrassing mistakes by misusing clichés, but just as importantly, you will be able to convey your thoughts more creatively and precisely.

Cliché (in Standard Form)	New Formation of the Cliché
as dry as a bone	as dry as a rock in the desert
as happy as a clam	as happy as a mouse in a grain silo
like a fish out of water	like a cat at the Westminster Dog Show

When you use a cliché, your readers will understand the meaning of the phrase, but you will have missed an opportunity to write in a fresh, original way. A much better option is create a new phrase.

Slang

Humans are very imaginative when it comes to language. Every culture and each new generation finds a way to bend linguistic rules a bit, and what results from that bending is *slang*. Slang is simply language used in a nonstandard way. For example, *croak* is a standard word when it refers to the sound a frog makes; however, when it is used as a synonym for *die*, the word is slang. (Example: "The old buzzard finally croaked.") Other slang words have no standard meaning; they are directly created as slang words. The word *scuzzy* is an example; its only use is as a slang word meaning "dirty" or "shabby in condition or character." (Example: "If you don't shave and do something with your hair, you'll just look scuzzy.")

Linguists, people who study language, will be quick to tell you that there is nothing wrong with slang. Most English professors agree. Slang wording becomes a problem when people use it in the wrong places. Most employers, for example, expect their employees to avoid slang in written communication and, in some work settings, in spoken communication also. Additionally, academic writing should never contain slang, and e-mails and other correspondence between students and instructors should be slang-free. In general, anytime you wish to establish a tone of seriousness, avoid slang.

So, what fits into that category we call *slang*? In "What Is Slang?" Robert Beard, a linguist, calls slang

> a code in which one vaguely related or unrelated word or phrase is substituted for a more common one. The words that are replaced in slang are the most common ones: good (*cherry, boss, phat, da bomb*), bad (*icky, yucky, jankety*), crazy (*nuts, bananas, crackers, bonkers*), smart (*brainy, savvy, sharp*), fast (*scream, tear out, fly, like greased lightning*), slow (*dragging, poky, crawling, creeping*).

One point Beard makes about slang is that it functions as a code: it separates the in-crowd from the outsiders. Because slang is a cultural code, its most appropriate use is within a particular cultural context. If you are hanging out with friends, using slang is probably not only common but actually expected.

If you are unsure whether a term is considered slang, look it up in a dictionary. Almost every dictionary will identify slang words in some fashion.

Punctuation marks are like road signs. They prepare people for what is ahead and point them in the right direction.

Punctuation and Mechanics

Punctuation is a tool that helps writers communicate their thoughts. End punctuation signals the end of a complete thought and comes at the end of a complete sentence. Commas group sets of words together so readers can grasp the meaning of a sentence as well as the importance of certain elements in the sentence. In this unit, we will discuss the various types of punctuation available to writers, when to use each type, and how to use each type correctly.

UNIT OBJECTIVES

After completing this unit, students will be able to do the following:

- **Use end punctuation correctly.**
- **Use commas correctly.**
- **Use apostrophes, colons, and semicolons correctly.**
- **Use hyphens, parentheses, dashes, quotation marks, and ellipses correctly.**

USING END PUNCTUATION CORRECTLY

A sentence is a complete thought. End punctuation shows readers where one thought ends and where the next thought begins. Sentences can end in periods, question marks, or exclamation marks.

TYPE	EXPLANATION	EXAMPLES
Period	A declarative (ordinary) sentence ends with a period.	*The sky is deep blue* *She cooks lunch daily.*
Question mark	A question is a sentence that asks something and ends with a question mark.	*How are you?* *What time is it?*
Exclamation mark	A sentence that emphasizes a point or strongly expresses an emotion ends with an exclamation mark. An interjection or command also ends with an exclamation mark.	*My way is right!* *I am so happy!* *Wow! That's cool.* *Clean your room!*

Connect IRW LearnSmart Achieve: Assign the topics "End Punctuation: Periods, Question Marks, Exclamation Points," "Commas," "Apostrophes and Quotation Marks," "Colons and Semicolons," and "Other Punctuation" for adaptive learning to accompany this unit.

Particular situations pose special problems for each of the three types of end punctuation, as the chart below illustrates.

TYPE	TROUBLE SPOTS	EXAMPLES
Period	Two complete thoughts that are combined without proper punctuation between them are called *run-on sentences*. This form is grammatically incorrect.	*The workers are drained they have labored all night.* (Period needed between *drained* and *they*.)
Question mark	Sentences in which the subject is wondering or asking about something should not end with a question mark. A question mark is only used when a question is being asked directly.	*I wonder if it will rain today.* *Ty asked whether the mail had come.* (No question mark needed.)
Exclamation mark	A sentence that is merely *reporting* strong emotion does not need an exclamation mark.	*Mira was excited about the news. Indeed, she was ecstatic.* (No exclamation mark needed.)

PRACTICE ❶ Using End Punctuation Correctly

Read the paragraph below, adding the appropriate end punctuation to each sentence. (Capital letters indicate where new sentences begin.)

Close the door! How many times do I have to tell you that? Whether it's cold or hot outside doesn't matter. You need to close the door regardless. Have you ever looked at our utility bills? Do you realize how much of our income goes to pay for heating and cooling? Think! If you would just think before you act, things would be so much better around here.

USING COMMAS CORRECTLY

Commas are primarily used to separate or to join elements within a sentence.

Commas after Introductory Elements

A comma should follow several types of words, phrases, and clauses that are used to begin a sentence.

USE	EXAMPLES
After a prepositional phrase of 3 + words	After the Saint Patrick's Day parade , we had lunch at a pub. On my birthday , my mom always bakes a special cake.
After an introductory verbal phrase	Talking rapidly , the agent described every detail about the house. Tired to the bone , the rangers collapsed in the cabin.
After some single words to clarify meaning or insert a useful pause	Yes , I did think her apology was sincere. However , I have enjoyed staying at this hotel.
After a dependent clause that begins a sentence	Although my family was out of town , I still enjoyed the holidays. Until he left , no one realized how much of a pest he had been.

See the Instructor's Manual (IM) for Connect IRW assignments that support the objectives of this unit.

Note that when a dependent clause is placed at the *end* of a sentence, no comma is needed.

Examples: I still enjoyed the holidays <u>although my family was out of town</u>.

No one realized how much of a pest he had been <u>until he left</u>.

PRACTICE ② Adding Commas after Introductory Elements

Read the paragraph below and consider the introductory elements in each sentence. If commas are needed, add them. Circle each comma you add.

By 4:00 p.m., the town was deserted. Across from Seawall Boulevard, businesses had boarded up their windows and doors. Although the storm was not supposed to make landfall until the next day, most people were not waiting around. However, a few people intentionally remained on the island. Seeking one last bit of adventure before heading for the mainland, the surfers stayed to ride the waves a last time. Scared though they were, their excitement trumped their common sense.

Commas with Conjunctions

If two sentences are joined together with a FANBOYS conjunction (*for, and, nor, but, or, yet, so*), a comma is needed before the conjunction.

CONJUNCTION	EXAMPLES
for	The parrot chattered constantly (,) for it hoped that a cracker would be presented.
and	The two boxers shook hands (,) and then they returned to their corners.
nor	The windows were not locked (,) nor were the curtains drawn shut.
but	Mr. Li wants to go the beach (,) but Ms. Li prefers taking a trip to the mountains.
or	He must do the assignment (,) or he will surely suffer the consequences.
yet	The heat was intense (,) yet the firefighters continued to battle the fire all night.
so	Tissa completed her homework (,) so she decided she could take time for some fun.

PRACTICE ③ Using Commas and Conjunctions to Join Sentences

Guided by the examples in the chart above, write two sentences using each conjunction. Add commas appropriately.

Answers will vary.

for 1 a. _____

b. _____

and 2 a. _____

b. _____

nor 3 a. _____

b. _____

but 4 a. _____

b. _____

(continued)

or	5 a. _____
	b. _____
yet	6 a. _____
	b. _____
so	7 a. _____
	b. _____

Commas in a Series

Use commas to separate elements in a series.

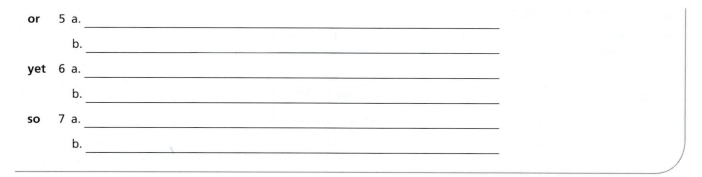

TYPE OF SERIES	EXAMPLES
adjectives	The cake is moist (,) sweet (,) and delicious.
nouns	The Broncos (,) the Panthers (,) the Redskins (,) and the Cowboys are the best teams in the league.
verbs	The mayor ran for reelection (,) won the race (,) and continued his political career.

Note that omitting the comma before the word *and* or *or* in a series is grammatically acceptable in journalism and other types of writing. However, because leaving out the comma can sometimes cause confusion, many writers include it. In academic writing, a comma is always used before *and* or *or.*

Commas between Dual Adjectives

Sometimes a noun is preceded by two adjectives that modify the noun separately. A comma between such dual adjectives is required.

Examples: The grand (,) glorious staircase makes the home seem regal.

Sweet (,) sticky cakes were served with the tea.

She freely offered advice to the sincere (,) curious girl.

PRACTICE ❹ Using Commas in a Series and between Dual Adjectives

Read the paragraph that follows, and add commas where necessary. Circle each comma you add.

I needed to take three science courses in college, so I chose to take anatomy(,) physiology(,) and microbiology. The intriguing(,) stimulating courses provided me with information I use to this day. I learned about the bones in the human body(,) the major body systems(,) and the principal types of diseases. My interesting(,) witty professor for all three courses was a retired cardiologist. He had years of surgical experience from which to draw wonderful stories, so he made the classes very entertaining. His classes convinced me that I would love to become a certified nursing assistant(,) a licensed vocational nurse(,) or a registered nurse, and so I am very glad that I took those courses.

Other Uses of Commas

Some commas are required simply as technical punctuation details based on rules developed by printers, who desired consistency in producing published works.

FUNCTION	EXAMPLES
To separate elements in addresses	811 Martin Drive (,)Richmond (,)VA
To separate the day of the month from the year and the year from whatever follows (when needed)	Wynn was born on May 16 (,)1887 (,)and he died on May 17 (,)1989. The battle on March 3 (,)1777 (,)was especially brutal.
To separate the day of the week from the month	I arrived on Tuesday (,)April 18.
To set off dialogue	Jayne said (,)"I wish I knew how to ice skate." "I took a year of lessons and then dropped out (,)" Ashley replied.
To introduce a quotation from a written source	In the words of Enrique Marquez (,)"An epidemic is a disease gone rogue."
To separate a person's name from a title that follows it	Soo Kim (,)mayor of Yuma (,)is the host for the week. Carrie Garza (,)MD (,)was the speaker at the conference.

Several situations involving comma usage require special attention, as the chart below illustrates.

TYPICAL USAGE	TROUBLE SPOT
To separate the day of the month from the year **Example:** Wynn was born on May 15, 1887.	Do *not* use a comma to separate the month from the year. **Example:** He died in May 1989.
To set off dialogue **Example:** Jayne said, "I wish I knew how to skate!"	Do *not* use a comma when dialogue is described but not quoted directly. **Example:** Jayne said that she wished she knew how to skate. (Note the use of the word *that* and the absence of quotation marks.)
To introduce a quote from a written source **Example:** The CDC report stated, "No significant outbreak of the virus has occurred."	Do *not* use a comma when the word *that* is used to transition into a quotation. **Example:** The CDC report stated that no significant outbreak of the virus had occurred. (Note the use of the word *that* and the absence of quotation marks.)

PRACTICE ⑤ Using Commas Correctly

Read the paragraph below, and add commas where necessary. Circle each comma you add.

Selena walked hurriedly into the classroom. She quickly took the nearest seat, quietly unzipped her backpack, and noiselessly removed her textbook. Opening her book, she sighed anxiously. The test would be extremely difficult, and she knew that she had not studied enough. Throughout the entire semester, Biology 101 had been a tough course for her. Her professor, Sue McGee, MD, was a retired surgeon, and she was very demanding. Professor McGee had told the class that the exam would be challenging, and Selena knew that she meant it.

Selena glanced backward and saw classmates studiously reading their notes. Her heart slowly sank as she realized that she had put herself into a very difficult situation. Nevertheless, she summoned her inner strength, closed her eyes, and said to herself, "Sellie, you can do this. You know you can."

USING APOSTROPHES, COLONS, AND SEMICOLONS CORRECTLY

Apostrophes, colons, and semicolons play important roles in sentences.

Apostrophes

Apostrophes are used for two principal reasons: to create contractions and to show possession by a noun.

Apostrophe Use in Contractions

A **contraction** is a word formed by the merging of two other words. When the words are merged, one or more letters are dropped. An apostrophe's role is to stand in the spot that the dropped letters have vacated. The key to forming contractions correctly is to use the apostrophe in *the very place* that the omitted letters once stood. Generally speaking, contractions should be used sparingly in academic or formal writing.

ORIGINAL WORDS	LETTERS OMITTED	CONTRACTION
do + not	*o* (in *not*)	don't
should + have	*ha*	should've
he + will	*wi*	he'll

Apostrophe Use to Show Possession

For a singular noun, simply add -'s to the noun in order to show possession. Names are treated in the same manner as other nouns.

SINGULAR NOUN	POSSESSIVE
the coach	the coach's cap
a truck	a truck's tires
a New York Yankee	a New York Yankee's hits
the scientist	the scientist's graph
a city	a city's schools

For a plural noun, follow these rules to show possession:

1. If the plural noun ends in -*s*, add only an apostrophe.
2. If the plural noun does not end in -*s*, add -'*s*.

PLURAL NOUN	POSSESSIVE
coaches	coaches' caps
scientists	scientists' graphs
New York Yankees	New York Yankees' infield
children (no -*s*)	children's toys
women (no -*s*)	women's vote

PRACTICE **6** Using Apostrophes Correctly

Read the paragraphs below, and add apostrophes where necessary. Circle each apostrophe you add.

Men's involvement in the construction industry is long established. However, women's participation is on the rise, so much so that some people have replaced the word *tradesmen* with *tradesworkers* because they don't want to suggest a gender bias.

Various members of the workforce are involved in the construction of a house. They specialize in various areas, and workers' tools vary from trade to trade.

Concrete finishers' principal role in building a house is pouring a foundation. Driveways and sidewalks are also the fruit of their labor. A concrete finisher has a tool called a "screed"; he'll use that to level and smooth poured concrete.

Carpenters' tasks primarily involve the "framing" of a house. Carpenters build the wooden structures that support the house's walls, ceilings, and roof. Hammers, saws, and measuring tapes are probably the most important tools for carpenters.

Masons lay brick and do other kinds of stonework. Masons use mortar as a type of adhesive between the bricks. A mason's number one tool is a trowel.

Wiring houses is electricians' assignment. An electrician relies on a special kind of pliers that can be used to cut, strip, and crimp wire; she'll never go to a job site without this special tool.

The responsibility of carpet layers is evident in the name of their trade. Carpet layers use a special tool called a "knee kicker" to stretch carpet for wall-to-wall installation.

A plumber's job in a house's construction is to install the pipes that carry water and the fixtures that provide outlets for water. Plumbers carry with them a set of tools that includes a propane torch, a hacksaw, and various wrenches.

Colons and Semicolons

Colons and semicolons help writers create interesting and varied sentences.

Colons

A colon's function is to introduce an explanation, a list, or a long quotation.

FUNCTION OF COLON	EXAMPLES
To introduce explanations	I decided to stay home for one good reason (:) the roads were frozen and the bridges icy. The result of the survey was clear (:) students want more parking.
To introduce lists	Campers will need the following (:) a flashlight, a backpack, and a knife. The car certainly had problems (:) bent frame, bad brakes, and bald tires.
To introduce long quotes	Mark Twain had this to say about books (:) "In a good bookroom you feel in some mysterious way that you are absorbing the wisdom contained in all the books through your skin without even opening them."

Semicolons

A semicolon is used to connect two complete sentences. Its function is similar to that of a FANBOYS conjunction (*for, and, nor, but, or, yet, so*): it joins two complete thoughts that are equally weighted in the mind of the writer. The two most common situations in which semicolons are properly used are described below.

FUNCTION OF SEMICOLON	EXAMPLES
To connect clauses that are clearly related in meaning or content	The plane was delayed (;) the airport was packed. The judge looked at the defendant (;) the defendant looked at his attorney.
To connect clauses using a conjunctive adverb	I took a wrong turn (;) consequently, I arrived at the party late. We slowly learned the truth (;) thus, we began to take action.

Note that each clause connected with a semicolon must be an *independent clause*—a complete thought capable of standing alone as a sentence. A comma used in place of a semicolon results in a *comma splice error*.

PRACTICE 7 Using Commas, Colons, and Semicolons Correctly

Insert the appropriate punctuation—comma, semicolon, or colon—in the sentences below. If no punctuation is needed, write *NP* in the blank.

1. We went to eat after the play (;) we went home after we ate.

2. The instructions indicated (NP) that each piece needed to be thoroughly cleaned before assembly.

3. Even though the theater company's interpretation of *Hamlet* was highly unusual (,) I found the performance to be superb.

4. The types of art that could be submitted in the contest were strictly limited (:) oil paintings, watercolors, pastels, or charcoal sketches.

5. We sailed for a day on rough seas (NP) because a storm had just passed through our sea route.

6. The restaurant specializes in ham and beans (,) buttermilk pie (,) and grits casserole.

7. The play lasted for two hours (;) consequently, we didn't get home until late.

8. The surgeons continued the operation (NP) even though the outlook for the patient seemed grim.

9. This is one of my favorite lines from Jack Kerouac's *On the Road* (:) "Why think about that when all the golden lands ahead of you and all kinds of unforeseen events wait lurking to surprise you and make you glad you're alive to see?"

10. The surface of the road ahead is smooth enough (;) however, the curves and the ice and the wind will make it treacherous indeed.

USING HYPHENS, DASHES, PARENTHESES, QUOTATION MARKS, AND ELLIPSES CORRECTLY

Hyphens, dashes, parentheses, quotation marks, and ellipses are used less frequently than the punctuation marks covered above.

Hyphens

The hyphen, which is a small horizontal mark, has three main uses, as shown in the following table.

USE	EXAMPLES	TIP
In some compound nouns	mother-in-law six-pack	The rules about when to use hyphens with compounds are inconsistent, so check a dictionary if in doubt.
In fractions and numbers that consist of two words	two-thirds twenty-seven	Numbers higher than one hundred are usually written with numerals: 101, 237, and so on.
In ranges of numbers or years	pp. 25-32 1920-2011	Do not use a hyphen to replace *to* in a construction with *from*: "The civil unrest took place *from* 2010 *to* 2014."

Dashes and Parentheses

A dash is a horizontal mark that is longer than a hyphen. Both dashes and parentheses set off material that interrupts a sentence but adds to its meaning. The principal difference between dashes and parentheses is how they focus the reader's attention. Dashes highlight an interruption; parentheses deemphasize it.

PUNCTUATION TYPE	FUNCTION	EXAMPLES
Dash	To set off emphasized information	The tiger —furious and roaring— leaped toward the tourists. The song —wistful and tender— touched his soul.
Parentheses	To set off understated information	The bus (which had seen better days) rolled along. Sammy (who had never liked school) joined the army.

Note that with word-processing software, you create a dash by typing two hyphens (--) without any spaces between them or on either side of them. Some word-processing software will automatically change the two hyphens into a dash (—). Both styles (two hyphens and a long dash) are acceptable, so there is no need to worry about this detail.

Quotation Marks

Double and single quotation marks serve different purposes.

TYPE	FUNCTION	EXAMPLES
Double quotes	To indicate a word-for-word quotation	According to Confucius, "Everything has beauty, but not everyone sees it."
Double quotes	To indicate dialogue in a narrative	They asked, "So what are you?" The Buddha simply replied, "I am awake."
Double quotes	To set off special terms	The term "scientific method" refers to a specific procedure used for investigation in the natural sciences.
Single quotes	To indicate a quote *within* a quote	The patient complained, "I told the doctor I was ill, but he muttered, 'It's probably all in your head.' Then he just walked away."

When you write, place periods and commas *inside* quotation marks, even inside single quotes.

Ellipses

In formal and scholarly writing, an ellipsis consists of three spaced periods that indicate the omission of words from quoted material. As a student writing academic papers, you may want to shorten a long quotation by using ellipses to show where you have omitted words. When the omission is at the end of a quoted sentence, the ellipsis is preceded by a period.

In informal writing and in some forms of literature, an ellipsis indicates a pause. Although you may never use an ellipsis for that purpose as a writer, you should be aware of this use as a reader. Why does the author want the reader to pause at the designated place? How does the pause affect the meaning being conveyed?

The chart below provides examples of different uses of ellipses.

FUNCTION	EXAMPLES
To show that words have been omitted from quoted material	"On the voyage . . . illness was a common cause of death." "With little to no medicine available, not much could be done. . . . The captain decided to head for port."
To show a pause in thinking or to show hesitation or uncertainty	I was wondering if maybe you'd be willing to loan me ten bucks . . . I was dreaming of a time long ago . . .

PRACTICE 8 Using Hyphens, Dashes, Parentheses, Quotation Marks, and Ellipses Correctly

In the sentences below, insert the appropriate punctuation.

1. Millions of Americans who are living with chronic pain rely on opioids—available only by prescription—to improve their lives. [dashes]

2. Recently, though, the Food and Drug Administration has noticed increased abuse and misuse of opioids (that is, hydrocodone combination drugs, such as Vicodin). [parentheses]

3. Many drug-dependent people are now obtaining opioids illegally. [hyphen]

4. The FDA announced, "Due to the unique history of this issue and the tremendous amount of public interest, we are announcing the agency's intent to recommend to HHS that hydrocodone combination products should be reclassified to a different and more restrictive schedule." [quotation marks]

5. The agency consulted a wide range of interested parties—health-care providers, patients, experts, and other agencies—before making the recommendation. [dashes]

6. Changing the classification of opioids from Schedule III to Schedule II would, according to the announcement, "increase the controls on these products." [quotation marks]

7. "I hope this doesn't make it harder for me to get my prescription," said one patient. She added, her voice trailing off, "To deal with the pain . . ." [quotation marks and ellipsis]

PART 6

Thematic Anthology of Readings

THEME | Triumphing over Adversity

We all face times of adversity, moments when obstacles of different kinds threaten to ruin our happiness or keep us from realizing our dreams. For some people, adversity is a stepping-stone to success. Why are some people successful at overcoming hard times while other people are crushed by them?

The four readings that follow present ideas about the difficulties we might encounter in life and how we handle them. As you read, think about your own experiences with adversity. Are there lessons in these readings that can help you overcome your own difficulties?

AUTHOR AND CONTEXT Melissa Balmain is a journalist whose writing has appeared in a variety of publications, including *The New Yorker, The New York Times,* and *McSweeney's.* "Bouncing Back" appeared in *Success* magazine in 2012.

PREVIEWING Have pen and paper (or a computer) on hand as you read. Think about the title, and then study the author's biography and the contextual information about the reading. Next, preview the selection. From the information you have gathered, determine the topic. What predictions can you make about the reading's content? Jot down your answers.

READING CRITICALLY AND ANNOTATING As you read, annotate the main idea, the major supporting points, key words, and a few passages that would make good quotations. Either write in your book or make annotations on sticky notes.

As you find key ideas, annotate them. Do Balmain's suggestions sound reasonable? Does Balmain support her suggestions with information that convinces you to try them? While you read and question content, also notice Balmain's writing choices. How does she organize her essay? What role do illustrations play in her essay? What is effective about her writing? Use annotations to record your observations and questions.

After reading and annotating, create an information sheet on which you record and organize your annotations as well as your thoughts about the content of the reading.

Teaching Resources: See the Instructor's Manual (IM) for instructions to set up this assignment in Connect IRW. Alternatively, this reading assignment and the writing prompts that follow have been pre-loaded into the Connect IRW *Common Places* Master Course.

Bouncing Back BY MELISSA BALMAIN

Lexile: 1040L

No matter what troubles you face, at work or at home, it's worth asking yourself one question: What would Howie Truong do? 1

In 1977, as Truong fled postwar Vietnam with his wife, baby son and several other people, their motorboat was captured by pirates. The pirates forced everyone aboard their own boat; although brusque toward the adults, they doted on the baby and tried to buy him. After a few days, they shoved Truong into the sea. He nearly drowned before he was rescued by fishermen. Weeks later, in Thailand, he learned that his wife's body had washed ashore; he would spend 34 years wondering what had happened to his son. 2

How in the world did Truong survive the grief that followed his ordeal? How did he move to America, become an expert metalworker, remarry, raise four more children, and eventually find his firstborn? Truong, handsome and dark-haired at 54, smiles in his living room in West Henrietta, N.Y. "I told myself, 'Get going,'" he replies emphatically. "'Life has to go on.'" 3

If you think Truong's story has little to do with your own, think again. Resilience like his can be learned, experts say. And it can help you through just about any setback—a blow to your business or health, for instance; a death, a divorce, a disaster. 4

"Resilience is very important in today's uncertain world," says Harvard psychologist Robert Brooks, Ph.D., author of *The Power of Resilience: Achieving Balance, Confidence, and Personal Strength in Your Life.* It's a trait worth nurturing even when all is well, he believes, so you'll be better prepared for a crisis. But if hard times have already knocked you down, it's not too late to bounce back. "There are certain outlooks and skills we can develop," Brooks says, "so that regardless of what the adversity or challenge may be, we are able to deal with it." 5

And who better to coach us than Truong and others who have endured life at its worst? 6

Pulling Yourself Forward

Getting flattened by adversity is, of course, as common as adversity itself. Inertia, self-pity, junk-food binges: All are par for the course, experts say, and nothing to beat yourself up about. "I think of grief as ebbing and flowing rather than as a distinct phase that ends," says Karen Reivich, Ph.D., co-director of the Penn Resiliency Project at the University of Pennsylvania, which trains soldiers and others to manage stress. The more time passes after a major loss—of a job, a loved one, or home—the more you'll feel able to get up and at 'em, Reivich says. "The good periods get longer and the others, shorter." The trick is to take advantage of those good periods. "If there's that voice inside you that says, 'I don't want to get out of bed, but I probably could,' listen to that voice," Reivich says. "Sometimes you may need to give yourself a little pep talk—'I know I don't feel like getting up, but if I get going it's going to feel better than if I don't get going.'" 7

Listening to those who love you is important, too: the buddy who says, "Grab your coat—we're taking you out." The brother who insists you start writing a new résumé. "Rely on people that you trust, who know you and know your style, to help pull you forward a bit," Reivich says. 8

Another powerful pulling force: obligation. For many who find themselves unemployed or bereaved, a desire to "be strong" for children or a spouse can help. 9

For Truong, what yanked him free of despair—and of drinking himself to sleep—was remembering his role in his family. "In my country, the big brother is the main guy to take care of sisters and brothers," he says. After his nightmare at sea, he went to a Thai refugee camp. Then an uncle sponsored him to come to Louisiana. Within seven months of losing his wife and son, Truong was studying welding in upstate New York (home of his in-laws), determined to earn money, and bring his parents and seven siblings from Vietnam to live with him. "Sometimes I would buy beer, try to forget the past, but then that wasn't good," he says. "I said to myself, 'Go out, learn something. Keep busy.'" Burying himself in his studies—and, later, his career—distracted him from his woes for long stretches and filled him with hope.

Taking Control

Any positive step you take after a major loss, in fact, can curb anxiety and keep you moving forward. "One basic finding in resilience research is that resilient people will focus on what they have control over," Brooks says.   10

Something as simple as cooking a good meal can make you feel less helpless. So can taking a brisk walk, playing a musical instrument or writing a step-by-step plan for getting what you want. "When people feel overwhelmed, being able to break up a task in shorter- or longer-term goals is very important," says Brooks, who has known plenty of overwhelming times himself. "I've always liked to put a couple of easy things at the top of my to-do lists, so I could check them off quickly. I know it's only a mind game, but seeing a few things checked off, I could say, 'OK! At least I got this out of the way.'" Making backup plans and lists is important as well, to buoy your spirits if Plan A doesn't pan out.   11

Even at the most basic level, seizing control may help. Three years ago, financial planner Carl Richards found himself—ironically—in financial hot water after the stock market crashed and the housing bubble popped. He and his family wound up losing their $575,000 house in Las Vegas. Richards' main way of handling the stress was to ride his mountain bike—and focus on his breathing. "It was kind of empowering to realize everything else may be out of control, but I can control my breath," says Richards, who has since written *The Behavior Gap: Simple Ways to Stop Doing Dumb Things with Money,* and moved with his family to a rented home in Park City, Utah. "It gave me a sense of stability and 'I can do this the next minute and the next, and doors will keep opening for me.' It gave me the ability to say, 'I can make the tough decisions. I can face this other stuff.'"   12

Finding a Team

When dealing with your own problems, resist the urge to isolate yourself. Join a support group. Keep up your social life. Don't be shy about asking a neighbor to watch your kids while you go to an interview. "The myth of resilience is you go it alone," Reivich says. "But resilience is really a team sport rather than an individual sport. Those people who have a board of advisers, a close-knit group—those people do better."   13

No one knows this more than Jennifer Loredo, a master sergeant in the Army. In 2010, while she and her husband, Edwardo, were serving in Afghanistan, a roadside bomb left her a single mother of two. Back in the United States, Loredo began seeking other widows to talk with; some were part of a military support group, some   14 not. "It just felt really like a relief almost, like I'm not alone in this—other people are going through it and they're OK," says Loredo, who lives in Fayetteville, N.C. "It kind of confirmed that my kids and I were going to come out OK."

Counting Your Blessings

Odd as it may sound, something else that has helped Loredo—and countless others in desperate straits—is gratitude. Each night before bed, Loredo takes a few minutes to recall three pleasant moments of her day. She often jots notes on how they made her feel, what made them happen and how she might make such things happen again. One recent note was about learning that her 14-year-old daughter had aced an English test, another about hearing her 4-year-old son say, "Mommy, you're beautiful." Research suggests that this habit of reflection, taught to her by Reivich (from the Penn Resiliency Project), reduces symptoms of depression. "In the beginning it's kind of hard to come up with three good things that happened every day," Loredo says. "But after you do it for a while, you find yourself realizing there is a lot of good in your life and it definitely out-weighs the bad." Partly as a result, she now tries harder to let family and friends know she treasures them: "It could be something as little as telling my mom that I love her and I appreciate the time we spent together the last time I was home." 15

All of which fits a common and welcome pattern known as "post-traumatic growth." "We're all familiar with post-traumatic stress," Reivich says. "But in post-traumatic growth, when people emerge on the other side of something horrible, they know what their passions are. They have a new commitment to life and a greater sense of spirituality and faith. It doesn't take away the suffering they feel, but some people experience this renewed sense of going after what matters in life. Research would support that that's a critical part of healing and resilience." 16

Post-traumatic stress disorder, often shortened to PTSD, is a type of anxiety disorder that results from exposure to serious trauma, such as sexual assault, serious injury, the witnessing of traumatic events, or the threat of death. The disorder is charac-terized by severe anxiety symp-toms, including panic attacks, inability to tolerate stressful situations, and suicidality.

Lending a Hand

For Celeste Peterson, what matters in life is what mattered to her daughter. Erin Peterson was among 32 students and faculty shot to death in 2007 by a deranged student at Virginia Tech. More than anything, Erin—who died at 18—had wanted to work for a nonprofit that improves people's lives. So now that's what Peterson does. With donations that poured in after Erin's death, she co-runs a program for at-risk boys who attend Erin's high school in Fairfax County, Va. She takes the boys on outings, brings in speakers to inspire them, and gives them scholarships for books if they're accepted to college. "It keeps my mind going," she says. "I don't just sit there and act pitiful. I don't have the time to just feel sorry for myself." 17

Helping others is a great way to boost your resilience, studies show. Like religion and spirituality, it can give you a sense of community. Like paid work, it can bolster your belief that you have a positive effect on the world. "This belief reinforces a sense of purpose to one's existence," Brooks has written, "thereby impacting positively on emotional and physical health." 18

Peterson says amen to that: "Working with the boys does give me a sense of pur-pose. It's like I can hear Erin in my head, saying, 'Come on, Mom, we've got a job to do.'" 19

Accepting and Adapting

Another key to climbing beyond self-pity, experts say, is a willingness to reinvent yourself. Anna Hovind of Atlanta learned the truth of this six years ago, after losing 20 her longtime position as a newsroom manager at CNN. Although her layoff came soon after her 25-year marriage dissolved, she found the divorce from her job even harder. And it wasn't just because she missed the office camaraderie and excellent health benefits. "Before I got downsized, all I had to do was say, 'I work at CNN,' and people were like, 'Wow'—and all of a sudden I didn't have that," she says. "I was just like an ordinary Joe on the street and that was a little bit of a challenge." After she found a new job in broadcast public relations, she continued struggling with her relative obscurity. But as she mastered the duties of an unfamiliar field, Hovind found a fresh identity to take pride in: that of the plucky middle-aged professional who could compete with people in their 20s. "I kind of shook the dust of CNN off my sandals," she says. "I said, 'I'm done grieving for what I lost, and this is my new reality.'"

Tricia Downing can relate. In 2000, she was a cyclist who rode in races throughout the country. Then a bike accident left her paralyzed from the chest down. Downing threw herself into rehab and—on top of learning how to care for herself—mastered the challenge of using a handcycle and a racing chair. As a para-athlete, she finished 68 marathons and triathalons and many other races between 2001 and 2011. Now she's training to make the U.S. Paralympic rowing team. "If I had thought, 'Gosh, I can never come back from this injury,' I probably wouldn't have," says Downing, who lives in Denver and has become a motivational speaker. "In the beginning I did have those thoughts, but I let them dissipate. I realized, 'I can't do things the same way I used to do them—I just have to find different ways.' Telling yourself, 'I can do this' is really important to being resilient." Another mantra that keeps her going on the racecourse and off: "Ride your own race." Instead of comparing herself to others, Downing takes pride in beating personal records. "What it comes down to is focusing on what you do have and not what you don't have," she says. And by her own estimation, she has a lot: A nice house. Lucrative work. A loving husband she met seven years ago. And, of course, the biceps of an Amazon. "I feel accomplished," Downing says. "I feel like I stared down a demon and I won." 21

Forgiving, but Not Necessarily Forgetting

It's easy after a major setback to be angry—at the spouse who dumped you, the driver who hit you, the boss who derailed your career. Yet one of the most important parts of resilience, experts say, is deciding to forgive. This shouldn't be confused with forgetting, minimizing or denying hurtful actions, Brooks says. "Rather," he explains, "forgiveness ensures that our lives are not dominated by intense anger and thoughts of revenge that lessen our own happiness." 22

And here, again, we look to Howie Truong. 23

As the decades passed, he couldn't shake the feeling that his stolen child, Khai, was still alive. The pirates had been too fond of the boy to have killed him, he believed. Last summer, after years of fruitless attempts to find him long-distance, Truong got his family's blessing to take an extended trip to Thailand. Incredibly, thanks in large part to his dogged questioning of strangers and to help from Thai officials and media, he found Khai in a month. He turned out to be a father of two known as Samart Khumkhaw, who worked on a rubber plantation near the home of the couple who—apparently ignorant of his kidnapping—had adopted him when he was a baby. 24

Now Khumkhaw, on his first visit to the United States, sits with Truong in his living room. Father and son have matching eyes, matching mustaches, and, above all, matching infectious grins. Truong, the only one adept at English, does most of the talking. 25

One thing he realized during his trip to Thailand, he says, is he could easily track   26
down the pirates and press charges against them. But he won't. "I figure if I forgive
them now," he says, "later somebody will forgive me for something." He glances at
his recovered son, eyes widening as if he still can't believe he is right beside him. "He
was lost for 34 years. It's time for me to make up for that."

Five More Secrets of Resilient People

1. Keep a journal and read through it now and then. You'll spot trends you may   27
   want to address ("I'm always sad around 6 p.m."), and feel proud when you read
   of obstacles you've since overcome.
2. Think about what your greatest strengths of character are—from kindness to persistence to a knack for humor. Then brainstorm approaches to your problems that
   revolve around those strengths.
3. Don't shield your partner or spouse from hard decisions you face. If you make
   them together, it will be easier for you both to live with the consequences.
4. As much as possible, even when times are hard, lift your spirits by keeping up
   with favorite hobbies or pastimes.
5. Stop asking, "Why me?" and start asking, "Why not me? How am I going to
   handle this? How do I help other people handle it?"

─────────────────────○○○─────────────────────

Using Your Annotations

Use your annotations and key words to write a one-page summary of the reading. In your summary, identify the writer's thesis statement, the major supporting points, the support for the major
supporting points, and any other information needed to complete the summary.

Thinking about the Text

1. What is Balmain's purpose for this article?
2. For what audience is this piece composed?
3. What does the writer mean by "pulling yourself forward"?
4. The writer shares the stories of several people who have overcome adversity. What character
   traits or behaviors do these people have in common?
5. Why do you think Howie Truong decided to forgive the pirates who killed his wife and stole
   his child?

The Writer's Techniques

1. Look at your annotations. Which of the following types of supporting details does Balmain
   use—comparison and contrast, cause and effect, definition, process analysis, classification, or
   illustration?
2. What method does Balmain use to introduce and conclude her essay? How might you use
   Balmain's introduction and conclusion methods in your own writing?
3. The writer uses illustrations extensively. Identify at least two illustrations. What effect does
   the use of illustrations have on you as a reader? What do you think the essay would be like
   without the illustrations? Explain.

Brief-Response Assignments

1. Write a paragraph defining *resiliency* in your own words. To support your definition, describe
   the characteristics of resilient people.
2. What role does forgiveness have in resiliency? Explain your answer, and provide an example.
3. Write a paragraph in which you explain this assertion: *Overcoming adversity requires intentional
   actions and intentional thoughts.*
4. What is the role of work in overcoming adversity? In other words, how does working or staying busy contribute to overcoming adversity?

Essay Assignments

1. Imagine you are writing an essay to be published in *Success*, the magazine that published Balmain's essay. Write a detailed account of someone who has overcome adversity. The person can be a family member, a friend, or a public figure from the past or present. What situation did the person face? What approach helped the person successfully overcome the situation's challenges? Why do you think this approach was successful? Your essay should present the person, the problem, the person's method for handling the problem, and the outcome.

2. Write an essay in which you classify responses to a particular adverse situation, such as losing a loved one or being in a car accident. First, discuss the event. Next, discuss the types of reactions people have to the event. Finally, explain the consequences of each type of reaction. For example, consider the ways people react to failing a class. Some students overcome the situation and emerge stronger and more determined to pass classes in the future; other students give up and drop out or get angry and blame others for their failure.

3. When we face adversity, our lives feel out of control. Adversity reminds us that we truly cannot control everything that happens to us or to those we love. Dealing with adversity requires us to confront this lack of control. One way to be successful is to control that which we can control. Using the ideas in this article and other ideas you develop through prewriting, write an essay about how people triumph over adversity by taking steps to regain control of their lives. Explain the methods they use to regain such control. Explain how these steps are effective at helping people overcome their difficulties. You might find it helpful to use process analysis as a text pattern for this assignment. ↻

Connect IRW Writing Assignments: You may assign any of these essay prompts in Connect IRW; the toolset supports options such as assigning peer review or building your own rubric to gather reporting around student writing outcomes.

AUTHOR AND CONTEXT Carlos C. Huerta is a major and a chaplain (rabbi) in the US Army 1st Battalion, 320th Field Artillery, 101st Airborne Division (Screaming Eagles). "Leaving the Battlefield" appeared as a news article on the US Army's Web page in April 2012.

PREVIEWING Have pen and paper (or a computer) on hand as you read. Think about the title, and then study the author's biography and the contextual information about the reading. Next, preview the selection. From the information you have gathered, determine the topic. What predictions can you make about the reading's content? Jot down your answers.

READING CRITICALLY AND ANNOTATING As you read, annotate the main idea, the major supporting points, key words, and a few passages that would make good quotations. Either write in your book or make annotations on sticky notes.

As you find key ideas, annotate them. When you read the essay, note the writer's occupation and think about how it may have affected him. Note any questions that come to mind.

After reading and annotating, create an information sheet on which you record and organize your annotations as well as your thoughts about the content of the reading.

Teaching Resources: See the Instructor's Manual (IM) for instructions to set up this assignment in Connect IRW. Alternatively, this reading assignment and the writing prompts that follow have been pre-loaded into the Connect IRW *Common Places* Master Course.

Leaving the Battlefield: Soldier Shares Story of PTSD BY CHAPLAIN (MAJ.) CARLOS C. HUERTA

Lexile: 970L

My name is Huerta. I am an American Soldier and I have PTSD [post-traumatic stress disorder]. I refused to admit it to myself even when the Army doctors told me I had it in 2004. I refused to talk to anyone about it even when Army health professionals told me I needed to in 2005. I was afraid how Army leadership would react if I had that on my record. I was a Soldier, I was tough, I just needed to rub the patch and drive on. 1

And drive on I did until one day in September 2010, five years after I last left the battlefield. I don't know what the trigger was. Maybe it was the young Soldier, a mother of two who was just redeployed, who I watched cut down after she hanged 2 herself weeks after returning from battle earlier. Maybe it was the faces of the children I saw behind all the doors I knocked on to tell them their father or mother was not coming home. Maybe it was because it was the same time of year when my uniform was covered with the blood and brains of a 6-year-old Iraqi child who was caught in an IED during Ramadan.

I don't know what the trigger was, but it hit me hard. I went home one evening 3 and all of a sudden, I felt a tightness in my chest, it was hard to breathe, and I felt closed in and panicky. I bolted out of bed thinking I was dying. I paced the room in the dark for hours before I exhausted myself. I almost went to the ER that night, but the Soldier in me said to stick it out.

The morning came and it hit again, a panic, a fear of being closed off, claustro- 4 phobia, and pains in the chest. I thought maybe I was having a heart attack and, if I was, I needed to see a doctor.

A heart attack was honorable, [but] PTSD was not. I went to sick call and they 5 ordered a battery of tests to exclude any heart condition. When my heart was cleared, the doctors recommended I see someone in CMHS [Community Mental Health Services]. I thought to myself, "I wasn't crazy, why do I need to see them? If I see them, I know the 'big' Army will find out and tag me as 'broken.'"

I went home that night and the same thing happened. I knew I could not live 6 like this so I talked, off the record, to someone in mental health. They looked at my records and after talking with me, said I had PTSD. They said there was probably some trigger that set it off. I did not want to believe it, but I knew that I needed something or I would face the same thing again that evening. I then "officially" saw them and was prescribed some psychotropic medication to help with the anxiety in order to help me function.

I thought when I got off the battlefield that I could heal and place the war behind 7 me. As a chaplain, I soon realized that I could not. Within weeks of getting back in 2004, I was knocking on doors telling families a husband, wife, a father or mother, a daughter or son was not coming home. In 2008, I knocked on a door to tell a family that their husband, a father of three, was lost to them. To this day I can close my eyes and see the face of a teenage daughter who looked at me with hatred. She looked deep into my soul and said that she would never forget what I did to her and her family that day and turned away, too destroyed to even cry.

Even though I was home, I never left the battlefield. I brought the war home and 8 it took a toll on me, my family, wife and children. I got to be good friends with Jim and Jack. You may know them as Mr. Beam and Mr. Daniels.

I did not want to get close to my new babies for fear I may get deployed again. 9 A big piece of me wanted to go back to battle because the battlefield made sense; coming home to emails, memorandums and unit "politics" did not. I also knew that if I went back, a bigger piece of me would not want to come back home again.

The home I came back to was not the one I left. My family was not the same, I 10 was not the same. I felt that something important was stolen from me and there was nobody I could talk to about it, nobody except the guys I was over there with. I would look for combat patches, look for buddies to talk to, look for the Soldiers who went through what I went through and felt the same way I did. There were many of us. Our experiences were very different but we had one thing in common. We felt different, but we were not crazy and we did not have some defective genetic failing.

It just was hard for us to come to terms with all the death, destruction and pain 11
we had participated in and witnessed. We were all reluctant about "officially" talking
to someone. Even if we needed help, we would not go to it as we thought leadership
would use that against us for assignments and promotions.

We felt we were alone. We were trapped in our own memories, sometimes trying 12
to ignore them and often not being able to. We watched as our suicide numbers went
up and are still going up.

The Army leadership has tried and is trying to change this trend and is having 13
some success. I cannot say that a piece of me at one time did not wonder if the world,
my family, would have been better off without me.

For Soldiers with PTSD, we often felt the very act of seeking help from a mental 14
health professional could be information that could be used against us, to target us,
and make us feel we were burdens to the system. I felt that way and was afraid to get
the help I needed. I now fear that the problem may be made worse with the so-called
discovery of a PTSD gene. If this data is used wrong or misinterpreted, those of us
with PTSD now could be considered genetically dysfunctional.

Instead of being a burden to the Army, I ended up being a burden to the most 15
important people in my life, my wife and children. Fearing being minimized as a
Soldier, I, like so many others, went underground. It seemed the very thing that leadership was using to try to help me actually worked against me.

When I close my eyes at night, sometimes I still see myself picking up the body 16
parts of my Soldiers. I still see myself holding my Soldiers as they die in my arms on the
battlefield. I still see the blood of Iraqi children spattered all over my uniform as they
take their last breaths due to no fault of their own. In the quiet moments of the day,
when I am with my family, I see the faces of all the wives, children, husbands, mothers
and fathers whose lives I destroyed with the notifications I made.

My mind tells me that I did not cause their pain and grief, but my heart tells me 17
otherwise. I know I can't change their pain, but I can change mine and the pain I
inflicted on my family due to war. Only a Soldier understands that physically being
home doesn't mean coming home.

Coming home from battle seemed to be one of the easiest things to do. It seemed 18
that you just get on a plane. After spending hours, weeks and months getting help
and talking to someone about my wounds, I am only beginning to understand how
to come home.

I am, in our Army culture, what some would identify as a broken or deadwood 19
Soldier. I have no bullet holes to show my wounds. I will not get any medal that will recognize them. If I did, I would be afraid and ashamed to wear it in our present culture. As
with so many of us, my wounds are the invisible kind, the type we bear in our souls. I am
not ashamed of them. For me and others like me, they are just as real as one that bleeds.

I am getting help because I'm tired of not being home. I am tired of being on the 20
battlefield I brought back with me. It is time for me to come home. It is time for all
of us to come home. My name is Huerta and I am a wounded American Soldier, and I
am not ashamed of my wounds and I have no genetic failing. I am proud of my service
and I am going home. Let's go home together.

Using Your Annotations

Use your annotations and key words to write a one-page summary of the reading. In your summary, identify the writer's thesis statement, the major supporting points, the support for the major supporting points, and any other information needed to complete the summary.

Thinking about the Text

1. What obstacles is Huerta facing as he seeks to recover from PTSD?
2. How did the writer's particular job in the army contribute to his stress?
3. What message does he hope to send to other veterans and soldiers?
4. Based on Huerta's article, what are some of the steps one should take to overcome PTSD?
5. What is the writer's main idea? What major details does he use to support his main idea?

The Writer's Techniques

1. How does Huerta use transitions in his essay to move from one point to the next? Explain, and provide some examples.
2. Which supporting details most effectively help you understand the pain Huerta is facing?
3. Reread the conclusion of Huerta's essay. Is the positive tone convincing? Explain your answer.

Brief-Response Assignments

1. What is PTSD? What situations other than combat might cause PTSD? Explain.
2. Explain this statement: *Because he was a soldier, Huerta had a more difficult time dealing with PTSD than he would have had dealing with a physical injury.*
3. What role does shame play in Huerta's struggle to overcome his wartime experiences? Explain in a paragraph.

Essay Assignments

1. Thousands of soldiers have returned from the wars in Afghanistan and Iraq with PTSD as well as other injuries, both physical and mental. Based on Huerta's essay, what are some solutions that can help soldiers come home? How can civilians help make the transition easier for these soldiers? Write an essay in which you explain the methods soldiers can use as well as the ways civilians can help.
2. Because soldiers are trained to be tough, they sometimes use ineffective coping mechanisms to deal with adversity. How does a soldier's training actually become a barrier to dealing with PTSD or other physical or mental problems? Write an essay in which you explain how the qualities of a strong warrior might lead soldiers to select ineffective coping mechanisms to deal with stress.
3. Interview a person who has successfully coped with a major change, such as coming back from war, surviving a life-threatening situation, or learning to live with the loss of a loved one or a significant disability. What coping mechanisms helped the person adjust? What lessons can be learned from this person's story? Write an essay in which you present the person's story and the lessons or insights the story provides. ↻

Connect IRW Writing Assignments: You may assign any of these essay prompts in Connect IRW; the toolset supports options such as assigning peer review or building your own rubric to gather reporting around student writing outcomes.

AUTHOR AND CONTEXT Benjamin B. Lahey is the Irving B. Harris Professor of Epidemiology, Psychiatry, and Behavioral Neuroscience at the University of Chicago. He is interested in the genetics, measurement, taxonomy, and behavioral neuroscience of child and adolescent psychopathology. The selection "Coping with Stress" is from Lahey's textbook *Psychology: An Introduction.*

PREVIEWING Have pen and paper (or a computer) on hand as you read. Think about the title, and then study the author's biography and the contextual information about the reading. Next, preview the selection. From the information you have gathered, determine the topic. What predictions can you make about the reading's content? Jot down your answers.

READING CRITICALLY AND ANNOTATING As you read, annotate the main idea, the major supporting points, key words, and a few passages that would make good quotations. Either write in your book or make annotations on sticky notes.

As you find key ideas, annotate them. Which methods have you used to cope with stress? Which methods are new to you? What kinds of events produce stress? Note any insights or questions you have as you read.

After reading and annotating, create an information sheet on which you record and organize your annotations as well as your thoughts about the content of the reading.

Teaching Resources: See the Instructor's Manual (IM) for instructions to set up this assignment in Connect IRW. Alternatively, this reading assignment and the writing prompts that follow have been pre-loaded into the Connect IRW *Common Places* Master Course.

Lexile: 1340L

Coping with Stress BY BENJAMIN B. LAHEY

We cannot always avoid stress in our lives. What are the best ways of coping with stress when we experience it? 1

Effective Coping

Effective methods of coping either remove the source of stress or control our reactions to it: 2

1. **Removing or reducing stress.** One effective way of dealing with stress is to remove or to reduce the source of stress from our lives. If an employee holds a job that is stressful, discussions could be held with the employer that might lead to a reduction in the pressures of the job, or the employee could resign. If the stress stems from an unhappy marriage, either marriage counseling could be sought or the marriage could be ended. In a variety of ways, effective coping with stress can take the form of reducing it. For example, Taylor and her colleagues randomly assigned college students to two groups at the beginning of the term. One group was asked to imagine themselves beaming with success when they received high marks in the class. The second group was asked to think of practical steps they could take to avoid failure and get a good grade (getting the book, reading assignments, studying in advance, and so on). They actually studied more and received higher grades, and as a result of reducing the stressful threat of failure, felt less anxious. 3

2. **Cognitive coping.** Our cognitions are intimately linked to our reactions to stressful events and a number of effective methods of coping involve cognitive strategies. Three effective cognitive coping strategies involve changing how we think about the stressful event, focusing attention away from stressful events that cannot be changed, and religious coping: 4

- Reappraisal can be an effective method of coping. This refers to changing how we think about—or interpret—the stressful events that push and shove our lives. For example, I know a musician who had a successful first record, but his second album was a flop—the critics panned it and the public didn't buy it. At first, he saw this as a sign that the first record was a fluke and that he had no real talent. As a result, the failure of the second album was a huge stress. However, a veteran musician convinced him that having an unsuccessful second album is a common "sophomore slump" among musicians who go on to be very successful. This conversation changed his interpretation of his unsuccessful album and allowed him to view it as a challenge to do better next time. Finding an interpretation that is realistic and constructive minimizes the stressfulness of negative events. 5

- In some cases, stressful events cannot be changed and reappraising their meaning is of limited help. For example, losing a spouse to death must be coped with in some other way. Focusing attention away from the death and moving on with life is associated with less depression and better physical health.

- Many individuals cope effectively by interpreting events in terms of their religious beliefs. For example, a study of Latinos with arthritis found that individuals who viewed their painful condition as being *en las manos de Dios* (in God's hands) experienced greater psychological well-being than did individuals who engaged in less religious coping.

3. Managing stress reactions. When the source of stress cannot realistically be removed or changed, another effective option is to manage our psychological and physiological reactions to the stress. For example, an individual may decide to start a new business, knowing full well that the first year or two will be hectic. She would be unwilling, then, to remove the source of the stress (the new business) but could learn to control her reactions to the stress. One strategy might be to schedule as much time as possible for relaxing activities, such as aerobic exercise, hobbies, or time with friends. Another would be to seek special training from a psychologist in controlling the body reactions to stress by learning to deeply relax the large body muscles. Happily, psychological counseling that encourages all three methods of effective coping has even been successful in changing the Type A behavior pattern. Indeed, treated patients showed a 50% reduction in heart attacks and deaths compared with Type A individuals who did not receive treatment.   6

Ineffective Coping

Unfortunately, many of our efforts to cope with stress are ineffective. They may provide temporary relief from the discomfort produced by stress but do little to provide a long-term solution and may even make matters worse. Three common, but ineffective, coping strategies are as follows: 7

1. Withdrawal. Sometimes we deal with stress by withdrawing from it. Many students encounter courses in college that are far more difficult than anything they had experienced in high school. Attempting to study difficult material can be highly stressful, and that stress can lead to a withdrawal from studying—by playing electronic games, talking on the telephone, partying, and the like. Similarly, a husband may ineffectively cope with the stress of an unhappy marriage by withdrawing to the refuge of a bar every day after work.   8

Note that it is not what you do, but how and why you do it, that makes a coping strategy effective or ineffective. Spending your time playing electronic video games actually may be an effective coping strategy if you only do it for reasonable periods of time to relax. It becomes withdrawal if you use it excessively as a way to avoid the necessity for more effective coping (studying).   9

In this context, it is also important to recognize that there is a big difference between actually removing a source of stress and withdrawing from it. If you find that you have signed up for an extremely difficult course for which you are not prepared, dropping that class until you are ready to take it would be an effective way to remove the stress. However, simply not studying for the tests in that course because you have withdrawn to the refuge of long philosophical discussions with friends would obviously be an ineffective solution.   10

2. Aggression. A common reaction to frustration and other stressful situations is aggression. The woman who has tried unsuccessfully to create romantic interest in a man   11 may suddenly become hostile toward him. The man who cannot get a screw to fit into a curtain rod may throw a temper tantrum and hurl the rod to the floor in disgust.

3. Self-medication. It appears that many individuals cope ineffectively with stress   12
by using tobacco, alcohol, and other drugs to soothe their emotional reactions to stress. For example, a study in which participants' emotions were measured daily showed that higher levels of anxiety during the day increased the likelihood of drinking alcohol later that day. Although alcohol temporarily reduces anxiety for some people, it does nothing to remove the source of stress and often creates additional problems in relationships, studying, job performance, and health that make things worse in the long run. Self-medication with alcohol or street drugs is a very poor method of coping indeed. It does seem clear, however, that some individuals benefit from professionally prescribed medications that reduce anxiety and depression far more effectively and safely than from alcohol and street drugs. Perhaps because of the stigma associated with mental health "problems," far too many people self-medicate instead of seeking medication from a competent physician in conjunction with assistance from a psychologist in developing effective coping strategies.

Defense Mechanisms

According to Freud, one of the key functions of the ego is to "defend" the person   13
from a buildup of uncomfortable tension. Freud believed that the ego possesses a small arsenal of defense mechanisms that are unconsciously used to cope with tension. There is evidence that we use cognitive coping strategies that are very similar to the defense mechanisms described by Freud over 100 years ago. When they are not overused, such defense mechanisms can effectively reduce stress, but they create problems when they are overused. The major defense mechanisms identified by Freud:

Displacement: When it's unsafe or inappropriate to express aggressive or sexual   14
feelings toward the person who is creating stress (such as a boss who pressures you), that feeling can be directed toward someone safe (such as yelling at your friend when you are really angry with your boss).

Sublimation: Stressful conflicts over dangerous feelings or motives are reduced by converting the impulses into socially approved activities, such as schoolwork, literature, and sports.

Projection: One's own dangerous or unacceptable desires or emotions are seen not as one's own but as the desires or feelings of others. A person who has stressful conflicts about sex might perceive himself as having little sexual desire but might view other people as being "obsessed" with sex.

Reaction formation: Conflicts over dangerous motives or feelings are avoided by unconsciously transforming them into the opposite desire. A married man with strong desires for extramarital sex might start a campaign to rid his city of massage parlors and prostitutes. A woman who wishes her hateful mother would die might devote herself to finding ways to protect her mother's health.

Regression: Stress may be reduced by returning to an earlier pattern of behavior, such as a business executive who has a stomping, screaming temper tantrum when her company suffers a major setback.

Rationalization: Stress is reduced by "explaining away" the source of stress in ways that sound logical. A man who is rejected by his lover may decide that he is glad because she had so many faults or because he really did not want to give up the single life.

Repression: Potentially stressful, unacceptable desires are kept out of consciousness without the person being consciously aware that the repression is occurring.

Denial: The conscious denial of upsetting feelings and ideas. For example, in an argument, an obviously angry person may shout: "I am not angry at you!" Similarly, a cigar smoker who was shown widely endorsed research on the dangers of all forms of tobacco use would be using denial if he or she flatly rejected the validity of the evidence.

Intellectualization: The emotional nature of stressful events is lessened at times by reducing it to cold, intellectual logic. For example, the person who learns that he has lost a large sum of money in an overly risky investment may think about it in a detached way as a temporary debit in a successful lifelong program of investment, rather than as a painful financial mistake that should be avoided in the future through more careful planning.

When overdone, defense mechanisms can inhibit long-term solutions to stress if   15 they distort reality. For example, suppose that a student copes reasonably well with the stress of failing a course in college by deciding that her instructor graded her test papers unfairly because she asks too many questions in class. If her instructor is actually fair and competent, she would be distorting reality by using the defense mechanism of rationalization. A simple change in study habits or test-taking strategies might make a big difference in her grades, but she will never see the need for change if she distorts reality through rationalization. The other defense mechanisms can be harmful in similar, reality-distorting ways.

Using Your Annotations

Use your annotations and key words to write a one-page summary of the reading. In your summary, identify the writer's thesis statement, the major supporting points, the support for the major supporting points, and any other information needed to complete the summary.

Thinking about the Text

1. What is Lahey's main idea? What major supporting points does the writer use to support his main idea?
2. Why is withdrawal an ineffective way of dealing with stress? Explain.
3. Choose three of the defense mechanisms the writer discusses. Provide an example of a time when you used each one.
4. Lahey says, "Note that it is not what you do, but how and why you do it, that makes a coping strategy effective or ineffective." What does he mean by this? Make up an example to add to your explanation, and explain your example.
5. What is self-medication? What does the writer say about this method of reducing stress?

The Writer's Techniques

1. In what ways does Lahey use examples? Cite some of the examples he uses.
2. How does the writer organize his essay? What method does he use to present the content early in the essay, and how does he organize the remaining information?
3. Does this reading fit a specific text pattern, such as cause and effect, classification, or process analysis? Explain your answer.

Brief-Response Assignments

1. Imagine that a student fails an exam. Discuss an ineffective coping mechanism the student might use to deal with the stress of failure. What might be the negative results of using this coping mechanism?
2. Give an example of how displacement is used to deal with stress. What other methods of coping might be more beneficial when dealing with stressful situations?
3. Discuss a time in your life when you used an unhealthy method for dealing with stress. What method would have been a better choice?

Essay Assignments

1. Imagine that a tornado destroys a person's home, leaving him with only a box of personal belongings. Everything else is gone. Write an essay in which you present three or more effective coping mechanisms this person could use to deal with the stress of his situation.
2. Write a self-analysis. What is the greatest source of stress in your life right now? Explain. Now, imagine that you can see yourself from a friend's perspective. What methods would she say you have used to deal with your stress? Would she think your methods have been effective? Why or why not? Based on your analysis, what new methods should you use to handle the particular stress you are dealing with? Why might these new methods be more effective?
3. In stressful situations, we tend to think about our own pain and suffering. However, those around us often suffer also. How are people affected by the stress of a close friend or family member? What are some methods for reducing the effects of your stress on others? What advice would you offer to a person who lives with someone who is constantly stressed out? ↻

Connect IRW Writing Assignments: You may assign any of these essay prompts in Connect IRW; the toolset supports options such as assigning peer review or building your own rubric to gather reporting around student writing outcomes.

AUTHOR AND CONTEXT Andria Ramon is a professor of political science at McLennan Community College, where she has also served as a sponsor of the Hispanic Student Association. She is the recipient of an Excellence Award from the National Institute for Staff and Organizational Development (NISOD).

PREVIEWING Have pen and paper (or a computer) on hand as you read. Think about the title, and then study the author's biography and the contextual information about the reading. Next, preview the selection. From the information you have gathered, determine the topic. What predictions can you make about the reading's content? Jot down your answers.

READING CRITICALLY AND ANNOTATING As you read, annotate the main idea, the major supporting points, key words, and a few passages that would make good quotations. Either write in your book or make annotations on sticky notes.

As you find key ideas, annotate them. Why do some people find Justice Sotomayor remarkable? In what way is Sotomayor like many other Americans? Note any insights or questions that come to mind as you read.

After reading and annotating, create an information sheet on which you record and organize your annotations as well as your thoughts about the content of the reading.

Teaching Resources: See the Instructor's Manual (IM) for instructions to set up this assignment in Connect IRW. Alternatively, this reading assignment and the writing prompts that follow have been pre-loaded into the Connect IRW *Common Places* Master Course.

"To Do for Others": The Dream of Justice Sonia Sotomayor BY ANDRIA RAMON

Lexile: 1210L

"After completing this exhaustive process, I have decided to nominate an inspiring   1 woman who I believe will make a great justice: Judge Sonia Sotomayor of the great state of New York" (White House, 2009). With these words, President Barack Obama, himself a trailblazer, nominated the first Hispanic, and only the third woman, to the U.S. Supreme Court. President Obama called Sotomayor an example of the American dream who had "sterling credentials." Justice Sotomayor's compelling background, sheer dedication, resolute commitment to the law, and selfless love led to her position on one of the greatest judicial bodies in the world.

Sonia Maria Sotomayor was born in 1954 in New York City. Her Puerto Rican father, Juan Sotomayor, was a factory worker whose work ethic and love for his children—in spite of his alcoholism—influenced Sonia throughout her life. Sonia's mother, Celina Sotomayor, also born in Puerto Rico, was orphaned at the age of 9. She had come to New York through the U.S. military's Women's Army Corps at age 17. When Sonia was a child, Celina was a somewhat distant mother, no doubt in part because of her own difficult background. Celina had grown up in dire poverty and had not experienced the benefits of a warm and supportive family.

2

Juan and Celina married and struggled through poverty, Juan's alcoholism, and the demands of a large extended family. These situations created the self-sufficient person that Sonia became. As a young child, she acquired the nickname Aji, or "hot pepper" in English, for her curious and boisterous behavior. Aji was never shy and had an adventurous personality. Sometimes that led to mischief, as when she put a bucket on her head to listen to her voice, and her head got stuck (Sotomayor, 2013, p. 5).

3

A dramatic display of self-sufficiency came at a young age, when Sonia was diagnosed with type 1 diabetes. Daily insulin shots are required for type 1 diabetics. Although by this point Sonia's mother was working as a nurse in a local hospital, Celina could not bear giving her daughter the insulin shots she needed to stay alive. She simply could not endure hurting her daughter in that way. So, at the age of 6, little Aji began giving herself her own insulin shots.

4

Sotomayor later admitted that the primary reason for her perseverance was actually fear. She feared that she would not be able to sleep over at her grandmother's house unless she learned to administer her own insulin injections. Coping with diabetes helped her develop the discipline and self-awareness that she later credited in part with enabling her to achieve her life goals.

5

Juan Sotomayor eventually succumbed to his alcoholism; he died when Sonia was only 9 years old. His death strained the family but strengthened the relationship between Sonia and her grandmother, her *abuelita* (literally, "little grandmother," a term of endearment). Sonia's grandmother had always provided a safe haven from the frequent arguments at her parents' house. Even when Sonia left her Bronx neighborhood to attend Princeton University, her grandmother sent her one dollar every week until the day she died (Sotomayor, 2013, p. 137). The relationship between the two of them had a profound effect on Justice Sotomayor. The nurture she received from her grandmother provided the sense of protection Sonia needed to defend herself against the cruelty of her neighborhood and the dysfunction of her family.

6

Sonia spoke primarily Spanish at home, loved the traditions of her Puerto Rican heritage, and visited Puerto Rico when her family could afford to make the trip. However, she experienced prejudice at the hands of those who did not understand her culture or who felt threatened by the advancements of Hispanic women. Her mother's answer to these difficulties and the impoverished world in which they lived was education. Sonia had what, as far as she knew, was the only set of encyclopedias in her neighborhood. Her mother purchased books with every little bit of extra money they acquired. Sonia read them insatiably, as well as any other books she could obtain. Reading transformed her world from the Bronx projects into a fantasy land created by words. Unfortunately, Sotomayor's poor neighborhood did not afford her the opportunity to read many classical works, nor did the poor private Catholic school that she attended. Only while attending Princeton did she realize that her exposure to the great literary works was deficient. In keeping with her self-reliant character,

7

Justice Sotomayor found the time despite her academic requirements to read the classics while in college. She also challenged herself to learn and use ten new vocabulary words every day during summer vacations (Sotomayor, 2013, p. 135).

After graduating first in her eighth-grade class, Sonia attended Cardinal Spellman 8 High School in the northeast Bronx. There, she enjoyed participating on the debate team and found that doing so helped her develop the skills necessary for structuring a good argument. Her teachers became her mentors and advisers. They pushed her to think critically and persuaded her to go to college. She graduated first in her high school class in 1972. A close friend suggested that she apply to the Ivy League school that he attended, and with the encouragement of her family, she did and was accepted into Princeton.

At Princeton, Sotomayor was one of the few minority students, as well as one of 9 the few women, on the campus. (Princeton had only just become coeducational in the fall of 1969.) As the valedictorian of her high school class, she was a qualified applicant. However, she has made no secret of her belief that affirmative action played a role in her Princeton admittance. "It was a door opener that changed the course of my life" ("Sotomayor on Role," 2013). She wrote in her memoir that affirmative action students were routinely criticized for taking the place of a "deserving student":

> [T]here were vultures circling, ready to dive when we stumbled. The pressure to succeed was 10 relentless, even if self-imposed out of fear and insecurity. For we all felt that if we did fail, we would be proving the critics right, and the doors that had opened just a crack to let us in would be slammed shut again. (Sotomayor, 2013, p. 145)

Sotomayor's initial semesters at Princeton revealed to her that, compared with 11 her classmates' educations, her own suffered from several gaps. Her limited English, lack of writing skills, and dearth of exposure to critical thinking, together with the amount and level of academic work required, posed a major challenge for her. Her Princeton mentor, Peter Winn, recalled, "She was not the best student I taught in my seven years at Princeton—though she certainly was high on the list—but she was the one who took greatest advantage of the opportunities there and emerged most transformed by her experience" (Winn, 2009). Sotomayor's determination was the key to her success. Winn writes, "By graduation, Sonia could compete with anyone and succeed anywhere—including on the Supreme Court" (Winn, 2009). Sotomayor graduated from Princeton *summa cum laude* (with highest honor) in 1976.

Notwithstanding her impoverished upbringing and limited exposure to advanced 12 academic experiences, her time at Princeton and her internal drive provided her with a strong sense of belonging at Yale Law School. She married her high school sweetheart and surrounded herself with a dynamic, diverse group of fellow-student friends, which contributed to her integration into the Yale environment.

Graduating from Yale Law School (in 1979) and passing the bar exam enabled 13 Sotomayor to reach a lifelong dream. Since her childhood days watching *Perry Mason* (a dramatized courtroom television series broadcast in the 1950s and 1960s), Sotomayor had dreamed of being a lawyer. In 1979, the district attorney in Manhattan offered her a job prosecuting criminals, many of whom were not unlike people she had known in her Bronx neighborhood. Her experiences in the Bronx enabled her to recognize the decency of many of these defendants, and this realization motivated her to protect her clients from overly aggressive prosecution (Stolberg, 2009). She received praise and at times criticism for her stalwart efforts to follow the rule of law and not be "pushed around" by judges or others (Stolberg, 2009).

For Justice Sotomayor, the "idea of heroism in action was a lawyer, the judge   14
being a kind of superlawyer" (Sotomayor, 2013, p. 255). Her captivation with the
concept of justice had grown during her adolescent years as she watched the nightly
news depictions of courageous Southern judges defying mobs to improve civil rights.
Her fighting spirit, her mother's humanity as a nurse, her grandmother's nurture, and
her community and educational mentors' support combined to produce her desire
to become a judge. Her goal was attained when she was nominated to the federal bench by President George H.W. Bush in 1991. Her judicial nomination received
unanimous consent from the U.S. Senate, and Judge Sotomayor became the first
Hispanic federal judge in the state of New York (Collins, 2010). After years of sterling
performance in that role, Sotomayor was nominated by President Bill Clinton to the
U.S. Court of Appeals for the Second Circuit, where she served from 1998 to 2009.
President Obama nominated Sotomayor to serve on the U.S. Supreme Court in May
2009. Sotomayor's nomination was approved by the Senate on August 6, 2009, by a
68–31 vote, and thus she became the first Hispanic to serve on the Supreme Court
("Sonia Sotomayor," n.d.).

What insights can be gained from Justice Sotomayor's ascension to the Supreme   15
Court? Of course, there are the usual lessons that one should have high aspirations and big dreams. Having those dreams—even though the odds are that they
are unlikely ever to come true—is an essential ingredient for accomplishing remarkable feats. But as Sotomayor herself says, her success was more than just the result
of having a dream. Was it her will, determination, and dedication to succeed that
propelled her to accomplish her goal? Certainly, these attitudes were necessary. But
Justice Sotomayor explains that something deeper than all those factors motivated
her. She had "the desire to do for others." She saw this selfless love demonstrated by
her *abuelita,* her mother, her helpful doctors, and her friends. This "synergy of love
and gratitude, protection and purpose" planted and cultivated in her the desire to
serve (Sotomayor, 2013, p. 255). That synergy eventually led her to assume one of
the most prestigious and important positions in the world: associate justice of the
Supreme Court of the United States.

References

Collins, L. (2010, January 11). Sonia Sotomayor's high-profile debut. *The New Yorker.* Retrieved from
    http://www.newyorker.com/reporting/2010/01/11/100111fa_fact_collins?currentPage=all
Sonia Sotomayor. (n.d.). The Oyez Project at IIT Chicago-Kent College of Law. Retrieved from
    http://www.oyez.org/justices/sonia_sotomayor
Sotomayor, S. (2013). *My Beloved World.* New York, NY: Knopf.
Sotomayor on role affirmative action played in her life. (2013, January 11). Retrieved from http://
    www.cbsnews.com/news/sotomayor-on-role-affirmative-action-played-in-her-life
Stolberg, S. G. (2009, May 26). Sotomayor, a trailblazer and a dreamer. *The New York
    Times.* Retrieved from http://www.nytimes.com/2009/05/27/us/politics/27websotomayor.html
    ?pagewanted=all
The White House, Office of the Press Secretary. (2009, March 26). Remarks by the president in
    nominating Judge Sonia Sotomayor to the United States Supreme Court (Press Release).
    Retrieved from http://www.whitehouse.gov/the_press_office/Remarks-by-the-President-in
    -Nominating-Judge-Sonia-Sotomayor-to-the-United-States-Supreme-Court
Winn, P. (2009, July 12). Mentor at Princeton recalls Sotomayor's evolution. *The Washington
    Post.* Retrieved from http://www.washingtonpost.com/wp-dyn/content/article/2009/07/09
    /AR2009070902391.html?sid=ST2009071302618

This reading and its references
can be used to show students
the features of APA style.

Using Your Annotations

Use your annotations and key words to write a one-page summary of the reading. In your summary, identify the writer's thesis statement, the major supporting points, the support for the major supporting points, and any other information needed to complete the summary.

Thinking about the Text

1. What does Ramon hope to accomplish by writing this article?
2. What does she mean when she writes that "the primary reason for [Sotomayor's] perseverance was actually fear"?
3. Why was Sotomayor's diabetes diagnosis a turning point for her in her childhood?
4. What are some of the adversities Sotomayor had to overcome in her life?
5. Based on the text, how do you think a friend might describe Justice Sotomayor?

The Writer's Techniques

1. Why do you think the author uses quotes throughout her essay? What do these quotes add to readers' understanding of Justice Sotomayor?
2. What method of ordering information did the writer use to present Sotomayor's story?
3. Which parts of the reading did you find the most interesting? Why? What can you learn—as a writer—from analyzing the parts of the reading that you found interesting? Explain.

Brief-Response Assignments

1. The reading makes connections between events in Sotomayor's life and the effects of those events. Select one event in her life and discuss its effects, according to the reading.
2. How did the support that Sotomayor received from her grandmother translate into feelings of security and strength?
3. Write a paragraph in which you discuss what it means to persist even when facing adversity. Use an example from the reading to explore this subject.

Essay Assignments

1. Write an essay in which you identify three or four of the character traits that made Sotomayor successful in life.
2. Sotomayor had a dream and worked hard to achieve it. Most children start life with dreams, but many of them eventually give up on their dreams and accept a life different from what they had planned. What enables some people to achieve their dreams while others never do? Write an essay in which you explore this topic.
3. Sotomayor believes affirmative action is a helpful policy. What is affirmative action? Why was it implemented? What is the controversy about affirmative action? Finally, how does Sotomayor defend affirmative action? Write an essay in which you answer these questions. If you use sources for ideas or quotes, be sure to give credit to the sources. ↻

Connect IRW Writing Assignments: You may assign any of these essay prompts in Connect IRW; the toolset supports options such as assigning peer review or building your own rubric to gather reporting around student writing outcomes.

THEMATIC ASSIGNMENT

Use the readings in this thematic unit to write an essay that answers one of the following questions.

a. Read the following explanation of *resilience* from the American Psychological Association's Practice Central Web site:

> Resilience is the process of adapting well in the face of adversity, trauma, tragedy, threats or significant sources of stress—such as family and relationship problems, serious health problems, or workplace and financial stressors. Resilience is not a trait that people either have or do not have. It involves behaviors, thoughts and actions that anyone can learn and develop.

The Web address http://www.apapracticecentral.org/outreach/building-resilience.aspx

Teaching Resources: See the IM for suggestions of other readings within Connect IRW Power of Process that may be used with this theme.

Resilience is not something people are born with; it is something that they can develop. Write an essay in which you explain how to develop resilience. Use the sources in this thematic unit for information. Provide concrete examples, and consider using hypothetical examples if you do not have real-life examples that fit your purpose.

b. Thousands of soldiers have returned from the wars in Afghanistan and Iraq with PTSD as well as other injuries, both physical and mental. Read the article entitled "Bouncing Back" in this section. Which of the suggestions Balmain presents might be helpful for soldiers who return with PTSD? Write an essay in which you present methods soldiers might use to overcome the stress that accompanies them as they return from war. Be sure to give credit to Balmain for each of the ideas you use from her essay.

c. Write an essay in which you present the best ideas you encountered in the readings about dealing with adversity. Select three to four ideas, and argue why they would be effective in dealing with adversity.

d. Write an argument essay on when *accepting* is the best way to deal with adversity and when *fighting back* is the best way. Which kinds of situations should be accepted, and which kinds of adversity are best met with resistance? Alternatively, when might a response include both acceptance and resistance? Write an essay in which you discuss hypothetical situations that fit into each of these three categories.

Be sure to cite any sources from which you obtain ideas or quotes. Include a works cited or references page with your essay. For additional information on source-based writing, follow the steps in the Quick Start Guide to Integrated Reading and Writing Assignments.

More than sixty years after the landmark US Supreme Court decision in *Brown v. Board of Education,* which made segregation in public schools illegal, the issue of segregation is still being debated. One question under debate is whether self-segregation in education and elsewhere holds advantages for minority groups in particular and society in general.

Self-segregation by race or ethnic group shows up in lunchrooms across America; it is seen in churches, prisons, college classrooms, and almost anywhere groups of people congregate. Is this common and sometimes unconscious separation good for minority groups in particular and society as a whole? Is it simply a natural impulse to segregate, and if so, are there any reasons for resisting this impulse?

These are the questions explored in the four readings that follow. As you read, think about your own experiences and the self-segregation you have participated in or observed.

AUTHOR AND CONTEXT Debra Humphreys received her BA from Williams College and her PhD in English from Rutgers University. Dr. Humphreys is currently the vice president for policy and public engagement at the Association of American Colleges and Universities. "Campus Diversity and Student Self-Segregation: Separating Myths from Facts" appeared on Diversity Web (www.diversityweb.org) in December 2008.

PREVIEWING Have pen and paper (or a computer) on hand as you read. Think about the title, and then study the author's biography and the contextual information about the reading. Next, preview the selection. From the information you have gathered, determine the topic. What predictions can you make about the reading's content? Jot down your answers.

READING CRITICALLY AND ANNOTATING As you read, annotate the main idea, the major supporting points, key words, and a few passages that would make good quotations. Either write in your book or make annotations on sticky notes.

As you find key ideas, annotate them. In the article that follows, Debra Humphreys weighs in on the issue of segregation on college campuses. Determine Humphreys's viewpoint as you read.

After reading and annotating, create an information sheet on which you record and organize your annotations as well as your thoughts about the content of the reading.

Teaching Resources: See the Instructor's Manual (IM) for instructions to set up this assignment in Connect IRW. Alternatively, this reading assignment and the writing prompts that follow have been pre-loaded into the Connect IRW *Common Places* Master Course.

American society. It also requires an appreciation of how white American higher education still is, despite its increasing diversity. Most students of color who do not attend historically black colleges or universities attend overwhelmingly white institutions.

A 1991 study of student life at [the University of California at] Berkeley, an unusually diverse college campus, describes the experience of campus life as a complex phenomenon that encompasses both some student-initiated racial/ethnic clustering and substantial amounts of interracial interactions. 21

This study also found, however, that 70% of all undergraduates agreed with the statement, *I'd like to meet more students from ethnic and cultural backgrounds that are different from my own.* 22

A forthcoming book by Richard Light of Harvard University also suggests that students from a wide array of racial/ethnic groups desire intergroup contact and see the educational and social benefits of such interactions. 23

The widespread segregation by race that still characterizes much of the rest of American life is, however, having an impact on how students interact with one another on college campuses. 24

A 1997 study at the University of Michigan found that students' friendship patterns closely reflected the make-ups of their high schools and home neighborhoods. This study confirmed that a majority of all students, but a very high percentage of white students, came from highly segregated high schools and neighborhoods. 25

The Michigan study also found that white students had the most segregated friendship patterns on campus of all ethnic groups. 26

The reality is that students of color have much more intergroup contact than do white students, but their patterns of interaction need to be understood in light of their psychological development. Research by psychologist Beverly Daniel Tatum, Dean of the College at Mt. Holyoke College, suggests that there are complex psychological reasons why college students may choose to cluster in racial/ethnic groups. She argues that racial grouping is a developmental process in response to an environmental stressor, racism. Joining with one's peers for support in the face of stress is a positive coping strategy. There is a developmental need on the part of many college students to explore the meaning of one's identity with others who are engaged in a similar process. 27

What difference does racial/ethnic clustering make when it does occur?

Recent research, including Tatum's and that of others, suggests that racial/ethnic clustering can be an important component contributing to the psychological health and educational success of many students. Research also suggests that this clustering need not prevent students from achieving the educational benefits of intergroup contact within college classrooms and on college campuses. 28

The 1991 study of 390 institutions cited above found that ethnic-specific activities were not impeding intergroup contact for the students who participated in them. Programs like racial/ethnic theme houses and study groups seem to help students of color persist and succeed in college and seem to increase their involvement overall with other areas of college life in which they interact frequently across racial/ethnic lines. 29

Impede: to obstruct, hinder, or hamper.

Other studies confirm these findings: 30

A 1994 study of Latino students suggests that students belonging to Latino organizations increased their adjustment and attachment to their colleges and universities. 31

Two other studies, one in 1994 and another in 1996, also found positive benefits   32
of participation in racial and ethnic groups and that these groups also fostered rather
than impeded intergroup contact.

Another 1989 study found that a targeted student support program was positively   33
related to African American students' persistence in college and their degree status.

Given the relatively high level of intergroup contact and the existence of some racial/ethnic clustering, what is the impact of campus diversity on today's college students?

Research suggests a variety of positive educational outcomes that result from being   34
educated in a diverse environment. It also suggests a positive impact for those students with high degrees of intergroup contact.

Patricia Gurin, professor of psychology at the University of Michigan, recently   35
compiled a report summarizing three parallel empirical analyses of university
students. Her report suggests that,

> A racially and ethnically diverse university student body has far-ranging and significant bene-   36
> fits for all students, non-minorities and minorities alike. Students learn better in such an envi-
> ronment and are better prepared to become active participants in our pluralistic, democratic
> society once they leave school. In fact, patterns of racial segregation and separation histori-
> cally rooted in our national life can be broken by diversity experiences in higher education.

Pluralistic: having multiple aspects or parts. In this context, the term is a synonym for *diverse.*

Gurin's research demonstrates that the diverse environment provided by many   37
colleges today contributes to students' intellectual and social development. She suggests that racial diversity in a college or university student body provides the very
features that research has determined are central to producing the conscious mode of
thought educators demand from their students.

Gurin also found that these positive effects of campus diversity extend beyond   38
graduation.

> Diversity experiences during college had impressive effects on the extent to which gradu-   39
> ates in the national study were living racially and ethnically integrated lives in the post-
> college world. Students with the most diversity experiences during college had the most
> cross-racial interactions five years after leaving college.

The study by Antonio mentioned above also confirms that campus diversity is   40
having a positive impact on today's college students.

Antonio examined the impact of the diverse friendship groups he found to be   41
common at UCLA. Controlling for important background information such as gender,
socio-economic status, and the racial diversity of pre-college friendship groups, Antonio
found that friendship group diversity contributed to greater interracial interaction outside the friendship group and stronger commitments to racial understanding.

Another important arena of college life, of course, is the classroom. On diverse   42
campuses, many students are now being educated in highly diverse classrooms in
which they are studying a much wider array of subjects that include content about
previously neglected groups. These classes are also having a significant positive educational impact on both majority and minority students as well.

Conclusions: Is there cause for alarm, hope, or celebration?

There is little cause for alarm, some cause for celebration and much hope for what lies   43
ahead. The reality is that while there is still a long way to go before American higher

education will truly reflect the full diversity of American society, college campuses are becoming much more diverse and their diverse campus environments are having a significant positive effect on this generation of students.

College campuses are not dominated by widespread racial/ethnic segregation and   44 the racial/ethnic clustering that does occur isn't impeding intergroup contact. In fact, the existence of racial/ethnic groups and activities, along with other comprehensive campus diversity initiatives, is contributing to the success of today's college students and preparing them to help build a healthier multicultural America for the future.

Using Your Annotations

Use your annotations and key words to write a one-page summary of the reading. In your summary, identify the writer's thesis statement, the major supporting points, the support for the major supporting points, and any other information needed to complete the summary.

Thinking about the Text

1. What is Humphreys's position on self-segregation?
2. What educational or social benefits might college students gain by self-segregating into ethnic groups?
3. What does the writer say about the differences between self-segregation in high schools and self-segregation on college campuses?
4. What would the writer like to see campuses do about self-segregation?
5. How common is racial self-segregation, according to Humphreys?

The Writer's Techniques

1. Humphreys cites a variety of sources to provide proof for her claims. What kind of information does she quote from these sources? What function does she hope each type of information will serve?
2. Look at your annotations. Which of the following types of supporting details does the writer use—comparison and contrast, cause and effect, definition, process analysis, classification, illustration, or narrative?
3. What ordering strategy does the writer use to present the information in this reading?

Brief-Response Assignments

1. Write a paragraph discussing how college students might consciously try to be more inclusive of others outside their own racial group.
2. What can colleges do to encourage more intergroup interaction? Explain.
3. Have you ever observed or participated in self-segregation? If so, reflect on your observation or experience. If you are writing about your observations, why do you think some people choose to self-segregate? If you are writing about your experience, why did you choose to self-segregate? Explain.

Essay Assignments

1. Write an essay in which you discuss the self-segregation you have observed on your college campus or elsewhere. Discuss the potentially positive and potentially negative effects of the self-segregation you have observed.
2. People who are critical of self-segregation claim that it limits a person's full development. What, exactly, is their argument? What are the problems of self-segregation? Write an essay in which you explain the problems fully.
3. Write an essay in which you present ways to add diversity to one's college experience. What can students do to try to experience more than their own culture? ↻

Connect IRW Writing Assignments: You may assign any of these essay prompts in Connect IRW; the toolset supports options such as assigning peer review or building your own rubric to gather reporting around student writing outcomes.

AUTHOR AND CONTEXT As a contributing writer for *USA Today* and *The Huffington Post,* Ernest Owens writes on a range of social issues, including race relations, social media and policy, and entertainment. His work has also appeared on the Good Men Project, Al Jazeera English, *The Root,* and the Oprah Winfrey Network. "Equal When Separate" appeared in *The Daily Pennsylvanian* on September 13, 2012.

PREVIEWING Have pen and paper (or a computer) on hand as you read. Think about the title, and then study the author's biography and the contextual information about the reading. Next, preview the selection. From the information you have gathered, determine the topic. What predictions can you make about the reading's content? Jot down your answers.

READING CRITICALLY AND ANNOTATING As you read, annotate the main idea, the major supporting points, key words, and a few passages that would make good quotations. Either write in your book or make annotations on sticky notes.

As you find key ideas, annotate them. What is Owens's opinion on the topic of self-segregation? What are his reasons for his opinion? Note any questions that come to mind as you read.

After reading and annotating, create an information sheet on which you record and organize your annotations as well as your thoughts about the content of the reading.

Teaching Resources: See the Instructor's Manual (IM) for instructions to set up this assignment in Connect IRW. Alternatively, this reading assignment and the writing prompts that follow have been pre-loaded into the Connect IRW *Common Places* Master Course.

Equal When Separate BY ERNEST OWENS

Lexile: 1060L

1   Some of my favorite moments at Penn have happened at 1920 Commons—most of them on a Saturday morning over brunch with friends.

Penn: University of Pennsylvania.

2   We usually laugh loudly and take comical jabs at one another—each more intense than the last. But then comes a moment when our antics dim and someone in the group points out the fact that we're the only black students in the room and shouldn't be so loud about it.

3   Someone usually says, "I wonder what they think about us being so loud and black over here . . . we are being so self-segregating."

4   For a long time, I felt the same way. Was I being culturally limiting by eating brunch every weekend with my black peers? Was this self-segregation?

5   Then I looked around the other tables at Commons and saw separate groups of white students and Asian students congregated over waffles and bacon. That made me wonder: do they ever have the same discussion that I just had with my friends?

6   I bet they don't. Otherwise, we would all mingle over pancakes every weekend like they do at the United Nations cafeteria. Fantasy aside, minorities on campus shouldn't feel a sense of guilt when they choose to hang out with friends from a similar background.

7   It didn't take a UMOJA, Makuu or Black Student League event for me to get together with my friends. We just found each other as a group of black students looking to kick start the weekend together.

These are names of African-American student organizations.

8   Debates about self-segregation are nothing new. W.E.B. Du Bois, Penn's honorary emeritus professor of sociology and Africana studies, was a strong proponent of developing economic enterprises exclusive to blacks.

9   Coretta Scott King, however, spoke out vocally against the practice when she said that segregation "is still wrong when it is requested by black people."

10   This idea is also explored at length in one of my favorite novels, *Invisible Man* by Ralph Ellison, published in 1952.

11   While the media and politicians attempt to convince us that we live in a post-racial society, the truth is, self-segregation persists and is a natural instinct.

Not everyone is going to get along all the time. It is normal for people to gravi- 12 tate toward those who are similar. It is necessary for each of us to find a "safe space" where we feel accepted and immune from misunderstandings.

Most Quakers devote a substantial amount of their time and energy to others. 13 We're always working on group projects with people we'd rather never see again. Or we're involved in six different student groups where we have to interact with students from all walks of life.

> *Quakers* is the name that the athletic teams of the University of Pennsylvania use, and so the word is used to refer to Penn students in general.

While there is a lot to be learned from interacting with diverse people, the ques- 14 tion arises: when can we take a step back from the face we strive so hard to display and be ourselves?

The fabric of Penn life is woven by strings of separate communities. While we 15 work together to produce equality, especially in an academic setting, each community is distinct. Most of our successes have come from different groups that worked hard to achieve a goal.

There is something aesthetically and socially pleasing about seeing the internal 16 workings of these individual groups. When I go to Hillel for lunch, it always amazes me to see a close-knit circle of Jewish students. I also appreciate the ability to see groups of exchange students from Germany, Israel and China occupy the floors of Du Bois College House every semester.

In essence, we should stop attempting to sacrifice our identities and embrace 17 self-segregation.

By virtue of being members of the Penn community, we have already made strides 18 to produce a more equal society. But in the words of Malcolm X, "We cannot think of uniting with others until after we have first united among ourselves."

Using Your Annotations

Use your annotations and key words to write a one-page summary of the reading. In your summary, identify the writer's thesis statement, the major supporting points, the support for the major supporting points, and any other information needed to complete your summary.

Thinking about the Text

1. What does Owens say about self-segregation on college campuses?
2. Explain what the writer means by "culturally limiting."
3. For what purpose did Owens write this article? Explain your answer.
4. For whom did he write the article? Explain your answer.
5. The writer contends that self-segregation is a natural instinct. What reasons does he give for this belief?

The Writer's Techniques

1. How does Owens use quotations in his essay? What purposes do these quotes serve?
2. The writer uses first and third person in this essay. What is the effect of using first person where the writer does? What would be the effect of using only third person? Is the writer's choice to use first person in some places a good choice?
3. The writer uses an extended anecdote in his introduction. How does this anecdote set the tone for the rest of the essay?

Brief-Response Assignments

1. Based on this essay, define *self-segregation*.
2. The author presents one side of the self-segregation argument. Write a paragraph presenting the other side.

3. Write a paragraph in which you agree or disagree with this statement: *Minorities on campus shouldn't feel a sense of guilt when they choose to hang out with friends from a similar background.*

Essay Assignments

1. The writer quotes Malcolm X as saying, "We cannot think of uniting with others until after we have first united among ourselves." What do you think would be the long-term impact of following this rationale? Would it result in a greater sense of cooperation with others or a deeper entrenchment in our own social groups? Why? Write an essay explaining the potential effects of Malcolm X's idea.
2. Some people are hesitant to move out of their self-segregated groups, not because they have prejudices against others but because moving out of one's group means moving out of one's comfort zone. Why is this so? What particular barriers must individuals address if they want to move out of their self-segregated circles? Write an essay explaining the causes.
3. What is the difference between self-segregation and the kind of segregation that used to be legal in the United States? Write an essay in which you contrast these two types of segregation. ↻

Connect IRW Writing Assignments: You may assign any of these essay prompts in Connect IRW; the toolset supports options such as assigning peer review or building your own rubric to gather reporting around student writing outcomes.

AUTHOR AND CONTEXT   The Australian journalist Michael Gawenda served as editor of *The Age* from 1997 to 2004. He was named the first director of the Centre for Advanced Journalism at the University of Melbourne in 2009. "What Happened to the Dream?" appeared in *The Age* in October 2005.

PREVIEWING   Have pen and paper (or a computer) on hand as you read. Think about the title, and then study the author's biography and the contextual information about the reading. Next, preview the selection. From the information you have gathered, determine the topic. What predictions can you make about the reading's content? Jot down your answers.

READING CRITICALLY AND ANNOTATING   As you read, annotate the main idea, the major supporting points, key words, and a few passages that would make good quotations. Either write in your book or make annotations on sticky notes.

As you find key ideas, annotate them. As an Australian, Gawenda can look at the United States from a unique perspective. How does his vantage point affect his ability to assess race relations in the United States? What insights does he have to offer? Make a note of these insights as you read.

After reading and annotating, create an information sheet on which you record and organize your annotations as well as your thoughts about the content of the reading.

Teaching Resources: See the Instructor's Manual (IM) for instructions to set up this assignment in Connect IRW. Alternatively, this reading assignment and the writing prompts that follow have been pre-loaded into the Connect IRW *Common Places* Master Course.

What Happened to the Dream?   BY MICHAEL GAWENDA

Lexile: 1520L

In Anacostia, on the street corners, outside the storefronts, along the littered pavements and in front of the rundown row houses, the young men of Washington's underclass spend their days. They do business, they huddle in groups. They look to outsiders dangerous and menacing; this is a place where whites are unwelcome. Here, in Washington's south-east, away from the grandeur of Capitol Hill or the simple, soaring optimism of the Washington Memorial, is one metaphor for race relations in America.

Travel a few kilometers north, through neighborhoods once like Anacostia but now gentrified, overwhelmingly white, inner-city suburbs, and you get to the Gold Coast, with its tree-lined streets and substantial houses and pretty gardens. This wealthy black neighborhood of Washington is another metaphor for America's race relations.

1

2

Gentrification occurs when people buy inner-city properties and transform them into high-income residences or businesses.

Washington and its surrounding suburbs in the adjacent states of Virginia and   3
Maryland is, in some ways, a microcosm of race relations in America. In this imperial
capital of the world's greatest power, more than 50 years after the US Supreme Court
ended school segregation—ruling that the concept of "separate but equal" when it
came to education was unconstitutional—the city's public schools have virtually no
white children.

It is a segregated city, with perhaps Silver Spring, one small neighborhood near   4
the Maryland-DC border approaching something like an integrated community.

This segregation is not a matter of class; Washington's growing black middle-class   5
lives in either the Gold Coast area of DC or, if they have children and want a suburban
life, in Montgomery County where they send their children to predominantly black
schools. They are a world away from the schools where the black and mostly poor
children of DC go.

Across America, somewhere between 5 and 10 percent of American families live   6
in integrated communities, and across America, the public school system is almost
totally segregated. What does this mean and what does it say about race relations in
America? More than 300 years after the first African slaves were brought here, black
and white Americans, in the main, exist in parallel universes, separated by culture,
language and history.

Like everything in this country where dreams and ideals bump up against harsh   7
reality yet remain as potent as ever, where neighborhood still means something,
where guns are invested with almost spiritual meaning, and where America as the
promised land remains the country's great unifying myth, no single metaphor can
encompass relations between blacks and whites. When New Orleans was drowned by
Hurricane Katrina a month ago, the most shocking and shaming images for Americans were of black poverty, helplessness and abandonment.

The New Orleans police chief and the city's mayor appeared on *The Oprah*   8
Winfrey Show and told of murders, rapes and bodies stored in the basement of the
Superdome while no one came to rescue the people inside. Mayor Ray Nagin told
tales of armed gangs roaming the streets, looting and shooting anyone, including
police, who stood in their way. Where, he cried, was the national guard? Where was
the army, the marines?

Police Chief Eddie Compass, who has since resigned, Nagin and, of course, Win-   9
frey are black, though her audience is predominantly white. Not once did she ask
Compass or Nagin whether they had credible eyewitness testimony to all this horror.
Like a game of broken telephone, the stories became increasingly lurid—and were
mostly untrue.

There were no murders and no rapes in the Superdome. There were no bodies   10
stacked in the basement. There were no armed gangs shooting at police and members
of the Army Corps of Engineers. These were fantasies retold, without much checking,
by hundreds of reporters in the chaos of Katrina's aftermath, in the rush to be first
with the story and, crucially, because these fantasies played into half-conscious but
widely held racial and class stereotypes.

Indeed the Katrina disaster offers a neat but ultimately simplistic and distorted   11
encapsulation of black-white relations in America: poor and powerless African-Americans
are left to suffer and die, preyed on by their own violent and lawless underclass, while
their white compatriots look the other way.

Broken telephone: a game in
which one person whispers
a message to another per-
son, who then whispers it to
another, and so on. At the end
of the game, the message is
announced, and usually the
message is different from the
one that the first person whis-
pered. The point of the game is
to show how inaccuracies occur
in the communication process.

In the days and weeks after Katrina, on cable television talk shows, on newspaper op-ed pages, even in Congress, race and poverty, for the first time in years, was a major issue.   12

When he gave his televised address to the nation from New Orleans, George Bush, for the first time in his presidency, said poverty and race were connected. Americans had seen that there was a "deep, persistent poverty and that poverty has roots in a history of racial discrimination which cuts off generations from the opportunity of America."   13

Both *Newsweek* and *Time,* for the first time since the O. J. Simpson trial, carried cover stories on race and poverty in America; all the major TV networks had current affairs specials on the subject; in Congress, politicians from both parties expressed dismay over what Katrina had revealed about the lives of the poor. But there is a weariness about all this talk, a lack of confidence that the intractable problems that Katrina revealed have solutions or even that there can be agreement across the great conservative-liberal divide on just what those problems might be.   14

Intractable: impossible to solve; incurable.

Ten years ago this month, Louis Farrakhan, the Nation of Islam leader, led his Million Man March to Washington, and 10 years ago this month, in Los Angeles, O. J. Simpson was acquitted of the murder of his white wife Nicole and her friend Ronald Goldman.   15

The Simpson trial divided Americans along racial lines; 83 percent of blacks agreed with the verdict compared with 37 percent of whites. Farrakhan's march attracted hundreds of thousands of black men to Washington, despite the fact that he was seen as an extremist, a sexist and some argue, an anti-Semite. It was a powerful statement by black men that they wanted to take responsibility for their lives and the lives of their children.   16

Ten years on, the Simpson anniversary has passed without much notice; the trial and verdict, which many thought would have a profound effect on race relations, has been virtually forgotten and Simpson, living in obscurity in Florida, is the occasional butt of jokes by black stand-up comedians.   17

And 10 years on, Farrakhan's Millions More protest, . . . to mark the anniversary of the Million Man March, attracted just 20,000 people, in the main to protest the Bush Administration's response to Hurricane Katrina.   18

Polls show that support for Bush is down about the 2 percent mark among African-Americans, compared with the 11.9 percent of the black vote he received at November's presidential election, a 3 percent increase compared with 2000, mostly because of conservative African-Americans who shared his views on gay marriage and "culture of life" issues. Now, black leaders from Jesse Jackson to Al Sharpton to Farrakhan argue that in New Orleans, the world saw that if you're poor and black in the US, you end up invisible and abandoned.   19

But the black and poor of New Orleans were invisible not just to America's white middle-class and the conservative and liberal elites, but to the essentially black leadership of the city and to the growing black middle-class in the country, which now represents almost 40 percent of America's 39 million African-Americans.   20

The life journey of Reverend Charles White, the regional head of the National Association for the Advancement of Colored People, based in Atlanta, Georgia, and covering most of the Deep South encapsulates the success and the failure of 40 years of civil rights activism, of landmark civil rights legislation and of government   21 programs that were meant to bridge the racial and economic divide between black and white America.

White is in his early 40s, passionate and outgoing, and articulate in the way peo- 22 ple of great conviction often are, and he is both angry and optimistic about the future. The child of farm laborers in the rural hinterland of Charleston, South Carolina, White calls himself a poster child for what can be achieved through government programs and by building on the legacy of the great civil rights leaders of the '60s.

Hinterland: a remote or outlying area.

"We are the first generation of African-Americans afforded opportunities and 23 access to institutions that were closed to African-Americans just a generation ago," he says. "We have made giant strides. Look at me. Were it not for the civil rights movement and the federal government programs that followed the big civil rights changes, I would never have had the chance to go to college.

"Those programs gave me simple things like milk and cheese, took me out of my 24 poor segregated high school on weekends to Charleston College, where a whole new world opened up for me and where I was shown that I could be more than a farm laborer like generations of farm laborers in my family.

"Those programs have been cut during the Bush presidency. There are a thousand 25 young men like me wandering around in Charleston County and tens of thousands across the South who would give anything to have the opportunities I had who simply won't be afforded them."

Atlanta was the birthplace of Martin Luther King, Jr., the city where the first sit- 26 ins by blacks at all-white lunch counters were held in the early '60s, and where King preached his message of non-violent protest at the Ebenezer Baptist Church. It was in Atlanta where he was arrested for the first time and jailed for breaking the city's rigidly enforced color bar.

This is no longer the Atlanta where King's great crusade for black civil rights 27 began. It is a big, sprawling, growing city, the headquarters for a number of multi-national corporations, including Coca-Cola, a magnet for mostly small-town white southern middle-class go-getters, young northerners and increasingly, Latinos attracted by job opportunities, low state taxes and relatively cheap housing.

Some time in the next few years, Atlanta will cease to be a majority black city, and 28 when that happens, the political dynamics will change and a predominantly black city government, which has ruled Atlanta for decades, will be replaced by a white mayor and a majority white city council.

All over the south, this growing urbanization is changing the demographics and the 29 economy of what has been America's poorest region and where black Americans, for more than a hundred years after the civil war freed them from slavery, lived like serfs, without rights, without economic opportunities, abused and discriminated against, at best patronized and treated like children and at worst, lynched and humiliated by an overwhelming racist white population.

Serf: a slave who was attached to the lord's land and trans-ferred with it from one owner to another.

On the streets surrounding the Martin Luther King Centre, just beyond the 30 Martin Luther King museum and gift shop, past the Martin Luther King Memorial Pool in the center of which is King's white marble tomb and just beyond the reno-vated Ebenezer Baptist Church, there is black despair.

Panhandlers, unemployed young black men, young black women with ancient 31 faces, battered apartment blocks, menace and hopelessness—indeed this could be Anacostia in Washington or the battered heart of Detroit or perhaps the 9th district of

New Orleans before the great flood. For all the changes in Atlanta, the violent crime rate remains the highest in the country, just ahead of Detroit, and Atlanta has the third highest murder rate behind the black-majority cities of Baltimore and New Orleans.

Things change and things stay the same. Or get worse. More than 37 million   32 Americans live below the official poverty line, set at $19,500 for a family of four and just under $9000 for people living alone; during every year of the Bush Administration, on average an extra 1 million people joined the ranks of the poor.

While the poverty rate for white Americans is about 8 percent, for African-   33 Americans it is close to 25 percent. Most of that poverty is concentrated in the inner-city neighborhoods of America's cities from which the whites fled to the suburbs after the black riots of the '60s and which newly middle-class blacks abandoned as soon as they had the means to do so.

Professor Michael Giles is a political scientist at Emory University in Atlanta, who   34 has worked on inner-city renewal programs and who is pessimistic about the prospect of solving the multitude of problems that afflict the mostly black inner-city communities that, in many ways, are the casualties of globalization and the decline of unskilled manufacturing jobs.

"There has been a huge growth in the black middle class, basically because of the   35 good economic times in the '90s, but at the same time, all the government programs, all the development of so-called enterprise zones in our inner-city areas, all the work on addressing generational poverty and family dysfunction in these communities has been only marginally successful," he says.

"You know, there's been lots of talk after New Orleans about how the Federal   36 Government was slow to respond because most of the victims in that city of Hurricane Katrina were poor and black. We were shocked by what we saw. We had developed amnesia about poverty in our country.

"But a lot of black middle-class people had amnesia as well. The leadership of New   37 Orleans was black and they had amnesia. We have had black leadership in Atlanta for a long time but they have not significantly improved the lives of poor black people here."

Giles considers himself to be a liberal. The department of political science at   38 Emory has several black professors. Giles tells of how delighted he is that some of his regular tennis partners are black—engineers, academics, businessmen.

Asked whether beyond playing tennis together, he meets his tennis partners   39 socially, Giles pauses and then says, no, he does not.

"Middle-class blacks mix with middle-class whites in the workplace but there's   40 still a comfort-level issue, a fear of being slighted, of racial put-downs that means middle-class blacks prefer to live and even worship among their own.

"We have wonderful African-American middle-class communities here, with   41 great amenities, great homes, great schools. Yes, more than four decades after desegregation, self-segregation rules so that our schools and our churches and our neighborhoods remain as segregated as they ever were."

Eleanor Holmes Norton was a civil rights leader in the '60s and now represents   42 Washington DC in Congress. She worries that in the poorer black areas of Washington, and in similar areas across America, a sea-change is taking place, a change that if it continues, will mean "we will have whole non-viable communities."

"It is impossible to overestimate what has happened to our community in only a   43
couple of generations and what might happen to the next generation if it continues
at this pace," she says.

What she means is that there has been a fundamental breakdown of family life in   44
these communities—about 70 percent of babies are born outside marriage, to young
single mothers, many of them teenagers who are invariably abandoned by the fathers
of their children.

"Disintegration of the family is the greatest problem facing the African-American   45
community," she says. "And there are no simple, easy answers to this. Government
has a role, but you have to be careful. How do you get into someone's family and
try and save it, convince young men that they have responsibilities, young men who
often feel they have no future and no hope?"

Farrakhan's Million Man March was meant to inspire young black men to take   46
responsibility for their children, their families and perhaps it worked for some. What
cannot be denied is that more than a century-and-a-half after the end of slavery,
more than 50 years after the end of legal segregation, more than 40 years after landmark civil rights legislation ended legal discrimination, black and white Americans
live in separate worlds, informed by their different histories and life experience, their
different takes on what it means to be American.

For all the high-profile blacks in American life, the athletes, the black success sto-   47
ries in politics such as Condoleezza Rice and Colin Powell, the genius of black music
and the success of black writers such as Alice Walker and Toni Morrison and a host of
others, blacks and whites in America do not, it seems, really want to share their lives
with each other.

In Atlanta, walking through the exhibits at the Martin Luther King Center that   48
mark the often bloody and yet inspiring history of the civil rights movement, listening
to King's mesmerizing speeches, his dream of an America where skin color no longer
mattered and where all Americans shared common dreams and aspirations, it was
impossible not to wonder what he would have thought of all this.

Chances are he would have been gratified and disappointed. Chances are that he   49
would have thought that America had not yet become the promised land.

— OOO —

Using Your Annotations

Use your annotations and key words to write a one-page summary of the reading. In your summary, identify the writer's thesis statement, the major supporting points, the support for the major
supporting points, and any other information needed to complete the summary.

Thinking about the Text

1. According to Gawenda, what role does self-segregation play in the cycle of poverty?
2. Why does the writer believe race and poverty became newsworthy again after Hurricane
   Katrina?
3. What does Gawenda believe about race relations in the United States? Express his beliefs in
   a paragraph.
4. In what ways was Charles White's upbringing different than that of young African Americans
   today, according to Gawenda?
5. The writer mentions globalization. What is globalization? Explain in a paragraph.

The Writer's Techniques

1. Why does Gawenda use a question for his title? What possible functions might such a title have?
2. How does the writer sequence his essay? Is it organized by time, by importance, or by some other method? Explain and cite examples of his ordering strategy.
3. The writer uses several quotes. Select one of these quotes, and write a paragraph about the person being quoted. What is the person's reputation, expertise, and status? You may need to do an Internet search to learn about the person.

Brief-Response Assignments

1. What is Gawenda's point about the aftermath of Hurricane Katrina? Explain.
2. According to a source quoted in the article, "Disintegration of the family is the greatest problem facing the African-American community." What does this sentence mean? Explain in a paragraph.
3. Gawenda points out a number of problems but does not discuss many solutions. What is one solution the writer might offer for a problem he discusses?

Essay Assignments

1. The writer states, "Blacks and whites in America do not, it seems, really want to share their lives with each other." Is this true? Write an essay in which you support, qualify, or refute Gawenda's statement based on the evidence you have seen in your community. Do not write a first-person essay explaining your own point of view. Rather, use observations of race relations to support your point.
2. Write an essay in which you explain this quote from the reading: "America as the promised land remains the country's great unifying myth." In what ways is the idea of America as a promised land a myth? Is it a myth for all people or for only some people? For whom is it a myth? Explain.
3. Gawenda's essay presents his point of view on the status of segregation in the United States, but he is not from the United States; he is an Australian journalist, viewing the situation as an outsider. Does his position as an outsider help him form a more accurate view of the American situation, or does it limit his knowledge of what life here is really like? Write an essay in which you answer this question. Defend your answer by analyzing Gawenda's observations. ↺

Connect IRW Writing Assignments: You may assign any of these essay prompts in Connect IRW; the toolset supports options such as assigning peer review or building your own rubric to gather reporting around student writing outcomes.

AUTHOR AND CONTEXT Brett Buckner is an award-winning freelance writer in Alabama. Previously, Buckner, a graduate of Troy University, was a features writer (with a focus on religion) for *The Anniston Star* in Anniston, Alabama. "Color Blind: Is Sunday Morning Still the Most Segregated Hour in America?" first appeared in *The Anniston Star* in May 2011. A slightly shortened version appears here.

PREVIEWING Have pen and paper (or a computer) on hand as you read. Think about the title, and then study the author's biography and the contextual information about the reading. Next, preview the selection. From the information you have gathered, determine the topic. What predictions can you make about the reading's content? Jot down your answers.

READING CRITICALLY AND ANNOTATING As you read, annotate the main idea, the major supporting points, key words, and a few passages that would make good quotations. Either write in your book or make annotations on sticky notes.

The essay contains five sections. Write a sentence that expresses the main idea of each one.

After reading and annotating, create an information sheet on which you record and organize your annotations as well as your thoughts about the content of the reading.

Teaching Resources: See the Instructor's Manual (IM) for instructions to set up this assignment in Connect IRW. Alternatively, this reading assignment and the writing prompts that follow have been pre-loaded into the Connect IRW *Common Places* Master Course.

Color Blind: Is Sunday Morning Still the Most Segregated Hour in America? BY BRETT BUCKNER

Lexile: 1070L

1   As a black woman in Anniston during the 1960s—a time of racism, segregation and bus burnings—Jean Martin knew what it was like to live in fear because of the color of her skin. "She saw and survived a lot of awful stuff," said her son, Marcus Dunn. "But she never put that poison in me to hate people just because they were different from me."

2   In 1962, when her son was 2 years old, Martin left Anniston "for a better life" in Oakland, Calif. She taught her son a simple rule: "Every white person isn't bad. Every black person isn't good. Good people come in all colors."

3   When Dunn returned to Anniston in 1989, her words still resonated.

4   Twelve years later, when he founded Kingdom Place Ministries, one of his main aspirations was to build a diverse congregation where people worshipped colorblind.

5   "We have an ingrained fear," Dunn said. "We fear loving one another outside of race, outside of culture, outside of tradition. We go to church where we're comfortable. That's not good enough. Too many of us have been raised in the church, when what we need is to be born into the kingdom of God. In the kingdom of God, we should only see God's people."

6   With a congregation that runs 80 percent black, 20 percent white, Dunn is working to achieve what he believes is the biblical mandate of "Love thy neighbor as thyself"— that the only way to truly worship God is to learn from all people of faith, no matter their race, culture, tradition, social or financial background.

7   "Since this ministry began, God has wanted us to be diversified . . . it's the only way to learn from one another," Dunn said. "We've done that by displaying love to one another or whoever comes through that door. If we show love in the church, we can't help but come together as men and women of God."

8   True diversity in Christian pews is a dream still under construction. The largest obstacles are differing opinions on music and style of worship, especially in the South, where the ghosts of racism and segregation linger just below the surface.

9   In order to exorcise those demons of the past, pastors must aggressively pursue diversity, rather than praying it will resolve itself, said Carlton Weathers, pastor of Grace Fellowship in Anniston, which in addition to a dozen or so black members also numbers Hispanic, Indian and Japanese among its nearly 200 members.

10   "Racism is a sin," Weathers said. "To me, diversity is a gospel issue rather than a social issue. Christians must be on the forefront of integration by attempting to bring racial harmony to the community, but too often the church has been on the wrong side of the issue. Sure, we've come a long way, but there's still a long way to go."

"The Most Segregated Hour"

11   It's been 53 years since Martin Luther King Jr. wrote in *Stride Toward Freedom: The Montgomery Story* "that the most segregated hour in Christian America is 11 o'clock on Sunday morning, the same hour when so many are standing to sing, 'In Christ there is no East nor West.' Equally appalling is the fact that the most segregated school of the week is Sunday school. How often the church has had a high blood count of creeds and anemia of deeds."

King's indictment still rings true. According to a recent study conducted at Baylor   12
University, nine out of 10 congregations have a single racial group that accounts for
more than 80 percent of their membership.

"Socially, we've become much more integrated in schools, the military and busi-   13
nesses," said Kevin Dougherty, assistant professor of sociology at Baylor University,
who co-authored the study. "But in the places where we worship, segregation still
seems to be the norm. And it's not just an issue of attraction, of getting them into
the door, but of retention. Can we keep them? Our research indicates that we've not
been able to."

It is a challenge that all mainstream Christian denominations must acknowledge,   14
said Will Willimon, bishop for the North Alabama Conference of the United Methodist Church.

"Look at the numbers and what Martin Luther King said still rings true," he said.   15
"Attending church tends to be one of the most culturally specific things we do. In
most of our churches where there is tension, it's usually over style of worship and
music, things that are as much generational as racial."

One big difference in worship styles is the length of the service. At black churches,   16
music, prayer, the reading of Scripture and other activities can run upwards of an
hour before the preacher starts preaching.

Some 20 years ago, Willimon served as a guest pastor at a historically black   17
church in South Carolina where the service lasted more than two hours. Afterwards,
Willimon asked the pastor why worship at black churches lasts so long. The answer
was, simply put, some black people have more to deal with come Sunday mornings.

"Male unemployment is running about 30 percent in this neighborhood. Young   18
male unemployment is running about 50 percent. That means when my people are
outside the church, every signal they receive from the culture is saying, 'You're nothing.
You're nobody.' Then I get them into church and tell them, 'Jesus died for you. You're
God's people.' It takes about two hours for them to get their heads on straight."

Seeking Something Different

Tyler McDaniel's parents never sat in a pew beside a white person.   19

Having been raised in Oxford [Mississippi] at a time when it was dangerous to   20
be black, they attended a tiny C.M.E. [Christian Methodist Episcopal] church less than
a mile from their home. Every Sunday for as long as he could remember, McDaniel
went to that church, surrounded by friends and relatives. But when his parents died,
McDaniel, then 27, did something they never would have considered.

"I went to a white church . . . several, in fact," he said. "It was a different gen-   21
eration. I had white friends and co-workers, went to a racially mixed school at JSU
[Jacksonville State University]. I even dated a white girl, so going to church with white
people wasn't that big a deal."

At first, he felt a bit out of place, McDaniel admitted. Not because anyone in the   22
pews treated him differently, but because he was in such a "total minority practically everywhere I went." There were other black members at Word Alive, the church
he most frequently attended—"quite a few," in fact. But then he started talking to
friends who still attended predominantly black churches.

"It was about going where they were raised," he said. "It wasn't just that I was in   23
the minority in terms of where I went to church, I was also in the minority as someone
who wasn't afraid to seek out something different. And I think that's the problem for

both blacks and whites. True diversity on Sunday mornings will forever be a problem because we never stop to consider that where we are might not be where we belong.

"Faith is supposed to challenge us. We'll never really learn anything if we're 24 always surrounded by people who think and act just like we do . . . it's a dead end."

Church Leaders Encourage Diversity

Willimon and other United Methodist Church leaders have encouraged diversity by 25 making cross-racial appointments—placing a black minister in charge of a predominately white congregation, or vice versa. They have met with only limited success.

"Unfortunately, we can't point to a case where it dramatically energized or grew a 26 congregation, at least not repeatedly," Willimon said. "That's terribly disappointing."

Genia Garrett was one of those cross-racial appointments. Today, Garrett, who is 27 black, is the minister at the predominantly black Glen Addie Community Church—which also has eight white members. For the previous three years, however, she was minister at four churches in Iowa where she was the only black person in the congregation.

"I think sometimes we get too hung up on tradition, on what we think is right 28 or 'normal,' and that means being surrounded by people who look and act like us," Garrett said. "In doing that, we can block out the power of what God is trying to do. You can't keep God in a box. When it comes to worship, when it comes to getting closer to God, we've all got to think outside the box we were raised in."

Born in Birmingham and raised in the Baptist church, Garrett felt called to preach 29 from a young age, but because she was Baptist her options were limited. Now, as a Methodist, she has come to understand and respect various forms of worship, from the conservative traditionalism common to white congregations to the enthusiastic worship of black churches.

At Glen Addie Community Church, the most important thing is the music, 30 Garrett said. "We have different members of various denominations—Holiness, Baptist, Pentecostal—but they all want vibrant praise, especially in the music. They expect the songs to take them off to heaven and just be off the chain, and they expect the preacher to bring the word—dynamic with fire and brimstone," she said.

"I think blacks have been given the gift of freedom of worship, the power and 31 the gift of feeling the music and using that in their worship to God," Garrett said. "And while that might look more dynamic, it's just different—not necessarily better."

"They Were Just Like Me"

Nita Jones considers herself to be quiet and reserved most of the time, but that all 32 changes when she steps into Kingdom Place Ministries, where she is one of a handful of white members. Raised Methodist, Jones attended mostly nondenominational churches before being invited by a friend to visit Kingdom Place five years ago. She never went anywhere else. During services, she claps, raises her hands to the heavens and praises the Lord "loudly."

It was the first time she'd ever been in the minority during worship services—but 33 she didn't really notice. "It didn't really register," she said with a laugh. "I know it sounds strange, but color didn't exist for me. Everybody was kind and I felt right at home. The way I saw it, they were just like me. Inside, Christians are all the same . . . at least they should be." . . .

Using Your Annotations

Use your annotations and key words to write a one-page summary of the reading. In your summary, identify the writer's thesis statement, the major supporting points, the support for the major supporting points, and any other information needed to complete the summary.

Thinking about the Text

1. What is the main idea of this article?
2. Buckner suggests that one difference between white and black churches is the typical length of worship services. He says that Will Willimon asked the pastor of a black church why worship there lasts so long. What answer did the pastor offer?
3. The writer quotes Tyler McDaniel as saying that his experience regarding race and church has been very different than that of his parents. What reason does McDaniel give for his being so much more comfortable in attending a predominantly white church than his parents would have been?
4. The author says that Willimon and other United Methodist Church leaders have encouraged diversity by making "cross-racial appointments." What does the expression "cross-racial appointments" mean?
5. According to Willimon, how successful have "cross-racial appointments" been in promoting racial diversity?

The Writer's Techniques

1. What text pattern best fits this article? Explain.
2. What is the purpose of this article—to inform, analyze, evaluate, or persuade? Explain your answer.
3. Analyze the article's conclusion, paying particular attention to the quotes in the last paragraph. Why do you think Buckner ends his article with these quotes? Explain.

Brief-Response Assignments

1. In the body of the essay, Buckner provides the context for the title of the essay. What was the source? Why is it important to note the source?
2. Included in the quotation from Martin Luther King, Jr., at the beginning of the essay is this expression: "How often the church has had a high blood count of creeds and anemia of deeds." The word *anemia* is used in this context to mean the opposite of *high blood count*. What does King mean? Use a dictionary to look up *creed* and *anemia* and any other words in that sentence that are unfamiliar.
3. Several churches are mentioned in the article: Kingdom Place Ministries, Word Alive International Outreach, Grace Fellowship, and Glen Addie Community Church. Do an Internet search for each church, and determine where it is located. (For best results, enclose the church's name in quotation marks, and include the pastor's name, if provided.) Identify the location by city and state. Once you have done that, answer this question: Why are their locations relevant to this particular article?

Essay Assignments

1. Most of the voices heard in this essay suggest that racially integrated worship is a very desirable goal. However, some arguments for blacks worshipping with blacks and whites worshipping with whites are implied, if not explicitly stated. Using these implicit perspectives, construct an argument that the self-segregation of worshippers not only is understandable but also can be a positive practice.
2. The writer includes stories of white people attending black churches and vice versa. Locate one of each story type, and compare and contrast the descriptions of the experiences each person had.
3. Select another religious tradition, such as Islam, Buddhism, or Orthodox Judaism. Is segregation a problem for the religious tradition you have selected? Write an informative essay explaining how integration issues exist or have been resolved in the religious tradition in question. ↻

Connect IRW Writing Assignments: You may assign any of these essay prompts in Connect IRW; the toolset supports options such as assigning peer review or building your own rubric to gather reporting around student writing outcomes.

THEMATIC ASSIGNMENT

Use the readings in this thematic unit to write an essay that answers one of the following questions.

Teaching Resources: See the IM for suggestions of other readings within Connect IRW Power of Process that may be used with this theme.

   a. Write an essay discussing the advancements that have been made regarding race relations in the United States. Also discuss ways in which progress has been slow in coming.
   b. Is self-segregation something we should eliminate? Should self-segregation be eliminated in some places and allowed in others? Defend your answer.
   c. Describe various steps mentioned in the readings in this thematic unit that might be taken to actively encourage desegregation.
   d. Analyze the self-segregation practices at your college or university by observing and making notes about classroom and lunchroom behaviors. Write an essay about your observations, and evaluate your college. Is self-segregation prevalent on your campus? If it is, what are the effects of such segregation? What insights can you draw from your observations? Present them in your essay.

Be sure to cite any sources from which you obtain ideas or quotes. Include a works cited or references page with your essay. For additional information on source-based writing, follow the steps in the Quick Start Guide to Integrated Reading and Writing Assignments.

DANGER
BE CAREFUL
WHEN BELT
IS IN MOTION.

THEME | Is Comedy Central?

Comedy has always been a form of entertainment—from the comedy plays of the ancient Greeks to modern film comedies like *Ghostbusters*. Is comedy good for more than giving us a laugh?

We have all heard the adage that laughter is the best medicine, but is this really true? What makes some people hilarious and others not so much? Can those who lack a well-developed sense of humor learn to be funnier? How can we incorporate laughter and humor into our everyday lives?

These are the questions explored by the writers of the four selections that follow. As you read, think about your own experiences. What can you learn from these selections that can help you better understand your world?

AUTHOR AND CONTEXT An assistant professor of communication at Washington State University Vancouver, Brett Oppegaard is an expert in mobile place-based media. In 2012, he received the George and Helen Hartzog Award for his research into mobile application development and media delivery systems within the National Park Service. "Anatomy of a Laugh: Amusing Analysis" appeared in *The Columbian* in September 2006.

PREVIEWING Have pen and paper (or a computer) on hand as you read. Think about the title, and then study the author's biography and the contextual information about the reading. Next, preview the selection. From the information you have gathered, determine the topic. What predictions can you make about the reading's content? Jot down your answers.

READING CRITICALLY AND ANNOTATING As you read, annotate the main idea, the major supporting points, key words, and a few passages that would make good quotations. Either write in your book or make annotations on sticky notes.

As you find key ideas, annotate them. What is the role of laughter in life, according to Oppegaard? How might laughter make a family closer? Note any insights or questions that come to mind as you read.

After reading and annotating, create an information sheet on which you record and organize your annotations as well as your thoughts about the content of the reading.

Teaching Resources: See the Instructor's Manual (IM) for instructions to set up this assignment in Connect IRW. Alternatively, this reading assignment and the writing prompts that follow have been pre-loaded into the Connect IRW *Common Places* Master Course.

Anatomy of a Laugh: Amusing Analysis BY BRETT OPPEGAARD

Lexile: 1160L

1. When Glynda and Pat Hamilton celebrated their 38th wedding anniversary recently, Pat gave his wife a dozen roses. He told her those were for the 12 good years.

2. The Vancouver couple have been in Texas much of the summer, helping Pat's ill 91-year-old mother, Kathrin. During their stay, Glynda was giving her mother-in-law a sponge bath, when the matriarch quipped, "I bet when you and Pat came down the hall to tell us you were engaged, you didn't know you would be doing this."

3. In the Hamilton household, Glynda says, humor is the preferred method of handling most situations—no matter how joyous or difficult. Such an approach has changed their lives, and Glynda has become a modern mirth missionary, joining a growing chorus of people who think humor is hardly trivial.

4. As scientists amass quantifiable evidence of the health benefits of laughter, humor-based social organizations such as the Laughter Club are rapidly gaining members. It all plays into the Mark Twain remark: "The human race has only one really effective weapon and that is laughter."

5. A broad social movement in support of such an idea started about a decade ago in a public park in Bombay. Dr. Madan Kataria, a physician in India, noticed that his more jovial patients seemed to heal faster and stay healthier. So he went to a park and simply stood around with a few people and told jokes.

6. The program he developed around that concept combines laughter and childish exercises with gentle breathing and other yoga techniques. The first club to practice this technique had five people. Today, there are reportedly more than 5,000 of these clubs of various sizes throughout the world—in [places] such as Australia, France, Switzerland, Hungary, Singapore, Hong Kong and Dubai—including 2,000 American organizations, with both Portland and Vancouver in the fold. The movement's Mecca, Matlani Garden in India, now hosts eight laughter sessions a day, year-round, starting as early as 5:45 a.m. and lasting until after 7 p.m.

Mecca: the holiest city in Islam. The term is used figuratively here to mean a place of geographic importance to the movement.

7. Glynda Hamilton, the local proponent of the idea, has been preaching a lighter perspective on life for a long time, she says. But being certified as a laughter leader through the international group, plus the experiences she has had making people around her laugh, has inspired her to take her quirky sense of humor to the masses. The Hamiltons, who are retired, now are trying to sell their east Vancouver house to spend the next few months driving cross-country in a motor home. Glynda wants to stop along the way in Wal-Mart parking lots and make even more people laugh.

8. This idea has gone well beyond a trivial whim, she says. Academics and scientists in the fields of humor and laughter have been gradually revolutionizing alternative medicine.

9. One of the top physicians in the field is Lee Berk, associate director of the Center for Neuroimmunology and an associate research professor of pathology and human anatomy in the school of medicine at Loma Linda University in California.

Neuroimmunology: a branch of science that deals with connections between the brain and immunity.

10. He and colleagues have gathered numerous studies over the years that indicate tangible benefits of humor and laughter in such areas as cardiac rehabilitation, pain perception, discomfort thresholds, coping with stress and boosting immune systems. Research also shows that laughter goes beyond muscular and vocal behavior, according to work by Berk and others.

"We seek humor and laughter because it feels good," Berk says. "It feels good 11 because it's triggering the entire limbic system."

Like listening to a beloved piece of music, humor ignites activity throughout the 12 mind and body as it is interpreted by the brain. Blood flow increases. Positive hormones and endorphins are released. Energy grows, and negative chemicals, interpreted as stress, are suppressed.

Endorphin: a chemical in the brain that, when released, produces pleasant feelings.

"The joy of the world can't be experienced at the same time as the pain," says 13 Steven Sultanoff of Pepperdine University in Malibu, Calif. The psychologist has been incorporating therapeutic humor into his work for 20 years. He says that the clearly established connection between negative thinking and poor health has convinced him that the opposite is true.

Sultanoff says that he's not naturally a funny person but that he works on his 14 humor capacity, like honing any other skill. He watches comedies. He reads jokes. He carries around props, such as a clown nose, wind-up toys and an Elvis Presley driver's license. When a clerk asks him for identification, he gives that mock card, then a few seconds later quips, "You didn't say it had to be mine."

He suggests to clients that they dedicate a portion of each day to being funny. 15

"Medical science is starting to get serious about positive emotions," Berk says. 16 "For the most part, medical care is concerned with disease and dysfunction. Not about the positive stuff. But the public increasingly has been demanding that we look at those things that are good for us. Things that keep us healthy, well and happy."

He adds, "Religion and spirituality have some health benefits. Optimists versus 17 pessimists. Happiness versus sadness. There's a biology involved, and it appears that humor and laughter are significant components in keeping things in balance."

Glynda Hamilton says she instinctively used comedy as a coping technique while 18 growing up. Her father's Air Force career moved their family 12 times before Glynda graduated from high school, constantly making her the new kid in class.

"'We laugh to survive' has been my motto for years," she says. 19

That kind of attitude has been particularly helpful in dealing with the deteriora- 20 tion of Glynda's elderly mother-in-law. After a sponge bath recently, Kathrin perked up and told Glynda that she had just needed to be watered. When Kathrin does arm exercises, the family jokes that she's building her bust. She had a double mastectomy years ago.

After Glynda's children were born, she started keeping a journal of everyday hap- 21 penings on her calendars. The Hamiltons now look those over and laugh together about the notes every Thanksgiving.

Glynda recalls that her son TJ, at 5, told her that all he wanted for Christmas was 22 to be an only child. When she told him that she couldn't do that, he asked to be a foster child. Glynda told him she would work on it.

Daughter Stacia, when she was in high school, asked if she could help with dinner. 23 Glynda told her to boil some carrots, and when she did, Glynda heard the teen saying softly over the pot, "Hey, you sexy little carrots. You're really looking hot tonight."

When TJ was in high school, he was being lectured by Glynda about his behavior 24 when he told her, "I've never done anything as bad as what Dad did when he was a teenager." So Glynda turned to Pat, still shaking her finger, and said, "Quit telling him what (you) did as a teenager."

Glynda was visiting Stacia in Florida a couple of years ago when she heard about 25 a three-day Laughter Club certification that was taking place in a nearby city. So she enrolled. Now she's become one of the group's advocates. She's led dozens of free sessions throughout Clark County [Washington] at churches, family reunions, birthday parties, schools and community festivals.

The first time she taught the techniques in a nursing home, about a year ago in 26 Brush Prairie, Glynda encouraged everyone to get involved. That included a feeble woman with a walker and oxygen tank. By the end of the session, the elderly woman was standing and clapping her hands and laughing. She made sure to thank Glynda afterward, and that appreciation resonated.

"When I believe in something, I want to share," Glynda says. "And it's fun. . . . It's 27 the way of getting away from thinking about whatever it is that's bringing you down. The stresses of life. Or the pains of the body. If you can find a way to laugh, it can pull you out of that. It can bring you up."

Using Your Annotations

Use your annotations and key words to write a one-page summary of the reading. In your summary, identify the writer's thesis statement, the major supporting points, the support for the major supporting points, and any other information needed to complete the summary.

Thinking about the Text

1. What is the main idea of this article?
2. Explain the relationship between humor and health, according to Oppegaard.
3. Why might someone be interested in joining a "laughter club"?
4. Why is the medical community interested in researching the role that laughter plays in our lives?
5. What does laughter add to the lives of Glynda and Pat Hamilton, according to the article?

The Writer's Techniques

1. Look at your annotations. Which of the following types of supporting details does Oppegaard use—comparison and contrast, cause and effect, definition, process analysis, classification, or illustration?
2. Find two or three anecdotes the writer uses to illustrate points about humor. As a reader, what effect did the use of anecdotes have on you?
3. The writer uses quotes from both experts and ordinary people. Would his essay be better if he had *not* included quotes from ordinary people? Explain your answer.

Brief-Response Assignments

1. Write a paragraph about why having a sense of humor can be advantageous.
2. What do Glynda and Pat Hamilton believe about the humor in their lives?
3. Since humor is so important in health and healing, why do you suppose doctors do not typically prescribe it as a form of treatment? Explain your answer.

Essay Assignments

1. The author quotes Steven Sultanoff as saying, "The joy of the world can't be experienced at the same time as the pain." Write an essay in which you explain the meaning of this quote. Consider using illustrations to assist your explanation.
2. In what ways can a sense of humor add value to one's life? Write about at least three ways that humor enriches our lives.
3. According to the article, humor and laughter help keep your health in balance. Write an essay in which you present methods for incorporating humor into one's life. If you use ideas from the reading, give credit to the source.

Connect IRW Writing Assignments: You may assign any of these essay prompts in Connect IRW; the toolset supports options such as assigning peer review or building your own rubric to gather reporting around student writing outcomes.

AUTHOR AND CONTEXT Vicki Haddock is a staff writer for the *San Francisco Chronicle*. "What Makes Us Laugh—And Why?" appeared in the June 10, 2007, issue of the *San Francisco Chronicle*.

PREVIEWING Have pen and paper (or a computer) on hand as you read. Think about the title, and then study the author's biography and the contextual information about the reading. Next, preview the selection. From the information you have gathered, determine the topic. What predictions can you make about the reading's content? Jot down your answers.

READING CRITICALLY AND ANNOTATING As you read, annotate the main idea, the major supporting points, key words, and a few passages that would make good quotations. Either write in your book or make annotations on sticky notes.

As you find key ideas, annotate them. Have you ever found something incredibly funny, only to show it to a friend who failed to see the humor? What makes certain things funny to certain people? Think about these questions as you read the selection. Note any insights or questions that come to mind.

After reading and annotating, create an information sheet on which you record and organize your annotations as well as your thoughts about the content of the reading.

Teaching Resources: See the Instructor's Manual (IM) for instructions to set up this assignment in Connect IRW. Alternatively, this reading assignment and the writing prompts that follow have been pre-loaded into the Connect IRW Common Places Master Course.

What Makes Us Laugh—And Why? Scientists Delve into Our Brains to Figure Out Funny BY VICKI HADDOCK

Lexile: 1180L

What does it take to be funny? [1]

The question is simple, but the answer is not, as attested to by legions of scientists trying to pinpoint the brain's "laugh zone" and decipher how wit works. [2]

Consider this snippet from recent Stanford research: "Our analysis showed extroversion to positively correlate with humor-drive blood oxygenation level-dependent signal in discrete regions of the right orbital frontal cortex, ventrolateral prefrontal cortex, and bilateral temporal cortices. Introversion correlated with increased activation in several regions, most prominently the bilateral amygdala . . ." [3]

On second thought, perhaps E. B. White was onto something when he once noted that analyzing humor is like dissecting a frog. The procedure kills the essence of both the frog and the funny—and then what's the point? [4]

But humor research remains a fast-growing area of inquiry, with neurologists mapping areas of the brain that oxygenate to register and respond to puns, slapstick and other forms of wit. The solution potentially carries a big payoff: Social scientists and surveyors have long documented that people who are perceived as witty, clever and funny are destined for popularity and greater success in work and relationships. [5]

A sense of humor may indeed be the most necessary ingredient to transform a romantic attraction into a flourishing long-term relationship, but research published last year in the journal *Evolution and Human Behavior* found a distinction. Women say they want someone who makes them laugh. Men say they want someone whom they can make laugh. [6]

A survey released by the Menlo Park temp agency Robert Half International found that 91 percent of top executives surveyed consider humor important to career advancement. [7]

What's more, scientists report that a robust sense of humor speeds healing and reduces the risk of suicide, depression and heart disease. It is humanity's ultimate coping mechanism, the lubricant that smooths the abrasive frictions of modern life. [8]

E. B. White: an American writer, who co-authored The Elements of Style as well as the amusing children's stories Charlotte's Web and Stuart Little.

Scientists map the brain by using a functional MRI (fMRI) machine, which shows which parts of the brain receive oxygen and thus "light up" when provoked. For example, an fMRI will show that when a person laughs at a particular type of joke, a certain location of the brain receives oxygen and appears lit on a computer screen readout.

A thriving International Society for Humor Studies . . . defines itself as a "scholarly   9
and professional organization dedicated to the advancement of humor research,"
and routinely solicits proposals for studies and papers on what prompts the teeth-
revealing curvature of the naso-labial furrows (what we call a smile) and the way
neural-path action triggers the involuntary expulsion of air and sound (otherwise
known as a laugh).

For anyone who had trouble following all that neurological nomenclature, fear   10
not. You can purchase humor how-to for lay people from the late TV host Steve Allen
and the late science fiction writer Isaac Asimov, as well as creators of *Saturday Night
Live* sketches. The market overflows with books, tapes and seminars purporting to
teach everyday people how to be funny.

But is such a thing really possible? Can people "learn" humor? Can it be reduced   11
to its essence and bottled for mass consumption? Is humor really a science, or something more ephemeral?

Perhaps you can no more teach yourself to be witty than you can teach yourself   12
to fall in love. Maybe a sense of humor is akin to a sense of rhythm: You either got it
or you ain't. The task of harnessing humor is daunting, calling to mind the classic Bob
Monkhouse line: "They all laughed when I said I wanted to be a comedian. They're
not laughing now . . ."

But there is hope for the seemingly witless, insists Malcolm Kushner of Santa   13
Cruz, a humor consultant, Webmaster of an online humor museum and author of
Public Speaking for Dummies.

"This is the most common question I get, and I've always hedged by saying that   14
everyone can learn to better communicate the sense of humor they already have," he
said. "Actually, I've never met anyone who didn't think they had a sense of humor.
Most people have had the experience of writing off someone they know as completely humorless—unfortunately this is usually their boss—and then one day they'll
say something funny or laugh, and everyone around them immediately re-evaluates
the whole situation.

"Not everybody is born hilarious. There's Robin Williams and Jonathan Winters   15
and then there's the rest of us. But we all can learn some specific techniques to make
the most of the sense of humor we have."

As the human brain develops into adulthood, studies suggest, it comes to appre-   16
ciate different kinds of jokes, which are processed in different parts of the brain.

Using a functional MRI—a brain scan that takes rapid-fire images of the brain to   17
reflect activity—researchers at York University in Toronto and the Institute of Neurol-
ogy in London observed reactions to two kinds of jokes. Half were "semantic," such
as "Why don't sharks bite lawyers? Professional courtesy." The other half were puns,
such as "Why did the golfer wear two pairs of pants? He had a hole in one."

The unexpected results, published in the journal *Nature Neuroscience,* were   18
that semantic jokes activated a bilateral network in the temporal lobes, whereas
the puns used areas only on the left side, around the brain's headquarters for
speech-production.

But either way, if people found the joke funny, it invariably activated the same   19
"funny zone" in the brain: the medial ventral prefrontal cortex. The funnier they
found the joke, the more that area of the brain lit up like a pinball machine.

So scientists are refining their understanding of how humor works—the impor-   20
tance of incongruity (Dave Barry: "Never take a sleeping pill and a laxative on the

same night."), shifting point of view (Paul Klee: "A line is a dot that went for a walk."), revelations of unspoken truth (George Carlin: "Why is it that anyone who drives slower than you is an idiot and anyone who drives faster is a maniac?") and the defusing of anxiety (Rita Rudner: "Those oxygen masks on airplanes? I don't think there's really any oxygen. I think they're just to muffle the screams.").

But science is nowhere near distilling the formula for funny. For that, we are left   21
with humor consultants, who offer these tips:

One: Share funny stories from your own life experience. We all have a few weird   22
relatives, haywire vacations and other wacky experiences along life's trajectory.

A long-suffering mother of three, for example, might share how she agreed to   23
let her toddler use her ChapStick as long as he replaced it every time. Weeks later, she was mortified to discover him meticulously rubbing her ChapStick to the family cat's butt. Pointing, he declared, "Chapped." Nothing left for her to do but decide whether to ask if this was the first time her ChapStick had been applied to the cat's butt . . . or the hundredth.

Two: Use your wry tales to make a larger point. Kushner tells of a previously   24
humor-challenged computer programmer who learned to deliver speeches that opened with a tale of his weird uncle daring tipsy relatives at family gatherings to insert large objects into their mouths. After describing in detail how a family member had to be rushed to the ER with a sawed-off bedpost stuck in his mouth, the program-mer could make a serious point, such as "Don't bite off more than you can chew."

Three: Follow the "rule of threes." For some reason, there's something magic about   25
triples. Comedy Professor and author Melvin Helitzer characterizes them as firecrackers on the way to a big blast. His example: "My wife's an angel: She's constantly up in the air, continually harping on something and never has anything to wear."

Four: Humor requires a target. If you make a bull's-eye out of someone weaker,   26
particularly if you initiate the attack, you come off like a bully. Far better to take aim at the powerful and mighty—and better still for someone else to make you a target first. "Then it is lunge-and-riposte," Asimov observed, "and at the riposte we can laugh with a clear conscience."

But the best strategy of all is to make yourself a target. As all successful politicians   27
know, the most effective way to disarm a potential weapon against you is to use it first. One such turnaround was executed by former President Ronald Reagan's wife, Nancy, who decided to neutralize caustic criticism about her extravagant spending after being photographed on a trip to England wearing 15 couture outfits. After she appeared at a press dinner dressed in rags and belted out a parody of "Second Hand Rose," her approval ratings rebounded.

Five: Know your audience. Crude, stereotypical, sexist jokes can be oh so unfunny.   28
Just ask Chevron Corp., which was ordered to pay $2.2 million in damages after four female workers sued over male co-workers' circulation of an e-mail joke that began "25 reasons why beer is better than women . . ."

Six: If you regularly find yourself in an awkward conversation, have a funny   29
response prepared. Waiters who know they will occasionally screw up orders, sin-gle people who are routinely interrogated about whether they're ever going to get married, defense attorneys who are asked how they can possibly defend a guilty client—all could save themselves trouble with a ready-to-go retort. As old comedians advise, the best ad libs are written down in advance.

Using Your Annotations

Use your annotations and key words to write a one-page summary of the reading. In your summary, identify the writer's thesis statement, the major supporting points, the support for the major supporting points, and any other information needed to complete the summary.

Thinking about the Text

1. Can people develop their ability to be funny, or is the gift of making others laugh something people are born with? Explain what the article says.
2. In what ways is humor an important part of career advancement?
3. For what purpose did Haddock write this article? For whom did she write it? Explain your answer.
4. What do you think the writer means when she writes that humor is "humanity's ultimate coping mechanism"?
5. Do you think the writer believes it is wise to spend money on humor research? Use passages from the article to explain your answer.

The Writer's Techniques

1. How does Haddock introduce her essay? Is her method of introduction effective?
2. The writer uses several examples of different types of jokes in this essay. How do these examples help the reader understand what Haddock is trying to say?
3. Did you understand the scientific information presented in the essay? If so, what writing techniques did the author use to help you understand it? If not, how could she have improved her explanation of the neuroscience?

Brief-Response Assignments

1. Haddock says that "humor requires a target." What advice does she give about choosing a target for humor?
2. The writer provides scientific information about how humor affects the brain and body. Why should readers care about the physical effects of humor?
3. How can a person develop a better sense of humor?

Essay Assignments

1. According to the article, "people who are perceived as witty, clever and funny are destined for popularity and greater success in work and relationships." Write an essay discussing what it means to *not* be funny. What impact do you think a lack of humor might have on one's relationships or career or other aspects of one's life?
2. Social scientists have determined that humor is an important part of a romantic relationship. Why does humor play a part in romantic relationships? Write an essay in which you answer this question. Consider interviewing couples who have stayed together a long time. Ask them about the role of humor in their lives together.
3. Analyze the humor of a popular comedian. What makes this person funny? Which elements of humor does the person use? Haddock mentions four: incongruity, shifting point of view, revelations of unspoken truth, and the defusing of anxiety. Write an essay in which you discuss the kind of humor the comedian uses and why he or she is successful. ↻

Connect IRW Writing Assignments: You may assign any of these essay prompts in Connect IRW; the toolset supports options such as assigning peer review or building your own rubric to gather reporting around student writing outcomes.

AUTHOR AND CONTEXT Tait Trussell has written for *The Wall Street Journal, The Saturday Evening Post, Congressional Quarterly, Nation's Business,* and *FrontPage.* He was vice president of the American Enterprise Institute, a Washington public policy think tank, and served on the Bicentennial Commission on the Constitution. "Healing Humor" appeared in the July/August 2008 edition of *The Saturday Evening Post.*

PREVIEWING Have pen and paper (or a computer) on hand as you read. Think about the title, and then study the author's biography and the contextual information about the reading. Next, preview the selection. From the information you have gathered, determine the topic. What predictions can you make about the reading's content? Jot down your answers.

READING CRITICALLY AND ANNOTATING As you read, annotate the main idea, the major supporting points, key words, and a few passages that would make good quotations. Either write in your book or make annotations on sticky notes.

As you find key ideas, annotate them. Why is Trussell interested in humor? In what aspects of humor is he most intrigued? Note any questions that come to mind as you read.

After reading and annotating, create an information sheet on which you record and organize your annotations as well as your thoughts about the content of the reading.

Teaching Resources: See the Instructor's Manual (IM) for instructions to set up this assignment in Connect IRW. Alternatively, this reading assignment and the writing prompts that follow have been pre-loaded into the Connect IRW *Common Places* Master Course.

Healing Humor BY TAIT TRUSSELL

Lexile: 1030L

Research is showing that laughter is good medicine. 1

It was a remarkable case, a generation or so ago. Norman Cousins, the editor and researcher, found laughter to be a cure for a serious disease he had contracted. 2

Cousins was editor of *The Saturday Review of Literature*. He was diagnosed in 1964 with spondylitis, an acute inflammation of the spine. He was given only a few months to live. Cousins was sure that negative thoughts can cause illness. So, he reasoned that positive thoughts could have the opposite effect. 3

He left the hospital and checked into a hotel where he watched humorous movies and shows. He found that 10 minutes of hearty laughter resulted in at least two hours of pain-free sleep. He continued this "treatment" until he recovered. He wrote a widely read book about his amazing recovery. 4

But he was not the first to believe in laughter as a form of medication. A French surgeon, Henri de Mondeville, in the 13th century wrote: "Let the surgeon take care to regulate the whole patient's life for job and happiness, allowing his relatives and special friends to cheer him, and by having someone tell him jokes." 5

"No man who has heartily and wholly laughed can be altogether irreclaimably depraved," quipped the Scottish essayist Thomas Carlyle, using humor to praise that ability of practically the only species that can laugh—humans. 6

Stanford School of Medicine studies have reported that the average kindergarten student laughs 300 times a day. But adults average only 17 laughs a day. You might say: "We don't stop laughing because we grow old. We grow old because we stop laughing." 7

When we laugh our heads off, changes occur in many parts of our body. Some people slap their knee, as if to hurt themselves to restrain the laughter. Others double up, as if in pain. 8

We love to laugh, especially at the antics of our children or grandchildren or dogs, as well as the telling and retelling of tales of bygone years, some of the crazy things we did as youngsters. 9

People are much more likely to laugh in social settings than when they are alone, even watching a funny TV program. 10

Those of us who have several decades of marriage can appreciate such jokes as the one about the couple who went to counseling after 35 years of marriage. The wife went into a tirade. There was no intimacy, an emptiness, a loneliness, she lamented. 11

The therapist finally got up, asked the woman to stand, embraced her and kissed her passionately. The therapist then turned to the husband and said: "This is what your wife needs at least three times a week. Can you do this?" 12

The husband thought for a moment, then replied: "Well, I can drop her off here 13 on Mondays and Wednesdays. But on Fridays, I'm busy playing golf."

Laughter is said to rid us of tension, stress, anger, anxiety, grief, and depression. 14 Something like crying, in a way, laughter releases our pent-up emotions. Someone said a person devoid of a sense of humor is like a car without shock absorbers. Laughter is said to release endorphins, which relieve pain. Endorphins are neurotransmitters in the brain. Humor is supposed to integrate both hemispheres of the brain. The left hemisphere helps decipher the verbal part of a joke. The right hemisphere determines whether it is funny.

Medical researchers have discovered that laughter also boosts your immune 15 system. The study of this subject is gaining more and more attention as we try to understand mind-body relationships.

According to a study by cardiologists at the University of Maryland Medical Center 16 in Baltimore, laughter, plus an active sense of humor, can help guard you against a heart attack. The study, said Dr. Michael Miller, "has recently shown for the first time that laughter is linked to healthy functioning of blood vessels. The old saying that laughter is the best medicine definitely appears to be true when it comes to protecting your heart."

He added, "We don't know yet why laughing protects the heart; but we know 17 mental stress is associated with impairment of the endothelium, the protective barrier lining our blood vessels. This can cause a series of inflammatory reactions that lead to fat and cholesterol build-up in the coronary arteries and ultimately to a heart attack."

Dr. Miller said his study showed that people with heart disease responded less 18 humorously to everyday life situations. They laughed less, he said, and generally displayed more anger and hostility.

"The ability to laugh—either naturally or as a learned behavior—may have impor- 19 tant implications . . . in the U.S. where heart disease remains the number-one killer."

In a study published in the *Journal of Holistic Nursing,* patients were told funny 20 one-liners after surgery and before pain medication was administered. Those who were exposed to humor said they felt less pain, compared with patients who didn't get a dose of humor as part of their therapy.

At Loma Linda University in California, Dr. Lee Berk and his fellow researcher, 21 Dr. Stanley Tan, have studied the effects of laughter on the immune system. They have found that laughter lowers blood pressure, reduces stress hormones, increases muscle flexibility, and boosts the immune function. It does this by raising the levels of infection-fighting proteins and cells that produce disease-destroying antibodies.

A good belly-laugh seems to tell the immune systems to "turn it up a notch." The 22 results of the study also supported research indicating a decrease in hormones that constrict blood vessels and suppress immune activity. These decreased in the study group exposed to humor.

For instance, levels of epinephrine were lower in the group both in anticipation 23 of humor and after being exposed to humor.

In addition, the researchers said that laughing is aerobic, providing a workout for 24 the diaphragm and increasing the lungs' ability to use oxygen in a positive manner.

You might say that: "He who laughs . . . lasts." 25

Using Your Annotations

Use your annotations and key words to write a one-page summary of the reading. In your summary, identify the writer's thesis statement, the major supporting points, the support for the major supporting points, and any other information needed to complete the summary.

Thinking about the Text

1. What is Trussell's main idea? What support does he use as evidence for his main idea?
2. What is the connection between laughter and health?
3. Explain one physical process that occurs when we laugh.
4. According to the writer, can humorless people learn to laugh?
5. What does the story of Norman Cousins suggest?

The Writer's Techniques

1. What is Trussell's tone in this essay? Is it serious, scientific, or something else?
2. To support his point, the writer uses scientific information, personal stories, and historical information. Which types of support do you believe most effectively help him make his case? Why?
3. Does the writer use statistics as a type of support? Explain.

Brief-Response Assignments

1. Write a paragraph discussing one way in which laughter can affect one's health.
2. What was the most surprising insight you gained from this essay? Explain.
3. What are some practical things a person can do to increase the amount of laughter in his or her life, according to Trussell?

Essay Assignments

1. Write an essay in which you argue that laughter is serious medicine, so "laughter therapy" should be covered by health-care plans as a medical expense. Provide support for your assertion.
2. Consider these sentences from the essay: "Laughter is said to rid us of tension, stress, anger, anxiety, grief, and depression. Something like crying, in a way, laughter releases our pent-up emotions." Choose three or four of the benefits of laughter, and discuss them in an essay.
3. Imagine a friend has been diagnosed with heart disease and needs to make some serious—and difficult—changes in his lifestyle, such as eating a healthier diet and exercising more often. Write an essay about the ways he can add humor to his life as another method for controlling heart disease. Provide practical suggestions. ↻

Connect IRW Writing Assignments: You may assign any of these essay prompts in Connect IRW; the toolset supports options such as assigning peer review or building your own rubric to gather reporting around student writing outcomes.

AUTHOR AND CONTEXT   Phillip Perry is a freelance writer based in New York City. "Laughter in the Workplace" appeared in the March 2005 issue of *Focus: Journal for Respiratory Care and Sleep Medicine*.

PREVIEWING   Have pen and paper (or a computer) on hand as you read. Think about the title, and then study the author's biography and the contextual information about the reading. Next, preview the selection. From the information you have gathered, determine the topic. What predictions can you make about the reading's content? Jot down your answers.

READING CRITICALLY AND ANNOTATING   As you read, annotate the main idea, the major supporting points, key words, and a few passages that would make good quotations. Either write in your book or make annotations on sticky notes.

As you find key ideas, annotate them. Why is laughter in the workplace so important? Why are some employers afraid to introduce laughter and fun into the workplace? Note any questions or insights that come to mind as you read.

Teaching Resources: See the Instructor's Manual (IM) for instructions to set up this assignment in Connect IRW. Alternatively, this reading assignment and the writing prompts that follow have been pre-loaded into the Connect IRW *Common Places* Master Course.

After reading and annotating, create an information sheet on which you record and organize your annotations as well as your thoughts about the content of the reading.

Laughter in the Workplace   BY PHILLIP PERRY

Lexile: 1000L

Work, especially patient care, is no laughing matter, right? That's the common wisdom. But managers everywhere are discovering something else: Some lighthearted play at work can boost the bottom line of morale and productivity.   1

"Humor is a great management tool," says Jeff Slutsky, president of Fighter Marketing in Columbus, Ohio. "It's a critical technique for increasing employee morale, productivity and effectiveness in communication."   2

How so? For starters, says Slutsky, laughter can defuse tense or sensitive situations. It can relieve the stress that often drains energy and restrains productivity. It can help people feel less threatened about sharing their ideas, thus invigorating the creative process, and laughter can help employees retain information longer and apply it better. "It's been proven in studies that when a teacher uses humor four to five times an hour the students like the teacher more, retain their knowledge longer and are more willing to do as they are told," says Allen Klein, president of the Association for Applied and Therapeutic Humor, Princeton, NJ. "Now translate that to the workplace. The fact is that laughter helps people think more clearly and do better work." Humor is especially effective in reaching certain people who might not respond to standard management approaches.   3

Suppose your own workplace is more gloom and doom than laughter and light. How can you encourage your employees to lighten up? Before answering that, let's pause for a caveat: Some individuals may feel threatened by any overt attempt to introduce humor into their environment. "People get very nervous about the potential for politically incorrect and racist and sexist humor," warns Robert Shaw, Professor Emeritus of Psychology and Education at the University of Wisconsin–La Crosse. Not only that, but the abstract concept of "humor" can be a difficult one for people to understand in practical ways.   4

A much better approach, says Shaw, is to encourage your employees to engage in behaviors that represent humor: "Focus on laughter and joy and fun."   5

Start by establishing a "fun committee" of volunteers. "I teach managers to put people in small groups and ask one simple question: 'What activities would you suggest to increase joy and laughter in the workplace?'" To get the ball rolling encourage the group members to identify the parts of their jobs that make their work experiences less than positive. Then find ways to use humor to lessen the negative impact of those activities.   6

Encouraging this kind of "group think" is smart for several reasons. First, people will develop more effective ideas by brainstorming than by thinking alone. Second, with peer support, individuals will gain the courage to introduce outrageous ideas.   7

Last but not least, by laughing together the group members will learn an important lesson: Humor is very often less about jokes and more about social interaction. Indeed, improving employee relationships and communications is one of the most productive results of a joyful workplace.   8

Laughter's great, but make sure everyone stays within the bounds of good taste. "Early on I'd make sure everyone knows the rules or guidelines of what they're   9 not allowed to do," cautions Slutsky. "You can't encourage people to use humor then reprimand them when it goes too far and still expect them to put a humorous effort forward."

And the rules are? First, be prudent. Too much humor can backfire. "There are 10 many serious parts of health care delivery," says Slutsky. "A manager who uses humor all the time will eventually not be taken seriously. It works best when you pick and choose the most appropriate times to use humor."

Second, humor has to be of the positive kind. "No sexual, off color, or racial humor, 11 under any circumstances," says Slutsky. "Even if someone is laughing on the outside, you still might have hurt their feelings. Plus, it can be illegal." Don't target other people for humor. "You should be the brunt of your jokes, not coworkers or customers."

A sense of humor is subjective, says Slutsky. And it's a tough thing to teach if 12 someone doesn't have the knack. But keeping vigilant watch and consulting with individuals who cross the line will keep things from getting out of hand.

Boss Clown

When it comes to job behavior, employees take cues from their bosses. Indeed, sour-puss 13 supervisors are very often the cause of poor employee attitudes. "The shame is that managers usually shun laughter," says Steve Rizzo, a Wading River, N.Y. based speaker and consultant who helps business organizations promote workplace humor. "They believe that employees who are laughing are not getting their work done. That's far from true."

Set the example for your employees by being an individual who uses productive, 14 non-threatening humor. Klein suggests starting a meeting with a joke or a cartoon.

One final caveat. Avoid pressuring reluctant employees to hop aboard the laugh- 15 ter bandwagon. "Mandatory policies generally fail," says Shaw. "Don't make any fun activity a job requirement." The good news is that people who resist fun activities often come around over time.

Productive Employees

The tips in this article can help you establish a more joyful workplace. The greatest 16 benefit of humor, perhaps, is the improved morale that helps your employees work together more enthusiastically, deal more productively with patients and colleagues and develop creative solutions to problems.

Finally, consider this bonus: Humor will help you and your employees deal with 17 the inevitable crises that occur in your organization and in your department. "The most important thing in the workplace is how you cope with challenge," says Klein. "If you can find something to laugh about in a situation you get a different perspective and do your job better. Humor can help you maintain balance when the going gets tough."

—○○○—

Using Your Annotations

Use your annotations and key words to write a one-page summary of the reading. In your summary, identify the writer's thesis statement, the major supporting points, the support for the major supporting points, and any other information needed to complete the summary.

Thinking about the Text

1. What is the main idea of this article?
2. According to the article, why is humor a "great management tool"?
3. What risks does a manager run by incorporating humor into the workplace?
4. Perry claims that humor in the workplace results in greater productivity. How can this be? Explain.
5. The writer suggests that a "bonus" results if a manager intentionally includes humor in the workplace. What is that "bonus"? Explain.

The Writer's Techniques

1. Who do you think Perry's audience is for this essay? How do you know? Explain.
2. The writer gave a lot of advice, but he did not use many illustrations. Where might the writer have inserted illustrations showing humor used in a business setting? How might illustrations have changed your reading experience?
3. What text pattern or patterns does the writer use to present the information? How can you tell?

Brief-Response Assignments

1. Write a paragraph discussing how encouraging a culture of "laughter and joy and fun" might have both positive and negative consequences for a business.
2. Reflect on your work experiences (either working at a job or with family members on tasks). Write a paragraph on a work experience that was either pleasant because of humor while working or unpleasant because of a lack of humor and fun. Describe your experience and how you felt about the work you were doing.
3. Is humor a *necessary* part of a productive work environment? Explain your answer.

Essay Assignments

1. Write an essay describing the positive benefits that might be achieved by incorporating humor into the workplace. If you use ideas from the reading, give credit to the source.
2. The writer says, "Humor is very often less about jokes and more about social interaction." Write an essay in which you explain and discuss at least three ways in which humor aids social interaction. Use illustrations to demonstrate your point.
3. Think of a class, a job, or a work experience (perhaps with family members) in which you experienced fun and laughter. Now think of a class, job, or work experience that included no laughter. Write a comparison and contrast essay in which you discuss the effects of both experiences. ↻

Connect IRW Writing Assignments: You may assign any of these essay prompts in Connect IRW; the toolset supports options such as assigning peer review or building your own rubric to gather reporting around student writing outcomes.

THEMATIC ASSIGNMENT

Use the readings in this thematic unit to write an essay that answers one of the following questions.

a. Write an essay in which your goal is to convince people with serious illnesses to include laughter as a part of the healing process. Use evidence from the sources in this thematic unit, making sure you give credit appropriately.

b. What role does laughter serve in families? Write an essay explaining your answer. Use the essays in this thematic unit to answer this question. Add to your knowledge by interviewing three families and asking them to explain the role of laughter in their lives.

c. What kinds of things make people laugh? In other words, why are certain things funny? Write an essay in which you classify types of laughter. Provide explanations and examples for each type.

Teaching Resources: See the IM for suggestions of other readings within Connect IRW Power of Process that may be used with this theme.

d. Select a situation in which you have not experienced or might not expect to experience much humor and laughter. For example, in some college classes, there is little humor. Some work environments seem not to lend themselves to humor and laughter. Write an essay explaining what the effects would be if humor became a part of the environment. Explain at least three effects that might result from infusing humor into the scene.

Be sure to cite any sources from which you obtain ideas or quotes. Include a works cited or references page with your essay. For additional information on source-based writing, follow the steps in the Quick Start Guide to Integrated Reading and Writing Assignments.

The American inventor and engineer Charles Franklin Kettering said, "We should all be concerned about the future because we will have to spend the rest of our lives there." What responsibilities do we have, to ourselves and to the rest of the world, to take care of the future?

THEME | Planning for the Future

Mass exterminations, super volcanoes, nuclear holocaust! Is it time to settle down in our bomb shelters, or are we making mountains out of nanobot hills?

In the following selections, you will read about what some people believe the future holds and how we should plan for it. Some of the writers bemoan the advent of technology and fear what future generations of supercomputers may mean for the human race. Other writers are optimistic about our ability to prepare for and handle the challenges of the future. As you read these selections, keep an open mind so you can look at the future in a new way.

nanobot: an incredibly tiny, self-propelled machine. The word is a blend of *nano-* (tiny, literally one-billionth) and *robot.*

AUTHOR AND CONTEXT Cahal Milmo, chief reporter of *The Independent,* has been with the London newspaper since 2000. He was born in London and previously worked at the Press Association news agency. "*Google* Search and Destroy" was published in *The Independent* on December 16, 2013.

PREVIEWING Have pen and paper (or a computer) on hand as you read. Think about the title, and then study the author's biography and the contextual information about the reading. Next, preview the selection. From the information you have gathered, determine the topic. What predictions can you make about the reading's content? Jot down your answers.

READING CRITICALLY AND ANNOTATING As you read, annotate the main idea, the major supporting points, key words, and a few passages that would make good quotations. Either write in your book or make annotations on sticky notes.

As you find key ideas, annotate them. If you think of robots as toys, you will be surprised to learn about how far robotics technology has advanced. As you read, make notes about any questions or insights you have.

After reading and annotating, create an information sheet on which you record and organize your annotations as well as your thoughts about the content of the reading.

Teaching Resources: See the Instructor's Manual (IM) for instructions to set up this assignment in Connect IRW. Alternatively, this reading assignment and the writing prompts that follow have been pre-loaded into the Connect IRW *Common Places* Master Course.

Google Search and Destroy: Rise of the Machines BY CAHAL MILMO

Lexile: 1530L

Big Dog is capable of many things of interest to its new owners at *Google.* What remains to be seen is whether the quadruped robot's ability to pick up a breeze block and hurl it across a warehouse with impressive dexterity and speed is among them. 1

Breeze block: British term for cinder block.

The computer search giant has completed the purchase of Boston Dynamics, the maker of a cutting-edge menagerie of walking and crawling robots including Big Dog, which counts America's Department of Defense (DoD) among its major sources of income. 2

The robotics firm is the eighth company in the same field to be snapped up by *Google* in the past six months under a project headed by Andy Rubin, the executive responsible for turning Android into the world's most widely used smartphone software and whose first love is robots. Mr. Rubin, an engineer by training, last week used Twitter to declare that "the future is looking awesome!" 3

But what is as yet unclear is just to what use *Google,* whose motto is famously "Don't be evil," plans to put its new stable of walking, sprinting and rock-throwing machines. 4

Boston Dynamics has won contracts worth $140m (£86m) since 2000 from the DoD and its agencies. The company boasts that it advises and assists the "US Army, Navy and Marine Corps" on developing "the most advanced robots on earth." By comparison, *Google*'s income from defense work over the same period was $300,000. 5

Experts and campaigners yesterday voiced concern that despite *Google*'s insistence that it does not intend to become a defense contractor, the acquisition of a company with established links to the military might make such work hard to resist in the future. 6

With inventions such as Big Dog, which is primarily designed to carry loads over rough terrain and has the uncanny ability to recover from a human kick, Boston Dynamics could move into the sphere of transporting weaponry rather than producing it. Professor Noel Sharkey, the leading artificial intelligence and robotics expert, based at the University of Sheffield, told *The Independent:* "I would like to think that *Google* will actually use the advanced technology to build an astonishing civil robot—maybe one that can deliver parcels or help in the home. But the multi-million dollar lure of military contracts may push them into the dark side. Let us hope not." 7

The Boston Dynamics deal, for an undisclosed sum, brought inevitable—if overblown—comparisons between *Google* and Skynet, the rogue computer system which manages to wipe out much of humanity in the *Terminator* film series. The robotics company has blazed a trail in producing some extraordinary machines capable of operating in harsh environments, including the Cheetah, which can run at 29 mph—faster than Usain Bolt—and Atlas, a humanoid robot built under a $10.8m deal with the Pentagon's Defense Advanced Research Projects Agency. 8

But rather than hunting down hapless *Homo sapiens* for some sort of robotic genocide, the maker of Atlas and its stablemates insists they are designed to help humanity out of self-inflicted disasters such as the Fukushima nuclear meltdown by working in environments where people would perish. 9

Dr. Marc Raibert, a former professor at the Massachusetts Institute of Technology who became fascinated with re-creating animal biology in mechanical form and 10 founded Boston Dynamics, has insisted his company does not exist to be a military contractor and is motivated by advancing robotics. For his part, Mr. Rubin has described his project as a "moonshot"—the term *Google* applies to its slightly more outlandish schemes, such as self-driving cars and using a network of blimps to bounce Internet signals to remote regions. But while a world of autonomous cars remains some way off, it is likely *Google* is expecting a quicker return on its robotic investments. Amazon has already spent nearly £500m [$852m] on automating its warehouses and announced earlier this month—amid a lot of skepticism about the feasibility of such a scheme—that it is developing delivery drones designed to drop a package on doorsteps for use within the next five years.

11 Amid such accelerating interest in the potential of what Mr. Rubin has described as computers that are "starting to sprout legs," it is likely that *Google* will focus its attentions on manufacturing and logistics, with its first products ready within several years. While it is unclear whether the *Google* robotics venture will sail forth under the name of the mother ship or be hived off as a separate subsidiary, the pattern of spotting an everyday need—such as Internet search—and expanding dynamically to fulfill it may sound familiar.

12 Mr. Rubin told *The New York Times:* "I feel with robotics it's a green field. We're building hardware, we're building software. We're building systems, so one team will be able to understand the whole stack."

13 The question is whether the company avowed to "make money by doing good things" can finesse Big Dog and its brethren sufficiently to assist an old person out shopping or run to a stricken hiker's aid, rather than launching bits of masonry like a siege engine.

Siege engine: an ancient machine, such as a catapult, used to sling stones and other projectiles over fortified walls.

Boston Dynamics: The Brains behind the Beasts

14 They sound like characters from a sci-fi series: SandFlea can leap 30 ft into the air; Big Dog can lug a 340 lb load up steep slopes and muddy trails, moving mammal-like on its four legs; LS3 can do even better, with the strength to shoulder 400 lb cargos; and the tiny claws in RiSE's feet allow it to crawl up walls, trees and fences.

15 But they are, in fact, the eerily agile robotic creations of Boston Dynamics, the Massachusetts-based company that's been snapped up by *Google.* Its roots lie at MIT, where founder Marc Raibert first worked on machines that could mimic the movement of animals. Spun off from the university in 1992, the business has since produced a line-up of robots that can leap and bound with astonishing nimbleness.

MIT: Massachusetts Institute of Technology, a highly respected research university.

16 Though the company doesn't sell its creations to the public, it does upload videos of its robotic army on *YouTube*. One, showing the four-legged Cheetah, a machine that Boston Dynamics says can run faster than Usain Bolt, has been viewed over seven million times. Another, demonstrating the agility of WildCat, a bulkier quadruped that is shown darting around what appears to be a car park, has received close to 15.8 million hits. Among the company's collaborators is the Defense Advanced Research Projects Agency, or DARPA, which was involved in the creation of the Internet.

Car park: British term for *parking lot.*

17 Earlier this year, Boston Dynamics unveiled Atlas, an advanced humanoid robot created for a DARPA-run competition that is meant to spur the development of robots that can help in responding to natural disasters.

18 Mr. Raibert was quizzed about the company's association with the military in 2010, when *The Engineer* magazine asked him if he had any concerns over how his

creations might be deployed in the future. "I'm an engineer who builds robots; I don't know why people would be interested in my views on the ethical question," he replied.

"The big thing is that some people think the designer should be responsible for   19 all possible uses of the system, and others think that the designer is just building a platform and someone else is responsible for the ethics of how it's used. I look at our systems and I say they're vehicles. You could put sacks of rice on them. You could put bullets on them. Their use is to go to places on Earth where you can't put vehicles now—and there are a lot of uses that can be put to."

——————————————————— ⦿⦿⦿ ———————————————————

Using Your Annotations

Use your annotations and key words to write a one-page summary of the reading. In your summary, identify the writer's thesis statement, the major supporting points, the support for the major supporting points, and any other information needed to complete the summary.

Thinking about the Text

1. What are Milmo's main idea and major supporting points?
2. Why are some people concerned with the potential uses of robotics?
3. How might robots help humankind, according to this article?
4. What is the relationship between the military and Boston Dynamics?
5. Based on the information in this essay, explain why a company like *Google* might be interested in robotics.

The Writer's Techniques

1. Is the subject presented in a biased way, or does Milmo attempt to present the information objectively? Explain your answer, using examples from the text as support.
2. How does the essay's title help readers anticipate the content?
3. What is the primary type of support the writer uses in this article? Which text pattern or patterns does the writer use?

Brief-Response Assignments

1. Reread the section called "Boston Dynamics: The Brains behind the Beasts." Write a paragraph to explain how robots could be used for malevolent or criminal purposes.
2. In one or two paragraphs, explain some of the potentially positive uses of robots. Use the article for ideas, and come up with some ideas of your own.
3. When asked about his personal responsibility to create technologies that do no harm, Raibert said he is merely an engineer who builds robots; how people use them is not his concern. Does the person who builds a potentially harmful machine have any responsibility if someone uses that machine for criminal purposes? Write two or three paragraphs defending your point of view.

Essay Assignments

1. If you have never seen one of the robots referred to in this article, go to *YouTube* and do a search for the "Cheetah robot" or the "Big Dog robot." From what you see in the videos and what you have read in this article, do you think there should be rules that govern the things people can program robots to do? Defend your position.
2. How would the use of robots in warfare transform the rules of war? Explain some of the new issues that would arise from using robots, including advantages, disadvantages, and ethical issues.
3. Make a list of the potential evil that robots could do. Make another list of ways robots could help the human race. Compare and contrast your lists and decide whether developing robots is a good idea. Write a paper arguing your position. ↻

Connect IRW Writing Assignments: You may assign any of these essay prompts in Connect IRW; the toolset supports options such as assigning peer review or building your own rubric to gather reporting around student writing outcomes.

AUTHOR AND CONTEXT As a Los Angeles–based journalist and writer, Andrew Gumbel has been a longtime foreign correspondent for British newspapers. After covering the collapse of communism in eastern Europe, the wars in Yugoslavia, and the rise of Silvio Berlusconi in Italy—mostly for *The Independent* of London—he came to the United States in 1998 and has written extensively about politics, the criminal justice system, and pop culture. The following article appeared in *The Independent* in March 2000.

PREVIEWING Have pen and paper (or a computer) on hand as you read. Think about the title, and then study the author's biography and the contextual information about the reading. Next, preview the selection. From the information you have gathered, determine the topic. What predictions can you make about the reading's content? Jot down your answers.

READING CRITICALLY AND ANNOTATING As you read, annotate the main idea, the major supporting points, key words, and a few passages that would make good quotations. Either write in your book or make annotations on sticky notes.

As you find key ideas, annotate them. Which of the issues are you most interested in? Which ones do you think are important enough to prepare for? Make a note of any questions or insights that come to mind as you read.

After reading and annotating, create an information sheet on which you record and organize your annotations as well as your thoughts about the content of the reading.

Teaching Resources: See the Instructor's Manual (IM) for instructions to set up this assignment in Connect IRW. Alternatively, this reading assignment and the writing prompts that follow have been pre-loaded into the Connect IRW *Common Places* Master Course.

Homo Sapiens RIP (or Why One of the Leading Gurus of the Technological Age Believes That the Future Doesn't Need Us) BY ANDREW GUMBEL

Lexile: 1350L

Bill Joy is not a Luddite. He is not afraid of new technology. On the contrary, as chief scientist at Sun Microsystems, the Silicon Valley company that devised JavaScript and countless other Internet-era computer innovations, he has been in the vanguard of the high-tech revolution for more than 20 years: a geek's geek if ever there was one. But recently Joy took a glimpse into the future and it scared him to death.

Luddite: a person who is opposed to technological changes.

What he saw was a world in which humans have been effectively supplanted by machines; a world in which super-powerful computers with at least some attributes of human intelligence manage to replicate themselves and develop their own autonomy; a world in which people become superfluous and risk becoming extinct.

What he saw, in short, was something resembling the nightmare universe of the *Terminator* movies. Previously, Joy had dismissed such scenarios as sci-fi fantasy, but then he listened to his friends who were experts in robotics and realized that this brave new world is much closer than any of us might imagine—as close as 30 years away. What spooked him most was this passage, quoted in a book called *The Age of Spiritual Machines* by the computing innovator Ray Kurzweil: "As society and the problems that face it become more and more complex and machines become more and more intelligent, people will let machines make more of their decisions for them, simply because machine-made decisions will bring better results than man-made ones. Eventually a stage may be reached at which the decisions necessary to keep the system running will be so complex that human beings will be incapable of making them intelligently. At that stage the machines will be in effective control. People won't be able to just turn the machines off, because they will be so dependent on them that turning them off would amount to suicide."

The way Kurzweil's book was laid out, Joy did not know who had written this 4 passage until he had read most of it and found himself nodding in agreement. As he turned the page, however, he realized with a start that the author was Theodore Kaczynski, the notorious Unabomber who so hated technology that he sent mail-bombs to leading scientists to try to deter them from furthering their research. Joy had spent most of his professional career bitterly opposed to everything the Unabomber stood for.

"Kaczynski's actions were murderous and, in my view, criminally insane," Joy 5 writes in a remarkable explanation of his misgivings in this April's *Wired* magazine. "He is clearly a Luddite, but simply saying this does not dismiss his argument; as difficult as it is for me to acknowledge, I saw some merit in the reasoning in this single passage. I felt compelled to confront it."

And confront it he did. The further Joy dug into the cutting edge of research 6 in the new technologies—robotics, genetic engineering and nanotechnology—the more horrified he became. He began thinking about what would happen to the mass of humanity if labor became obsolete (the scenarios he read about ranged from mass extermination, Nazi style, to a world in which most human beings would be reduced to the level of domestic animals). In a book by Hans Moravec, a leading researcher in robotics at Carnegie Mellon University, he read how "in a completely free marketplace . . . robotic industries would compete vigorously among themselves for matter, energy and space, incidentally driving their price beyond human reach. Unable to afford the necessities of life, biological humans would be squeezed out of existence."

Not only did he see scenarios in which robots would take on a life of their own 7 and exterminate the human race, but he began to perceive ways in which other staples of sci-fi horror might come to pass: the ability to download consciousness into a computer and so effectively merge human beings and machines into a new organism; the proliferation of so-called White Plagues, in which malevolent scientists or governments could unleash diseases that would strike widely but selectively; genetically engineered bacteria or plants that could dominate and wipe out existing species.

In fact, Joy argues, the technological age could usher in the same terror of human 8 self-destruction as the nuclear age did 55 years ago, with one crucial difference. While the 20th-century weapons of mass destruction required the sponsorship of governments and highly skilled scientists to become a reality, the nightmares of the 21st century will be accessible to anyone with the educational skills to know how to manipulate them. Joy describes this as the potential for "knowledge-enabled mass destruction."

"We have yet to come to terms with the fact that the most compelling 21st- 9 century technologies . . . pose a different threat than the technologies that have come before," Joy writes. "Specifically, robots, engineered organisms, and nanobots share a dangerous amplifying factor: they can self-replicate. A bomb is blown up only once—but one bot can become many, and quickly get out of control. . . .

"I think it is no exaggeration to say we are on the cusp of the further perfection 10 of extreme evil, an evil whose possibility spreads well beyond that which weapons of mass destruction bequeathed to the nation-states, on to a surprising and terrible empowerment of extreme individuals."

Using Your Annotations

Use your annotations and key words to write a one-page summary of the reading. In your summary, identify the writer's thesis statement, the major supporting points, the support for the major supporting points, and any other information needed to complete the summary.

Thinking about the Text

1. According to this article, what is Bill Joy afraid of?
2. How does Gumbel feel about artificial intelligence? Use portions of the article to identify his fears.
3. Why did Gumbel write this article? For whom did he write it? Explain your answer.
4. Explain what *artificial intelligence* is, based on this article.

The Writer's Techniques

1. What is Gumbel's purpose in writing this article—to inform, analyze, evaluate, or persuade? Explain your answer.
2. How does the writer present Bill Joy as a credible source? What information does he include that demonstrates Joy's credibility?
3. Would the article have been as effective if Gumbel had given the information without presenting Bill Joy's ideas? Explain.

Brief-Response Assignments

1. Why was Bill Joy reluctant to recognize the insights of Theodore Kaczynski?
2. What does it mean to be a Luddite? Does our culture revere or revile Luddites (or neither)? Explain in a paragraph.
3. Write a paragraph in which you discuss how the world would be different today without the proliferation of machine intelligence.
4. What do you think Joy means when he says, "We are on the cusp of the further perfection of extreme evil"?

Essay Assignments

1. Write an essay discussing the development of artificial intelligence. Discuss three areas in which artificial intelligence has replaced human intelligence.
2. Bill Joy believes that teaching computers to "think" may be opening up a world that could destroy us. Should we be performing research regarding self-replication and nanotechnology? Why or why not?
3. The writer quotes Ray Kurzweil as saying, "Machine-made decisions will bring better results than man-made ones." Write an essay comparing and contrasting decisions that are better made by machines and those in which a human's experience is beneficial. ↻

Connect IRW Writing Assignments: You may assign any of these essay prompts in Connect IRW; the toolset supports options such as assigning peer review or building your own rubric to gather reporting around student writing outcomes.

AUTHOR AND CONTEXT Jon Talton is the economics columnist for *The Seattle Times,* the editor and publisher of the blog *Rogue Columnist,* and the author of nine novels. He was a Knight Western Fellow in Journalism at the University of Southern California and a community fellow at the Morrison Institute at Arizona State University. This article appeared in *The Seattle Times* in January 2013.

PREVIEWING Have pen and paper (or a computer) on hand as you read. Think about the title, and then study the author's biography and the contextual information about the reading. Next, preview the selection. From the information you have gathered, determine the topic. What predictions can you make about the reading's content? Jot down your answers.

READING CRITICALLY AND ANNOTATING As you read, annotate the main idea, the major supporting points, key words, and a few passages that would make good quotations. Either write in your book or make annotations on sticky notes.

As you find key ideas, annotate them. What does Talton think will happen in the future? What is his attitude toward preparedness? Note any questions that come to mind as you read.

After reading and annotating, create an information sheet on which you record and organize your annotations as well as your thoughts about the content of the reading.

Teaching Resources: See the Instructor's Manual (IM) for instructions to set up this assignment in Connect IRW. Alternatively, this reading assignment and the writing prompts that follow have been pre-loaded into the Connect IRW *Common Places* Master Course.

○

In a World of Challenges, It's Time to Look at Possibilities BY JON TALTON

Lexile: 980L

I was born for apocalypse.   1

A child of the Cold War, I ducked and covered, watched a grim President   2
Kennedy on television during the Cuban Missile Crisis—when the world came very close to thermonuclear destruction—and always felt an icy stab in my middle when the air-raid sirens were tested every Saturday at noon.

And in my hometown, which didn't get tornadoes or tsunamis, those sirens   3
existed for one reason: To warn of fiery holocaust in 30 minutes or less.

Some precocious children of my generation built primitive computers. I learned   4
everything I could about intercontinental ballistic missiles, bombers, fallout, blast waves and the difference between counterforce and counter-value targeting. I could read a Geiger counter at age 7. None of it abated my terror.

Geiger counter: a device that measures radiation.

This experience helped make me a natural-born worrier. Because things turned   5
out well, it also instilled a certain worry skepticism. After all, if we avoided a very real threat of annihilation by hydrogen bombs, it was difficult to get my pulse up over Y2K or the Mayan calendar.

I have a high bar for doomsday.   6

These have been difficult years for most Americans: Not just the worst recession   7
since the Great Depression, but evidence that the American promise itself is at risk. We've come through a bitter presidential campaign that illuminated how polarized we have become.

The Year 2000 problem—also known as Y2K—was primarily a computer programming issue. Y2K, along with fears of the new millennium, prompted some people to speculate about widespread devastation in the year 2000.

Even so, we didn't suffer a second Great Depression. The economy is healing   8
slowly and actually doing better than Europe and Japan. America remains prosperous and powerful. We are living through the longest period of peace between major nations in centuries. Seattle is booming again and continuing to attract some of the most talented and innovative people in the world.

Because of a misinterpretation of the Mayan calendar, some people believed that December 21, 2012, would be the end of the world.

Yet every minute of every day, if one knows where to look, a fire hose of alarm-   9
ing predictions and information bombards us.

The social critic James Howard Kunstler and Soviet émigré Dmitry Orlov warn   10
that we're headed for societal collapse. *Collapse* was the title of Jared Diamond's cautionary best-seller. A few years ago, Cullen Murphy wrote the book, *Are We Rome?* The "we" being the United States.

A few scary notches down, Northwestern University economist Robert Gordon   11
published a widely discussed paper last year warning that the United States could face prolonged slow growth: We're out of the revolutions that create so many new industries and jobs and face severe "headwinds" in righting ourselves.

And these are serious thinkers, not reality TV's doomsday preppers. 12

What, us worry? 13

Take a deep breath: 14

Debt. Deforestation. Environmental degradation. Financial-market meltdowns. 15
Freak weather events. Food shortages. Geopolitical destabilization. Global unemployment. Governing paralysis. Inequality. Mass migrations. Mideast conflict. Middle-class decline.

Hang with me: 16

Melting Arctic icecap and glaciers. Nuclear terrorism. Ocean acidification. Over- 17
population. Pakistan instability. Peak oil. Permafrost melting. Political extremism.
Resource scarcity. Rising temperatures. Sea-level rise. Species extinction. Tropical diseases moving north. Tribalism. War with China.

It almost makes you pine (almost) for the seeming simplicity of two superpowers 18
facing off with thousands of nukes.

Unfortunately, every one of the challenges listed above is real. Some will be the 19
hinge upon which the history of the 21st century turns.

Little of this was discussed in the presidential debates. Outside of doomsday 20
porn, such as potential asteroid strikes, "bad news" about the real risks facing us is
unpopular.

In general, we're a nation with two emotional speeds: Irrational optimism 21
and incapacitating depression. Majorities in much of Red State America are highly
mistrustful of science, especially the driver of many of these dangers: Climate change.
And they believe an unfettered market will fix the rest.

All around is a condition of crisis fatigue. How far we have come from the opti- 22
mism of the 1980s and 1990s. How often have I heard people say, "I just can't bear to
read the newspaper. It's too depressing."

In little more than a decade, we've been through 9/11, two recessions, two wars, 23
middle-class free-fall and the routine of boarding an airplane turned into an experience similar to being booked into jail.

Better to sublimate our anxieties in the telling zombie craze or ever-present irony. 24

Nobody knows the future. History does provide a toolbox, of sorts, for under- 25
standing the path ahead. It can give plenty of ammunition to skeptics—and cause
for hope.

For example, 40 years ago the Club of Rome, an influential think tank, released 26
a report warning that the decline of oil reserves and other resources would severely
limit growth. It didn't happen. Nearly two centuries before, the gloomy Rev. Thomas
Malthus predicted that overpopulation would make progress impossible. At the time
Malthus was writing, the world had one-seventh the number of humans it holds today.

Technology can change the arc of the future. American cities enjoy much cleaner 27
air and water than they did just a few decades ago, thanks to innovations and regulation. The so-called Green Revolution resulted in dramatic increases in food production
worldwide, although not without unintended environmental consequences.

Sometimes we muddle through. The United States was able to postpone the Civil 28
War, albeit at a horrendous human cost to those enslaved, for some 30 years after it
became clear that the house, to use Lincoln's metaphor, was divided against itself.

Prepper: a person who focuses on preparedness, typically with the expectation that some catastrophic event is likely to occur relatively soon.

Green Revolution: an increase in agricultural production by means of research and technological advances in the period between the 1940s and the late 1960s.

We muddled through the Cold War. As with all successful muddling involving big   29
stakes, this also required leadership, wisdom, compromise and luck.

But today's challenges shouldn't be lightly dismissed. Many are backed by much   30
more robust science than that used by the Club of Rome. Americans should be wary of
a childlike faith in technology-as-savior.

We should be wary of muddling. We were muddling when the 2001 presidential   31
daily brief stated, "bin-Laden determined to strike in U.S."

It's enough to make a skeptical worrier worry. The 21st century is a different game.   32

When I gave a speech last November to the Ballard Rotary Club, the very emblem   33
of Main Street respectability, one of the members asked, "When do you think the
food riots will begin?" He was not joking.

The issues and challenges we face are hugely complex. Some of their details are   34
open to debate, and their effects are being felt only slowly in most places. They do
not comprise a single doomsday.

But at the core are three things we must address if we want for our grandchil-   35
dren the better future that our grandparents handed on to us.

First is climate change, the greatest challenge to face humanity. It's real. It's   36
human-caused. It's happening at a faster rate than scientists feared, and will bring
astronomical economic and human costs. This is our reality that cares not a whit
whether oil-company propaganda or denial dead-enders believe it or not.

Hurricane Sandy, with its unprecedented storm surge into lower Manhattan, was   37
a reminder that climate change will not just affect poor people in the Third World.
If we do nothing, if we continue to drill, baby, drill, and dump evermore greenhouse
gases into the atmosphere, future generations will attempt to inhabit a planet out of
a science-fiction nightmare by the end of the century.

Drill, baby, drill: a 2008 Republican campaign slogan advocating that the United States increase its effort to find oil on U.S. lands.

Second is regaining effective self-government in the United States. This challenge   38
goes beyond a partisan divide that is the worst since the eve of the Civil War.

To put it in a non-Seattle-nice way, an oligarchy has taken over our government.   39
The "financial services industry." The Military-Industrial Complex. Big Oil and King
Coal. Highly consolidated industries that have created proto-monopolies and cartels.

Oligarchy: control by a small group of people.

While it's comforting to see that their hundreds of millions of dollars failed to   40
unseat President Obama, they firmly control Congress and most state legislatures.
They heavily influence regulation and the courts, gaming the system for their benefit
and calling it "the free market."

Third, we must get the world economy growing again. Prosperous nations tend   41
not to go to war with each other (a big exception happened nearly a century ago) or
see civil unrest. This, along with unseating the oligarchs, is important to rebuilding
the American middle class and closing historic income inequality.

But it is also critical for developing nations. Look at any image of global con-   42
flict on the television and you're likely to see a mob of hopeless, unemployed young
men. Last year, the United Nations estimated that 202 million people worldwide
were unemployed. In addition, rising prosperity usually empowers women. Better-off
nations have lower birthrates.

This is the point in a magazine article where the writer is expected to lay out solu-   43
tions. I'm not sure that's realistic.

Not that we lack for sound policy suggestions. On climate change, for example,   44
we could institute a carbon tax, rebuild our passenger rail system, begin a "Manhattan
Project" on clean energy and expand transit where demand is high or promising.

Intelligent responses, if not "solutions," exist for every challenge we face.   45

But the status quo is strong. Its supporters aren't confined to a moneyed elite. 46 The average American isn't yet willing to contemplate how to make different living arrangements for a truly sustainable future. The very word "sustainability" has been hijacked to mean spending big sums to preserve the unsustainable.

Meanwhile, President Obama, contrary to the caricature of the right, is a cau- 47 tious, small-c conservative, unlikely to lead bold change. Thus far, he hasn't even had a serious conversation with the American people about necessary transitions that might require lead times of 15 years or more. One of our fundamental problems: Our leaders won't tell us the truth.

Excuses are legion: China won't reduce its greenhouse gases, so why should we, 48 especially in a hurting economy? I would argue that if America truly is exceptional, this is the moment to show it. We emit huge amounts of carbon on our own, and leaping ahead on clean tech and conservation would be a beacon to the world.

On the most basic level, social customs change slowly. A reset of this magnitude could 49 take a generation or more. And indeed, college-educated young people are flocking to quality city cores and shunning automobiles—a sea change, perhaps, but only a start.

Unfortunately, we don't have that time on climate change. Some climate scien- 50 tists say our window to head off the worst consequences is five years. Yet most of what we hear or read is about extracting and burning more fossil fuels, which in fact are only safe for the climate if left in the ground.

So I'm worrying again, and not the immature panic of a duck-and-cover child. 51

"We need to be the change we wish to see in the world." Gandhi probably didn't 52 actually say that, but it's a good sentiment. Even when circumstances seem overwhelming, individuals can vote, become involved, learn and talk to their neighbor. Plant a tree.

Seeing what I call the Great Disruption coming, I chose Seattle five years ago as a 53 safer harbor than most in America. Among other things, it offered a literate population, environmental ethic, culture, transportation choices, civic stewards and a vibrant downtown and city neighborhoods. It is a "we society."

I live in Belltown and don't need a car. My Walk Score is 97, and my Transit Score 54 is 100. I can take trains to Portland, San Francisco, Vancouver or Chicago. The downtown retail district and Pike Place Market are close by. I shop with local companies and buy the produce of Washington farmers. I write about the uncomfortable reality confronting us.

Cities are rated in terms of how easily people can walk to places they need to go (grocery stores, schools, health-care facilities, and so on).

This is not moral greatness, and I don't claim all the answers. It is one person's 55 attempt to do something for a better future.

Others may see their true north elsewhere. Across the country, people are work- 56 ing and living in ways to address the storms ahead.

My younger worrier roots remind me of the power of individuals. 57

In 1983, during one of the tensest moments of the Cold War, a Soviet early warn- 58 ing center detected an incoming American missile. This might well have caused the Soviet Union to launch its own missiles against the United States before they could be destroyed in their silos.

At no small professional risk, the duty officer at the command center, Lt. Col. 59 Stanislav Petrov, decided it must be a false alarm and didn't sound a general alert.

We're here today because of Petrov's good judgment. 60

Let's hope people alive in the decades ahead might say the same about us. 61

Using Your Annotations

Use your annotations and key words to write a one-page summary of the reading. In your summary, identify the writer's thesis statement, the major supporting points, the support for the major supporting points, and any other information needed to complete the summary.

Thinking about the Text

1. What is the main idea of this essay?
2. What does Talton mean when he writes, "We're a nation with two emotional speeds: Irrational optimism and incapacitating depression"?
3. What does the writer mean by "crisis fatigue"?
4. According to the article, what are the three things that we must address for a better future?
5. What has the author personally done to take responsibility for the future?

The Writer's Techniques

1. What is Talton's purpose? Does he hope to inform, analyze, evaluate, or persuade, or does he have more than one purpose? Explain your answer.
2. Is humor a part of the writer's strategy? Did you find any parts of the writing entertaining? Explain.
3. What kind of proof does the writer offer for his assertions?

Brief-Response Assignments

1. What future crisis is the most alarming to Talton? Explain why he finds this crisis the most serious one.
2. Explain what the writer means when he says, "Our leaders won't tell us the truth."
3. On the whole, do you think that the writer is more optimistic or more pessimistic about civilization's future? Explain your thoughts.

Essay Assignments

1. Talton states that "'bad news' about the real risks facing us is unpopular." Why are many people uninterested in serious issues, such as the ones raised in this article? Write an essay explaining the causes of such apathy.
2. The writer discusses some ways in which he attempts to make a difference for a better future. Write an essay to identify and present small changes that people could make today that would positively affect future generations.
3. The writer advocates urban life—living in cities—as a solution to some of the problems we are facing. Why would living in cities be advantageous for the future of the earth and environment? How might urban life be advantageous to us as individuals? Discuss this topic in an essay. ↻

Connect IRW Writing Assignments: You may assign any of these essay prompts in Connect IRW; the toolset supports options such as assigning peer review or building your own rubric to gather reporting around student writing outcomes.

AUTHOR AND CONTEXT The American Preppers Network (APN) is a nonprofit corporation and part of a growing international movement of people who call themselves preppers. The social network is organized by state and regional blogs and forums. The members are volunteer contributors who are dedicated to providing free information on survival, preparedness, self-sufficiency, and sustainability. "The Five Principles of Preparedness," inspired by a talk by James E. Faust, appears on the APN Web site (americanpreppersnetwork.com). It was written by Phil Burns, a co-owner of the APN.

PREVIEWING Have pen and paper (or a computer) on hand as you read. Think about the title, and then study the author's biography and the contextual information about the reading. Next, preview the selection. From the information you have gathered, determine the topic. What predictions can you make about the reading's content? Jot down your answers.

READING CRITICALLY AND ANNOTATING As you read, annotate the main idea, the major supporting points, key words, and a few passages that would make good quotations. Either write in your book or make annotations on sticky notes.

Teaching Resources: See the Instructor's Manual (IM) for instructions to set up this assignment in Connect IRW. Alternatively, this reading assignment and the writing prompts that follow have been pre-loaded into the Connect IRW *Common Places* Master Course.

As you find key ideas, annotate them. What is "prepping"? Why do people participate in it? Is prepping something that everyone should do? Think about these questions as you read and annotate the selection.

After reading and annotating, create an information sheet on which you record and organize your annotations as well as your thoughts about the content of the reading.

The Five Principles of Preparedness

BY PHIL BURNS, THE AMERICAN PREPPERS NETWORK

Lexile: 1220L

There are basic principles that keep us and our families grounded that are key to our   1
happiness as a family unit while we walk the path of the prepper. By getting started in prepping, or continuing in prepping as the case may be, and following these five principles of preparedness we can provide our families with the assurance that we will be able to maintain a certain standard of living. This standard of living is dictated by the level of preparedness we are able to achieve and maintain.

Principle 1: Practice Thrift and Frugality

The depression era saying of "Use it up, wear it out, make it do, or do without" sums   2
up the practice of thrift. Living thriftily is not a popular concept in our "staying up with the Joneses" mentality, but the folly of that mentality is that if one thing goes wrong and your family slips into crisis, you will have to learn all about "staying above water." Living thriftily is a very simple, effective and immediate method to increase your spending power. Imagine being, instead of a consumer, a creator, a repairer, or simply abstaining. Thrift is a practice of not wasting anything including time and money.

Why do Americans work themselves so hard and as soon as the paycheck comes   3
in, throw it to the wind as quickly as they can—leaving themselves with no reserves, no safety and no peace? It is because we have come to accept abundance as our standard. We foolishly assure ourselves that there will be a check next pay period—and there normally is—until there is not. It is the high possibility that at some point something critical will happen in our lives that brings us to the conclusion that it is very likely that at some point, that check will not be there.

One massive waste that Americans have become very comfortable with is living   4
on credit. We have become extremely complacent with our finances in this regard. Instead of doing without for a short time while we save, we finance everything and as a consequence, pay financing fees and interest that we somehow justify as necessary. It is not necessary that we ever pay financing fees or interest for anything, even a house, if we are willing to be prudent.

Preppers who successfully follow this principle for a few years will find them-   5
selves in a position where they are able to spend time not working without affecting their families in an adverse manner.

Principle Two: Seek to Be Independent

Debt can be crippling and crushing to a family, making them unable to move forward   6
due to the demands of making payments on things they potentially don't even own anymore. Seek to become independent from debt. Learn to abhor the idea of being forced to labor and earn money that is not yours as a consequence of choosing to "live a little better" by going into debt. Living independently means being free to choose what is pertinent for you and your family to do with your money. Establish savings that will grow and serve you as you become the master of your money. Learn

to budget and responsibly manage your money as it is a very powerful tool to either enslave or empower you.

Independence doesn't just mean money though. Seek to be independent of the   7
influences of the world such as caffeine, alcohol, drugs, tobacco, unhealthy yet addictive food, medications (where possible) and so on. All of these things not only make you a personal slave to addictions, but indenture your wallet and cause you to spend wasteful amounts of money to satiate your personal weaknesses. Strive to become independent of all these things and you will not only be healthier, but you will also increase your income as you free a daily outgo to servicing your demons.

Live independent of the entrapping influences of society as much as possible.   8
Free your mind of thinking you need a better looking car, a prettier house or better clothes. Do what works for *you,* not what you think others will think highly of. Live independently of the fear of judgment of others and become secure in your own person. Prepper families who learn to live independently will find themselves prospering greatly—in ways that may not be apparent to the enslaved masses of society.

Principle Three: Become Industrious

Learn, explore, do. When opportunity presents itself, work hard at redefining and   9
reshaping yourself, your position and your knowledge to be worthy of the success that opportunity can provide. Be resourceful, always looking for a new way to create what you need in order to succeed.

Common ways to be industrious include furthering your education and constantly   10
working to develop new skills. By exploring opportunities, we are able to assess their potential, weigh risks and make decisions as to whether our conclusions merit committing to an opportunity or walking away from it. By improving ourselves constantly, we open up even more opportunity; and opportunities can potentially bring success.

Idly standing by and waiting for success to land in your lap is a poor strategy.   11
Being industrious means getting up and attempting something, even if it has the potential to fail. The farmer who fails to put in a crop because he doesn't think there was enough snowfall during the winter loses out when spring rains finally bring plenty of water. When you commit to something, work hard at it; throw in everything you've got. Getting up and going is truly the only way to end up somewhere else.

Preppers who industriously seek out opportunity will soon find the one that will   12
create a change in the direction their lives have been heading.

Principle Four: Strive Towards Self-Reliance

The principle of self-reliance is predicated by and builds upon the first three principles. Self-reliance is, in its simplest form, being able to create or provide all needed   13
things as the result of labor using a developed skill or talent and being able to provide resources as a result of a judicious practice of storing needful things. Therefore, becoming self-reliant is the actual process of developing skills and talents while putting away resources.

When combined with thrift and frugality, self-reliance helps you to obtain what   14
you need without having to pay exorbitant amounts of money for those things such as growing a garden, sewing or repairing clothes, building furniture, building a home, fixing your vehicle and so on. It is being willing to enjoy the fruits of your labor versus the blandness of buying something commercially produced. It is accepting things for

their functionality, not for the logo that was stamped on them in a plant somewhere. It is being willing to use something that may be less than perfect in its manufacture but is functional.

Self-reliance, when combined with independence, drives us to be truly reliant 15 on ourselves in all areas. Self-reliance can involve learning how to make soap, grow your own food, provide your own energy, defend yourself, and create the things you need and so on. It requires research, learning, experimenting, failing, experimenting more and finally succeeding. By being self-reliant, you succeed in gaining a new skill, accomplishing something new or developing a new vocation. An industrious and self-reliant person is truly a creator and experiences the joy of creation on a daily basis.

Principle Five: Aspire to Have a Year's Supply of Every Needful Thing

The natural outgrowth of becoming truly self-reliant is to feel compelled to store 16 things up that are essential for our family's ensured safety, comfort and existence. The "every needful thing" concept teaches us to consider the possibility of storing up a supply of every item that we purchase which we truly need. What is a need? Simply put, it is something that it would be difficult to not have or to live without. This includes food, clothing, water, heat, power, home medical supplies, fire starters, and so on.

It is obviously not prudent to simply purchase a year's supply of every needful thing. 17 For example, it is quite inexpensive and easy to acquire a year's supply of ketchup; at most a family will use two bottles a month. Therefore, purchasing 24 bottles would give you a year's supply. However, a year's supply of something like water, which is consumed every day, requires a very different approach. It is not feasible to store a year's supply of water unless you have your own water tower. There are other options available, though, which include such things as drilling a well, installing a rain catchment system, or being situated near a body of water.

Preppers who are striving to build a year's supply of every needful thing will 18 experience a dramatic reduction in stress and an increase in peace as they begin meeting goals on the path to achieving this principle.

The Impact of Living the Principles of Preparedness

When teaching these principles, the question is inevitably asked: "What if nothing ever happens that I need my supplies for?" To which I respond, "That would be wonderful!"

As you live by these principles, you will experience breaking free of the slavery of 20 debt, a "career," of "keeping up with the Joneses" and most importantly, the stress of trying to live month to month. What you will find instead is that you are able to fully experience life and truly enjoy the blessings of your family, all the while knowing that the secret to a happy life is wrapped up in a little concept called being a "prepper"!

—○○○—

Using Your Annotations

Use your annotations and key words to write a one-page summary of the reading. In your summary, identify the writer's thesis statement, the major supporting points, the support for the major supporting points, and any other information needed to complete the summary.

Thinking about the Text

1. What is the main idea of this essay?
2. What does the writer mean in stating that "we have come to accept abundance as our standard"?
3. Why does the writer believe the elimination of debt is so important?
4. What is self-reliance, according to the essay?
5. What does the writer say are the benefits of becoming industrious?

The Writer's Techniques

1. Preppers are sometimes thought of as radical people who have outlandish ideas. How does this article help to change that stereotype?
2. Think of some examples the writer could use to enhance the article. Where would examples make the writer's ideas clearer?
3. How does the writer conclude the essay? What is the conclusion trying to convey?

Brief-Response Assignments

1. Of the five principles mentioned in the essay, which one would be the most difficult for most people to accomplish? Why?
2. Reflect on what the average American might need for a year's worth of supplies. What would be the most important supplies to have on hand to be self-reliant?
3. In what ways would a prepper's lifestyle be different from the lifestyle of most Americans today?

Essay Assignments

1. The writer suggests that a key to living a happy life is being a prepper. Write an essay discussing how being a prepper could make one's life either happier or more miserable.
2. This writer, as well as other famous writers in history, discusses the importance of self-reliance. What is self-reliance, and how can the average American become more self-reliant?
3. Select one of the principles offered in this essay that would improve the lives of Americans if followed. Write an essay defending your advocacy of this principle. Provide reasons for your belief, and include examples. You may use hypothetical examples. ↻

Connect IRW Writing Assignments: You may assign any of these essay prompts in Connect IRW; the toolset supports options such as assigning peer review or building your own rubric to gather reporting around student writing outcomes.

THEMATIC ASSIGNMENT

Use the readings in this thematic unit to write an essay that answers one of the following questions.

Teaching Resources: See the IM for suggestions of other readings within Connect IRW Power of Process that may be used with this theme.

a. To what extent should all Americans become "preppers"? What prepping behaviors are reasonable? Write an essay in which you answer these questions. Provide proof for your point of view, and provide examples of the kinds of prepping you believe people should undertake, based on your understanding of the articles in this chapter. Use two or more of the readings as support for your point of view.

b. We have limited time, limited resources, and limited energy to solve the problems of the future. Thus, we have to prioritize the projects that need our attention. Many of the articles in this section emphasize problems: a divided government, global warming, consumer debt, the potential dangers of computer technology, and more. Select the three most important issues we should tackle. Use the readings in this unit to support your assertion that these are the three most important issues.

c. The essays in this unit present at least two responses to the future: one is to withdraw to an extent and become a prepper, and the other (represented by Jon Talton) is to move to a city, reduce one's environmental footprint, and advocate for change. Compare and contrast these two responses. In what ways are they similar? In what ways are they different? Write an essay presenting your comparison.

d. The articles in this thematic unit present both problems and prospects for the future. How can some of the ideas presented here—such as robots and prepping—solve some of the problems we are facing? For example, can robots solve any climate change problems? Select a problem presented in this unit that may be solved by one of the prospects presented here. Explain how the prospect may affect the problem.

Be sure to cite any sources from which you obtain ideas or quotes. Include a works cited or references page with your essay. For additional information on source-based writing, follow the steps in the Quick Start Guide to Integrated Reading and Writing Assignments.

CREDITS

Text Credits

Chapter 2

Page 27: Larry Roberts, John Janovy, Jr., and Steve Nadler, *Foundations of Parasitology*, 9th ed. New York: McGraw-Hill, 2013, p. 2; p. 29: William Cunningham and Mary Ann Cunningham, *Principles of Environmental Science*, 7th ed. New York: McGraw-Hill, 2013, pp. 267–268; p. 30: Fish Consumption Advisory from William Cunningham and Mary Ann Cunningham, *Principles of Environmental Science*, 5th ed., Figure 10.17 (p. 246). Copyright © 2009 by McGraw-Hill Education. Reprinted with permission; p. 46: "the ability to perceive . . . " is from *Managing Stress*. MTD Training and Ventus Publishing, 2010, p. 48.

Chapter 3

Page 51: Textbook chapter headings from William Cunningham and Mary Ann Cunningham, *Principles of Environmental Science*, 5th ed. New York: McGraw-Hill, 2009, pp. 25, 36; p. 51: Food Chain figure from William Cunningham and Mary Ann Cunningham, *Principles of Environmental Science*, 5th ed., Figure 2.2. Copyright © 2009 by McGraw-Hill Education. Reprinted with permission; p. 53: Chapter Outline and caption from Charles R. Swanson, Neil Chamelin, and Leonard Territo, *Criminal Investigation*, 11th ed. New York: McGraw-Hill, 2012, from Chapter 4; p. 64: Eldon D. Enger and Bradley F. Smith, *Environmental Science: A Study of Interrelationships*, 13th ed., pp. 382–383. Copyright © 2013 by McGraw-Hill Education. Reprinted with permission.

Chapter 4

Page 81: Paragraphs A-C in Practice 5 are from Judith A. Boss, *THINK: Critical Thinking and Logic Skills for Everyday Life*, 2nd ed. New York: McGraw-Hill, 2012, p. 277; p. 89: Kathryn Rentz, Marie E. Flatley, and Paula Lentz, *Lesikar's Business Communication: Connecting in a Digital World*, 12th ed., p. 3. Copyright © 2011 by McGraw-Hill Education. Reprinted with permission; p. 101: Peter J. McDonnell, MD, "Adapting to the Situation." Reprinted with permission from *Ophthalmology Times*, January 15, 2010. *Ophthalmology Times* is a copyrighted publication of Advanstar Communications Inc. All rights reserved.

This article was originally published with the title "Viewpoint: Key Is Learning To Be Successful Wherever You Land in Your Profession."

Chapter 5

Page 111: Bryce Covert, "Four Ideas for How Obama Could Really Transform the Cost of College." This article was published by ThinkProgress, August 21, 2013. Reprinted with permission; p. 126: Excerpt from Brittany Horn, "Recovery Is Slow in Rural China's 'Cancer Villages'." © 2013 by Brittany Horn. Reprinted by permission of the author. From McClatchyDC.com, August 19, 2013; p. 136: Brett and Kate McKay, "Coming of Age: The Importance of Male Rites of Passage." Copyright © 2008 The Art of Manliness. Reprinted with permission. http://www.artofmanliness.com

Chapter 6

Page 148: Adapted from http://starchild.gsfc.nasa.gov/docs/StarChild/questions/question6.html; p. 151: Laura Cunningham, "The Chosen One." © 1994 by Laura Cunningham. Reprinted by permission of the author. From *New York Times Magazine*, April 17, 1994; p. 161: Mary Ann Bell, "What I Really Meme Is. . . Anatomy of a Happenin' Thing," *Internet@Schools*, vol. 20, Issue 2 (March/April 2013), p. 24. © Copyright 2013 Information Today, Inc. Reprinted with permission; p. 167: Bill W. Tillery, *Physical Science*, 9th ed., excerpt and Figure 2.19 from p. 41. Copyright © 2012 by McGraw-Hill Education. Reprinted with permission; p. 171: Table "Identified Prevalence of Autism Spectrum Disorders" from U.S. Centers for Disease Control and Prevention, http://www.cdc.gov/ncbddd/autism/data.html#prevalence; p. 178: Excerpts from G. Michael Maddock and Raphael Louis Vitón, "Three Types of People to Fire Immediately," Businessweek.com, November 8, 2011. © 2011 Bloomberg L.P. All rights reserved. Reprinted with permission; p. 194: Patrick Leon Abbott, *Natural Disasters*, 8th ed., pp. 338–339. Copyright © 2012 by McGraw-Hill Education. Reprinted with permission; p. 200: *A Guide to Naturalization*. Washington, DC: U.S. Citizenship and Immigration Services, M-476 (rev. 03/12), p. 31; p. 213: Dennis Henigan, "Keep Guns

Off Campus." Reprinted by permission of the author. From *Huffington Post*, March 3, 2011.

Chapter 7

Page 241: *Antibiotic Resistance Threats in the US*. Atlanta, GA: Centers for Disease Control and Prevention, September 16, 2013. www.cdc.gov; p. 242: Conrad Phillip Kottak, *Mirror for Humanity*, 9th ed., pp. 36–37. Copyright © 2014 by McGraw-Hill Education. Reprinted with permission.

Chapter 8

Page 250: Reprinted with permission from "Campus Diversity and Student Self-Segregation: Separating Myths from Facts," by Debra Humphreys. Copyright 1999 by the Association of American Colleges and Universities; p. 253: Stanley J. Baran, *Introduction to Mass Communication: Media Literacy and Culture*, 8th ed., p. 394. Copyright © 2014 by McGraw-Hill Education. Reprinted with permission; p. 254: Janet Shibley Hyde and John DeLamater, *Understanding Human Sexuality*, 11th ed., p. 275. Copyright © 2011 by McGraw-Hill Education. Reprinted with permission; p. 256: From Larry D. Rosen, "Driven to Distraction: Our Wired Generation." © 2012 Larry D. Rosen, Ph.D. Reprinted by permission of the author. From *St. Paul Pioneer Press*, November 12, 2012; p. 258: Tait Trussell, "Healing Humor." © 2008 by Tait Trussell. Reprinted by permission of the author. From *Saturday Evening Post*, vol. 280, no. 4 (July/August 2008); p. 259: From Mitch Renkow, "Wal-Mart and the Local Economy," *NC State Economist*, November/December 2005. Reprinted by permission of the author; p. 260: From Tom Fitzgerald, "Probing Question: Is 'Just Say No' an effective anti-drug approach?" *Penn State News*, January 23, 2006; p. 260: From Christine VanDeVelde Luskin, "Mark Lepper: Intrinsic Motivation, Extrinsic Motivation and the Process of Learning," *Bing Times Online*, Stanford University, 2003; p. 262: From Mitch Renkow, "Wal-Mart and the Local Economy," *NC State Economist*, November/December 2005. Reprinted by permission of the author; p. 264: reprinted with permission from "Campus Diversity and Student Self-Segregation: Separating Myths from Facts," by Debra Humphreys.

Copyright 1999 by the Association of American Colleges and Universities; p. 266: Andrew Gumbel, "Homo Sapiens RIP," *The Independent*, March 15, 2000. Reprinted with permission. © independent .co.uk. http://www.independent.co.uk; p. 267: David Croteau and William Hoynes, *Experience Sociology*, 1st ed., pp. 213–214. Copyright © 2013 by McGraw-Hill Education. Reprinted with permission.

Chapter 9

Page 279: Em Griffin, *A First Look at Communication Theory*, 1st ed. New York: McGraw-Hill, 1991; p. 282: From Dorothy Foltz-Gray, "What Really Makes Us Happy," *Prevention* 58.2 (2006): 156–163; p. 291: Passage A is from Amit Shah, *Business Now*. New York: McGraw-Hill, 2011, p. 79; p. 296: From Tom Orsborn, "'Brick Layer' Ready to Replace Spencer Full-Time," MySanAntonio.com, September 25, 2013; p. 303: Map from Althea Arnold et al., *Out of Reach 2014*. Washington, DC: National Low Income Housing Coalition, p. 14. © 2014 National Low Income Housing Coalition. Reprinted with permission; p. 304: Vincent Ryan Ruggiero, *Beyond Feelings: A Guide to Critical Thinking*, 9th ed., pp. 103–105. Copyright © 2012 by McGraw-Hill Education. Reprinted with permission.

Chapter 10

Page 339: Benjamin Percy, "Home Improvement: Revision as Renovation," *Poets & Writers Magazine*, May/June 2010. Reprinted with permission of the publisher, Poets & Writers, Inc., 90 Broad Street, Suite 2100, New York, NY 10004, www.pw.org

Chapter 11

Page 352: Larry D. Rosen, "Driven to Distraction: Our Wired Generation." © 2012 Larry D. Rosen, Ph.D. Reprinted by permission of the author. From *St. Paul Pioneer Press*, November 12, 2012; p. 361: Jim Taylor, "The Bad, the Ugly, and the Good of Kids' Use of Social Media," The Blog of Dr. Jim Taylor, www.drjimtaylor.com, posted May 28, 2013. Copyright © Jim Taylor, Ph.D. Reprinted by permission of the author; p. 365: Stanley J. Baran, *Introduction to Mass Communication: Media Literacy and Culture*, 8th ed., p. 394. Copyright © 2014 by McGraw-Hill Education. Reprinted with permission.

Chapter 12

Page 383: Eldon D. Enger and Bradley F. Smith, *Environmental Science: A Study of Interrelationships*, 13th ed., pp. 333–334. Copyright © 2013 by McGraw-Hill Education. Reprinted with permission; p. 389: Adapted from "Biodiversity: the magic of our planet!" World Wildlife Fund, http://wwf.panda.org/about_our_earth/biodiversity. Creative Commons Attribution-ShareAlike 3.0 Unported (CC BY-SA 3.0) http://creativecommons .org/licenses/by-sa/3.0/deed.en; p. 393: William P. Cunningham and Mary Ann Cunningham, *Environmental Science*, 13th ed., pp. 135–139. Copyright © 2015 by McGraw-Hill Education. Reprinted with permission; p. 397: Craig Welch, "Sea Change: Food for Millions at Risk," *Seattle Times*, December 21, 2013. Copyright © 2013 The Seattle Times. Reproduced by permission of The Seattle Times via Copyright Clearance Center.

Chapter 13

Page 415: Liza Featherstone, "Watching Wal-Mart." Copyright © 2006 by Liza Featherstone. Reprinted by permission of the author. From *Columbia Journalism Review*, vol. 44, no. 5 (January/February 2006), pp. 58–62. Liza Featherstone is the author of *Selling Women Short: The Landmark Battle for Workers' Rights at Wal-Mart*; p. 421: Mitch Renkow, "Wal-Mart and the Local Economy," *NC State Economist*, November/December 2005. Reprinted by permission of the author; p. 424: Joseph DesJardins, *An Introduction to Business Ethics*, 5th ed., pp. 49–52. Copyright © 2014 by McGraw-Hill Education. Reprinted with permission; p. 429: John Semmens, "Wal-Mart Is Good for the Economy," *The Freeman*, vol. 55, no. 8 (October 1, 2005), p. 8. © 2005 Foundation for Economic Education. Reprinted by permission of Foundation for Economic Education (FEE).

Chapter 14

Page 447: Joe and Teresa Graedon, "How Safe Is Aspartame?" The People's Pharmacy®, January 9, 2006. Reprinted with permission. www.peoplespharmacy .com. Appeared in *Buffalo News*, January 4, 2006; p. 452: This content is excerpted with permission from *Controlling Anger Before It Controls You*, http://www.apa .org/topics/anger/control.aspx. Copyright © 2005 by the American Psychological Association. No further reproduction or distribution is permitted without written permission from the American Psychological Association; p. 454: "Commentary. Concussions in Football," by Miller, Michael Craig. Excerpted from the *Harvard Mental Health Letter*, vol. 26, no. 7 (January 2010). © 2010, Harvard University. For more information visit: http://www.health.harvard.edu/ Note: Harvard Health Publications does not endorse any products or medical procedures; p. 460: This content is excerpted with permission from *Controlling Anger Before It Controls You*, http://www.apa .org/topics/anger/control.aspx. Copyright © 2005 by the American Psychological Association. No further reproduction or distribution is permitted without written permission from the American Psychological Association; p. 464: From Pamela Cantor, "Police and Punishment: Strategic Alternatives for Schools," *District Administration*, August 2013. http://www .districtadministration.com

Theme: Triumphing over Adversity

Page 555: Melissa Balmain, "Bouncing Back." Copyright © 2012 Melissa Balmain; first published in *Success Magazine* (April 2012); p. 560: Chaplain (Maj.) Carlos C. Huerta, "Leaving the Battlefield: Soldier Shares Story of PTSD," www .army.mil, The Official Homepage of the United States Army, April 25, 2012; p. 564: Benjamin B. Lahey, *Psychology: An Introduction*, 10th ed., pp. 456–459. Copyright © 2009 by McGraw-Hill Education. Reprinted with permission; p. 568: "'To Do for Others': The Dream of Justice Sonia Sotomayor." Written by Andria Ramon for *Common Places*. Copyright © 2015 by Lisa and Kent Hoeffner.

Theme: Self-Segregation

Page 575: Debra Humphreys, reprinted with permission from "Campus Diversity and Student Self-Segregation: Separating Myths from Facts," by Debra Humphreys. Copyright 1999 by the Association of American Colleges and Universities; p. 580: Ernest Owens, "Equal When Separate," *The Daily Pennsylvanian*, September 13, 2012. Reprinted by permission of The Daily Pennsylvanian; p. 582: Michael Gawenda, "What Happened to the Dream?" © 2005 by Michael Gawenda. Reprinted by permission of the author. From *The Age* (Melbourne, Australia), October 22, 2005; p. 589: Brett Buckner, "Color Blind: Is Sunday Morning Still the Most Segregated Hour in America?" © 2011 by Brett Buckner. Reprinted by permission of the author. From *The Anniston Star*, May 28, 2011.

Theme: Is Comedy Central?

Page 595: Brett Oppegaard, "Anatomy of a Laugh—Amusing Analysis," *The Columbian* (Vancouver, WA), September 17, 2006. Reprinted by permission of the publisher; p. 598: Vicki Haddock, "What Makes Us Laugh—And Why?" *San Francisco Chronicle*,

June 10, 2007. © 2007 The Hearst Corporation. Reprinted with permission; p. 602: Tait Trussell, "Healing Humor." © 2008 by Tait Trussell. Reprinted by permission of the author. From *Saturday Evening Post*, vol. 280, no. 4 (July/August 2008); p. 605: Phillip Perry, "Laughter in the Workplace," *Focus: Journal for Respiratory Care & Sleep Medicine*, March 22, 2005. Reprinted by permission of the publisher.

Theme: Planning for the Future

Page 610: Cahal Milmo, "*Google* Search and Destroy: Rise of the Machines," *The Independent*, December 16, 2013. Reprinted with permission. © independent.co.uk. http://www.independent.co.uk; p. 613: Andrew Gumbel, "Homo Sapiens RIP; (or Why One of the Leading Gurus of the Technological Age Believes That the Future Doesn't Need Us)," *The Independent*, March 15, 2000. Reprinted with permission. © independent.co.uk. http://www.independent.co.uk; p. 616: Jon Talton, "In a World of Challenges, It's Time to Look at Possibilities." © 2013 by Jon Talton. Reprinted by permission of the author. From *Seattle Times*, January 4, 2013; p. 621: Abridged from Phil Burns, "The Five Principles of Preparedness," American Preppers Network, http://americanpreppersnetwork.com. © American Preppers Network. Reprinted with permission.

Photo Credits

Part Openers

1: © Doug Steakley/Lonely Planet Images/Getty Images; 2: © Radius Images/Corbis RF; 3: © Mark Sykes/JAI/Corbis; 4: © Dean Uhlinger/Corbis RF; 5: © Digital Vision/Getty Images RF; 6: © Don White/SuperStock

Chapter 1

Opener (top): © Blend Images/Getty Images RF; (middle): © BananaStock/PunchStock RF; (bottom): © Stockbyte/Getty Images RF; (right): © Purestock/SuperStock RF; p. 3: © Margie Hoeffner; p. 4 (left): © Granger Wootz/Blend Images/Corbis RF; p. 4 (right): © Barry Howe/Corbis RF; p. 6: © Jose Luis Pelaez Inc/Blend Images LLC RF; p. 8 (top): © Halfdark/Getty Images RF; p. 8 (bottom): © Hero/age fotostock RF

Chapter 2

Opener: © Hero Images/Getty Images RF

Chapter 3

Opener: © Ana Abejon/E+/Getty Images RF; p. 52: CDC; p. 53: © Dr. Richard Souviron; p. 56 (left): © Dieter Melhorn/Alamy RF; p. 56 (top right): © Stockbyte/Getty Images RF; p. 56 (bottom right): Walt Jennings/FEMA

Chapter 4

Opener: © Michael Babwahsingh; p. 97: Photographs in the Carol M. Highsmith Archive, Library of Congress, Prints and Photographs Division; p. 108: © Image Source/Digital Images/Getty RF

Chapter 5

Opener: © Calle Montes/Photononstop/Corbis

Chapter 6

Opener: (left): © Design Pics/Bilderbuch RF; (middle): © Ingram Publishing RF; (right): © Creatas/PunchStock RF; p. 149: Library of Congress Prints and Photographs Division LC-DIG-ppmsca-26286; p. 191: © Digital Vision/PunchStock

Chapter 7

Opener: © ZUMA Press, Inc./Alamy

Chapter 8

Opener: © Felix Behnke/Cultura/Getty Images RF; p. 250: © The Palma Collection/Getty Images RF; p. 261: © Comstock Images RF

Chapter 9

Opener: © Terry J. Alcorn/Photodisc/Getty Images RF; p. 278: © Roy McMahon/Corbis RF

Chapter 10

Opener: © Stockbyte/Getty Images RF; p. 324: © Ocean/Corbis RF; p. 344: © John Lund/Sam Diephuis/Blend Images LLC RF; p. 345 (top): © The John B. Lovelace Collection Photographs in Carol M. Highsmith's American Project, LOC; p. 345 (bottom): © Radius Images/Getty Images RF

Chapter 11

Opener: © Csondy/Getty Images RF

Chapter 12

Opener: © Comstock Images/PictureQuest

Chapter 13

Opener: © Robyn Beck/AFP/Getty Images

Chapter 14

Opener: © McGraw-Hill Education/Christopher Kerrigan, photographer; p. 443 (top): © C. Sherburne/PhotoLink/Getty Images RF; p. 443 (middle): © Brand X Pictures/Getty Images RF; p. 443 (bottom): © Purestock/SuperStock RF; p. 444 (top): © Rich Legg/E+/Getty Images RF; p. 444 (bottom): © Andrew Penner/E+/Getty Images RF; p. 444 (left): © Laurent Hamels/PhotoAlton/Corbis RF; p. 445: © Jupiterimages RF

Grammar Units

Unit 1 p. 480: © Digital Vision/Getty Images RF; Unit 2 (left) p. 520: © Imagestate Media (John Foxx)/Image State RF; Unit 2 (right) p. 520: © Dusty Pixel photography/Getty Images RF; Unit 3 p. 572: © Image 100/Corbis RF

Themes

p. 554: © Ingram Publishing RF; p. 574: © iStock/360/Getty Images RF; p. 594: © CBS Photo Archive/Getty Images; p. 609: © Fotosearch/SuperStock RF

Opener images for content available only in Create™

"Reading and Writing Summaries": © Stockbyte/Getty Images RF; "Reading and Writing to Solve Problems": © Buzzshotz/Alamy RF; "Reading and Writing Persuasive Responses": © Bloomberg via Getty Images; "Strategies for Reading and Writing Exams": NASA; "Editing and Revising Practice": © Jupiterimages/Photolibrary/Getty Images RF; "Television and Stereotypes": © AP Photo; "The Rules of Attraction": © iStock/360/Getty Images RF

INDEX

Note: Page numbers in italics refer to illustrations; page numbers in boldface refer to plates; page numbers followed by a "t" refer to tables.

A

Academic writing
  as formal writing, 292
  present tense in, 156–157
  third-person point of view in, 293–294
accept/except, 522–523
Active voice, 219–221, 333–334
Adages, 257–258
"Adapting to the Situation" (McDonnell), 100–102
Addresses, commas in, 546t
Adjectives, commas between, 545
advice/advise, 522–523
affect/effect, 522–523
Agreement, subject-verb, 335–338
all, 337
allot/a lot, 523–524
all ready/already, 524
although, 509
American Preppers Network, 621–623
among/between, 537–538
Amount/number, 538
Analogies, 27, 217–218, 370
Analysis, causal, 191
Analysis and evaluation texts, 378
  developing the essay, 402–407, 404t
  identifying, 146–147
  reading process for, 380–382
  readings for, 382–402
  revising and formatting, 407–410
"Anatomy of a Laugh: Amusing Analysis" (Oppegaard), 595–597
and
  in combining sentences, 496–497
  commas with, 544t
  subject-verb agreement with, 335
Anecdotes, 27, 28t
Annotation, 24–29
  of readings, 26–29, 28t, 446
  in revision, 324–325
  tips on, 24–25, 24t–25t
Antecedents of pronouns, 318–321
any, 337
APA (American Psychological Association) style
  formatting a paper in, 471–472, 473–477

in-text references in, 463–464
for long quotations, 474
references lists in, 472–473, 477
Apostrophes, 547, 547t
Argument, 209–218
  elements of, 209–212
  logical errors in, 217–218
  using, in writing, 215–216
Argument texts, 413–438
  formatting, 438
  reading and annotating, 212–215, 413–414
  readings for, 414–431
  recognizing, 212
  revising, 436–438
  writing, 431–436
Assignments
  assignment page creation, 55
  checking requirements of, 374, 407–408, 436
  from employers, 329–331
  purpose in, 131, 350, 367–368, 380
  reading and analyzing, 55, 131, 367–368, 379–380, 412
  tone for, 295–296
Assumptions, 281–287
  analyzing, 286–287
  inferences and, 281–283
  negative implications of, 284–286
Attributive tags, 457, 457t, 458–459
Audience
  anticipating questions from, 133
  in argument essays, 215–216
  in drafting, 372
  employer as, 329–331, 330t
  in revising, 317, 329–331
  selecting supporting details for, 130, 369–370
  for sources, 441–442
audience, 336
Awkward expressions, 316

B

"The Bad, the Ugly, and the Good of Kids' Use of Social Media" (Taylor), 361–364
Balmain, Melissa, 555–559
Baran, Stanley J., 364–366
bare/bear, 524
believe/feel, 538
between/among, 537–538
Bias, in sources, 441, 442–443, *443, 444, 445*
Bibliographic information, 236, 350
Block arrangement, 184–185, *185,* 187–188, 189–190

board, 336
Body paragraphs, 372–373
"Bouncing Back" (Balmain), 555–559
Brainstorming, 56–57
brake/break, 524–525
breath/breathe, 525
Buckner, Brett, 589–591
but, 499, 544t

C

"Campus Diversity and Student Self-Segregation: Separating Myths from Facts" (Humphreys), 575–579
can/may, 538–539
casual/causal, 539
Causal analysis, 191
Cause and effect, 191–198
  analyzing texts, 193–196
  faulty causes or effects, 217
  recognizing, 191–193, *193*
  using, in writing, 196–198, 197t
Chronological order, 224, *225,* 226t, 370
Circular definitions, 165
cite/sight/site, 525–526
Claims, 74, 209–210, 411
Classification, 175–182
  analyzing texts, 178–180
  recognizing, 175–177, 175t, *176*
  using, in writing, 180–182
Clauses, 492–515. *See also* Sentence combining
  dependent, 506–510, 507t, 543t, 544
  essential and nonessential, 508
  independent, 506, 549t
  punctuation of, 494, 509, 543t, 549t
  sentences and, 492–494
Clichés, 540
Closed thesis statement, 96, *96,* 132, 404
Closure, in conclusions, 261
clothes/cloths, 526
Cloud accounts, 376
Clustering, 61–62, *62,* 102, *102*
coarse/course, 526
College success, 7–13
Colons, 248, 548, 548t
"Color Blind: Is Sunday Morning Still the Most Segregated Hour in America?" (Buckner), 589–591
Combining sentences. *See* Sentence combining
"Coming of Age: The Importance of Male Rites of Passage" (McKay and McKay), 136–138

board, 336
Commands, 293, 542t
Commas
  in addresses, 546t
  between adjectives, 545
  after clarifying single words, 543t
  after conjunctive adverbs, 513–514
  after dependent clauses, 509, 543t, 544
  after introductory elements, 543–544, 543t
  after prepositional phrases, 483, 543t
  after verbal phrases, 543t
  with conjunctions, 544, 544t
  in dates, 546t
  to introduce quotations, 546t
  between names and titles, 546t
  in series, 545
  to set off dialogue, 546t
Comma splices
  coordinating conjunctions and, 494–495
  quotations and, 407, 458–459
  semicolons to correct, 549t
"Commentary: Concussions in Football" (Miller), 454–455
committee, 336
Compare, 183
Comparison-contrast, 183–190
  analyzing, 186–188
  recognizing, 183–185, *185*
  using, in writing, 189–190
complement/compliment, 526–527
Compound nouns, 550t
Conclusions, 261–266, 373
Concrete examples, 370
Conjunctions, commas with, 544, 544t
Conjunctive adverbs, 512–515, 513t, 549t
Connotations, 296
conscience/conscious, 527
Content resources, 9–10
Context, 36, 49, 49t
Context clues, 36–38, *37*
Contractions, apostrophes in, 547, 547t
Contrast, 183. *See also* Comparison-contrast
Coordinating conjunctions (CC), 494–506
"Coping with Stress" (Lahey), 564–567
Correlations, 196–197
council, 336
Counterarguments, 210, 216
course/coarse, 526
Credibility, of sources, 442, 443–445, *443, 444, 445*
Criteria list, 403, 404t